Somos así

LISTOS

Second Edition

ANNOTATED TEACHER'S EDITION

James F. Funston

Contributing Writers

Rolando Castellanos
Paul J. Hoff
Sandra Martín Arnold
Daphne Sherman

EMC/Paradigm Publishing, Saint Paul, Minnesota

ISBN 0-8219-1914-8

Published by EMC/Paradigm Publishing
875 Montreal Way
St. Paul, Minnesota 55102
800-328-1452
www.emcp.com
E-mail: educate@emcp.com

Printed in the United States of America
1 2 3 4 5 6 7 8 9 10 X X X 05 04 03 02 01 00

CONTENTS

SCOPE AND SEQUENCE

Capítulo	Communicative Functions	Topics	Readings	Idioma
Capítulo 1 **Un nuevo año** Lección 1	• talk about technology • seek and provide personal information • describe the weather • state what is happening right now • talk about everyday activities • discuss ecological problems • talk about the future • discuss schedules • compare quantity, quality, age and size • talk about the past • refer to what just happened	Spanish-speaking world Technology and communications Weather School Environmental problems Schedules	Conectados con el mundo La mejor compañera	Repaso rápido: el presente del indicativo I Repaso rápido: el presente progresivo El presente de los verbos *seguir* y *conseguir* Repaso rápido: el presente del indicativo II El comparativo y el superlativo
Lección 2		Spanish-speaking world Vacations Newspapers Current events Everyday activities Shopping	Escuela virtual Después de clases	Repaso rápido: el pretérito Repaso rápido: los pronombres de complemento directo e indirecto Usando los dos complementos
A leer	Estrategia para leer: *using cognates to determine meaning* En la Internet			
A escribir	Estrategia para escribir: *keeping your reader in mind*			
Capítulo 2 **Todos los días** Lección 3	• talk about everyday activities • seek and provide personal information • discuss personal grooming • compare and contrast • recognize and identify Hispanic influence in the United States • state when things are done	Influence of Spanish in the United States Daily routine Food Items in a bathroom	Somos muy diferentes Una toalla, por favor	Los verbos reflexivos La palabra *se* Repaso rápido: los adjetivos demostrativos Los pronombres demostrativos
Lección 4	• express past actions and events • identify items in a bathroom • point something out • write about everyday activities • discuss health • give and take instructions • identify parts of the body	Hispanic influence in the United States Jobs Health Parts of the body Doctor's office	No me siento bien El cuerpo En el médico	Otras construcciones reflexivas Repaso rápido: las preposiciones Los verbos después de las preposiciones
A leer	Estrategia para leer: *drawing on background information* La vida de un atleta profesional			
A escribir	Estrategia para escribir: *organizing information chronologically*			

Algo más	Conexión cultural	Oportunidades	Estrategia	Para ti
Expresiones adicionales Más sobre el comparativo y el superlativo	El mundo y la tecnología La contaminación ambiental	Aprender ofreciendo servicios a otros *(Service learning)*		¿Inglés o español? En los Apéndices Más para hablar del tiempo Proverbios y dichos: El que persevera alcanza. *Ir a*
¿Qué te interesa? Expresiones afirmativas y negativas	Los periódicos en los países de habla hispana	El periódico de la escuela		*Acabar de* Más quehaceres en la casa
Todos los días El artículo definido con verbos reflexivos El pretérito de los verbos reflexivos	Lugares en los Estados Unidos con nombres en español ¿Qué es la comida?	El español en tu comunidad	Para aprender mejor: *comparing to English*	Hablando del pelo Proverbios y dichos: Vísteme despacio que tengo prisa. Otras palabras y expresiones
¿Qué oyes en el consultorio del médico?; ¿Qué puedes contestar? Más sobre los verbos reflexivos Verbos similares	Aquí se habla español	¿Qué valor hay en ser bilingüe?		La palabra *pescar* Más palabras del cuerpo ¿Doctor?

Capítulo	Communicative Functions	Topics	Readings	Idioma
Capítulo 3 **¡Vamos a la ciudad!** Lección 5 Lección 6	• ask for and give directions • identify places in the city • discuss what is sold in specific stores • tell someone what to do • order from a menu in a restaurant • advise and suggest • discuss whom and what people know • talk about everyday activities • tell others what not to do • identify parts of a car • advise others in writing	Mexico Places in the city Directions Specialty stores Restaurants Food Mexico Directions Everyday activities Parts of a car City signs	En la ciudad ¿Qué te gustaría ordenar? En el barrio Las Lomas En casa de Pablo ¡Qué coches! Las señales de tráfico	El mandato afirmativo informal El mandato afirmativo formal y el mandato plural El mandato con *nosotros/as* Los verbos *conocer* y *saber* El mandato negativo
A leer	Estrategia para leer: *using format clues to predict meaning* ¡Conozca México!			
A escribir	Estrategia para escribir: *appealing to your reader's sense*			
Capítulo 4 **¡Qué divertido!** Lección 7 Lección 8	• seek and provide personal information • describe in the past • talk about activities at a special event • identify animals • express quantities • provide background information about the past • indicate past intentions • discuss nationality • add emphasis to a description • recognize and express size • state possession • identify sounds that animals make	El Salvador Amusement park Zoo Animals Nationalities Honduras Circus Animals Farm	Un día en el parque de atracciones Una visita al jardín zoológico El Gran Circo de las Estrellas ¿Qué pasó en la finca? Lo que los animales dicen	El imperfecto de los verbos regulares El imperfecto de los verbos *ser, ir* y *ver* Repaso rápido: *Ser* vs. *estar* *¡Buenísimo/a!* Repaso rápido: *-ito* e *-ita* Los adjetivos y su posición Los adjetivos posesivos: formas largas
A leer	Estrategia para leer: *guessing meaning from context* ¡El gran circo de los Hermanos Suárez!			
A escribir	Estrategia para escribir: *writing a cinquain poem*			

Algo más	Conexión cultural	Oportunidades	Estrategia	Para ti
Las tiendas de la ciudad Los cambios ortográficos	México Las comidas tradicionales		Para aprender mejor: *using the ending* -ería	Más tiendas de la ciudad Proverbios y dichos: Haz el bien y no mires a quien. Más palabras
Los puntos cardinales Verbos como *conocer* Más sobre el mandato negativo	México hoy	Pedir ayuda		Más palabras para el coche
Los usos del imperfecto ¿Qué es América? ¿Los nombres de animales o de personas? Las nacionalidades	El Salvador	El Salvador	Para hablar mejor: *using the expression* más de	Más animales Los monos
Lo que los animales hacen Los pronombres posesivos *Lo* con adjetivos/adverbios ¡Qué vaca tan grande!	Honduras			Los adjetivos como sustantivos Proverbios y dichos: Perro que ladra no muerde.

Algo más	Conexión cultural	Oportunidades	Estrategia	Para ti
Hay, había o *hubo*	Cuba: El Caribe a todo sol El sistema métrico	El menú		El pretérito de *conocer* Más comida en el supermercado Los grados centígrados Más palabras en el menú
El progresivo: un poco más *Lo*: un poco más	El Caribe	Viajando al Caribe		Expresiones adicionales Más palabras en la joyería Proverbios y dichos: A buen hambre no hay pan duro.

El subjuntivo con mandatos
   indirectos
 La familia: un poco más
 Más sobre el subjuntivo
   con mandatos indirectos
 Verbos de causa sin el
   subjuntivo
	Bolivia			Los quehaceres
				 Palabras de cariño
				 La arquitectura hispana

Otros verbos de emoción
 El subjuntivo con
   expresiones impersonales
	Los países bolivarianos	Carreras que usan
		   el español
			Para leer mejor: *observing
			 contextual cues*
				Proverbios y dichos: Más
				   vale tarde que nunca.
				 Otros aparatos de la casa

Capítulo	Communicative Functions	Topics	Readings	Idioma
Capítulo 7 **Las noticias** Lección 13	• express events in the past • talk about the news • discuss what has happened • discuss a television broadcast • talk about everyday activities • describe people and objects • write about what someone has done • identify sections of newspapers and magazines	Uruguay News Television programs Everyday activities	Las noticias Las noticias (continuación) En la televisión En la televisión (continuación)	El pretérito perfecto y el participio
Lección 14	• relate two events in the past • discuss a radio broadcast • talk about soccer • add emphasis to a description • express wishes	Paraguay Newspapers News Radio Soccer	En el periódico Las noticias se escuchan por Radio Ñandutí El fútbol	El pretérito pluscuamperfecto Repaso rápido: la voz pasiva La voz pasiva: un poco más
A leer	Estrategia para leer: *distinguishing the main theme from the supporting information* Ayuda para las víctimas del terremoto			
A escribir	Estrategia para escribir: *modeling a style of writing*			
Capítulo 8 **Las vacaciones** Lección 15	• seek and provide personal information • plan vacations • talk about the future • express emotion • talk about everyday activities • express uncertainty or probability • make travel and lodging arrangements	Spain Vacations Travel agency Food	Las próximas vacaciones Las próximas vacaciones (continuación) Las reservaciones En la agencia de viajes	Repaso rápido: el futuro con *ir a* El futuro El futuro de los verbos irregulares
Lección 16	• identify people and items associated with travel • state wishes and preferences • talk about schedules • use the twenty-four-hour clock • express logical conclusions • write about hopes and dreams	Spain Travel Airport Twenty-four-hour clock schedules Hotels	En el mostrador de la aerolínea Bienvenidos a su vuelo 108 En taxi al hotel En la recepción del hotel	El condicional
A leer	Estrategia para leer: *utilizing a combination of reading strategies* Lázaro cuenta su vida y de quién fue hijo			
A escribir	Estrategia para escribir: *arranging an itinerary in chronological order*			

Algo más	Conexión cultural	Oportunidades	Estrategia	Para ti
Para hablar de las noticias Participios irregulares El pretérito perfecto: los verbos reflexivos El participio pasivo como adjetivo	El Uruguay	El español y la televisión		Más sobre las noticias Proverbios y dichos: A buen entendedor pocas palabras bastan.
¿Qué hay en los periódicos y en las revistas? Para hablar del fútbol	Paraguay	Los periódicos en español	Para hablar mejor: *applying prefixes*	Más palabras de los periódicos
El futuro de probabilidad El futuro: los verbos reflexivos	La tortilla española	En la agencia de viajes		La corrida de toros Otras palabras y expresiones
La hora de veinticuatro horas El condicional de los verbos irregulares ¿Dónde nos alojamos? El condicional de probabilidad	España La diversidad cultural española	En el aeropuerto Los hoteles		Proverbios y dichos: ¡No dejes para mañana lo que puedes hacer hoy! ¿A qué hora?

Algo más	Conexión cultural	Oportunidades	Estrategia	Para ti
Más sobre los empleos	Nuestros sueños para el planeta	Las carreras Ayudando a solucionar los problemas del mundo		Más empleos
¿Adónde te gustaría viajar?; Algunos países del mundo	El mundo		Para hablar mejor: *using body language*	Proverbios y dichos: Soñar no cuesta nada. Más países del mundo
	E-mail, la aplicación más popular del mundo	Amigos en el cyberespacio	Para hablar mejor: *usando proverbios y dichos*	Proverbios y dichos: Lo que bien se aprende nunca se olvida.
	¿Dónde puedo seguir estudiando?	Sin límites Estudiando en un país de habla hispana		Quisiera ¡Ojo!

INTRODUCTION

Somos así LISTOS was created to make teaching and learning in the 21st century an enjoyable and rewarding experience. The emergence of information-based technologies such as the Internet and World Wide Web has rocked the world, much as space travel did in the 1960s. The resulting global economy has engendered new standards. The international marketplace now requires a workforce with a wider range of competencies and knowledge. In addition, skills and abilities that are being sought shift quickly, requiring today's student to acquire a global mind-set of continuous self-development in order to compete and excel.

Personal responsibility for career development has been just one of many changes that has taken place in language education in recent years. Students also must acquire a different set of communicative skills and a broader understanding of how to use technology. The increased emphasis on teamwork and interpersonal skills now requires that students demonstrate competence in the area of intercultural communication with its concomitant underlying requirement of an appreciation for different cultures.

Somos así LISTOS is designed to support and advance the vision described by the writers of the national standards, blending the five Cs of communication, cultures, connections, comparisons and communities with pedagogically sound content, fun activities and an ongoing discussion of the wealth of opportunities available to students. The series provides a map for learning that empowers students to learn to speak, read, write and comprehend spoken Spanish, and to do so in a culturally authentic manner. Varied dialogs and readings (such as collages, letters, recipes, signs and articles from magazines and newspapers) on diverse topics will stimulate students to look beyond the classroom at real life in the Spanish-speaking world. Clear and comprehensive explanations about grammar guide students to understand and use Spanish with increasing accuracy. Activities are both creative and communication-oriented, allowing students to use Spanish in meaningful, everyday circumstances. In addition, the textbook provides a visual context for learning through abundant text-related photographs and illustrations.

The accompanying components of the series, which are described in this front section, have been carefully designed and written to provide instructors with an effective, flexible and manageable program for teaching students to communicate in Spanish. Whether an instructor prefers additional writing or listening practice, videos or some other means of addressing student needs, materials for tailoring lesson plans are available to reinforce, recycle and expand upon the textbook content, thus allowing the teacher to decide which components and activities to use on a day-to-day basis.

As we begin the new millennium, *Somos así LISTOS* offers exciting opportunities to address the multiple intelligences, workplace readiness skills, critical thinking, creative problem solving and the ability to work cooperatively with others in the world community. The series' textbooks and extensive ancillaries offer teachers and students alike a comprehensive step-by-step instructional program that interrelates and presents culture, grammar and vocabulary in a communicative manner, thus enabling students to understand and use authentic Spanish.

Perhaps the greatest challenge that educators face today is the need to reach a large number of students, each with individual interests and learning styles. A comprehensive, flexible instructional program allows educators and students to meet the challenge together. With *Somos así,* students will enjoy using Spanish while becoming familiar with the culture of the many Spanish-speaking parts of the world.

PHILOSOPHY AND GOALS

Somos así LISTOS is a reflection of extensive research and the efforts of many dedicated professionals. Several important developments in language teaching and learning influenced the writing and design of the series. Many of the guiding principles and motivating forces in the creation of both the textbook and the supplemental materials are outlined in the following pages.

NATIONAL STANDARDS

When the *Goals 2000: Educate America Act* provided funding for improving education in 1994, a K-12 Student Standards Task Force was formed to establish content standards in foreign language education. The National Standards in Foreign Language Education Project brought together a wide array of educators, organizations and interested individuals to discuss and establish a new national framework of standards for language education in the United States. The resulting document, titled *Standards for Foreign Language Learning: Preparing for the 21st Century,* provides a bold vision and a powerful framework for understanding language learning that will help shape instruction and assessment for years to come.

Specifically, the National Standards for Foreign Language Learning identify and describe eleven content standards that correspond to the organizing principle of five interconnected Cs: **Communication, Cultures, Connections, Comparisons** and **Communities.** The eleven standards follow:

COMMUNICATION

Communicate in Languages Other Than English

Standard 1.1: Students engage in conversations, provide and obtain information, express feelings and emotions and exchange opinions.

Standard 1.2: Students understand and interpret written and spoken language on a variety of topics.

Standard 1.3: Students present information, concepts and ideas to an audience of listeners or readers on a variety of topics.

CULTURES

Gain Knowledge and Understanding of Other Cultures

Standard 2.1: Students demonstrate an understanding of the relationship between the practices and perspectives of the culture studied.

Standard 2.2: Students demonstrate an understanding of the relationship between the products and perspectives of the culture studied.

CONNECTIONS

Connect with Other Disciplines and Acquire Information

Standard 3.1: Students reinforce and further their knowledge of other disciplines through the foreign language.

Standard 3.2: Students acquire information and recognize the distinctive viewpoints that are only available through the foreign language and its cultures.

COMPARISONS

Develop Insight into the Nature of Language and Culture

> **Standard 4.1:** Students demonstrate understanding of the nature of language through comparisons of the language studied and their own.
>
> **Standard 4.2:** Students demonstrate understanding of the concept of culture through comparisons of the cultures studied and their own.

COMMUNITIES

Participate in Multilingual Communities at Home and around the World

> **Standard 5.1:** Students use the language both within and beyond the school setting.
>
> **Standard 5.2:** Students show evidence of becoming lifelong learners by using the language for personal enjoyment and enrichment.

Note: This list of goals and standards has been cross-referenced in the lower left- and right-hand corners of the pages of *Somos así LISTOS,* using the numbering system as it appears in the standards, e.g., **C1.1** stands for **Standard 1.1:** Students engage in conversations, provide and obtain information, express feelings and emotions and exchange opinions.

CROSS-CURRICULAR LEARNING

As detailed in the National Standards for Foreign Language Learning, the foreign language classroom provides a powerful avenue for connecting language study with other academic disciplines. Such connections serve to make language learning interesting and meaningful via relevant topics and a wide variety of resources for obtaining and sharing information. Students can identify and enjoy the real-life application of their language learning as they relate the study of Spanish to geography, history, mathematics, art, literature, music, social studies and science.

Somos así offers a wealth of activities for connecting Spanish with other disciplines. To this end, the margins of the ATE provide cross-curricular activities titled "Connections," and the student textbook includes cross-curricular activities titled *Cruzando fronteras*

SERVICE LEARNING/MENTOR PROGRAMS

Service learning and mentor programs are two ways students can make connections with the community. Service learning consists of volunteering time in order to learn about an organization, gain experience and make a positive contribution. A mentor is a person with considerable experience who offers to work with and help a student learn about an organization. Students benefit by gaining firsthand experience while learning about themselves and an organization in their community. The organization and the community benefit by saving resources, generating new ideas and involving future leaders.

Teachers in schools wishing to promote service learning or a mentor program should encourage students to talk with their parents about their desire to volunteer in the community. For example, students may wish to volunteer with an organization where they are able to use Spanish with customers, such as at a library, in a museum or in organizing a *Cinco de mayo* festival. Brainstorm with the class other ways students might participate in community service or find a mentor.

The following are some suggestions teachers can offer students who have decided they would like to explore service learning or a mentor program for school-aged volunteers: 1) Explore the available options; 2) select a job that is interesting; 3) talk with people in a few of the organizations being considered in order to gather information; 4) be realistic about the time available to volunteer; 5) consider whether transportation to the site will be a problem; 6) visit the site and talk with members of the organization to answer concerns; 7) make a decision.

CAREER AWARENESS/WORKPLACE READINESS SKILLS

In today's global economy, it is increasingly important to develop an awareness of the impact that learning a language can have on young people's lives. If in the past the desire to enter college was sufficient reason for taking a second language, today there are more opportunities than ever to apply language skills on the job and elsewhere outside the classroom. For example, international pacts such as NAFTA have made it more important than ever for graduates from high schools and colleges in the United States to improve their language skills in order to compete in the international marketplace.

To address employment opportunities, *Somos así* uses a strand approach to career awareness. While students are learning the skills and knowledge that are necessary for them to become proficient in Spanish, they also discuss and learn how Spanish can be beneficial when looking for employment.

Career awareness is integrated regularly through the *Oportunidades* section of *Somos así*. Activities for introducing students to this significant benefit of learning another language can be found in both the Pupil's Edition of the book and in the margins of the ATE.

PARENTAL INVOLVEMENT

Parental involvement in the classroom is an ongoing concern in education and a point of increased discussion. The benefits of having students, parents, teachers and the community involved in supporting one another are undeniable. Teachers can do many things to encourage parents to have a larger role in their child's classroom education. The margins of the *Somos así LISTOS* ATE and accompanying ancillaries offer suggestions for encouraging parental support for classroom learning, strengthening communication and improving parental awareness of how a student is doing and how the student can do better.

SPANISH FOR SPANISH-SPEAKING STUDENTS

Given the growing Hispanic population in the United States, it is more and more common to find native speakers or heritage speakers of Spanish in the Spanish classroom. Such students may present special needs as they formally study a language that they have acquired or experienced to varying degrees. In order to address this reality, the *Somos así LISTOS* ATE includes a variety of suggestions and activities for teaching Spanish to Spanish-speaking students.

THE MULTIPLE INTELLIGENCES

Many factors affect learning. For years classroom teachers have recognized that intelligence, social environment and motivation all need to be considered when teaching. In addition, not all students learn the same way. Students display diverse learning styles that need to be addressed in different ways in order to maximize individual potential.

Research on how the brain works has provided language teachers with additional information about intelligence and the learning process. One study that has drawn wide attention is Howard Gardner's theory of multiple intelligences. The theory poses the notion that people have different abilities in many different areas of thought and learning, and that these varying abilities affect people's interests and how quickly they assimilate new information and skills. This pluralistic view of intelligence suggests that all people possess at least eight different intelligences, which operate in varying degrees depending upon each person's individual profile. The eight intelligences identified by Gardner include the following: bodily-kinesthetic, interpersonal, intrapersonal, linguistic, logical-mathematical, musical, naturalist and spatial (visual) intelligence.

The general characteristics associated with each of these intelligences are described below along with suggested instructional strategies:

- **Bodily-Kinesthetic:** Students who are athletic may demonstrate bodily-kinesthetic intelligence. They learn best by doing what they enjoy, and want to learn through movement and touch and express their thoughts with body movement. They are good with hands-on activities such as sewing, woodworking, dancing, athletics and crafts.

  Teaching Strategies:
  Perform a dance from a Spanish-speaking country
  Act out a part from a play
  Build a housing structure that is reminiscent of one that appears in the textbook
  Perform an activity as directed by a classmate or the teacher (TPR)
  Create artwork that represents some aspect of the Spanish-speaking world

- **Interpersonal:** Students with interpersonal intelligence are natural leaders. They communicate well, empathize with others and often know what someone is thinking or feeling without having to hear the person speak.

  Teaching Strategies:
  Role-play a vendor making a sale
  Lead a discussion
  Debate an issue
  Organize and direct a poll
  Negotiate a settlement

- **Intrapersonal:** People with intrapersonal intelligence may appear to be shy. They are self-motivated and are very aware of their own thoughts and feelings about a given subject.

  Teaching Strategies:
  Write answers to questions about personal life
  Prepare a written plan for a career path
  Determine the pros and cons of an issue
  Create a list of favorite activities
  Write a poem expressing feelings

- **Linguistic:** This type of student demonstrates a strong appreciation for and fascination with words and language. People who display linguistic intelligence enjoy writing, reading, word searches, crossword puzzles and storytelling.

  Teaching Strategies:
  Tell a story
  Summarize a magazine or newspaper article
  Write a poem

Discuss the meaning of a song
Write to a key pal on the Internet
Do a crossword puzzle

- **Logical-Mathematical:** This type of student likes establishing patterns and categorizing words and symbols. Students with logical-mathematical intelligence enjoy mathematics, experiments and games that involve strategy or rational thought.

  Teaching Strategies:
  Calculate the temperature in degrees Fahrenheit and in Celsius equivalents
  Figure changes in ingredient amounts to double or triple a recipe
  Write an analysis of an event
  List the reasons why something happened
  Tabulate the total cost of a shopping trip

- **Musical:** These students can be observed singing or tapping out a tune on a desk or other nearby object. They are discriminating listeners who can hear a song once and then are able to play or sing the tune. Students who demonstrate musical intelligence catch what is said the first time, whereas others around them may need to hear the same thing repeated a number of times.

  Teaching Strategies:
  Write a song
  Listen to and describe a musical piece
  Perform a song
  Identify musical styles of several musicians from the Spanish-speaking world
  Prepare a comparison of the music of two or more musicians

- **Naturalist:** Students with naturalist intelligence might have a special ability to observe, understand and apply learning to the natural environment. For example, students with naturalist intelligence may collect data about the environmental conditions for a particular place and instinctively know what crop would grow best there.

  Teaching Strategies:
  Draw or photograph and then present to the class an object found in nature
  Collect and categorize objects from the natural world
  Do research and present findings about a wildlife protection project
  Keep a notebook of observations of nature
  Go on a nature hike or field trip

- **Spatial (Visual):** These students think in pictures and can conceptualize well. They often like complicated puzzles and may be seen drawing a picture, doodling, constructing something from the objects that surround them or daydreaming. They are able to imagine how something would look from a verbal description.

  Teaching Strategies:
  Write a summary comparing the artistic styles of two paintings
  Draw the ideal house
  Design a building
  Identify a shape based upon a classmate's description
  Prepare a Cad-Cam design

Benefits of Using the Multiple Intelligences—Since every individual is different, we all possess different combinations of intelligences. The multiple intelligences theory reflects a way of thinking about people that not only allows for similarities, but also differences. It fosters inclusion, increases opportunities for enrichment, builds self-esteem and develops respect for individuals and the gifts they bring to the classroom. Teachers who employ multiple intelligences research create an environment that allows all students to learn through their strengths and to share their expertise with others.

Gardner's research has provided us with a wealth of information and a clear message: Educational designers should develop teaching materials that motivate a greater number of students and, in turn, teachers should select teaching and assessment materials that are geared to maximizing student potential. To this end, *Somos así* has been created to address the benefits of teaching to students' multiple intelligences.

SCANS

Research by the Secretary of Labor's Commission on Achieving Necessary Skills (SCANS) indicates that productivity and good jobs depend on people who can put knowledge to work. The SCANS report identifies eight areas considered essential preparation for all students, whether going directly to work or planning a future education.

The SCANS report was used as a basis for curricular development of *Somos así.* To aid teachers in understanding and applying the educational focus provided by SCANS, the eight areas considered essential preparation for all students (as presented in the SCANS report for *Goals 2000*) are summarized here. The eight areas consist of a three-part foundation of skills and qualities, which in conjunction with five competencies, are an integral part of the education of every young person in America today.

THREE-PART FOUNDATION

BASIC SKILLS: Reads, writes, performs arithmetic and mathematical operations, listens and speaks

  A.   *Reading*—locates, understands, and interprets written information in prose and in documents such as manuals, graphs and schedules

  B.   *Writing*—communicates thoughts, ideas, information and messages in writing; and creates documents such as letters, directions, manuals, reports, graphs and flow charts

  C.   *Arithmetic/Mathematics*—performs basic computations and approaches practical problems by choosing appropriately from a variety of mathematical techniques

  D.   *Listening*—receives, attends to, interprets, and responds to verbal messages and other cues

  E.   *Speaking*—organizes ideas and communicates orally

THINKING SKILLS: Thinks creatively, makes decisions, solves problems, visualizes, knows how to learn and reasons

  A.   *Creative Thinking*—generates new ideas

  B.   *Decision Making*—specifies goals and constraints, generates alternatives, considers risks, and evaluates and chooses the best alternative

  C.   *Problem Solving*—recognizes problems and devises and implements plan of action

  D.   *Seeing Things in the Mind's Eye*—organizes and processes symbols, pictures, graphs, objects and other information

E. *Knowing How to Learn*—uses efficient learning techniques to acquire and apply new knowledge and skills

F. *Reasoning*—discovers a rule or principle underlying the relationship between two or more objects and applies it when solving the problem

PERSONAL QUALITIES: Displays responsibility, self-esteem, sociability, self-management, and integrity and honesty

A. *Responsibility*—exerts a high level of effort and perseveres toward goal attainment

B. *Self-Esteem*—believes in own self-worth and maintains a positive view of self

C. *Sociability*—demonstrates understanding, friendliness, adaptability, empathy and politeness in group settings

D. *Self-Management*—assesses self accurately, sets personal goals, monitors progress and exhibits self-control

E. *Integrity/Honesty*—chooses ethical courses of action

FIVE COMPETENCIES

RESOURCES: Identifies, organizes, plans and allocates resources

A. *Time*—selects goal-relevant activities, ranks them, allocates time and prepares and follows schedules

B. *Money*—uses or prepares budgets, makes forecasts, keeps records and makes adjustments to meet objectives

C. *Material and Facilities*—acquires, stores, allocates, and uses materials or space efficiently

D. *Human Resources*—assesses skills and distributes work accordingly, evaluates performance and provides feedback

INTERPERSONAL: Works with others

A. *Participates as Member of a Team*—contributes to group effort

B. *Teaches Others New Skills*

C. *Serves Clients/Customers*—works to satisfy customers' expectations

D. *Exercises Leadership*—communicates ideas to justify position, persuades and convinces others, responsibly challenges existing procedures and policies

E. *Negotiates*—works toward agreements involving exchange of resources, resolves divergent interests

INFORMATION: Acquires and uses information

A. *Acquires and Evaluates Information*

B. *Organizes and Maintains Information*

C. *Interprets and Communicates Information*

D. *Uses Computers to Process Information*

SYSTEMS: Understands complex inter-relationships

A. *Understands Systems*—knows how social, organizational, and technological systems work and operates effectively with them

B. *Monitors and Corrects Performance*—distinguishes trends, predicts impacts on system operations, diagnoses deviations in systems' performance and corrects malfunctions

C. *Improves or Designs Systems*—suggests modifications to existing systems and develops new or alternative systems to improve performance

TECHNOLOGY: Works with a variety of technologies

A. *Selects Technology*—chooses procedures, tools or equipment including computers and related technologies

B. *Applies Technology to Task*—understands overall intent and proper procedures for setup and operation of equipment

C. *Maintains and Troubleshoots Equipment*—prevents, identifies , and solves problems with equipment, including computers and other technologies

COMPONENTS

Somos así consists of a comprehensive three-level Spanish language program. Components of the second-level textbook, *Somos así LISTOS,* include the following:

- Textbook
- Annotated Teacher's Edition (ATE)
- ATE on CD-ROM
- Workbook
- Workbook Teacher's Edition
- Teacher's Resource Kit, or TRK (includes Quizzes/Listening Activities, Quizzes/Written Activities, Listening Activities Audiocassettes/Audio CDs, Quizzes/Activities Teacher's Edition, Workbook Teacher's Edition, Audiocassette/Audio CD Program Manual)
- Testing/Assessment Program (includes Test Booklet, Test Booklet Teacher's Edition, Oral Proficiency Evaluation Manual, Portfolio Assessment and Listening Comprehension Audiocassettes/Audio CDs)
- Test Generator
- Video Program (includes manual)
- Audiocassette/Audio CD Program (includes manual)
- Overhead Transparencies
- Internet Activities

TEXTBOOK

The completely revised and rewritten textbook contains ten chapters, an appendices section, a Spanish-English and English-Spanish glossary and an index. Chapters are arranged thematically and consist of two numbered lessons followed by a Spanish reading selection *(A leer)*, a writing activity *(A escribir)* and a review checklist. The first and last chapters offer special benefits to teachers and students alike:

- Chapter 1 offers a review and reintroduction to Spanish and the Spanish-speaking world. It is easy to teach, lively, communication-oriented and proficiency-based, encouraging students to use Spanish in enjoyable, authentic contexts while building confidence and positive motivation from the very first days of class.
- Chapter 10 is intended as a review chapter. It contains no new vocabulary or grammar. Teachers may select from the interesting and varied review activities and readings the chapter offers, or skip the chapter if they choose.

Vocabulary has been limited and grammatical structures are constantly reintroduced in order to further improve student mastery of the material. New active words and expressions appear in context within numbered lessons only and in various formats: Some words and expressions appear in bold within dialogs and other expository material, and students must discern their meaning from the context in which they are used; more difficult vocabulary appears in bold and is glossed for students; some words and expressions appear in illustrations; and yet other active vocabulary terms may appear in the section *Algo más,* which is explained in the section descriptions that follow. Regardless of where vocabulary occurs, all words and expressions that students must learn are listed for reference at the end of each lesson.

The choice of which words to illustrate, define or leave for students to discern the meaning of is obviously a subjective one. Every attempt has been made to present new vocabulary in the most pedagogically sound and most appropriate manner to encourage students to think in Spanish, but without making the presentation of new material too difficult for students to enjoy. Words that your students are unable to recognize can be found in the vocabulary glossary that appears at the end of the book.

Each chapter of *Somos así LISTOS* opens with two photo-illustrated pages that visually prepare students for the general cultural and communicative content of the corresponding thematic lessons that follow. Functional objectives and communicative skills that reflect the skills students will be learning in the chapter are also listed here.

Lessons begin with a contextualized presentation of new and review vocabulary and grammatical structures. These may take the form of a dialog, narrative or other expository material, accompanied by colorful photographs or illustrations depicting everyday life in the Spanish-speaking world. The people in these scenes represent a cross section of age groups, although the emphasis is on young adults. Be sure to encourage students to read for content and not to rely on glossed vocabulary to translate word for word. In the ATE the audiocassette/compact disc icons indicate which of these items have been recorded as part of the Audiocassette/Audio CD Program.

Following the introductory material are explanatory notes, activities and readings that provide the background necessary to enable students to act and react competently using Spanish in real-life situations. These sections interrelate culture, vocabulary and grammar while inducing students to practice and thus internalize new concepts and skills doing activities that are carefully graded from manipulative (focusing on receptive skills) to personalized and communicative (with an emphasis on productive skills). The main textbook sections include the following:

- *Oportunidades*—Randomly occurring, these notes provide thoughtful insights on the subject of what doors open to students because they know Spanish and are familiar with the culture of the Spanish-speaking world. The section addresses issues such as careers, travel, college and lifelong study in the field of languages and cultures.

- *¿Qué comprendiste?*—Expository content such as dialogs and readings are followed by related questions in the section *¿Qué comprendiste?,* which is designed to check student comprehension. The questions, completions, matching, true/false and other comprehension-based formats of the *¿Qué comprendiste?* review the vocabulary, grammatical structures and cultural themes of the preceding narrative and serve as an introduction to the thematic content of the lesson.

- *Charlando*—This section offers open-ended and personalized questions that provide a realistic and natural motivation for students to write and talk about a variety of everyday topics. Questions in the *Charlando* require thoughtful responses that employ a general understanding of the content of the previous dialog, reading, realia selection and so on, as well as a specific understanding of Spanish vocabulary, culture and grammar. Students are encouraged to apply what they have just learned while simultaneously drawing upon their own experiences to analyze situations and offer personal opinions about the content. The section is intended to help students internalize new vocabulary and structures while concentrating on the communicative aspect of offering opinions and solving problems in Spanish.

- *Conexión cultural*—The *Conexión cultural* expands the cultural theme of the lesson. These commentaries are intended to heighten the students' appreciation of the target-language culture and to provide insight into daily aspects of Hispanic life. Additional ideas for expanding upon the core content may be suggested in accompanying annotations. The section often presents the opportunity for creative out-of-class projects. Topics covered in the *Conexión cultural* include history, geography, nonlinguistic behavioral cues, the arts and cultural details from different countries in keeping with the authors' goals of providing relevant information that students will find both appealing and useful.

- *Cruzando fronteras*—These cross-curricular activities (highlighted in blue in the student textbook) require students to apply Spanish skills while focusing attention on another curricular area (i.e., mathematics, geography, music, art, history, culinary arts, etc.).

- *Algo más*—The section *Algo más* provides linguistic notes and additional required vocabulary that expands upon the lesson content.

- *Idioma*—The *Idioma* section summarizes the main grammatical points of *Somos así LISTOS*. The clear and concise explanations (often with the addition of colorful charts for easy reference) are followed by activities that practice key grammatical structures and vocabulary in a functional context. These activities have been developed to allow for maximum flexibility, since they may be done orally or in writing. For easy identification, activities with answers that have been recorded on audiocassette/audio CD are indicated in the ATE by an audiocassette/audio CD icon.

- *Estrategia*—This section offers strategies for learning. Included are pointers on such topics as how to be successful learning Spanish vocabulary and how students can improve their skills in reading, speaking, writing and so forth.

- *Para ti*—The *Para ti* section provides notes and asides to help students feel successful, much like the side notes for teachers in the ATE. The contents of the *Para ti* are not required, and thus are not addressed in the accompanying Testing/Assessment Program.

- *¡La práctica hace al maestro!*—The section *¡La práctica hace al maestro!* (Practice makes perfect!) combines both speaking skills (in the section *Comunicación*) and the ability to use technology (in the section *Conexión con la tecnología*) and provides students with personalized opportunities to develop these abilities using the functions, grammar, vocabulary and cultural content of the preceding lesson. Many of the activities involve cooperative learning in which students must work in pairs or small groups in order to accomplish a task. The *Conexión con la tecnología* encourages students to develop the ability to apply technology to communicating in Spanish.

  Consider using some of the activities from the *¡La práctica hace al maestro!* as a quiz or for prescriptive testing in order to determine deficiencies in student understanding of the lesson content, thus allowing time for remediation before end-of-lesson testing/assessment. The section also may be used to replace part of, or along with the

Testing/Assessment Program, for end-of-lesson summative testing/assessment.

- *Autoevaluación*—This section offers students an opportunity to review some of the more important content of a lesson before having to take the lesson test/assessment. Although the section is titled *Autoevaluación*, answers were not included in the student textbook so teachers can choose how and when they wish to offer feedback about student answers.

- *Vocabulario*—Active vocabulary is introduced in context throughout the lesson in various formats, such as illustrations, dialogs, readings, collages and so forth, and is listed for reference at the end of every lesson. The list of active vocabulary includes only the words that students must be able to speak, read, write and understand. Words from the list are included in other components in this Spanish program (i.e., workbook, testing/assessment, videos, etc.).

  Remind students how to use the *Vocabulario,* which is intended as a tool to help students distinguish new words and expressions in a lesson: Students may review the list, quizzing themselves to see how many words and expressions they recall. The list also helps teachers hold students accountable for their own learning. English transla tions are not given here since the list is for reference only. English equivalents may be found in the vocabulary glossary.

- *A leer*—The *A leer* provides a formal opportunity for students to improve their ability to read in Spanish. Note for students that it is not essential to understand every word in order to read in Spanish. Equivalents for most unknown words have been provided to help students enjoy the content of the readings without having to look up important but passive vocabulary. All highlighted vocabulary is intended to expand student receptive skills and is not intended for active use at this point.

  The presentation of the *A leer* section is similar to that of the dialogs. There are a variety of possible techniques. You should choose the one that is the most effective for you. It is a good idea to warm students to the particular content of a reading by completing the section titled *Preparación.* Begin by having students read the *Estrategia* that appears before every *A leer* in *Somos así.* Then have students complete the warm-up activities as preparation for starting to read. Next, play the first paragraph of the recording of the *A leer,* using the corresponding audiocassette/audio CD from the Audiocassette/Audio CD Program. As an alternative, you may choose to read the first paragraph yourself. Read the paragraph again with students following along in the book. Give students a moment to look over the paragraph silently on their own and ask questions. Ask for a student to volunteer to read the paragraph aloud. Continue in this way for subsequent paragraphs.

- *A escribir*—The *A escribir* consists of a writing strategy, which is followed by a theme that encourages students to apply what they learned in the chapter. The *A escribir* provides a formal opportunity for students to improve their Spanish skills by providing developmental practice in creative writing.

- *Repaso*—The section *Repaso* consists of a checkoff list of the communicative functions for a chapter (see page 39), along with additional objectives that students can use as a self-check to evaluate their own progress.

ANNOTATED TEACHER'S EDITION (ATE)

The Annotated Teacher's Edition, or ATE, offers an in-depth and complete guide to using *Somos así LISTOS* and accompanying ancillaries, including the following:

Front Section—The front section of this ATE contains a scope and sequence chart for each chapter; the philosophy and goals of the series; a description of all components; an introductory explanation of the methodology used in the textbook; a section on using the Internet and computers; a sample step-by-step approach model lesson plan for teaching *Capítulo 3;* a comprehensive section offering suggestions for additional activities and games; and a list of useful classroom expressions.

Margin Icons—Located at the top of left- and right-hand pages of the ATE, the following icons denote additional ancillaries that support the contents of a given page.

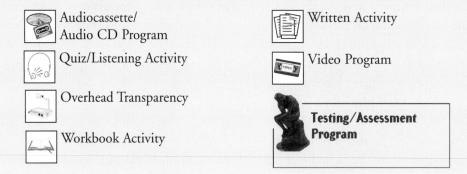

Audiocassette/
Audio CD Program

Written Activity

Quiz/Listening Activity

Video Program

Overhead Transparency

Testing/Assessment
Program

Workbook Activity

Margin Activity Answers—The ATE consists of an annotated full-size version of the student textbook containing answers to close-ended activities in the left- and right-hand ATE margins.

Margin Notes—The ATE left- and right-hand margins also provide additional teaching suggestions and cultural notes that expand on the lesson content.

Margin Activities—A fourth element in the left- and right-hand margins on many ATE pages consists of additional activities that will help teachers better address individual learner needs. Included in these helpful activities are the following:

- **Communities** addresses connections with the community and provides students with suggestions on how they may participate in service learning.

- **Connections** indicates an activity that is cross-curricular.

- **Cooperative Learning** denotes an activity that is intended to offer students additional opportunities for cooperative learning beyond the textbook content. The activities require students to cooperate with one another in pairs or small groups using Spanish for authentic communication.

- **Critical Listening** activities are provided to promote listening comprehension. They require that students learn not only the sounds of the language, but also the meaning behind them. Ultimately, students will reach a point where they are able to correct their own errors.

- **Critical Thinking** activities are designed to enhance the higher order thinking skills of the student. Educators have increasingly encouraged emphasis on critical thinking. The authors and publisher consider critical thinking an essential part of the total academic development of students. For this reason we have included a thorough and systematic program of higher order thinking skill activities that address comprehension, application, analysis, synthesis and evaluation, along with many of the skills involved in each of these categories.

- **Expansion** activities offer enrichment. They allow students' personal interests and creativity to take over, empowering them to discover a wealth of information about the language and the cultures studied in *Somos así LISTOS*.

- **Language through Action** indicates activities that require students to combine Spanish speaking or listening skills with physical movement. The suggestions enhance student learning while relieving the teacher of the time required to prepare such activities.

- **Multiple Intelligences** indicates an activity is appropriate for dealing with individual student intelligences in the eight areas identified by brain research, including linguistic intelligence, logical-mathematical intelligence, spatial intelligence, bodily-kinesthetic intelligence, musical intelligence, interpersonal intelligence, intrapersonal intelligence and natural intelligence.

- **Prereading Strategy** activities include questions pertaining to the subject matter being taught that prepare students for what is ahead. They might be asked to look at an illustration and guess what the theme of that dialog is. Students are encouraged to guess the meaning of words they do not recognize, and are taught that they need not understand all the vocabulary to discern the main theme of an activity.

- **Pronunciation** activities allow students to practice pronunciation. Have students break down sentences into individual words and sounds and then have them use the words you have practiced in meaningful sentences. In addition, after presenting the initial dialog (or other expository material) and accompanying activities, have students work in pairs practicing the activity and focusing on the new pronunciation point. Circulate and assist with pronunciation and intonation.

- **Spanish for Spanish Speakers** activities are designed especially for students who are native speakers of Spanish. These activities allow students to examine their cultural heritage and to increase their Spanish skills.

- **Students with Special Needs** activities have been provided for students who need extra help. These activities allow students to practice areas they are having difficulty with in new and interesting ways, and facilitate the ability to acquire new skills and improve comprehension of various subject matters.

- **Technology** activities require students to use the Internet, e-mail or another medium in combination with their knowledge of Spanish to complete an activity.

- **TPR** denotes activities that involve Total Physical Response (TPR). Whereas many teachers have used TPR either extensively or on a limited basis, these activities often require an extra effort on the part of the teacher to prepare for and use TPR in the classroom.

Margin Codes—The lower left- and right-hand margins of the ATE provide a correlation to the national standards. The coding system uses the letter **C** for **Communication, Cultures, Connections, Comparisons** and **Communities.** The number that follows the **C** indicates which standard is covered on the given page. (See the section in the ATE Introduction "Philosophy and Goals" for specific numbers that were used for cross-referencing the national standards to the content of the pages of *Somos así LISTOS.*)

ATE ON CD-ROM

The complete Annotated Teacher's Edition is available on CD-ROM. This handy version of the ATE offers a convenient alternative medium for displaying the wealth of information contained in the ATE, along with pop-up versions of ancillaries indicated by icons in the ATE margins.

WORKBOOK

The Workbook provides reinforcement and expansion of the functions, grammar, readings and cultural points presented in the textbook. Basic skills are augmented through interesting written activities that emphasize both communication and structural production. The Workbook includes a variety of practice in several different formats to maintain student interest. The level of difficulty of the activities ranges from rote practice of vocabulary and basic activities emphasizing receptive skills in reading, to more challenging, open-ended items that emphasize productive skills in writing.

The Workbook presents students with an assortment of activities: reading passages taken from actual newspaper and magazine articles with follow-up questions and exercises; sentence completion; guided compositions; matching activities; practice in geography in mapping activities; word searches; crossword puzzles; and more. Reading, writing, grammar, vocabulary and culture are all given thorough attention in the Workbook.

WORKBOOK TEACHER'S EDITION

The Teacher's Edition of the Workbook includes an overprint that provides answers to close-ended activities in the Workbook.

TEACHER'S RESOURCE KIT

The Teacher's Resource Kit (TRK) is a handy and practical tool that organizes supplemental teaching materials and keeps them at teachers' fingertips. Items contained in the TRK include the following:

- **Quizzes/Listening Activities (on duplicating masters)**—These quizzes/activities may be used either for testing student listening comprehension practice over isolated content before giving the lesson test, or for offering students additional listening practice using the vocabulary and structures of the corresponding textbook lessons. They are to be used with the Listening Comprehension Audiocassettes/Audio CDs, which have been recorded by native speakers and which can be found in the Teacher's Resource Kit.

- **Quizzes/Written Activities (on duplicating masters)**—These quizzes/activities have been provided to increase the convenience and flexibility of teaching with *Somos así LISTOS*. The coordinated quizzes/activities are sequenced with the content of the textbook and may be used either for testing reading and writing skills or as written practice that you may choose to use for enrichment or as a text-related reinforcement of the content of the textbook.

- **Quizzes/Listening Activities Audiocassettes/Audio CDs**—These audiocassettes/audio CDs are contained in the Teacher's Resource Kit. They offer the recorded version of the Listening Activities.

- **Quizzes/Activities Teacher's Edition**—This booklet contains the answers to the additional Quizzes/Listening Activities and Quizzes/Written Activities, as well as a transcript of the recorded version of the Quizzes/Listening Activities.

- **Workbook Teacher's Edition**—The Workbook Teacher's Edition provides an overprint of the answers for the Workbook activities.

- **Audiocassette/Audio CD Program Manual**—The Audiocassette/Audio CD Program Manual provides a script of the recorded material along with the questions and answers included after the expository material for each lesson.

TESTING/ASSESSMENT PROGRAM

A proficiency-based curriculum requires a way of testing/assessing an individual's attainment of stated objectives. The *Somos así LISTOS* Testing/Assessment Program offers comprehensive means for evaluating student performance. The basic program consists of the following components:

- **Test Booklet**—The Test Booklet contains tests for each of the lessons. In addition, there are comprehensive midyear and year-end tests. Student answer sheets for listening comprehension tests and for written tests are included in the Test Booklet.

- **Test Booklet Teacher's Edition**—The Test Booklet Teacher's Edition includes the text of the material recorded on audiocassettes/audio CDs for the listening comprehension tests, along with an answer key to these tests. It also includes an answer key for the written tests.

- **Listening Comprehension Audiocassettes/Audio CDs**—The *Somos así LISTOS* Testing/Assessment Program also contains listening comprehension tests. The material for testing listening skills is included on audiocassettes/audio CDs. Student answer sheets are provided in the Test Booklet.

- **Oral Proficiency Evaluation Manual**—The Testing/Assessment Program can be expanded by evaluating student oral proficiency using the activities included in the Oral Proficiency Evaluation Manual. The materials for the evaluation of oral proficiency consist of three parts or types of activities: communicative interaction between teacher and student, paired activities calling for student-to-student interaction and illustrations with related questions that students must answer orally in Spanish.

- **Portfolio Assessment**—Intended as an alternative to traditional evaluation tools, and as an extension of the Testing/Assessment Program and the Oral Proficiency Evaluation Manual, the Portfolio Assessment includes a variety of activities for monitoring student progress.

TEST GENERATOR

The Test Generator allows teachers to select and modify sections from the existing Testing/Assessment Program in order to generate tests that reflect what they have taught.

VIDEO PROGRAM

The Video Program was filmed in various parts of the Spanish-speaking world using professional actors. The ten episodes, which vary in length from five to eight minutes per chapter, consist of a continuous story line that is carefully coordinated with each chapter of the textbook. The videos depict native speakers in authentic situations that reflect the content of *Somos así LISTOS,* thus allowing students an opportunity to see and hear Spanish used in a carefully controlled but realistic and enjoyable context. The few unknown words that are used can be easily understood by the context (motion, action, gestures, background) of the material presented. An accompanying Video Program Manual contains a transcript of the videos, notes about using the program and numerous activities on duplicating masters.

AUDIOCASSETTE/AUDIO CD PROGRAM

The Audiocassette/Audio CD Program is an integral part of *Somos así* since it exposes students to a variety of native speakers' voices with different accents, pronunciation and intonation. The following material has been recorded on audiocassettes/audio CDs and is indicated in this ATE by a cassette/compact disc icon: dialogs, readings and other expository material for listening practice and for dictation; *¿Qué comprendiste?* questions and answers; *Charlando* questions; selected activities related to the *Idioma;* and questions and answers in the end-of-chapter section titled *A leer.*

Although the text for many of these activities is contained in the textbook itself, a separate manual provides an exact transcript of the recordings, many of which have been modified so they are more appropriate for speaking and listening practice.

OVERHEAD TRANSPARENCIES

A set of sixty-four full-color overhead transparencies, coordinated with the ten chapters, is also available. The transparencies can be used for a variety of activities, including the rote review of discreet vocabulary and grammar, mapping activities of the countries students are studying and comprehensive scenes that encourage creative self-expression. Use the transparencies to review and expand the cultural content, grammar, vocabulary and functions that are presented in the textbook and to encourage students to apply their knowledge of Spanish and the Spanish-speaking world.

INTERNET ACTIVITIES

The *Somos así LISTOS* Internet Activities Web site features activities that are correlated to each chapter of the textbook. Students practice using their language skills as they explore authentic realia in Spanish and read up-to-the-minute information about Hispanic culture. They combine the use of technology and Spanish in real-life situations as they develop their Internet research skills.

METHODOLOGY

Language teaching has undergone many changes during the 20th century. The Grammar-Translation Approach was popular for the first half of the century. In 1958, space exploration and improved technology were factors that gave rise to the Audio-Lingual Approach for teaching languages. In the mid-1980s, the publication of the American Council on the Teaching of Foreign Languages (ACTFL) proficiency guidelines focused attention on proficiency in the four basic skills and increased cultural awareness. The *Standards for Foreign Language Learning: Preparing for the 21st Century* describe a new framework of communicative modes that will take language instruction forward. It is exciting to see the increased emphasis on improving students' abilities to use authentic language in more realistic situations.

Somos así LISTOS is a direct result of these initiatives and the concern to meet the growing need for a foreign language educational program that will serve teachers and students in the 21st century. As teachers deal with an ever more diverse student population, there is a greater demand for increased variety and for teaching materials that address a multiplicity of learning styles, interests and needs. There also is an ever-increasing need for educational materials that enable students to function using Spanish in a wider spectrum of situations. By introducing content and by putting students in real-life contexts, this proficiency-based program creates a positive learning spiral. The activities are structured to allow students to apply immediately what they have learned. The resulting feeling of accomplishment leads them back into the textbook where they acquire more skills and information and are then able to draw upon their own personal experience to communicate information, ideas and opinions in authentic Spanish.

The following methods and techniques reflect the approaches to language instruction found in *Somos así LISTOS* and will help maximize the use and benefits of both the textbook and supplementary materials.

Recognition vs. Production—It is natural that students are able to recognize new vocabulary and structures before they are able to produce them. The transition from recognition to production may cause errors, but this is an accepted occurrence in the language-learning process. *Somos así* presents new material and then recycles it in a number of different ways in each of the components of the program, thus aiding the transition from recognition to active use of the language. Some activities dealing with structures, for example, promote recognition more than production (especially in the activities immediately after concept presentation). Students will feel more comfortable at the productive levels of communication as they continue in the program and use materials that practice previously learned material.

Augmenting the textbook with the Audiocassette/Audio CD Program, Video Program, Workbook, Teacher's Resource Kit and other supplemental materials will prove helpful in developing the ability to produce Spanish in communicative contexts. In particular, paired and group activities, cooperative activities and the section *¡La práctica hace al maestro!* are intended to stimulate additional production on a communicative level; students may be encouraged further toward production of the target language if they are afforded extra time to prepare these activities. As a general homework assignment, have students scan each lesson for new vocabulary, grammar and the cultural theme. This will facilitate recognition and, hence, production.

Language through Action and Total Physical Response (TPR)—While many educators recognize the importance of the senses (sight, hearing and so forth) in the language-learning process, the use of physical action in response to verbal stimuli has not been thoroughly exploited as an asset to language acquisition. One excellent technique used in second-language learning is Total Physical Response (TPR). Since TPR involves a student's physical memory, it is an aid in internalizing new concepts or vocabulary and in recycling those already learned. In a typical TPR activity, the instructor first prepares a series of commands that are contextualized and based on material to be presented or practiced in class. The instructor then models and gives a series of commands to the students, who demonstrate comprehension by dramatizing the physical actions corresponding to the language they hear.

Many teachers have experimented successfully with TPR but found that it requires an extra effort to prepare activities. For this reason, *Somos así LISTOS* includes numerous TPR activities to help the instructor incorporate this effective learning technique on a regular basis. The activities will enhance student learning while relieving the teacher of the time required to prepare such materials.

Critical Listening—Perhaps the most basic of all language-learning skills is listening, first for recognition of sounds that convey meaning and later for error correction in pronunciation, structure and so on. Students can develop this skill by listening to the teacher, to the *Somos así* audio and video components, to themselves and to each other. (At this level, students are able to use critical listening skills such as identification of structures and self-correction.)

Critical Thinking—It is essential to develop higher-order thinking skills in our students if they are to succeed in school and later in life, therefore an abundance of activities in *Somos así LISTOS* practice critical thinking. The cognitive abilities and their associated critical thinking skills included in the program are: knowledge acquisition (locate, define, describe, identify, list, match, name, recite, recall); comprehension (explain, summarize, rewrite, convert, translate, rearrange, paraphrase); analysis (compare and contrast, interpret, outline, subdivide, order, categorize, distinguish); evaluation (criticize, conclude, support, justify); synthesis (associate, combine, compile, rearrange, plan, generalize); and application (compose, create, design, produce).

Pair Work, Group Work and Cooperative Learning—In *Somos así* every effort has been made to encourage students to express themselves creatively after adequate practice. An additional aim of the program is to broaden that horizon by taking the language-learning process out of the classroom context and into the world. One way to accomplish this goal is to decrease textbook dependency and remove the idea that Spanish is a language that exists only in a static environment. To this end, the abundant illustrations and photographs in *Somos así LISTOS* reveal Spanish in real-life situations and each *Capítulo* is organized around a theme that students may apply to their own lives.

Similarly, pair work and group work help encourage the internalization and application of the target language by providing students with authentic communicative settings with real communicative goals. Numerous activities in every lesson are structured for role-playing or for open-ended practice in pairs, while others are designed for groups of no more than five members. Such activities encourage proficiency in a number of ways: more students can use the target language for a longer period of time than is possible in a teacher-centered activity;

students have a feeling of accomplishment in this atmosphere since they are interacting successfully; the teacher is able to meet the needs of more students by circulating among students and correcting or directing where necessary; and most importantly, learning with one's peers results in a nonthreatening learning atmosphere, since the object is communication and not mere correction of errors.

To many, cooperative learning involves merely having students work in pairs or small groups practicing material that has been presented in class. This procedure is certainly one aspect of cooperative learning and it is extensively utilized in *Somos así LISTOS.* However, cooperative learning at a more significant level requires that one student relate or share information with another student (or with a small group or even the entire class) that the student has acquired through personal experience or from recent study. Numerous activities in the textbook and in the ATE address this issue and provide teachers with extensive opportunities to include this type of practice as a normal part of the curriculum.

Portfolio Assessment—Second-language instruction has undergone significant changes in recent years. This metamorphosis reflects the increased importance of using language in an ever wider range of communicative contexts. In keeping with this trend, once common practices such as grammar translation and substitution drills have been supplanted by teaching methods that place greater stress on much broader goals, such as communicative proficiency in the four basic language skills, increased cultural awareness and creative problem solving. In turn, it has become apparent that traditional written exams are not sufficient and that more elaborate tools for assessing and documenting student performance are required to reflect these philosophical and pedagogical changes. One such tool is the portfolio: a systematic, organized method of collecting data that offers teachers the ability to develop a composite chronicle of a student's performance in today's proficiency-based curriculum.

Portfolios that document student growth and performance consist of a variety of items that reflect the dynamic experience of studying a foreign language. Such items may include:
* videotaped skits that show students conversing and using appropriate paralinguistic behavior
* an oral interview
* results from listening comprehension activities
* a recorded audiocassette/audio CD containing a sample of the student speaking Spanish
* compositions about selected themes in Spanish
* art projects (such as a poster) depicting some aspect of a Spanish-speaking part of the world
* a written diary
* peer or self-assessment

Portfolios can also serve as a means of improving articulation between levels of a program of instruction for helping students to see personal growth, and for determining the efficacy of a student's progress toward specific language goals within a specific curriculum.

Somos así LISTOS offers a number of opportunities to collect and record student work for portfolios. Activities in the textbook, the Testing/Assessment Program and the Video Program (and its accompanying manual) provide opportunities for documenting listening comprehension. Paired, group and cooperative learning activities in the textbook, as well as

TE33

questions taken from the section *Charlando*, are ideal for developing a portfolio with speaking samples. In addition to content questions that appear after the reading selections in the textbook, the Workbook and Teacher's Resource Kit activities provide samples of a student's reading comprehension. Portfolio writing samples can be taken from a number of different activities that occur throughout the program, including the section titled *A escribir*. Finally, activities to document a student's cultural awareness abound in the textbook and in ancillaries such as the Workbook and TRK.

The portfolio is a multifaceted assessment tool. It encourages growth, monitors and records progress and promotes individual self-expression. In addition, portfolios improve data collection and add the dimensions of time and space to the evaluation process, thus enabling teachers to test what they teach. An integrated portfolio system is more than a collection of work, however, since assessment is inseparable from the curriculum. Portfolios can actually provide a structural reconfiguration of summative evaluation methods for formative monitoring of student growth in the areas of skills, knowledge, cultural awareness and attitudes. The *Somos así LISTOS* portfolio assessment materials have been developed to address these issues. Teachers should use the suggested activities as a guide for developing their own tasks in order to monitor student progress and to improve student learning in accordance with the local curriculum and desired course outcomes.

These are but a few of the language-teaching approaches and methods incorporated into *Somos así LISTOS*. A glance at the textbook, the Annotated Teacher's Edition and the wide array of ancillaries for each level of the program will indicate that every effort has been made to provide a comprehensive and effective program of instruction based on up-to-date language-teaching methods and techniques.

Note: In *Somos así LISTOS,* instructions for activities are given in the *tú* form. By requiring that students use the *Usted* form of verbs with you and by suggesting that they use *tú* with their peers, you will increase students' exposure to both the formal and informal forms. *Vosotros* is introduced as a word, but students are not required to actively use the *vosotros* form of verbs. If you decide to teach using *vosotros,* modify activities to include practice with both *ustedes* and *vosotros.*

USING THE INTERNET: SUGGESTIONS AND IDEAS

Because of its widespread and instantaneous nature, the Internet holds much promise as a tool for teaching and learning in our nation's schools. In foreign language instruction, the Internet can help teachers meet the challenge of providing students with materials that are up to date and culturally authentic. With scarcely a trace of lag time, information from the target culture can be accessed and utilized in a variety of ways. For example, in a lesson about Madrid you and your students can:

- access city and subway maps
- view photographs of major landmarks of the city
- obtain news from Spanish newspapers
- visit on-line museums and see famous paintings
- obtain tourist information
- participate in discussion groups on Spanish culture and civilization
- access current weather information and forecasts
- exchange e-mail correspondence

By using the Internet as a supplement to *Somos así*, you also will create exciting opportunities for teachers and students that simply did not previously exist. The activities you will be able to do with your students are limited only by your imagination. What follows are sample activities and a variety of supplementary materials that illustrate the vast possibilities of the Internet.

E-MAIL PROJECTS

Consider arranging e-mail (electronic mail) exchanges to complement the use of *Somos así*. For example, have students participate in a number of exchanges that allow them to apply the concepts, vocabulary and cultural information studied in a given lesson. Sample exchanges include:

1. After studying weather, students write a weather report for their state/city and send it to a collaborating class or key pals. They also inquire about the weather and climate in the region where the collaborating class is located or where the key pals live. Subsequent exchanges could deal with:
    - sports and activities related to different seasons of the year
    - outdoor activities that the students enjoy
    - the school calendar and how the local climate may affect it
    - weather conditions in different Spanish-speaking countries

2. In relation to a food unit, students develop an e-mail exchange sharing the following information about their culture/family:
    - a typical meal schedule at home
    - a traditional meal schedule in their country
    - a menu for a typical day and a special celebration

3. After learning about leisure-time activities, students share with their collaborating partners what they do on a typical weekend or during vacation.

4. Students write a description of a well-known individual in sports, music, politics or movies. Send the description to your collaborating classroom with an invitation to guess who the person is.

5. Students conduct surveys in order to explore cultural comparisons. Topics of interest include:
    - the level of independence given to adolescents
    - the access and admittance to discotheques
    - the legal age for driving
    - the number of students who work
    - the minimum wages paid to adolescents who work

6. Examples of other possible exchange topics for lower-level students include school, daily life, family, friends, travel, sports, clothing and popular music. More complex topics of interest may include current events, politics, household rules, curfew and educational aspirations.

A MODEL UNIT FOR AN E-MAIL EXCHANGE: MI FAMILIA

This unit allows students to share information about their families and learn about the families of their classmates and key pal friends. While the unit is appropriate for learners at various levels of proficiency, teacher expectations and student performance will vary accordingly.

ACADEMIC GOALS

Students will be able to:

1. Use vocabulary related to the family.
2. Use possessive and descriptive adjectives and appropriate verb structures.

SOCIAL GOALS

Students will be able to:

1. Share information about their families.
2. Find out about the families of their key pals.
3. Recognize similarities and differences between families in the United States and families in cultures where Spanish is spoken.

PROCEDURES FOR A BEGINNING LANGUAGE CLASS

1. Teach and practice specific vocabulary pertaining to family members. For example, the teacher shows pictures and begins by describing his/her real family or a fictitious family in terms of members, roles, names, ages, likes, dislikes and professions. After the description, the teacher checks to see what students are able to remember. This questioning gives students a chance to use basic expressions. Other practice follows.
2. The next step is for students to describe their own families. As preparation for class, students prepare notes about their families (real or imagined) according to the specifications given in advance.
3. After further practice in class, students write descriptions of their families. Possible information includes:
   * family name
   * number of people in the family (family makeup)
   * description of each member of the family (name, age, occupation, personality)
   * family activities and traditions
4. Once the documents are completed and revised using peer editing and student/teacher editing, the descriptions are sent to collaborating classes abroad and students wait for the responses from their key pals describing their families. When the correspondence is received, students compare families in both cultures and find similarities and/or differences.

LOCATING COLLABORATING COLLEAGUES AND KEY PALS

Possible collaborating partners can be found in the same school building or district, in another city or around the world. Here are some strategies for locating key pals:

* Place ads in professional organization newsletters and journals.
* Attend professional conferences and technology workshops in order to network with colleagues.
* Search the Net for Collaborating Classrooms, Cultural Classroom Connection or Exchanges.
* Post messages in Spanish newsgroups.
* Subscribe to listservs pertinent to Spanish or countries where Spanish is spoken.

- Check related WWW home pages or Internet Guides (a listing is included in the WWW section).
- Write to American Schools Abroad (a listing may be obtained from the Department of State in Washington, D.C.).

TIPS FOR USING E-MAIL

- Have students avoid tabs and foreign characters unless both groups are using compatible software.
- Write your introductory remarks for the collaborating teacher and then paste the letters of each student/group after your message. Separate each individual message using a line, a symbol or a character. This will make it easier for your collaborating teacher to separate the messages and distribute them to his/her students.
- Specify the font and size to use on a project.
- Clearly specify project checkpoints and deadlines.
- Give clear directions for minimum length and content to be included.
- Explain how you will evaluate a project.
- Explain how and where to save a project, including how to name it before saving.

E-MAIL PROJECTS: OVERCOMING E-MAIL LIMITATIONS

Hardware limitations: When a limited number of computers are available, students can work in pairs or individual students can access computers at other times (for example, while others in class are working on an assignment, after completing a test, or during lunch periods, study hall, or before and after school). Assignments made well in advance of their due date will allow students to choose their work time and produce final products of high quality.

Time limitations: When computer lab time is limited, schedule individuals or groups in such a way that at least one exchange can be completed per quarter, trimester or semester.

Access limitations: If you have one computer with access to the Internet using a modem and a single phone line, get the project ready and transmit it when the line is available. A designated student can be the mailer. If there is no access in school, a teacher or student who has access to the Internet or other commercial service can be the mailer for the group. This will ensure that the outgoing and incoming mail will involve one e-mail account.

Students with computers at home also can do their work on their own time. Today's computers and word processors allow texts created on one platform to be read by computers on another. For example, using Microsoft Word 5.0 or later, you can open just about any type of text file. In addition, there are software programs such as **Access PC** and **PC Exchange** that allow the exchange of files written using computers of different platforms.

SURFING THE INTERNET

To search the Internet—or surf the Net, as it is commonly called—use the latest version available of the Web browser of your choice. Web browsers provide a harmonious interface for text and graphics.

You have different options for search engines. Some search titles or headers of documents, others search the documents themselves, and still others search indexes or directories. To locate a desired resource, do a Net Search. The following are some popular and powerful search engines:

(**Note:** The following addresses may change at any time. Visit sites to verify they are active before using them in class.)

Lycos	http://www.lycos.com/
Yahoo	http://www.yahoo.com/
Yahoo Español	http://espanol.yahoo.com/
Webcrawler	http://www.webcrawler.com/
InfoSeek	http://infoseek.go.com/
AltaVista	http://www.altavista.com/

Sample Web Sites and Activities
City Net is a World Wide Web home page that archives or stores information about cities around the world. This resource can be particularly helpful in creating cultural units because the information found at this site might include historical events, transportation, maps, pictures and sites of interest (including schedules, addresses and telephone numbers). Once the user has clicked on the city of choice, user-friendly graphics and text that support these categories are accessible by clicking on highlighted areas on the screen.

Virtual City Tour
Take students on a virtual city tour using the City Net home page. First, determine your objectives for this activity: What will your students learn and gain from this work? What cultural awareness and knowledge will be developed? What language skills will be practiced? How will students practice critical thinking and problem solving? How will they further process their conclusions and share what they have learned with others?

Procedures for initiating a virtual city tour
1. Open the Web browser and go to City Net by keying *http://www.city.net*.
2. Select the desired city, either through the alphabetical listing of the grouping or by continent.
3. Locate a map of the city; identify specific sites of interest that your students might "visit" during a virtual tour of the city.
4. If the city has a subway system, find a subway map or a subway planner (this option allows you to enter specific points of origin and destination and receive a routing path and duration of the trip).

Three alternatives for the virtual city tour
A. In small groups, students visit a city that you have chosen. Each group of four students visits a different section of the city. Their task is to determine what sites to visit during a 48-hour period on a given budget. For example, one group may visit museums while another group may travel to a park to see sculptures and attend a particular event that has been planned by the Office of Tourism.
B. Each group visits different cities in the same country. When each group has processed the information, a class presentation is given to highlight the attractions of the various

cities. As a further activity, the information is shared with the class in written form and each group designs a quiz pertaining to its city.

C. In small groups, students design a travel brochure for their city that includes information on some of the following topics:
- entertainment opportunities
- shopping and dining
- brief historical facts about the city
- airlines serving the city
- special events
- weather
- typical cuisine

When doing Web-based activities, keep in mind specific language-practice targeting tasks; vocabulary and structures will vary according to level. For example, you may ask beginning students to identify numbers, times, days of the week, cognates and vocabulary related to daily life activities. In turn, more advanced students may be asked to imagine and narrate a special experience from their virtual city tour.

CULTURAL/HISTORICAL STUDIES AND PRESENTATIONS

Students work in small groups to become "experts" on a country where Spanish is spoken. The objectives of the activity are to help students get acquainted with the history, geography, economics, climate, attractions and current events of the target country and culture. Working in groups, students search for information pertaining to a country that is assigned or chosen. Once the search is completed, the groups summarize the information and present it to the class. The information can be found by doing searches using the browser of your choice:

Lycos	http://www.lycos.com/
Yahoo	http://www.yahoo.com/
Yahoo Español	http://espanol.yahoo.com/
Webcrawler	http://www.webcrawler.com/
InfoSeek	http://infoseek.go.com/
AltaVista	http://www.altavista.com/

The search starts by selecting the name of the country and browsing through the results. Another place to search is Electronic Embassies. Once a site with relevant information is found, it may be possible to do searches within that site. The information found may differ from country to country, but suggest to students information that should be included in their presentation. Such content may include:
- geography
- maps
- history
- climate/weather
- major cities and tourist attractions
- popular events
- airlines serving the country
- economic activity and exchange rate
- major newspapers (include a copy of recent headlines)

In addition to sharing their findings with the class, students should submit to you the following:

1. A printed copy of the material found and used for the presentation.
2. A copy of the final presentation.
3. A reading/listening comprehension quiz prepared by the group and based on the presentation. The quiz should also include a key with the correct responses. In order to complete the quiz, the class either does a listening comprehension exercise while the presentation is given or a reading comprehension exercise at the conclusion of the presentation when printed copies of the presentation are made available to the class.

VIRTUAL MUSEUMS AND WORKS OF ART

When teaching colors, emotions, description and even history, works of art may be downloaded to teach, illustrate and reinforce a variety of concepts. For example, students may be assigned to search for works of given artists to illustrate the concepts and/or vocabulary studied in class. When considering the works of given artists, students also may be assigned to give a presentation on a given artist that includes the following:

- Country of origin
- Biographical information about the artist
- Period of time in history when the artist lived
- Style of work
- Colors and shapes used by the artist
- Feelings and aspects of life represented by his/her work
- Examples of his/her work

WEATHER REPORTS

Weather reports, including satellite and infrared maps, are available through the Net. When teaching about weather and weather conditions, have students access weather reports from Spanish-speaking countries and regions of the United States. The students then use this information to give weather reports or forecasts to the class. If used throughout the year, such information can be included in different units of the curriculum to link weather conditions with seasons, clothing, sports, outdoor activities and other topics.

As with other projects, the level of the students will be a factor in assigning specific tasks and content. For example, beginning students may give simple weather reports, including temperatures and precipitation, while advanced students may explore the relationship between weather conditions and lifestyle, tourism and the economy.

NEWSPAPERS AND MAGAZINES

The many newspapers and magazines on the World Wide Web are another outstanding resource for students and teachers in the language classroom. One possible activity involves these steps:

1. Locate appropriate newspapers and magazines from countries where Spanish is spoken.
2. Familiarize yourself with their format and content.
3. Divide the class into small groups.
4. Assign a content area to each member of the group or allow the students to choose an area of interest. Possible areas include international news, national news, politics, entertainment, weather and sports.

5. According to the number of groups in class, the level and the time allotted, develop a schedule that allows each group to present news from its newspaper or magazine on a regular basis. For example, a different group can do this at the beginning of class every day or you may want to identify a day of the week for several group presentations. However done, the activity should not take more than 5-10 minutes per group. It is helpful to give specific instructions about the content, length and depth you expect of the presentations and to post a calendar of presentation dates in the classroom.

A variation of this activity is to divide students in small groups and have them summarize the school newspaper in the target language. Once done, the newspaper and/or summary are sent via e-mail to a collaborating class with which you have contact. Such an exchange of news can become an activity to be done throughout the year.

ASSESSING INTERNET PROJECTS

The following guidelines may be helpful when developing and assessing e-mail and Web projects:

1. Give specific instructions in writing about the project.
2. Post a calendar or time line corresponding to the project.
3. Remember that some flexibility may be necessary if students encounter difficulties (for example, with access or printing).
4. Develop clear criteria for grading and evaluation. Depending on the project, factors to consider may include:
   - meeting guidelines for content, length, etc.
   - completing the project on time
   - the quality of the presentation and/or written assignment(s)
   - printed copies of the materials used from the Net
   - participation

Being specific about how student work will be evaluated will make it easier to assign a grade that will require very little explanation at the end of the project. Again, it is a good idea to post the requirements, the deadlines and the evaluation procedures of the project.

TEACHER RESOURCES ON THE WORLD WIDE WEB

Search engines:

Lycos	http://www.lycos.com/
Yahoo	http://www.yahoo.com/
Yahoo Español	http://espanol.yahoo.com/
Webcrawler	http://www.webcrawler.com/
InfoSeek	http://www.infoseek.com/
AltaVista	http://www.altavista.com/

Newspapers and magazines:

http://www.mediainfo.com/emediajs/html
http://libraries.mit.edu/humanities/flnews
http://yahoo.com/news/
http://cnnespanol.com/

City/country information:

City Guide	http://cityguide.lycos.com/
City Guide	http://www.city.net./
Lycos Travel	http://www.lycos.com/travel/
Embassies	http://www.embassy.org
Ciudad virtual	http://www.laeff.esa.es/~crb/

Weather:

http://cnnespanol.com/tiempo/
http://cnn.com/weather/
http://www.intellicast.com/search/

Culture/education:

Latin American Studies Virtual Library	http://www.lanic.utexas.edu/las.html
Classroom Connections for E-mail Partners	http://www.stolaf.edu/network/iecc/
Food (Spanish recipes)	http://www.recetario.com/recetari

Foreign language professionals:

FLTEACH is designed to facilitate networking and dialog among foreign language professionals. To subscribe to the list, send the following message: SUBSCRIBE FLTEACH first name last name to: LISTSERV@UBVM.CC.BUFFALO.EDU.

Other sites of interest:

- Virtual Tourist
  http://www.vtourist.com/
- TravNet Menu
  http://www.sky.net/~eric/
- Electronic Embassy
  http://www.embassy/org/
- The Tecla Home Page from Birkbeck College London (Teaching resources)
  http://www.bbk.ac.uk/Departments/SpanishTecla/
- Intercultural E-Mail Connections
  http://www.stolaf.edu/network/iecc/
- WorldWide Classroom
  http://www.worldwide.edu/index.html
- Web 66: International WWW School Registry
  http://web66.coled.umn.edu/schools.html
- The World Wide Web Virtual Library: Latin American Studies
  http://www.lanic.utexas.edu/las.html
- La Cocina Mexicana (Mexican cooking)
  http://mexico.udg.mx/Cocina/
- Spanish for Travelers
  http://www.travlang.com/
- Univision (television station from Miami)
  http://www.univision.net/startpage.html

GLOSSARY OF TECHNOLOGY TERMS

account	e-mail address of a subscriber
application	software program
BBs	same as Newsgroup
bookmark	a marked location on the Web for easier future access
download	to copy a file from a distant location
e-mail	electronic message sent via the network
e-mail address	electronic mailbox on the server
gopher	program that allows one to locate files and servers on the Net
home page	location on the World Wide Web
http	hypertext transfer protocol
Internet	a worldwide network of interconnected computers
key pal	an electronic "pen pal"
Listserv	electronic mailing list; need to subscribe and unsubscribe
modem	electronic device that connects computers via phone lines
Newsgroup	an electronic bulletin board where messages are posted and read
PC	personal computer (commonly referred to as an IBM-compatible)
platform	Macintosh or IBM (IBM-compatible computers)
server	a host computer providing access to the Internet
slip connection	access to the Internet via a phone line and modem
surfing the Net	searching the network for files/information
URL	universal resource locator
user	a subscriber
Web browser	software that allows you to locate files on the Net
www	World Wide Web; a web of computers interconnected

POLICY AND GUIDELINES FOR COMPUTER USERS

It is essential to create an acceptable use policy before giving students access to the Internet. The development of such a policy should include all interested parties, such as school administrators, faculty, students, parents and members of the school board. The following policy and guidelines are an example created by one school. They were presented as a "working document" to allow for revisions and additions.

ACCEPTABLE USE POLICY

The major school rules provide the basic structure for the Acceptable Use Policy. All users must be honest and respectful of others. Their work must meet the school-wide guidelines for appropriate language and subject matter; it must not violate the school's harassment policy.

All use of the computers must be within the law. Copyright laws must be observed. Only software licensed to the school may be put on school computers. Copyrighted files cannot be sent or received from school computers without permission of the copyright owner.

Users may access only their own files and programs or those intended for their use. Access to another's account or files without authorization is forbidden. Students must not attempt to access administrative files.

Those using the school's computing resources for classroom use and school-related projects have priority for use of the lab and/or equipment. School facilities may not be used for commercial purposes. Individuals are expected to use the resources thoughtfully. Use that unnecessarily slows access to the network, wastes storage or wastes other resources is forbidden.

Students who violate these policies will be subject to the school's disciplinary process. Students will be asked to read and sign a list of additional guidelines before being given access to the school's computers. These guidelines will give students additional information about safe and respectful use of the school's computing resources.

GUIDELINES FOR COMPUTER USERS

Permission to use the school's computing facilities is granted to those who agree to use it thoughtfully and respectfully. The following guidelines should be followed:

All use of school's computers must be consistent with the school's Acceptable Use Policy. You are expected to be honest, respect others, follow the school's rules about harassment and do nothing illegal.

Access only those files for which you are authorized. You must not use or attempt to use any other person's files or programs without permission. Attempting to access administrative files, even for fun, will be viewed as a serious offense.

Do not use offensive language, which includes both vulgar or insulting language and derogatory language.

Do not monopolize the use of the equipment. Users working on class-related projects have priority for the use of the facilities.

Do not give your home address or phone number over the Net. If you need to give someone an address or phone number, use the school's. If in doubt, check with a teacher.

Be a positive member of the school's computer-using community. Be helpful to those less knowledgeable than you. Avoid activities that earn some computer users their bad reputation: Do not "hack," "spam," "flame," introduce viruses and so on.

Keep the system running legally and efficiently. Get rid of unwanted programs, files, and e-mail that take up valuable storage. "Unsubscribe" from mail lists that no longer interest you. Do not use illegal software. Do not store your own personal software at school.

Student use of the Internet is limited to the computers in the student computer lab unless they are working under the supervision of a faculty member.

TEACHING SUGGESTIONS

Model Chapter (*Capítulo 3*)

Somos así LISTOS is a flexible program that allows you to cover material in the textbook and ancillaries with the degree of thoroughness suggested by student needs, time and your own personal teaching style or school resources. In general, try to vary your presentations by using as many different resources as possible in order to recombine similar material for your students' diverse learning styles. For example, the Audiocassette/Audio CD Program and the Teacher's Resource Kit offer listening comprehension practice; the Video Program provides students with an opportunity to observe native speakers using Spanish in contexts that require skills your students are learning; overhead transparencies offer visual support of spoken Spanish and can serve to practice both rote material as well as to provide situational contexts for conversations; the textbook, Workbook and TRK activities all offer additional writing practice.

Capítulo 3 (Lecciones 5, 6) has been selected as the model chapter, since it contains all elements of a typical chapter. Two models are provided: one for a 50-minute class period meeting 180 days per year, and another for a 90-minute block meeting 90 days per year. Some activities and *Conexión cultural* notes may be omitted, depending upon the needs and time limitations set by individual circumstances. The reading section titled *A leer* is optional, thus offering you additional flexibility in matching content to the needs, interests and curriculum requirements of your own particular situation.

Dialogs, other narrative material and many activities in *Somos así LISTOS* have been recorded and thus offer you additional choices about how to present or review the chapter content. For example, you may choose to have students listen to a recorded activity before going to the textbook, or you may choose instead to use the audiocassette/audio CDs as additional reinforcement after having completed the activity in the textbook. Recorded activities are indicated by an audiocassette/audio CD icon in the margins of the ATE.

In addition, the many ancillaries already discussed in this front section are available to supplement the textbook. These program components provide an abundance of textbook-related activities to provide teaching formats that will enable you to customize your teaching to the many and varied learning styles and needs of your students.

Since every teacher has his or her own approach to the subject of homework, and due to the extensive variety offered by the *Somos así LISTOS* support materials, specific homework assignments are not provided. However, suggestions for including activities from the accompanying ancillaries have been offered to give you an idea of the possible variations the teaching program offers. You should try to include an assortment of different activities, choosing some from the textbook and others from the ancillaries (such as the Workbook, the ATE, etc.).

REGULAR CLASS PERIOD (50 MINUTES)

Day 1

Textbook	Support Materials
Warm-up: Review everyday activities, commands (used in a doctor's office), foods Review test on *Lección 4* Chapter preview: Discuss chapter opener, pp. 82-83 *En la ciudad*, p. 84 Activities 1-2, p. 85 *Conexión cultural*, p. 86 Activity 3, p. 87 *Estrategia*, p. 87 *Algo más*, p. 87 Activity 4, p. 88	AC/CD: *En la ciudad* AC/CD: *México* AC/CD: Activities 1-4 Transparencies 17-19 Quizzes/Listening Activities 1-3 Workbook Activities 1-3 Quizzes/Written Activities 1-2

Day 2

Textbook	Support Materials
Warm-up: Review *Estrategia*, p. 87 Activities 5-6, p. 88-89 *Idioma*, p. 89 *Para ti: Haz el bien y no mires a quién*, p. 90 Activities 7-8, p. 90	AC/CD: Activities 5-6 Quiz/Listening Activity 4 Workbook Activities 4-6 Quizzes/Written Activities 3-4

Day 3

Textbook	Support Materials
Warm-up: Review dialog, p. 84 and affirmative informal commands, p. 89 Activities 9-12, p. 91-92	*En la ciudad*

Day 4

Textbook	Support Materials
Warm-up: Talk with students about Mexican-American foods they have eaten *¿Qué le gustaría ordenar?*, p. 93 Activity 13, p. 93 *Para ti*, p. 93 *Conexión cultural*, pp. 94-95 *Oportunidades*, p. 96 Activities 14-15, p. 96	AC/CD: *¿Qué le gustaría ordenar?* AC/CD: Activities 13-14 Workbook Activity 7 Quiz/Written Activity 5

Day 5	Textbook	Support Materials
	Warm-up: *¿Qué le gustaría ordenar?*, p. 93 *Idioma,* p. 97 Activities 16-19, pp. 98-99	AC/CD: *¿Qué le gustaría ordenar?* AC/CD: Activity 19 Quizzes/Listening Activities 5-6 Workbook Activities 8-9 Quiz/Written Activity 6

Day 6	Textbook	Support Materials
	Warm-up: Review affirmative formal commands, p. 97 *Algo más,* p. 100 Activities 20-22, pp. 100-101	AC/CD: Activities 20-21 Workbook Activity 10

Day 7	Textbook	Support Materials
	Review affirmative informal and formal commands, p. 89, 97 *Idioma,* p. 101 Activities 23-25, pp. 102-103	AC/CD: Activity 23 Quiz/Listening Activity 7 Workbook Activity 11 Quiz/Written Activity 7

Day 8	Textbook	Support Materials
	Review affirmative commands, pp. 89, 97, 101 *Autoevaluación,* p. 103 *¡La práctica hace al maestro!,* Activity A, p. 104	Workbook Activity 12

Day 9	Textbook	Support Materials
	Review for the test on *Lección 5* *¡La práctica hace al maestro!,* Activity B, p. 104	Oral Proficiency Evaluation Manual, Portfolio Assessment

Day 10	Textbook	Support Materials

	Test on *Lección 5*	Student Test Booklet, Test Booklet Teacher's Edition,
		    Listening Comprehension Audiocassette/Audio
		    CD, Oral Proficiency Evaluation Manual,
		    Portfolio Assessment

Day 11	Textbook	Support Materials
	Warm-up: Review places in the city, affirmative commands Review test on *Lección 5* *En el barrio Las Lomas*, p. 106 Activity 1, p. 106 *Algo más*, p. 107 Activity 2, p. 107 *Oportunidades*, p. 107	AC/CD: *En el barrio Las Lomas* AC/CD: Activities 1-2 Quiz/Listening Activities 1-2 Workbook Activities 1-2

Day 12	Textbook	Support Materials
	Warm-up: Review *En el barrio Las Lomas*, p. 106 *Conexión cultural*, p. 108 Activity 3, p. 109 *Idioma*, p. 110 Activities 4-6, p. 111	AC/CD: *México hoy* Quiz/Listening Activity 3 Workbook Activities 3-5 Quiz/Written Activity 1 AC/CD: Activities 5-6

Day 13	Textbook	Support Materials
	Warm-up: Review *conocer* and *saber*, p. 110 Activities 7-9, p. 112 *Algo más*, p. 113 Activities 10-11, pp. 113-114	AC/CD: Activities 9, 11 Workbook Activity 6 Quiz/Written Activity 2

Day 14	Textbook	Support Materials
	Warm-up: Review the formation of affirmative commands *En casa de Pablo*, p. 115 Activities 12-13, p. 115 *Idioma*, p. 116 Activities 14-16, pp. 116-117	AC/CD: *En casa de Pablo* AC/CD: Activities 12-13, 15-16 Quiz/Listening Activity 4 Workbook Activities 7-8 Quiz/Written Activities 3-4

Day 15	Textbook	Support Materials
	Warm-up: Review negative commands, p. 116 Activities 17-20, pp. 118-119 *Algo más*, p. 119 Activities 21-22, p. 120	AC/CD: Activity 21 Quiz/Listening Activity 5 Workbook Activity 9 Quizzes/Written Activity 5

Day 16	Textbook	Support Materials
	Warm-up: Review negative commands, pp. 116, 119 Activities 23-24, p. 121 *¡Qué coches!,* p. 122 Activities 25-27, pp. 122-123	AC/CD: *¡Qué coches!,* p. 122 AC/CD: Activities 25, 27 Quiz/Written Activity 6 Transparencies 20-21 Workbook Activities 10-11

Day 17	Textbook	Support Materials
	Warm-up: Discuss vocabulary associated with getting around in a city *Las señales de tráfico,* p. 124 Activities 28, p. 124 *¡La práctica hace al maestro!,* Activities A-B, p. 126	AC/CD: *Las señales de tráfico* AC/CD: Activity 28 Quiz/Listening Activity 6 Transparencies 22-26 Workbook Activity 12

Day 18	Textbook	Support Materials
	Warm-up: Conduct a discussion about Mexico *Estrategia,* p. 128 *¡Conozca México!,* p. 128 Activities A-B, p. 129	AC/CD: *¡Conozca México!* AC/CD: Activities A-B Quiz/Listening Activity 7 Quiz/Written Activity 7

Day 19	Textbook	Support Materials

	Warm-up: Review what students have
	   learned about Mexico
	Autoevaluación, p. 125
	Review for test on *Lección 6*
	Estrategia, p. 130
	A escribir, p. 130
		Oral Proficiency Evaluation Manual,
		   Portfolio Assessment

Day 20	Textbook	Support Materials

	Test on *Lección 6*	Student Test Booklet, Test Booklet Teacher's Edition,
		   Listening Comprehension Audiocassette/Audio
		   CD, Oral Proficiency Evaluation Manual,
		   Portfolio Assessment, Video Program
		   (Episode 3)

BLOCK SCHEDULE (90 MINUTES)

Day 1

Textbook	Support Materials
Warm-up: Review everyday activities, commands (used in a doctor's office), foods	AC/CD: *En la ciudad*
Review test on *Lección 4*	AC/CD: *México*
Chapter preview: Discuss chapter opener, pp. 82-83	AC/CD: Activities 1-6
En la ciudad, p. 84	Transparencies 17-19
Activities 1-2, p. 85	Quizzes/Listening Activities 1-4
Conexión cultural, p. 86	Workbook Activities 1-6
Activity 3, p. 87	Quizzes/Written Activities 1-4
Estrategia, p. 87	
Algo más, p. 87	
Activities 4-6, p. 88-89	
Idioma, p. 89	
Para ti: Haz el bien y no mires a quién, p. 90	
Activities 7-10, p. 90-91	

Day 2

Textbook	Support Materials
Warm-up: Review dialog, p. 84 and affirmative informal commands, p. 89	AC/CD: *¿Qué le gustaría ordenar?*
Activities 11-12, p. 92	AC/CD: Activities 13-14, 19
¿Qué le gustaría ordenar?, p. 93	Workbook Activities 7-9
Activity 13, p. 93	Quizzes/Written Activities 5-6
Para ti, p. 93	Quizzes/Listening Activities 5-6
Conexión cultural, p. 94-95	
Oportunidades, p. 96	
Activities 14-15, p. 96	
Idioma, p. 97	
Activities 16-19, p. 98-99	

Day 3

Textbook	Support Materials
Warm-up: Review affirmative formal commands, p. 97	AC/CD: Activities 20-21, 23
Algo más, p. 100	Workbook Activities 10-12
Activities 20-22, pp. 100-101	Quiz/Listening Activity 7
Idioma, p. 101	Quiz/Written Activity 7
Activities 23-25, pp. 102-103	
Autoevaluación, p. 103	
¡La práctica hace al maestro!, Activity A, p. 104	
Review for the test on *Lección 5*	

Day 4	Textbook	Support Materials
	Warm-up: Review *for test* Test on *Lección 5* *¡La práctica hace al maestro!,* Activity B, p. 104	Student Test Booklet, Test Booklet Teacher's Edition, Listening Comprehension Audiocassette/Audio CD Program, Oral Proficiency Evaluation Manual, Portfolio Assessment

Day 5	Textbook	Support Materials
	Warm-up: Review places in the city, affirmative commands Review test on *Lección 5* *En el barrio Las Lomas,* p. 106 Activity 1, p. 106 *Algo más,* p. 107 Activity 2, p. 107 *Oportunidades,* p. 107 *Conexión cultural,* p. 108 Activity 3, p. 109 *Idioma,* p. 110 Activities 4-6, p. 111 Activities 7-9, p. 112 *Algo más,* p. 113 Activity 10, p. 113	AC/CD: *En el barrio Las Lomas* AC/CD: Activities 1-2, 5-6, 9, 11 AC/CD: *México hoy* Quizzes/Listening Activities 1-3 Workbook Activities 1-6 Quizzes/Written Activities 1-2

Day 6	Textbook	Support Materials
	Warm-up: Review the formation of affirmative commands *En casa de Pablo,* p. 115 Activities 12-13, p. 115 *Idioma,* p. 116 Activities 14-16, pp. 116-117 Activities 17-20, pp. 118-119 *Algo más,* p. 119 Activities 21-22, p. 120 Activities 23-24, p. 121 *¡Qué coches!,* p. 122 Activities 25-27, pp. 122-123	AC/CD: *En casa de Pablo* AC/CD: *¡Qué coches!,* p. 122 AC/CD: Activities 12-13, 15-16, 21, 25, 27 Quizzes/Listening Activities 4-5 Workbook Activities 7-11 Quizzes/Written Activities 3-6 Transparencies 20-21

Day 7	Textbook	Support Materials
	Warm-up: Discuss vocabulary associated with getting around in a city	AC/CD: *Las señales de tráfico*
		AC/CD: *¡Conozca México!*
	Las señales de tráfico, p. 124	AC/CD: Activity 28, A-B
	Activity 28, p. 124	Quizzes/Listening Activities 6-7
	¡La práctica hace al maestro!, Activities A-B, p. 126	Transparencies 22-26
	Estrategia, p. 128	Workbook Activity 12
	¡Conozca México!, p. 128	Quizzes/Written Activity 7
	Activities A-B, p. 129	
	Autoevaluación, p. 125	
	Review for test on *Lección 6*.	

Day 8	Textbook	Support Materials
	Test on *Lección 6*	Student Test Booklet, Test Booklet Teacher's Edition,
	Estrategia, p. 130	Listening Comprehension Audiocassette/
	A escribir, p. 130	Audio CD, Oral Proficiency Evaluation Manual,
		Portfolio Assessment, Video Program (Episode 3)

Personal Notes

ADDITIONAL ACTIVITIES AND GAMES

ACTIVITIES

The activities that follow offer additional opportunities to enrich and supplement the lessons in *Somos así LISTOS*. The section provides additional support for teaching the following: dictionary skills, mapping, charting, the multiple intelligences, Total Physical Response (TPR), cooperative learning, critical thinking and so forth. Pick and choose from the activities throughout the school year as needed.

SKILL DEVELOPMENT

Dictionary: Show students the vocabulary appendices in the back of the book. Then teach some important dictionary skills by having them find the meaning of two or three new words. This activity can be used in any lesson, as often as you like.

Have students identify several infinitives in a Spanish dictionary. (The glossary at the end of the textbook can serve as the dictionary.)

Mapping: Teach mapping skills every chance you have. For example, use the map transparencies to practice the names of the Spanish-speaking parts of the world. Ask students *¿Cómo se llama?* while pointing to one of the countries on a map transparency; students should answer with *Es* (name of the country).

Say the name of a country, have a student point to the country on a map transparency or on a wall map and then ask the student to write the country's name on the board. (You may choose to have various students direct the class to add variety.)

Use a wall map of South America or an overhead transparency of the map in the front of this book to review Colombia and Venezuela. Have individual students go to the map *(Ve or Camina al mapa)*. Have students touch *(toca)* or point to *(señala)* the items you mention: *toca la capital de Venezuela, toca el país que produce mucho café* and so forth.

Reading: Prepare students for the content of a reading by asking some general questions on the reading topic, such as the questions found in the section *Preparación*. Next, play the first paragraph of the recorded reading using the corresponding audiocassette/audio compact disc that is part of the Audiocassette/Audio CD Program. As an alternative, you may choose to read the first paragraph yourself as students follow along in the book. Give students a moment to look over the paragraph silently on their own and then have them ask questions. Ask for a student to volunteer to read the paragraph aloud. Continue in this way for subsequent paragraphs.

Discuss the following after the reading: principal ideas and themes, secondary ideas and themes, climax of the story, characters' physical appearance, intellectual traits, cultural practices, etc.

Research: Assign research projects, allowing students to choose to research one of the many fascinating native cultures in the Spanish-speaking world. You may want to divide the class into three groups, each group working on a particular culture (Aztec, Mayan, Inca). You might assign one or two individuals in each group to prepare reports on subthemes such as religion, art and architecture, principal sites, government, social customs and current cultural traits, for example.

Listening: Before any dialog or other oral activity, have students use cues from accompanying illustrations in order to make an educated guess about the content of what they are about to hear. Students may be able to determine such things as how many people are speaking, whether the speakers are young or old, male or female. Have students try to determine if they are hearing questions or just statements. Then play the audiocassette or audio CD as students listen with their books closed.

Play a recording of people who are speaking Spanish. Encourage students to learn to become good listeners by asking follow-up questions to listening activities: What are the speakers talking about? Are they angry with each other? Did students notice any names in the dialog? Play the audiocassette/audio CD again with books open, having students read along silently. Have students repeat after you as you read the content in short phrases. You may choose to act out or paraphrase the meanings of words and expressions, avoiding word-for-word translations (for instance, *¿Cómo te llamas?* is the question used to find out someone's name; *me llamo...* is the phrase used to state your name, and so forth).

COOPERATIVE LEARNING

When students finish school and enter the workforce, the knowledge they will have acquired will be complemented by the socialization skills they have learned. Encourage the ability to work cooperatively to solve problems in Spanish using the following activities:

Information Exchange: 1) Have students find out information about other students in class by pairing up or working in small groups asking and answering questions about one another's lives. For example, students create a name tag for the student behind them (or in front of them, beside them, etc.) by having them spell their names in Spanish, using the expressions *¿Cómo te llamas?, ¿Cómo se escribe?* and so on. 2) Have students write a description of themselves in Spanish as well as information about where they live and their interests. Then have students photograph themselves with an item showing their hobby or interest. Number each of the photos and have the class try to match the descriptions to the photo. As an extension of the activity, mail the descriptions and photos to a partner school for them to read and match. Based on the descriptions, the partner school could try to guess the location too (unless it's a well-established partnership and they already know which school it is and where it is located). If the schools are connected by Internet, follow-up communication could include the correct match-up and any additional questions and information to establish long-term communication between the students and schools.

Concentric Circles: Students form two concentric circles. Students in the inner ring pair up with students in the outer ring, each student asking the other for information (for example, his or her name and how it is spelled). Students in the outer ring move one student to their right and begin the process again.

CRITICAL THINKING

It is important for students to develop skills that go beyond the four basic skills of listening, speaking, reading and writing. As students go out into the workplace, they will need to have the ability to think critically and solve problems. Some possible activities for developing critical thinking skills in Spanish include the following:

Analysis—comparing and contrasting: Have students pick out names that are unlike names they know in English: *Domingo, Luz* and so forth. Then have students select several names that are similar to names they know in English, while pointing out any spelling differences: *Alicia—* Alice.

Analysis—distinguishing: Have students point out the letters that are not in the English alphabet: *ñ, rr* and differences in punctuation between English and Spanish.

Evaluation—concluding, comparing, appraising: Discuss student conclusions about Hispanic culture based upon the cultural information they learn in *Somos así LISTOS* (gestures, the embrace or a kiss on the cheek for greeting others or for saying farewell). Then have students tell how the culture they are learning about is similar to or different from their own culture. Finally, ask how students feel about the similarities and/or differences.

ENCOURAGING THE MULTIPLE INTELLIGENCES

Educators have long agreed that not everyone learns in the same way. Equally so, not everyone is intelligent in the same way. One person might have verbal or mathematical ability, whereas another may demonstrate musical ability. These intelligences, along with abilities in other areas such as music, interpersonal relationships and so on, must be developed so that students can achieve their full potential. Some activities that address the multiple intelligences follow:

Spatial Intelligence: Have students prepare maps of the Spanish-speaking world in Spanish, adding any details they wish to borrow from the color maps at the beginning of the textbook or from an atlas.

Logical-Mathematical: This activity involves critical thinking and will develop your students' logical-mathematical intelligence. After students have studied the days and months, ask the class some questions that require your students to do some calculations with the days and months of the year. Call on a student to answer each question. Then, in order to keep everyone involved, call on another student to confirm whether the answer given was correct and to give the correct answer if it was not. Begin with some of the following questions: *¿Cuántos minutos hay en un cuarto de hora?; ¿Cuántos días hay en una semana?; ¿En tres semanas?; ¿Cuántos minutos hay en cuatro horas y media?; ¿Cuántos segundos hay en cuarenta y siete minutos?; ¿Cuántos meses hay en siete años?; ¿Cuántos meses hay en dos siglos?; ¿Cuántos meses hay en siete siglos?*

TOTAL PHYSICAL RESPONSE

Plural Commands: Practice the *Uds.* forms of the commands by having the entire class perform certain actions or gestures as you say them aloud in Spanish. The commands should be presented in as many logical pairs as possible *(abran, cierren; escriban, borren; escuchen, repitan)*. Practice the action or gesture two or three times with students, then repeat the pair of commands one or two times with no actions or gestures.

Singular Informal Commands: After students are adequately familiar with the *Uds.* commands, you may want to use the *tú* forms of a few verbs for TPR activities. Ideally, the *Uds.* and the *tú* forms should be presented on separate days. Before proceeding to the familiar commands, briefly review the *Uds.* forms of the verbs you plan to use by having students perform several actions. For example, *Abran Uds. los libros; Cierren Uds. los libros; Toquen Uds. los libros.* Then select several students to react to the informal commands of the corresponding verbs: *Abre el libro; Cierra el libro; Toca el libro.* Work with one verb several times before going to another verb. To avoid monotony, vary the commands slightly: (student's name), *abre el libro;* (student's name), *abre el cuaderno.* Perform the action or use gestures only if a student does not respond.

Colors: Combine the teaching of colors with teaching/reinforcing some common commands. For example, say *Toca algo azul (rojo, verde, etc.)* and observe to see that students respond appropriately. Then broaden the activity to include clothing (or other objects). You may choose to bring in a bag of old clothing, especially items that are out of style, awful colors, extra large and so forth, as a humorous way to allow students to find and point out colors and items of clothing that you name or describe.

GAMES

Games, mnemonic devices and similar activities are excellent educational tools, giving students the opportunity to learn in a context that varies the daily routine. All games and activities can be modified to suit the needs of your students or to support your particular approach to teaching.

I Spy: Have students work in pairs to play guessing games. Students take turns describing an object they see (being certain to describe the colors, the size, what it is made of), mentioning one clue at a time while the partner guesses what the object is.

Streetcar (vocabulary review): Prepare file cards with the words you want to practice in Spanish on one side (it may be helpful to indicate infinitives with an asterisk and include articles with nouns) and in English on the reverse side. You may extend this game by using synonyms and antonyms. Your list could develop from the active vocabulary words listed at the end of each lesson. Decide whether you want the students to produce the English or the Spanish. Students should study the vocabulary before playing Streetcar. The object of this game is to get all the way back to one's seat. The teacher may direct the game or have a student do it.

Begin on the left side of class with the first row. The first student stands up next to the second who remains seated. Show a card to these students while saying the word. The first student to respond correctly moves on to compete with the third student.

Whoever answers correctly stands next to the third student; for example, if the second student wins the round, he or she moves on to the third student and the first student sits down in the second student's seat. If neither of the first two students can answer after five seconds, the third student is given an opportunity to respond. If there is still no answer, use the card as a free review, ask the class to define the problem word and choose a new card. This should be a relatively fast-paced game. By saying the target word as you show it, students practice assigning sound to visual cues as well.

Rhythm/Concentration (verbs): This game can be used for practicing numbers or for reviewing or practicing verbs. The same rhythm is maintained: Students tap the tops of their desks twice, clap their hands twice and snap their fingers twice—words may be called out only during the snapping of fingers. For verb practice, for example, the first student in each row gives an infinitive *(hablar)* on the first snapping of fingers, the next student gives a subject pronoun *(tú)* on the second, and the third student must respond with the appropriate answer *(tú hablas)* on the third snapping of fingers. Students who make an error move to the end of the row and the other students move up. Try to have an uneven number of students in each row so that every student will have the opportunity to match subject pronoun and verb ending. All the students in each row monitor each other for errors. You also may have the entire class participate rather than play the game by rows. In this case you may want to point to students for verb infinitive, subject pronoun and response.

Jeopardy (general review): This game is especially good as a review before the midyear or final exam, but it can be used at almost any time in many different ways. Write a series of categories horizontally on the board (to review *Capítulo 3*, for example, write the words *food, Mexico, commands, city, car)*. Write the numbers ten through fifty by tens under each category. Prepare questions in advance; unlike the television game show, students need not respond with a question. Questions may be completions, synonyms or antonyms, translations, direct questions, matching and so forth. Divide the class into three or four teams and tell students that each team has an imaginary buzzer they must use if they wish to participate.

To see which team will go first, ask a question that may be answered by any student. The first student who sounds the buzzer gets a chance to answer. The team that correctly answers the opening question has the opportunity to choose a category and a dollar amount. Read the question, allowing that team to respond within a time limit (ten or fifteen seconds). If not answered within the specified time limit, the question is open to the entire class, but buzzers must be used; that is, students should not randomly blurt out answers.

Prepare several *Daily Double* questions, as well. Use these when enthusiasm for the game wanes. Whatever the dollar amount in the chosen category is at that moment, double it. These questions may be answered by any team, not just the team that chose the category. (**Note:** If you wish to practice numbers while playing the game, the dollar amounts may be given in odd numbers.)

When a question is answered correctly, write the answer in the space left by the erased dollar amount as you keep score. This will provide students with visual reinforcement of the material. When the entire board is filled with answers, total the scores. You may wish to offer prizes as an incentive.

Stop-the-Clock (vocabulary review): Make up a series of small cards with pictures on one side and their Spanish definition on the other and distribute them to the class. Divide the class into two groups and choose one person to be *It* for each group (you will have two games going at once). The rest of the students sit at their desks (or stand in from of them) in a circle, holding their cards with the picture facing out. The person who is *It* stands in the center.

To begin the game, pick one student in each group. Those students must say the name in Spanish of the pictures on the cards they are holding and the name of the picture on another student's card. (It makes it harder on the person who is *It* to not be looking at the person whose card is named. Thus, you may wish to advise students to name a second card that is to the side or behind *It*.) The person in the center of the circle must find the second person and point at the corresponding picture, thus "stopping the clock," before the second student can name both his or her picture and another person's picture. Make sure the person in the center is accurately pointing at or preferably touching the picture. If someone's clock is stopped, that person is then *It*.

¿Dónde está? (directional vocabulary and commands): Choose a small object such as a piece of chalk, show it to the students and ask them to hide it somewhere in the room. Go out of the room for a few minutes while they hide the item. When you return, they will help you find it by giving you directional commands or indicating direction *(Doble a la derecha, está cerca, mire arriba, etc.)*.

Next, divide the class into groups of four or five, choose one person from each group to leave the room and then repeat the game, this time with familiar commands.

El Detective (general review): This game may be played with a number of different objectives: to help students get to know one another, to practice specific vocabulary, to practice different verb tenses and so forth. Make a number of lists with five to ten different items on each list. If the object is for students to get to know each other, include items such as *le gusta el fútbol, el béisbol*, etc. (a different sport on each list); *come pollo, ensalada, hamburguesas*, etc. (a different food on each list); *mañana va a la playa, al concierto, al cine*, etc. (a different place on each list); and so on. It is fun to include an unusual category to make the activity more interesting. Copy the lists to equal the number of students you have so that each group (of five, for example) has the same list and different groups have different lists. *El detective* must fill in his or her list by asking fellow students if certain categories apply to them and if so, they sign the list by the appropriate category. Students will practice the *tú* form while asking classmates questions *(¿Te gusta el fútbol?)*, and may practice third-person singular by reporting the findings to the class after all students have completed the activity.

Hot Potato: This simple game will help beginning students gain confidence in speaking because it occupies students with a physical activity while they are conversing in Spanish, thus reducing their inhibitions about making an error. Hot Potato is played as follows: Students stand in a circle in the classroom. One student, who is holding a nerf ball (nerf footballs work well because they are soft and yet still easy to throw), asks a question of another student in the circle, and then calls the student by name. The first student then carefully tosses the ball to the second student, who must start answering the question before he or she catches the ball. Allow students ten to fifteen seconds to finish answering each question. The student who catches the ball and answers a question then asks a question and passes the ball to another student and so on. The game continues until all students have had at least two chances to answer a question. Questions can be based on chapter vocabulary and grammar, cultural topics or a textbook story. The teacher serves as the moderator.

Vary the game by restricting the amount of time a student can hold the ball. For example, tell students they cannot hold the ball for more than twenty seconds before beginning to ask or answer a question, or they will have to sit down. The last person standing wins the game.

The game eliminates a student's natural inclination to think in English before saying something in Spanish; thinking in Spanish becomes a natural reflex. An added benefit is that all students actively participate in the activity since they are not just responding to the teacher's questions while passively sitting at their seats.

¿Qué pasa, calabaza?: Students prepare a short list of action verbs, which they must act out in front of the class. Classmates then try to guess which Spanish verbs are being acted out. Limit the time to encourage presenters to act out the list as quickly as possible.

Ganar, perder o empatar: This game incorporates the rules and objectives of Charades. The class is split up into teams. Give one member of each group a list of words or phrases. The team member with the word or phrase then draws clues for his or her team members. Each team has one minute to guess the word or phrase from the drawn clues. Award points to the fastest team and continue until a team reaches a point total determined in advance by the teacher.

El recado: This enjoyable activity is useful for reviewing vocabulary and serves to reinforce listening, writing, reading and speaking skills. Provide students with a list of the names of all the students in class. The list can be in alphabetical or random order. As you hand out the list of names, inform students that they will be leaving phone messages with one another in Spanish and should hold on to this phone list in order to know whom to call with messages. Then on a day when you would like to review vocabulary (or just to vary the routine), start several phone calls by whispering to several students a word or expression in Spanish that they must write down and then whisper to the next student on the list. Give students a set time when you will be collecting all phone messages (five minutes, for example). Compare what the final person wrote down to the "phone message" you whispered to the first person for each vocabulary word or expression.

CLASSROOM EXPRESSIONS

Apunta/Señala (Apunten Uds./Señalen Uds.)....	Point at....
Borra (Borren Uds.) la pizarra.	Erase the board.
Cierra (Cierren Uds.) el libro/cuaderno.	Close your book/notebook.
Contesta/Responde (Contesten Uds./Responden Uds.).	Answer.
Continúa/Sigue (Continúen Uds./Sigan Uds.).	Continue.
Copia (Copien Uds.)....	Copy....
Da (Den Uds.) la vuelta.	Turn around.
Dibuja (Dibujen Uds.)....	Draw....
Dime (Díganme Uds.)....	Tell me....
Empieza (Empiecen Uds.) ahora.	Begin now.
Escoge (Escojan Uds.)....	Choose....
Entrégame (Entréguenme Uds.) la tarea.	Hand in your homework to me.
Escribe (Escriban Uds.)	Write....
Escribe (Escriban Uds.) a máquina....	Type....
Escucha (Escuchen Uds.).	Listen.
Estudia (Estudien Uds.)....	Study....
Formen Uds. grupos de....	Form groups of....
Habla (Hablen Uds.) en español.	Speak in Spanish.
Inserta (Inserten Uds.) el diskette en la computadora.	Insert the diskette into the computer.
Levanta (Levanten Uds.) la mano (para contestar).	Raise your hand (to answer).
Lee (Lean Uds.)...en voz alta.	Read...out loud.
Levántate (Levántense Uds.).	Stand up.
Llévate (Llévense Uds.)....	Take...with you.
Mira (Miren Uds.)....	Look....
Mira (Miren Uds.) el vídeo.	Look at the video.
Oye (Oigan Uds.).	Listen.
Para (Paren Uds.).	Stop.
Pasa (Pasen Uds.) a la pizarra.	Go to the board.
Piensa (Piensen Uds.).	Think.
Pon (Pongan Uds.)....	Put/Place....
Presta (Presten Uds.) atención a....	Pay attention to....
Pronuncia (Pronuncien Uds.)....	Pronounce....
Recoge (Recojan Uds.)....	Pick up....
Recuerda (Recuerden Uds.)....	Remember....
Repite (Repitan Uds.).	Repeat.
Revisa (Revisen Uds.)....	Review....
Quita (Quiten Uds.) todo de encima de sus pupitres.	Take everything off the top of your desks.

Saca (Saquen Uds.) una hoja de papel/un bolígrafo/un lápiz.	Take out a sheet of paper/a pen/a pencil.
Siéntate (Siéntense Uds.).	Sit down.
Toca (Toquen Uds.)….	Touch….
Trabajen Uds. en parejas en….	Work in pairs on….
Trae (Traigan Uds.)….	Bring….
Trata (Traten Uds.).	Try.
Ve (Vayan Uds.) a….	Go to….
Ven (Vengan Uds.) aquí.	Come here.
Muy bien.	Very good.
Excelente.	Excellent.
Para mañana….	For tomorrow….
Más alto/bajo.	Louder/Softer.
Silencio.	Quiet.
Otra vez.	Once more.
Vamos a tener una prueba/un examen.	We're going to have a quiz/a test.
¿Quién sabe (la respuesta)?	Who knows (the answer)?
¿Alguien?	Anyone?
Todos juntos.	All together.
¿Hay preguntas?	Are there any questions?
¿Cómo se dice…(en español)?	How do you say…(in Spanish)?
¿Cómo se escribe…?	How do you write…?
¿Qué quiere decir…?	What does…mean?
Repita Ud., por favor.	Repeat, please.
No sé.	I don't know.
No comprendo/entiendo.	I don't understand.
No recuerdo.	I don't remember.
Tengo una pregunta.	I have a question.
Bueno, pues, este….	Okay (Well, Um)….
Yo creo/pienso que….	I believe/think that….

Learning a language has always meant more than merely memorizing words and structures and then putting them together with hopes of actually being able to communicate. Just as language is inseparable from culture, so is it inseparable from the authentic communication of thoughts and emotions. The culture of the Spanish-speaking world varies from moment to moment and from one place to the next. Language and culture cannot be segmented and learned out of context if students are ever going to become proficient. As students use *Somos así* they will have exciting opportunities to learn about culture and to use language for obtaining and communicating information. In *Somos así,* students will cross several disciplines and will use a wide variety of resources for obtaining and sharing information, ideas and feelings, including the Internet, newspapers, magazines and libraries, to name just a few. These authentic learning experiences will introduce them to and expand their knowledge of language, mathematics and science, social sciences and the arts and humanities. In *Somos así* students will learn not only academic skills, but also problem solving, survival and employment skills so that when they walk out of the classroom they will be able to communicate confidently using authentic Spanish.

Somos así

LISTOS

Second Edition

James F. Funston
Alejandro Vargas Bonilla
Daphne Helms Sherman

Contributing Writer
Rolando Castellanos

CONSULTANTS

Lourdes C. Adams
Niceville High School
Niceville, Florida

Sandra Martin Arnold
Palisades Charter High School
Palisades, California

Washington B. Collado
Broward County Public Schools
Ft. Lauderdale, Florida

Nancy S. Hernández
Simsbury High School
Simsbury, Connecticut

Paul J. Hoff
University of Wisconsin—Eau Claire
Eau Claire, Wisconsin

Emily S. Peel
Wethersfield High School
Wethersfield, Connecticut

Jane S. Stevens
Niceville High School
Niceville, Florida

EMC/Paradigm Publishing, Saint Paul, Minnesota

Credits

Assistant Editor
Yuri M. Guerra Guerra

Editorial Consultants
Carlos Calvo
Judy Cohen
Amy Dorn-Fernández
Guilherme P. Kiang-Samaniego
Sharon O'Donnell
Eliana Silva Premoli
David Thorstad

Editorial Assistance
Glenndell Larry

Illustrator
Tune and Khet Insisiengmay

Photo Research
Jennifer Anderson

Design and Production
Leslie Anderson
Julie Hansen
Joan D'Onofrio
Jennifer Wreisner

EMC/Paradigm World Language Consultants
Dana Cunningham
Robert Headrick
Sarah Vaillancourt

We have attempted to locate owners of copyright materials used in this book. If an error or omission has occurred, EMC/Paradigm Publishing will acknowledge the contribution in subsequent printings.

ISBN 0-8219-1913-X

Published by EMC/Paradigm Publishing
875 Montreal Way
St. Paul, Minnesota 55102
800-328-1452
www.emcp.com
E-mail: educate@emcp.com

Printed in the United States of America
1 2 3 4 5 6 7 8 9 10 X X X 05 04 03 02 01 00

About the Cover

Do you know what dance the couple on the cover of *Somos así LISTOS* is doing? It's the tango, a romantic dance associated with Buenos Aires, Argentina, the city often called the "Paris of South America." Buenos Aires, as its nickname suggests, has always imitated European culture, transforming it into something unique. The tango became the embodiment of Buenos Aires, what gave the city its cosmopolitan character. The music originated in the nineteenth century when European immigrants joined immigrants from *las pampas* in search of work in the bustling metropolis. But these lonely men often found solace in the arms of lonely women as they danced the tango, "a sad thought that can be danced." This dance is a deep, beautiful and tragic depiction of the mystery and misery of urban life.

In her original acrylic, *The Tango,* Kelly Stribling Sutherland captures the elegance, romance and intrigue of Buenos Aires in the 1940s. To set her painting in this period, the artist has created a background of collaged photographs of the city. We see a sophisticated scene of skyscrapers and scurrying businessmen. Against this backdrop she places a couple, intensely focused as they face us head-on. The woman holds a red rose between her lips, a stereotypical image of a tango dancer. The roses on the front cover contribute to the swirling, romantic atmosphere Ms. Sutherland has painted, a musical mirror of the urban soul. Two solitary people become one as they dance the tango.

Table of Contents

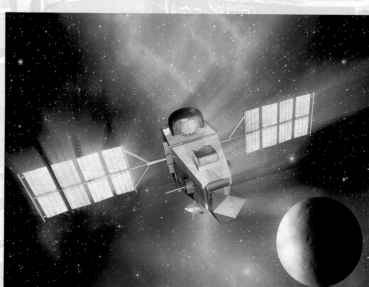

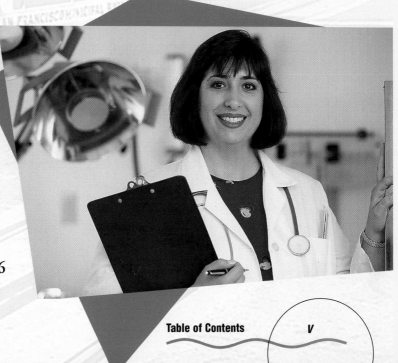

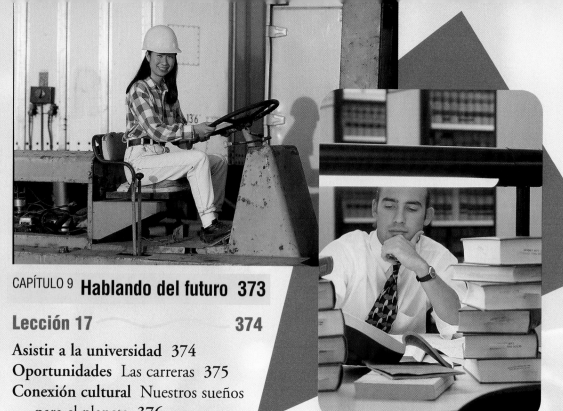

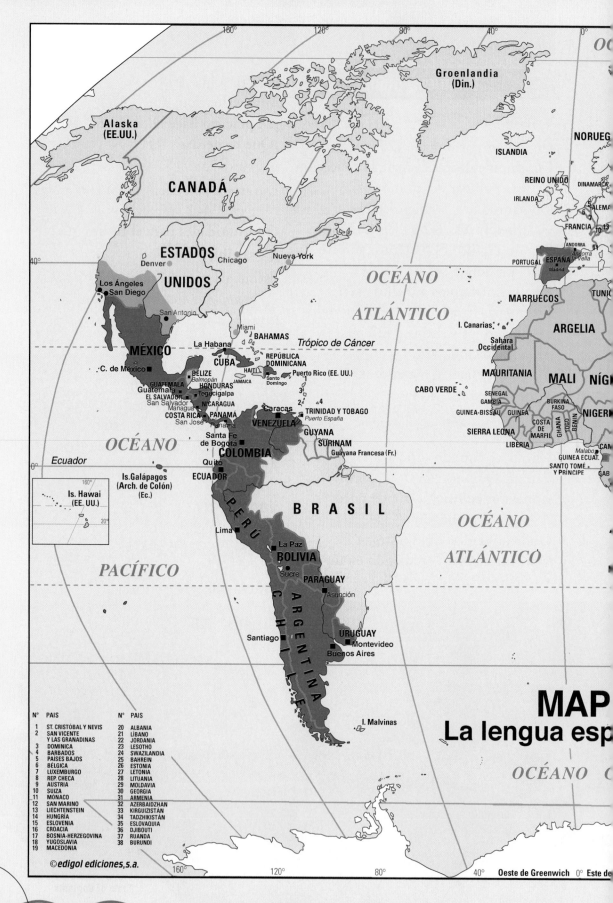

Groenlandia
(Din.)

Alaska
(EE.UU.)

CANADÁ

ESTADOS
UNIDOS

Denver
Chicago
Nueva York
Los Ángeles
San Diego
San Antonio

Miami

BAHAMAS
Trópico de Cáncer

MÉXICO
La Habana
CUBA
REPÚBLICA
DOMINICANA
C. de México
BÉLIZE
Belmopán
HAITÍ
Puerto Rico (EE. UU.)
GUATEMALA
HONDURAS
Santo
Domingo
JAMAICA
Guatemala
Tegucigalpa
EL SALVADOR
San Salvador
NICARAGUA
Managua
Caracas
TRINIDAD Y TOBAGO
COSTA RICA
PANAMÁ
Puerto España
San José
Panamá
VENEZUELA
GUYANA
Santa Fe
de Bogotá
SURINAM
COLOMBIA
Guayana Francesa (Fr.)

Ecuador
Quito
ECUADOR

OCÉANO

Is. Galápagos
(Arch. de Colón)
(Ec.)

BRASIL

Is. Hawai
(EE. UU.)

PERÚ
Lima

La Paz
BOLIVIA
Sucre

PACÍFICO
PARAGUAY
Asunción

ARGENTINA
URUGUAY
Santiago
CHILE
Montevideo
Buenos Aires

I. Malvinas

OCÉANO

ATLÁNTICO

I. Canarias
Sahára
Occidental

ISLANDIA

NORUEG

REINO UNIDO
DINAMARCA
IRLANDA
ALEMA
6
7
FRANCIA
10 13
ANDORRA
Andorra
la Vella
11
PORTUGAL
ESPAÑA
Madrid

MARRUECOS

TUN

ARGELIA

MAURITANIA
MALI
NÍG

CABO VERDE
SENEGAL
GAMBIA
BURKINA
FASO
GUINEA-BISSAU
GUINEA
NIGER
COSTA
DE
MARFIL
GHANA
TOGO
BENIN
SIERRA LEONA
LIBERIA
Malabo
CAN
GUINEA ECUAT.
SANTO TOMÉ
Y PRÍNCIPE
GAB

OCÉANO

ATLÁNTICO

MAP
La lengua esp

OCÉANO C

N°	PAIS	N°	PAIS
1	ST. CRISTÓBAL Y NEVIS	20	ALBANIA
2	SAN VICENTE Y LAS GRANADINAS	21	LÍBANO
		22	JORDANIA
3	DOMINICA	23	LESOTHO
4	BARBADOS	24	SWAZILANDIA
5	PAÍSES BAJOS	25	BAHREIN
6	BÉLGICA	26	ESTONIA
7	LUXEMBURGO	27	LETONIA
8	REP. CHECA	28	LITUANIA
9	AUSTRIA	29	MOLDAVIA
10	SUIZA	30	GEORGIA
11	MÓNACO	31	ARMENIA
12	SAN MARINO	32	AZERBAIDZHAN
13	LIECHTENSTEIN	33	KIRGUIZISTAN
14	HUNGRÍA	34	TADZHIKISTÁN
15	ESLOVENIA	35	ESLOVAQUIA
16	CROACIA	36	DJIBOUTI
17	BOSNIA-HERZEGOVINA	37	RUANDA
18	YUGOSLAVIA	38	BURUNDI
19	MACEDONIA		

Oeste de Greenwich 0° Este de

GLACIAL ÁRTICO

RUSIA

KAZAJSTÁN

MONGOLIA

Alaska
(EE.UU.)

SIA

RANIA

UZBEKISTÁN 33

30 31 32

TURQUÍA

TURKMENISTÁN 34

REP. POP. CHINA

CÓREA
DEL NORTE

40°

HIPRE 21

SIRIA

IRAK

IRÁN

AFGANISTÁN

CÓREA
DEL SUR

JAPÓN

OCÉANO

ISRAEL 22
Jerusalén

KUWAIT

PAKISTÁN

PACÍFICO

GIPTO

ARABIA
SAUDITA

25

QATAR
EMIRATOS
ÁRABES UNIDOS

NEPAL

BHUTAN

BANGLA-
DESH

TAIWÁN

OMÁN

INDIA

BIRMANIA

LAOS

VIETNAM

ERITREA

SUDÁN

YEMEN

THAILANDIA

Manila

CAMBOYA

FILIPINAS

REP. DE PALAOS

ETIOPÍA

SOMALIA

36

SRI LANKA

BRUNEI

MALASIA

CA

UGANDA

KENYA

MALDIVAS

SINGAPUR

0°

CA 37
38

SEYCHELLES

OCÉANO

I N D O N E S I A

PAPÚA
NUEVA GUINEA

TANZANIA

ÍNDICO

SALOMÓN

COMORES

MALAWI

BIA

MAURICIO

MBABWE

MOZAMBIQUE

VA

MADAGASCAR

AUSTRALIA

24

Trópico de Capricornio

23

NA

NUEVA

40°

UNDI

ZELANDA

a en el mundo

Línea internacional
de cambio de hora

AL ANTÁRTICO

Países donde el español es la lengua oficial o co-oficial	**Madrid** Ciudad de más de 1 millón de hab.
	Panamá Ciudad de 100.000 a 1 millón de hab.
	Malabo Ciudad de menos de 100.000 hab.
Zonas donde el español es hablado por una parte de la población	Límite de Estado
	■ ∎ Capital de Estado
	● Otras ciudades

RTIDA

80°

120°

160°

160°

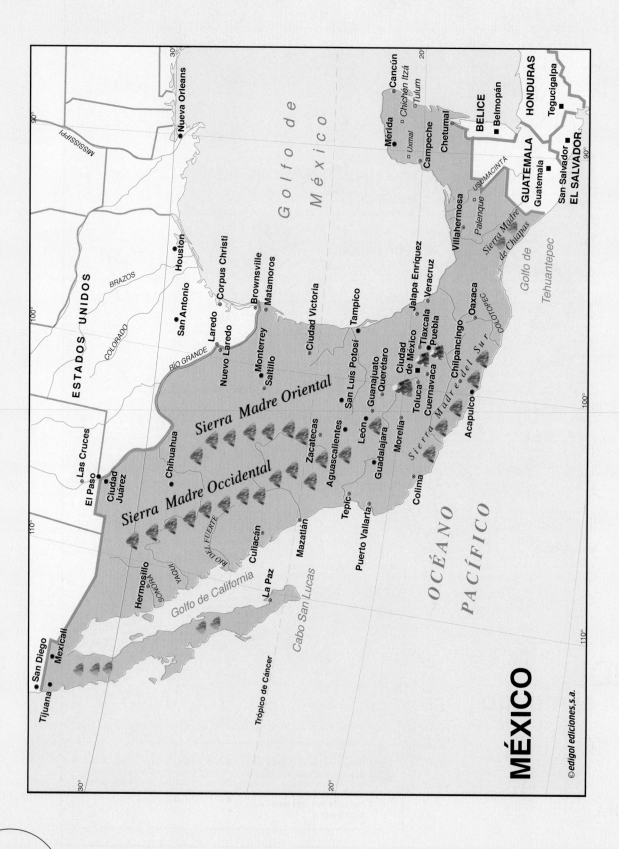

MÉXICO

ESTADOS UNIDOS

MISSISSIPPI

Nueva Orleans

90

Houston

BRAZOS

COLORADO

San Antonio

Corpus Christi

Brownsville

Matamoros

Laredo

Nuevo Laredo

RÍO GRANDE

Monterrey

Ciudad Victoria

Saltillo

Las Cruces

El Paso

Ciudad
Juárez

Chihuahua

Sierra Madre Oriental

San Luis Potosí

Tampico

Sierra Madre Occidental

Zacatecas

Querétaro

Aguascalientes

Guanajuato

León

Guadalajara

Morelia

Tepic

RÍO DEL FUERTE

Culiacán

YAQUI

Hermosillo

SONORA

Mazatlán

Puerto Vallarta

Colima

Golfo de California

La Paz

Cabo San Lucas

Trópico de Cáncer

San Diego

Mexicali

Tijuana

OCÉANO

PACÍFICO

110

30

100

Golfo de México

Mérida

Cancún

Chichén Itzá

Tulum

Uxmal

Campeche

Chetumal

Villahermosa

Palenque

USUMACINTA

Sierra Madre
de Chiapas

Golfo de
Tehuantepec

BELICE

Belmopán

HONDURAS

Tegucigalpa

GUATEMALA

Guatemala

San Salvador

EL SALVADOR

Jalapa Enríquez

Veracruz

Oaxaca

COLOTEPEC

Ciudad
de México

Tlaxcala

Puebla

Toluca

Cuernavaca

Chilpancingo

Acapulco

Sierra Madre del Sur

20

90

100

110

20

30

© edigol ediciones, s.a.

xviii

AMÉRICA CENTRAL Y EL CARIBE

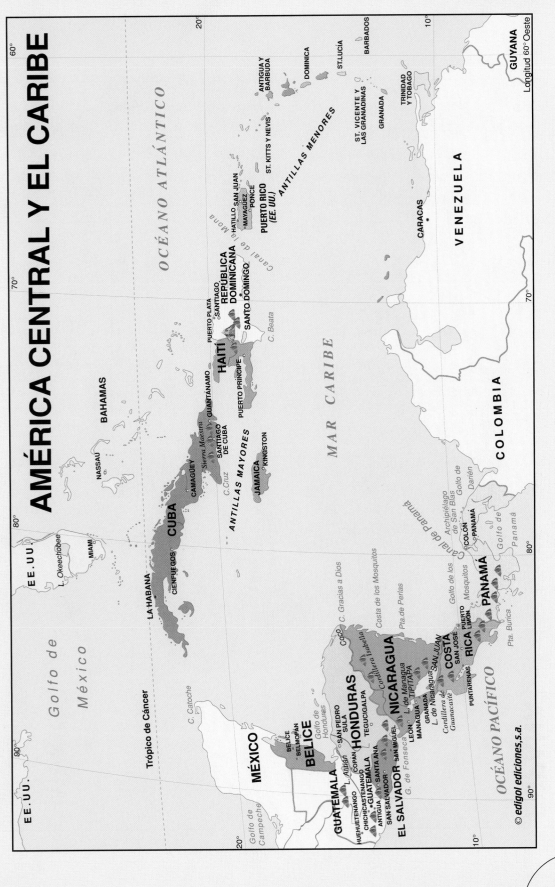

EE.UU.

EE.UU.

Golfo de México

Trópico de Cáncer

OCÉANO ATLÁNTICO

L. Okeechobee

MIAMI

C. Catoche

Golfo de Campeche

MÉXICO

BAHAMAS

NASSAU

BELICE

BELICE

BELMOPÁN

Golfo de Honduras

GUATEMALA

HUEHUETENANGO

CHICHICASTENANGO

ANTIGUA

SAN PEDRO SULA

COPÁN

GUATEMALA

SANTA ANA

SAN SALVADOR

SAN MIGUEL

EL SALVADOR

L. Atitlán

G. de Fonseca

HONDURAS

TEGUCIGALPA

Cordillera Isabella

LEÓN

MANAGUA

L. de Managua

GRANADA

L. de Nicaragua

Cordillera de Guanacaste

NICARAGUA

TIPITAPA

SAN JUAN

COSTA RICA

SAN JOSÉ

PUNTARENAS

PUERTO LIMÓN

OCÉANO PACÍFICO

Pta. Burica

CUBA

LA HABANA

CIENFUEGOS

CAMAGÜEY

Sierra Maestra

C. Cruz

SANTIAGO DE CUBA

GUANTÁNAMO

ANTILLAS MAYORES

JAMAICA

KINGSTON

HAITÍ

PUERTO PRÍNCIPE

PUERTO PLATA

SANTIAGO

REPÚBLICA DOMINICANA

SANTO DOMINGO

C. Beata

Canal de la Mona

MAYAGÜEZ

HATILLO

SAN JUAN

PONCE

PUERTO RICO (EE. UU.)

ANTILLAS MENORES

ST. KITTS Y NEVIS

ANTIGUA Y BARBUDA

DOMINICA

ST. LUCÍA

ST. VICENTE Y LAS GRANADINAS

BARBADOS

GRANADA

TRINIDAD Y TOBAGO

MAR CARIBE

COCO

C. Gracias a Dios

Costa de los Mosquitos

Pta. de Perlas

Golfo de los Mosquitos

Archipiélago de San Blas

Golfo de Darién

PANAMÁ

COLÓN

PANAMÁ

Canal de Panamá

Golfo de Panamá

PANAMÁ

CARACAS

VENEZUELA

COLOMBIA

GUYANA

Longitud 60° Oeste

© edigol ediciones, s.a.

xix

ESPAÑA

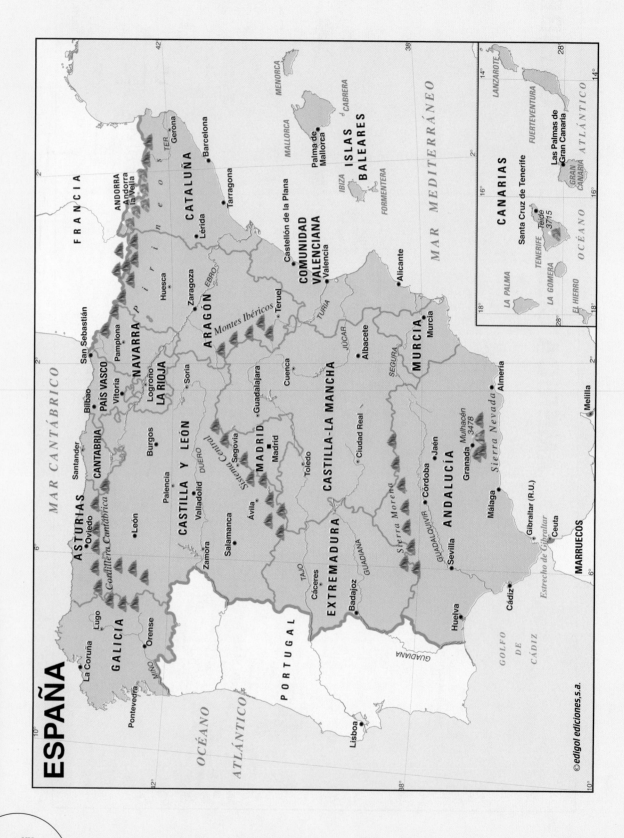

OCÉANO ATLÁNTICO

MAR CANTÁBRICO

GALICIA
La Coruña
Lugo
Pontevedra
Orense
MIÑO

ASTURIAS
Oviedo
Cordillera Cantábrica

CANTABRIA
Santander

PAÍS VASCO
Bilbao
San Sebastián
Vitoria

NAVARRA
Pamplona
LA RIOJA
Logroño

FRANCIA

ANDORRA
Andorra la Vella

P i r i n e o s

TER
Gerona
Barcelona

CATALUÑA
Lérida
Tarragona

Huesca
Zaragoza
EBRO
ARAGÓN
Teruel
Montes Ibéricos

CASTILLA Y LEÓN
León
Burgos
Palencia
Valladolid
DUERO
Zamora
Salamanca
Ávila
Soria
Segovia
Sistema Central

MADRID
Madrid
Guadalajara
Cuenca
Toledo

CASTILLA-LA MANCHA
Ciudad Real

COMUNIDAD VALENCIANA
Castellón de la Plana
Valencia
TURIA
Alicante
JÚCAR
Albacete
SEGURA

MURCIA
Murcia

EXTREMADURA
Cáceres
Badajoz
GUADIANA
TAJO

Sierra Morena

ANDALUCÍA
GUADALQUIVIR
Córdoba
Jaén
Sevilla
Granada
Mulhacén 3478
Sierra Nevada
Almería
Huelva
Málaga
Cádiz
Gibraltar (R.U.)
Ceuta
Estrecho de Gibraltar

GOLFO DE CÁDIZ
GUADIANA

PORTUGAL
Lisboa

MARRUECOS

Melilla

MAR MEDITERRÁNEO

MENORCA
MALLORCA
Palma de Mallorca
ISLAS BALEARES
IBIZA
CABRERA
FORMENTERA

CANARIAS
LANZAROTE
FUERTEVENTURA
LA PALMA
TENERIFE
Santa Cruz de Tenerife
Teide 3715
LA GOMERA
EL HIERRO
GRAN CANARIA
Las Palmas de Gran Canaria
OCÉANO ATLÁNTICO

XX

AMÉRICA DEL SUR

MAR CARIBE

BARRANQUILLA
CARTAGENA
G. de Venezuela
MARACAIBO   CARACAS
L. de
Maracaibo
VENEZUELA
Delta del
Orinoco
BUCARAMANGA
MÉRIDA
ARAUCA
ORINOCO
GEORGETOWN
PARAMARIBO
GUYANA
SURINAM
CAYENA
GUAYANA
FRANCESA
(Fra.)
MEDELLÍN
SANTA FE
DE BOGOTÁ
VILLAVICENCIO
CALI
PASTO
COLOMBIA
QUITO
ECUADOR
Cotopaxi
5896
Chimborazo
6267
CAQUETÁ
GUAYAQUIL
Golfo de
Guayaquil
CUENCA
IQUITOS
AMAZONAS
AMAZONAS

OCÉANO
ATLÁNTICO

Estuario del
Amazonas
Ecuador   0

FORTALEZA

B R A S I L

Pta. Negra
PERÚ
CHICLAYO
TRUJILLO
Los Andes

RECIFE

SAN FRANCISCO

CALLAO
LIMA
Machu Picchu
ICA
CUZCO
JULIACA
L. Titicaca
LA PAZ
BOLIVIA
COCHABAMBA
L. de Poopó
SUCRE
POTOSÍ
ARICA

SALVADOR

PARAGUAY

BRASILIA

BELO HORIZONTE

OCÉANO

Trópico de Capricornio   ANTOFAGASTA

PACÍFICO

CHILE

Gran Chaco
PILCOMAYO
Los Andes
SAN MIGUEL
DE TUCUMÁN
PARAGUAY
CONCEPCIÓN
Itaipú
ASUNCIÓN
Cataratas
del Iguazú
RESISTENCIA
CORRIENTES
URUGUAY
PARANÁ
PARANÁ

SÃO PAULO
RÍO DE JANEIRO   20

ARGENTINA

Aconcagua
6959
Los Andes
CÓRDOBA
SAN JUAN
VIÑA DEL MAR
VALPARAÍSO
SANTIAGO
DE CHILE
TALCA
MENDOZA
SALADO
Pampas
ROSARIO
BUENOS
AIRES
LA PLATA
PARANÁ
URUGUAY
SALTO
URUGUAY
MONTEVIDEO
RÍO DE LA PLATA
Pta. Norte

OCÉANO

ATLÁNTICO

IS. JUAN FERNÁNDEZ
(Chile)

CONCEPCIÓN
COLORADO
NEUQUÉN
NEGRO
BAHÍA BLANCA
MAR DEL PLATA

VALDIVIA

PUERTO
MONTT
SAN CARLOS DE
BARILOCHE

Patagonia

Golfo de Penas

C. Tres Puntas

Bahía
Grande
Estr. de Magallanes
ISLAS MALVINAS (R.U.)
PUERTO STANLEY

PUNTA ARENAS
USHUAIA
Cabo de Hornos
Estr. de Drake
TIERRA DEL
FUEGO

GEORGIA DEL SUR (R.U.)

©edigol ediciones,s.a.

Connections with Parents

The first month of school can form a foundation for success throughout the rest of the year. In order to encourage parents to play a larger part in their child's classroom education, try the following: During the first few days of class, send a letter home explaining objectives and expectations for the course; make phone calls to students' homes with some bit of good news before you have to call about poor grades or misbehavior. The margins of the Annotated Teacher's Edition and accompanying ancillaries provide suggestions and reminders for establishing and maintaining good parental support.

Notes

The National Standards in Foreign Language Education Project consisted of educators, organizations and interested individuals who met to establish a new national framework of standards for language education in the United States. Their work is summarized in the resulting document, titled *Standards for Foreign Language Learning: Preparing for the 21st Century*, which discusses philosophical issues, implications and strategies for maximizing proficiency and for empowering all students to become successful learners and users of world languages.

Somos así was created to support and advance the vision described by the writers of the national standards, blending the five Cs of communication, culture, connections, comparisons and communities with pedagogically sound content, fun activities and an ongoing discussion of the wealth of opportunities that learning a world language opens up for students.

NATIONAL STANDARDS
C1.2

Un nuevo año

CAPÍTULO 1

A/V TV/SAT
Sistemas de Audio y Video
Vía Satélite

GauchoNet
argentina en internet

In this chapter you will be able to:

- talk about technology
- seek and provide personal information
- describe the weather
- state what is happening right now
- talk about everyday activities
- discuss ecological problems
- talk about the future
- discuss schedules
- compare quantity, quality, age and size
- talk about the past
- refer to what just happened

1

Notes

The National Standards have been correlated to the content of the pages of *Somos así* in the lower left- and right-hand pages of the ATE (Annotated Teacher's Edition). The Introduction to the ATE provides a key for using the correlation.

Communicative functions are provided with the opening two pages along with accompanying visuals to whet students' appetites for the chapter they are about to begin. A checkoff list of the functions appears at the end of the chapter (see page 39), along with additional objectives that students can use as a self-check to evaluate their own progress.

Activities

Critical Thinking. Authentic materials serve to further student awareness of and connections to how Spanish is used outside the controlled environment of the classroom. Try to employ these supportive visuals on a regular basis. For example, ask students to try the following: 1) Guess what the word *GauchoNet* means in the realia on page 1; 2) tell what the phrase *Sistemas de Audio y Video Vía Satélite* on page 1 means.

Communities. Have a short classroom discussion about the various ways students were in touch with the Spanish-speaking world last summer. They should consider such possibilities as travel, food, media, music and products they purchased.

NATIONAL STANDARDS
C1.2, C5.2

Content reviewed in *Lección 1*
- present tense
- numbers
- weather
- the present progressive
- comparisons

Notes

It has been said there are six degrees of separation between any two people on earth. In today's technologically advanced world, we can communicate on a moment's notice, or transport ourselves quickly anywhere in the world. And yet, with all our advances, the world has become a complex labyrinth that young people are faced with navigating. That is the future our students face and preparing them for that future is a goal of *Somos así LISTOS*.

Deciding which words to illustrate, define or leave for students to discern the meaning of is obviously a subjective one. Every attempt has been made to present new vocabulary in the most pedagogically sound and most appropriate manner to encourage students to think in Spanish, but without making the presentation of new material too difficult for students to enjoy. Words that your students are unable to recognize can be found in the vocabulary glossary that appears at the end of the book.

Somos así stresses the use of authentic Spanish by students from the first day of class. Therefore, vocabulary is introduced lexically, in context, along with appropriate cultural background notes and with a minimal explanation of grammar.

Lección 1

Contexto cultural
EL MUNDO HISPANO

Conectados con el mundo

Enrique González, Nueva York, Estados Unidos

Sigue haciendo frío.

No puedo conseguir la dirección de correo electrónico de Mario.

Carlos E. Segura, San José, Costa Rica

*Con la **tecnología** de hoy estamos **conectados°** con cualquier parte del **mundo°** en forma muy rápida. En los países de habla hispana los chicos también usan la tecnología para estar conectados.*

Navego en la Internet. Hay mucha información de todo el mundo aquí.

Rosario Edelman, Buenos Aires, Argentina

National Standards
C1.2, C4.1

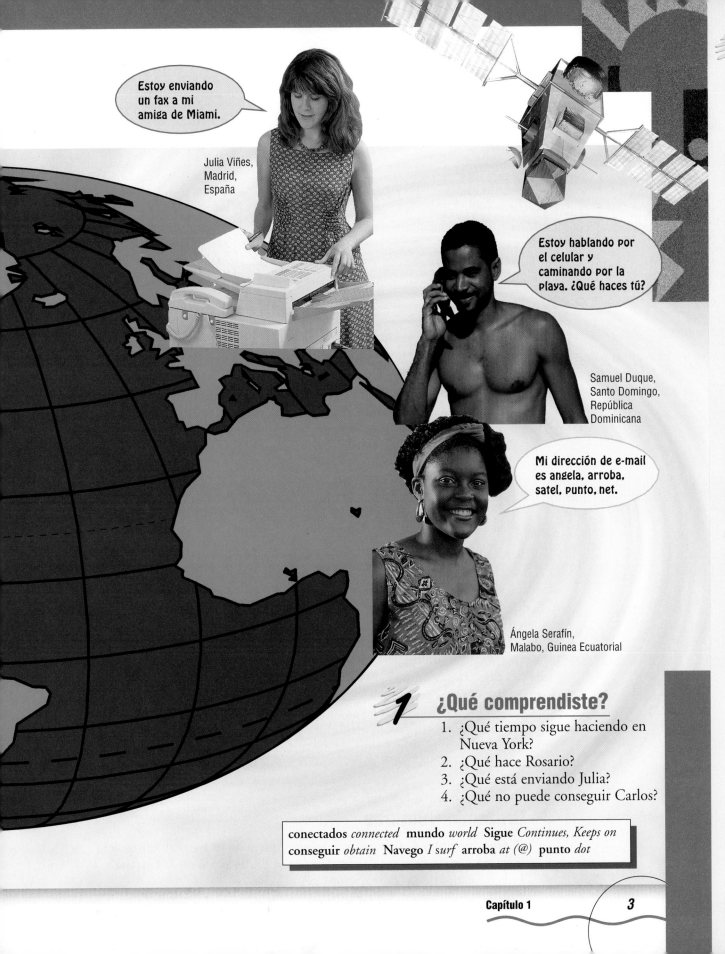

Estoy enviando un fax a mi amiga de Miami.

Julia Viñes,
Madrid,
España

Estoy hablando por el celular y caminando por la playa. ¿Qué haces tú?

Samuel Duque,
Santo Domingo,
República
Dominicana

Mi dirección de e-mail es angela, arroba, satel, punto, net.

Ángela Serafín,
Malabo, Guinea Ecuatorial

1 ¿Qué comprendiste?

1. ¿Qué tiempo sigue haciendo en Nueva York?
2. ¿Qué hace Rosario?
3. ¿Qué está enviando Julia?
4. ¿Qué no puede conseguir Carlos?

conectados *connected* mundo *world* Sigue *Continues, Keeps on* conseguir *obtain* Navego *I surf* arroba *at (@)* punto *dot*

Answers

1. 1. Sigue haciendo frío.
   2. Rosario navega en la Internet.
   3. Está enviando un fax a su amiga de Miami.
   4. No puede conseguir la dirección de correo electrónico de Mario.

Notes

The CD/cassette symbol in the margins of the Annotated Teacher's Edition (ATE) indicates an activity that has been recorded by native speakers as part of the audiocassette/audio compact disc program. Have students listen to the recording of these sections first in order to practice listening skills and then to practice speaking Spanish.

Detailed suggestions for using *Somos así* can be found in the Introduction to the ATE.

Icons in the side margins of the ATE indicate components with additional activities to reinforce and expand upon the content taught in *Somos así*.

Encourage students to refer to the maps at the beginning of the book to see where the places mentioned in the textbook are located.

Cultures. *Somos así LISTOS* reflects the practices, perspectives and products of people throughout the Spanish-speaking world so students can learn that language does not occur in a vacuum.

Activities

Expansion. Additional questions (*¿Qué comprendiste?*): *Si en Nueva York están ahora en invierno, ¿en qué estación están en Argentina?; ¿Dónde está Samuel?; ¿Qué está haciendo?; ¿Cómo están conectados los chicos con el mundo?*

Language through Action. Have students greet several classmates in Spanish. They should introduce themselves (being sure to shake hands!) and say they are pleased to meet one another. Then encourage students to ask each other about their interests and weekly activities.

NATIONAL STANDARDS
C1.1, C1.2, C4.1

Answers

2 Answers will vary.

3 Answers will vary.

Notes

The section *Algo más* consists of handy linguistic tips and required vocabulary to further improve students' language skills. Students are required to know the details spelled out in the section and to learn any new vocabulary presented here.

Vocabulary pertaining to technology varies from country to country. For example, in Spain *la computadora* is commonly called *el ordenador* while *el teléfono celular* is *el teléfono móvil*.

Remind students that English words that end in -**tion** have Spanish equivalents that end in -*ción*. Similarly, English words that end in -**ty** often end in -*dad* in Spanish.

The National Standards (i.e., Communication, Cultures, Connections, Comparisons and Communities). The National Standards are practiced and supported in activities and narratives throughout *Somos así LISTOS*. For example, activities on pages 3 and 4 require students to understand and interpret written and spoken language and to make curricular connections to other disciplines (technology). In addition, the *Para ti* on page 4 encourages students to make comparisons between English and Spanish.

Algo más

Expresiones adicionales

bajar un programa	*download a (software) program*
la comunicación	*communication*
el cuarto de charla	*chatroom*
el motor de búsqueda	*search engine*
la red	*net*
la Red Mundial de Información	*World Wide Web*
surfear	*to surf*
la Web	*Web*

¿Inglés o español?
You have learned to recognize Spanish cognates such as: *cero, comunicación* and *programa*. Do you remember any word endings in English that have Spanish equivalents? Can you give any examples? You may have even noticed that English words that end in -**tion** often have Spanish cognates that end in -*ción*. Other words are identical in both English and in Spanish, especially technology-related and scientific terms.

English	**Spanish**
Internet	*la Internet*
fax	*el fax*

2 Charlando

1. ¿Cómo estás conectado con el mundo?
2. ¿Qué tipo de información te gusta buscar en la Internet?
3. ¿Consigues toda la información que te gusta en la Internet?
4. ¿Bajas programas de la Internet? ¿De qué tipo?
5. ¿Usas los cuartos de charla? Explica.

Conexión cultural

El mundo y la tecnología

El mundo de habla hispana es tan grande que a veces nos parece difícil tener comunicación e información inmediata de lo que pasa en muchos de sus lugares. Sin embargo, hoy, gracias a la tecnología tenemos formas de comunicación que nos permiten estar en contacto con personas y obtener información de otros países en cualquier momento y en forma muy rápida. El teléfono celular, por ejemplo, nos permite llamar a otra persona desde cualquier lugar. Por el correo electrónico o e-mail podemos escribir cartas en la computadora y enviarlas a cualquier país del mundo en forma inmediata y por Internet podemos conseguir información del mundo y hacer compras sin salir de la casa. ¿Cómo piensas tú que la tecnología va a cambiar tu estilo de vida?

EL PACTO ANDINO PREFIERE A PORTA.

NORTEL
NORTHERN TELECOM

La Cumbre de Presidentes Andinos ha confiado su comunicación a la avanzada tecnología de **PORTA** *y* **Nortel.**

PORTA
COMUNICACION TOTAL

CONEXIONES 3 Cruzando fronteras

¿Cómo funciona el aparato tecnológico que más te gusta? Consigue la información en tu clase de ciencias, en la biblioteca o en la Internet. Luego, comparte la información con la clase.

Repaso *rápido*

Vamos a la escuela.

El presente del indicativo I
Verbos regulares
hablar: hablo, hablas, habla, hablamos, habláis, hablan
comer: como, comes, come, comemos, coméis, comen
vivir: vivo, vives, vive, vivimos, vivís, viven

Algunos verbos irregulares
estar: estoy, estás, está, estamos, estáis, están
hacer: hago, haces, hace, hacemos, hacéis, hacen
ir: voy, vas, va, vamos, vais, van
ser: soy, eres, es, somos, sois, son
tener: tengo, tienes, tiene, tenemos, tenéis, tienen

PARA ti

En los Apéndices
The Appendices at the end of *Somos así LISTOS* provide a comprehensive verb reference. Use the section any time you would like to review the formation of a regular or irregular verb.

 ## 4 Una entrevista

Completa la siguiente entrevista con la forma apropiada del verbo indicado.

ENTREVISTADOR: ¿*1. (Tener)* correo electrónico?
LUZ CONSUELO: Sí. Yo *2. (tener)* e-mail.
ENTREVISTADOR: ¿Cuál *3. (ser)* la dirección de tu correo electrónico?
LUZ CONSUELO: Mi dirección *4. (ser)* consuelo, arroba, yahoo, punto, com.
ENTREVISTADOR: ¿*5. (Navegar)* en la Internet?
LUZ CONSUELO: Sí, mi hermana y yo *6. (navegar)* mucho en la Internet.
ENTREVISTADOR: ¿*7. (Saber)* Uds. bajar programas de la red?
LUZ CONSUELO: Sí, yo *8. (saber)* pero mi hermana no *9. (saber)*.
ENTREVISTADOR: ¿*10. (Hacer)* amigos en los cuartos de charla?
LUZ CONSUELO: No, no *11. (hacer)* amigos en los cuartos de charla.
ENTREVISTADOR: Gracias por tu tiempo.
LUZ CONSUELO: Con mucho gusto.

consuelo@yahoo.com

Activity 2

Answers

5 Answers will vary.

6 Answers will vary.

7 Answers will vary. Make sure students use the word *arroba* (@) when giving the e-mail address.

8 Answers will vary.

Notes

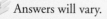

Pair and group activities are indicated in the Pupil's Edition by the symbol ▮.

As part of your classroom management, consider setting a time limit for each pair or group activity. You can hold students accountable by selecting pairs or groups to perform the task they are practicing or by having students select one person from each group to give a summary of the group's work to the class.

Communities. Ask your students how they think new means of communication (e-mail, cellular phones, etc.) can improve their lives and the communities where they live.

For a comprehensive reference list of the numbers, turn to the Appendices at the back of the book.

Review the following weather expressions before assigning activity 9 on page 7: *¿Qué tiempo hace?; Hace buen (mal) tiempo/ frío/sol/calor/fresco/viento/ sol.; Hay neblina.; Está soleado/ nublado.; Llueve.; Nieva.; ¿Qué temperatura hace?; Hace (number) grados.*

Connections. Another way to ask the temperature is *¿Cuál es la temperatura?*

Convert Fahrenheit to centigrade using the formula:

$$C° = 5/9 \times (F°-32°).$$

NATIONAL STANDARDS
C1.1, C1.2, C1.3, C4.1, C5.2

5 Encuesta

Responde afirmativamente (sí) o negativamente (no) a las siguientes oraciones.

Encuesta
Conectados con el mundo

		sí	no
1.	La tecnología es importante en mi vida.	[ ]	[ ]
2.	Sé navegar en la Internet.	[ ]	[ ]
3.	En mi casa tenemos los siguientes equipos:		
	A. Computadora	[ ]	[ ]
	B. Fax	[ ]	[ ]
	C. Celular	[ ]	[ ]
4.	Uso la computadora para enviar correo electrónico.	[ ]	[ ]
5.	La computadora está conectada con la Internet.	[ ]	[ ]
6.	Sé cómo bajar programas de la Internet.	[ ]	[ ]
7.	Uso la Internet para hacer compras.	[ ]	[ ]
8.	Puedo conseguir información importante en la Red Mundial de Información.	[ ]	[ ]
9.	Me gusta usar los cuartos de charla.	[ ]	[ ]
10.	Mi vida es mejor porque uso la tecnología.	[ ]	[ ]

6 Presentación a la clase

Trabajando en grupos pequeños, hablen de sus encuestas. Escriban un resumen *(summary)* de los resultados. Luego, una persona debe presentar la información a la clase.

7 Un e-mail

Consigue *(obtain)* la dirección de e-mail (correo electrónico) de tres compañeros de clase. Luego, escríbeles un mensaje, diciendo cinco cosas que vas a hacer el próximo fin de semana.

8 Consiguiendo información personal

Habla con tres compañeros/as de clase, para pedir *(ask for)* la siguiente información, si la tienen: número de teléfono, número de fax, número de celular, motor de búsqueda favorito.

Lección 1

9 Usando la Internet para conseguir información

Mira esta página web del clima en la Argentina y da un reporte del tiempo.

Hay niebla.

San Miguel de Tucumán •

80/62° F
26/16° C

Corrientes

80/66° F
26/19° C

Córdoba •

78/55° F
25/13° C

Mendoza •

75/47° F
23/8° C

Buenos Aires •

74/53° F
23/12° C

Mar del Plata

70/46° F
21/7° C

San Carlos de Bariloche

43/22° F
6/-5° C

El tiempo en Argentina

PARAti

Más para hablar del tiempo

el estado del tiempo	*weather conditions*
el aguacero	*rain shower*
la humedad	*humidity*
la niebla	*fog*
la nube	*cloud*
el relámpago	*lightning*
el trueno	*thunder*

10 El estado del tiempo en...

Busca información en la Internet sobre el estado del tiempo en un país (o ciudad) de habla hispana que te gustaría visitar. Prepara un informe *(report)* del tiempo en ese lugar, la ropa que debes llevar y las actividades que puedes hacer.

Nieva y hace frío en el invierno.

11 ¿Qué estación es?

Trabajando en parejas, alterna con tu compañero/a de clase en describir el tiempo durante una estación del año mientras que la otra persona adivina qué estación es.

A: Nieva y hace frío.
B: Es el invierno.

Answers

9 Answers will vary.
10 Answers will vary.
11 Answers will vary.

Notes

The National Standards (i.e., Communication, Cultures, Connections, Comparisons and Communities). The National Standards are practiced and supported in the activities on pages 6-7, which require students to make curricular connections with technology and science (meteorology).

Remind students that the seasons of the year south of the equator are the opposite of the United States . Thus, summer in the United States is winter in Argentina.

Activities

Critical Thinking. After reviewing the weather map, have students predict the month of the year and season. Next, have them describe the current weather conditions and state the type of outdoor activities people participate in on a day like the one shown on the map.

Expansion. After completing activity 9, ask students the following questions: *¿Hace buen tiempo hoy?*; *Cuando es invierno en los Estados Unidos, ¿qué estación es en Córdoba, Argentina?*; *¿Cuándo hace mucho frío y nieva?*; *¿Cuándo hace mucho calor?*; *¿Cuándo hace un poco de frío y viento?*; *¿Cuándo hay muchas flores?*; *¿Cuándo hay mucha nieve?*

NATIONAL STANDARDS
C1.1, C1.2, C1.3, C4.1, C5.1

Activity 12

Quiz/Activity 2

Activities 5-6

Answers

12 Possible answers:
1. Están navegando en la Internet.
2. Estamos saliendo/diciendo "adiós".
3. Está hablando por el celular.
4. Está enviando un fax.
5. Está leyendo el correo electrónico.
6. Están viendo televisión.

Notes

Stress that the present progressive describes an action in progress at the moment of speech.

Related activities can be found in the *Somos así LISTOS* ancillaries, which include the following: Workbook, Testing/Assessment Program, Oral Proficiency Evaluation Manual, Portfolio Assessment, Live-Action Video Program, Audiocassette/Audio CD Program, Overhead Transparencies and Teacher's Resource Kit (TRK).

Activities

Critical Thinking. Ask students to imagine it is 7:30 on a typical Saturday night. What are they doing? What are their family and friends doing? Ask them to write a composition of at least eight sentences, describing what people they know are doing at this imaginary moment. Give students a model for the first line of the composition.

Repaso *rápido*

El presente progresivo

The present progressive tense indicates what is happening at this very moment. It is formed by combining the present tense of *estar* and the present participle *(gerundio)* of a verb: *estoy estudiando, estás comiendo, está viviendo.*

| estar | + | gerundio |

The present participle of most Spanish verbs is formed by replacing the infinitive ending *-ar* with *-ando* and by replacing the infinitive endings *-er* or *-ir* with *-iendo*.

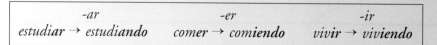

-ar	-er	-ir
estudiar → *estudiando*	*comer* → *comiendo*	*vivir* → *viviendo*

Some stem-changing verbs require a different change in the present participle. This change is indicated by the second letter or set of letters shown in parentheses after infinitives in *Somos así LISTOS*.

verbo	presente	gerundio
dormir (ue, u)	*duermo*	*durmiendo*
sentir (ie, i)	*siento*	*sintiendo*

but:

pensar (ie)	*pienso*	*pensando*
volver (ue)	*vuelvo*	*volviendo*

The following are some irregular present participles:

decir	→	*diciendo*	*poder*	→	*pudiendo*
leer	→	*leyendo*	*traer*	→	*trayendo*
oír	→	*oyendo*	*venir*	→	*viniendo*

Iván está durmiendo en clase.

 12 Todos hacen algo

¿Qué están haciendo las personas en las ilustraciones?

Sonia
Está oyendo música.

1. María y Fernando   2. nosotros   3. Teresa

8   **Lección 1**

4. Alejandro

5. Gabriela

6. Quique y Luis

El presente de los verbos *seguir* y *conseguir*

The verbs *seguir (i, i),* "to continue, to follow, to keep on," and *conseguir (i, i),* "to obtain," are conjugated following the pattern of *pedir (i, i).* However, *seguir* and *conseguir* require a spelling change, dropping the *u* before the letter *o.*

conseguir	
consigo	conseguimos
consigues	conseguís
consigue	consiguen

seguir	
sigo	seguimos
sigues	seguís
sigue	siguen

The verb *seguir* is usually followed by *a* when indicating motion or when stating that one thing (or one person) follows another.

Seguimos a Samuel en el carro.
We follow Samuel in the car.
Una página web **sigue** a otra.
One web page follows another.

Combine *seguir* with a present participle to say that someone keeps on doing something.

Julio **sigue buscando** información en la Web.
Julio keeps on looking for information in the Web.

¿Por qué me sigues?

13 En la Internet

Las siguientes personas están navegando en la Internet. Usando las pistas, haz oraciones completas para decir si consiguen la página web que están buscando.

 Patricia (sí)
Consigue la página web que está buscando.
Carlos (no)
No consigue la página web que está buscando.

1. yo (sí)
2. Pedro y Clara (no)
3. el profesor (sí)
4. Margarita (no)
5. nosotros (no)
6. tú (sí)

Patricia consigue la página web que está buscando.

 Activity 13

 Activity 7

 Quiz/Activity 2

Answers

13 1. Consigo la página web que estoy buscando.
2. No consiguen la página web que están buscando.
3. Consigue la página web que está buscando.
4. No consigue la página web que está buscando.
5. No conseguimos la página web que estamos buscando.
6. Consigues la página web que estás buscando.

Notes

Remind students that the second form of the verb on the right side of the paradigm for *conseguir* and *seguir* corresponds to the plural subject pronouns *vosotros* and *vosotras,* which are used in Spain.

Activities

Language through Action. Have students prepare a list of Spanish verbs that represent actions they can act out. Then ask for volunteers to say the first-person singular form of verbs from the list, while they perform the action in front of the class: *camino* (student walks), *canto* (student sings), etc.

NATIONAL STANDARDS
C1.2, C4.1

Answers

14
1. No sigo buscando.
2. Siguen buscando.
3. No sigue buscando.
4. Sigue buscando.
5. Seguimos buscando.
6. No sigues buscando.

15
1. Busca información para su asignatura de ecología.
2. No, no lo consigue.
3. Gloria es la mejor para encontrar información en la Internet.
4. Contiene información sobre la contaminación ambiental.
5. Sí, tiene muchos vínculos.
6. Answers will vary.

Notes

Narrative material as well as dialogs in *Somos así* provide spoken exposure to authentic Spanish in specific contexts. Explain to students that they will hear Spanish speakers that have been recorded on audiocassette/audio compact discs. They are not expected to understand everything they hear. However, students should listen carefully to the sounds, tone and rhythm of the language while trying to guess what topics are being discussed.

Students may find it interesting that a spider's web is a *telaraña*. In Spanish the word Web refers only to the World Wide Web.

Remind students that close cognates will not be defined in *Somos así LISTOS*.

Point out to students that the new verb *encontrar* is conjugated like the verb *contar*.

Activities

Prereading Strategy. Instruct students to cover up the dialog with one hand and look at the illustration. Ask them to imagine where the conversation takes place and what the people are saying to one another.

---

14 Siguen o no siguen buscando

Haz oraciones completas para indicar quiénes de las personas de la actividad anterior siguen buscando y quiénes no siguen buscando páginas web en la Internet.

Patricia (no)
No sigue buscando.

Carlos (sí)
Sigue buscando.

1. yo (no)
2. Pedro y Clara (sí)
3. el profesor (no)

4. Margarita (sí)
5. nosotros (sí)
6. tú (no)

La mejor compañera

GLORIA: ¡Hola, Javier! ¿Qué haces?

JAVIER: Busco información para mi **asignatura**° de **ecología**, pero no consigo nada.

GLORIA: ¿Te puedo ayudar? Soy la mejor para **encontrar**° información en la Internet.

JAVIER: Pues, necesito información sobre la **contaminación ambiental.**°

GLORIA: Mira, esta página web **contiene**° más información que las otras, y tiene muchos **vínculos.**°

JAVIER: Gracias, Gloria. ¡Eres la mejor compañera de la clase!

GLORIA: De nada, Javier. Ahora, ¿por qué no apagas la computadora y vamos al parque?

JAVIER: De acuerdo. Quiero salir por un momento y puedo continuar más tarde.

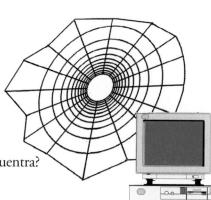

> Soy la mejor para encontrar información en la Internet.

asignatura *subject* **encontrar** *to find* **contaminación ambiental** *environmental pollution*
contiene *contains* **vínculos** *links*

15 ¿Qué comprendiste?

1. ¿Qué hace Javier?
2. ¿Consigue Javier lo que busca?
3. ¿Quién es la mejor para encontrar información en la Internet?
4. ¿Qué información contiene la página web que Gloria encuentra?
5. ¿Tiene vínculos la página web que Gloria encuentra?
6. ¿Qué va a hacer Javier?

16 Charlando

1. ¿Te gusta la ecología? ¿Por qué?
2. ¿Hay contaminación donde vives?
3. ¿Eres bueno/a para navegar en la Internet? ¿Puedes encontrar la información que buscas?
4. ¿Qué haces cuando no puedes conseguir lo que quieres? ¿Buscas en los vínculos?

Proverbios y dichos

A person who follows through usually succeeds. Dedication and devotion are key elements to achievement. If you fail at something you believe in, do not quit trying. You can even learn from mistakes and they can put you one step closer to your goal. As the saying goes in Spanish: *El que persevera alcanza* (Perseverance leads to success).

Conexión Cultural

La contaminación ambiental

Uno de los problemas más importantes que afectan hoy a los países de habla hispana y en general a todo el mundo es la contaminación ambiental. El humo *(smoke)* de las industrias y de los carros, y la destrucción de los bosques, son factores que contribuyen día a día al aumento de la contaminación. La situación es muy difícil, y mientras que algunos grupos ecologistas tratan de hacer algo por el planeta, muchos de nosotros no hacemos nada.

Todos debemos ayudar a la solución de la contaminación ambiental. ¿Y qué podemos hacer? No debemos tirar basura en la calle, en los parques o en los ríos. Debemos cuidar las plantas, los árboles y los animales. Podemos usar menos el carro y caminar más o usar la bicicleta cuando vamos a una tienda que está cerca. Con la tecnología de hoy, podemos crear un club de ecología virtual en una página web. Así muchachos y muchachas de todo el mundo pueden participar en la protección del medio ambiente *(environment)* y enseñar a otros a hacerlo. De esta manera podemos mejorar nuestro planeta y la vida de los que vivimos en él.

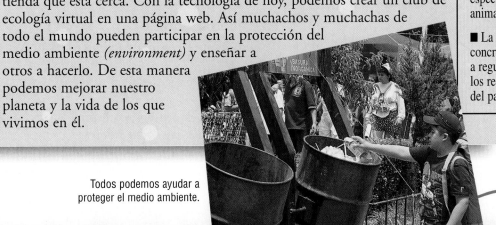

Todos podemos ayudar a proteger el medio ambiente.

Problemas Ambientales

La lista de problemas que atentan contra el medio ambiente es alarmante:

■ La tala indiscriminada de árboles.

■ Alto índice de contaminación de vertientes naturales.

■ Aire contaminado por el humo de automotores.

■ Exterminio de especies vegetales y animales.

■ La falta de una ley concreta que ayude a regular y conservar los recursos naturales del país.

11

Quiz/Activity 3

Activities 9-10

Quiz/Activity 3

Answers

17 Answers will vary.

Notes

Activity 17 addresses cross-curricular learning (ecology), the multiple intelligences (intrapersonal) and critical thinking (problem solving).

The section *Oportunidades* appears in every chapter of *Somos así*, addressing the future opportunities that learning Spanish will provide for students in the areas of careers, travel, college, success, personal fulfillment, etc.

Remind students that the present tense is generally used to say what people are doing now or what they do frequently. However, the present tense can also be used to refer to the not-too-distant future as long as a future time expression is used: *Puedo continuar más tarde.*

Service Learning Volunteers. An important aspect of learning Spanish is making real-life connections to what students are learning in class. Service learning volunteer activities provide students the opportunity to see what work is all about while contributing to their school or community. In this way, students engage in meaningful real-life work experiences within the classroom or in their own community while simultaneously engaging their minds and thinking capabilities in work that is specifically connected to the skills and knowledge they are learning in school.

NATIONAL STANDARDS
C1.2, C3.1, C3.2, C4.1, C4.2, C5.1

CONEXIONES

17 Cruzando fronteras

Estudia la contaminación ambiental en algunas ciudades de los Estados Unidos o de los países de habla hispana. Luego, di qué piensas tú que podemos hacer para ayudar con este problema. Busca información en la biblioteca o en la Internet si es necesario.

Oportunidades

Aprender ofreciendo servicio a otros *(Service learning)*

Most people recognize the importance of classroom learning. However, it is equally important to make real-life connections by using your knowledge in the community as actively involved citizens. One way you can do this is to exercise your right to vote. Another way to demonstrate good citizenship on a local, national or international level is by volunteering to serve others. For example, would you like to do something about the problem of environmental pollution? Instead of talking about the problem, make some calls around your community, or try searching the World Wide Web to find a group with similar interests. If there are no local organizations you can join, organize an ecology club. Then make a few calls or ask around (your teacher or the school counselor can probably help) to find out who in your community needs volunteers testing the water, picking up trash or helping with any number of other environmental problems that people talk about every day.

Repaso *rápido*

Juegan a las maquinitas cuando llueve.

El presente del indicativo II

Verbos con cambios en la raíz

cerrar: cierro, cierras, cierra, cerramos, cerráis, cierran
(Verbos similares: empezar, encender, nevar, pensar, preferir, querer, sentir)

pedir: pido, pides, pide, pedimos, pedís, piden
(Verbos similares: seguir, conseguir, repetir)

poder: puedo, puedes, puede, podemos, podéis, pueden
(Verbos similares: colgar, contar, costar, dormir, encontrar, llover, volver)

jugar: juego, juegas, juega, jugamos, jugáis, juegan

Tres verbos con acento

esquiar: esquío, esquías, esquía, esquiamos, esquiáis, esquían

enviar: envío, envías, envía, enviamos, enviáis, envían

continuar: continúo, continúas, continúa, continuamos, continuáis, continúan

¿Esquías con tus amigos en el invierno?

18 La clase de ecología

Haz oraciones completas en el presente para decir lo que hacen las personas indicadas, añadiendo las palabras necesarias.

>   Eliana/conseguir/información/sobre ecología
>   Eliana consigue información sobre ecología.

1. Alejandro y Conchita/empezar/leer/ sobre/contaminación ambiental
2. yo/pedir/hacer/club de ecología
3. mis compañeros/pensar/ser/buena idea
4. profesora/contar/algo de/historia/contaminación ambiental
5. Jennifer/continuar leyendo sobre/contaminación
6. nosotros/empezar/comprender/problema
7. Yuri/encontrar/otro club de ecología/Internet
8. Keeley/enviar/e-mail/otro club de ecología
9. tú/pensar hablar con tu clase/ problema/contaminación

www.greenpeace.es/
www.greenpeace.org/

EN LA RED DE GREENPEACE

No podíamos terminar el año sin manifestar nuestro espíritu ecológico, por eso te recomendamos las páginas oficiales de *Greenpeace* y *Greenpeace España*. En ellas encontrarás noticias sobre atmósfera, biodiversidad, basura tóxica y campañas ecológicas, así como la posibilidad de entrar en contacto con estas organizaciones.

INTERNET

19 El horario de Eliana

Eliana va a estar muy ocupada la semana que viene. Di qué va a hacer cada día, según el siguiente horario.

>   El lunes que viene va a enviar un fax al club de ecología.

lunes	enviar un fax al club de ecología
martes	ir al club de ecología
miércoles	navegar en la Internet
jueves	escribir a mis amigos por e-mail
viernes	conseguir información sobre la contaminación ambiental
sábado	ir de compras al centro comercial
domingo	llamar a mi tía Carmen al celular

PARA ti

Ir a
Remember that you can use the present tense of *ir* followed by *a* and an infinitive to talk about what is or is not going to happen in the not-to-distant future.

ir + a + infinitivo

¿Qué **vas a hacer?** What **are you going to do?**

Voy a buscar unos vínculos en la Web. **I am going to look** for some links on the Web.

20 Tu horario

Prepara tu horario para la semana que viene, usando el horario de Eliana como modelo (inventa la información si quieres). Luego, trabajando en parejas, alterna con tu compañero/a de clase en preguntar y contestar qué van a hacer, según sus horarios.

>   A: ¿Qué vas a hacer el lunes que viene?
>   B: Voy a comprar un celular.

Answers

18 Possible answers:
1. Alejandro y Conchita empiezan a leer sobre la contaminación ambiental.
2. Yo pido hacer un club de ecología.
3. Mis compañeros piensan que es una buena idea.
4. La profesora cuenta algo de la historia de la contaminación ambiental.
5. Jennifer continúa leyendo sobre la contaminación.
6. Nosotros empezamos a comprender el problema.
7. Yuri encuentra otro club de ecología en la Internet.
8. Keeley envía un e-mail a otro club de ecología.
9. Tú piensas hablar con tu clase del problema de la contaminación.

19 1. El martes que viene va a ir al club de ecología.
2. El miércoles que viene va a navegar en la Internet.
3. El jueves que viene va a escribir a sus amigos por e-mail.
4. El viernes que viene va a conseguir información sobre la contaminación ambiental.
5. El sábado que viene va a ir de compras al centro comercial.
6. El domingo que viene va a llamar a su tía Carmen al celular.

20 Creative self-expression.

Notes

The construction consisting of *ir* + *a* + infinitive is commonly heard as a substitute for the future tense, to the extent that it virtually replaces the ordinary future-tense form in the speech of many people, especially in Latin America.

Activities

Cooperative Learning. Practice the comparatives and superlatives with simple illustrations, such as one person labeled with a name, a dollar symbol and an amount; another person labeled with a name and the same amount; and a third labeled with a name and a higher amount: Pilar, 200 *pesetas*; Carlos, 200 *pesetas*; Andrés, 500 *pesetas*. Then hold up pictures of Pilar and Andrés and say, *"Pilar tiene 200 pesetas y Andrés tiene 500 pesetas. Pilar tiene menos pesetas que Andrés. Andrés tiene más pesetas que Pilar. ¿Quién tiene menos pesetas?"* (Ask a student to respond.) Continue with *"¿Quién tiene más pesetas?"* (Ask for a response.) Next ask a student to describe Pilar in relation to Andrés: *"Tiene menos pesetas que Andrés."* Ask a student to describe Andrés in relation to Pilar: *"Tiene más pesetas que Pilar."* Hold up pictures of Pilar and Carlos while making statements and asking questions to elicit responses: *"...tiene tanto dinero como..."* and *"...tiene tantas pesetas como..."* In similar fashion, use three illustrations of people with an item that may be described as larger or smaller, for example, and ask questions for responses that include the following: *más grande que, menos grande que, más pequeño que, menos pequeño que, tan grande como, tan pequeño como.*

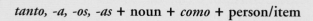

IDIOMA

El comparativo y el superlativo

Use the following patterns when making comparisons in Spanish:

> **más/menos + noun/adjective/adverb + *que* + person/item**

*Hay **más/menos** gente aquí hoy **que** ayer.*	There are **more/fewer people** here today **than** yesterday.
*Este celular es **más pequeño** que ese celular.*	This cellular phone is **smaller than** that cellular phone.
*Puedo escribir un e-mail **más rápidamente que** tú.*	I can write an e-mail **faster than you.**

> **tanto, -a, -os, -as + noun + *como* + person/item**

*No tengo **tanta información** como tú.*	I do not have **as much information as you.**

> **tan + adjective/adverb + *como* + person/item**

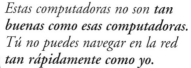

Tú no puedes ir tan rápidamente como yo.

*Estas computadoras no son **tan buenas como** esas computadoras.*	These computers are not **as good as** those computers.
*Tú no puedes navegar en la red **tan rápidamente como** yo.*	You do not surf the net **as quickly as I do.**

> **verb + *tanto como* + person/item**

*Yo estoy haciendo **tanto como** tú.*	I am doing **as much as you.**

Use the following patterns when singling out one person, group, object, group of objects or attribute as the best (most, least):

> **definite article (+ noun) + *más/menos* + adjective (+ *de* + person/item)**

*Es **la chica más baja** (de la clase).*	She is **the shortest girl** (in the class).
*Mi cuarto es **el cuarto más grande** (de la casa).*	My room is **the largest room** (in the house).

> **verb + *lo* + *más/menos* + adverb + *posible***

*Debes llegar **lo más temprano** posible.*	You should arrive **as soon as** possible.

21 La tecnología moderna

Haz oraciones completas usando el comparativo y el superlativo y las indicaciones que se dan. Añade las palabras que sean necesarias.

 fax/ser/más rápido/correo
El fax es más rápido que el correo.

1. correo electrónico/ser/tan rápido/fax
2. e-mail/no tomar/tanto/tiempo/fax
3. teléfono celular/ser/más cómodo/teléfono normal
4. Internet/ser/mejor/red de comunicaciones
5. correo normal/ser/más lento/correo electrónico

Un teléfono celular es más cómodo que un teléfono normal.

22 Los compañeros de clase

Trabajando en parejas, alterna con tu compañero/a de clase en hacer y contestar preguntas, según las indicaciones que se dan.

 alto
A: ¿Quién es la persona más alta de la clase?
B: La persona más alta de la clase es *(name of the person)*.

1. cómico   3. rubio   5. viejo
2. bajo   4. moreno   6. joven

Algo más

Más sobre el comparativo y el superlativo

Some adjectives/adverbs have irregular comparative forms:

peor	worse/worst	*mejor*	better/best
menor	younger/youngest	*mayor*	older/oldest

*El primer motor de búsqueda es **bueno,** pero el segundo es **mejor** y este motor de búsqueda es **el mejor** de todos.*

That first search engine is **good,** but the second one is **better** and this search engine is **the best of all.**

In order to state that there are "fewer than" or "more than" the number of items indicated, use *menos de* or *más de* followed by a number.

*Veo **menos de/más de** veinte computadoras.*

I see **fewer than/more than** twenty computers.

Veo más de tres computadoras.

NATIONAL STANDARDS
C1.1, C1.2, C4.1

Answers

23 Creative self-expression.

24 Creative self-expression.

25 Possible answers:
1. ...va a ser mejor.
2. ...va a ser peor.
3. ...van a ser más rápidos.
4. ...tanto como hoy.
5. ...va a ser (Answers will vary).
6. ...va a ser (Answers will vary).

Notes

With the exception of *bueno, malo, pequeño, grande, poco* and *mucho*, all adjectives form the comparative with *más...que* ("more than") or *menos que* ("less...than").

Activities

Multiple Intelligences (logical-mathematical). Have students work in small groups surveying their classmates about their schedule of activities for the week, using *ir a* + infinitive or using the present tense to talk about the future. They must then summarize the results. As a final step, one student from each group should present the information to the class.

TPR. Students prepare two columns of names of imaginary people and place a number next to each name to indicate how much money each person has. Working in pairs, have students make statements comparing how much the named people have as they point at the name of the person. Circulate to keep students on task and to offer assistance. You may wish to contribute to some of the conversations by stopping for a moment and asking or answering a question or two for each pair of students.

 23 En tu clase

Haz seis comparaciones entre tus compañeros de clase.

 Jorge es mayor que Ana.

Catalina es más alta que Yolanda.

 24 La vida de hoy

Trabajando en parejas, hablen de la tecnología y la vida de hoy. Deben usar *más que, menos que, tan...como* o *tanto...como*.

A: ¿Qué es más importante en la vida de hoy, el fax o el e-mail?
B: En la vida de hoy el e-mail es tan importante como el fax.

 25 El mundo del futuro

¿En qué va a ser diferente el mundo del futuro? Completa las siguientes oraciones, usando el comparativo y el superlativo para dar tu opinión.

Voy a tener....
Voy a tener <u>tanto dinero como Bill Gates.</u>

1. La comunicación electrónica....
2. El tráfico en las ciudades....
3. Los aviones....
4. Voy a navegar en la Internet....
5. Lo peor....
6. Lo mejor....

Universidad de Chile
Facultad de Ciencias
Programa de Postítulo en Contaminación Ambiental

Bienvenido
INSTITUTO DE ECOLOGIA, A.C.
Descripción
Acontecer IdeE
Investigación
Jardín Botánico
Posgrado
Biblioteca
Correo electrónico

Es importante cuidar el medio ambiente.

¿Por qué es la contaminación como una bola de nieve?

LA CONTAMINACIÓN ES COMO UNA BOLA DE NIEVE
TIRÁ LOS RESIDUOS AQUÍ

PAPERA BAKARRIK SOLO PAPEL

Estoy navegando en la Internet.

Autoevaluación. Como repaso y autoevaluación, responde lo siguiente:

1. In Spanish, name three or four technologies that you have used.
2. State in Spanish your e-mail address or the e-mail address of someone you know.
3. What season is it now?
4. What is the weather like today?
5. Name two things that are happening at this very moment.
6. Name one thing that you obtain on the Internet.
7. What do you know about environmental pollution?
8. What are some things you can do to help solve environmental problems?
9. List three things you are going to do this week.
10. Make three comparisons about yourself and your best friend.

Hay sol y hace calor. ¿Qué estación es?

Answers
Autoevaluación
Possible answers:
1. la computadora, la web/la Internet, el teléfono celular, el correo electrónico/el e-mail, el fax
2. Answers will vary.
3. Estamos en otoño/ invierno/primavera/verano.
4. Hace frío/sol/calor/fresco/ viento.
5. Estoy leyendo este libro. Mis amigos están hablando español.
6. Consigo amigos que hablan español en los cuartos de charla.
7. Answers will vary.
8. Answers will vary.
9. Voy a ir al colegio todos los días. Mi familia y yo vamos a ir al cine el viernes. Voy a jugar al fútbol este fin de semana.
10. Answers will vary.

Notes
The *Autoevaluación* activity provides an opportunity for students to measure their own progress learning the main elements of the lesson. The section also serves to prepare students for the lesson test.

Activities
Critical Thinking. Have students make a list of the sports that are offered at your school. Under each sport, students should state the following: month(s) the sport is played, what the weather is like during the time the sport is played, how many people participate in each activity and any other information they are able to provide.

NATIONAL STANDARDS
C1.2, C3.1, C4.1, C4.2

Activity 14

Answers

A Creative self-expression.

B Creative self-expression.

Notes

www

Intercultural E-Mail connections
http://www.stolaf.edu/network/iecc
Search Engines
www.webcrawler.com
www.yahoo.com
www.excite.com
www.magellan.com

Before having students use e-mail, the Internet or the World Wide Web (WWW), discuss the issue with your school media specialist in order to obtain guidelines for using them in connection with school assignments. Explain the procedures and requirements to all students before allowing them to use these technological resources for any work related to Spanish class. For example, students should not give out their home address or telephone number to any unknown person or organization. (All contacts and communication should be limited to e-mail only). The Introduction to the ATE offers additional tips on using technology in the classroom, including additional specific Internet addresses.

Communication. Lessons conclude with two activities in *¡La práctica hace al maestro!* that combine the themes and content of the lesson. By completing the *Comunicación* and *Conexión con la tecnología* activities students demonstrate they are acquiring skills specified in the National Standards that enable them to function in an ever-shrinking world.

NATIONAL STANDARDS
C1.1, C1.2, C1.3, C2.1,
C3.1, C3.2, C4.1, C4.2,
C5.1, C5.2

¡La práctica hace al maestro!

A Comunicación

Working in pairs, prepare a conversation on a cellular telephone. Ask what your partner is doing. The person must answer, making up an appropriate activity he/she is doing and what he/she is going to do afterwards. Next, even though your partner already has plans, invite him/her to do something. The person should refuse the invitation and must suggest another time when he/she can go with you to do the activity.

A: ¿Qué estás haciendo?
B: Estoy navegando en la Internet y luego voy a enviar un fax.
A: ¿Puedes ir al parque a las cinco?
B: No, no puedo ir hoy, pero el sábado sí puedo ir.

B Conexión con la tecnología

Using the Internet, go to one of the Internet search engines and look for sources for Spanish-speaking key pals (electronic pen pals). You can find this information by requesting a search about key pals and the word Spanish or Intercultural e-mail connections. Print out the results you think are most promising and share them with the rest of the class.

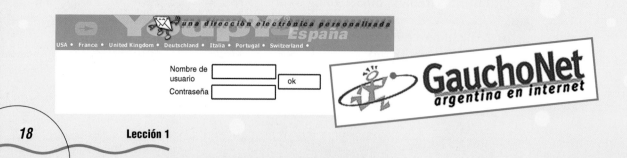

© Youpi® España
USA • France • United Kingdom • Deutschland • Italia • Portugal • Switzerland •

Nombre de usuario
Contraseña
ok

GauchoNet
argentina en internet

VOCABULARIO

La tecnología

- la arroba
- el celular
- conectado,-a
- el correo electrónico
- el cuarto de charla
- el e-mail
- el fax
- la Internet
- el motor de búsqueda
- el programa
- la Red Mundial de Información
- la tecnología
- el vínculo
- la Web

Verbos

- bajar
- conseguir (i, i)
- contener
- encontrar (ue)
- navegar
- seguir (i, i)
- surfear

Expresiones y otras palabras

- la asignatura
- la comunicación
- la contaminación ambiental
- la ecología
- la información
- el mundo
- el punto

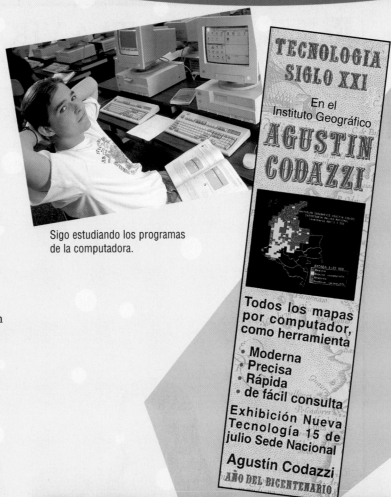

Sigo estudiando los programas
de la computadora.

**TECNOLOGIA
SIGLO XXI**

En el
Instituto Geográfico

**AGUSTIN
CODAZZI**

**Todos los mapas
por computador,
como herramienta**

- **Moderna**
- **Precisa**
- **Rápida**
- **de fácil consulta**

**Exhibición Nueva
Tecnología 15 de
julio Sede Nacional**

Agustín Codazzi

AÑO DEL BICENTENARIO

Notes

Evaluating the multiple intelligences: The Testing/ Assessment Program (Test Booklet, Oral Proficiency Evaluation Manual and Portfolio Assessment) provides a variety of activities to evaluate the multiple intelligences.

As part of your classroom management on the first day of school, explain to students that the *Vocabulario* is intended to help them identify the active vocabulary (words they must learn) for a lesson. Then demonstrate how to use this reference list of words and expressions as a self-test of the new active vocabulary for a lesson: Select two or three words that students do not know; return to where the word was first introduced to see how it was used; encourage students to try to determine what the word means. Finally, teach dictionary skills by having students find the meaning of any unknown words in the dictionary at the back of the book.

The singular definite articles *el* and *la* (and later the plural forms *los* and *las*) are frequently used with the nouns listed here. Learning them simultaneously will help students as they continue to learn to communicate more extensively in Spanish.

Both *navegar* and *surfear* are common ways in Spanish of saying someone is surfing the Internet.

Cuando estudiamos, buscamos
información en la Internet.

**NATIONAL STANDARDS
C1.2, C4.1, C5.2**

Escuela virtual

Activities 6-7

Contexto cultural
EL MUNDO HISPANO

Content reviewed in *Lección 2*
- preterite tense
- family
- household chores
- object pronouns
- telling time
- negative expressions

Notes

Explain that México, D.F., in Mexico is the approximate equivalent of Washington, D.C.

The official status of Puerto Rico is that of a U.S. Commonwealth (*Estado Libre Asociado*).

Explain that *un camping* is a **campground**; *ir de camping* is **to go camping**.

Activities

Critical Listening. Play a recorded version of statements made by these people. Have several individuals state what they believe the main theme of the conversation is.

Expansion. Practice the use of *acabar de* with the preterite tense (which is reviewed in this lesson) using the following sentences and the context **What had the following people just finished doing the last day of vacation?**: *Pedro/arreglar/cuarto (Pedro acabó de arreglar su cuarto); Elena y Marta/llegar/crucero (Elena y Marta acabaron de llegar de un crucero); tú/instalar/programa (Tú acabaste de instalar un programa); don Santiago/pintar/casa (Don Santiago acabó de pintar la casa).*

Prereading Strategy. Ask students about their favorite activities. Have them read the title of the online newspaper article. Then instruct students to cover up what the four people are saying with one hand and look at the illustrations. Finally, ask students if they can tell which activities each person is describing.

NATIONAL STANDARDS
C1.2, C4.1

chismes *gossip* noticias *news* países *countries* últimas *last* solo *alone*

¿Qué comprendiste?

1. ¿Qué encuentras en el artículo?
2. ¿Qué tomó Rosario?
3. ¿Qué acabó de pintar Raúl en junio solo?
4. ¿En qué montó Raúl?
5. ¿Adónde fue Raúl?
6. ¿Qué instaló Marcos?
7. ¿A quién visitó Silvia?
8. ¿Adónde fue Silvia?

Charlando

1. ¿Qué hiciste tú el pasado mes de junio?
2. ¿Instalaste algún programa nuevo en tu computadora?
3. ¿Fuiste a algún picnic? ¿A cuántos?
4. ¿Pintaste algo? ¿Qué pintaste?
5. ¿Hay algún periódico en tu escuela? ¿Está en la Internet?

PARA ti

Acabar de
Remember you can tell what someone has just done recently by using the expression *acabar de* followed by an infinitive.

$$acabar + de + infinitivo$$

Pedro **acaba de comprar un** programa nuevo.
Acabo de venir de camping.

Pedro **just bought (has just bought)** a new software program.
I just came (have just come) from camping.

Conexión Cultural — Diario del Caribe

Los periódicos en los países de habla hispana

Los periódicos tienen una gran tradición en los países de habla hispana. Algunos tienen hasta cien años de historia y muchos son de gran importancia e influencia en el continente americano. La gran mayoría de estos periódicos tienen hoy en día una página web en la Internet y permiten el acceso de todo el mundo.

Aquí tienes una lista de algunos periódicos que puedes leer en la red, si quieres saber lo que está pasando en el mundo, conocer más de la cultura y costumbres de otros países y practicar tu español.

Argentina
Clarín
La Nación
Chile
El Mercurio
Colombia
El Espectador
El Heraldo
El Tiempo
Costa Rica
La Nación

Ecuador
Diario Hoy
El Universo
España
ABC
El Mundo
El País
México
El Excelsior
El Universal

Paraguay
ABC Color
Diario Última Hora
Perú
La República
Puerto Rico
El Nuevo Día
La Estrella de Puerto Rico
Venezuela
El Nacional
El Universal

Activities 1-2

Activity 1

Answers

1. 1. Encuentro chismes de lo que hicieron cuatro estudiantes de diferentes países hispanos en sus vacaciones de junio.
   2. Tomó un crucero.
   3. Acabó de pintar la casa solo.
   4. Montó en bote.
   5. Raúl fue a muchos picnics.
   6. Marcos instaló un programa nuevo.
   7. Silvia visitó a su tía.
   8. Silvia fue a un camping.

2. Answers will vary.

Notes

The expression *acabar de* is usually taught in the present tense. However, it also may be used in the past when indicating that an action was just completed by a certain time. (Raúl states here that he just completed painting the house last June.)

Activities

Spanish for Spanish Speakers. Since some of your students may have celebrated fifteenth birthdays over the summer, ask if any celebrated a *fiesta de quince años*. Have your Spanish-speaking native students describe the event for the class: The *fiesta de quince años* consists of a party with a band; the *quinceañera* customarily wears a long white or pastel-colored dress and may be accompanied by a court of other girls; the family often hires a professional video camera operator to record the occasion; sometimes photographs of the event are published in the newspaper.

NATIONAL STANDARDS
C1.1, C1.2, C2.1, C4.1, C5.1, C5.2

Answers

3 Answers will vary.

Notes

CONEXIONES 3 Cruzando fronteras

Selecciona un periódico de habla hispana, búscalo en la Internet y mira sus páginas. Prepara un informe diciendo de qué ciudad y país es, algo que te gustó en el periódico y algo que te pareció diferente de los periódicos de tu ciudad. Luego, presenta la información a la clase.

EL MERCURIO

EL HERALDO
DE MEXICO

Oportunidades

El periódico de la escuela

Do you enjoy writing? Have you ever thought of pursuing a career as a journalist? Consider writing articles in Spanish for your school newspaper or a local Spanish-language newspaper. The opportunity would allow you to improve your writing skills, and you just may find out that you enjoy sharing your opinions, telling stories or relating news about school, local or world events.

Estoy escribiendo un artículo en español para el periódico.

Repaso *rápido*

El pretérito

Verbos regulares

pintar: pinté, pintaste, pintó, pintamos, pintasteis, pintaron
comer: comí, comiste, comió, comimos, comisteis, comieron
salir: salí, saliste, salió, salimos, salisteis, salieron

Verbos con cambios radicales

sentir (ie, i): sentí, sentiste, sintió, sentimos, sentisteis, sintieron
dormir (ue, u): dormí, dormiste, durmió, dormimos, dormisteis, durmieron
pedir (i, i): pedí, pediste, pidió, pedimos, pedisteis, pidieron

La profesora le pidió a Carmen hacer unas fotocopias.

Verbos con cambios ortográficos

buscar: **busqué**, buscaste, buscó, buscamos, buscasteis, buscaron
navegar: **navegué**, navegaste, navegó, navegamos, navegasteis, navegaron
empezar: **empecé**, empezaste, empezó, empezamos, empezasteis, empezaron

Verbos irregulares

dar: di, diste, dio, dimos, disteis, dieron
decir: dije, dijiste, dijo, dijimos, dijisteis, dijeron
estar: estuve, estuviste, estuvo, estuvimos,
   estuvisteis, estuvieron
hacer: hice, hiciste, hizo, hicimos, hicisteis, hicieron
ir: fui, fuiste, fue, fuimos, fuisteis, fueron
ser: fui, fuiste, fue, fuimos, fuisteis, fueron
tener: tuve, tuviste, tuvo, tuvimos, tuvisteis, tuvieron
ver: vi, viste, vio, vimos, visteis, vieron

Ayer buscamos zapatos.

4 Las vacaciones de verano

 Escribe oraciones completas para decir lo que hicieron Rogelio y sus amigos durante las vacaciones de verano. Añade las palabras que sean necesarias.

yo/visitar/mis abuelos/México
Yo visité a mis abuelos en México.

1. yo/comer/mucha comida/picnics
2. Amalia/navegar/Internet todos los días
3. Marta/pintar/solo/puertas de la casa
4. Tomás/escribir/e-mails/amigos
5. Ricardo, Nicolás y su papá/montar/bote/fines de semana
6. señora Campos y su esposo/tomar/crucero/el Caribe

Notes

The international marketplace demands that employees demonstrate a wider range of competencies and knowledge. Skills and abilities that are being sought are dynamic and ever changing, requiring today's student to develop the ability to adapt quickly to new workplace requirements in order to compete and excel. The ability to take personal responsibility for career development has been just one of many changes that is occurring in language education in recent years.

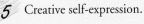

5 Las vacaciones pasadas

Trabajando en parejas, alterna con tu compañero/a de clase en decir cinco actividades que hicieron durante las vacaciones pasadas. Puedes inventar la información, si quieres.

 Las vacaciones pasadas monté en bote con mis amigos, instalé un programa nuevo en la computadora, limpié mi cuarto, escribí e-mails a unos parientes y alquilé varias películas.

NATIONAL STANDARDS
C1.1, C1.2, C1.3, C4.1, C5.1, C5.2

La familia Miranda

Todos en la familia Miranda hicieron algo diferente en las vacaciones pasadas. Di qué hizo cada uno de ellos según las ilustraciones. Añade las palabras que sean necesarias.

Sr. y Sra. Miranda/ir a nadar
El Sr. Miranda y la Sra. Miranda fueron a nadar a la playa.

1. el abuelo/dar un paseo

2. Catalina/ir con sus amigas

3. Danielito/pedir muchos

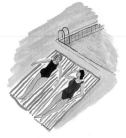  

4. las tías/dormir mucho

5. mis primos y yo/ir a dos

6. los tíos/hacer un viaje

Tus vacaciones

Describe las últimas vacaciones con tu familia. Escribe los verbos en el pretérito y completa las oraciones con más información. Puedes inventar la información, si quieres.

En las últimas vacaciones nosotros *(ir)*....
En las últimas vacaciones nosotros *fuimos* a un hotel en el Caribe.

1. Mis padres *(estar)*....
2. Mis hermanos *(hacer)*....
3. Mi hermana *(tener)*....
4. Mi padre *(dormir)*....
5. Nosotros *(ver)*....
6. Yo *(buscar)*....

Fuimos a un hotel en el Caribe.

24   Lección 2

8 Una entrevista para el periódico

Trabajando en parejas, hazle cinco preguntas a tu compañero/a de clase para saber lo que hizo durante el fin de semana pasado. Luego, tu compañero/a debe hacerte cinco preguntas a ti.

A: ¿Qué hiciste el fin de semana pasado?
B: Visité a mis abuelos.

Visitamos a los abuelos el fin de semana pasado.

Después de clases

la camiseta
las pantuflas
las bermudas
los shorts
Bienvenidos
la gorra
las gafas de sol
Puerto Rico

Sergio y Sofía son de Puerto Rico. Ahora hablan de lo que hacen después de sus clases.

SERGIO: Hoy después de clases le ayudo a Clara, la hermana de mi **novia,°** a arreglar su casa.

SOFÍA: ¡No lo puedo **creer!°** ¿**Se°** la arreglas toda tú solo?

SERGIO: No, yo sólo voy a limpiar el **polvo°** y hacer otros quehaceres.

SOFÍA: Pues, yo no voy a hacer nada en casa. Voy de compras con mi **novio.°** **Quisiera°** comprar una **camiseta**, unas **pantuflas**, unos **shorts** y quizás unas **bermudas.**

SERGIO: Yo quiero comprar una **gorra** y unas **gafas de sol**, pero hoy no puedo.

SOFÍA: ¡Yo te las compro!

SERGIO: No te preocupes. Yo voy luego.

novia *girlfriend* **creer** *believe* **Se** *For them* **polvo** *dust* **novio** *boyfriend* **Quisiera** *Me gustaría*

 Después de clases

 Activities 8-9

Answers
8 Creative self-expression.

Notes
Listen for the correct pronunciation and determine if students appear to understand what they are saying and hearing. Have students personalize the dialogs by role-playing the parts using their own names.

Remind students that clothing vocabulary may vary from country to country. For example, *shorts* are also referred to as *pantalones cortos.*

Activities
Communities. Have students talk with foreign exchange students at your school, or have them locate someone from another country to ask for his/her impressions about how life in the person's home country is similar to or different from life in the United States. Have some students present their findings to the class.

Critical Listening. Play the audiocassette/audio CD version of the dialog. Next, tell students to look at the illustration while they imagine what the people are discussing. Finally, have several individuals state what they believe the main theme of the conversation is.

Prereading Strategy. Instruct students to cover up the dialog with one hand and look at the illustration. Ask them to imagine where the conversation takes place and what the people are saying to one another.

Spanish for Spanish Speakers. Pair bilingual and nonbilingual speakers for activity 8.

NATIONAL STANDARDS
C1.1, C1.2, C4.1

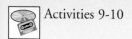

Answers

1. Sergio le ayuda a Clara, la hermana de su novia, a arreglar la casa.
2. No puede creer que Sergio va a arreglar la casa de la hermana de su novia.
3. No. Sólo le limpia el polvo y hace otros quehaceres.
4. No, no va a hacer nada en casa.
5. Sofía va a comprar una camiseta, unas pantuflas, unos shorts y quizás unas bermudas.
6. Sergio quiere comprar una gorra y unas gafas de sol.
7. No. Sergio va a ir luego.

Answers will vary.

Notes

Use this opportunity to review the present tense of the verbs that are part of the *Algo más*.

Remind students that the expressions they hear in Spanish will vary as they travel from one place to the next. For example, some people say *ver televisión* (with no article); other people may say *mirar (la) televisión*.

Activities

Language through Action. Have volunteers go to the front of the room to act out several common everyday activities. The student volunteers should then call on classmates to guess aloud in Spanish what activity the person is performing, using the present progressive: *escribir (Marta, ¿qué estoy haciendo?/Estás escribiendo en la pizarra.).*

¿Las gafas de sol?
Las compré ayer.

---

9 ¿Qué comprendiste?

1. ¿Qué hace Sergio hoy después de las clases?
2. ¿Qué no puede creer Sofía?
3. ¿Le arregla Sergio toda la casa?
4. ¿Va Sofía a hacer algo en casa después de las clases?
5. ¿Qué va a comprar Sofía?
6. ¿Qué quisiera comprar Sergio?
7. ¿Va Sofía a comprarle algo a Sergio?

10 Charlando

1. ¿A quién le ayudas tú a arreglar la casa?
2. ¿Limpias el polvo?
3. ¿Te gusta ir de compras? ¿Qué fue lo último que compraste?
4. ¿Cuántas gorras tienes?
5. ¿Tienes novio o novia?

PARA ti

Más quehaceres en la casa

brillar/pulir el piso	to polish the floor
planchar	to iron
secar los platos	to dry the dishes
trapear	to mop

Algo más

¿Qué te interesa?

Para divertirte

jugar al béisbol

ver la televisión

navegar en la Internet

ir de compras

patinar sobre el hielo

esquiar

ir al cine

dar un paseo en bicicleta

Para ayudar en la casa

barrer

cocinar

hacer las camas

poner la mesa

recoger la mesa

pasar la aspiradora

lavar la ropa

limpiar el polvo

Repaso *rápido*

Los pronombres de complemento directo e indirecto
Do you remember the direct and indirect object pronouns?

los pronombres de complemento directo			
me	*me*	**nos**	*us*
te	*you* (tú)	**os**	*you* (vosotros,-as)
lo	*him, it, you* (Ud.)	**los**	*them, you* (Uds.)
la	*her, it, you* (Ud.)	**las**	*them, you* (Uds.)

¿Me ayudas a instalar los programas?   *¿Estoy instalándolos ahora.*

los pronombres de complemento indirecto			
me	*to me, for me*	**nos**	*to us, for us*
te	*to you, for you* (tú)	**os**	*to you, for you* (vosotros,-as)
le	*to you, for you* (Ud.) *to him, for him* *to her, for her*	**les**	*to you, for you* (Uds.) *to them, for them*

¿Me compras un regalo?   *Voy a comprarte dos.*

Note: In Spanish, direct and indirect object pronouns usually precede conjugated verbs, but also may be attached to an infinitive or a present participle. When attaching an object pronoun to the end of a present participle, add an accent mark to maintain the original stress of the present participle.

11 ¿Qué más puedo hacer?

Sergio terminó de limpiar el polvo y le pregunta a Clara qué más puede hacer. Completa las siguientes oraciones, para decir lo que ella responde, usando los pronombres de complemento directo. Sigue el modelo.

     ¿La sala? <u>La</u> voy a arreglar yo.

1. ¿Las ollas? <u>(1)</u> voy a lavar yo.
2. ¿El mantel? Yo <u>(2)</u> voy a poner en la mesa.
3. ¿Los pisos? <u>(3)</u> voy a limpiar yo.
4. ¿Los platos? Yo <u>(4)</u> voy a poner en su lugar.
5. ¿La basura? Yo <u>(5)</u> voy a sacar.

Después, los voy a poner en su lugar.

NATIONAL STANDARDS
C1.2, C4.1

Answers

11
1. Las
2. lo
3. Los
4. los
5. la

Notes

Although the object pronoun *os* (comparable to the subject pronouns *vosotros* and *vosotras*) is reviewed here in the chart on page 27, you should decide what role these words will have in your class. In *Somos así*, verb paradigms include the *vosotros, vosotras* verb forms and pronouns for recognition. However, the forms are not practiced in *Somos así LISTOS* and they are not tested in the Testing/Assessment Program.

You may want to explain the following to students who do not know what direct and indirect objects are: A direct object is the person or thing that receives the action of the verb directly and answers the question **whom?** or **what?** For example, Sandra sees **whom?** (Sandra sees **him**.); They see **what?** (They see **the boats**.). Similarly, just as the direct object in a sentence answers the question **who?** or **what?**, the indirect object is the person in a sentence **to whom** or **for whom** something is said or done: Rosa is writing **to whom?** (He is cleaning the house **for whom?**); Rosa is writing **to him**. (He is cleaning the house **for her**.) Finally, be sure students understand that object pronouns replace direct and indirect objects.

Notes

Offer some additional examples of object pronoun placement: *La voy a abrir (la página web)* → *Voy a abrirla; Lo quisiera bajar (el programa)* → *Quisiera bajarlo; Los puedo encontrar (los shorts)* → *Puedo encontrarlos; ¿Lo estás visitando? (el tío)* → *¿Estás visitándolo?; Lo estamos leyendo (el e-mail)* → *Estamos leyéndolo; La estoy comprando (la gorra)* → *Estoy comprándola.*

Before assigning activity 14 on page 29, review with students how to tell time in Spanish.

Remind students they may use the object pronouns either before *estar* or after and may attach them to a present participle (in which case they must add a written accent mark).

Set a time limit for each pair or group activity.

Cómo Cuidar Sus Gafas

GENERAL OPTICA

12 La ayuda de Javier

Javier prometió ayudar a su compañera de clase con su trabajo. Completa el diálogo usando los pronombres de complemento directo apropiados.

ANA: Oye Javier, ¿(1) ayudas a buscar información en la Internet para mi clase de biología.

JAVIER: ¿Cuándo quieres que (2) ayude?

ANA: Esta noche.

JAVIER: Esta noche no (3) puedo ayudar. Mi novia y yo vamos a salir. Sus padres (4) invitaron a los dos a comer. Tú (5) comprendes, ¿verdad?

ANA: Sí, claro. ¿Qué te parece si (6) hacemos mañana por la tarde?

JAVIER: Está bien. Hasta luego.

13 De compras

Sofía y su novio fueron al centro comercial después de las clases. Acaban de comprarles algo a varias personas. Haz oraciones completas para saber qué acaban de comprarle a cada persona, usando los pronombres de complemento indirecto. Sigue el modelo.

Teresa
Acaban de comprarle un sombrero.

1. Sergio

 2. Uds.

3. Gloria

 4. nosotros

5. tú

 6. yo

¿Cuándo vas a hacer las tareas?

14 Después de las clases

Hoy hay muchas cosas por hacer en casa después de las clases. Contesta las siguientes preguntas, usando las pistas y cambiando *(changing)* las palabras en itálica a pronombres de complemento directo o indirecto. Sigue el modelo.

> ¿Cuándo vas a hacer *las tareas*? (3:30 P.M.)
> Voy a hacerlas a las tres y media.
>
> ¿Cuándo vas a pintar el bote a *tu papá*? (4:30 P.M.)
> Voy a pintarle el bote a las cuatro y media.

1. ¿Cuándo vas a preparar la comida a *tus hermanos*? (5:00 P.M.)
2. ¿Cuándo vas a sacar *la basura*? (7:00 P.M.)
3. ¿Cuándo vas a lavar las camisetas a *tu abuelo*? (7:15 P.M.)
4. ¿Cuándo vas a limpiar *el polvo en tu cuarto*? (7:30 P.M.)
5. ¿Cuándo vas a ayudar a *tu hermana* con las tareas? (8:45 P.M.)
6. ¿Cuándo vas a llamar a *tus amigos*? (9:30 P.M.)

15 Todos están haciendo algo

¿Qué están haciendo tú y otros miembros de la familia? Alterna con tu compañero/a de clase en hacer y contestar preguntas. Usa un pronombre de complemento directo o indirecto en las respuestas según las palabras indicadas en itálica en las pistas. Sigue el modelo.

> tu padre/lavar *los platos*
> A: ¿Está lavando los platos tu padre?
> B: Sí, (No, no) está lavándolos./Sí, (No, no) los está lavando.
>
> tu hermano/lavar la ropa a *tu madre*
> A: ¿Está tu hermano lavando la ropa a tu madre?
> B: Sí, (No, no) está lavándole la ropa./Sí, (No, no) le está lavando la ropa.

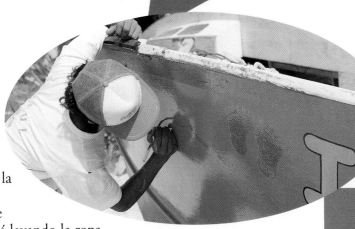

Le estoy pintando el bote a mi papá.

1. tu hermano/pintar la casa a *tu padre*
2. tu madre/limpiar *el polvo*
3. tu tío/visitar a *sus sobrinos*
4. tus hermanas/comprar unas pantuflas para *ti*
5. tus abuelos/ver *la televisión*
6. tú/instalar un programa a *tus amigos*

Answers

14 1. Voy a prepararles la comida a las cinco.
2. Voy a sacarla a las siete.
3. Voy a lavarle las camisetas a las siete y cuarto.
4. Voy a limpiarlo a las siete y media.
5. Voy a ayudarle con las tareas a las ocho y cuarenta y cinco.
6. Voy a llamarlos a las nueve y media.

15 1. ¿Está...pintando...?/...está pintándole la casa./...le está pintando la casa.
2. ¿Está...limpiando...?/...está limpiándolo./...lo está limpiando.
3. ¿Está...visitando...?/...está visitándolos./...los está visitando.
4. ¿Están...comprando...?/...están comprándome unas pantuflas./...me están comprando unas pantuflas.
5. ¿Están...viendo...?/...están viéndola./...la están viendo.
6. ¿Estás...instalando...?/...estoy instalándoles un programa./...les estoy instalando un programa.

Activities

Multiple Intelligences (interpersonal). After students have worked on activity 14, have them work in pairs writing their schedules for the week both in and out of school. They should include ten or twelve activities. (Help them with Spanish words for subjects or activities they may wish to include.) Students should then exchange schedules and ask *¿A qué hora es tu clase de...?* (Since A has B's schedule, A can verify if B answers correctly.) Students should take turns asking and answering questions about their schedules until all subjects on each schedule have been included.

NATIONAL STANDARDS
C1.1, C1.2, C4.1, C5.1

Activity 9

Quiz/Activity 3

Answers

16 1. Se las arreglan a ellos.
2. Se la cuelgas a ella.
3. Se los saca a caminar a él.
4. Se lo lavo a él.
5. Se las subimos a ellas.
6. Se la preparamos a ellos.

Notes

The use of a direct and indirect object pronoun in the same sentence sometimes can be difficult for students to master in Spanish. However, because double object pronouns are often used in conversation by native speakers, the concept has been introduced here primarily for recognition. Double object pronouns are used sparingly throughout the remaining chapters of *Somos así LISTOS*. The concept is reviewed in lessons 5 and 6 (where commands are taught) and reviewed again in *Somos así ¡YA!* This reentry offers you the flexibility of teaching the double object pronouns now and reviewing them later, or you may choose to delay teaching the concept until you feel students are better prepared. For the time being, consider introducing the use of double object pronouns for recognition.

In addition to using the pronouns, the person(s) receiving the action may be named specifically in the clarifying or emphasizing phrase.

Activities

Students with Special Needs. Model a second example for activity 16.

NATIONAL STANDARDS
C1.2, C4.1

Usando los dos complementos

When a sentence has two object pronouns in one sentence in Spanish, the indirect object pronoun occurs first. As you already learned, it is equally acceptable to place the object pronouns before a conjugated form of the verb, or after and attached to an infinitive or a present participle. When adding two object pronouns to an infinitive or a present participle, an accent mark must be added to the infinitive or present participle in order to maintain the correct pronunciation.

¿Quieres pintársela a tus padres?

*¿**Me la** puedes traer?*
*¿Puedes traér**mela**?*

Can you bring **it** *(la gorra)* **to me?**

The indirect object pronouns *le* and *les* become *se* when used together with *lo, la, los* or *las.*

¿Quieres pintarle la silla a tus padres? → *¿Quieres pintár**sela**?/¿**Se la** quieres pintar?*

You can clarify the meaning of *se* by adding *a Ud., a él, a ella, a Uds., a ellos* or *a ellas,* if needed.

Se la pinto a ellos.

I paint it for them.

16 Los quehaceres

Todos ayudan con los quehaceres en la casa de Sergio. Escribe de nuevo *(again)* las siguientes oraciones, usando *se* y el complemento directo apropiado. Sigue el modelo.

Yo le traigo las pantuflas a su madre.
Se las traigo a ella.

1. Carlos y Esteban les arreglan las sillas a sus padres.
2. Tú le cuelgas la gorra a su hermana.
3. Gabriela le saca los perros a caminar a su hermano.
4. Yo le lavo el bote a su padre.
5. Nosotros les subimos las camisetas a sus hermanas.
6. Uds. les preparan la comida para el picnic a sus primos.

Yo le traigo las pantuflas a ella.

¿Te puedo ayudar?

 Trabajando en parejas, alterna con tu compañero/a de clase en preguntar y contestar lo que tú puedes hacer para ayudar, usando los dos pronombres de complemento. Sigue el modelo.

> sacar la basura
> **A:** ¿Te puedo sacar la basura?
> **B:** Sí, (No, no) puedes sacármela.

1. limpiar el polvo
2. lavar las camisetas
3. hacer las camas
4. barrer la cocina
5. limpiar el bote
6. poner los cubiertos

18 ¿Qué están haciendo todos ahora?

Después de las clases todos van a hacer algo a sus casas. Añade los pronombres de complemento indirecto a las siguientes oraciones. Sigue el modelo.

> Yolanda le está lavando los platos
> *a ella.*
> *Se* los está lavando./Está lavándo*se*los.

1. Pedro y Julio le están pintando las puertas a él.
2. Marcos le está instalando el programa a ella.
3. Yo le estoy limpiando el bote a ellos.
4. Nosotros les estamos trayendo las gafas de sol a ellas.
5. Tú le estás lavando las camisetas a él.
6. Uds. les están comprando unas bermudas a ellos.

19 Preguntas personales

 Contesta las siguientes preguntas, usando los pronombres de complemento apropiados.

 ¿Les arreglas la casa a tus padres?
Sí, (No, no) se la arreglo.

1. ¿Le preparas la comida a tu familia?
2. ¿Les recoges la mesa a tus padres?
3. ¿Le limpias la cocina a tu madre los fines de semana?
4. ¿Le haces la cama a tu hermano/a?
5. ¿Le lavas el carro a tu madre?
6. ¿Les haces compras en el supermercado a tus padres?

Le estamos lavando el carro a nuestra madre.

Answers

17
1. ¿...limpiar el polvo?/...limpiármelo.
2. ¿...lavar las camisetas?/...lavármelas.
3. ¿...hacer las camas?/...hacérmelas.
4. ¿...barrer la cocina?/...barrérmela.
5. ¿...limpiar el bote?/...limpiármelo.
6. ¿...poner los cubiertos?/...ponérmelos.

18
1. Se las están pintando./Están pintándoselas.
2. Se lo está instalando./Está instalándoselo.
3. Se lo estoy limpiando. /Estoy limpiándoselo.
4. Se las estamos trayendo. /Estamos trayéndoselas.
5. Se las estás lavando. /Estás lavándoselas.
6. Se las están comprando. /Están comprándoselas.

19
1. ...se la preparo.
2. ...se la recojo.
3. ...se la limpio.
4. ...se la hago.
5. ...se lo lavo.
6. ...se las hago.

Notes

The following verbs are likely to use both indirect and direct object pronouns together: *comprar, contestar, dar, decir, dejar, enseñar, escribir, hacer, mandar, pedir, presentar, prestar, traer, vender.*

NATIONAL STANDARDS
C1.1, C1.2, C4.1

Answers

20
1. alguien
2. nada
3. siempre
4. nadie
5. también
6. algo
7. Todavía
8. algo
9. siempre

Notes

Introduce the topic of affirmatives and negatives by telling students some things that you always do on certain days and some others you never do on certain others. Then ask students to say something they always do on weekends and something they never do on weekdays.

Have students notice that *nada* and *nadie* precede the verb when they are the subjects of the verb.

Help students with the meaning of the examples.

Give several sentences and have students practice using the negative expressions.

Algo más

Expresiones afirmativas y negativas

Unlike English, sentences in Spanish may contain two negatives. Often *no* is used before the verb and another negative expression follows the verb. How many of the following do you remember?

Expresiones afirmativas	Expresiones negativas
sí *(yes)*	no *(no)*
algo *(something, anything)*	nada *(nothing, anything)*
alguien *(somebody, anybody)*	nadie *(nobody, anybody)*
algún, alguna *(some, any)*	ningún, ninguna *(none, not any)*
siempre *(always)*	nunca *(never)*
también *(also, too)*	tampoco *(neither, either)*
ya *(already)*	todavía no *(not yet)*
todavía *(still)*	ya no *(not yet)*

¿No vas nunca a un camping?

The words *nada, nadie, nunca* and *tampoco* may precede the verb, and *no* may be omitted. However, when these words follow the verb, another negative is needed before the verb.

Nunca voy a un camping. → *No voy a un camping nunca.*
No voy nunca a un camping.

Todavía is sometimes used at the beginning or at the end of a negative sentence when it is the equivalent of **yet**. When used without a verb, *todavía* must be used with the word *no*, which most commonly follows *todavía*.

Todavía no lo consiguen.
Todavía no. → *No lo consiguen todavía.*

20 Solas en casa

Rosario está limpiando su cuarto con su amiga Andrea. Completa su diálogo para saber lo que pasa en casa de Rosario, escogiendo las palabras apropiadas.

ANDREA: Oye, Rosario, creo que hay *1. (nada/alguien)* en el otro cuarto. ¿Oyes?

ROSARIO: No, no oigo *2. (algo/nada)*. Creo que tú *3. (siempre/nunca)* oyes cosas que *4. (nada/nadie)* más oye. *(Ahora Rosario oye algo en el otro cuarto.)* ¿Qué fue eso?

ANDREA: Sí, ves. Ahora *5. (tampoco/también)* oyes lo que yo oigo. Bueno, voy a ver qué es.

ROSARIO: Ay, espera Andrea, ¿te puedo decir *6. (alguien/algo)*?

ANDREA: *7. (Todavía/Ya)* no. ¡Silencio! Primero debemos mirar quién está en el otro cuarto.

ROSARIO: ¡Pero es que es *8. (alguien/algo)* muy importante!

ANDREA: Está bien, ¿qué es?

ROSARIO: Yo sé quién está en el otro cuarto. Es mi perro Titán. Mis padres no lo sacaron a pasear y *9. (siempre/todavía)* le gusta jugar.

ANDREA: ¡Qué bueno! Entonces, vamos a sacarlo.

21 Sin ganas de hablar

Trabajando en parejas, alterna con tu compañero/a de clase en preguntar y contestar en forma negativa las siguientes preguntas, usando *nada, nadie, no, nunca* o *tampoco*.

A: ¿Quién te escribió un e-mail?
B: Nadie.

1. ¿Qué compraste ayer?
2. Yo no sé ningún chisme. ¿Y tú?
3. ¿Cuándo vas a tomar un crucero?
4. ¿Qué le quieres dar a tu novio/a de cumpleaños?
5. ¿Quién te visitó el domingo?
6. ¿Te gusta navegar en la Internet?
7. ¿Cuándo vas a comprarte unas gafas de sol?
8. ¿Limpiaste el polvo de tu cuarto hoy?

22 No y no

Repite con tu compañero/a de clase la actividad anterior, pero ahora usando negativos dobles.

A: ¿Quién te escribió un e-mail?
B: Nadie me escribió nada.

1. ¿Qué compraste ayer?
2. Yo no sé chismes. ¿Y tú?
3. ¿Cuándo vas a tomar un crucero?
4. ¿Qué le quieres dar a tu novio/a de cumpleaños?
5. ¿Quién te visitó el domingo?
6. ¿Ya tienes Internet?
7. ¿Cuándo vas a comprarte unas gafas de sol?
8. ¿Ya limpiaste el polvo de tu cuarto hoy?

Nadie me escribió un e-mail.

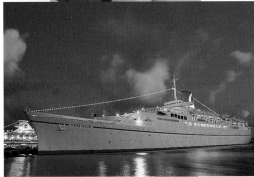

¿Cuándo vas a tomar un crucero?

Autoevaluación. Como repaso y autoevaluación, responde lo siguiente:
1. Name two things you did last summer.
2. What do you know about newspapers in Spanish-speaking countries?
3. Describe what you did on your last vacation.
4. Name one thing you just did last weekend.
5. What things do you do to help out at home?
6. What are some of your favorite pastime activities?
7. Imagine you just purchased a new computer program. How would you say that you installed it on your computer last weekend.
8. Imagine you cannot find several pairs of shorts you are looking for and the store clerk says there are more in the storage area. Ask the clerk in Spanish to please bring them to you.

Answers

21
1. Nada.
2. Tampoco.
3. Nunca.
4. Nada.
5. Nadie.
6. No.
7. Nunca.
8. No.

22
1. No compré nada.
2. No sé tampoco.
3. No voy a tomar nunca un crucero.
4. No le quiero dar nada de cumpleaños.
5. No me visitó nadie.
6. Todavía no.
7. No voy a comprar nunca unas gafas de sol.
8. Todavía no.

Autoevaluación
Possible answers:
1. Answers will vary.
2. Answers will vary.
3. Fui de camping con mi familia. Hicimos muchos picnics y monté en bote.
4. Instalé un programa nuevo en la computadora después de visitar a mis abuelos.
5. Para ayudar en casa yo barro el piso de la cocina, hago mi cama, pongo la mesa y a veces también cocino.
6. Answers will vary.
7. Lo instalé el fin de semana pasado.
8. ¿Puede Ud. traérmelos, por favor?

Notes

By assigning the *Autoevaluación* students may measure their own progress learning the main elements of the lesson. The section also serves to prepare students for the lesson test.

NATIONAL STANDARDS
C1.1, C2.1, C3.1, C4.1, C4.2, C5.1, C5.2

Activity 12

Answers

A Creative self-expression.

B Creative self-expression.

Notes

Connections. Use this *Conexión con la tecnología* as a cross-curricular opportunity for students to learn about journalism.

Many students today have computers at home. For this reason, you may want those students to use their home computers to search the World Wide Web (WWW). Talk with the librarian, computer science teacher and other colleagues to locate computers in your building or community that you can have students work on. If your students do not have access to the Internet, an alternative would be for them to use the library or media center materials available in your school or district.

WWW

City/Country information
City Guide
http://cityguide/lycos.com/
City Guide
http://www.city.net.com/
Lycos Travel
http://www.lycos.com/travel/
Embassies
http://www.embassy.org
Latin American Studies
Virtual Library
http://lanic.utexas.edu:80/las.html
Organization of
American States
http://www.oas.org

NATIONAL STANDARDS
C1.1, C1.2, C2.1, C3.1,
C4.1, C5.1, C5.2

¡La práctica hace al maestro!

A Comunicación

Working in pairs, talk with a classmate about the household chores or fun activities you do after school. Say when, with whom or for whom you do each chore or activity. Try to use as many direct and indirect object pronouns as possible. You may make up any information you wish.

A: Bueno, después de las clases hago las tareas y luego, les ayudo a mis padres a limpiar la casa.
B: ¿Se la limpias toda?
A: No, no la limpio toda. Sólo les ayudo a limpiar la cocina.

B Conexión con la tecnología

Use a computer to write an article for your electronic version of the school newspaper. Decide whether you want to write about *chismes* or about *noticias* such as an event or something you did last summer. If your school has a web page, ask for assistance to put your article on the Internet.

Vamos a escribir un artículo para el periódico.

Testing/Assessment
Test Booklet
Oral Proficiency
   Evaluation Manual
Portfolio Assessment

Actividades
el camping
el crucero
el picnic

La ropa
las bermudas
la camiseta
las gafas de sol
la gorra
las pantuflas
los shorts

Verbos
creer
instalar
pintar
quisiera
visitar

Expresiones y otras palabras
el bote
el chisme
la noticia
la novia
el novio
el país
el polvo
solo,-a
último,-a

Somos novios.

Te voy a contar unos chismes.

¿Qué llevan para ir a la playa?

35

Notes
Evaluating the multiple intelligences: The Testing/Assessment Program (Test Booklet, Oral Proficiency Evaluation Manual and Portfolio Assessment) provides a variety of activities to evaluate the multiple intelligences.

Compararisons. Have students compare English and Spanish using some of the cognates introduced in this lesson.

Activities
Cooperative Learning. Have students work in small groups to do a survey of the class about what they did yesterday or during the weekend. Then have members of each group tabulate their findings, and select one student to report to the class a summary of what people did and did not do. Encourage students to use the preterite tense in their summaries.

Expansion. Model each word or expression and have students repeat. Then call on students to use the words or expressions in sentences. This activity would be appropriate for all lists of vocabulary found in *Somos así*.

Multiple Intelligences (interpersonal/intrapersonal). Talk with students about some activities they participate in every day, such as household chores or recreational activities. For example, ask if students do the family shopping. How often? Then ask what activities students like to do for fun.

Spanish for Spanish Speakers. Ask your bilingual students to write a short composition in Spanish about an activity or event last summer that stands out for some reason, i.e., something really enjoyable that happened.

NATIONAL STANDARDS
C1.2, C4.1

a leer

Estrategia

Preparación

Estrategia para leer: *using cognates to determine meaning*
When reading a selection in Spanish for the first time, it is helpful to take advantage of words that are similar in both Spanish and English (cognates). Spanish has adopted many words from English relating to the rapidly advancing field of technology and the Internet.

Conecta las palabras de la columna A con los cognados de la columna B, como preparación para la lectura.

A	B
1. categoría	A. area
2. servicios	B. parts
3. exportar	C. services
4. dólares	D. dollars
5. información	E. information
6. partes	F. lottery
7. área	G. category
8. agencia	H. agency
9. lotería	I. virtual
10. virtual	J. export

Es un satélite.

En la Internet

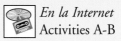

```
┌──────────────────────────────────────────────────────────────┐
│  📄 Internet                                                   │
│  ┌──────────────────────────────────────────────────────┐  ▲ │
│  │  http://languageresource.com/spanish/classifieds      │  │ │
│  └──────────────────────────────────────────────────────┘    │
│  ─────────────────────────────────────────────────────────── │
│  N  Netscape                                                  │
│     Netcenter  ──────────────────────────────────────────── │
│                                                                │
│  Categoría: Servicios              País: Estados Unidos       │
│  Servicio de Internet y venta de equipo                       │
│  Fecha: Miércoles 6 de enero                                  │
│     International Computer, ubicada en la Florida. Exportamos  │
│     equipos completos y partes. Ofrecemos servicio de         │
│     Internet en el área de Miami por $15,95 al mes.           │
│     No se necesita tarjeta de crédito.                        │
│        international@computer4u.com                            │
│  ─────────────────────────────────────────────────────────── │
│  Categoría: Negocios               País: España               │
│  OBTENGA SU AGENCIA DE LOTERÍA VIRTUAL                         │
│  Fecha: Viernes 22 de enero                                   │
│     ¡¡¡GANE MUCHO DINERO EN LA RED!!! Ésta es su oportunidad  │
│     de ¡¡¡GANAR MILES DE DÓLARES!!! ¡Un trabajo como pocos    │
│     para realizar a tiempo parcial o a tiempo completo! Tenga │
│     su propia AGENCIA DE LOTERÍA virtual, en un programa      │
│     oficial autorizado y controlado por el gobierno alemán.   │
│     ¡¡¡Solicite información AHORA!!!                           │
│        tgsgroup@SmartBot.net                               ▼  │
└──────────────────────────────────────────────────────────────┘
```

¿Qué comprendiste?

1. ¿Dónde está la compañía International Computer?
2. ¿Qué exportan ellos?
3. ¿Dónde ofrecen servicio de Internet?
4. ¿Sus clientes tienen que usar tarjeta de crédito?
5. ¿Cuánto dinero se puede ganar con una agencia de lotería virtual?
6. ¿Quién autoriza y controla estas agencias de lotería virtual?

Charlando

1. ¿Tienes servicio de Internet en casa?
2. ¿Buscas productos o servicios por la Internet?
3. ¿Compras cosas por la Internet?
4. ¿Tienes tarjeta de crédito?

a escribir

Estrategia

Estrategia para escribir: *keeping your reader in mind*

When you start to write an e-mail note or a letter, it is a good idea to keep your reader in mind. You can do this by writing about things you think the person will find interesting. In addition, your targeted reader will be more motivated to answer your correspondence if you include some personal questions about the person's interests.

Write to a key pal and begin an e-mail exchange in which you talk about one another's lives. Be sure to include the following in your e-mail exchange:

- **personal biographical information (name, date of birth, age, etc.)**
- **description of yourself, your family and your friends (names, descriptions, where people live)**
- **after-school activities (*ver televisión, hacer quehaceres, navegar en la Internet* etc.).**
- **questions asking for similar information about the key pal**

¿Te gusta escribir e-mails?

Portfolio Assessment
Select an activity from
Capítulo 1 to include in the
Somos así Portfolio
Assessment.

Notes

Tips for school-aged volunteers
and students with mentors:
Students should: 1) explore the
available options; 2) select a job
that is interesting; 3) talk with
people in the organization being
considered to gather information;
4) be realistic about the time
available to volunteer; 5) consider
whether transportation to the site
will be a problem; 6) visit the site
and talk with members of the
organization to answer concerns;
7) make a decision.

Portfolio Assessment. Select an
activity from the chapter to
include in the *Somos así LISTOS*
Portfolio Assessment.

repaso

Now that I have completed this chapter, I can...
- ✓ talk about technology.
- ✓ seek and provide personal information.
- ✓ describe the weather.
- ✓ state what is happening right now.
- ✓ talk about everyday activities.
- ✓ discuss ecological problems.
- ✓ talk about the future.
- ✓ discuss schedules.
- ✓ compare quantity, quality, age and size.
- ✓ talk about the past.
- ✓ refer to what just happened.

¡Llueve mucho!

I can also...
- ✓ give an e-mail address in Spanish.
- ✓ read about environmental contamination and some solutions in Spanish.
- ✓ identify opportunities to volunteer and use Spanish in my community.
- ✓ use the Internet to find electronic key pals.
- ✓ learn new words in Spanish through context.
- ✓ read about newspapers from Spanish-speaking countries that are available on the Internet.
- ✓ talk about what I did last summer.

NATIONAL STANDARDS
C1.1, C1.2, C1.3, C3.2,
C4.1, C4.2, C5.1, C5.2

Connections with Parents

During the first week or two of class, note at least one good thing that each student has done in Spanish class. Then as soon as you are able to fit it in your schedule, call the individual's parents/guardians to inform them what their child did that merited a call home. The call does not have to be long. (As an alternative, if you are unable to reach the home by phone, send a note home.) Doing so will break the mold of calling only when there is a problem and you will find that both parents/guardians and students will better understand and accept future calls that involve a problem, because you will have already established that you do not just call with bad news. Try to make at least five to ten connections per week.

Notes

Note that the United States is the fifth largest Spanish-speaking country in terms of population (after Mexico, Spain, Colombia and Argentina).

Activities

Critical Thinking. The visuals that appear on the opening two pages of the chapter depict the functions, cultural setting and themes of the chapter ahead. Ask students what conclusions they can draw from the information, and so forth. For example, ask students the following: 1) In what country or part of the world does the chapter take place?; 2) What are students in the photographs doing?

NATIONAL STANDARDS
C1.2, C4.1, C5.2

Todos los días

CAPÍTULO 2

Estados Unidos

Over twenty million people use Spanish in the United States every day. In fact, in some parts of the United States, such as in Florida, Arizona, Colorado and Texas, knowing Spanish may not always be a job requirement but it certainly can prove advantageous because Spanish is spoken by so many people for both pleasure and for business.

Notes

Cultures. Review these two pages, asking students what country they think they will be studying in the chapter. Then discuss what students know about the country (i.e., the country is the United States; Spanish is widely spoken in the United States).

Communicative functions are provided with the opening two pages along with accompanying visuals to mentally and visually whet students' appetites for the chapter they are about to begin. A checkoff list of the functions appears at the end of the chapter (see page 81), along with additional objectives that students can use as a self-check to evaluate their own progress.

Activities

Communities. Ask students which cities and states have a large number of Spanish-speaking inhabitants. Discuss why the number of people who speak Spanish might be larger in some states than in others. Finally, ask students if they can name any well-known Spanish-speaking citizens of the United States.

Multiple Intelligences (linguistic). Ask students to identify some words that are commonly used in the United States that are Spanish: *plaza, fiesta, taco, poncho, patio.*

In this chapter you will be able to:

- talk about everyday activities
- seek and provide personal information
- discuss personal grooming
- compare and contrast
- recognize and identify Hispanic influence in the United States
- state when things are done
- express past actions and events
- identify items in a bathroom
- point something out
- write about everyday activities
- discuss health
- give and take instructions
- identify parts of the body

41

National Standards
C1.2, C5.2

Content reviewed in *Lección 3*
- stating who you are
- asking for and stating place of origin
- everyday activities
- Spanish in the United States
- telling time
- colors
- clothing
- demonstrative adjectives

Lección 3

Contexto cultural

ESTADOS UNIDOS

Somos muy diferentes

afeitarse · el pelo · peinarse · ducharse · cepillarse · maquillarse · levantarse · acostarse · vestirse · bañarse

Notes

The reflexive *Me llamo* comes from the reflexive verb *llamarse*, which students learned in the present-tense expression: *¿Cómo te llamas?* Reflexive verbs are explained in this lesson.

Acostarme comes from *acostarse (ue)*, which changes in the present tense from *o* to *ue*. Compare this change to the infinitive *volver (ue)*, which students already have learned.

Point out that *me despierto* comes from the infinitive *despertarse (ie)* and requires the same stem changes as *pensar (ie)*, which students already have learned. Similarly, *me visto* comes from the infinitive *vestirse (i, i)* and requires the same stem changes as *seguir (i, i)*, which students already have learned.

Activities

Communities. Lapaz is located in northern Indiana. It is similar to many other geographical sites throughout the United States in that the town's name is Spanish. This would be an appropriate time to discuss the influence that Spanish has had in the United States (Los Angeles, Santa Fe, El Paso, Colorado, Nevada, Sierra Madre, Alamo), especially in your community or state.

Me llamo Araceli Martínez. Vivo en Lapaz, Indiana, con mi madre y mi hermano Miguel. Miguel y yo somos muy diferentes. Cuando estamos juntos, no somos muy felices porque no tenemos mucha **paz.°** A mí me gusta **levantarme°** temprano y **acostarme°** temprano; a él le gusta levantarse **tarde°** y acostarse tarde. Le gusta **quedarse°** en la cama. **Desde luego,°** cuando tenemos que salir juntos, es un problema. Yo **me despierto°** y en menos de media hora **me baño,° me visto,° me cepillo°** el **pelo, me maquillo,°** y voy a la cocina para **desayunarme.°** Y él, ¿dónde está? Está **duchándose°** o quizás está **quitándose°** una camisa que no le gustó para hoy, y **poniéndose°** otra. Como siempre, yo estoy aquí **esperándolo,°** y él **no se preocupa°** por nada. ¿Cómo puede él ser **así?°**

paz *peace* **levantarme** *to get up* **acostarme** *to go to bed, to lie down* **tarde** *late* **quedarse** *to remain, to stay* **Desde luego** *Of course* **me despierto** *I wake up* **me baño** *I bathe* **me visto** *I get dressed* **me cepillo** *I brush* **me maquillo** *I put on makeup* **desayunarme** *to have breakfast* **duchándose** *taking a shower* **quitándose** *taking off* **poniéndose** *putting on* **esperándolo** *waiting for him* **no se preocupa** *he does not worry* **así** *thus, that way*

1 ¿Qué comprendiste?

1. ¿Por qué no son felices Araceli y Miguel?
2. ¿Cuándo le gusta levantarse a Araceli?
3. ¿Cuándo le gusta acostarse a Miguel?
4. ¿En cuánto tiempo se baña, se viste, se cepilla el pelo y se maquilla Araceli?
5. ¿Qué piensa Araceli de Miguel?

Hablando del pelo
Sometimes you may hear the word *cabello* instead of *pelo*. Both words refer to **hair.** However, do not confuse *cabello* with *caballo* because they have two different meanings. Do you remember what a *caballo* is?

para su cabello Solamente

BONA-CURE

2 Charlando

1. ¿Tienes tiempo para desayunarte?
2. ¿En cuánto tiempo te bañas y te vistes?
3. ¿Te gusta acostarte temprano? ¿A qué hora?
4. Miguel no se preocupa por nada. ¿Hay alguien en tu casa que es así?

3 Todos los días

1. Me despierto a las....
2. Me gusta levantarme....
3. Me visto en....
4. Me gusta desayunarme con....
5. Me gusta acostarme....

8:00 A.M.

¿jugo de naranja?

en quince minutos

11:30 P.M.

Capítulo 2 43

Answers

1. 1. No son felices porque no tienen mucha paz.
   2. Le gusta levantarse temprano.
   3. Le gusta acostarse tarde.
   4. Ella se baña, se viste, se cepilla el pelo y se maquilla en menos de media hora.
   5. Araceli piensa que él no se preocupa por nada.

2. Answers will vary.

3. Answers will vary.

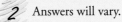

Notes

Make adjectives and nouns that end in a vowel plural by adding *-s* to the end of the word. Make adjectives and nouns that end in a consonant plural by adding *-es.* For nouns that end in *-z,* change the *-z* to *-c* before adding *-es: feliz* → *felices; luz* → *luces.*

Remind students that a *caballo* is a horse.

Activities

Critical Thinking. Have students make the following sentences plural: *La chica vive en Indiana; La luz está encendida; Hay un lápiz en el escritorio; La muchacha es muy feliz; La familia vive en paz; Los chicos oyeron una voz muy dulce; Comemos una vez al día.*

Expansion. Additional questions (*¿Qué comprendiste?*): *¿Cómo se llama la muchacha? ¿Y el muchacho?; ¿Qué son Araceli y Miguel?; ¿Cuándo tienen problemas?; ¿Qué puede estar haciendo Miguel mientras Araceli está esperándolo?*

Additional questions (*Charlando*): *¿Tienes hermanos o hermanas? ¿Cuántos?; ¿No se preocupa(n) por nada?; ¿Es tu vida diferente o similar a la vida de Araceli y Miguel? Explica.*

NATIONAL STANDARDS
C1.2, C2.2, C3.2, C4.2, C5.2

Activity 11

Activity 2

Quiz/Activity 2

Answers

4 Answers will vary.

Notes

Connections. Note for students that there is a significant Hispanic influence in the states named in this *Conexión cultural*, along with parts of New York, Illinois, Indiana, Ohio, New Jersey and several other states. In addition, there are considerable Spanish-speaking populations in these states, as well. Give the meanings and origins of the sites mentioned in this *Conexión cultural*: *Arizona* (arid land), *Colorado* (red-colored, referring here to the earth), *Florida* (land of flowers), *Montana* (land of mountains), *Nevada* (snow-covered, referring to mountains) and *Nuevo México* (New Mexico).

Activities

Communities. Have students prepare a list of geographical sites, businesses, etc., in your community that have Spanish names.

Critical Thinking. Ask students to search the Internet for a newspaper from a Spanish-speaking country that contains an article about the United States. Then have them compare the coverage of that news story with the coverage of the same story by a newspaper published in the United States. Have them tell the class how the coverage is the same or different.

Spanish for Spanish Speakers. Have students research a particular aspect of your community that is Hispanic in origin.

Conexión Cultural

La misión San Miguel en Santa Fe, Nuevo México.

Lugares en los Estados Unidos con nombres en español

Araceli Martínez vive en Lapaz, Indiana. El nombre *Lapaz* viene de dos palabras españolas: la paz *(peace)*. ¿Qué influencia tiene el español donde vives tú? Mira un mapa y vas a ver cuerpos de agua, ciudades, montañas *(mountains)* y otros lugares geográficos con nombres en español. Por ejemplo, los estados *(states)* de Arizona, Colorado, Florida, Montana, Nevada y Nuevo México tienen nombres de origen español. ¿Puedes ver esta influencia en tu comunidad o en tu estado?

Arizona

COLORADO

CONEXIONES
4 **Cruzando fronteras**

Mira un mapa o un atlas de los Estados Unidos y haz una lista de quince lugares o puntos geográficos con nombres en español.

Lista de lugares

1. *Lapaz*

2. *San Francisco*

Oportunidades

El español en tu comunidad

How can you use Spanish in your community?
Have you ever considered offering your services as
a volunteer at one of the many organizations where
you live? Many groups could use the help of
someone who speaks Spanish.

Usamos español en nuestra comunidad.

 **En la comunidad**

5

**Trabajando en grupos pequeños preparen una lista de organizaciones que
puedan necesitar la ayuda de alguien que hable español.**

IDIOMA

Los verbos reflexivos

Some verbs in Spanish have *se* attached to the end of the infinitive. The *se* is a
reflexive pronoun *(pronombre reflexivo)* and the verb is called a reflexive verb
(verbo reflexivo) because it reflects action back upon the subject of the sentence.
For example, adding the reflexive pronoun *se* to the infinitive *peinar* (to comb
another person's hair) forms the reflexive verb *peinarse* (to comb one's own hair).

no reflexivo · reflexivo

peinar · peinarse

Reflexive verbs are conjugated the same as nonreflexive verbs; however, they are
used with a corresponding reflexive pronoun.

peinarse			
yo	**me** pein**o**	nosotros nosotras	**nos** pein**amos**
tú	**te** pein**as**	vosotros vosotras	**os** pein**áis**
Ud. él ella	**se** pein**a**	Uds. ellos ellas	**se** pein**an**

Answers

5 Community-based learning.

Notes

The *vosotros,-as* verb endings are
included for passive recognition.
Decide if you want to teach the
vosotros,-as form of verbs. Then
include these verb forms in class
work, as required.

Before teaching the reflexive verbs,
remind students that Spanish
infinitives may end in *-ar, -er* or *-ir.*

Use a comb to introduce reflexive
pronouns in order to contrast *Me
peino* and *Peino a* (name of a person).

Activities

Connections. Discuss the
meanings and origins of the
Spanish names for the
geographical sites your students
have selected on page 44.

Critical Thinking. Have students
use the provided cues to give
complete sentences in the present
progressive, saying what the
following people are doing right
now: *Carlos/peinarse/baño; Gloria/
peinar/su hermanita; Fabiola/
lavarse/pelo; la abuela/poner/su
nieto en la cama; Javier/vestir/su
hermanito; el tío Jorge/ponerse/
camisa nueva; ellos/ lavar/carro a su
papá; Uds./vestirse/ahora.*

Language through Action. Have
students point out geographical
names in Spanish on a map of the
United States.

Students with Special Needs.
Review with students some
present-tense stem-changing
(cerrar, conseguir, acostarse) and
orthographic-changing *(conseguir,
dirigir)* verbs.

NATIONAL STANDARDS
C1.2, C4.1, C5.1

Quiz/Activity 2

 Activity 12

Activity 5

Quiz/Activity 3

Answers

6 A, D, G, I, J

Notes

Point out that a *churro* (in the realia next to activity 6) is a donut-like pastry that is sometimes eaten at breakfast or as a snack with hot chocolate.

From this point forward, verbs that have been introduced previously in their nonreflexive form and verbs that have been introduced in their reflexive form will not be listed again as new words unless their meanings change significantly.

These are only a few of the verbs that have both reflexive and nonreflexive forms. You may wish to give students practice making some already-learned nonreflexive verbs reflexive by reminding students that these verbs follow the pattern of *peinar (peinarse): arreglar (arreglarse), comprar (comprarse), lavar (lavarse), mirar (mirarse), preparar (prepararse), ver (verse)* and so forth.

Note for students the present-tense stem changes that occur for the verbs *acostar(se), despertar(se), sentar(se)* and *vestir(se)*.

Activities

Students with Special Needs. As an oral warm-up activity before assigning the written activities that practice the reflexive, ask students several questions that use the reflexive and nonreflexive verbs in the list. After practicing several verbs, have students ask classmates the questions in order to practice the *tú* form of the verbs.

NATIONAL STANDARDS
C1.2, C4.1, C5.2

Much like direct and indirect object pronouns, reflexive pronouns may precede a verb, or they may be attached to the end of an infinitive or a present participle.

Se va a peinar.	→	*Va a peinarse.*
Se está peinando.	→	*Está peinándose.*

6 La vida diaria

Di cuáles de las siguientes oraciones o preguntas usan el reflexivo.

A. Nos desayunamos a las ocho.
B. ¿No la viste ayer?
C. **Los voy a despertar ahora.**
D. ¿Te estás quitando los calcetines?
E. ¿Estás esperándome?
F. Tengo sed.
G. *Me levanté temprano hoy.*
H. **Comemos juntos.**
I. ¿No se va a duchar?
J. ¿A qué hora se acuestan Uds.?

Desayuno con Churros

Algo **más**

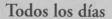

Me baño todos los días.

Todos los días

The following verbs refer to everyday actions and have both reflexive and nonreflexive forms.

no reflexivo	*reflexivo*
acostar (ue) to put (someone) in bed	*acostarse (ue)* to go to bed
afeitar to shave (someone)	*afeitarse* to shave (oneself)
bañar to bathe (someone)	*bañarse* to bathe (oneself)
calmar to calm (someone) down	*calmarse* to calm down
cepillar to brush (someone, something)	*cepillarse* to brush (one's teeth, hair)
despertar (ie) to wake (someone) up	*despertarse (ie)* to wake up
lavar to wash (clothes, dishes)	*lavarse* to wash (oneself)
levantar to raise, to lift (a hand)	*levantarse* to get up
llamar to call (someone)	*llamarse* to be called
maquillar to put makeup on (someone)	*maquillarse* to put on makeup
mirar to look at (someone, something)	*mirarse* to look at (oneself)
peinar to comb (someone's hair)	*peinarse* to comb (one's own hair)
quemar to burn	*quemarse* to get burned
sentar (ie) to seat (someone)	*sentarse (ie)* to sit down
vestir (i, i) to dress (someone)	*vestirse (i, i)* to get dressed

7 En la casa de Quique

Muchas cosas pasan en la casa de Quique ahora. Di lo que pasa, decidiendo qué oración describe mejor la acción en cada una de las siguientes ilustraciones.

A. El chico se calma.
B. El chico lo calma.

1.

A. Los cepillo antes de salir.
B. Me cepillo antes de salir.

2.

A. Despierto temprano a mi hermano.
B. Me despierto muy temprano.

3.

A. Estoy poniéndome los calcetines azules.
B. Estoy poniéndolos en la cama.

4.

A. Ella le está lavando el pelo.
B. Ella está lavándose el pelo.

5.

A. Estoy acostándolo.
B. Me estoy acostando.

6.

A. Me despierto temprano.
B. Lo despierto temprano.

8 Todos los días

Trabajando en parejas, alterna con tu compañero/a de clase en hacer y contestar preguntas, usando las pistas.

despertarse temprano los sábados
A: ¿Te despiertas temprano los sábados?
B: Sí, (No, no) me despierto temprano los sábados.

1. cepillarse el pelo por las mañanas
2. vestirse rápidamente
3. bañarse todos los días
4. acostarse tarde
5. levantarse tarde los domingos
6. sentarse a comer a las ocho

NATIONAL STANDARDS
C1.1, C1.2, C1.3, C2.2

Answers

7
1. A
2. B
3. A
4. B
5. A
6. B

8
1. ¿Te cepillas...?/...me cepillo....
2. ¿Te vistes...?/...me visto....
3. ¿Te bañas...?/...me baño....
4. ¿Te acuestas...?/...me acuesto....
5. ¿Te levantas...?/...me levanto....
6. ¿Te sientas...?/...me siento....

Notes

Reflexive verbs often correspond to daily routines. Thus, you may wish to review expressions such as *por la mañana/tarde/noche*.

Ask students in English to identify the main actions in the illustrations before assigning activity 7.

Activities

Critical Listening. Read sentences A and B from activity 7. Students must raise their left hand if you say sentence A; they must raise their right hand if you say sentence B.

Students with Special Needs. Model a second example for activity 8.

TPR. Reflexive verbs are easily introduced with physical actions and corresponding language. Consider using TPR as a means of introduction and review.

Answers

9 1. ¿...te levantas?/Me levanto....
2. ¿...te bañas?/Me baño....
3. ¿...te vistes?/Me visto....
4. ¿...te desayunas?/Me desayuno....
5. ¿...te acuestas?/Me acuesto....
6. ¿...te sientas...?/Me siento....

10 1. ...se está afeitando./...está afeitándose.
2. ...se está bañando./...está bañándose.
3. ...se está quemando..../...está quemándose....
4. ...se están poniendo..../...están poniéndose....
5. ...se está quitando..../...está quitándose....
6. ...se están sentando..../...están sentándose....
7. ...no se está calmando..../...no está calmándose....

11 Answers will vary.

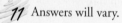

Notes

Review telling time with students before beginning activity 9.

Activities

Students with Special Needs. Model a second example for activities 9-11.

9 Un sábado típico

Alterna con tu compañero/a de clase en preguntar y contestar a qué hora Uds. hacen las siguientes actividades en un sábado típico.

  despertarse
A: ¿A qué hora te despiertas?
B: Me despierto a las nueve de la mañana.

1. levantarse
2. bañarse
3. vestirse
4. desayunarse
5. acostarse
6. sentarse para comer

Me despierto a las ocho. ¿Puedo dormir un poco más?

10 El domingo por la mañana

Todos hacen algo en casa el domingo por la mañana. Haz oraciones completas para decir lo que está pasando. Sigue el modelo.

  mamá/maquillarse
Mamá se está maquillando./Mamá está maquillándose.

1. papá/afeitarse
2. tía Teresa/bañarse
3. tío Manuel/quemarse la mano cuando prepara unos huevos
4. mis abuelos/ponerse los abrigos antes de salir
5. mi hermana Araceli/quitarse el collar de perlas
6. mis primos/sentarse a la mesa para comer
7. el perro/no calmarse después de ver a mi gato

11 La rutina familiar

Combinando palabras de cada una de las tres columnas haz oraciones completas, añadiendo más información para decir cómo es la rutina de los miembros de tu familia en un día de fiesta.

  Mi hermana se viste muy elegante.

A	B	C
mi mamá	nos	bañar
mi hermana	me	poner
mi hermano	te	maquillar
mis padres	se	levantar
mis hermanos		lavar
mis hermanos y yo		vestir
mi papá		afeitar
yo		despertar

Estrategia

Para aprender mejor: *comparing to English*

English often uses a form of **to get** where Spanish uses a reflexive verb. Knowing this may help you decide when to use a reflexive or a nonreflexive verb to state an action. Compare the following:

levantarse	→	*Ellos se levantan.*	They get up.
vestirse	→	*Ella se viste.*	She gets dressed.

Proverbios y dichos
Have you ever rushed to finish something and then discovered you made many mistakes and needed to take time to go back and fix them? Often it is better to slow down and do things right the first time than to go back and fix what you did wrong because you rushed. Take your time and carefully complete a task by paying attention to the quality of the work, and not the speed, and you will save yourself time in the end. As the saying goes in Spanish: *Vísteme despacio que tengo prisa* (Dress me slowly because I am in a hurry).

12 ¿De qué color se visten?

Haz oraciones, usando la forma apropiada del verbo *vestirse* y las pistas indicadas para decir de qué color se visten hoy tú y tus amigos.

 Luis
Luis se viste de amarillo.

1. Vivina y Sonia   2. Uds.   3. tú   4. nosotros

5. Eduardo   6. yo   7. José   8. Clara

Answers

12
1. Viviana y Sonia se visten de rojo.
2. Uds. se visten de anaranjado.
3. Tú te vistes de negro.
4. Nosotros nos vestimos de azul.
5. Eduardo se viste de gris.
6. Yo me visto de blanco.
7. José se viste de verde.
8. Clara se viste de rosado.

Notes

Review colors with students before doing activity 12.

Review the *Para ti* with students, explaining how the saying is used.

Activities

Critical Thinking. Ask students for some additional examples of verbs that are used reflexively in English. Find out how many of the verbs students are able to give equivalents for in Spanish.

Expansion. Have students look around the classroom and identify the color of clothing classmates are wearing today. Encourage students to use the reflexive verb *vestirse* in their statements.

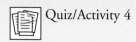
Notes

Review the content of the *Algo más* with students before assigning activity 13. Be sure they use the article in place of a possessive pronoun in their conversation about what they do after getting up. For students who are having difficulty, give a few examples comparing to English: wash **the** face *(lavarse la cara)*, brush **the** teeth *(cepillarse los dientes)*, etc.

Get students thinking about their daily routine before beginning activity 13 by talking with the class about some of their daily rituals (i.e., eat breakfast, go to school).

Activities

Spanish for Spanish Speakers. Try to include at least one bilingual speaker in each group for activity 13.

Cooperative Learning. For variety, have students pair up and do activity 14 orally, one asking the question and the other providing the logical response. Hold students accountable for their own work by assigning the activity as a quick written check of how well they understood what they did orally. Finally, after writing out the answers to the activity, students should switch roles and do the activity again orally.

13 Después de levantarse

En grupos pequeños, hablen Uds. de las cinco primeras cosas que hacen después de levantarse. Luego, un estudiante del grupo debe reportar la información a la clase, diciendo cuáles son las cosas más populares que los miembros del grupo hacen para empezar el día.

Después de levantarme, me cepillo los dientes.

Algo más

El artículo definido con verbos reflexivos

In Spanish a definite article is generally used instead of a possessive adjective when using a reflexive verb to talk about personal items, such as clothing and parts of the body.

*Me pongo **el** suéter.*	I put on **my** sweater.
*¿Quieres lavarte **las** manos?*	Do you want to wash **your** hands?

14 Hay que ser cortés

Si invitas a otras personas a tu casa, tienes que ser cortés *(courteous)*. Completa las siguientes oraciones, escogiendo la palabra apropiada.

   Tienes frío. ¿Deseas ponerte *(tu/la)* chaqueta?
Tienes frío. ¿Deseas ponerte *la* chaqueta?

1. ¿Puedo llevarte *(el/tu)* abrigo para el cuarto?
2. ¿Te gustaría cepillarte *(tus/los)* dientes?
3. ¿Quieres esperar a *(los/tus)* hermanos?
4. Por favor, ¿puedes quitarte *(los/tus)* zapatos?
5. ¿Quieres ir a lavarte *(tus/las)* manos antes de comer?
6. ¿Te gustaría quitarte *(tu/el)* abrigo?

15 ¿Qué están haciendo?

Todos se preparan para salir. Di lo que está haciendo cada una de las siguientes personas, según las ilustraciones. Sigue el modelo.

 Ella se está maquillando.

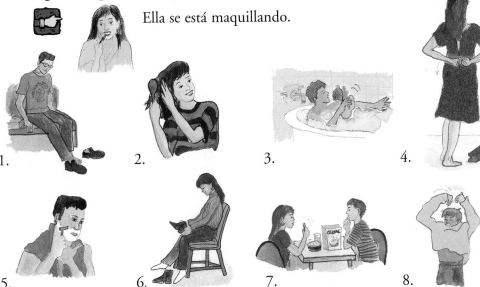

1.   2.   3.   4.

5.   6.   7.   8.

16 De otra manera

Haz las oraciones de la actividad anterior de otra manera, siguiendo el modelo.

Ella está maquillándose.

17 ¿Cómo se preparan para salir?

Imagina que varias personas de tu familia están preparándose para salir juntas. Trabajando en parejas, alterna con tu compañero/a de clase en hacer y contestar preguntas para decir cómo se preparan para salir. Sigue el modelo.

quitarse las botas/ponerse otros calcetines
A: ¿Vas a quitarte las botas?
(¿Te vas a quitar las botas?)
B: No, voy a ponerme otros calcetines.
(No, me voy a poner otros calcetines.)

1. cepillarse el pelo/lavarse el pelo
2. desayunarse con café/desayunarse con chocolate y huevos
3. bañarse/vestirse
4. lavarse las manos/ponerse el abrigo
5. afeitarse/peinarse
6. vestirse/maquillarse
7. ponerse el impermeable/ponerse el abrigo

¿Prefiere simplemente bañarse... o también eliminar las bacterias que causan el mal olor del sudor?

el jabón antibacterial y desodorante Protex elimina las bacterias que causan el mal olor del sudor.

Usando diariamente Protex protege la salud de su familia.

Jabón **Protex**
Antibacterial y Desodorante

Protege diariamente la salud de su familia

¿Te vas a afeitar?

Answers

15 Possible answers:
1. Él se está poniendo los zapatos.
2. Ella se está cepillando el pelo.
3. Él se está bañando.
4. Ella se está vistiendo.
5. Él se está afeitando.
6. Ella se está quitando las botas.
7. Ellos se están desayunando.
8. Él se está quitando el suéter.

16 1. Él está poniéndose los zapatos.
2. Ella está cepillándose el pelo.
3. Él está bañándose.
4. Ella está vistiéndose.
5. Él está afeitándose.
6. Ella está quitándose las botas.
7. Ellos están desayunándose.
8. Él está quitándose el suéter.

17 1. ¿Vas a cepillarte el pelo? (¿Te vas a cepillar el pelo?)/No, voy a lavarme el pelo. (No, me voy a lavar el pelo.)
2. ¿Vas a desayunarte con café? (¿Te vas a desayunar con café?)/No, voy a desayunarme con chocolate y huevos. (No, me voy a desayunar con chocolate y huevos.)
3. ¿Vas a bañarte? (¿Te vas a bañar?)/No, voy a vestirme. (No, me voy a vestir.)
4. ¿Vas a lavarte las manos? (¿Te vas a lavar las manos?)/No, voy a ponerme el abrigo. (No, me voy a poner el abrigo.)
5. ¿Vas a afeitarte? (¿Te vas a afeitar?)/No, voy a peinarme. (No, me voy a peinar.)
6. ¿Vas a vestirte? (¿Te vas a vestir?)/No, voy a maquillarme. (No, me voy a maquillar.)
7. ¿Vas a ponerte el impermeable? (¿Te vas a poner el impermeable?)/No, voy a ponerme el abrigo. (No, me voy a poner el abrigo.)

Quiz/Activity 3

 Activity 6

Quiz/Activity 5

Answers

18 1. me desperté
2. me bañé
3. me peiné
4. desperté
5. se afeitó
6. se lavó
7. se levantó
8. se maquilló
9. se cepilló
10. nos desayunamos
11. nos quedamos

Notes

Let students know that the preterite tense of *vestirse (i, i)* in this *Algo más* uses the second stem change indicated in parentheses, as is shown in this example: *vistió.*

Review telling time with students before assigning activity 18.

The abbreviated form of *el cuarto de baño* is *el baño.* Other expressions for *el baño* include *los servicios, el W.C.* and *el toilette.*

Activities

Cooperative Learning. Have students work in pairs asking and answering whether the following people completed the mentioned activities: *1) tus hermanos/ya/ levantarse; 2) Uds./ya/quitarse los pijamas; 3) Uds./ya/bañarse; 4) tú/ya/lavarse el pelo; 5) tus primos/ya/vestirse; 6) tu hermana/ ya/quitarse la falda sucia; 7) tu abuela/ya/desayunarse.*

Spanish for Spanish Speakers. Have students write a short composition in Spanish summarizing their day yesterday, using activity 18 as a model.

Algo
más

El pretérito de los verbos reflexivos

Reflexive and nonreflexive verbs follow the same patterns you have learned for forming the preterite tense, with the exception that reflexive verbs require an appropriate reflexive pronoun. Compare the following:

no reflexivo		*reflexivo*	
Bañé al perro.	I gave the dog a bath.	*Me bañé.*	I took a bath.
Ella vistió a su hermanita.	She dressed her little sister.	*Ella se vistió.*	She got dressed.

 18 **Una nota de Marta**

Ésta es una nota que Marta está escribiendo sobre lo que pasó ayer en su casa. Ayúdala a completarla, usando la forma apropiada del pretérito de los verbos entre paréntesis.

Primero, yo 1. (despertarse) a las 6:30 y fui al baño donde 2. (bañarse) y 3. (peinarse). Luego, yo 4. (despertar) a mi hermano Juan. Entonces, él fue al baño y 5. (afeitarse) y 6. (lavarse) el pelo. Cuando Juan estuvo listo, mi hermana, Natalia, 7. (levantarse) y entró en el baño donde 8. (maquillarse) y 9. (cepillarse) el pelo. A las 7:45, nosotros tres 10. (desayunarse) y, luego, fuimos para el colegio. Nosotros 11. (quedarse) en el colegio hasta las 3:00, que es cuando siempre regresamos a casa.

Tinta china

19 ¿Qué pasó ayer?

Tu amigo/a está muy curioso/a *(curious)* hoy y te pregunta sobre algunas cosas que pasaron ayer. Trabajando en parejas, alterna con tu compañero/a de clase en hacer y contestar preguntas, usando las pistas indicadas. Sigue el modelo.

> tu hermano/bañarse ayer por la noche
>
> **A:** ¿Se bañó tu hermano ayer por la noche?
>
> **B:** Sí, (No, no) se bañó ayer por la noche.

1. tu papá/afeitarse ayer después de desayunarse
2. nosotros/vestirse ayer con el mismo color de pantalón
3. tú/peinarse ayer antes de salir para el colegio
4. tú/lavarse el pelo ayer
5. él/quemarse con agua caliente
6. tus padres/despertarse ayer a las cinco de la mañana
7. tú/quedarse ayer en la cama hasta que mamá vino para despertarte
8. tu mamá/cepillarse el pelo ayer por la mañana
9. tu hermana/maquillarse ayer por la mañana
10. Uds./desayunarse ayer con huevos y chocolate

IDIOMA

La palabra *se*

In Spanish, when the person who is doing something is indefinite or unknown (where in English one might say "one," "people" or "they"), *se* is sometimes combined with the *él/ella/Ud.* or the *ellos/ellas/Uds.* form of a verb in order to express the action. In such cases the subject (which may precede or follow the verb) indicates whether the verb should be singular or plural. If the subject is singular, the verb is singular. Likewise, if the subject is plural, so is the verb.

Se habla español aquí.	Spanish **is spoken** here.
Las verduras se comen muchas veces para el almuerzo.	**People** often **eat** vegetables for lunch.

Se come comida mexicana en los Estados Unidos.

20 El horario de los Martínez

Las siguientes oraciones describen algunas de las actividades de un sábado típico de la familia Martínez. Cámbialas, usando una construcción con *se*.

> Empiezan el día a las ocho.
> Se empieza el día a las ocho./El día se empieza a las ocho.

1. Arreglan la casa a las nueve.
2. Lavan el carro a las diez y media.
3. Preparan el almuerzo a las once.
4. Cepillan el perro a las cuatro.
5. Preparan la comida a las seis.
6. Ponen la mesa a las siete.
7. Comen la comida a las siete y media.

Activity 20

Quiz/Activity 4

Activities 7-8

Answers

19 1. ¿Se afeitó...?/...se afeitó....
2. ¿Nos vestimos...?/...nos vestimos....
3. ¿Te peinaste...?/...me peiné....
4. ¿Te lavaste...?/...me lo lavé....
5. ¿Se quemó...?/...se quemó....
6. ¿Se despertaron...?/...se despertaron....
7. ¿Te quedaste...?/...me quedé....
8. ¿Se cepilló...?/...se cepilló....
9. ¿Se maquilló...?/...se maquilló....
10. ¿Se desayunaron...?/...nos desayunamos....

20 1. Se arregla la casa./La casa se arregla a las nueve.
2. Se lava el carro./El carro se lava a las diez y media.
3. Se prepara el almuerzo./El almuerzo se prepara a las once.
4. Se cepilla al perro./Al perro se le cepilla a las cuatro.
5. Se prepara la comida./La comida se prepara a las seis.
6. Se pone la mesa./La mesa se pone a las siete.
7. Se come la comida./La comida se come a las siete y media.

Notes

Explain that the article *los* plus a last name can be used to refer to a group of family members: *la familia Martínez* is the equivalent of *los Martínez*.

Activities

Students with Special Needs. Model a second example for activities 19-20.

NATIONAL STANDARDS
C1.1, C1.2, C4.1, C5.2

Notes

Remind students that *almorzar* has a change in its present-tense stem from *o* to *ue*. This same change occurs in the infinitive *volver (ue)*, which students already have learned.

Connections. Inform students that mealtimes and foods vary greatly from one country to another. For example, in Colombia people sometimes have a light snack around 10:30 A.M., called *las onces*, and a second one around 4:00 P.M., called *las medias nueves*. They consist of tea, coffee or hot chocolate, with bread, cookies or pastry.

Point out that the typical schedule of a late lunch and dinner may cause someone to feel hungry at certain times of the day. Two solutions are a *merienda* (snack) or *tapas* (appetizers) typically found in Spanish cafes.

Activities

Communities. Start a discussion about meals students eat at home and away. Finish by comparing their eating habits with the content of the *Conexión cultural*.

Critical Thinking. Ask if students can read the sign on the right side of the page. Ask what the words *comedor, desayuno, cena* and *agua mineral* mean. Ask students what they think an *almuerzo ejecutivo* is in the sign on the left.

Multiple Intelligences (intrapersonal): *¿Quién prepara el almuerzo los domingos?; ¿Con quién cenas?; ¿Comes siempre las tres comidas?*

Conexión Cultural

¿Qué es la comida?

You have already noticed that a word in Spanish can have more than one meaning. This is especially true for words dealing with the daily activity of eating. For example, you already know *la comida* may mean either **the food** or **the dinner**. But, what is **dinner**? Look at the following:

el desayuno	breakfast	desayunarse	to have breakfast
el almuerzo	lunch	almorzar (ue)	to have lunch
la cena	supper	cenar	to have supper
la comida	dinner, the main meal	comer (la comida)	to have dinner, the main meal

In some Spanish-speaking countries, the midday meal is considered to be the main meal—*la comida*—and is usually eaten between one and three o'clock. Families come home during these hours so this meal provides an opportunity for them to spend time together daily before returning to school or work. When the midday meal is the *comida*, then the *cena* is a light supper. However, some families' schedules allow time for only a light *almuerzo* in the middle of the day. For these people, the *cena* then becomes the large family *comida* at home in the evenings.

On weekends, family members usually have a midday *comida* where they gather to discuss important events. Then, *la cena*, which is the much lighter meal, is usually eaten around seven or eight o'clock. Dinner at a restaurant may be even later, beginning around ten o'clock and lasting until midnight or one in the morning.

Cenamos a las siete de la noche.

21 Preguntas personales

Contesta las siguientes preguntas en español. Puedes inventar la información si quieres.

1. ¿A qué hora te desayunas cuando vas al colegio?
2. ¿Qué comes para el desayuno?
3. ¿A qué hora almuerza tu familia los sábados? ¿Y los domingos?
4. ¿A qué hora es la comida en tu casa?
5. ¿Dónde se sientan para cenar?
6. ¿Cuál de las tres comidas es la más importante en tu casa?

22 Frijoles negros cubanos

Ésta es una receta que la familia Martínez prepara los sábados para el almuerzo. Haz una lista de todos los verbos que están en voz pasiva. No te preocupes si no sabes todos los significados.

Frijoles negros cubanos

8 porciones

1 libra de frijoles negros
10 tazas de agua
1 ají (pimiento verde), a la mitad
2/3 taza de aceite de oliva
1 cebolla grande, finamente picada
4 dientes de ajo machacados y cortados
1 ají (pimiento verde), machacado
1 cucharada de sal
1/4 de cucharadita de orégano
1 hojita de laurel
2 cucharadas de azúcar
2 cucharadas de vinagre
2-4 cucharadas de aceite de oliva

Se limpian y se lavan los frijoles y se ponen a remojar con el pimiento verde. Una vez hayan crecido, se cocinan en la misma agua hasta que estén blandos, unos **45** minutos. Se sofríe el pimiento verde machacado en una cacerola con aceite caliente hasta que esté suave. Se le añade una taza de frijoles ya cocidos y se machacan. Se agregan los frijoles restantes con el caldo, junto con la sal, el orégano, la hojita de laurel y el azúcar. Se deja hervir por una hora y se añade el vinagre. Se cocina despacio por otra hora. Si todavía hay mucho líquido se cocina sin tapar por un rato. Un momento antes de servirlos se le añaden de **2** a **4** cucharadas de aceite de oliva y se sirven calientes.

Una toalla, por favor

Answers

21 Answers will vary.

22 se limpian, se lavan, se ponen, se cocinan, se sofríe, se (le) añade, se machacan, se agregan, se deja, se añade, se cocina, se cocina, se (le) añaden, se sirven

Notes

Another word for *el lavabo* is *el lavamanos*. Some people use *el excusado*, while others prefer *el retrete* or *el W.C.* In addition, *el peine* is called *la peinilla* in some parts of the world.

Activities

Connections. Ask for volunteers to make the recipe to bring to class. As an alternative, talk with a knowledgeable foods instructor and make arrangements to go to the family and consumer sciences department area to prepare the recipe as a class project.

Prereading Strategy. Using transparency 14, preteach the bathroom vocabulary. Pronounce each of the words in the illustration and have students repeat them. Then use transparency 13 to point to some of the objects included in the illustration and ask students what they are.

Students with Special Needs. Read through the recipe as a class activity and answer questions to be certain all students understand the content before attempting activity 22.

NATIONAL STANDARDS
C1.1, C1.2, C2.2, C3.1, C3.2, C4.1, C4.2

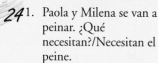

23 ## ¿Qué se vende?

Alterna con un(a) compañero/a de clase en preguntar y contestar si las siguientes cosas se venden o no en la tienda de la ilustración.

Nueva vida para el pelo seco.

champú
A: ¿Se vende champú en la tienda?
B: Sí, se vende champú.

lavaplatos
B: ¿Se venden lavaplatos en la tienda?
A: No, no se venden lavaplatos.

1. lavabos
2. peines
3. grifos
4. crema de afeitar
5. cepillos
6. toallas
7. desodorante
8. excusados
9. espejos
10. tinas

24 ## ¿Qué necesitan?

Trabajando en parejas, alterna con tu compañero/a de clase en hacer y contestar preguntas para decir lo que las siguientes personas necesitan, según lo que ellos van a hacer. Sigue el modelo.

Rosa/maquillarse
A: Rosa se va a maquillar. ¿Qué necesita?
B: Necesita el maquillaje.

1. Paola y Milena/peinarse
2. Ud./mirarse su nuevo color de pelo
3. yo/afeitarse
4. tú/lavarse el pelo
5. Sandra/cepillarse el pelo
6. Rodrigo y Alberto/bañarse

Rosa necesita comprar maquillaje.

25 ## ¡A adivinar!

En grupos de cuatro estudiantes, un estudiante debe representar con un dibujo, en un tiempo máximo de medio minuto, una acción o un objeto nuevo de esta lección. Los otros deben adivinar *(to guess)* lo que está dibujando esa persona. El estudiante que primero adivina la acción o el objeto tiene un punto y tiene el turno para dibujar. La persona con más puntos después de un período de juego de diez minutos, es la ganadora *(winner)*.

Repaso *rápido*

Los adjetivos demostrativos

Remember to use the demonstrative adjectives to indicate where someone or something is located in relation to the speaker. They include *este, esta, estos, estas, ese, esa, esos, esas, aquel, aquella, aquellos* and *aquellas*. Compare the following:

*No me gusta **este** jabón.*	I do not like **this** soap.
*Tampoco me gusta **ese** jabón.*	I do not like **that** soap either.
*Prefiero **aquel** jabón.*	I prefer **that** soap **over there**.

Los pronombres demostrativos

Demonstrative adjectives become demonstrative pronouns when they are used with a written accent mark and when they take the place of a noun.

los pronombres demostrativos

singular		plural	
masculino	**femenino**	**masculino**	**femenino**
éste	ésta	éstos	éstas
ése	ésa	ésos	ésas
aquél	aquélla	aquéllos	aquéllas

Note how demonstrative pronouns are used in the following sentences:

*Creo que **éste** es bueno*	I think **this one** is good and
*y **ése** es muy bueno, pero **aquél***	**that one** is very good, but **that one over**
es el mejor de todos.	**there** is best of all.

Three neuter demonstrative pronouns *(esto, eso, aquello)* refer to a set of circumstances or to very general nouns. The neuter demonstrative pronouns do not require an accent mark.

***Esto** no es bonito.*	**This** is not pretty.
*Me gustaría ver **eso**,*	I would like to see **that** (**stuff**),
por favor.	please.
***Aquello** fue imposible.*	**That** was impossible.

Aquéllos   *esto*   *Ésta*

Notes

In modern usage, demonstrative pronouns are sometimes spelled without an accent.

Point out that the distinction among the demonstratives that many Spanish-speakers make is to use forms of *este* for items near the speaker, forms of *ese* for items near the person spoken to and forms of *aquel* for items that are far from both.

When pointing out people or objects that are nearby, use *éste, ésta, éstos* or *éstas*: *Pienso comprar uno de éstos* (referring to *jabones,* for example). Use *ése, ésa, ésos* or *ésas* to call attention to people or objects that are farther away: *¿Qué piensas de ésas (toallas,* for example)?* Draw attention to people or objects that are even farther away (over there) by using the demonstrative pronouns *aquél, aquélla, aquéllos* or *aquéllas: Aquéllas (toallas) son bonitas.*

Activities

Critical Listening. Practice the demonstrative pronouns and review the demonstrative and possessive adjectives by asking questions containing a classroom object. Students must answer the questions, using an appropriate demonstrative pronoun or adjective: *¿De quién es ese libro?/Éste es mi libro. Ése es el libro de Juan. Aquel libro es su libro* (pointing to another student).

NATIONAL STANDARDS
C1.2, C4.1

26
1. ¿...cuesta esa crema de afeitar?/¿Esa crema de afeitar?/Sí, ésa./Esa crema de afeitar cuesta un dólar con sesenta centavos.
2. ¿...cuesta ese champú?/¿Ese champú?/Sí, ése./Ese champú cuesta dos dólares con cinco centavos.
3. ¿...cuesta aquel cepillo?/¿Aquel cepillo?/Sí, aquél./Aquel cepillo cuesta dos dólares con ochenta centavos.
4. ¿...cuesta este jabón?/¿Este jabón?/Sí, éste./Este jabón cuesta setenta y nueve centavos.
5. ¿...cuestan estos espejos?/¿Estos espejos?/Sí, éstos./Estos espejos cuestan tres dólares con noventa y seis centavos.
6. ¿...cuestan aquellos desodorantes?/¿Aquellos desodorantes?/Sí, aquéllos./Aquellos desodorantes cuestan dos dólares con setenta y tres centavos.
7. ¿...cuestan aquellas toallas?/¿Aquellas toallas?/Sí, aquéllas./Aquellas toallas cuestan ocho dólares con veinticinco centavos.

27 Possible answers:
1. aquél
2. ésta
3. ésta
4. Esto
5. éste
6. ése
7. ésta
8. éste

Activities

Language through Action. Have students clip advertisements for the items mentioned in activity 26. Then ask them to discuss the information in pairs or small groups, using activity 26 as a model.

NATIONAL STANDARDS
C1.1, C1.2, C4.1

---

26 ¿Cuánto cuesta eso?

Durante las vacaciones estás trabajando en una tienda y unos clientes te están preguntando por el precio de algunos objetos. Trabajando en parejas, alterna con tu compañero/a de clase en hacer y contestar preguntas, según las ilustraciones y las indicaciones. Sigue el modelo.

peines/$1.00
A: ¿Cuánto cuestan esos peines?
B: ¿Esos peines?
A: Sí, ésos.
B: Esos peines cuestan un dólar.

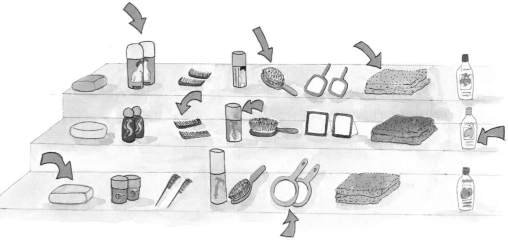

1. crema de afeitar/$1.60
2. champú/$2.05
3. cepillo/$2.80
4. jabón/$0.79

5. espejos/$3.96
6. desodorantes/$2.73
7. toallas/$8.25

27 Todos se preparan

Todos en la casa de Miguel se preparan para salir de viaje. Completa las siguientes oraciones con los pronombres demostrativos apropiados para decir qué hacen para prepararse.

 Quiero otro jabón; <u>éste</u> no me gusta.

1. Ese jabón no; yo quiero <u>(1)</u> que está allá.
2. Mi toalla es roja; <u>(2)</u> es rosada.
3. Aquélla no es mi crema de afeitar; es <u>(3)</u>.
4. ¡<u>(4)</u> es un desastre! Debes limpiar el baño ahora mismo.
5. ¿Es aquél tu desodorante? ¿Y <u>(5)</u> que está aquí?
6. ¿Qué champú es nuevo? <u>(6)</u> que está allí es nuevo.
7. Necesito otra toalla; <u>(7)</u> está sucia.
8. ¿Dónde está mi champú? No es <u>(8)</u> que está aquí.

Pasta de dientes

28 ¿De quién es?

Trabajando en parejas, alterna con tu compañero/a de clase en preguntar y contestar de quiénes son cinco cosas que tú señalas en la clase sin mencionarlas. Sigue el modelo.

A: ¿Es esto de Patricia?
B: No, esto es de Rafael.

¿esto?

¿eso?

¿aquello?

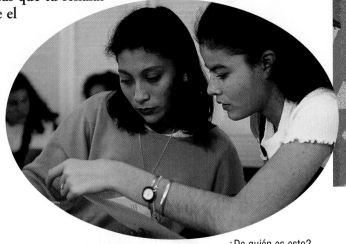

¿De quién es esto?

Autoevaluación. Como repaso y autoevaluación, responde lo siguiente:
1. In Spanish, state three activities you do every day.
2. Name three places in the United States with names that are derived from Spanish.
3. How might you use Spanish as a volunteer in your community?
4. Describe in Spanish how two people in the classroom are dressed.
5. What was the last thing you did last night?
6. At what time do you eat breakfast on Sundays?
7. What is the first thing you do each morning after you wake up?
8. Imagine you are traveling and see a swimsuit you would like to buy. How would you say "I want that one"?

San Diego, California.

Santa Fe, Nuevo México.

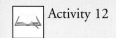

Activity 12

Answers

A Creative self-expression.

B Creative self-expression.

Notes

Technology. Suggest that students use one of many available Internet search engines to do their search for summer-abroad programs mentioned in activity B.

WWW

Lycos
http://www.lycos.com/
Yahoo
http://www.yahoo.com/
Yahoo Español
http://espanol.yahoo.com/
Webcrawler
http://www.webcrawler.com/
Infoseek
http://www.infoseek.com/
Altavista
http://www.altavista.digital.com/

Activities

Expansion. Make a bulletin board of information about summer-abroad programs students find during their search.

Students with Special Needs. You may wish to have some groups present their dialogs for activity A in front of the class after adequate practice.

¡La práctica hace al maestro!

A Comunicación

Working with a partner, ask questions about one another's daily routine. Compare how your schedules and activities vary on school days and over the weekend or during holidays. (You may wish to discuss how your routine varies for certain special holidays, for example.)

B Conexión con la tecnología

Search the Internet to find summer-abroad programs that offer opportunities for students to stay in Spanish-speaking countries. Then imagine you are a participant in the program and share your findings with the class about the following: what a typical school day is like; when you wake up; at what time you get out of bed; how you prepare for the day; when and with whom you eat meals; how you get to school; at what time you go home; and how you finish the day. Make up any of the information you wish, but try to keep it culturally accurate.

Siempre desayunamos en este café antes de ir a la escuela.

VOCABULARIO

En el baño
- el cepillo
- el champú
- la crema de afeitar
- el desodorante
- la ducha
- el espejo
- el excusado
- el grifo
- el jabón
- el lavabo
- el maquillaje
- el peine
- la tina
- la toalla

Comidas
- la cena
- la comida
- el desayuno

Verbos
- acostar(se) (ue)
- afeitar(se)
- almorzar (ue)
- bañar(se)
- calmar(se)
- cenar
- cepillar(se)
- desayunar(se)
- despertar(se) (ie)
- duchar(se)
- esperar
- lavar(se)
- levantar(se)
- llamar(se)
- maquillar(se)
- peinar(se)
- poner(se)
- preocupar(se)
- quedar(se)
- quemar(se)
- quitar(se)
- sentar(se) (ie)
- vestir(se) (i, i)

Expresiones y otras palabras
- aquél, aquélla (aquéllos, aquéllas)
- aquello
- así
- desde luego
- ése, ésa (ésos, ésas)
- eso
- éste, ésta (éstos, éstas)
- esto
- la paz
- el pelo
- tarde

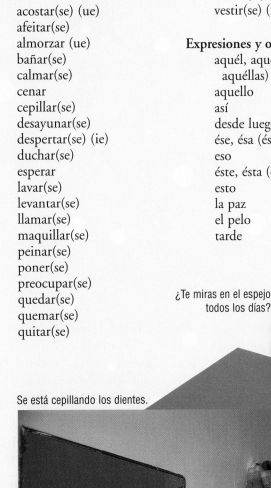

¿Te miras en el espejo todos los días?

Se está cepillando los dientes.

Se llama Hernán.

NATIONAL STANDARDS
C1.2, C4.1

No me siento bien
Activity 1

Activity 1

Contexto cultural
ESTADOS UNIDOS

Answers

1. Va a ver a la doctora Morales.
2. No, no sabe.
3. Le parece que sólo tiene un resfriado.
4. No quiere estar enfermo porque él y su familia van a irse de viaje.
5. Van a visitar a sus tíos en Chicago y a pescar en el Lago Michigan.

Content reviewed in *Lección 4*
- Hispanic influence in the United States
- parts of the body
- health
- prepositions

Notes

Explain that *me siento* comes from the infinitive *sentirse (ie, i)* and requires the same stem changes as *sentir (ie, i)*, which students already have learned. Similarly, *divertirnos* comes from the infinitive *divertirse (ie, i)* and requires the same stem changes as *sentir (ie, i)*.

You may choose to note for students that *doler (ue)* follows the pattern of *gustar* and usually is used with an indirect object pronoun. This will be explained more thoroughly later in the lesson.

Activities

Cooperative Learning. After introducing the dialog (playing the audiocassette/compact disc, modeling words and phrases for student repetition, reviewing parts of the body, etc.), have students work in pairs practicing the dialog. Circulate and assist with pronunciation and intonation.

DRA. MORALES:	¿Qué te **duele?**°
MIGUEL:	No sé, **doctora. No me siento**° bien.
DRA. MORALES:	Vamos a ver.... **Abre** la **boca** y **di** *aaaaa*.
MIGUEL:	¿Qué tengo? ¿**Gripe?**°
DRA. MORALES:	No, me parece que sólo es un **resfriado.**°
MIGUEL:	¡Eso no puede ser!
DRA. MORALES:	¿Por qué no?
MIGUEL:	Vamos a **irnos de viaje**° el fin de semana.
DRA. MORALES:	¿De viaje? ¿Adónde van?
MIGUEL:	Vamos a **visitar** a mis tíos en Chicago y a **pescar** en el **Lago**° Michigan. Vamos a **divertirnos**° mucho.
DRA. MORALES:	Bueno, debes **descansar**° por dos días. Si descansas un poco, no vas a tener ningún problema.

duele *hurts* **no me siento** *I do not feel* **gripe** *flu* **resfriado** *cold* **irnos de viaje** *go away on a trip* **Lago** *Lake* **divertirnos** *have fun* **descansar** *to rest, to relax*

¿Qué comprendiste?

1. ¿A qué médico va a ver Miguel?
2. ¿Sabe Miguel qué le duele?
3. ¿Qué cree la doctora Morales que tiene Miguel?
4. ¿Por qué Miguel no quiere estar enfermo?
5. ¿Adónde van Miguel y su familia?

PARA ti

La palabra *pescar*
The word *pescar* (to fish, to catch) changes meaning according to the context:

Mañana, voy a pescar en ese lago.	Tomorrow, I am going **to fish** in that lake.
Voy a pescar un resfriado.	I am going **to catch** a cold.

2 Charlando

1. ¿Cómo te sientes ahora?
2. ¿Qué haces cuando estás enfermo/a?
3. ¿Cuánto tiempo descansas en un día?
4. ¿Qué crees que debes hacer cuando tienes gripe?
5. ¿Cuándo fue la última vez que pescaste un resfriado?

Conexión cultural

Aquí se habla español

La población *(population)* de hispanohablantes *(Spanish-speaking people)* en los Estados Unidos es muy grande. Por ejemplo, las ciudades de Santa Fe, Nuevo México y Miami son un cincuenta por ciento hispanas. Además, en Los Ángeles la población es de un cuarenta por ciento hispana y en Nueva York es de un treinta por ciento. En los estados de California, Arizona, Florida, Colorado y Texas el número de hispanohablantes y su influencia son muy grandes. Por esta razón, en cada uno de estos estados es posible encontrar desde periódicos hasta programas de televisión y de radio en español.

Como hay muchas personas de habla hispana en los Estados Unidos, el ser bilingüe *(bilingual)* puede ser importante. Por ejemplo, en muchos lugares, como en los hospitales, las clínicas, los restaurantes y los hoteles, o en cualquier otro lugar, el comunicarse en español es muy común y necesario. ¿Qué influencia hispana hay donde tú vives?

En este lugar se habla español. (San Francisco, California.)

Answers

2 Answers will vary.

Notes

Cultures. Point out that Hispanics in the United States have many different countries of origin and that some families have resided in the United States for decades while others arrived more recently. The three largest U.S. Hispanic groups are of Mexican, Puerto Rican and Cuban origin.

Activities

Prereading Strategy. This *Conexión cultural* provides an opportunity for students to improve their ability to acquire information in Spanish about some places where Spanish is used in the United States. The vocabulary and structures have been controlled to enable individuals to read in the target language and enjoy the experience. Note for the class that it is not essential to understand every word in order to read Spanish; the meaning of important but unknown passive vocabulary has been provided to facilitate an enjoyable experience. Before beginning the *Conexión cultural*, consider asking some general preparation questions about the theme of the reading: What are the names of some cities in the United States where there are large Spanish-speaking populations? Then have students skim the *Conexión cultural* for cognates and any words or expressions they already know.

NATIONAL STANDARDS
C1.1, C1.2, C3.2, C4.1,
C4.2, C5.2

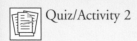
Answers

3 Answers will vary.

4 Creative self-expression.

Notes

You may want to give the Spanish terms for the jobs named in this *Oportunidades*: physician *(médico/médica)*, court reporter *(reportero/reportera de tribunal)*, lawyer *(abogado/abogada)*, customs agent *(agente de aduana)*, bilingual administrative assistant *(asistente administrativo/a bilingüe)*, nurse *(enfermero, enfermera)*.

Activities

Spanish for Spanish Speakers. Discuss cultural pluralism in your community, particularly in the Spanish-speaking community. Try to develop the leadership and public-speaking skills of the Hispanic/Latin American/ bilingual students you may have in class by involving them in the discussion. Encourage them to talk about their family and community, allowing them to develop greater pride in their ancestry.

Communities. Additional well-known people (past and present) you may choose to name include the following: Jennifer López, María Conchita Alonso, Jimmy Smits, actors; Ricky Martin, Gloria Estefan, singers; Rubén Blades, singer of popular contemporary music and actor; Sammy Sosa, Tony Fernández, baseball players. You may wish to have students find out more about these or other famous Spanish-speaking people. Draw upon your students' interests and reinforce their knowledge of the Spanish-speaking people in your community.

NATIONAL STANDARDS
C1.1, C2.2, C3.1, C5.1

3 Cruzando fronteras

En cinco minutos, haz una lista de lugares geográficos en los Estados Unidos con nombres en español. Trata de incluir por lo menos quince lugares. Sigue el modelo.

Cuerpos de agua	Ciudades	Estados	Otros lugares
Río Grande	Lapaz	Colorado	Sierra Nevada

Oportunidades

¿Qué valor hay en ser bilingüe?

You are already aware that knowing how to communicate in a second language can enhance your career opportunities, especially in areas where there are large Hispanic populations. The following are some interesting careers where being bilingual may offer a distinct advantage:

Soy operadora.

physician

NURSE

court reporter

bilingual administrative assistant

lawyer

CUSTOMS AGENT

OFFICIAL

4 Las personas famosas

Trabajando en parejas, hagan una lista de por lo menos cinco personas hispanas famosas que viven en los Estados Unidos. Deben decir lo que hace cada una de estas personas. También deben decir de dónde son y dónde viven, si es posible. Puedes buscar información usando la Internet.

El cuerpo

la niña
la espalda
el niño
la oreja
el oído
el cuello
el ojo
la nariz
el diente
la lengua
la cara
la garganta

el corazón
el brazo izquierdo
el hombro
el pecho
el codo
el estómago
la rodilla
la pierna derecha

5 ¿Qué hacemos con...?

Conecta las frases de la columna A con las partes del cuerpo apropiadas de la columna B en forma lógica.

A	B
1. Vemos con...	A. el pelo.
2. Oímos con...	B. los pies.
3. Mi amigo escribe con...	C. los oídos.
4. Comemos con...	D. los dedos.
5. Tocamos algo con...	E. la boca.
6. Caminamos con...	F. la cara.
7. A veces mi amiga se maquilla...	G. los ojos.
8. A mi amigo no le gusta cepillarse...	H. la mano izquierda.

PARA ti

Más palabras del cuerpo

la ceja	eyebrow
la cintura	waist
la frente	forehead
el labio	lip
la mejilla	cheek
la pestaña	eyelash
la uña	nail

¿ESTA USTED PERDIENDO EL PELO?

Solo para sus ojos

EYE QUITA EL ROJO DE LOS OJOS

GOTAS OFTALMICAS

 El cuerpo

 Quiz/Activity 1

 Activities 15-16

Activities 3-4

Answers

5.
1. G
2. C
3. H
4. E
5. D
6. B
7. F
8. A

Notes

Review previously learned parts of the body: *el cuerpo, la cabeza, el brazo, la mano, el dedo, la pierna, el pie.*

Remind students that just as some words in Spanish that end in *-a* require a masculine article (*el problema, el programa, el mapa, el día*), some words that end in *-o* are feminine and thus require a feminine article *(la mano)*.

Activities

TPR. Use TPR to teach and reinforce the parts of the body. Teach the following commands, combining them with the appropriate parts of the body: *toca, mueve, ráscate, tira, levanta, baja, abre, cierra.* You can review the present progressive by asking individual students questions after each command: (name), *¿qué estás tocando?;* (name), *¿qué está tocando* (second student's name)?

Multiple Intelligences (linguistic). Ask students to tell you what the two items at the bottom of page 65 say.

NATIONAL STANDARDS
C1.1, C1.2, C1.3, 4.1, C4.2

Answers

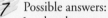

6
1. cabeza y cara
2. pierna y rodilla
3. codo y brazo
4. mano y dedo
5. boca y dientes
6. enfermero y médico
7. niño y niña
8. resfriado y gripe
9. izquierdo y derecho
10. ojos y orejas

7 Possible answers:
1. el codo
2. el hombro
3. la lengua
4. la espalda
5. la nariz
6. el estómago
7. el ojo
8. la garganta
9. el brazo izquierdo
10. la pierna derecha

8
1. Es la nariz.
2. Son los ojos.
3. Son las piernas.
4. Son los dedos.
5. Son los dientes.
6. Son los brazos.
7. Es el cuello.
8. Es el codo.
9. Es el corazón.
10. Es la lengua.

Notes

Review. In activity 7 the name *Pedrito* is the diminutive form of *Pedro*. Based on this example, ask students to give the diminutive forms of *Pablo, Teresa* and *Ana*.

Activities

Connections. Have students investigate which bone *(hueso)* corresponds to each part of the body.

Multiple Intelligences (linguistic). Have students look in a dictionary for equivalents in Spanish for bones they know in English.

Cooperative Learning. Have students work in pairs to invent their own *adivinanzas* (activity 8).

 **Las partes del cuerpo**

En cada grupo escoge las dos palabras que están relacionadas *(related)* de alguna forma.

1. cabeza	cara	pie	cinturón
2. gripe	pierna	rodilla	cena
3. codo	brazo	lago	cita
4. mano	doler	tina	dedo
5. boca	pescar	dientes	espalda
6. enfermero	espejo	dedo	médico
7. niño	visitar	niña	sentirse
8. resfriado	irse	gripe	corazón
9. izquierdo	niño	derecho	resfriado
10. lago	ojos	orejas	peine

Tengo un resfriado.

 Un examen médico

Pedrito está en la oficina de la doctora para un examen. Identifica las siguientes partes del cuerpo.

 el corazón

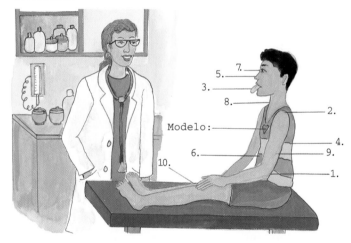

 Adivina, adivinador/a

Adivina a qué partes del cuerpo se refieren las siguientes oraciones.

1. Está entre los ojos.
2. Están en la cara y los usas para ver.
3. Son largas y las usas para correr.
4. Están en los pies y las manos y son veinte en total.
5. Son de color blanco y están en la boca.
6. Son largos y los usas para dar abrazos.
7. Está entre la cabeza y los hombros.
8. Está entre el hombro y la mano.
9. Está en el pecho. No podemos vivir sin él.
10. Es de color rosado y está en la boca.

Sonrisas del Corazón

Algo más

¿Qué oyes en el consultorio del médico?

Siéntate.	*Sit down.*
Abre la boca.	*Open your mouth.*
Saca la lengua.	*Stick out your tongue.*
Di *aaaaa.*	*Say aaaaa.*
Tócate la nariz.	*Touch your nose.*
¿Cómo te sientes?	*How do you feel?*
¿Qué te duele?	*What hurts?*

¿Qué puedes contestar?

Me siento cansado/a.	*I feel tired.*
No me siento bien.	*I do not feel well.*
Me duele/Me duelen....	*My...hurts/hurt.*

¿Qué te duele?

ABRE Bien LOS OJOS

9 En el médico

Yolanda fue al médico. Completa el siguiente diálogo de una manera lógica.

YOLANDA:	¡Hola, doctor Rojas!
MÉDICO:	¡Hola, Yolanda! (1), por favor.
YOLANDA:	Muchas gracias, doctor.
MÉDICO:	¿Qué te (2)?
YOLANDA:	Me duele mucho la (3).
MÉDICO:	Bueno, vamos a mirar. (4) la boca. (5) la lengua. (6) *aaaaa.* Parece que tienes un (7).
YOLANDA:	¿Qué debo hacer?
MÉDICO:	Debes (8) y tomar mucha agua.

Aaaaa.

¡NO DESCUIDE SU ESPALDA...!

¿Es dolor de estómago?

10 Tócate...

Trabajando en parejas, alterna con tu compañero/a en decirle qué parte del cuerpo debe tocar. Mira para ver si tu compañero/a toca la parte del cuerpo correcta. Cada estudiante debe mencionar ocho partes del cuerpo.

A: Tócate la cara.
B: *(Student B should touch his/her face.)*

—

Answers

9 Possible answers:
1. Siéntate
2. duele
3. garganta
4. Abre
5. Saca
6. Di
7. resfriado
8. descansar

10 This is a TPR activity. Students should observe one another as they give their commands to be sure their classmates have responded correctly. Circulate and spot-check student work for problems. (You may wish to inform students that you will select two or three pairs of students to perform several commands for the class.)

Activities

Cooperative Learning. Working in pairs, have students play the part of a doctor *(médico/médica)* and a patient *(paciente)*. The doctor should question the patient about how he or she has been feeling and what hurts. The doctor should instruct the patient what he or she should do during the examination and, then, should recommend what the patient can do to get better. Finally, have students switch roles and start over.

Critical Thinking. As explained in the *Estrategia* for the *A leer* on page 78, background knowledge can be helpful in facilitating listening and reading comprehension. To illustrate this point, ask students to identify topics and expressions typical of a visit to the doctor.

NATIONAL STANDARDS
C1.1, C1.2, C3.1, C4.1, C5.1, C5.2

Answers

11 Creative self-expression.

12
1. ¿Vas a dormir mucho?/No, voy a dormir poco.
2. ¿Vas a llevarte mal con tus amigos?/No, voy a llevarme bien con mis amigos.
3. ¿Vas a comerte todo en el viaje?/ No, voy a comerme casi todo.
4. ¿Vas a dormirte temprano?/No, voy a dormirme tarde.
5. ¿Vas a llevar mucha ropa?/No, voy a llevar poca ropa.
6. ¿Vas a irte de vacaciones a Chicago?/No, voy a irme de vacaciones a Los Ángeles.
7. ¿Vas a comer poco en el viaje?/No, voy a comer mucho.

Notes

Other verbs that have changes in meaning when used non-reflexively are *enfermarse* (to get sick) → *enfermar* (to make someone else sick) and *preocuparse* (to worry) → *preocupar* (to worry someone else).

11 ¡Eres artista!

Imagina que eres artista. Haz un dibujo de un monstruo *(monster),* **usando las siguientes indicaciones.**

El monstruo tiene una cabeza pequeña y un corazón pequeño. En la cara, tiene tres ojos grandes de color azul. La nariz es fea, y el monstruo tiene una boca grande con cuatro dientes y una lengua delgada y larga. A los lados de la cabeza tiene dos orejas grandes y sobre la cabeza tiene sólo tres pelos. El cuello es delgado y largo y el pecho es grande. Tiene cuatro brazos largos y en cada brazo tiene una mano con tres dedos. Las piernas no son muy largas y tiene dos pies con cuatro dedos cada uno.

IDIOMA

Otras construcciones reflexivas

Some verbs in Spanish have a different meaning when they are used reflexively.

comer to eat	→	*comerse* to eat up
dormir (ue, u) to sleep	→	*dormirse (ue, u)* to fall asleep
ir to go	→	*irse* to leave, to go away
llevar to take, to carry	→	*llevarse* to take away, to get along
preguntar to ask	→	*preguntarse* to wonder, to ask oneself

Compare the following:

*Isabel **duerme** mucho.*   Isabel **sleeps** a lot.
*Muchas veces **me duermo***   I often **fall asleep** before nine.
antes de las nueve.

12 ¿Qué planes tienes?

Imagina que ya tienes planes para las vacaciones y tu compañero/a te hace preguntas sobre tus planes. Trabajando en parejas, alterna con tu compañero/a de clase en hacer y contestar preguntas, según las indicaciones. Sigue el modelo.

irse con tus hermanos/mis amigos
A: ¿Vas a irte con tus hermanos?
B: No, voy a irme con mis amigos.

1. dormir mucho/poco
2. llevarse mal con tus amigos/bien
3. comerse todo en el viaje/casi todo
4. dormirse temprano/tarde
5. llevar mucha ropa/poca ropa
6. irse de vacaciones a Chicago/Los Ángeles
7. comer poco en el viaje/mucho

DE VACACIONES

13 En Chicago

Cuando Miguel visita a sus tíos, muchas cosas pasan. Di lo que pasa, completando las siguientes oraciones con la forma apropiada de los verbos entre paréntesis.

Chicago.

El tío de Miguel *(llevar)* a los chicos en su carro nuevo.
El tío de Miguel *lleva* a los chicos en su carro nuevo.

Miguel *(dormirse)* temprano para despertarse temprano.
Miguel *se duerme* temprano para despertarse temprano.

1. Todos *(ir)* al Lago Michigan a las cinco y media de la mañana.
2. Ramiro siempre *(preguntarle)* a él todo lo que Miguel sabe sobre cómo pescar.
3. Miguel y sus primos *(irse)* a pescar al Lago Michigan bien temprano.
4. Los tíos de Miguel *(dormir)* muy poco.
5. Miguel *(llevarse)* muy bien con Ramiro.
6. Ellos *(comer)* perros calientes.
7. La tía de Miguel siempre *(preguntarse)* a qué hora van a volver de pescar.
8. A la hora de la comida, Miguel y sus primos *(comerse)* todo el pescado.

14 Preguntas personales

Contesta las siguientes preguntas. Puedes inventar la información si quieres.

1. ¿Adónde vas a ir?
2. ¿Cuándo piensas irte de viaje?
3. Cuando viajas, ¿qué te divierte a ti?
4. ¿Qué tipo de comida comes cuando viajas?
5. Cuando en un viaje vas a un restaurante, ¿te comes siempre todo lo que pides? Explica.

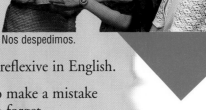

Nos despedimos.

Algo más

Más sobre los verbos reflexivos

Some verbs are reflexive in Spanish that do not appear at all reflexive in English.

acostumbrarse	to get used to	*equivocarse*	to make a mistake
broncearse	to tan	*olvidarse*	to forget
caerse	to fall down	*reunirse*	to get together
despedirse (i, i)	to say good-bye	*sentirse (ie, i)*	to feel

Note: The verb *caer(se)* is regular in the present tense, except for the first-person singular form *(me) caigo*. The preterite tense of *caer(se)* is conjugated following the pattern of the verb *leer: caí, caíste, cayó, caímos, caísteis, cayeron.* The present participle of *caer (caerse)* is *cayendo (cayéndose)*.

 Activity 14

 Activity 7

 Quiz/Activity 5

Answers

13
1. van
2. le pregunta
3. se van
4. duermen
5. se lleva
6. comen
7. se pregunta
8. se comen

14 Answers will vary.

Activities

Students with Special Needs. In order to familiarize students with the present tense, the preterite tense and the present progressive forms of the verb *caer(se)*, try this simple rote practice: Name a verb and a verb tense. Then give several students various subject pronouns (or people's names) that they must use to conjugate correctly the named verb in the stated tense: *caerse*, present tense, *tú*. The student must respond with *te caes*. Add a creative element by having students use *caer(se)* in a sentence. You may wish to give some examples: *¿Cuándo te caes? Yo me caigo cuando esquío.*

1. B
2. F
3. C
4. E
5. D
6. A

1. se compran
2. se compra
3. bañarse
4. se despide
5. acostumbrarme
6. me olvido
7. nos olvidamos
8. me olvido
9. se equivoca
10. se broncean
11. me voy
12. se preocupa
13. nos divertimos

Notes

Point out for students that *me siento* (activity 15) can mean **I feel** or **I sit down**. As is often the case, the context provides the clue as to the meaning here: *Me siento muy bien.* (I feel very well.)

Activities

Critical Listening. Inform the class you will be playing a recorded version of the dialog on page 71. (The dialog has been recorded by native speakers as part of the *Somos así LISTOS* Audio cassette/Audio CD Program.) Instruct students to cover the words with one hand since you want them to develop good listening skills before learning how to read Spanish. Next, tell students you would like them to look at the illustration while they imagine what the people are saying to one another. Finally, have several individuals state what they believe the main theme of the conversation is.

Expansion. Have students invent their own responses to the questions that appear in column A of activity 15: *¿De qué te preocupas?/Me preocupo de no despertarme a tiempo.*

---

15 ¿Cuál es la respuesta?

Selecciona de la columna B una respuesta apropiada para cada una de las preguntas de la columna A.

A	B
1. ¿De qué te preocupas?	A. Sí, los vamos a visitar a su casa.
2. ¿Te bronceas?	B. No me preocupo de nada.
3. ¿Se divierten mucho o me equivoco?	C. Te equivocas, estamos muy aburridos.
4. ¿Me siento allí?	D. Me siento muy bien.
5. ¿Cómo te sientes?	E. No. Siéntate aquí.
6. ¿Nos reunimos con nuestros abuelos después del viaje?	F. No. Sólo tomo un poco de sol.

16 El diario de Miguel

Miguel escribió en su diario *(diary)* sobre los viajes con su familia. Completa el siguiente párrafo con la forma apropiada de los verbos entre paréntesis.

Mi familia y yo viajamos mucho. Antes de viajar, nosotros vamos al médico sólo para saber que estamos bien. También, antes de viajar, nos gusta ir de compras. Mis hermanos 1. *(comprarse)* algo para broncearse y mi hermana 2. *(comprarse)* algo para 3. *(bañarse)* en la playa. A la hora de salir, mi hermana 4. *(despedirse)* de su perro. Yo no puedo 5. *(acostumbrarse)* a eso. Mi padre siempre me pregunta si yo no 6. *(olvidarse)* de nada. Él dice que nosotros siempre 7. *(olvidarse)* de algo. Es verdad, yo siempre 8. *(olvidarse)* de algo. Él casi nunca 9. *(equivocarse)* cuando dice algo. Cuando vamos a una playa, mis hermanos 10. *(broncearse)* y yo 11. *(irse)* a nadar porque a mí no me gusta broncearme. Mi madre siempre 12. *(preocuparse)* cuando no estamos todos juntos, pero yo le digo que no debe preocuparse. Lo mejor de todo, cuando viajamos, es que nosotros 13. *(divertirse)* mucho.

17 En Los Ángeles

Imagina que tú y tu familia fueron de vacaciones a Los Ángeles el verano pasado. Haz oraciones completas con las indicaciones que se dan para decir lo que pasó.

> mi tía/no/equivocarse al decir que la ciudad es bonita
> Mi tía no se equivocó al decir que la ciudad es bonita.

1. nosotros/reunirse con nuestros parientes en Los Ángeles
2. yo/sentirse un poco resfriado el primer día
3. mis hermanas/no/broncearse mucho en la playa
4. mi papá/olvidarse de llevar ropa de verano
5. mi abuela/no/acostumbrarse a tantos carros
6. nosotros/despedirse de nuestros tíos el último día

Los Ángeles, California.

En el médico

el enfermero

la enfermera

DR. DÍAZ: ¿Qué sientes?
RAÚL: Me duele el pecho y me siento mal.
DR. DÍAZ: ¿Tú **fumas?**°
RAÚL: A veces.
DR. DÍAZ: ¡Tu problema son esos **cigarrillos!**
RAÚL: ¿Debo tomar alguna **medicina?**
DR. DÍAZ: Sí. Antes de acostarte debes tomar esto y debes **dejar de**° fumar. Tienes que hacer más **ejercicio** y **cuidarte**° mejor. La **enfermera** te va a dar otra **cita.**° Quiero verte en un mes.
RAÚL: Muchas gracias, doctor. Adiós.

fumas *smoke* **dejar de** *to stop, to quit* **cuidarte** *take care of yourself* **cita** *appointment*

Answers

17 1. Nos reunimos con nuestros parientes en Los Ángeles.
2. Yo me sentí un poco resfriado el primer día.
3. Mis hermanas no se broncearon mucho en la playa.
4. Mi papá se olvidó de llevar ropa de verano.
5. Mi abuela no se acostumbró a tantos carros.
6. Nos despedimos de nuestros tíos el último día.

Notes

¿Qué tienes?, ¿Qué te duele?, ¿Te duele algo?, ¿No te sientes bien? and *¿Te sientes mal?* are all expressions used to ask about a person's health.

The word *cita* may refer to an appointment, such as a visit to the doctor or a social date. Context will make the meaning clear.

Activities

Critical Thinking. Take this opportunity to discuss the hazards of smoking. Talk to a school counselor for suggestions. In addition, you may be able to contact a local health organization and request materials in Spanish on the dangers of smoking.

Expansion. Additional questions (*¿Qué comprendiste?*): *¿Qué tiene Raúl?; ¿Fuma Raúl?; ¿Qué debe hacer Raúl?; ¿Cuándo quiere ver el médico a Raúl?*

Prereading Strategy. Instruct students to cover up the dialog with one hand and look at the illustration. Ask them to imagine where the conversation takes place and what the people are saying to one another. Finally, have students look through the dialog quickly to find cognates and any words or expressions they already know.

NATIONAL STANDARDS
C1.2, C4.1

Activities 18-19

Answers

18 1. A Raúl le duele el pecho.
2. Él se siente mal.
3. Los cigarrillos son su problema.
4. Raúl debe dejar de fumar.
5. Raúl debe tomar la medicina antes de acostarse.
6. La enfermera le va a dar una cita a Raúl.

19 Answers will vary.

20 1. Mi última cita fue....
2. Me siento....
3. Sí, (No, no) fumo.
4. Tengo....
5. Sí, (No, no) estoy tomando medicina.
6. Sí, (No, no) hago ejercicio.
7. Sí, algunas veces./No, nunca dejo de tomar el desayuno.

Notes

The terms *médico* and *médica* usually are used to refer to a person's profession, whereas *doctor (Dr.)* and *doctora (Dra.)* are usually used as a term of address with the person's name. This custom is changing, however, and more and more people are beginning to use *doctor (Dr.)* and *doctora (Dra.)* interchangeably with *médico* and *médica*.

Activities

TPR. Name various body parts in Spanish while students point to the part named.

NATIONAL STANDARDS
C1.1, C1.2, C2.1, C3.1, C4.1

---

18 **¿Qué comprendiste?**

1. ¿Qué le duele a Raúl?
2. ¿Cómo se siente Raúl?
3. ¿Cuál es el problema de Raúl?
4. ¿Qué debe dejar Raúl?
5. ¿Cuándo debe tomar la medicina Raúl?
6. ¿Quién le va a dar una cita a Raúl?

19 **Charlando**

1. ¿Cómo te sientes ahora?
2. ¿Crees que fumar cigarrillos es malo para el corazón? Explica.
3. ¿Haces algún ejercicio? ¿Cuál?
4. ¿Qué haces para cuidarte?
5. ¿Cuándo tienes una cita con el/la médico/a?

20 **El doctor Díaz**

Imagina que vas al consultorio del doctor Díaz y las siguientes son algunas preguntas que te hace. Contesta sus preguntas.

DR. DÍAZ:	¿Cuándo fue tu última cita?
TÚ:	(1)
DR. DÍAZ:	¿Cómo te sientes?
TÚ:	(2)
DR. DÍAZ:	¿Tú fumas?
TÚ:	(3)
DR. DÍAZ:	¿Cuántos años tienes?
TÚ:	(4)
DR. DÍAZ:	¿Estás tomando alguna medicina?
TÚ:	(5)
DR. DÍAZ:	¿Haces ejercicio?
TÚ:	(6)
DR. DÍAZ:	¿Algunas veces dejas de tomar el desayuno?
TÚ:	(7)

¿Doctor?

Although the term *doctor(a)* is commonly used in Spanish to refer to medical doctors, dentists and other professionals with doctoral degrees, in some places (i.e., Colombia) the term can be used to address any person with a professional degree as a sign of respect. In fact, sometimes the term is used as a joke when talking with a friend who happens to be wearing a tie and a suit.

¿Haces ejercicio?

Soy doctora.

Algo más

Verbos similares

You may encounter some verbs in Spanish that may seem like they should be reflexive, but they are not. They follow the pattern you have learned for *gustar* and are normally used with an indirect object pronoun.

- *doler (ue)* (to hurt, to suffer pain from)
  *A Diego **le duele** la espalda.*   Diego's back hurts.

- *hacer falta* (to be necessary, to be lacking)
  ***Les hace falta** divertirse mucho.*   They need to have a lot of fun.

- *importar* (to be important, to matter)
  *No **me importa**.*   It does not matter to me.

- *parecer* (to seem)
  *¿**Te parece** difícil?*   Does it seem difficult (to you)?

A Marcos le duele el codo.

 21 ## ¿Qué les duele?

Trabajando en parejas, alterna con tu compañero/a de clase en preguntar y contestar lo que les duele a las siguientes personas.

Ana
A: ¿Qué le duele a Ana?
B: Le duele el dedo del pie.

1. Nicolás   2. Isabel   3. ellos   4. Juan y Graciela

5. tú   6. nosotros   7. Antonio   8. yo

Capítulo 2   73

Quizzes/Activities 5-6

Activity 10

Quiz/Activity 6

Answers

22 1. me duele
2. le duele
3. le parece
4. le duele
5. le importa
6. le duelen
7. nos hace falta
8. Te parece
9. te hace falta

Notes

Review. Be certain students know the meaning of the prepositions on page 74.

Note for students before they begin activity 25 on page 75 that the verb *hacer* often appears in a question but is then replaced by a different verb (a specific action) in a response.

Activities

Cooperative Learning. Have students do activity 24 on page 75 in pairs.

22 Nadie se siente muy bien

Hoy todos se sienten enfermos en la familia de Raúl. Completa el siguiente párrafo con la forma apropiada de *doler, hacer falta, importar* o *parecer* y el complemento directo o indirecto apropiado, según las indicaciones.

Nadie se siente muy bien hoy en mi familia. Yo tengo gripe y 1. *(doler)* todo el cuerpo. Mi hermana cantó mucho ayer y hoy a ella 2. *(doler)* la garganta. Pablo, mi hermano, también cree que está enfermo. A él 3. *(parecer)* que tiene un resfriado. A mi padre 4. *(doler)* la cabeza, pero dice que a él no 5. *(importar),* y a mi madre 6. *(doler)* mucho los pies. Creo que a todos nosotros 7. *(hacer falta)* descansar mucho. Y tú, ¿cómo estás? ¿8. *(parecer)* que hoy hay alguien enfermo en tu familia? ¿A ti también 9. *(hacer falta)* descansar?

Repaso *rápido*

Las preposiciones

Look at the following list of prepositions in Spanish and see how many you remember. Look up any you do not recognize.

a	cerca de	desde	hasta	por
al lado de	con	después de	lejos de	sin
antes de	de	en	para	sobre

IDIOMA

Los verbos después de las preposiciones

In Spanish an infinitive (the form of the verb that ends in *-ar, -er* or *-ir*) is the only form of a verb that can be used after a preposition.

*Voy a estudiar **después de** descansar media hora.*	I am going to study **after resting** for a half hour.
*Miguel nunca va a Chicago **sin pescar** en el Lago Michigan.*	Miguel never goes to Chicago **without fishing** in Lake Michigan.

If the verb after the preposition is reflexive, the reflexive pronoun must be attached to the end of the infinitive and must agree with the subject.

Después de levantarte, debes bañarte.	**After getting up,** you should bathe.
Después de bañarme, yo me visto.	**After bathing,** I get dressed.
*Nosotros salimos **sin almorzar**.*	We left **without having lunch.**

23 ¿Qué van a hacer?

¿Qué van a hacer las siguientes personas después de levantarse, según las indicaciones? Sigue el modelo.

 mis tías (cepillarse el pelo)
Mis tías van a cepillarse el pelo después de levantarse.

1. tú (leer el periódico)
2. mi hermana (maquillarse)
3. mi madre (preparar el desayuno)
4. mi abuela (hacer la cama)

5. yo (desayunar)
6. nosotros (ducharse)
7. mis hermanos (afeitarse)
8. mi papá y mi tío (vestirse)

 ## 24 Un sábado típico

Imagina que es un sábado típico. Contesta las preguntas para decir lo que haces los sábados antes o después de las siguientes situaciones. Puedes inventar la información si quieres.

1. ¿Qué haces después de levantarte?
2. ¿Qué haces antes de bañarte?
3. ¿Qué haces después de vestirte?
4. ¿Qué haces después de desayunarte?
5. ¿Qué haces antes de acostarte?

 ## 25 Los domingos

 Trabajando en parejas, habla de lo que hacen varios miembros de tu familia los domingos por la mañana, usando las preposiciones *antes de*, *después de* y *sin*, y el infinitivo apropiado para esa situación. Trata de usar algunos verbos reflexivos si es posible.

A: ¿Qué hace tu padre antes de bañarse?
B: Mi padre lee el periódico antes de bañarse.

Después de levantarme, hago la cama.

Autoevaluación. Como repaso y autoevaluación, responde lo siguiente:

1. Imagine you have finished your internship and are starting a medical practice. How can you ask your new patients what hurts?
2. How would you tell the doctor that you have the flu?
3. What parts of the United States have large Spanish-speaking populations?
4. Why is it advantageous to be bilingual?
5. Say in Spanish what you would expect to hear if the doctor wants you to open your mouth.
6. Imagine you are at the beach with friends. How do you say in Spanish that you forgot your bathing suit?
7. Name one thing you do before going to bed.

Answers

23 1. Tú vas a leer el periódico después de levantarte.
2. Mi hermana va a maquillarse después de levantarse.
3. Mi madre va a preparar el desayuno después de levantarse.
4. Mi abuela va a hacer la cama después de levantarse.
5. Yo voy a desayunar después de levantarme.
6. Nosotros vamos a ducharnos después de levantarnos.
7. Mis hermanos van a afeitarse después de levantarse.
8. Mi papá y mi tío van a vestirse después de levantarse.

24 The second part of each of the following answers will vary:

1. Después de levantarme, yo....
2. Antes de bañarme, yo....
3. Después de vestirme, yo....
4. Después de desayunarme, yo....
5. Antes de acostarme, yo....

25 Creative self-expression.

Autoevaluación
Possible answers:
1. ¿Qué te/le duele?
2. Tengo gripe.
3. Answers will vary.
4. Answers will vary.
5. Abre la boca.
6. ¿Te olvidaste de traer el traje de baño?
7. Antes de acostarme, me cepillo los dientes.

Activities

Spanish for Spanish Speakers.
After completing activity 25, have students write a short composition in Spanish summarizing the events at their home on a typical Sunday morning.

 NATIONAL STANDARDS
C1.1, C1.2, C2.1, C3.1,
C4.1, C4.2, C5.1

Activity 11

Notes

Try the following address or search the words **pen pal** or **key pal** for activity B:

WWW

Intercultural E-Mail connections
http://www.stolaf.edu/network/iecc

Technology. Make certain to explain any Web-use policies your school may have before assigning this project. The ATE Teacher's Introduction offers tips and guidelines for using technology in the classroom.

Activities

Multiple Intelligences (interpersonal/intrapersonal). Have students make a list of sites they would like to visit in the Spanish-speaking world. Then ask them to search for information about what they can do when visiting the places on their lists (i.e., Isla de Pascua in Chile, the *Palacio de Bellas Artes* in Mexico). Extend the activity by having students write to key pals telling about their travel plans to the chosen sites they listed.

Technology. If you have located a class with which to do e-mail projects in a Spanish-speaking country or in another city in the United States, have students exchange and compare their schedules. You may wish to try the following sources before assigning the activity to students: Intercultural E-mail Exchanges and Intercultural E-mail Connections. Also, the State Department is a good source for American schools abroad.

NATIONAL STANDARDS
C1.1, C1.2, C1.3,
C2.1, C3.1, C4.1,
C5.1, C5.2

¡La práctica hace al maestro!

A Comunicación

Working in small groups, create a dialog in which you discuss preparations for a trip to visit someone in California. Include whom you are going to visit, what things you are going to do before the trip *(ir al médico, comprarse algo, despedirse de alguien)*, and how you are planning to have fun and relax during the trip *(pescar, broncearse, olvidarse del colegio por unos días)*. Try to use as much new vocabulary and as many new expressions from this lesson as you can. *¡Sean creativos!* (Be creative!)

B Conexión con la tecnología

Write a key pal in Spanish telling about your plans for this Saturday or Sunday. Include what time you are going to wake up, your morning preparations, some activities during the day and what you are going to do to prepare for bed. Then be sure to ask about your key pal's weekend plans.

Este sábado, voy a divertirme con mis amigos.

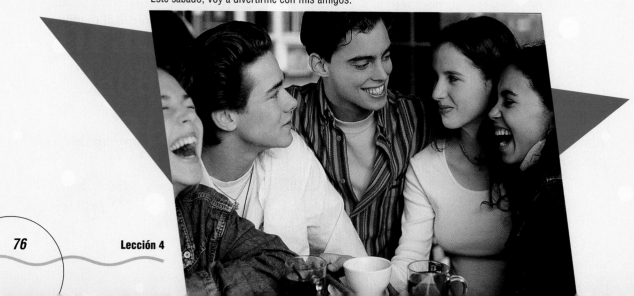

Testing/Assessment
Test Booklet
Oral Proficiency
Evaluation Manual
Portfolio Assessment

El cuerpo

la boca
la cara
el codo
el corazón
el cuello
el diente
la espalda
el estómago
la garganta
el hombro
la lengua
la nariz
el oído
el ojo
la oreja
el pecho
la rodilla

Verbos

abre *(command)*
acostumbrar(se)
broncear(se)
caer(se)
comer(se)
cuidar(se)
dejar (de)
descansar
despedir(se) (i, i)
di *(command)*
divertir(se) (ie, i)
doler (ue)
dormir(se) (ue, u)
equivocar(se)
fumar
ir(se)
llevar(se)
olvidar(se)
pescar
preguntar(se)
reunir(se)
saca *(command)*
sentir(se) (ie, i)
siéntate *(command)*
toca *(command)*
visitar

Expresiones y otras palabras

el cigarrillo
la cita
derecho,-a
el doctor, la doctora
el ejercicio
el enfermero, la
 enfermera
la gripe
irse de viaje
izquierdo,-a
el lago
la medicina
el niño, la niña
el resfriado

Nos gusta pescar en el verano.

El ejercicio es bueno
para el corazón.

Notes

Vocabulario. Point out that *doler* has a change in its present-tense stem from *o* to *ue*. This same change occurs in the infinitive *volver (ue)*, which students already have learned.

Activities

Cooperative Learning. Ask students to say a word they have learned in Spanish and then select someone else to spell the word. Have them check their spelling and then switch roles.

Critical Thinking. Write several words on the board or on an overhead transparency (i.e., *boca, pie, doctor, Estados Unidos*). Ask students to write or say words that are related to the words you wrote down (they should be ready to justify their answers in English): *boca, ojo* (both are parts of the face); *pie, zapato* (both have to do with the foot). As an alternative, have students do the activity in pairs while you spot-check their answers.

Language through Action. Use this Spanish version of Simon Says, titled *El rey manda* (The King Orders) as a paired or group activity to practice the parts of the body. Say (or have a student say) *"El rey manda...* (name a verb and an appropriate part of the body)." The person making the statements should then watch to see that the other person does what "the king orders": *El rey manda (tocar la cabeza/cerrar los ojos/tocar la pierna derecha/etc.).*

Pronunciation. To ensure proper pronunciation, model each word or expression and have students repeat after you.

NATIONAL STANDARDS
C2.1, C4.1

La vida de un atleta profesional

Quiz/Activity 7

Quiz/Activity 7

Answers

Preparación
Statement 3 best describes what the reading is about.

Notes

In this chapter students have learned to use reflexive verbs to talk about their daily routine. As an additional help, have students locate the reflexive verbs used in the following reading *(Se levantan, se desayunan, divertirse, mantenerse)* before selecting the statement that best describes what they predict the reading is about.

Activities

Expansion. Bring newspapers or magazines published in Spanish to class. Ask students to look at the advertisements to identify cognates. Next, ask students to identify three Hispanics mentioned in the newspapers or magazines. Who are they? Where are they from? Why are they in the news?

Multiple Intelligences (linguistic). Write a composition of at least ten sentences in Spanish, telling what you are going to do this Saturday. Include what time you will wake up, what you will do to prepare for the day, what you will do during the day and how you will finish the day.

a leer

Estrategia

Preparación

Estrategia para leer: *drawing on background information*
Understanding a reading in a second language is a process made up of a series of steps. One of the first steps in the process is to use the background knowledge you already have about the topic to predict what the reading is about.

Basado en lo que conoces, y como preparación para la lectura, decide cuál de las siguientes tres ideas representa mejor el contenido de lo que vas a leer.
1. Los atletas profesionales son populares y tienen una vida muy fácil.
2. Los atletas profesionales son pobres y tienen una vida aburrida.
3. Los atletas profesionales son famosos y ricos pero tienen una vida difícil.

La vida de un atleta profesional

¿Te gustaría ser un atleta profesional? ¿Crees que ellos tienen una vida estupenda? Claro, los atletas profesionales son famosos y populares. **Además,** ganan mucho dinero y viajan por todas partes del mundo. ¡Qué vida tan fantástica! ¿Verdad?

La realidad es que la vida de un atleta profesional no es tan divertida. Muchas veces su vida es difícil. Los tenistas profesionales, como Kristina Brandi de Puerto Rico y Marcelo Ríos de Chile, tienen un horario muy **duro.** Se levantan muy temprano para correr y para hacer aeróbicos. Después, practican el tenis de dos hasta cuatro horas al día. Cuando se desayunan o cenan, tienen que comer bien porque es muy importante estar en excelente condición física.

Marcelo Ríos practica todos los días.

Conchita Martínez

En España, las tenistas Conchita Martínez y Arantxa Sánchez-Vicario son **idolatradas** por muchas personas. Pero, ellas no tienen mucho tiempo libre porque tienen que viajar de seis hasta diez meses al año y por ese tiempo no pueden ver a sus familias. Para estar en contacto con sus familiares y sus amigos, ellas viajan con sus computadoras: Son ciberchicas de la Internet.

Aun para divertirse, los tenistas no descansan. Siguen siendo energéticos para **mantenerse** en perfecto estado físico. Montan en bicicleta, juegan al golf, nadan, bailan con sus amigos y, **por supuesto**, practican el tenis.

Pues, ahora, ¿te gustaría tener la vida de un atleta profesional?

Además *Besides* **duro** *hard* **idolatradas** *idolized* **Aun** *Even* **mantenerse** *to keep oneself* **por supuesto** *of course*

 ## ¿Qué comprendiste?

1. ¿Cuáles son algunos beneficios de la vida de un atleta profesional?
2. ¿Qué aspectos de sus vidas son difíciles?
3. ¿Qué hacen las tenistas para estar en contacto con sus familias y sus amigos?
4. ¿Cómo se divierten los tenistas?

 ## Charlando

1. ¿Te despiertas tarde o temprano?
2. ¿Practicas deportes para divertirte? ¿Cuáles practicas?
3. ¿Te gusta la vida de un atleta profesional? Explica.
4. ¿Qué haces para estar en contacto con tus amigos?

Answers

A Answers will vary.

B Answers will vary.

Notes

The *A leer* provides a formal opportunity for students to improve their ability to read in Spanish. Equivalents for most unknown words have been provided to help students enjoy the content of the readings without having to look up important but passive vocabulary. All highlighted vocabulary is intended to expand students' receptive skills and is not intended for active use at this point.

Communities. The choices for obtaining information in Spanish about the Spanish-speaking world (and news and entertainment in general) are growing greater every year. Television stations that broadcast in Spanish across the world include cable stations, such as *Univisión*, *CBS Telenoticias*, *CNN En Español*, and so forth.

Activities

Expansion. Additional questions (*¿Qué comprendiste?*): *¿Por qué tienen que comer bien los tenistas todos los días?*; *¿Quiénes son las tenistas puertorriqueñas?*; *¿De dónde son Conchita y Arantxa?*

Additional questions (*Charlando*): *¿Cuáles son otros dos tenistas famosos que conoces?*; *¿En qué se diferencia tu vida de la de un atleta profesional?*; *¿Qué deportes te gustan? ¿Es tu vida fácil o difícil?*

NATIONAL STANDARDS
C1.1, C1.2, C2.1, C4.1 C5.2

Answers

Creative writing practice.

Notes

The section *A escribir* provides students with an opportunity to demonstrate proficiency in writing, using the functions, grammar, vocabulary and cultural content of a lesson. In addition to providing students with developmental practice in creative writing, the section may be used as a quiz on writing, as a replacement or addition to the end-of-lesson summative testing of writing skills or for prescriptive testing in order to provide remediation.

Activities

Multiple Intelligences (linguistic). Have students practice organizing their thoughts by having them do the following writing practice activity: Students must write a six- or seven-sentence paragraph in Spanish telling six or seven things they did yesterday in chronological order. Ask them to include some of the following items in their composition: when they woke up, ate breakfast, went to school, ate lunch, returned home, ate dinner and went to bed. Have them add a visual such as a photograph or drawing to decorate the compostion. Display the final products on a bulletin board for parents to see when they visit the classroom.

Technology. Suggest to students that they send a copy of the composition for the *A escribir* section by e-mail to another person (a key pal or friend). Remind them that using electronic mail for communicating saves paper and provides students with an opportunity to become comfortable with the technology they will need to survive and do well in the future.

a escribir

Estrategia

Estrategia para escribir: *organize information chronologically*

When you are writing about a series of events occurring in a given time frame, first organize your composition in chronological order. Then, to make your sentences flow smoothly from one to another, include some of the following transition words.

entonces	then, next
por eso	therefore
sin embargo	however
a causa de	because of
después	later
y	and
pero	but
también	also

Manuel Vázquez Montalbán es un escritor español.

Choose a famous person that you would like to be for a day and assume the person's identity for this activity. Then write a composition of at least ten sentences in Spanish telling what your routine is for tomorrow (as that famous person). Include what time you wake up, what you eat, what you do to prepare for the day, what you do during the day and how you finish your day. Make up any of the information you wish. Be creative!

VÁZQUEZ MONTALBÁN
ESCRITOR

Premio Nacional de las Letras 1995, su último gran éxito es *Un polaco en la corte del Rey Juan Carlos.* Se despierta a las 6,30. Pone la radio en la cama y se levanta a las 7. "Me aseo, tomo la medicación de cardiopatía que tengo prescrita y saco a los perros y a la gata a la calle". Toma un zumo de naranja, sigue escuchando la radio y "casi sin darme cuenta, me pongo a escribir".

repaso

Now that I have completed this chapter, I can...

✓ talk about everyday activities.
✓ seek and provide personal information.
✓ discuss personal grooming.
✓ compare and contrast.
✓ recognize and identify Hispanic influence in the United States.
✓ state when things are done.
✓ express past actions and events.
✓ identify items in a bathroom.
✓ point something out.
✓ write about everyday activities.
✓ discuss health.
✓ give and take instructions.
✓ identify parts of the body.

Se habla español en Nueva York.

I can also...

✓ name some cities and states that have names that are derived from Spanish.
✓ identify some professions that use Spanish.
✓ recognize the importance of taking the time to do something right.
✓ compare meals in the United States and the Spanish-speaking world.
✓ talk about opportunities to study in another country.
✓ recognize some benefits of being bilingual.
✓ recognize and use appropriate expressions in a doctor's office.
✓ read in Spanish about a typical day in the life of a professional athlete.
✓ write a short composition in Spanish about a typical day.

Notes

Communities. Point out that Spanish is used extensively on Spanish radio and television programs, for business and for pleasure in such diverse places as California and the Southwest, Denver, Chicago, Miami, New York and numerous other major cities and small towns throughout the United States.

Activities

Cooperative Learning. Have students work in pairs asking and answering questions about when they do several everyday activities on any typical weekday. Then modify the activity and have students answer the questions as if it were a typical Sunday: *¿A qué hora se empieza el día?; ¿A qué hora se desayuna?; ¿A qué hora se empieza a preparar el almuerzo?; ¿A qué hora se almuerza?; ¿A qué hora se empieza a preparar la comida?; ¿A qué hora se cena?*

Pronunciation. Have students correctly pronounce several cities in the United States that have Spanish names: *San Diego, California; Las Vegas, Nevada; Amarillo, Texas; Boca Ratón, Florida.*

Spanish for Spanish-speakers. Ask students to research their own family histories. When did their relatives come to the United States and why? Where were they originally from?

NATIONAL STANDARDS
C1.1, C1.2, C1.3, C2.1, C2.2, C3.1, C3.2, C4.1, C4.2, C5.1, C5.2

Notes

Cultures. Review the contents of these two pages with students. See if students can guess what country they think they will be studying in the chapter. Then ask what students know about the country (i.e., Spanish is Mexico's official language; the capital is Mexico City; the country is a favorite vacation spot for many Americans). Point out that Mexico is the United States' nearest neighbor to the south. It is a country with a rich and varied history.

Activities

Critical Thinking. The photographs and other selected visuals that appear on pages 82-83 depict the functions, cultural setting and themes of the chapter ahead. Ask about any similarities and differences students observe, what words students are able to understand, what conclusions students can draw from the information, and so forth. For example, ask students to answer the following: 1) What is shown in the photograph in the upper left-hand corner of page 82?; 2) In what Spanish-speaking country does this chapter take place?; 3) What is the theme of the chapter?

NATIONAL STANDARDS
C1.2, C4.1

¡Vamos a la ciudad!

CAPÍTULO 3

México

Nombre oficial: Estados Unidos Mexicanos

Población: 93.008.000

Capital: México, D.F.

Ciudades importantes: Monterrey, Guadalajara

Unidad monetaria: el peso

Fiesta nacional: 16 de septiembre, Día de la Independencia

Gente famosa: Luis Miguel (cantante); Frida Kahlo y Diego Rivera (artistas); Octavio Paz (escritor); Emiliano Zapata (líder popular)

Notes

The communicative functions on this page and accompanying visuals mentally and visually whet students' appetites for the chapter they are about to begin. A checkoff list of the functions appears at the end of *Capítulo 3* (see page 131), along with additional objectives that students can use as a self-check to evaluate their own progress.

Activities

Connections. First, call on students to identify some cities in Mexico. Next, ask what places in Mexico students or their friends have visited. Finally, conduct a class discussion about what students know about Mexico.

Multiple Intelligences (linguistic). Play a CD or audiocassette of some of Luis Miguel's songs and have students identify and write down words they recognize.

Golfo de México

Los Cabos
Puerto Vallarta
Guadalajara •Guanajuato
•Querétaro
Manzanillo
•Cd. de México
Puebla
Ixtapa-Zihuatanejo
•Oaxaca
Acapulco
Huatulco
Mérida • Cancún
Cozumel

México Océano Pacífico

In this chapter you will be able to:

* ask for and give directions
* identify places in the city
* discuss what is sold in specific stores
* tell someone what to do
* order from a menu in a restaurant
* advise and suggest
* discuss whom and what people know
* talk about everyday activities
* tell others what not to do
* identify parts of a car
* advise others in writing

83

NATIONAL STANDARDS
C1.2, C1.4, C5.2

Content reviewed in *Lección 5*
- places in a city
- asking and answering questions
- telling time
- double object pronouns

Notes

Point out that whereas in *Lección 4* the adjective *derecho,-a* was the equivalent of **right**, here *derecho* is the equivalent of **straight ahead** or **straight**.

Activities

Connections. Make a cross-curricular connection to geography by showing students where some of the places mentioned in *Capítulo 3* are located using the maps in the front of the book or a wall map.

Critical Listening. Preteach the new vocabulary with transparencies 17 and 18. Next, play the *Somos así LISTOS* audiocassette/audio compact disc version of the dialog. Remember to instruct students to cover the words with one hand since you want them to concentrate on developing good listening skills. Tell students to look at the illustration while they imagine what the speaker is saying. Have several individuals state what they believe the main theme of the conversation is. Finally, ask if students can guess where the dialog takes place (in Mexico City).

Critical Thinking. Encourage your students to guess the meaning of the command forms: *sigue* (continue, keep on), *ve* (go) and *camina* (walk). The informal affirmative commands are explained later in this lesson.

NATIONAL STANDARDS
C1.2, C4.1

Lección 5

En la ciudad

Contexto cultural
MÉXICO

*Carlitos, un muchacho **mexicano** del D.F., está pidiendo **direcciones** a un **policía**....*

CARLITOS: Perdón señor, ¿sabe Ud. dónde hay una **dulcería**? Quiero comprar unos **dulces°** con estas **monedas.°**

POLICÍA: Sí, hay dos dulcerías. Sigue **derecho°** hasta **la próxima° esquina°** y **para°** allí. Pasa la calle y luego, ve **a la derecha°** y camina un poco por esa **cuadra.°** Hay una **a la izquierda°** y si sigues un poco más **adelante,°** hay otra al lado derecho.

CARLITOS: Ah, muchas gracias.

dulces *candy (candies)* **monedas** *coins* **derecho** *straight ahead* **próxima** *next* **esquina** *corner* **para** *stop* **a la derecha** *to the right* **cuadra** *city block* **a la izquierda** *to the left* **adelante** *ahead, farther on*

1 ¿Qué comprendiste?

1. ¿De qué país es Carlitos?
2. ¿A quién le está pidiendo direcciones?
3. ¿Qué tienda busca Carlitos? ¿Qué quiere comprar allí?
4. ¿Qué debe hacer el chico para llegar a la dulcería?
5. ¿Cuántas dulcerías hay en la cuadra? ¿Dónde están?
6. ¿Dónde está la oficina de correos?
7. ¿Qué venden o qué hacen en los diferentes edificios que ves en el dibujo?
8. ¿Qué hay en el edificio alto que está al lado de la florería?

2 Charlando

1. ¿Qué tiendas hay en tu ciudad?
2. ¿Hay almacenes cerca de tu casa? ¿A cuántas cuadras?
3. ¿Qué otros edificios hay en tu ciudad?
4. ¿Qué es lo que más te gusta de una ciudad? ¿Qué te gusta de tu ciudad?
5. ¿Qué es lo que menos te gusta? ¿Qué no te gusta?
6. ¿Vives en un apartamento o en una casa?

¿Qué se vende en una pescadería?

Compro todos mis dulces en esta dulcería.

Floristería Carmenza

TEL. 864-3214

Arreglos para toda ocasión
Cumpleaños, Bautismos,
Funeral, Decoración de
Bodas y Quinceañeros.

México

Quiz/Activity 2

Activity 2

Notes

Connections. Make a geographical connection for students by pointing out that the Mayan influence can be seen in the ruins at Chichén Itzá, Tulum and Uxmal.

It is uncertain exactly when these civilizations originated in Mexico. Approximate dates are as follows: *la olmeca, 1500-1000 a.C.* (B.C.); *la maya, 100-500 d.C.* (A.D.); and *la tolteca, 900 d.C.* (A.D.)

Connections. The Mexican town of Taxco is well known for its silver mines and its colonial architecture.

Population experts predict that by the first decade of the 21st century, Mexico City will have a population of 35 million people.

It is interesting to note that Mexico is divided into thirty-two states.

Activities

Prereading Strategy. Prepare students for this cultural reading in Spanish by making a list of information that students know about Mexico. Write the list on the board for students to add to after they have read the *Conexión cultural.* Next, show students a map of Mexico and surrounding countries and bodies of water and discuss where the named countries and cities are located.

Spanish for Spanish Speakers. As enrichment, consider having one or more students do a report on a topic of interest that was mentioned in this *Conexión cultural.*

NATIONAL STANDARDS
C1.2, C3.2, C4.1, C5.2

Conexión cultural

México

México es el segundo país más grande de todos los países de habla hispana después de la Argentina. Su nombre oficial es los Estados Unidos Mexicanos. Está ubicado *(located)* entre los Estados Unidos al norte, los países de Guatemala y Belice al sur, el Océano Pacífico al suroeste y el Golfo de México al este. La Ciudad de México, D.F., también conocida *(known)* como el D.F. o el Distrito Federal, es la capital del país. Otras ciudades principales son Guadalajara, Monterrey, Puebla y Ciudad Juárez.

México tiene una historia muy vasta. Sus primeros habitantes estuvieron en la región hace más de doce mil años. Otras civilizaciones importantes llegaron después, como la olmeca, la maya y la tolteca.

Un ejemplo del arte olmeca.

Más tarde vinieron los aztecas (o mexicas). Fundaron *(They founded)* la ciudad de Tenochtitlán en 1325, lo que hoy es la Ciudad de México. Al noreste de la capital está Teotihuacán, donde fueron construidas *(constructed)* muchos años antes dos grandes pirámides, la del Sol y la de la Luna *(moon).*

El conquistador español, Hernán Cortés, llegó a la costa del Golfo de México en 1519. Luego, tomó control de la ciudad de Tenochtitlán en 1521, empezando así el período de colonización por los españoles. México consiguió su independencia de España en 1821. La revolución mexicana de 1910 continuó la evolución cultural e histórica del país.

Como las ruinas de las civilizaciones antiguas, las pirámides de los aztecas y la arquitectura colonial española, las obras *(works)* de artistas como Diego Rivera (1886-1957), Frida Kahlo (1910-1954), José Clemente Orozco (1883-1949) y David Alfaro Siqueiros (1898-1974) mantienen *(maintain)* hoy viva *(alive)* la historia de México.

Parte de una obra de Diego Rivera en el Palacio de Gobierno. (México, D.F.)

Teotihuacán, México.

PUEBLA

Guía turística
Tourist guide

CIUDADES COLONIALES

GUADALAJARA
Jalisco

Cruzando fronteras

¿Qué sabes sobre México? Contesta las siguientes preguntas.

1. ¿Qué quieren decir las letras *D.F.*?
2. ¿Cuál es el nombre oficial de México?
3. ¿Cuáles son algunas ciudades principales de México?
4. ¿Qué civilizaciones importantes estuvieron en México?
5. ¿Quiénes fundaron la ciudad de Tenochtitlán?
6. ¿Qué fueron construidas en Teotihuacán?
7. ¿En qué año consiguió México su independencia?
8. ¿Quiénes son algunos artistas mexicanos importantes?

¿D.F.?

Estrategia

Para aprender mejor: *using the ending -ería*

In Spanish adding the ending *-ería* to a word will often tell you where that item can be purchased. For example, you can buy flowers *(flores)* in a *florería*. In a *papelería* you will find *papel* (paper). Of course, there are exceptions and variations to this rule (if a word ends in a vowel, drop the vowel before adding *-ería*).

Algo más

PAPELERIA EL ...
PAPELERIA
LIBRERIA

PARA ti

Más tiendas de la ciudad

camisería	*shirt store*
ferretería	*hardware store*
joyería	*jewelry store*
juguetería	*toy store*
peluquería	*hairstylist's*
relojería	*watchmaker's shop*
tintorería	*dry cleaner's*

Las tiendas de la ciudad

The following is a list of other specialty stores that you will encounter in Spanish-speaking parts of the world. Can you find a connection between the name of the store and what is sold there?

la **carnicería** *(carne)*   la **lechería** *(leche)*
la **dulcería** *(dulces)*   la **panadería** *(pan)*
la **frutería** *(fruta)*   la **sombrerería** *(sombreros)*
la **heladería** *(helados)*   la **zapatería** *(zapatos)*

CAFETERIA • CONFITERIA
PANADERIA
JOSBEL
DESAYUNOS Y MERIENDAS
CUMPLEAÑOS Y FIESTAS INFANTILES
CELEBRACIONES
TORRECERREDO, 33 • TEL. 511 25 40 • OVIEDO

La Cevichería
Ceviche de camarón, Langostino,
Bombas, Ostras, Palmitos de cangrejo,
Cazuelas, Ensaladas de fruta,
Servicio a domicilio:
Tel: 2156508 Cra. 7 No. 121-09

• **Siempre la mejor** •
El Buen Gusto
Confitería
Cafetería
Bombonería
Boutique de pan
AURELIANO SAN ROMAN, 33 • TEL. 529 17 12 • OVIEDO

 Activity 3

 Quiz/Activity 3

 Activity 19

 Activity 3

Quiz/Activity 2

Answers

3
1. Quieren decir "Distrito Federal".
2. El nombre oficial de México es los Estados Unidos Mexicanos.
3. Algunas ciudades principales de México son Guadalajara, Monterrey, Puebla y Ciudad Juárez.
4. Las civilizaciones olmeca, maya, tolteca y azteca estuvieron en México.
5. Los aztecas fundaron la ciudad de Tenochtitlán.
6. Fueron construidas la pirámide del Sol y la pirámide de la Luna.
7. México consiguió su independencia en 1821.
8. Diego Rivera, Frida Kahlo, José Clemente Orozco y David Alfaro Siqueiros son importantes artistas mexicanos.

Notes

While supermarkets do exist in Spanish-speaking countries, specialty food stores reflect the custom of buying fresh food nearly every day.

Activities

Expansion. Additional questions (activity 3): *¿Qué lugar en tamaño tiene México entre los países de habla hispana?; ¿Qué países están al sur de México?; ¿Qué país está al norte de México?; ¿Qué hay al este de México?; ¿Cómo se llama el conquistador que llegó a las costas del Golfo de México en 1519?*

NATIONAL STANDARDS
C1.1, C1.2, C3.1, C4.1, C5.2

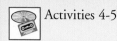

Activities 4-5

Answers

4 Answers will vary.

5
1. La puedo conseguir en la carnicería.
2. Las puedo conseguir en la florería.
3. Las puedo conseguir en la frutería.
4. La puedo conseguir en la lechería.
5. Los puedo conseguir en la papelería.
6. Los puedo conseguir en la sombrerería.

Notes

Explain that students may sometimes hear regional variations of these words, such as *floristería (florería)*. Other specialty shops include the following: *huevería (huevos), choricería (chorizos), corbatería (corbatas), pollería (pollos), relojería (relojes).*

Activities

Language through Action.
Working in pairs, student A asks student B to touch the item sold in the store that student A names: *la librería* (student B touches the book). Have students alternate between naming the store and responding.

Multiple Intelligences (spatial).
Have students make a drawing of a city street in one of the Spanish-speaking countries they have studied. Have students label different types of stores in the drawings.

Students with Special Needs.
Have students repeat activity 5, attaching the direct object pronoun to the infinitive: *Puedo conseguirlo en la heladería.*

 4 **¿Qué hacen?**

Haz seis oraciones completas para decir lo que hacen las siguientes personas en el centro de la ciudad. Usa elementos de cada columna.

 Yo compro carne en la carnicería.

A	B	C
yo	comprar flores	el aeropuerto
ellos	tomar el avión	la estación del tren
Uds.	enviar cartas	la florería
María y Pedro	tomar el autobús	la carnicería
Andrés	comprar carne	la dulcería
nosotros	buscar dulces	la estación de autobuses
don Juan	tomar el tren	los monumentos
Carmen y Alicia	mirar	la oficina de correos

5 **¿En dónde se consiguen?**

Di en qué lugares puedes conseguir las siguientes cosas.

Lo puedo conseguir en la heladería.

1.   2.   3.

4.   5.   6.

6 ¿Dónde se...?

Trabajando en parejas, alterna con tu compañero/a de clase en hacer y en contestar preguntas, según las indicaciones. Sigue el modelo.

comprar/fruta
A: ¿Dónde se compra fruta?
B: Se compra en una frutería.

1. vender/dulces
2. hacer/pan
3. vender/papel
4. conseguir/libros
5. comprar/leche
6. vender/zapatos
7. buscar/flores

LAVANDERÍA en 40 MINUTOS

Un servicio fuera de este mundo

IDIOMA

El mandato afirmativo informal

Use a command *(el imperativo)* to give advice and to tell people what you would like them to do. In Spanish, commands may be either informal or formal, singular or plural. Singular informal affirmative commands normally use the present-tense *él/ella* form of a verb. Verbs that require a spelling change and verbs with changes in their stem in the present tense usually have the same change in the informal singular command. The following are just some of the singular informal commands you already have heard or seen.

Habla en español. — Speak in Spanish.
Escribe en el cuaderno. — Write in the notebook.
Abre la ventana. — Open the window.

and:

Cierra la ventana. — Close the window.
Continúa escribiendo. — Continue writing.
Sigue caminando derecho. — Keep walking straight ahead.

A few verbs have irregular affirmative *tú* commands.

| decir | **di** | ir | **ve** | salir | **sal** | tener | **ten** |
| hacer | **haz** | poner | **pon** | ser | **sé** | venir | **ven** |

Object and reflexive pronouns follow and are attached to affirmative informal commands: *dime* (tell me). Add an accent mark to most commands with more than one syllable that have an attached pronoun: *siéntate* (sit down). When using two object pronouns with the same verb, remember that the indirect object pronoun occurs first: *préstamelo* (lend it to me).

Haz de la limpieza tu ritual de belleza.

TELEFONO

Pon más monedas.

ponte al día

Answers

6
1. ¿Dónde se venden dulces?/Se venden en una dulcería.
2. ¿Dónde se hace pan?/Se hace en una panadería.
3. ¿Dónde se vende papel?/Se vende en una papelería.
4. ¿Dónde se consiguen libros?/Se consiguen en una librería.
5. ¿Dónde se compra leche?/Se compra en una lechería.
6. ¿Dónde se venden zapatos?/Se venden en una zapatería.
7. ¿Dónde se buscan flores?/Se buscan en una florería.

Notes

Tell students that many of the irregular verbs with irregular *tú* commands are the same as those with a *yo* form ending in -*go* in the present tense: *decir, tener, poner, hacer, salir, venir.*

Activities

TPR. Practice the *tú* forms of a few verbs using TPR. Select several students to react to the informal commands of the corresponding verbs: *Abre el libro; Cierra el libro; Toca el libro.* Work with one verb several times before going to another verb. To avoid monotony, vary the commands slightly: (student's name), *abre el libro*; (student's name), *abre el cuaderno.* Perform the action or use gestures only if a student does not respond.

NATIONAL STANDARDS
C1.1, C1.2, C4.1, C5.2

7 ¿Acento o no?

En una hoja de papel escribe los siguientes mandatos y pon los acentos que sean necesarios.

dimelo	hablame	cierra	sigue	continua
hazla	compraselas	abremelos	esperanos	se

2 mini-jeeps con motor de gasolina
Gáneselos
¡ BÚSQUELA EN LOS PUNTOS DE VENTA !

8 Dando direcciones

Teresa le dice a su amigo Gabriel cómo llegar a la estación del metro. Completa el siguiente diálogo con los mandatos informales de los verbos entre paréntesis.

GABRIEL: ¿Tú sabes si la estación del metro está cerca de aquí?

TERESA: Sí, está cerca.

GABRIEL: Bueno, por favor, *1. (decirme)* cómo llegar a la estación del metro.

TERESA: Sí, claro. Bueno, *2. (hacer)* lo siguiente: Primero, *3. (salir)* del edificio. Luego, *4. (ir)* a la derecha y *5. (caminar)* tres cuadras hasta la esquina donde está la iglesia. Luego, ve a la izquierda y *6. (continuar)* derecho hasta pasar el puente. Al final del puente vas a ver la estación a la derecha. *7. (Tener)* el dinero listo para pagar.

GABRIEL: Muy bien. Muchas gracias, Teresa. *8. (Venir)* a visitarme esta tarde.

TERESA: Bueno, no sé si puedo ir pero voy a ver.

GABRIEL: Está bien. Hasta luego. *9. (Ser)* buena.

TERESA: Siempre lo soy. Adiós, Gabriel.

9 ¿Qué mandatos das?

Conecta lógicamente los mandatos con las ilustraciones apropiadas.

 A.

 B.

 C.

 D.

 E.

 F.

 G.

 H.

1. Abre la ventana.
2. Cierra la puerta.
3. Escribe en el cuaderno.
4. Léelo.

5. Dibuja.
6. Siéntate.
7. Dime tu nombre.
8. Ve a la zapatería.

10 En la clase

Trabajando en parejas, alterna con tu compañero/a de clase en dar mandatos sobre actividades en la clase. Cada estudiante debe dar cinco mandatos, usando los complementos directos e indirectos apropiados. La otra persona debe hacer los mandatos.

A: *(Hand a closed notebook to B.)* Ábrelo.
B: *(Open the notebook.)*

B: *(Point at a door.)* Ciérrala.
A: *(Close the door.)*

Cuaderno de tareas

Answers

9 1. G
2. E
3. C
4. D
5. B
6. F
7. A
8. H

10 Creative self-expression.

Notes

The subject pronouns are not usually used with the *tú* commands.

Activities

Students with Special Needs. Review some of the commands students have learned to recognize in activity instructions. For example, point out to students that in activities 3 through 12 *contesta* (answer), *haz* (make, do), *di* (say), *alterna* (alternate), *sigue* (follow), *escribe* (write), *conecta* (connect) and *encuentra* (find) are singular informal (*tú*) commands. Ask if students can find any other commands in other activities.

TPR. Try doing activity 10 with the entire class, asking individuals to do each command. As an alternative, select individual students who must name other students and then give them a command. Listen to hear that each command is stated correctly and observe to see that the named student completes the command properly.

NATIONAL STANDARDS
C1.1, C1.2, C1.3, C4.1, C5.1, C5.2

Answers

11 planifica, revisa, lleva, examina, conduce

12
1. Léela a Laura.
2. Recuérdale visitar el monumento.
3. Límpialas a los abuelos.
4. Cómprame el sombrero en la sombrerería.
5. Danos el mapa de la ciudad.
6. Ciérrame la puerta del carro.
7. Dime cuánto dinero necesitas.

Notes

Although many affirmative *tú* commands use the present-tense *él/ella* form of a verb, point out that this does not cause confusion. Context and voice tone help to indicate what is a command, and the subject *tú* may follow the command form for added emphasis.

Activities

Multiple Intelligences (linguistic). Discuss with students the newspaper clipping at the top of the page. Ask what words students can recognize; find out if students can discern the general theme of the advertisement. What else can students make out in the clipping?

Students with Special Needs. Have students repeat activity 12, responding with two object pronouns *(Ciérramela, Límpiaselas, etc.)*.

Lección 5

...antes de salir de viaje

Repasemos la Lección

1 Planifica bien la ruta

2 Revisa tus documentos
- Cédula de Ciudadanía
- Tarjeta de Propiedad del vehículo
- Licencia de Conducción
- Seguro Obligatorio
- Certificado de Movilización

3 Lleva equipo de prevención y seguridad:
- Triángulos
- Tacos
- Extintor
- Cinturón de Seguridad
- Herramienta
- Gato
- Linterna
- Botiquín de primeros auxilios
- Llanta de repuesto

4 Examina el estado del vehículo:
- Frenos
- Llantas
- Luces
- Dirección
- Y el cinturón de Seguridad

5 y conduce con cuidado que te esperamos acá.

INTRA
CON SEGURIDAD

11 Antes de salir

Encuentra cinco mandatos informales en este aviso *(advertisement)*.

12 Preguntas y respuestas

 Trabajando en parejas, alterna con tu compañero/a de clase en hacer y en contestar las siguientes preguntas con mandatos informales, según el modelo y las indicaciones que se dan.

A: ¿A quién le pido ayuda? (al policía)
B: Pídela al policía.

1. ¿A quién le leo la lista? (a Laura)
2. ¿Qué le recuerdo a Edgar? (visitar el monumento)
3. ¿A quiénes les limpio las vitrinas? (a los abuelos)
4. ¿Dónde te compro el sombrero? (en la sombrerería)
5. ¿Qué les doy a Uds.? (el mapa de la ciudad)
6. ¿Qué te cierro? (la puerta del carro)
7. ¿Qué te digo? (cuánto dinero necesitas)

Pide ayuda al policía.

¿Qué le gustaría ordenar?

CAMARERO:	¿Qué le gustaría **ordenar,**° señorita?
PATRICIA:	No sé todavía. Jorge, ¿qué comemos?
JORGE:	Comamos comida mexicana.
PATRICIA:	Entonces, quiero unas **tortillas,**° una **enchilada** de pollo y un **jugo**° de naranja.
CAMARERO:	¿Y el señor?
JORGE:	Yo quiero unos **tacos,** una ensalada de aguacate y un vaso con agua.
CAMARERO:	¿Algo más?
JORGE:	Sí, **camarero.** Por favor, dígame, ¿dónde está el baño?
CAMARERO:	Siga derecho hasta esa puerta. El baño de los **caballeros**° está a la derecha por el **corredor.**

ordenar *to order* **tortillas** *cornmeal pancakes* **jugo** *juice* **caballeros** *gentlemen*

13 ¿Qué comprendiste?

1. ¿En qué lugar están los muchachos?
2. ¿Qué ordena Patricia?
3. ¿Qué pide Jorge?
4. ¿Qué más quiere saber Jorge?
5. ¿Dónde está el baño de los caballeros?

PARA ti

Más palabras
You just learned that for men's bathroom you use *el baño de los caballeros*. For the women's restroom you might use *el baño de las damas*. You can also say *el baño de los hombres* or *de las mujeres* when referring to the men's or women's restroom.

Por favor, quiero una sopa y un vaso con agua.

¿Qué le gustaría ordenar?
Activity 13

Answers
13
1. Están en un restaurante.
2. Patricia ordena unas tortillas, una enchilada de pollo y un jugo de naranja.
3. Jorge pide unos tacos, una ensalada de aguacate y un vaso con agua.
4. Quiere saber dónde está el baño de los caballeros.
5. El baño de los caballeros está a la derecha por el corredor.

Notes
Explain to students that many restaurants in Latin America offer a different menu each day. It is common practice to offer a complete lunch or dinner that includes two or three courses and a beverage for one fixed price.

Activities
Connections. *Tacos, tortillas* and *enchiladas* are commonly eaten in Mexico and in parts of Central America, but they are not common in Spain and South America. Begin a study of the typical dishes of various countries. Contact and maintain good relations with the home economics teacher(s) at your school in order to obtain valuable assistance with this cross-content teaching activity. In addition, you may choose to have students present reports or even prepare the dishes for class or for your Spanish club.

Expansion. Additional questions (*¿Qué comprendiste?*): *¿Cómo se llama la señorita?; ¿Quiere tomar Patricia un vaso con agua?; ¿Qué quiere tomar?; ¿Qué quiere tomar Jorge?*

NATIONAL STANDARDS
C1.2, C 2.1, C3.2, C4.1

Notes

Mexico has had a history of severe earthquakes. This has resulted in a severe problem in providing clean drinking water to all the city's residents and visitors. It is an enormous and costly job to constantly repair and improve the piping system that transports water throughout the city. However, the Mexican government is attempting to deal with the problem over time.

Activities

Communities. Take students on a field trip to a restaurant that serves some of the foods mentioned in the *Conexión cultural* titled *Las comidas tradicionales*. Consider requiring that students speak only Spanish during the trip.

Critical Thinking. Have students search in the library or on the Internet for *"comidas mexicanas por regiones."* Then compare and discuss the typical dishes of Mexico by regions in order for students to see the variety of foods and similarity of ingredients and spices used in Mexico's cuisine.

Prereading Strategy. As a prereading activity have students present reports on Hispanic foods, or have them prepare foods and discuss them in class. Some of the more unusual foods that students may find interesting include *menudo* (cow intestine soup—a broth made with beef entrails) and *hormigas fritas* (large deep-fried ants), which are popular in the Santander region of northeast Colombia.

Conexión cultural

Las comidas tradicionales

Los chiles se usan para hacer salsa picante.

The foods that are popular in one part of the world are often totally different from what is enjoyed elsewhere. For example, *tacos* and *enchiladas* are two foods that have their origins in Mexico. You already may have eaten one of these foods since they are also popular throughout the United States. However, you would be wrong to presume that these foods are the daily fare for everyone who speaks Spanish. Every country has its own unique cuisine.

The *tortilla* is almost a national food in Mexico. Although usually made from cornmeal *(masa de maíz)*, tortillas also may be made from wheat flour *(masa de trigo)*. This thin, breadlike pancake frequently is wrapped around various meats and vegetables to make tacos and other popular dishes. *Tortillas* are popular in Spain also, but there the word refers to an omelet. The traditional *tortilla española* is, in fact, an omelet with potatoes and onions. Sometimes it is referred to as *tortilla de patatas*.

Other common foods in Mexico include *tamales,* which consist of seasoned cornmeal *(masa)* that is wrapped and cooked in corn husks *(hojas de maíz),* a popular Mexican corn-based stew called *pozole* and *mole* (a spicy, bittersweet chocolate sauce often served over turkey or

Unos tamales mexicanos.

El mofongo es un plato muy popular en Puerto Rico.

NATIONAL STANDARDS
C1.2, C3.2, C4.2, C5.2

chicken). Many Mexican foods are served with *salsa picante* (a spicy sauce made of hot peppers, tomatoes and onions).

Sometimes foods with the same name in two countries may be prepared very differently. In Central America, corn serves as the main ingredient in several foods, much like in Mexico. However, *tamales* in Central America are made with plantain leaves *(hojas de plátano)* instead of corn husks, and *pozole* is a sweetened corn-based drink instead of a stew.

Popular foods vary elsewhere, too. In Cuba, *picadillo* is popular. This dish is made from ground beef *(carne molida)*, chopped onions, tomatoes and green peppers. In Puerto Rico, rice with beans *(arroz con habichuelas)* is a favorite food. In Colombia and Venezuela, *arepas* (similar to thin English muffins) are common. A favorite food of Argentineans is meat, especially beef *(carne de res)*. Meat turnovers *(empanadas)* are popular throughout South America, and each country offers its own variety and favorite ingredients. If you should travel to Peru, you will become familiar with the word *ceviche,* which is a typical dish made from cold raw fish that has been marinated in lime juice and then combined with onions and many different spices.

Every country in the Hispanic world offers many different and delicious foods. Dining out in any Spanish-speaking country can be a fascinating experience that can further broaden your understanding of Hispanic culture.

Arroz con frijoles negros.

La Cabaña
RESTAURANTE

Actualidades

EL resurgimiento de la cocina MEXICANA
Por Vicente Ochoa Leyzaola

El maíz es un ingrediente importante en muchas comidas de México y la América Central.

Notes

Point out that *picante* means spicy while *caliente* means hot in temperature. *Salsa picante* now outsells catsup in the United States!

Activities

Communities. Ask students when they last went to a restaurant that serves Mexican or Mexican-American food. Discuss some of the things the waiter/waitress said and how students replied.

Connections. Make a geographical connection by having students use a map or atlas to find the places mentioned in this *Conexión cultural.* Then as a follow-up activity, identify the various sites as a class activity.

Prereading Strategy. Before beginning the *Conexión Cultural,* consider asking some general preparation questions about the theme of the reading: What Mexican foods can students name? Do students eat any of those foods very often? Which ones? Where do they go to have the Mexican/Mexican-American foods they eat?

NATIONAL STANDARDS
C1.2, C3.2, C4.2, C5.2

Activity 14

Answers

14 Answers will vary.

15 Creative self-expression.

Activities

Communities. Have students make a list of a variety of foods as follows: 1) foods their families prepare and eat at home; 2) dishes from throughout the Spanish-speaking world that students have heard about but have never eaten; 3) foods students have tried in a Hispanic or Latin American restaurant. Have students compare the foods, saying what they do or do not like, and why, and what foods they would like to try, and why.

Cooperative Learning. Have students imagine that they are going to open a restaurant that sells only Hispanic meals. In groups of three, have students prepare a menu for their restaurant.

Expansion. Additional questions *(Charlando)*: *¿Te gusta la comida mexicana? Explica; En tu opinión, ¿cuál es comida americana típica?; ¿Hay muchos restaurantes mexicanos en tu ciudad? ¿Te gustan?; ¿Hay restaurantes españoles o hispanoamericanos donde vives? ¿Sabes qué sirven?; ¿Te gustaría comer ceviche? ¿Por qué sí o no?; ¿Quieres comer empanadas?; ¿Qué plato prefieres, la tortilla española o la tortilla mexicana?; ¿Qué diferencia hay entre los dos tipos de tortilla?*

14 Charlando

1. ¿Te gusta comer en restaurantes? ¿Por qué?
2. ¿Te gusta la comida mexicana? Explica.
3. ¿Qué ordenas de comer cuando vas a un restaurante mexicano?
4. ¿Qué pides de tomar?
5. ¿Te gustaría trabajar como camarero/a en algún restaurante? ¿En cuál?
6. ¿Pides ayuda cuando necesitas encontrar el baño o tratas de encontrarlo sin ayuda?

15 Las comidas en tu comunidad

En grupos pequeños, hagan una lista de comidas hispanas que hay en los restaurantes o en los supermercados de su comunidad. Luego, un representante del grupo debe reportar la información a la clase.

Vamos a ordenar en español.

Oportunidades

En el restaurante

The next time you eat in a Mexican restaurant, try to order your meal in Spanish. The staff will be pleased that you are making the effort to learn to speak their language, and practicing your Spanish with native speakers is a fun way to improve your comprehension.

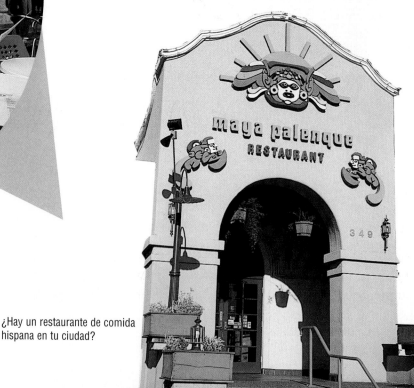

¿Hay un restaurante de comida hispana en tu ciudad?

NATIONAL STANDARDS
C1.2, C1.3, C2.1, C2.2, C4.1, C4.2, C5.1

96   Lección 5

IDIOMA

El mandato afirmativo formal y el mandato plural

To form an affirmative formal command, substitute the -*o* of the present-tense *yo* form of a verb with an -*e* for -*ar* verbs, or with an -*a* for -*er* and -*ir* verbs. Make the plural *(Uds.)* command by adding the letter -*n* to the singular formal command. Verbs with changes in their stem in the present tense usually have the same change in the formal command. **Note:** Like *tú* in singular informal commands, *usted (Ud.)* or *ustedes (Uds.)* are usually omitted from formal/plural commands.

infinitive	*yo* form	stem	singular formal command	plural commands
hablar	hablo	habl-	Hable Ud.	Hablen Uds.
comer	como	com-	Coma Ud.	Coman Uds.
escribir	escribo	escrib-	Escriba Ud.	Escriban Uds.
cerrar	cierro	cierr-	Cierre Ud.	Cierren Uds.
volver	vuelvo	vuelv-	Vuelva Ud.	Vuelvan Uds.
seguir	sigo	sig-	Siga Ud.	Sigan Uds.

MANTENGA EL AREA LIMPIA GRACIAS

MAINTAIN CLEAN THE AREA THANKS

Look at the following:

Mire Ud. (Miren Uds.) la pizarra. — Look at the blackboard.
Lea Ud. (Lean Uds.) el libro. — Read the book.
Repita Ud. (Repitan Uds.) la palabra florería. — Repeat the word *florería*.
Cierre Ud. (Cierren Uds.) la ventana. — Close the window.
Vuelva Ud. (Vuelvan Uds.) en cinco minutos. — Come back in five minutes.
Siga Ud. (Sigan Uds.) caminando derecho. — Keep walking straight ahead.

A few verbs have irregular formal and plural commands.

infinitive	*Ud.* command	*Uds.* command
dar	dé Ud.	den Uds.
estar	esté Ud.	estén Uds.
ir	vaya Ud.	vayan Uds.
saber	sepa Ud.	sepan Uds.
ser	sea Ud.	sean Uds.

Object and reflexive pronouns follow and are attached to affirmative formal commands. A written accent mark may be required in order to maintain the original stress of the verb: *dígame Ud.* (tell me), *escríbanlas Uds.* (write them), *levántense Uds.* (stand up).

Llénelo Ud., por favor.

Quizzes/Activities 5-6

Activities 8-9

Quiz/Activity 6

Notes

Explain that the verbs with irregular formal and plural commands have present-tense *yo* forms that end in a letter other than *o*.

If you wish to teach the *vosotros/as* command, explain the following: Form the affirmative *vosotros/as* command by dropping -*r* from the infinitive and by adding -*d* (hablar: hablad; comer: comed; escribir: escribid).

Note for students that the accent on *dé Ud.* will help students distinguish the command from the preposition *de*. Additional information about accentuation may be found on page 465 of the Appendices.

Explain that direct commands may be considered rude. For this reason, *por favor* is frequently added to soften them.

Activities

Critical Thinking. Have students identify commands given in exercises throughout the book. Then have them give the infinitives of each verb.

TPR. Practice the *Uds.* form of the commands by having the entire class perform actions or gestures as you read them aloud in Spanish. The commands should be presented in as many logical pairs as possible (*abran, cierren; escriban, borren; escuchen, repitan*). Model the action or gesture two or three times with students, then repeat the pair of commands one or two times with no actions or gestures as students do what you request.

16 Una receta

Encuentra los siete mandatos formales que hay en la siguiente receta de mousse de chile poblano.

MOUSSE DE CHILE POBLANO

Del menú de Rosa Mexicano
6 porciones

6 chiles poblanos
1 diente de ajo
1 cebolla blanca
1 taza de crema de leche de batir
aceite vegetal
agua suficiente

Preparación de los chiles: Precaliente el horno a 350°F. Ase los chiles poblanos sobre la llama del gas o el asador hasta que se les ennegrezca la piel. "Súdelos" por 55 minutos en una bolsa y pélelos. Córtelos a la mitad y quíteles las semillas y la membrana. Enjuáguelos bien. Córtelos en rajas y métalos dentro de un bol con agua caliente con sal durante una hora. Para chiles menos picantes, cambie el agua varias veces. Déjelos reposar 12 horas.

Preparación del mousse: Al día siguiente, en una sartén con aceite sofría las cebollas ligeramente. Añada las rajas de chile y cocínelas de 10 a 15 minutos sin dejar que se peguen. Quite el exceso de aceite y ponga el chile a un lado. Haga el mousse licuando las rajas y la cebolla. Pase la mezcla por un colador fino para obtener un puré muy suave. Bata la crema de leche hasta que espese y mézclela con el puré. Se puede usar para cubrir pescados y servida por sí misma en un recipiente de cristal. En ambos casos se debe refrigerar.

17 Un amigo de visita

Un amigo de tus padres está visitando a tu familia por dos semanas y quiere saber alguna información. Trabajando en parejas, alterna con tu compañero/a de clase en hacer y en contestar preguntas, usando las indicaciones que se dan. Sigue el modelo.

¿dónde/poder/comer comida mexicana? (en el restaurante Las Américas)
A: ¿Dónde puedo comer comida mexicana?
B: Coma (Ud.) en el restaurante Las Américas.

1. ¿en qué panadería/poder/comprar pan? (en la panadería de la Avenida Cruz)
2. ¿a quién/deber/escribir para conseguir información sobre el metro? (a la estación del metro)
3. ¿qué/poder/mirar en el centro? (el monumento del Ángel de la Independencia)
4. ¿dónde/poder/enviar cartas? (en la oficina de correos de la Avenida Juárez)
5. ¿dónde/deber/tomar el autobús para ir al centro? (en la Calle 8ª)
6. ¿a qué hora/deber/salir de casa para llegar al centro a las ocho? (a las siete)
7. ¿dónde/poder/correr? (en el parque de la esquina)
8. ¿cuándo/deber/visitar la catedral? (los martes por la mañana)

¿Dónde puedo comprar libros?

18 Dos amigos de visita

Haz otra vez la actividad anterior con tu compañero/a de clase, imaginando que estás hablando con dos amigos de tus padres. Sigue el modelo.

¿dónde/poder/comer comida mexicana?
(en el restaurante Las Américas)

A: ¿Dónde podemos comer comida mexicana?
B: Coman (Uds.) en el restaurante Las Américas.

Puedes comer unos huevos rancheros en un restaurante mexicano.

19 Una familia de otro país

Imagina que una familia de otro país (la familia Hofmann) te está visitando a ti y a tu familia y tú estás arreglando el horario. Usa el mandato apropiado para decirles a todos lo que deben hacer antes de visitar a tu ciudad mañana.

Sabrina/leer/este libro sobre la ciudad
Lee este libro sobre la ciudad.

Sr. Hofmann/mirar/este programa a las diez
Mire (Ud.) este programa a las diez.

Sabrina y Bianca/acostarse/temprano
Acuéstense (Uds.) temprano.

1. Sr. y Sra. Hofmann/levantarse/a las 6:15
2. Sr. Hofmann/ducharse/y/afeitarse/en este baño a las 6:20
3. Sra. Hofmann/bañarse/en el otro baño a la misma hora
4. Sr. y Sra. Hofmann/leer/el periódico en la sala después de estar listos
5. Sabrina y Bianca/despertarse/a las 7:00
6. Sabrina/ducharse/en este baño a las 7:05
7. Bianca/bañarse/en el otro baño a la misma hora
8. Uds./desayunarse/a las 8:00
9. Uds./tomar/nuestro carro para ir a la ciudad

Sabrina, lee este libro sobre la ciudad.

Answers

18 1. ¿En qué panadería podemos comprar pan?/Compren (Uds.)....
2. ¿A quién debemos escribir para conseguir información sobre el metro?/Escriban (Uds.)....
3. ¿Qué podemos mirar en el centro?/Miren (Uds.)....
4. ¿Dónde podemos enviar cartas?/Envíen (Uds.)....
5. ¿Dónde debemos tomar el autobús para ir al centro?/Tomen (Uds.)....
6. ¿A qué hora debemos salir de casa para llegar al centro a las ocho?/Salgan (Uds.)....
7. ¿Dónde podemos correr?/Corran (Uds.)....
8. ¿Cuándo debemos visitar la catedral?/Visiten (Uds.)....

19 1. Levántense (Uds.)....
2. Dúchese y aféitese (Ud.)....
3. Báñese (Ud.)....
4. Lean (Uds.)....
5. Despiértense (Uds.)....
6. Dúchate....
7. Báñate....
8. Desayúnense (Uds.)....
9. Tomen (Uds.)....

Notes

For activity 19, be sure students are aware that sentences may require singular or plural informal commands as well as singular or plural formal commands.

Activities

Communities. Using the telephone book, have students make a list of restaurants in their community that serve Hispanic food. What kinds of food do they serve?

Answers

20 1. Consígales (Ud.) unos mapas de la ciudad.
2. Apágueme (Ud.) las luces antes de salir.
3. Explíquele (Ud.) cómo llegar al aeropuerto.
4. Escójale un hotel.
5. Dígales (Ud.) dónde están los monumentos.
6. Tráigame (Ud.) dinero del banco.
7. Cómpreme (Ud.) papel en la papelería.
8. Ordénenos (Ud.) la comida por teléfono.
9. Búsqueme (Ud.) un bolígrafo.

21 1. Empiece (Ud.)....
2. Apague (Ud.)....
3. Busquen (Uds.)....
4. Escoja (Ud.)....
5. Busquen (Uds.)....
6. Vuelvan (Uds.)....
7. Recoja (Ud.)....

Notes

Review. Reinforce the content of the *Algo más* on page 100 by reviewing the formation of several commands that have orthographic changes: *almorzar, explicar, pagar, recoger.*

Activities

Cooperative Learning. Give students the task of preparing suggestions for a group of tourists who will be visiting the area and/or state. Small groups of students should prepare and then present their recommendations using logical *Uds.* commands.

Multiple Intelligences (spatial). Have students prepare a folding pamphlet for visitors to their city that tells what they must definitely see. Students should use commands in the flyer.

Students with Special Needs. Model a second example for activities 20-21.

Algo más

Los cambios ortográficos

Sometimes commands require a spelling change in order to maintain the original sound of the infinitive. Look at the following:

$c \rightarrow qu$ before the letter *e* (*buscar: busque Ud.*)
$g \rightarrow gu$ before the letter *e* (*apagar: apague Ud.*)
$z \rightarrow c$ before the letter *e* (*empezar: empiece Ud.*)
$g \rightarrow j$ before the letter *a* (*escoger: escoja Ud.*)

20 Tu primer día de trabajo

Hoy es tu primer día de trabajo en una oficina de turismo y tu jefa *(boss)* te está diciendo todo lo que debes hacer hoy. Haz oraciones completas, usando los complementos apropiados y los mandatos formales para saber lo que tú tienes que hacer.

 enseñar/a ellas/la ciudad
Enséñeles (Ud.) la ciudad.

1. conseguir/a ellos/unos mapas de la ciudad
2. apagar/a mí/las luces antes de salir
3. explicar/al señor López/cómo llegar al aeropuerto
4. escoger/a la señora Johnson/un hotel
5. decir/a Gloria y a Lupe/dónde están los monumentos
6. traer/a mí/dinero del banco
7. comprar/a mí/papel en la papelería
8. ordenar/a nosotros/la comida por teléfono
9. buscar/a mí/un bolígrafo

Enséñeles Ud. la ciudad. (Taxco, México).

21 ¿Qué tienen que hacer?

Imagina que trabajas en un nuevo hotel de la ciudad y tienes que arreglar un lugar para la fiesta de un cliente. Diles a las personas que trabajan contigo lo que tienen que hacer, usando los mandatos formales.

 Ud./cerrar todas las ventanas
Cierre (Ud.) todas las ventanas.

1. Ud./empezar a barrer allá
2. Ud./apagar esas luces
3. Uds./buscar los manteles para las mesas
4. Ud./escoger la música para la fiesta
5. Uds./buscar sillas para las mesas
6. Uds./volver a pasar la aspiradora
7. Ud./recoger esa basura

22 ¿Qué hacemos?

Trabajando en grupos pequeños, alternen Uds. en decirles a sus compañeros de grupo qué deben hacer. Miren Uds. para ver si los compañeros pueden hacer cada mandato. Cada estudiante debe decir tres mandatos.

Escriban (Uds.) su nombre en un papel.

Paremos aquí.

El mandato con *nosotros/as*

Another form of the command allows you to suggest that others do some activity with you and is equivalent to "Let's (do something)" in English. It is formed by substituting the *-o* of the present-tense *yo* form of a verb with an *-emos* for most *-ar* verbs, or *-amos* for most *-er* and *-ir* verbs. Stem-changing *-ar* and *-er* verbs do not require a stem change for the *nosotros/as* command. Stem-changing *-ir* verbs require a stem change that uses the second letter shown in parentheses after infinitives in this textbook. The affirmative *nosotros/as* command for the verb *ir* is irregular: *Vamos.* (Let's go.)

infinitive	*yo* form	*nosotros* **command**
hablar	hablo	Hablemos....
comer	como	Comamos....
escribir	escribo	Escribamos....
cerrar (**ie**)	cierro	Cerremos....
volver (**ue**)	vuelvo	Volvamos....
divertir (**ie, i**)	divierto	Divirtamos....

Object and reflexive pronouns follow and are attached to affirmative *nosotros/as* commands. However, when combining a direct object pronoun with the indirect object pronoun *se,* and for reflexive verbs, drop the final consonant *-s* before attaching the pronouns.

¿Cuándo vamos a cerrar la tienda? → *Cerrémosla en una hora.*

but:

¿Vamos a preparar las enchiladas a nuestros padres? → *Sí. Preparémoselas.*

¿Cuándo podemos sentarnos a comer? → *Sentémonos en quince minutos.*

The *nosotros/as* command is interchangeable with the construction "*Vamos a* (+ infinitive)."

Vamos a comer en un restaurante. → *Comamos en un restaurante.*

Answers
22 Answers will vary.

Notes
Point out that the *nosotros* command form is more frequently used to suggest than to command.

Activities
Cooperative Learning. Have students work in pairs or small groups discussing plans for the weekend or a special event. They should use *nosotros* commands and the construction *vamos a* + infinitive in order to express their ideas.

Language through Action. Have volunteers do activity 22 in front of the class.

Students with Special Needs. After discussing the *Idioma* titled *El mandato con nosotros/as,* practice the formation of several *nosotros* commands that have orthographic changes: *almorzar, explicar, pagar, recoger,* etc.

TPR. As an alternative, have representatives from several groups call on various students to perform the commands their groups prepared and practiced for activity 22.

NATIONAL STANDARDS
C1.1, C1.2, C1.3, C4.1, C5.1

Answers

23 1. Abramos....
2. Miremos....
3. Caminemos....
4. Corramos....
5. Tomemos....
6. Veamos....
7. Visitemos....
8. Visitemos....

24 1. ¿...nos bañamos...?/
Bañémonos....
2. ¿...salimos...?/Salgamos....
3. ¿...nos reunimos...?/
Reunámonos....
4. ¿...compramos...?/
Comprémoslos....
5. ¿...visitamos...?/
Visitémosla....
6. ¿...almorzamos...?/
Almorcemos....
7. ¿...conocemos...?/
Conozcámoslo....
8. ¿...vamos...?/Vamos....
9. ¿...cenamos...?/
Cenemos....
10. ¿...nos acostamos...?/
Acostémonos....

Activities

Communities. Using the Internet, the library and other sources, have students prepare a short report about pollution in Mexico City. In their report have them include the cause of the pollution, its consequences and what steps the Mexican government is taking to control it.

Connections. Have students prepare a report about the muralists and their importance in Mexican history and society, selecting from the following: Diego Rivera, José Clemente Orozco and David Alfaro Siqueiros.

Multiple Intelligences (spatial/linguistic). Have students imagine they work for the tourist office of Guadalajara, Mexico. Have them prepare a poster that tells visitors to the city what to see and do, for example: *Venga y vea la magnífica catedral.*

Vamos a mirar vitrinas el sábado.

23 ¡Vamos a la ciudad!

Escribe las siguientes oraciones de otra manera, usando los mandatos con *nosotros/as.* Sigue el modelo.

 Vamos a subir a la torre.
Subamos a la torre.

1. Vamos a abrir el almacén.
2. Vamos a mirar vitrinas.
3. Vamos a caminar por la carretera.
4. Vamos a correr hasta la esquina.
5. Vamos a tomar un refresco.
6. Vamos a ver los aviones en el aeropuerto.
7. Vamos a visitar la catedral.
8. Vamos a visitar el centro.

24 En la ciudad de Guadalajara

Imagina que tú y tu hermano están haciendo el horario para el viaje a la ciudad de Guadalajara mañana. Trabajando en parejas, alterna con tu compañero/a de clase en hacer preguntas y en contestarlas, usando mandatos y las indicaciones que se dan.

levantarnos/6:00
A: ¿A qué hora nos levantamos mañana?
B: Levantémonos a las seis.

tomar el desayuno/7:00
B: ¿A qué hora tomamos el desayuno mañana?
A: Tomémoslo a las siete.

1. bañarnos/6:35
2. salir del apartamento/7:30
3. reunirnos con nuestros amigos/8:20
4. comprar los regalos para la familia/9:00
5. visitar la catedral/10:45
6. almorzar/12:30
7. conocer el monumento/3:30
8. ir a la oficina de correos/4:10
9. cenar/8:00
10. acostarnos/10:30

guadalajara
MEXICO

25 En carro por la ciudad

Tú y tu amigo/a van en carro por la ciudad buscando la oficina de correos, pero no saben muy bien cómo llegar. Trabajando en parejas, alterna con tu compañero/a de clase en hacer y en contestar preguntas en forma afirmativa, usando las indicaciones. Sigue el modelo.

preguntar al policía/dónde está la oficina de correos
A: ¿Le preguntamos al policía dónde está la oficina de correos?
B: Sí, preguntémosle.

1. parar/en la esquina
2. buscar/la oficina de correos en el mapa
3. tomar/esa carretera
4. ir/a la derecha
5. ir/ahora
6. volver/a preguntarle dónde está
7. empezar/otra vez a buscar la estación
8. seguir/hasta la próxima cuadra

Preguntémosle al policía dónde está la oficina de correos.

Autoevaluación. Como repaso y autoevaluación, responde lo siguiente:

1. Name the store in Spanish in which you can purchase each of the following items: *fruta, zapatos, carne* and *leche*.
2. How would you tell a friend in Spanish to close the door?
3. Imagine a friend asks you for directions to the bus station. Give the following directions to the station in Spanish: Go to the right and walk four blocks to the corner where the bakery is. Then go left and you will see the station on the right.
4. Some Spanish-speaking friends from a different city are visiting and you tell them some things to see and do while they are in town. Tell them to do the following: get up early, take the bus to downtown, visit the cathedral and the museum, then eat lunch in the Mexican restaurant on the corner near the library.
5. Imagine you are visiting Mexico City with your family. Your mother says, "Let's go to the museum." Suggest three additional things to do.
6. What do the letters D.F. mean in the name of the capital city of Mexico?
7. Name two common foods from Mexico.

¿Qué comidas ves en esta foto?

ITO (*prohPOHseetoh*)

SOLUTION

ósitos tienes para Año Nuevo?

re your New Year's resolutions?

	LUNES/MONDAY
NGUAGE	**3**
	ENERO/JANUARY

Activities

Expansion. Have students redo activity 25 using *vamos a* in place of the *nosotros/as* command.

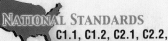

NATIONAL STANDARDS
C1.1, C1.2, C2.1, C2.2, C3.1, C4.1, C5.1

 Activity 12

Answers

A Creative self-expression.

B Creative self-expression.

Notes

www

Intercultural E-Mail connections
http://www.stolaf.edu/network/iecc
Search Engines
www.webcrawler.com
www.yahoo.com
www.excite.com
www.magellan.com

For all oral activities, listen for the correct pronunciation and determine if students appear to understand what they are saying and hearing. Also, be sure students personalize information so that it is meaningful to them.

Activities

Cooperative Learning. Working in small groups, have students alternate with their classmates giving directions how to go from school to various sites in their city or town, without naming the place. Others in the group must then identify the place where they would end up if they followed the directions.

Spanish for Spanish Speakers. Have students investigate the use of the Internet in their country of ancestry or in the country where their relatives live. They should find out how widespread its use is and what percentage of the population owns a personal computer.

¡La práctica hace al maestro!

A Comunicación

Prepare a list of ten commands, telling another person something you would like that person to do. Include five informal commands and five formal commands. Then, working with a partner, take turns telling one another your commands, watching to see if your partner does what you have requested.

B Conexión con la tecnología

Imagine you have a Hispanic friend who is new to your area and would like to visit some of the local attractions. Using an Internet search engine, select a website such as Mapquest or Mapblast that provides road maps to specific addresses. Follow their instructions to locate a map to a particular site in your city or town, such as a park, museum, or theater. Print out the map. Then, referring to the map, write directions in Spanish to tell your friend how to get to the site.

¿Cómo llegamos a la estación del metro? (México, D.F.)

NATIONAL STANDARDS
C1.1, C1.2, C1.3, C2.1, C5.1, C5.2

VOCABULARIO

Testing/Assessment
Test Booklet
Oral Proficiency
    Evaluation Manual
Portfolio Assessment

En la ciudad
el aeropuerto
el almacén
el apartamento
la carnicería
la carretera
la catedral
la cuadra
la dulcería
el edificio
la esquina
la estación
   (de autobuses/del
   metro/del tren)
la florería
la frutería
la heladería
la iglesia
la lechería
el monumento
la oficina de correos
la panadería
la papelería
el puente
la sombrerería
la torre
la vitrina
la zapatería

Direcciones
a la derecha (izquierda)
adelante
la derecha
derecho
la dirección
la izquierda
próximo,-a

En el restaurante
el camarero, la camarera
la enchilada
el jugo
el taco
la tortilla

Verbos
ordenar
parar

Expresiones y otras palabras
el caballero
el corredor
el dulce
mexicano,-a
la moneda
el policía, la policía

Estas flores artificiales son las flores más bonitas de la florería.

Una cuadra en el D.F.

Notes
Ask if students can see a logical pattern for some of the specialty shops: words that end in a consonant add -*ería*; words that end in -*a* and -*o* drop the vowel before adding -*ería*; words that end in -*e* add -*ría*. Explain that some words may follow no apparent rule at all.

Activities
Cooperative Learning. Ask students to say a word they have learned in Spanish and then select someone else to spell the word. Have them check their spelling and then switch roles.

Expansion. Select several words and phrases for individual students to use orally in sentences.

Pronunciation. To ensure proper pronunciation, model each word or expression and have students repeat after you.

Technology. Have students search the Internet or the library to find information about some of the archeological sites, the cities or the artists mentioned in the lesson. Using PowerPoint®, Hyper Studio® or other presentation software, students could prepare and present to the class the information they found about these places or people in order to reinforce their awareness about Mexican history and its people. Students presenting should create a questionnaire as a listening/reading comprehension check to be used at the end of the presentation, to check how much their classmates understood. In order to promote interest and responsibility, the results may be used as part of your grading.

NATIONAL STANDARDS
C1.2, C4.1

En el barrio Las Lomas

Activity 1

Quiz/Activity 1

Activity 1

Content reviewed in *Lección 6*
- places in the city
- foods
- object pronouns
- negative expressions

Answers

1. Vive en el barrio Las Lomas.
2. No tiene la dirección de la oficina de correos.
3. Le dijeron que la oficina de correos está hacia el este.
4. Debe manejar tres cuadras hacia el norte.
5. No, no debe tomar la curva, sino debe seguir derecho por una cuadra más hasta la señal de alto donde dobla a la izquierda.
6. Quiere tirar una lata a la basura.

Notes

Las Lomas is a neighborhood located in the southeast part of Mexico City along the famous *Avenida de la Reforma*.

Note for students that the infinitive for *maneje* is *manejar*.

Activities

Critical Listening. Play the audiocassette/audio compact disc version of the dialog. Have several individuals state what they believe the main theme of the conversation is.

Prereading Strategy. Instruct students to cover up the dialog with one hand and look at the illustration. Ask them to imagine where the conversation takes place and what the people are saying to one another.

Lección 6

En el barrio Las Lomas

Contexto cultural
MÉXICO

PABLO: Señora, ¿sabe Ud. dónde está la oficina de correos? No **conozco**° este **barrio**° y no tengo la **dirección**° de la oficina. Me dijeron que está **hacia**° el **este.**

SEÑORA: ¿Al este? Pues, no siga en esa **dirección** porque no hay ninguna oficina de correos. Ud. debe ir hacia el **norte.**

PABLO: ¿Hacia el norte? Entonces, ¿dónde está?

SEÑORA: Mire, **maneje**° tres cuadras hacia el norte por esta calle hasta llegar a la **curva.** No tome la curva, **sino**° siga derecho por una cuadra más hasta la **señal**° de **alto.**° Luego, **doble**° a la izquierda y la oficina está allí.

PABLO: ¡Ah, gracias! Perdón, ¿tiene dónde **tirar**° esta lata?

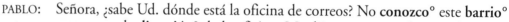

conozco *I know* **barrio** *neighborhood* **dirección** *address* **hacia** *toward* **maneje** *drive* **sino** *but (on the contrary)* **señal** *sign* **alto** *stop* **doble** *turn (a corner)* **tirar** *to throw away*

¿Qué comprendiste?

1. ¿En qué barrio vive la señora donde está Pablo?
2. ¿Qué no tiene Pablo?
3. ¿Qué le dijeron a Pablo?
4. ¿Cuántas cuadras hacia el norte debe manejar Pablo?
5. ¿Debe Pablo tomar la curva? ¿Qué debe hacer?
6. ¿Qué quiere tirar Pablo a la basura?

Algo más

Los puntos cardinales

You can tell someone how to go somewhere using the directions *(los puntos cardinales)* north *(el norte)*, south *(el sur)*, east *(el este)* and west *(el oeste)*.

Siga derecho al este.   Go straight (ahead) east.
Ve cinco cuadras al oeste.   Go five blocks to the west.

To be even more exact, these directions can be combined as shown here:

Charlando

1. ¿Cómo se llama el barrio donde tú vives?
2. ¿Sabes dónde está la oficina de correos en tu barrio? Explica.
3. Desde tu casa (o apartamento), ¿en qué dirección está la oficina de correos?
4. ¿Y en qué dirección está tu escuela?

Este lugar en el D.F. se llama la Zona Rosa.

Pedir ayuda

Have you ever visited a different city and been unable to find where you needed to go? When you are new to a city or lost, asking directions can be very helpful. With the Spanish language skills you have acquired you will be able to survive being lost in any city where Spanish is spoken. You have the skills to ask directions in Spanish and now you are also capable of giving directions to someone in Spanish if they approach you!

Sigan derecho.

 Activity 2

 Quiz/Activity 2

 Activity 2

Answers

2 Answers will vary.

Notes

Some people prefer the following for referring to directions: *oriente* (east); *occidente* (west); *nororiente* or *nordeste* (northeast); *suroriente* or *sudeste* (southeast); *noroccidente* (northwest); *suroccidente* or *sudoeste* (southwest).

Activities

Cooperative Learning. Have students prepare a map that shows the route between two places, such as school and the student's home. Then, working in pairs, students take turns explaining the directions to a classmate.

Expansion. Additional questions *(¿Qué comprendiste?)*: *¿Qué está haciendo la señora en la calle?; ¿Qué busca Pablo?; ¿Hacia qué dirección dice la señora que Pablo debe ir?; ¿Dónde está la oficina de correos?*

Additional questions *(Charlando)*: *¿Cuál es la dirección de tu casa?; Desde tu casa, ¿en qué dirección está el centro comercial? ¿Y el colegio? ¿Y la iglesia?; ¿Cuál es la dirección de la oficina de correos que está más cerca de tu casa?; ¿Qué tiendas hay en tu barrio?*

Multiple Intelligences (intrapersonal). Discuss travel with the class, calling on individuals to answer some of the following questions: *¿Usas folletos turísticos para planear tus viajes? Explica; ¿Conoces alguna ciudad de México? ¿Cuál conoces?; ¿Qué lugares te gustaría visitar en México? ¿Por qué?; ¿Te gustan los lugares históricos o los lugares modernos? Explica.*

NATIONAL STANDARDS
C1.1, C1.2, C3.2, C4.2

 *México hoy*

 Quiz/Activity 3

 Activity 3

Notes

In addition to the beach resorts mentioned in the reading, other popular destinations include Cozumel, Ixtapa and Cabo San Lucas. Ask students if they have visited any of these locations and/or where they would like to travel in Mexico.

The Aztecs founded and began to inhabit Tenochtitlán in what today is Mexico City beginning in 1325.

Activities

Prereading Strategy. Reading the *Conexión cultural* offers an opportunity for students to increase their knowledge about the Spanish-speaking world by reading about Mexico in Spanish. The vocabulary and structures have been controlled to enable individuals to read in the target language and enjoy the experience. Remind students that it is not essential to understand every word in order to read Spanish; the meaning of important but unknown passive vocabulary has been provided to facilitate an enjoyable experience. Before beginning the *Conexión cultural*, consider asking some general preparation questions about the theme of the reading: What is Mexico's capital? What else do students know about Mexico? What is NAFTA? Then have students skim the *Conexión cultural* for cognates and any words or expressions they already know.

NATIONAL STANDARDS
C1.2, C3.2, C4.1, C4.2

Conexión cultural

México hoy

México es hoy un país muy moderno, de buen desarrollo *(development)* económico y con una geografía muy variada *(diverse)*. Es también un país de muchos contrastes en donde se combinan la historia, la cultura y la vida moderna.

México, D.F., la capital del país, es una de las ciudades más grandes del mundo con más de veinte millones de habitantes. La vida moderna se ve en sus sistemas de transporte y en sus imponentes *(majestic)* rascacielos. En cada calle, museo y universidad está presente su vida cultural e historia.

La bandera mexicana.

Hacia el sur de la capital está Cuernavaca, la ciudad de la eterna primavera. Es una ciudad muy bonita con un clima excelente todo el año. Al este, en la península del Yucatán, está Mérida, que es un centro económico y comercial del país. Al noroeste está Guadalajara, una ciudad grande y cosmopolita. Un poco más lejos al noroeste está la península de Baja California. Esta región tiene costas espectaculares, grandes desiertos y lindas montañas.

México también tiene ciudades importantes por su turismo internacional. Entre las más populares, especialmente por sus playas bonitas, están las ciudades

La Universidad Nacional Autónoma de México (UNAM).

de Acapulco, Puerto Vallarta y Mazatlán en el Pacífico, y Cancún en el Mar Caribe.

La economía de México es muy variada. Su mayor producto de exportación es el petróleo. Otros productos de exportación son el maíz, los tomates y el gas natural. La importancia internacional de la economía mexicana se ve hoy en iniciativas como la del tratado de libre comercio *(free trade agreement)* entre México, los Estados Unidos y el Canadá.

El México de hoy disfruta *(enjoys)* de muchas cosas buenas, pero también tiene los problemas de todos los países modernos. La contaminación y el crimen son comunes hoy en sus grandes ciudades, pero también lo son sus grandes esfuerzos *(efforts)* para solucionar estos problemas.

Acapulco tiene playas muy bonitas.

CONEXIONES

3 Cruzando fronteras

Completa las siguientes oraciones sobre México, escogiendo la letra de la respuesta correcta.

1. Baja California es...
   A. un golfo con mucho petróleo y desiertos.
   B. una ciudad importante de México.
   C. una península con costas espectaculares y desiertos.

2. Las playas son muy bonitas en...
   A. Puerto Vallarta, Mazatlán y Cancún.
   B. Acapulco, Guanajuato y Cuernavaca.
   C. Puebla, Monterrey y Ciudad Juárez.

3. El D.F. es una de las ciudades...
   A. más pequeñas del mundo.
   B. más importantes de la América Central.
   C. más grandes del mundo.

4. La ciudad de la eterna primavera es...
   A. Mérida.
   B. Acapulco.
   C. Cuernavaca.

5. La ciudad de Mérida está...
   A. al sur del país.
   B. al este del país.
   C. al oeste del país.

6. El mayor producto de exportación de México es...
   A. el maíz.
   B. el gas natural.
   C. el petróleo.

7. Guadalajara está...
   A. al noroeste de la capital.
   B. al sureste de la capital.
   C. al suroeste de la capital.

en el d.f.

PLAYAS DE MAZATLÁN

OLAS ALTAS
Se encuentra ubicada en el paseo del mismo nombre. Es un paseo tradicional, donde se puede disfrutar de incomparables puestas del sol.

PLAYA NORTE
Se extiende a lo largo de la Avenida del Mar, donde está el monumento al "Pescador". Desde aquí se llevó a cabo la resistencia contra los franceses (1864).

PLAYAS GAVIOTAS Y CAMARÓN
Comprende lo correspondiente a la zona hotelera moderna. Ahí se encuentran las playas más arenosas de Mazatlán.

PLAYAS SABALO-BRUJAS-CERRITOS
Las más alejadas del centro. Se encuentran ubicadas al extremo norte de la zona hotelera; son extensas, poco concurridas y seguras para nadar.

Baja California tiene costas y desiertos espectaculares.

Answers
3 1. C
    2. A
    3. C
    4. C
    5. B
    6. C
    7. A

Notes
Mexico City is located in the southern portion of the Valley of Mexico at an altitude of 7556 feet.

Activities
Critical Thinking. Discuss the pros and cons of the North American Free Trade Agreement (NAFTA) between Mexico, the United States and Canada that took effect on January 1, 1994.

Language through Action. Have students locate and point to various sites in Mexico that are mentioned in activity 3.

Spanish for Spanish Speakers. Ask students to read the realia and then ask them questions to determine how much they understood: *¿De qué se trata?*; *¿Qué puede uno ver en el paseo Olas Altas?*; *¿Qué playa está lejos del centro?*; *¿Dónde se llevó a cabo la resistencia a los franceses?*

NATIONAL STANDARDS
C1.2, C2.1, C3.1, C4.1

Notes

Tell students that *saber* refers to factual knowledge of the type that can be imparted to someone else: names, addresses, subjects and abilities that can be taught. *Conocer* refers to knowledge in the sense of knowing a person, a place or a thing.

Some native speakers of Spanish use the personal *a* after conocer when referring to cities and countries: *¿Conoces a México?*

Activities

Critical Thinking. Describe situations and have students indicate whether *conocer* or *saber* should be used for each: You want to say you know the works of Frida Kahlo and Diego Rivera (*conocer*); you are saying you are familiar with the *barrio* someone is giving you directions to find (*conocer*); you are telling what you know about Mexico (*saber*); you are telling someone you know how to speak Spanish (*saber*).

Expansion. Ask the following questions to further practice using *conocer* and *saber: ¿Conoces México?; ¿Qué países/estados conoces?; ¿Conoces a alguien de un país hispanohablante?; ¿Sabes cuál es la población de México?; ¿Sabes cuántas personas viven en México, D.F.?; ¿Sabes dar mandatos en español?; ¿Sabes usar el pretérito en español?; ¿Sabes manejar?*

IDIOMA

Los verbos *conocer* y *saber*

Just as you have learned to use *ser* and *estar* in different situations as the equivalent of "to be," the Spanish verbs *saber* and *conocer* are used in very different situations for "to know." Both verbs are irregular in the present tense.

conocer	
conozco	conocemos
conoces	conocéis
conoce	conocen

saber	
sé	sabemos
sabes	sabéis
sabe	saben

Use *saber* to talk about facts that someone may or may not know. *Saber* followed by an infinitive indicates that someone knows how to do something.

¿Sabes jugar al básquetbol?

¿Conoces a la chica nueva?

¿Sabes dónde se puede comprar flores?	**Do you know** where one can buy flowers?
Sé dar direcciones en español.	**I know how** to give directions in Spanish.

Use *conocer* to discuss whether someone is familiar with (or acquainted with) people, places or things. Note that it is necessary to add the personal *a* after *conocer* when referring to people.

¿Conoces a tus vecinos?	**Do you know** your neighbors?
Conozco una florería cerca de la estación del metro.	**I know (am familiar with)** a flower shop near the subway station.

4 ¿Qué saben?

Completa las siguientes oraciones con la forma apropiada de *saber*.

 ¿Sabe tu amigo qué es la UNAM?

1. ¿(1) Uds. si la península de Baja California está al noroeste o al noreste de la Ciudad de México?
2. Yo (2) que la gente mexicana habla español.
3. ¿(3) el profesor mucho sobre México?
4. Nosotros (4) que Guadalajara está al noroeste de la capital.
5. ¿(5) ellos las direcciones para ir desde el Zócalo hasta el Palacio de Bellas Artes?
6. ¿(6) tú hablar español?
7. ¿Qué (7) Uds. sobre México?
8. ¿(8) Ud. qué quieren decir las letras *D.F.?*

¿Me conoces?

5 ¿Las conocen o no?

 Di si las siguientes personas conocen o no a las personas indicadas, según las pistas. Sigue los modelos.

 Juan/mi prima/sí
Juan conoce a mi prima.

Gloria/Juan/no
Gloria no conoce a Juan.

1. yo/esa mujer/sí
2. nosotros/ese futbolista famoso/sí
3. tú/aquellas muchachas/no
4. tus amigos/la profesora de inglés/sí
5. ellas/doña Elena/no
6. el profesor/los abuelos de Pablo/no

6 Algunos lugares de la ciudad

Trabajando en parejas, alterna con tu compañero/a de clase en preguntar y en contestar quién conoce los siguientes lugares. Sigue el modelo.

 la estación del tren/Mercedes
A: ¿Quién conoce la estación del tren?
B: Mercedes la conoce.

1. el nuevo almacén/Víctor
2. la nueva carretera/Yolanda y Esteban
3. la torre del reloj/nosotros
4. el aeropuerto/tú
5. la nueva heladería/Marisol
6. el apartamento del profesor/ellos
7. la vitrina del nuevo almacén/yo

 Activities 5-6

Answers

4
1. Saben
2. sé
3. Sabe
4. sabemos
5. Saben
6. Sabes
7. saben
8. Sabe

5
1. Yo conozco a esa mujer.
2. Nosotros conocemos a ese futbolista famoso.
3. Tú no conoces a aquellas muchachas.
4. Tus amigos conocen a la profesora de inglés.
5. Ellas no conocen a doña Elena.
6. El profesor no conoce a los abuelos de Pablo.

6
1. ¿...conoce...?/Víctor lo conoce.
2. ¿...conoce...?/Yolanda y Esteban la conocen.
3. ¿...conoce...?/Nosotros la conocemos.
4. ¿...conoce...?/Tú lo conoces.
5. ¿...conoce...?/Marisol la conoce.
6. ¿...conoce...?/Ellos lo conocen.
7. ¿...conoce...?/Yo la conozco.

Notes

Remind students to use the personal *a* after *conocer* when referring to people.

UNAM stands for the *Universidad Autónoma de México.*

Activities

Students with Special Needs. Model another example for activities 5 and 6.

NATIONAL STANDARDS
C1.1, C1.2, C4.1, C5.1

Activities

Communities. Ask students to list names of famous individuals (past or present) who played an important role in the history of your city or state. Then have students pair up and use *saber* and *conocer* to ask questions about the people: *¿Conoces a* (name of person)*? ¿Sabes qué hizo?*

Cooperative Learning. Pair students to discuss what they wrote for activity 8. Then ask for volunteers to summarize the information for the class.

Multiple Intelligences (intrapersonal/linguistic). *¿Cómo se llaman algunas tiendas cerca de tu casa?; ¿Qué se vende en esas tiendas?; ¿Cuál es tu tienda favorita? ¿Por qué?; ¿Te gusta ir al centro de la ciudad? Explica; ¿Cómo llegas al centro de la ciudad?; ¿Prefieres ir de compras solo/a o con amigos?; ¿Vives cerca o lejos del colegio?; ¿Hay muchos edificios donde vives?*

Students with Special Needs. Model another example for activities 8 and 9.

7 La estudiante nueva

Completa el siguiente diálogo con las formas apropiadas de *conocer* y *saber*.

A: Oye, ¿(1) tú a Catalina, la estudiante nueva?
B: Sí, la (2). ¿(3) dónde vive?
A: No, yo no (4) exactamente, pero (5) que es cerca del colegio.
B: ¿(6) tú a su hermano, Benjamín?
A: No, no lo (7), pero yo (8) que es muy simpático.
B: Yo no lo (9) tampoco, pero quiero (10).
A: ¿(11) tú el número de teléfono de Catalina y Benjamín?
B: No, yo no lo (12), pero la profesora debe (13).

¿Conoces tú a Catalina?

8 ¿Conoces donde vives?

Haz una lista de por lo menos ocho lugares que conoces de tu barrio o del lugar donde vives y di algo sobre cada lugar.

 Conozco el teatro.
Sé dónde está y sé que es muy popular.

9 ¿Lo sabes?

Escogiendo elementos de cada columna, escribe ocho oraciones diferentes. Añade las formas apropiadas de *saber* y *conocer*.

 Ricardo sabe la historia de la torre del parque.

A	B
Uds.	llegar a la estación del tren
nosotros	la dirección de ese monumento
tú	el aeropuerto de Guanajuato
Paloma y Pilar	dibujar un mapa de ese barrio
Ricardo	la historia de la torre del parque
Rafael y Mónica	manejar
el policía	todas las señales de alto en esta calle
yo	sus vecinos

Yo sé donde está el aeropuerto de Guanajuato.

¿Conoces este monumento? Se llama el Ángel de la Independencia. (México, D.F.)

Aeropuerto Internacional de Guanajuato

Algo más

Yo ofrezco todo tipo de pan en mi panadería.

Verbos como *conocer*

Other verbs like *conocer* that require the spelling change *c* → *zc* for *yo* in the present tense include the following: *conducir* (to drive, to conduct), *ofrecer* (to offer) and *traducir* (to translate).

*Nunca **conduzco** en el centro de la ciudad.*	I never **drive** in the downtown area.
*Siempre **ofrezco** ayuda a todo el mundo.*	I always **offer** help to everyone.
*Cuando estamos en Mazatlán, **traduzco** de español a inglés para mis amigos.*	When we are in Mazatlan, **I translate** from Spanish to English for my friends.

10 Somos traductores

Imagina que tú y tus amigos son los intérpretes *(interpreters)* de un grupo de turistas de los Estados Unidos que van a Mérida. Haz las siguientes oraciones para decir quién debe servir como traductor a las personas indicadas. Sigue el modelo.

Silvia/la familia Brown
Silvia le traduce a la familia Brown.

1. ellas/la familia Deyo
2. Sergio y Roberto/el señor y la señora Cliff
3. Uds./la familia Capecchi
4. Luis/el señor Spencer
5. tú/la señorita O'Reilly
6. yo/la señora Larry
7. Susana/doña Hansen
8. nosotros/las señoritas Morton

Una plaza en Mérida, México.

Activity 6

Quiz/Activity 2

Answers

10
1. Ellas le traducen a la familia Deyo.
2. Sergio y Roberto les traducen al señor y a la señora Cliff.
3. Uds. le traducen a la familia Capecchi.
4. Luis le traduce al señor Spencer.
5. Tú le traduces a la señorita O'Reilly.
6. Yo le traduzco a la señora Larry.
7. Susana le traduce a doña Hansen.
8. Nosotros les traducimos a las señoritas Morton.

Notes

Some other verbs that have the same spelling change as *conocer* include *complacer* (to please), *deducir* (to deduce) and *introducir* (to introduce).

Activities

Expansion. Ask students if they can name a synonym for *conducir: manejar.*

Spanish for Spanish Speakers. Pair bilingual and nonbilingual students for activity 10.

National Standards
C1.2, C4.1, C5.1

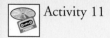

Answers

11
1. ...conduzco....
2. ...le traduce....
3. ...conoce....
4. ...les ofrecen....
5. ...le ofrece....
6. ...conducen....
7. ...traducimos....
8. ...traduces....
9. ...les ofrezco....
10. ...conocemos....

Notes

Mention that it is not unusual to see mothers and their teenage sons or daughters walking arm-in-arm as they attend the theater or tour ruins and museums. Also, two girls who are good friends commonly walk around arm-in-arm in parks and in other public sites of interest.

Explain to students that since personal space is more limited in some places in Spanish-speaking countries, they should not find it particularly surprising when they are jostled a bit in lines where they are making a purchase, such as purchasing admittance to a museum or theater.

Activities

Critical Thinking. Have students compare large cities in the United States and Mexico City (size, benefits of living in the city, problems).

NATIONAL STANDARDS
C1.2, C2.1, C4.1, C5.2

---

11 En Guadalajara

Imagina que estás con tus compañeros y algunos profesores del colegio en una excursión en Guadalajara. Haz oraciones completas para decir lo que pasa durante el viaje, usando las indicaciones que se dan.

 yo/no/conocer/las carreteras muy bien
Yo no conozco las carreteras muy bien.

1. yo/conducir/por cinco horas
2. Luz/traducirle/las señales a Pablo
3. Amalia/conocer/la ciudad mejor que todos
4. los muchachos/ofrecerles/unos refrescos a las muchachas
5. Francisco/ofrecerle/ayuda a su amiga
6. los profesores/conducir/cuando los estudiantes están cansados
7. nosotros/traducir/algunos periódicos y revistas
8. tú/traducir/lo que yo digo
9. yo/ofrecerles/unos dulces a los profesores
10. todos nosotros/conocer/lugares interesantes para visitar

Zona
Metropolitana
GUADALAJARA
ZAPOPAN
TLAQUEPAQUE
TONALA

FRAGMENTO MURAL J.C. OROZCO, PALACIO DE GOBIERNO

JALISCO • MEXICO

La catedral de Guadalajara.

El Teatro Degollado de Guadalajara.

En casa de Pablo

la galleta

RICARDO: Hola, doña Rosalba. ¿Está Pablo?

SEÑORA: No está, pero **no va a tardar en°** llegar. ¿Les puedo ofrecer unas **galletas mientras que°** esperan?

RICARDO: Bueno, muchas gracias.

MARTA: Ricardo, espera. No comas con las manos sucias.

PABLO: Hola a todos. Perdón por la **demora,°** pero tuve problemas para encontrar la oficina de correos. Bueno, vamos a la **exhibición** de **coches.°** ¿Quién conduce?

RICARDO: Yo conduzco... pero, un segundo, Pablo. No vayas tan rápido. Comamos primero estas galletas y, luego, nos vamos.

no va a tardar en *is not going to be long* **mientras que** *while* **demora** *delay* **coches** *carros*

 ## ¿Qué comprendiste?

1. ¿Va a llegar pronto Pablo o va a tardar en llegar?
2. ¿Cuándo pueden los muchachos comer las galletas?
3. ¿Quién dice que Ricardo no debe comer con las manos sucias?
4. ¿Adónde fue Pablo?
5. ¿Cuál fue la demora de Pablo?
6. ¿Adónde van a ir los muchachos?

 ## Charlando

1. ¿Cuál fue la última demora que tuviste?
2. ¿Das alguna explicación cuando tienes una demora? ¿Qué dices?
3. ¿Le ofreces algo de tomar o de comer a una persona cuando te visita en tu casa? ¿Qué le ofreces?
4. ¿Te gustan las exhibiciones de coches? ¿Por qué sí o no?

 En casa de Pablo
Activities 12-13

Answers

12
1. Pablo va a llegar pronto.
2. Pueden comer las galletas mientras que esperan.
3. Marta lo dice.
4. Pablo fue a la oficina de correos.
5. Tuvo problemas para encontrar la oficina de correos.
6. Van a ir a la exhibición de coches.

13 Answers will vary.

Notes

Galletas can refer to either cookies (*galletas dulces*) or crackers (*galletas saladas*).

Activities

Expansion. Additional questions (*¿Qué comprendiste?*): *¿Está Pablo en casa?*; *¿Quiénes llegan a la casa de Pablo?*; *¿Qué les ofrece la señora Rosalba a los muchachos?*; *¿Quién va a conducir?*; *¿Qué van a hacer primero Ricardo y Marta?*

Additional questions (*Charlando*): *¿Te gusta ir a visitar a tus amigos o prefieres invitarlos a tu casa? ¿Por qué?*; *¿En qué cuarto de la casa se sientan las personas que te visitan?*; *¿Sabes de alguna exhibición en tu ciudad? ¿De qué tipo?*

Pronunciation. After presenting and practicing the dialog (playing the audiocassette/audio compact disc, modeling words and phrases for student repetition, etc.), have students work in groups of three practicing the dialog. Circulate and assist with pronunciation and intonation. Encourage students to switch roles.

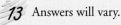 **NATIONAL STANDARDS**
C1.1, C1.2, C2.1, C4.1, C4.2

Quiz/Activity 4

Activities 7-8

Quizzes/Activities 3-4

Answers

14
1. No comamos tortillas.
2. No tomen (Uds.) el jugo.
3. No vayas más adelante.
4. No consigas galletas.
5. No dobles a la derecha.
6. No suban (Uds.) ahora.
7. No traduzcas esa palabra.
8. No hables con tu vecino.
9. No estén (Uds.) aquí temprano.
10. No cierre (Ud.) la puerta.
11. No volvamos mañana.
12. No continúen (Uds.) derecho.
13. No conduzca (Ud.).
14. No pare (Ud.) allí.
15. No ordenemos tacos.

Notes

If you are teaching the *vosotros/as* command, note the following: The negative *vosotros/as* command is formed by adding *-éis* to the formal command stem of *-ar* verbs, and by adding *-áis* to the formal command of *-er* and *-ir* verbs (*no habléis; no comáis; no escribáis*).

Activities

TPR. Use Total Physical Response to introduce the negative commands or to practice them after your introduction. For example, give a command orally. While the student is performing the action, interrupt or stop him/her with the negative of the same command.

IDIOMA

El mandato negativo

The formation of a negative *Ud.* or *Uds.* command or a negative *nosotros/as* command is the same as for an affirmative command, but with *no* before the verb. The negative *nosotros/as* command for *ir* is one exception: *¡Vamos!* → *¡No vayamos!*

Camine Ud. derecho. (Walk straight ahead.)	→	*No camine Ud. derecho.* (Don't walk straight ahead.)
Coman Uds. temprano. (Eat early.)	→	*No coman Uds. muy tarde.* (Don't eat too late.)
¡Salgamos! (Let's leave!)	→	*No salgamos todavía.* (Let's not leave yet.)

The negative *tú* command is different from the affirmative *tú* command. It is formed by adding an *-s* to the end of the formal *Ud.* command and by placing *no* before the verb.

Verónica, habla. (Verónica, talk.)	→	*Verónica, no hables.* (Verónica, don't talk.)
Ve hasta la esquina. (Go to the corner.)	→	*No vayas hasta la esquina.* (Don't go to the corner.)

14 Cambiando de opinión

Cambia los siguientes mandatos al negativo.

1. Comamos tortillas.
2. Tomen Uds. el jugo.
3. Ve más adelante.
4. Consigue galletas.
5. Dobla a la derecha.
6. Suban Uds. ahora.
7. Traduce esa palabra.
8. Habla con tu vecino.
9. Estén Uds. aquí temprano.
10. Cierre Ud. la puerta.
11. Volvamos mañana.
12. Continúen Uds. derecho.
13. Conduzca Ud.
14. Pare Ud. allí.
15. Ordenemos tacos.

No lleven estas cosas peligrosas en el avión.

Juega limpio, NO contamines

¡No continúen Uds. derecho, por favor!

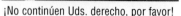

15 Cuidando niños

Imagina que cuidas a un grupo de niños de tu barrio y ahora caminas en la calle con ellos. Diles lo que no deben hacer, usando las indicaciones y mandatos informales.

Pepe/ir tan rápido
Pepe, no vayas tan rápido.

1. José/recoger esa basura
2. Enrique/hacer eso
3. Esteban/correr por la calle
4. Luisa/comer con las manos sucias
5. Eduardo/decir malas palabras
6. Pilar/ser mala con tu hermanito
7. Inés/caminar sobre el césped
8. Carmen/comprar galletas allí
9. Adolfo/tirar basura al piso

Felipe, ¡no juegues a las maquinitas todo el día!

16 En el restaurante Laredo

Ahora imagina que llevas a comer a los niños al restaurante Laredo. Diles lo que no deben hacer mientras que están en el restaurante.

Pepe/correr por ese corredor
Pepe, no corras por ese corredor.

1. chicos/pedir mucha comida
2. Luisa/comer la carne con las manos
3. Enrique/regañar a tu hermano
4. Pilar/ir al baño de las damas todavía
5. Esteban/jugar en la mesa
6. Inés/tirar la comida al piso
7. Carmen/escribir nada sobre la mesa
8. Adolfo y Esteban/ir al baño de los caballeros ahora
9. Pepe/hablar mientras que comes
10. José/tardar en venir

Sus padres siempre le dicen a Carlitos que no hable mientras que come.

Restaurante Laredo
Ya puede disfrutar
a diario de la buena cocina.

Ingredientes de primera calidad — Creatividad — Experiencia — Delicadeza — Y por supuesto, buen gusto

Answers

15
1. ...no recojas....
2. ...no hagas....
3. ...no corras....
4. ...no comas....
5. ...no digas....
6. ...no seas....
7. ...no camines....
8. ...no compres....
9. ...no tires....

16
1. Chicos, no pidan....
2. Luisa, no comas....
3. Enrique, no regañes....
4. Pilar, no vayas....
5. Esteban, no juegues....
6. Inés, no tires....
7. Carmen, no escribas....
8. Adolfo y Esteban, no vayan....
9. Pepe, no hables....
10. José, no tardes....

Activities

Cooperative Learning. Ask small groups of students to assume the role of dieticians and prepare appropriate negative and affirmative commands in order to suggest a healthy diet. Each group then presents its ideas to the class and discussion follows on what recommendations would be easy or difficult to follow.

Critical Thinking. If you are teaching students to recognize or to use *vosotros/as*, provide them with opportunities to practice the *vosotros/as* commands by adapting exercises such as this one. For example, ask students to first make all *tú* commands plural using *vosotros/as*, and then have them make the plural *vosotros/as* command negative.

NATIONAL STANDARDS
C1.2, C2.1, C4.1, C5.2

Answers

17 1. Quiere decir unas cortas vacaciones.
2. Possible answers: camino (carretera, calle); vehículo (coche, carro); conduzca (maneje)
3. Possible answer: Les debe importar a las personas que van a viajar en carro o en motocicleta.
4. Answers will vary.
5. El viaje más bonito es la vida.
6. Hay once mandatos. Son: disfrute, piense, siga, revise, abróchese, respete, mantenga, no adelante, no conduzca, póngase y siga (por segunda vez).
7. Los mandatos negativos en el aviso son: no adelante y no conduzca.

18 1. camina
2. jueguen
3. vayan
4. siga
5. pare
6. compren
7. Doblen
8. tardemos
9. ofrezca
10. sigamos

Activities

Pronunciation. You can ask one student or several to read the advertisement aloud.

Students with Special Needs. Read the article as a class activity and answer questions to be certain all students understand the content before attempting activity 17.

Spanish for Spanish Speakers. Pair bilingual and nonbilingual speakers for activity 17.

---

17 Un aviso de la Dirección General de Tráfico

Contesta las siguientes preguntas en español sobre el aviso.

1. ¿Qué quiere decir la palabra *puente* en este aviso?
2. ¿Qué otras palabras quieren decir lo mismo que *camino, vehículo* y *conduzca*?
3. ¿A quiénes les debe importar este aviso?
4. ¿Es este aviso importante para la gente que no tiene carro? Explica.
5. ¿Cuál es el viaje más bonito, según el aviso?
6. ¿Cúantos mandatos hay en el aviso? ¿Cuáles son?
7. ¿Cuáles son los dos mandatos negativos en el aviso?

18 Los vecinos de la cuadra

Imagina que es un día de verano y tú y tus vecinos están en la calle de tu cuadra. Escoge la forma correcta del mandato en las siguientes oraciones para ver qué están diciendo todos.

1. Carlota, *(camines/camina)* por la acera.
2. Julia y Sofía, no *(juegan/jueguen)* en la calle.
3. No *(vayan/vamos)* Uds. ahora.
4. No *(siga/sigas)* Ud. en esa dirección.
5. Sra. Barrios, *(para/pare)* un momento, por favor.
6. Muchachos, no *(compren/compran)* helados en esa heladería.
7. *(Doblen/Doblan)* Uds. a la derecha en la esquina.
8. No *(tardamos/tardemos).* Quiero volver temprano.
9. Sr. Rodríguez, no *(ofrece/ofrezca)* dulces a los niños, por favor.
10. No *(seguimos/sigamos)* por esta calle. Debemos continuar derecho.

ESTE PUENTE TIENE QUE CRUZARLO DOS VECES

Disfrute cuanto pueda de estas cortas vacaciones. Pero piense que el puente que le ha traído hasta aquí, es también el camino de vuelta a casa. Y al otro lado hay mucha gente que le espera.
Cuando llegue la hora de partir, siga nuestro consejo.
En los largos desplazamientos:
•Revise los puntos vitales de su vehículo.
•Abróchese siempre el cinturón.
•Respete los límites de velocidad.
•Mantenga la distancia de seguridad.
•No adelante sin visibilidad.
•Al mínimo síntoma de cansancio, no conduzca.
•Póngase el casco si viaja en moto o ciclomotor.
•**Siga estos consejos también en los trayectos cortos.**

LA VIDA ES EL VIAJE MAS HERMOSO

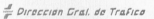
Dirección Gral. de Tráfico

Ministerio del Interior

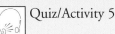

19 Un paseo por la ciudad

Tú y tres amigos van a dar un paseo en carro por los barrios de la ciudad. Están tratando de decidir qué dirección van a tomar. Trabajando en grupos de cuatro, hagan mini-diálogos con las indicaciones que se dan. Sigan el modelo.

 seguir/derecho

A: ¿Sigo derecho?   C: Sí, sigue derecho.
B: Sí, sigamos derecho.   D: ¡No! No sigas derecho.

1. doblar en la próxima calle
2. parar en la esquina
3. seguir hasta la señal de alto
4. conducir a la izquierda
5. ir al sur
6. buscar la carretera principal

20 Dando consejos

Imagina que un/a turista mexicano/a está visitando el lugar donde vives. Haz una lista de ocho consejos que le puedes ofrecer.

 No camine (Ud.) por las calles, sino por las aceras.

Algo más

Más sobre el mandato negativo

You have learned to attach object and reflexive pronouns to the end of affirmative commands. For negative commands, object and reflexive pronouns must precede the verb. When used together with the same verb, the indirect object pronoun precedes the direct object pronoun. Since the placement of object pronouns before the command does not affect the pronunciation of the word, it is not necessary to add a written accent mark to negative commands. Compare the following:

Tíralo al cesto de papeles.	→ *No lo tires al cesto de papeles.*
Ordénelas Ud.	→ *No las ordene Ud.*
Sentémonos allí.	→ *No nos sentemos allí.*
Prepárenmelas Uds.	→ *No me las preparen Uds.*
Cómanselos Uds.	→ *No se los coman Uds.*

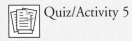

DESVIO!
AL BANCO DE COLOMBIA

SOLO ES NECESARIO UN PEQUEÑO DESVIO DESDE LA **OFICINA OCCIDENTE**, PARA PODER ATENDERLO MAS COMODAMENTE EN NUESTRA NUEVA SEDE.

LO ESPERAMOS A PARTIR DEL 2 DE ENERO/92 EN NUESTRA **NUEVA OFICINA CALLE 13 N° 68C-78.**

Banco de Colombia
Siempre adelante!

Answers

19 1. ¿Doblo...?/...doblemos ..../...dobla..../No dobles....
2. ¿Paro...?/...paremos..../...para..../No pares....
3. ¿Sigo...?/...sigamos..../...sigue..../No sigas....
4. ¿Conduzco...?/...conduzcamos..../...conduce..../No conduzcas....
5. ¿Voy...?/...vamos..../...ve..../No vayas....
6. ¿Busco...?/...busquemos..../...busca..../No busques....

20 Creative self-expression.

Activities

Critical Thinking. Discuss student responses for activity 20.

Spanish for Spanish Speakers. Ask volunteers to read the advertisement on page 119 and then tell the class what it says.

No me prepare Ud. más tortillas.

NATIONAL STANDARDS
C1.1, C1.2, C2.1, C1.3, C4.1, C5.1

Activity 21

21 Cambiando de opinión otra vez

Cambia los siguientes mandatos al negativo.

1. Ciérrela Ud.
2. Manéjalo hasta el puente.
3. Háblele Ud. en inglés.
4. Lávense Uds. las manos en el baño de los caballeros.
5. Comámoslas.
6. Busquémoslos en la florería.
7. Sentémonos a la derecha.
8. Ordenémoslos.
9. Pónganlas Uds. en el corredor.
10. Condúzcalo Ud.

22 De vacaciones en Cancún

Santiago y Guillermo están de vacaciones en Cancún con su familia, pero no están felices. Cada vez que dicen que van a hacer algo, sus padres se lo niegan *(tell them not to do it)*. Haz mandatos negativos para ver qué les dicen sus padres.

Voy a despertarme tarde mañana.
No te despiertes tarde mañana.

Vamos a broncearnos en la playa todo el día.
No se bronceen (Uds.) en la playa todo el día.

Santiago
1. Voy a acostarme tarde esta noche.
2. Vamos a irnos del hotel ahora.
3. Voy a quedarme en la cama mañana.

Guillermo
4. Voy a ducharme ahora.
5. Vamos a desayunarnos en la playa mañana.
6. Voy a levantarme tarde mañana.

¿Vas a ir de vacaciones a Cancún un día?

23 ¿De acuerdo?

Imagina que estás con dos amigos que nunca están de acuerdo en nada. Trabajando en grupos de tres, alternen Uds. en hacer preguntas y contestarlas, usando las pistas que se dan y un mandato afirmativo o negativo. Sigue el modelo.

Cómprame unos helados en esta heladería.

yo/comprar/a Uds./unos helados/en esta heladería

A: ¿Les compro (a Uds.) unos helados en esta heladería?

B: Sí, cómpranos unos helados en esta heladería.

C: No, no nos compres helados en esta heladería.

1. yo/leer/a Uds./las direcciones/para llegar/a la exhibición
2. yo/preparar/a Uds./enchiladas
3. yo/hacer/un mapa del barrio/a su amigo
4. nosotros/decir/la dirección/de ese edificio/a los vecinos
5. yo/dar/a Uds./las monedas
6. nosotros/esperar/a ella/en la esquina
7. nosotros/comprar/unas enchiladas/a los vecinos

24 Usando la imaginación

Trabajando en parejas, haz un diálogo con tu compañero/a de clase de por lo menos diez líneas, usando pronombres y mandatos afirmativos y negativos. Luego, tú y tu compañero/a deben presentar el diálogo a la clase.

A: Oye, ¿puedo manejar el carro de papá por el barrio?

B: Manéjalo, pero no vayas muy lejos.

El carro de papá.

Answers

23
1. ¿Les leo (a Uds.) las direcciones para llegar a la exhibición?/...léenos..../...no nos leas....
2. ¿Les preparo (a Uds.) enchiladas?/...prepáranos..../...no nos prepares....
3. ¿Le hago un mapa del barrio a su amigo?/...hazle..../...no le hagas....
4. ¿Les decimos la dirección de ese edificio a los vecinos?/...digámosles..../...no les digamos....
5. ¿Les doy (a Uds.) las monedas?/...danos..../...no nos des....
6. ¿La esperamos (a ella) en la esquina?/...esperémosla..../...no la esperemos....
7. ¿Les compramos unas enchiladas a los vecinos?/...comprémosles..../...no les compremos....

24 Creative self-expression.

Activities

Students with Special Needs. Repeat activity 23, having students change the direct object nouns to pronouns: *¿Les compro unos helados en esta heladería?* → *Sí, cómpranoslos./ No, no nos los compres.*

NATIONAL STANDARDS
C1.1, C1.2, C1.3, C2.1, C4.1

¡Qué coches!

Activity 25

Activities 20-21

Activities 10-11

Quiz/Activity 6

Answers

25
1. Son excelentes.
2. Quiere ver de cerca el coche.
3. Quiere ver la exhibición sobre las señales de tráfico.
4. Nadie sube al coche.
5. Los espejos no son muy deportivos.
6. Ricardo es muy exigente.
7. Answers will vary.
8. Answers will vary.

Notes

Note the use of the word *coche* in this dialog. Explain that *coche* is commonly used in Mexico instead of *carro*. In addition to *carro* and *coche*, students may encounter the words *automóvil* and *vehículo*.

Another word for *tráfico* is *tránsito*.

Activities

Critical Listening. Help students learn to become good listeners by asking follow-up questions to the dialog *¡Qué coches!*: What are the speakers talking about? Are they angry with each other? Did students notice any names in the dialog?

Expansion. Additional questions (*¿Qué comprendiste?*): *¿Dónde están los chicos?*; *¿Qué quiere ver Pablo primero?*; *¿Tiene el coche cinturones de seguridad?*

¡Qué coches!

el volante — el baúl — el claxon — la puerta — el parabrisas — el limpiaparabrisas — la rueda — el faro — el capó — la placa — el freno — la llanta — el guardabarros

RICARDO: ¡Qué coches!
PABLO: Ese coche tiene un **motor** y unos **frenos°** excelentes. Vamos a verlo **de cerca.°**
MARTA: ¡Miren! Allí hay una exhibición sobre las señales de **tráfico.** Vamos a verla.
PABLO: No la veamos todavía. Miremos este coche **moderno** primero. ¡**Sube°** al coche, Marta!
MARTA: No, gracias. Aquí estoy bien. Es muy bonito.
PABLO: ¡Tiene de todo! **Cinturones de seguridad,°** **alarma,** CD....
RICARDO: ¡Qué lástima! Los espejos no son muy **deportivos.°**
MARTA: ¡Qué **exigente°** eres!
PABLO: Sí, ¡eres muy exigente! ¡Vamos!

frenos *brakes* **de cerca** *close up, from a short distance* **Sube** *Get in* **Cinturones de seguridad** *seat (safety) belts* **deportivos** *sporty* **exigente** *demanding*

PARA ti

Más palabras para el coche

el asiento delantero/trasero	*front/back seat*
la barra de cambios	*stick shift*
el espejo retrovisor	*rearview mirror*
el gato	*jack*
la guantera	*glove compartment*
la direccional	*signal light*
la llanta de repuesto	*spare tire*
el parachoques	*bumper*
el techo corredizo	*sunroof*
el tablero	*dashboard*

25 ¿Qué comprendiste?

1. ¿Cómo son el motor y los frenos del coche?
2. ¿Qué quiere ver Pablo de cerca?
3. ¿Qué exhibición quiere ver Marta?
4. ¿Quién sube al coche?
5. ¿Qué no son muy deportivos, según Ricardo?
6. ¿Quién es muy exigente?
7. ¿Qué es lo que más te gusta de un coche moderno?
8. ¿Por qué crees que son importantes los cinturones de seguridad en un coche? Explica.

¿Dónde está el motor de este coche?

26 Un coche

En una hoja de papel, dibuja un coche. Luego, trabajando en parejas, alterna con tu compañero/a de clase en decir las partes del coche mientras que tu compañero/a señala cada parte que mencionas.

A: El capó.
B: (Point to the hood.)

¿Cuántas ruedas tiene mi coche?

REFACCIONARIA Y AUTO PARTES AUTOMOTRICES SANDOVAL, S.A. DE C.V.

REFACCIONES PARA TODA CLASE DE AUTOS Y CAMIONES

AV. INSURGENTES No. 91, OTE. TEPIC, NAY.

3-20-05

27 Adivina qué partes del coche son

Adivina cuáles son las siguientes partes del coche, de acuerdo con sus usos (uses).

 Úsalo para darle dirección a las ruedas.
El volante.

1. Ábrelo para poder mirar el motor.
2. Úsalo para llamar la atención a alguien que está en la carretera.
3. Límpialo para poder ver mejor.
4. Úsalos para parar el coche.
5. Enciéndelos para quitar la lluvia cuando está lloviendo.
6. Póntelo por seguridad antes de empezar a manejar.
7. Enciéndelos por las noches para poder ver.

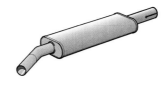

POR SU SEGURIDAD

USE EL CINTURON

¿Por qué es necesario usar los cinturones de seguridad?

Capítulo 3   123

 Activity 27

Answers

26 Creative self-expression. Check to be sure that students are able to properly identify the parts of the car in Spanish.

27 1. El capó.
2. El claxon.
3. El parabrisas.
4. Los frenos.
5. Los limpiaparabrisas.
6. El cinurón de seguridad.
7. Los faros.

Notes

Cars in Mexico have not always had seat belts or car alarms. In fact, few people used seat belts until recently. For this reason seat belts have just recently become a standard feature on cars, and alarms are more in demand as an add-on accessory.

Activities

Cooperative Learning. Have students do activity 27 in pairs.

Critical Listening. Note for students the hidden clues in the sentences in activity 27: Students can tell whether the car parts are masculine or feminine, according to the pronouns that are used with each command. You may wish to say the following to see how many students understand your advice: *Busca las pistas en los pronombres que hay en cada mandato.*

Prereading Strategy. Using transparencies 20 and 21, introduce the vocabulary used in the dialog *¡Qué coches!* (page 122). Then instruct students to cover up the dialog with one hand and look at the illustration. Ask them to imagine where the conversation takes place and what the people are saying to one another. Finally, have students look through the dialog quickly to find cognates and other words or expressions they already know.

NATIONAL STANDARDS
C1.1, C1.2, C1.3, C3.1, C4.1

Las señales de tráfico

A.   B.   C.   D.

E.   F.   G.   H.

28 Las señales de tráfico

Conecta lógicamente los siguientes mandatos con las señales de la ilustración anterior.

1. No vaya Ud. a más de cien kilómetros por hora.
2. Vaya Ud. a la izquierda.
3. Pare Ud.
4. No entre Ud.
5. Vaya Ud. a la derecha.
6. No doble Ud. a la derecha.
7. Tome Ud. la curva.
8. No doble Ud. a la izquierda.

¡No vaya Ud. a la izquierda!

¡Vaya rápido!

Por favor, no estacione Ud. en ese lugar.

¿Qué partes de este auto puedes nombrar?

Conozco esta calle muy bien. (México, D.F.)

Creo que Guadalajara está al noroeste de aquí.

Autoevaluación. Como repaso y autoevaluación, responde lo siguiente:
1. Name the four cardinal directions in Spanish.
2. In Spanish, how would you say that you know your neighbors?
3. How would you ask someone in Spanish if they know where the restroom is?
4. Imagine you are babysitting your little brother. He is very curious and does things he is not supposed to do. Tell him five things not to do.
5. Most public beaches post signs with rules for the beach. Make a list of three rules that you would include on such a sign.
6. Name five parts of a car that you have learned in Spanish.
7. Name two traffic signs in Spanish.
8. Name two cities in Mexico that are popular for tourists.

Answers

Autoevaluación
1. el norte, el sur, el este, el oeste
2. Conozco a mis vecinos.
3. ¿Sabes dónde está el baño?
4. No salgas de la casa. No subas la escalera. No toques la cocina. No corras en la casa. No comas la planta.
5. Answers will vary.
6. el baúl, el parabrisas, el limpiaparabrisas, la llanta, el faro, el freno, la rueda, el guardabarros, el volante, el claxon, el motor, el capó, la placa, la puerta, los cinturones de seguridad
7. Pare. No entre. No doble a la derecha. No doble a la izquierda. Tome la curva. Vaya a la derecha.
8. Acapulco, Puerto Vallarta, Mazatlán, Cancún

Notes

It is interesting to point out that several vocabulary items related to a car are compound words. For example, *parabrisas* (windshield) comes from *parar* (to stop) and *brisa* (wind).

Other words that pertain to cars that may be of interest to students include *el filtro* (filter) and *el aire acondicionado* (air conditioning).

Activities

Cooperative Learning. Working in pairs, one student describes his or her ideal car as the classmate draws the car. Have students switch roles. Take care with this activity as students will enjoy themselves and possibly get a little loud.

Multiple Intelligences (linguistic). Have students write a magazine column in which they provide helpful suggestions to people who are about to buy a car. Have them write an article consisting of at least ten lines in which they offer advice about what to do and what not to do when purchasing a new or used car. Remind them to use both affirmative and negative formal commands in their article.

NATIONAL STANDARDS
C2.1, C2.2, C3.1, C4.1, C4.2

Answers

A Answers will vary.

B Creative self-expression.

Notes

For all oral activities, listen for the correct pronunciation and determine if students appear to understand what they are saying and hearing. Also, be sure students personalize information so that it is meaningful to them.

Activities

Communities. If you live in an area that is visited by large numbers of Spanish-speaking people (for example, where there is a health care facility or government agency that is used by a large Spanish-speaking population), suggest to students that they investigate how they may be able to offer their services helping Spanish-speaking visitors (e.g., as a guide or as a translator). Check for a community organization that might already offer such help.

Technology. If there are no such opportunities in your community to offer volunteer services to Spanish-speaking visitors, have students use the Internet and print out a map of the subway of some major Hispanic cities (use **Subway Navigator**). Have them list some outings in the city. Then, working in pairs, have students use interrogatives asking for and giving directions to get to their selected destinations. In order to facilitate the activity, each person must have a copy of the map. One map will have the route marked while the other will not. Students then face each other and ask and answer questions until they get to their destinations.

¡La práctica hace al maestro!

A Comunicación

The following street map shows the route someone could follow to go from the word *aquí* to the letter *X*. Prepare two similar maps, but without adding the dotted line. Then, plot your own route between the two points on one copy of the map. Next, give the blank copy to another student. After deciding who will go first, describe the route you plotted between the word *aquí* and the letter *X* as your partner plots

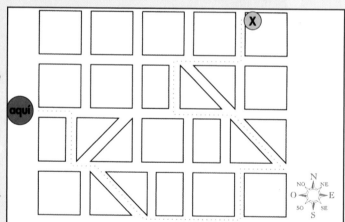

the course on the blank map. When you have finished, compare the routes that appear on both maps to see if they are the same. Switch roles.

B Conexión con la tecnología

Search the Internet for sources for renting a car in Mexico. Print out your findings. Report back to the class on the costs, the selection of vehicles to choose from, the cost of fuel, the cost of insurance, the availability of maps and directions to your destinations, the driver's license requirements, and any other interesting information you discovered.

Testing/Assessment
Test Booklet
Oral Proficiency
    Evaluation Manual
Portfolio Assessment

En la ciudad
la acera
el alto
el barrio
el césped
la curva
la señal
el tráfico
el vecino, la vecina

Partes del coche
la alarma
el baúl
el capó
el cinturón de seguridad
el claxon
el coche
el faro
el freno
el guardabarros
el limpiaparabrisas
la llanta
el motor
el parabrisas
la placa
la rueda
el volante

Puntos cardinales
el este
el noreste
el noroeste
el norte
el oeste
el sur
el sureste
el suroeste

Verbos
conducir
conocer
doblar
manejar
ofrecer
subir
tardar
tirar
traducir

Expresiones y otras palabras
de cerca
la demora
deportivo,-a
la dirección
la exhibición
exigente
la galleta
hacia
mientras (que)
moderno,-a
la seguridad
sino
tardar en
    (+ *infinitive*)

El perro de la vecina está en la acera.

Hay mucho tráfico hoy.
¡No puedo seguir
derecho!

127

Activities
Critical Thinking. *El verdugo.* The idea of the game is to guess a word. One student goes to the board and writes one blank for each letter of any word. The other students then begin to guess letters of the alphabet that might be in that word. Each correct letter is inserted into the proper blank. If the correct letter is not guessed, the student at the board draws in a part of a hanged person. The game continues until the word has been guessed or the complete hanged person has been drawn. You may want to make the game more challenging by drawing in a part of the hanged person for every vowel guessed, since the vowels first would probably make the entire word much easier to figure out. This game may be played with the class divided into two teams or with the entire class guessing the letters.

Expansion. Dictate a letter of the alphabet to the class. Give students three minutes to write any words they can think of in Spanish that begin with that letter. After calling time, ask students to read their lists aloud. The student with the longest list of correct words wins.

Pronunciation. To ensure proper pronunciation, model each word or expression and have students repeat after you.

Students with Special Needs. Students must say a word they have learned in Spanish and then select someone else to spell the word. Have them check their spelling and then switch roles.

NATIONAL STANDARDS
C1.2, C4.1

¡Conozca México!

 Quiz/Activity 7

Answers

Preparación

1. B
2. A
3. C
4. A

Activities

Communities. Ask students to plan a trip to Mexico or to research aspects of Mexican history, art, geography, music or politics. Such work may generate a special interest in the country and encourage a study/travel-abroad experience to be organized by your school and a student-oriented travel agency.

Critical Listening. Play the *Somos así LISTOS* audiocassette/audio compact disc version of the reading. Tell students to listen for the main ideas the speaker is addressing. Finally, have several individuals state what they believe the main theme of the reading is.

a leer
Estrategia

Preparación

Estrategia para leer: *using format clues to predict meaning*
Before you begin a reading, it is helpful to examine how it is formatted. Look at the title, the subtitles, the photos, the graphics and the layout to predict what the reading is about.

Mira la lectura y, luego, contesta las siguientes preguntas como preparación para la lectura, escogiendo la letra de la respuesta apropiada.

1. ¿Para qué es el folleto *(brochure)*?
   A. Para dar direcciones de cómo llegar a México.
   B. Para preparar un viaje a México.
   C. Para dar información sobre la historia de México.

2. ¿Quién hace este folleto?
   A. Lo hace Viajes Planeta.
   B. Lo hace La Ruta Indígena.
   C. Lo hacen en Puebla.

3. ¿Qué ofrecen para visitar México?
   A. No ofrecen nada.
   B. Ofrecen paseos a caballo.
   C. Ofrecen rutas.

4. ¿A qué tipo de lugares ofrecen viajes?
   A. A lugares donde hace sol.
   B. A lugares donde hay nieve.
   C. A y B.

La Quebrada está en Acapulco.

Las ruínas mayas de Tulúm están en la costa del Caribe.

¡Conozca México!

El mejor plan de excursiones a México lo tiene *Viajes Planeta*.
Viajes Planeta le ofrece cuatro rutas fascinantes para conocer México: La Ruta Indígena, La Ruta Colonial, La Ruta Moderna y La Ruta del Desierto.

 NATIONAL STANDARDS
C1.2, C2.1, C3.1, C4.1

Ruta: La Ruta Indígena
Duración: 15 días
Lugares de visita:  • Ciudad de México (el Zócalo, el Palacio de Bellas Artes)
• Mérida (la catedral)
• Cancún (las playas)
• Chichén Itzá (las ruinas mayas)
• Tulum (las ruinas mayas)
• Uxmal (las ruinas mayas)

Ruta: La Ruta Moderna
Duración: 20 días
Lugares de visita: • Ciudad de México (la Zona Rosa, la Torre Latinoamericana, la UNAM, la estación del metro, el monumento del Ángel de la Independencia)
• Guadalajara
• Puerto Vallarta (las playas)
• Monterrey
• Ciudad Juárez

Ruta: La Ruta Colonial
Duración: 8 días
Lugares de visita: • Ciudad de México (la Catedral, el Palacio Nacional)
• Puebla
• Cuernavaca (los Jardines de Borda, el Palacio de Cortés)
• Taxco
• Acapulco (playas)

Ruta: La Ruta del Desierto
Duración: 6 días
Lugares de visita: • Ciudad de México (el Parque de Chapultepec)
• Mazatlán (las playas)
• Baja California (el desierto, las montañas)

¿Qué comprendiste?

1. ¿Cuántas rutas diferentes ofrece este folleto turístico?
2. ¿Cuál es la ruta más larga?
3. ¿Cuántos días tiene el viaje más corto?
4. ¿Cuál es la única ciudad que está en todas las rutas?
5. ¿En qué viaje hay ruinas mayas y playas?
6. ¿En qué viaje puede la gente bañarse en la playa?
7. ¿Qué lugar ofrece desiertos?

Charlando

1. ¿Cuál de las rutas que ofrece *Viajes Planeta* te gustaría tomar? ¿Por qué?
2. ¿Te gustan los viajes cortos o largos? Explica.
3. ¿Qué lugares te gusta visitar cuando vas a una ciudad?
4. ¿Te gusta visitar ciudades grandes o pequeñas? Explica.
5. ¿Cuáles son los lugares más importantes para visitar donde tú vives?

 Activities A, B

Answers

 A
1. Ofrece cuatro rutas diferentes.
2. La ruta más larga es La Ruta Moderna.
3. El viaje más corto tiene seis días.
4. La ciudad de México es la única ciudad que está en todas las rutas.
5. En la Ruta Indígena hay ruinas y playas.
6. En todas las rutas la gente puede bañarse en la playa.
7. Baja California ofrece desiertos.

 B Answers will vary.

Notes

It is interesting to note that Mexico's indigenous heritage is reflected in names that are popular even today. For example, a leading Mexican politician is Cuauhtémoc Crdenas.

Activities

Prereading Strategy. Ask some general questions about this brochure and about Mexico, such as the questions found in the *Preparación,* in order to mentally prepare student for the reading *¡Conozca México!* Next, play the first paragraph of the recording of the *A leer* section, using the corresponding audiocassette or compact disc that is part of the Audiocassette/Audio CD Program. As an alternative, you may choose to read the first paragraph yourself. Read the paragraph again with students following along in the book. Give students a moment to look over the paragraph silently on their own and then have them ask questions. Ask for a student to volunteer to read the paragraph aloud. Continue in this way for the four *Rutas* outlined on page 129.

 **NATIONAL STANDARDS**
C1.2, C2.2, C3.1, C3.2, C4.1, C5.2

Answers

Creative writing practice.

Activities

Connections. Inform students that in many ways, the history of Mexico is closely connected to that of the United States. Have students choose one of the following topics and write a brief report (2–3 paragraphs) to share with the class. They may use an encyclopedia, books from the school library or the Internet to gather information for their reports. Some possible topics include the following: Pancho Villa, Mexico's struggle for independence, Gadsden Purchase, Treaty of Guadalupe Hidalgo, Constitution of 1917, Battle of the Alamo or NAFTA (North American Free Trade Agreement).

Cooperative Learning. As an alternative to the Connections activity suggestion, have a group of students research and write cooperatively about a specific topic to be sure all subjects are covered. Stress that each member of the group contribute information and ideas, and make each group responsible for submitting a final draft. Each group should elect one person to prepare a finished copy of the report on a typewriter or computer. Place the compositions in a folder or a binder marked *La historia de México*, or make enough copies to distribute so that each student receives one. Have students review their peer's work and offer suggestions for improving the compositions.

Multiple Intelligences (linguistic). If you have not yet done so, have students begin to create a Writer's Journal consisting of student writing activities. The Writer's Journal offers appropriate portfolio activities for assessing student writing skills and is an ideal opportunity for an on-going dialog with students about their writing progress. How to create a Writer's Journal is addressed more thoroughly in the *A escribir* section at the end of *Capítulo 2* of *Somos así EN SUS MARCAS*.

NATIONAL STANDARDS
C1.3, C4.2, C5.1, C5.2

a escribir

Estrategia

Estrategia para escribir: *appeal to your reader's senses*

You have already learned the importance of identifying your purpose for writing and the audience you are writing for. If your purpose is to attract and hold the reader's attention, it is a good idea to include details and descriptions that appeal to the reader's sense of sight, sound and taste.

Cabo San Lucas, Baja California, México.

Create a travel brochure for a location that you have always dreamed of visiting. Use commands (such as ¡*Diviértase Ud. mucho!*) and add description and details about the dream vacation that will appeal to the reader's senses of sight, sound and taste. Incorporate graphics and/or artwork to enhance the visual appeal of your brochure.

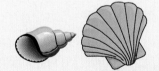

repaso

Now that I have completed this chapter, I can...
- ✓ ask for and give directions.
- ✓ identify places in the city.
- ✓ discuss what is sold in specific stores.
- ✓ tell someone what to do.
- ✓ order from a menu in a restaurant.
- ✓ advise and suggest.
- ✓ discuss who and what people know.
- ✓ talk about everyday activities.
- ✓ tell others what not to do.
- ✓ identify parts of a car.
- ✓ advise others in writing.

I can also...
- ✓ read in Spanish about Mexico.
- ✓ talk about foods in Spanish-speaking countries.
- ✓ identify opportunities to use Spanish in my community.
- ✓ read a recipe in Spanish.
- ✓ write in Spanish about where I live.

Este aeropuerto está en el D.F.

¿Conoces esta calle?
(Guanajuato, México.)

Episode 3

Activities

Critical Listening. Practice giving directions by using a map of your city or school and command forms of verbs such as *seguir, ir* and *doblar*. In order to practice both listening and speaking skills, place students in pairs and have one student give directions from a given starting point to an unknown destination. The partner must listen and follow on the map in order to identify the appropriate finishing point.

Multiple Intelligences (spatial). As an alternative activity, have artistically inclined students create a hanging mural, a poster or other artwork that depicts some aspect of what they have learned about Mexico.

Spanish for Spanish Speakers. Have students prepare a report about the city of Teotihuacán. The report should include photos and/or illustrations.

Students with Special Needs. Using overhead transparencies, review the city vocabulary students have learned in *Capítulo 3:* places in a city (transparencies 17-18), specialty shops (transparency 19); parts of a car (transparencies 20-21); traffic signs (transparencies 22-23) and map directions (transparencies 24-25).

TPR. In pairs or small groups, students prepare logical *tú* commands for some of the following people: a brother or sister, a best friend, a boyfriend or girlfriend, a parent. Ask students from different pairings to react to the commands while observing whether or not they seem to understand what they are supposed to do.

NATIONAL STANDARDS
C1.1, C1.2, C1.3, C2.1, C2.2, C3.1, C3.2, C4.1, C4.2, C5.1, C5.2

Notes

Communicative functions are provided with the opening two pages along with accompanying visuals to mentally and visually whet students' appetites for the chapter they are about to begin. A checkoff list of the functions appears at the end of the chapter (see page 183), along with additional objectives that students can use as a self-check to evaluate their own progress.

Activities

Critical Thinking. Photographs, maps and artwork appear here and are used throughout the book as a way to encourage students to connect with the countries and people they are studying. The photographs and other selected visuals that appear on pages 132-133 depict the functions, cultural setting and themes of the chapter ahead and serve to further student connections to how Spanish is used outside the controlled environment of the classroom. Try to employ these supportive visuals on a regular basis. Ask about any similarities and differences students observe, what words they are able to understand, what conclusions students can draw from the information, and so forth. For example, ask students to answer the following: 1) What does *El amigo de los animales* mean in the photograph on page 132?; 2) In what Spanish-speaking countries does this chapter take place?; 3) What is one theme in the chapter?

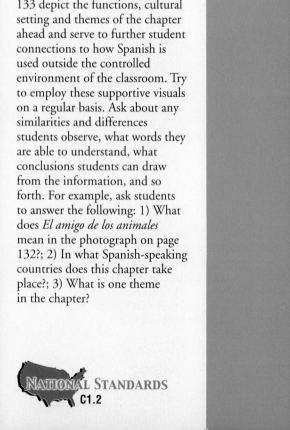

NATIONAL STANDARDS
C1.2

¡Qué divertido!

EL SALVADOR
P-56-001
CENTRO AMERICA

HONDURAS
P76445
CENTRO AMERICA

El Salvador
Nombre oficial:
República de El Salvador

Población: 5.750.000

Capital: San Salvador

Ciudades importantes:
Santa Ana, San Miguel,
Mexicanos

Unidad monetaria: el colón

Fiesta nacional: 15 de
septiembre, Día de la
Independencia

Gente famosa: Roque
Dalton (poeta); Francisco
Gavidia (dramaturgo)

Honduras
Nombre oficial: República
de Honduras

Población: 5.860.000

Capital: Tegucigalpa

Ciudades importantes: San
Pedro Sula, La Ceiba, El
Progreso

Unidad monetaria: el
lempira

Fiesta nacional: 15 de
septiembre, Día de la
Independencia

Gente famosa: José Antonio
Velázquez (pintor); Rafael
Heliodoro Valle (cronista)

Activities

Connections. Ask students to
name the countries of Central
America. Then discuss what
students know about the Central
American countries that are the
setting for *Capítulo 4.* For
example, have students name the
capitals of these two Central
American nations. Ask students to
name some other cities in El
Salvador and Honduras. Ask what
else students know about
the countries.

In this chapter you will be able to:
- seek and provide
  personal information
- describe in the past
- talk about activities
  at a special event
- identify animals
- express quantities
- provide background
  information about
  the past
- indicate past
  intentions
- discuss nationality
- add emphasis to a
  description
- recognize and
  express size
- state possession
- identify sounds that
  animals make

133

NATIONAL STANDARDS
C1.2, C5.2

Un día en el parque de atracciones

 Quiz/Activity 1

 Activities 26-27

 Activity 1

Content reviewed in *Lección 7*
• describing in the past
• numbers
• telling time
• Spanish-speaking countries
• *ser* vs. *estar*

Activities

Critical Listening. Play the audiocassette/audio compact disc recording of the dialog. Instruct students to cover the words as they listen to the conversation in order to develop good listening skills before concentrating on reading Spanish. Have students look at the illustration and imagine what the people are saying to one another. Ask several individuals to state what they believe is the main theme of the conversation.

Critical Thinking. Have students describe the illustration. As an alternative activity, have students make up a story about what they see in the amusement park.

Prereading Strategy. Use transparencies 26 and 27 to introduce students to the vocabulary used in this dialog. Then instruct students to cover up the dialog with one hand and look at the illustration. Ask them to imagine where the conversation takes place and what the people are saying to one another. Finally, have students look through the dialog quickly to find cognates and other words or expressions they already know.

NATIONAL STANDARDS
C1.2, C5.2

Lección 7

Contexto cultural
EL SALVADOR

Un día en el parque de atracciones

la montaña
los fuegos artificiales
el globo
la montaña rusa
la atracción
el globo
el desfile
el carro antiguo
la serpiente

*Luisa, una chica **salvadoreña**, habla con David sobre lo que hizo en sus últimas vacaciones.*

LUISA: Mi familia y yo fuimos de vacaciones a un parque de **atracciones** en los Estados Unidos.

DAVID: ¿En los Estados Unidos? ¡**Maravilloso**!

LUISA: Sí, en la Florida. El parque es **fascinante**. **Había°** mucho para ver y hacer, **como° fuegos artificiales**, carros **antiguos,°** atracciones.... Bueno, ya puedes **imaginarte**. También había muchas **golosinas,°** helados y refrescos.

DAVID: Y, ¿te pasó algo divertido?

LUISA: Sí, algo **chistoso°** pasó. Una vez, cuando yo comía un helado, oí que unas muchachas **gritaban.°** Entonces miré por todos lados para ver qué pasaba.

DAVID: Y, ¿qué pasaba?

LUISA: Bueno, mi hermano menor **molestaba°** con una **serpiente** de **plástico** a unas chicas que miraban el **desfile**.

DAVID: ¡Qué chistoso es tu hermano!

Había *There (was) were* **como** *like, such as* **antiguos** *antique, ancient, old* **golosinas** *sweets* **chistoso** *funny* **gritaban** *were shouting* **molestaba** *was bothering*

¿Qué comprendiste?

1. ¿De qué país es Luisa?
2. ¿Adónde fueron de vacaciones Luisa y su familia?
3. ¿Cómo es el lugar donde ellos fueron, según Luisa?
4. ¿Qué había allí para ver y hacer?
5. ¿Qué oyó Luisa?
6. ¿Quién molestaba a unas chicas?

Charlando

1. ¿Hay alguien chistoso en tu familia? ¿Quién?
2. ¿Comes muchas golosinas?
3. ¿Te gustan los parques de atracciones? Explica.
4. ¿Te gusta montar en la montaña rusa? Explica.
5. ¿Te puedes imaginar montando en globo? Explica.

Un día en el parque de atracciones

Trabajando en parejas, haz el papel de una de las personas del diálogo anterior.

Fueron a este parque de atracciones.

 Activities 1-2

Answers

1
1. Ella es de El Salvador.
2. Fueron a un parque de atracciones.
3. Es fascinante.
4. Había mucho para ver y hacer, como fuegos artificiales, carros antiguos y atracciones.
5. Oyó que algunas muchachas gritaban.
6. El hermano menor de Luisa molestaba a unas chicas.

2 Answers will vary.

3 Role-playing activity.

Notes

Inform students that as they travel they will hear some native speakers use *habían* as a plural form of the impersonal expression *había*.

Show students where El Salvador is located using the maps in the front of the book or the transparencies that are part of this program.

Activities

Cooperative Learning. After sufficient practice, have several pairs of students present their dialogs in front of the class.

Expansion. Additional questions (*¿Qué comprendiste?*): *¿Qué comía Luisa cuando algo chistoso pasó?; ¿Qué miraban las chicas?; ¿En dónde está el parque de atracciones?; ¿Qué había de tomar en el parque?; ¿Adónde miraba Luisa cuando oía que algunas personas gritaban?*

Additional questions (*Charlando*): *¿Cuándo fue la última vez que fuiste a un parque de atracciones? ¿En dónde?; ¿Te pasó algo chistoso? ¿Qué?; ¿Te gusta ver fuegos artificiales?; ¿Qué comes cuando vas a un parque de atracciones?; ¿Compras globos cuando vas al parque?*

National Standards
C1.2, C1.3, C2.1, C3.2, C4.1, C4.2

Notes

Students will find it interesting to note that a pre-Columbian village was discovered in El Salvador not long ago. The site is referred to as *Joya de Cerén* and it was found buried under lava and volcanic ash.

Activities

Multiple Intelligences (linguistic/spatial). Have students make a tourist pamphlet highlighting El Salvador's main attractions using information obtained by searching the Internet. When complete, students might share their work with the class (using PowerPoint® or HyperStudio®, if available). Then investigate placing the presentation on the school's Web page or in the school's newspaper for other students and parents to see.

Prereading Strategy. This *Conexión cultural* provides an opportunity for students to increase what they know about the Spanish-speaking world by reading about El Salvador in Spanish. The vocabulary and structures have been controlled to enable individuals to read in the target language and enjoy the experience. Note for the class that it is not essential to understand every word in order to read Spanish; the meaning of important but unknown passive vocabulary has been provided to facilitate an enjoyable experience. Before beginning the *Conexión cultural*, consider asking some general preparation questions about the theme of the reading: What is the capital of El Salvador? What else do students know about El Salvador? Where is El Salvador located? Then have students skim the *Conexión cultural* for cognates and any words or expressions they already know.

NATIONAL STANDARDS
C1.2, C3.2, C4.1

Conexión *cultural*

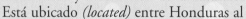

El Salvador

El Salvador es un país de contrastes. Es el país más pequeño de habla hispana de la América Central y a la vez es el país que tiene más densidad de población de todos los países latinoamericanos. Esta densidad de población produce grandes problemas de contaminación y destrucción de la naturaleza.

El palacio municipal en Santa Ana, El Salvador.

Está ubicado *(located)* entre Honduras al noreste, Guatemala al noroeste, y el Océano Pacífico al sur. La capital, San Salvador, es la ciudad más grande del país, con más de 500.000 habitantes. San Salvador y otras ciudades principales, como Santa Ana y San Miguel están en la región central. Esta región es de tipo volcánico y por lo tanto propensa a sufrir muchos temblores y terremotos *(earthquakes)*. Hay más de veinte volcanes activos en esta área.

Antes de la llegada de los españoles en el siglo XVI, la región era parte del territorio maya. En 1524, empezó la conquista española de la población indígena *(native)* para tomar posesión de las tierras *(land)* que hoy son El Salvador. En 1525, el conquistador español, Diego Alvarado, fundó la ciudad de San Salvador en el Valle de las Hamacas *(Valley of the Hammocks)*. El Salvador consiguió su independencia de España en 1821.

En la historia reciente de esta nación hay mucha violencia, problemas sociales y económicos, y una guerra civil *(civil war)*. Los problemas sociales existen por el gran contraste que hay entre los pocos ricos y los muchos pobres. Los problemas económicos se deben a que la mayor parte de su economía depende de la producción del café. Hoy El Salvador está tratando de solucionar estos problemas y de mejorar *(improve)* sus sistemas político y económico para dar a su gente un mejor futuro.

La producción de café es importante en la economía de El Salvador.

Cruzando fronteras

Haz un folleto *(brochure)* de una página para dar a conocer a la gente de otros países las cosas buenas y los puntos geográficos importantes de El Salvador. Busca información sobre El Salvador en la biblioteca o en la Internet, si es necesario.

Oportunidades

El Salvador

If you are interested in the field of environmental conservation, organizations from the United States, Europe and Australia are helping to rebuild El Salvador through programs devoted to education, agricultural reform and reforestation. There are a lot of different ways to volunteer in El Salvador, and many organizations exist to help. The *Centro Internacional de Solidaridad (CIS)* runs language schools in San Salvador that take English teachers as volunteers. And Green Arrow's Conservation Connection Placement Program, based in Costa Rica, places volunteers in work positions throughout Central America.

Tenemos que conservar los bosques del mundo. Muchos bosques como éste son quemados cada año.

If you are interested in the field of volcanology, El Salvador's volcanic terrain provides plenty of opportunities for hiking. You can trek around the rim of San Salvador's Boquerón volcano or follow a trail down into the crater itself.

IDIOMA

El imperfecto de los verbos regulares

Past events in Spanish usually are expressed using one of two tenses. You already have learned the *pretérito,* which expresses completed past actions. A second tense, the *pretérito imperfecto* (usually referred to as *el imperfecto*), also refers to the past, but without indicating specifically when the event or condition begins or ends.

Form the imperfect tense of regular verbs by dropping the *-ar, -er* or *-ir* ending from the infinitive and by adding the endings indicated in bold in the chart on the following page. All verbs in Spanish follow this pattern except for *ir, ser* and *ver,* which you will learn later in this lesson.

 Quiz/Activity 3

 Activities 3-4

 Quiz/Activity 1

Answers
4 Creative self-expression.

Notes
Technology. Have students use a program like HyperStudio® or PowerPoint® to create the brochure for activity 4. Then find out if it is possible to place some of the better brochures on the school's Web page.

Activities
Spanish for Spanish Speakers. In addition to or as an alternative to doing activity 4, have students write a short composition in Spanish of at least 100 words describing a trip they took to a local amusement park. They might tell whom they went with, what they saw and did, what they ate that day and any other details they wish.

NATIONAL STANDARDS
C1.2, C1.3, C3.1, C3.2, C4.1

Notes

Note that for *-ar* verbs only the *nosotros* form takes a written accent. For *-er* and *-ir* verbs all forms take a written accent.

Remind your students that they already have learned to use an impersonal form of the verb *haber: hay.* Students will learn other impersonal forms of *haber* in lesson 9. The use of *haber* as an auxiliary verb will be presented in chapter 7 of *Somos así LISTOS.*

Tell students that stem-changing verbs do not show a change in the imperfect since the imperfect is formed from the infinitive.

Sara estudiaba mucho.

el imperfecto de *hablar, comer* y *vivir*

hablar

yo	hab**laba**	*I was speaking (I used to speak)*	nosotros nosotras	hab**lábamos**	*we were speaking (we used to speak)*
tú	hab**labas**	*you were speaking (you used to speak)*	vosotros vosotras	hab**labais**	*you were speaking (you used to speak)*
Ud.		*you were speaking (you used to speak)*	Uds.		*you were speaking (you used to speak)*
él	hab**laba**	*he was speaking (he used to speak)*	ellos	hab**laban**	*they were speaking (they used to speak)*
ella		*she was speaking (she used to speak)*	ellas		*they were speaking (they used to speak)*

comer

yo	com**ía**	*I was eating (I used to eat)*	nosotros nosotras	com**íamos**	*we were eating (we used to eat)*
tú	com**ías**	*you were eating (you used to eat)*	vosotros vosotras	com**íais**	*you were eating (you used to eat)*
Ud.		*you were eating (you used to eat)*	Uds.		*you were eating (you used to eat)*
él	com**ía**	*he was eating (he used to eat)*	ellos	com**ían**	*they were eating (they used to eat)*
ella		*she was eating (she used to eat)*	ellas		*they were eating (they used to eat)*

vivir

yo	viv**ía**	*I was living (I used to live)*	nosotros nosotras	viv**íamos**	*were living (we used to live)*
tú	viv**ías**	*you were living (you used to live)*	vosotros vosotras	viv**íais**	*you were living (you used to live)*
Ud.		*you were living (you used to live)*	Uds.		*you were living (you used to live)*
él	viv**ía**	*he was living (he used to live)*	ellos	viv**ían**	*they were living (they used to live)*
ella		*she was living (she used to live)*	ellas		*they were living (they used to live)*

Note: The impersonal expression *había* is the imperfect tense of *haber* (to have) and is the equivalent of **there was/there were.**

5 Unas preguntas

Quieres saber qué hacían ayer por la tarde las personas indicadas. Haz preguntas, usando la forma apropiada del imperfecto de los siguientes verbos. Usa las pistas que se dan.

traducir (él)
¿Traducía él?

1. volver (ella)
2. viajar (nosotros)
3. trabajar (Uds.)
4. hablar (tú)
5. aprender (ellos)

6. conducir (yo)
7. entrar (ellas)
8. jugar (tú)
9. correr (tú)
10. dormir (yo)

11. leer (yo)
12. acostarse (Ud.)
13. divertirse (Uds.)
14. gritar (él)
15. escribir (nosotros)

6 En la montaña rusa

Usa el imperfecto de los verbos indicados para decir qué hacían las personas mencionadas cuando tú montabas en la montaña rusa.

unas chicas/cepillarse el pelo
Unas chicas se cepillaban el pelo.

1. un hombre chistoso/vender globos rojos y amarillos
2. una niña/molestar a todo el mundo con una serpiente de plástico
3. tú/mirar un desfile de carros antiguos y pequeños
4. yo/gritar en la montaña rusa
5. nosotros/comer unas golosinas
6. cuatro muchachos/subir por una escalera al globo

CATARINA VOLADORA

De pronto sientes que un rayo láser atraviesa tu cuerpo y te convierte en un diminuto ser, más pequeño que un insecto. Repentinamente una catarina voladora te atrapa entre sus alas y te lleva a viajar a través de una espesa maleza a una velocidad inexplicable. Vive y disfruta al máximo esta inolvidable experiencia.

¡Gritábamos mucho cuando estuvimos en la montaña rusa!

Answers

5
1. ¿Volvía ella?
2. ¿Viajábamos nosotros?
3. ¿Trabajaban Uds.?
4. ¿Hablabas tú?
5. ¿Aprendían ellos?
6. ¿Conducía yo?
7. ¿Entraban ellas?
8. ¿Jugabas tú?
9. ¿Corrías tú?
10. ¿Dormía yo?
11. ¿Leía yo?
12. ¿Se acostaba Ud.?
13. ¿Se divertían Uds.?
14. ¿Gritaba él?
15. ¿Escribíamos nosotros?

6
1. ...vendía....
2. ...molestaba....
3. ...mirabas....
4. ...gritaba....
5. ...comíamos....
6. ...subían....

Activities

Spanish for Spanish Speakers. Ask students to read the realia on page 139 that accompanies activity 6 and then ask them to summarize for the class what they understood.

NATIONAL STANDARDS
C1.2, C2.1, C4.1

Answers

 7 Times may vary. Verbs are as
follows: Dormía..., Me
despertaba..., Me levantaba...,
Me bañaba..., Me vestía...,
Me desayunaba..., Salía...,
Llegaba..., Almorzaba...,
Estudiaba..., Hacía..., Me
acostaba..., Me dormía....

 8 1. estaba
2. comía
3. dormía
4. pedía
5. miraba
6. molestaba
7. subían
8. hablaban
9. pasábamos
10. oíamos

Notes

Tell students the imperfect
describes an incomplete process.
The speaker does not know when
the process started, when or if it
ended or how many times it took
place. However, the speaker does
know that there was some
duration (but there are no limits
on the time) and the beginning
and the end are irrelevant. The
imperfect is used to refer to an
event that happened sometime in
the middle of the past.

Activities

Spanish for Spanish Speakers.
Have volunteers read the realia on
page 140 that accompanies
activity 8. Then ask students
questions to determine how much
they understood: *¿De qué se trata
el aviso?; ¿Reconocen algunos de los
sabores?; ¿Qué sabor(es) no
reconocen?*

---

7 A diferentes horas

Haz oraciones completas para decir lo que tú hacías ayer a diferentes
horas, usando los siguientes verbos y pistas: *dormir, despertarse, levantarse,
bañarse, vestirse, desayunarse, salir de la casa, llegar a la escuela, almorzar,
estudiar español, hacer la tarea, acostarse, dormirse.*

> Dormía a las seis.
> Me despertaba a las seis y media.

8 El fin de semana pasado

Imagina que el fin de semana pasado fuiste con la familia de tu vecino a un
parque de atracciones. Completa las siguientes oraciones con el imperfecto
de los verbos indicados para decir qué hacía cada persona todo el día.

> Las hermanas menores de mi vecino <u>tomaban</u> refrescos. (tomar)

1. Su hermana mayor <u>(1)</u> en la montaña rusa. (estar)
2. Su prima <u>(2)</u> golosinas. (comer)
3. Su abuelo <u>(3)</u>. (dormir)
4. Su hermano menor <u>(4)</u> monedas para montar en las
   atracciones. (pedir)
5. Su abuela <u>(5)</u> a la gente. (mirar)
6. Yo <u>(6)</u> a todo el mundo. (molestar)
7. Sus primos <u>(7)</u> a una montaña artificial. (subir)
8. Sus padres <u>(8)</u> con todo el mundo. (hablar)
9. Nosotros <u>(9)</u> un día maravilloso. (pasar)
10. Todos nosotros <u>(10)</u> música popular. (oír)

Refrescos
Jonlly
REFRESCOS DE FRUTA NATURAL AL POR MAYOR Y DETAL
ELABORADO CON AGUA PURIFICADA

- TORONJA
- ACEROLA
- TAMARINDO
- GUANABANA
- AJONJOLI
- FRUIT PUNCH
- COCO
- PARCHA
- CHINA
- LIMON
- MAVI
- UVA
- GUAVAPIÑA

Algo **más**

Los usos del imperfecto

The imperfect tense is used to describe an ongoing past action, a repeated
(habitual) past action or a long-standing situation.

Hablaba con mi vecino cuando....	**I was talking** with my neighbor when....
Comíamos a las dos todos los sábados.	**We used to/would eat** at two every Saturday.
Vivíamos en San Miguel.	**We were living** in San Miguel.

Siempre comíamos juntas
en la cafetería.

140

9 De vacaciones

Verónica y toda su familia estaban de vacaciones la semana pasada. Cambia los verbos en itálica de las siguientes oraciones al tiempo imperfecto para decir qué hacían todos en su familia durante la semana.

 Visitamos el parque de atracciones todos los días.
Visitábamos el parque de atracciones todos los días.

1. *Se levantan* a las siete todos los días para ir al parque.
2. El papá de Verónica *lee* el periódico en el parque todas las mañanas.
3. Dos hermanos de Verónica *montan* en la montaña rusa todos los días.
4. El hermano de Verónica *trabaja* en el parque.
5. La mamá de Verónica *grita* cuando *monta* en las atracciones.
6. La hermanita de Verónica *molesta* a una niña cuando todos *miran* el desfile.
7. Verónica y su hermana *comen* golosinas todas las noches.
8. *Duermen* en un hotel que *está* cerca del parque.
9. Verónica *se acuesta* todas las noches a las once.
10. *Se divierten* mucho todos los días.

Mi hermana y yo andábamos por el parque de atracciones.

10 Cuando tenía seis años

Completa el siguiente párrafo con las formas apropiadas del imperfecto de los verbos indicados para decir qué hacían Luisa y su hermano en el parque de atracciones cuando ella tenía seis años.

Mi hermano y yo siempre 1. *(visitar)* el parque de atracciones los fines de semana cuando yo 2. *(tener)* seis años. Nosotros 3. *(caminar)* por el parque y 4. *(hablar)* de nuestras vidas. Nosotros 5. *(parar)* muchas veces para comer algo y para tomar unos refrescos. Me parece que él siempre 6. *(comer)* en menos de cinco minutos. Yo 7. *(tardar)* más tiempo. Cuando nosotros 8. *(terminar)*, 9. *(montar)* en la montaña rusa varias veces y, luego, 10. *(salir)* para ir a casa. Mis padres también 11. *(hacer)* lo mismo a los seis años, pero ellos no 12. *(poder)* comer en el parque porque sus padres siempre los 13. *(esperar)* para comer en casa.

Cuando tenía seis años mi hermano y yo hacíamos muchas cosas juntos.

MÁS DE 50 ATRACCIONES
Adentro podrás pagar por las atracciones con grandes descuentos

9
1. Se levantaban....
2. ...leía....
3. ...montaban....
4. ...trabajaba....
5. ...gritaba...montaba....
6. ...molestaba...miraban....
7. ...comían....
8. Dormían...estaba....
9. ...se acostaba....
10. Se divertían....

10
1. visitábamos
2. tenía
3. caminábamos
4. hablábamos
5. parábamos
6. comía
7. tardaba
8. terminábamos
9. montábamos
10. salíamos
11. hacían
12. podían
13. esperaban

Activities

Cooperative Learning. Ask small groups of students to further reflect upon their lives when they were six, seven, eight, etc., years old: *¿Qué música escuchaban?; ¿Qué programas de televisión miraban?; ¿Qué comidas les gustaban?;* etc. Each group should then present a summary to the class.

Expansion. Discuss the realia that accompanies activity 10. Then ask students what they think it means.

Multiple Intelligences (linguistic/interpersonal). Give students the assignment of interviewing a favorite relative about his or her life at the age of ten. The student should then write a composition describing the relative and telling about the person's life in the past.

NATIONAL STANDARDS
C1.2, C4.1

Activity 11

Answers

11 1. ...escribía....
2. ...compraba....
3. ...corrían....
4. ...visitaba....
5. ...miraba....
6. ...comía....
7. ...leían....
8. ...llamaba....

12 Answers will vary.

Notes

Remind students that *don* and *doña* are titles of respect that are used with a first name to show respect toward a man or woman due to age or social position.

Activities

Multiple Intelligences (linguistic/spatial). Write a simplified version of a well-known fairy tale, leaving spaces for students to write the verbs in the imperfect. Then students must illustrate the fairy tale and write a short summary of the tale, using the imperfect tense.

Students with Special Needs. Model a second sentence for activity 11.

11 Luisa y su familia

Luisa y su familia vivían en otra ciudad antes de vivir en San Salvador. Trabajando en parejas, alterna con tu compañero/a de clase para decir lo que las siguientes personas hacían cuando vivían en la otra ciudad, según las indicaciones.

> Luisa/salir a comer golosinas con sus amigas
> Luisa salía a comer golosinas con sus amigas.

1. el hermano de Luisa/escribir a sus parientes en San Salvador
2. la abuela/comprar chocolates en la dulcería
3. los tíos/correr por el parque de atracciones
4. el abuelo/visitar los museos de historia
5. la tía Amalia/mirar las vitrinas de los almacenes nuevos
6. doña Clara/comer los viernes en un restaurante mexicano
7. los padres de Luisa/leer el periódico todos los días
8. don Diego/llamar a sus amigos todos los sábados

12 ¿Qué recuerdas?

Contesta las siguientes preguntas para decir qué recuerdas de cuando tenías seis años, usando el imperfecto.

1. ¿Te gustaba molestar a otras personas? ¿A quién? ¿Cuándo?
2. ¿Qué hacías con tu familia los domingos?
3. ¿A qué jugabas con tus amigos/as?
4. ¿A qué hora comía tu familia los domingos?
5. ¿A qué hora tenías que acostarte?
6. ¿Dónde vivías cuando tenías seis años?
7. ¿Qué hacías durante el verano a los seis años?
8. ¿A qué horas podías ver televisión?

¿Qué hacías con tu familia los domingos?

Una visita al jardín zoológico

el hipopótamo
el flamenco
la iguana
el mono
el elefante
la jirafa
el tigre
el zoológico
el camello
el león
la tortuga
la cebra
la pantera
el gorila

Bienvenidos al zoológico.

Una visita al jardín zoológico

 Quiz/Activity 4

 Activities 28-29

 Activities 7-8

 Quiz/Activity 3

GUÍA: Hola, amigos y amigas. **Bienvenidos°** al **zoológico.** Soy Josefina Toro Pombo y voy a ser su **guía** hoy. Este zoológico tiene **más de°** tres mil **animales.** ¿Pueden imaginarse? Todos los animales que Uds. van a ver hoy aquí son **salvajes.°** Muchos de ellos son **feroces,°** y casi todos vienen de las **selvas°** del **África** o de las **Américas.** Por ejemplo, los **leones** son **africanos** y las **iguanas** son americanas, de El Salvador. Bueno, tengan listas sus **cámaras** y diviértanse en su **visita.** ¿Alguna pregunta?

SEÑOR: Perdón, señorita, ¿no íbamos a ver la película sobre el zoológico primero? Cuando entré al zoológico, yo vi que algunas personas iban a ver una película.

GUÍA: Sí, señor. Vamos a ver una película primero.

Bienvenidos *Welcome* **más de** *more than* **salvajes** *wild* **feroces** *fierce, ferocious* **selvas** *jungles*

EL PARAISO DE LOS ANIMALES EN LIBERTAD

Este jaguar salvaje está cansado.

Capítulo 4   **143**

Notes

Remind students that Spanish speakers commonly use two last names. In the case of *Josefina Toro Pombo, Toro* is her father's first last name while *Pombo* is her mother's first last name.

In addition to *tomar fotos,* students may hear *sacar fotos* or *fotografiar.*

Activities

Critical Thinking. Remind students that they recently studied commands and ask them to identify the two *Uds.* commands found in the dialog on page 143. Then ask them to think of other commands that would be given by a tour guide.

Multiple Intelligences (linguistic). Ask students what the realia at the bottom of page 143 means. Then ask if students have ever been to a park or zoo where animals run free.

Prereading Strategy. Using transparencies 28 and 29, introduce the vocabulary used in this dialog. Then instruct students to cover up the dialog with one hand and look at the illustration. Ask them to imagine where the conversation takes place and what the people are saying to one another. Finally, have students look through the dialog quickly to find cognates and other words or expressions they already know.

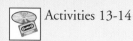

Activities 13-14

Answers

13 1. Tiene más de tres mil animales.

2. Hay camellos, cebras, elefantes, flamencos, gorilas, hipopótamos, iguanas, jirafas, leones, monos, panteras, tigres y tortugas.

3. Son salvajes y algunos son feroces.

4. Casi todos vienen de la América del Sur, de la América del Norte, de la América Central o de las selvas del África.

5. Iban a ver la película sobre el zoológico.

14 Answers will vary.

Notes

Point out that *estadounidense* is more specific than *norteamericano* because North America is actually comprised of Canada, the United States and Mexico.

Additional nouns/adjectives of nationalities are presented on page 151.

Activities

Expansion. Additional questions (*¿Qué comprendiste?*): *¿Cómo se llama la guía?; ¿De dónde son las iguanas?; ¿Qué deben tener listas las personas?; ¿Quiénes son bienvenidos?; ¿De dónde son los elefantes de este zoológico?; ¿Tiene alguien alguna pregunta? ¿Quién?; ¿Qué van a ver primero las personas que están de visita en el zoológico?*

NATIONAL STANDARDS
C1.2, C3.2, C4.1, C4.2

13 **¿Qué comprendiste?**

1. ¿Cuántos animales tiene el zoológico?
2. ¿Qué animales hay en el zoológico?
3. ¿Cómo son los animales?
4. ¿De dónde vienen casi todos los animales?
5. ¿Qué iban a ver algunas personas?

Algo más

¿Qué es América?

In the Spanish-speaking world, the word *América* refers to *la América del Sur, la América Central* and *la América del Norte*. Additionally, the adjective *americano,-a* refers to anyone from any part of *América*. For this reason, when traveling outside the United States, demonstrate good diplomacy and a knowledge of this cultural and linguistic difference by referring to yourself as a *norteamericano,-a* or *estadounidense*.

Había una cebra en el zoológico.

14 **Charlando**

1. ¿Te gustan los zoológicos? Explica.
2. ¿Cuándo fue la última vez que fuiste a un zoológico?
3. ¿Qué animales había? ¿Eran africanos?
4. ¿Conoces a alguna persona con un apellido de animal? ¿Cómo se llama?

Los rinocerontes son del África.

Me gustaba el tigre.

Las jirafas comían mucho.

144   Lección 7

Algo
más

¿Los nombres de animales o de personas?

Do you know any Birds? How about people who are named Wolf? In Spanish-speaking countries, it is fairly common to meet people with names that are the same as the names of animals. Do not be surprised, for example, if one day you are introduced to Mr. and Mrs. Lion *(el señor* and *la señora León),* or to their friend Miss Bull *(la señorita Toro),* whose first name is *Paloma* (Dove). For some people the use of an animal's name to refer to a person may seem odd. However, in many cultures you will find that animal names for people are quite common and very acceptable.

¿Cuál de ustedes es la señorita León?

Más animales

el águila	eagle
el avestruz	ostrich
la ballena	whale
el cocodrilo	crocodile
el delfín	dolphin
la foca	seal
el loro	parrot
el rinoceronte	rhinoceros
el tiburón	shark
el venado	deer

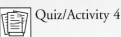

Quiz/Activity 4

Answers

15 1. Es una pantera.
2. Es una jirafa.
3. Es un león.
4. Es un elefante.
5. Es un tigre.
6. Es una iguana.

Activities

Critical Thinking. As an interesting means of dealing with cultural pluralism, discuss the meanings and origins of several names: Sitting Bull (Native American), Johnson (a Scandinavian name that originally meant "son of John"), Du Pont (a French name that originally meant "of the bridge"), Álvar Núñez Cabeza de Vaca (a Spanish name that means "cow's head").

Expansion. Additional questions *(Charlando): ¿Qué animales africanos conoces?; ¿Qué animales americanos conoces?; ¿Cuál es tu animal salvaje favorito?; ¿Te gustaría visitar la selva? ¿Por qué?; ¿Te gusta tomar fotos de animales?; ¿Crees que los zoológicos son lugares buenos o malos para los animales?*

15 En el jardín zoológico

Indentifica los animales que ves en estas ilustraciones.

  Es un camello.

1.

2.

3.

4.

5.

6.

NATIONAL STANDARDS
C1.2, C3.2, C4.1

Answers

16 Answers will vary according to individual research.

Notes

Point out that the students have already learned the imperfect endings for the verb *ver*. It is irregular only because it maintains the vowel *e*.

The *vosotros/as* verb endings are included for passive recognition. If you have decided to make these forms active, adapt the provided activities as required.

Activities

Multiple Intelligences (interpersonal/linguistic). Ask students to recall a favorite teacher from elementary school. Students should then write a composition describing both themselves and the instructor in the imperfect tense.

¿Es el elefante un carnívoro?

CONEXIONES
16 Cruzando fronteras

Estudia más sobre los animales salvajes que acabas de aprender. Di si son animales herbívoros o carnívoros; mamíferos *(mammals)* u ovíparos *(egg-laying animals)*; dónde viven comúnmente *(usually)*, qué comen y cualquier otra información que te interese. Busca información sobre estos animales en la biblioteca o en la Internet, si es necesario.

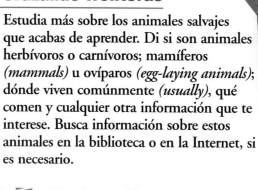

¿Es la tortuga un mamífero?

IDIOMA

El imperfecto de los verbos *ser, ir* y *ver*

There are only three irregular verbs in the imperfect tense in Spanish: *ser, ir* and *ver*.

ser		ir		ver	
era	éramos	iba	íbamos	veía	veíamos
eras	erais	ibas	ibais	veías	veíais
era	eran	iba	iban	veía	veían

Algo más

Más sobre los usos del imperfecto

In addition to describing an ongoing past action, a repeated (habitual) past action or a long-standing situation, the imperfect tense may be used in the following situations:

- to refer to a physical, mental or emotional characteristic or condition in the past

  Era alto y muy delgado. — **He was** tall and very thin.
  Tenían miedo a las serpientes. — **They were** afraid of snakes.

- to describe or provide background information about the past

  Eran las ocho de la mañana. — It was 8:00 a.m.
  Yo tenía diez años. — I was ten years old.
  Hacía mucho frío. — It was very cold.
  Había muchos animales. — There were many animals.

- to indicate past intentions

  Iba a ir al zoológico ayer. — **I was going to go** to the zoo yesterday.
  Queríamos ver la película sobre el zoológico. — **We wanted to see** the movie about the zoo.

17 En el parque con tu familia

Imagina que tú y tu familia visitaban un parque de atracciones ayer. Completa las siguientes oraciones con la forma apropiada del imperfecto de los verbos entre paréntesis para describir la visita.

Había muchos carros antiguos en la exhibición.

Las atracciones *(ser)* fascinantes.
Las atracciones eran fascinantes.

1. El parque *(ser)* maravilloso.
2. Yo *(ir)* a comprar una serpiente de plástico pero no tenía dinero.
3. Mi hermano y yo *(ver)* una exhibición de carros antiguos por la tarde.
4. Mi hermana menor *(ser)* la muchacha más simpática de todo el parque.
5. Mis hermanas *(ir)* sólo para montar en la montaña rusa.
6. Mucha gente *(ver)* los fuegos artificiales.
7. Nosotros *(ir)* a montar en globo pero tuvimos miedo.
8. Tú *(ver)* un desfile por más de una hora.
9. Cuando salíamos del parque *(ser)* las once de la noche.
10. Uds. *(ser)* los chicos más chistosos del parque.

18 Los animales salvajes

Imagina que el fin de semana pasado fuiste al jardín zoológico. Describe los animales que viste, tomando elementos de cada columna y haciendo los cambios necesarios.

La pantera era feroz.

A	B	C
la pantera		grande
los monos		feroz
los gorilas		lento y viejo
la jirafa		largo
la tortuga	era	chistoso
el tigre	eran	alto
los flamencos		rápido y negro
los elefantes		rosado y delgado
los hipopótamos		rápido
la cebra		gordo y lento
las serpientes		rápido y chistoso

Africam safari

¿Crees que este mono es mono?

Los monos
You might find it interesting to know that the word *mono* is used in Colombia to refer to blond people and in Mexico to refer to a good-looking person. In Spain the word *mono* is equivalent to "cute." To say "blond" in El Salvador, use the word *chele* for a man or *chela* for a woman.

147

Answers

17 1. era
2. iba
3. veíamos
4. era
5. iban
6. veía
7. íbamos
8. veías
9. eran
10. eran

18 Answers will vary.

Activities

Multiple Intelligences (bodily-kinesthetic). Divide the class into two groups. A person from each group imitates an animal found in the zoo. A person from the other team guesses the animal and says a sentence describing a physical attribute of the animal (e.g., *Es una jirafa; las jirafas tienen el cuello muy largo*).

NATIONAL STANDARDS
C1.2, C3.2, C4.1

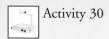 Activity 30

Answers

19 1. ¿...era...?/Era a las diez y
   media.

2. ¿...era...?/Era a las ocho.

3. ¿...era...?/Era a las nueve.

4. ¿...era...?/Era a la una y
   media.

5. ¿...eran...?/Eran a las once
   y media y a las cuatro.

6. ¿...era...?/Era al mediodía
   (a las doce).

7. ¿...eran...?/Eran a las once,
   a las tres y a las cuatro y
   media.

8. ¿...era...?/Era a las tres y
   media.

Activities

Critical Listening. Make several correct and incorrect statements about the schedule for several events at the Zoofari Zoo as students look at the realia on page 148. Students should raise their hands if the times you mention correspond to the events listed.

Prereading Strategy. Encourage students to find cognates and other words they are able to recognize and understand in the realia that accompany activity 19. Then ask students some questions to prepare them for what they will be reading: Have they ever been to a zoo? Which one?; What animals did they see at the zoo?; What were the exhibits like?

19 Zoofari

 Mira el siguiente horario del zoológico Zoofari. Luego, trabajando en parejas, alterna con tu compañero/a de clase en preguntar y contestar la hora en que ocurrían diferentes actividades ayer en el zoológico.

los fuegos artificiales
A: ¿A qué hora ayer eran los fuegos artificiales?
B: Eran a las siete.

Zoológico Zoofari
Horario de eventos y exhibiciones

9:00	Película: Bienvenidos a Zoofari
9:30	Exhibición: Las serpientes del desierto
10:30	Exhibición: Los monos de la América Central
11:00	Película: Los maravillosos animales de la América del Norte
11:30	Exhibición: Los animales salvajes africanos
12:00	Visita: El mundo de los hipopótamos
1:30	El desfile de la selva
2:30	Exhibición: Las serpientes del desierto
3:00	Película: Los animales salvajes de la América Central
3:30	Exhibición: Gatos grandes, los tigres
4:00	Exhibición: Los animales salvajes africanos
4:30	Película: Los fascinantes animales de la América del Sur
5:30	Exhibición: Las serpientes del desierto
7:00	Fuegos artificiales
8:00	Gran desfile

1. la exhibición de los monos de la América Central
2. el gran desfile
3. la película sobre el zoológico
4. el desfile de la selva
5. las exhibiciones de animales salvajes africanos
6. la visita al mundo de los hipopótamos
7. las películas sobre los animales de las Américas
8. la exhibición de los tigres

La exhibición de las serpientes era fascinante.

20 ¿Cuántos años tenían?

Las siguientes personas fueron al zoológico por última vez el año pasado. Di cuántos años tenían cuando fueron al zoológico el año pasado, según la edad que tienen hoy.

 Manuela tiene 20 años.
Manuela tenía 19 años el año pasado.

1. Doña Esperanza tiene 55 años.
2. Luisa y Francisco tienen 18 años.
3. La señorita León tiene 25 años.
4. Víctor tiene 14 años.

5. Tú tienes 17 años.
6. Pedro y yo tenemos 19 años.
7. Uds. tienen 21 años.
8. Yo tengo....

21 Tus animales favoritos

Las siguientes personas fueron contigo al zoológico la semana pasada para ver sus animales favoritos. Di qué animales iban a ver, según las ilustraciones.

 tú
Tú ibas a ver los gorilas.

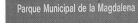

Parque Municipal de la Magdalena

LEON
Panthera Leo

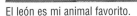

Excmo. AYUNTAMIENTO DE SANTANDER

El león es mi animal favorito.

1. nosotros

2. Rosa y Sergio

3. Claudia

4. Pedro y Pablo

5. Uds.

6. Jorge

7. Marcela y Natalia

8. yo

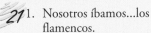

Answers

20 1. ...tenía 54....
2. ...tenían 17....
3. ...tenía 24....
4. ...tenía 13....
5. ...tenías 16....
6. ...teníamos 18....
7. ...tenían 20....
8. ...tenía....

21 1. Nosotros íbamos...los flamencos.
2. Rosa y Sergio iban...las jirafas.
3. Claudia iba...los tigres.
4. Pedro y Pablo iban...los hipopótamos.
5. Uds. iban...las tortugas.
6. Jorge iba...los leones.
7. Marcela y Natalia iban...las cebras.
8. Yo iba...los monos.

Activities

Spanish for Spanish Speakers.
Have students read the realia that accompanies activity 19. Then ask them questions to determine how much they understood: *¿Cómo se llama el zoo?; ¿Qué tipos de animales tienen en el zoo?; ¿De dónde son los animales?*

Students with Special Needs.
Read through the realia that accompanies activity 19 as a class activity and answer questions to be certain all students understand the content before attempting the activity.

NATIONAL STANDARDS
C1.2, C4.1

Activity 22

 Activity 12

Answers

22 1. Ellos veían los flamencos más de....
2. Yo veía más de....
3. Los niños comían más de....
4. Nosotros veíamos más de....
5. Uds. iban a ver los camellos más de....
6. El guía hablaba por más de....
7. Tú hacías más de....
8. Mi amiga veía más de....
9. Tú comías más de....

Activities

Multiple Intelligences (linguistic/intrapersonal/interpersonal). As a follow-up to activity 23 on page 151, ask pairs of students to compare their lives as children with their lives now. Examples should then be shared with the class.

Spanish for Spanish Speakers. Have students write a short composition describing a visit to the zoo. The zoo trip can be imaginary or real, past or future. The composition should discuss what students saw or would like to see and what activities the individuals did or would like to do during the trip.

National Standards C1.2, C4.1

Estrategia

Para hablar mejor: *using the expression* más de

To express "more than" before a number in Spanish, use the expression *más de*.

¿Había **más de** cien monos?
Ellos tenían **más de** veinte años.

Were there **more than** one hundred monkeys?
They were **more than** twenty years old.

Había más de veinte globos.

22 ¿Qué hacían?

 Haz oraciones completas en el imperfecto para decir lo que las siguientes personas hacían durante su visita al zoológico. Usa las indicaciones que se dan y la expresión *más de*.

mi amigo/tomar fotos de/veinte animales
Mi amigo tomaba fotos de más de veinte animales.

1. ellos/ver los flamencos/una vez
2. yo/ver/cinco elefantes
3. los niños/comer/diez golosinas
4. nosotros/ver/dos tigres
5. Uds./ir a ver los camellos/cinco veces
6. el guía/hablar por/dos horas
7. tú/hacer/cinco preguntas
8. mi amiga/ver/cien serpientes de plástico
9. tú/comer/dos helados

150   Lección 7

23 **¿Qué hacías cuando eras pequeño/a?**

Haz una lista de por lo menos ocho cosas que tú hacías cuando eras pequeño/a. Luego, trabajando en parejas, lean el uno al otro lo que escribieron y hagan una lista de las actividades que los dos tienen en común en sus listas. Por último, da un reporte de estas actividades a otra pareja de estudiantes.

A: Cuando era pequeño/a montaba en la montaña rusa con mis hermanos y comía muchos dulces.

B: Cuando era pequeño/a comía muchos dulces de chocolate y montaba en bicicleta con mis amigos del barrio.

A/B: Cuando *A/B* y yo éramos pequeños/as comíamos muchos dulces.

Cuando era pequeño/a:
1. Comía muchos dulces de chocolate.
2. Montaba en bicicleta con mis amigos del barrio.

Cuando era pequeño/a:
1. Montaba en la montaña rusa con mis hermanos.
2. Comía muchos dulces.

Algo más

Las nacionalidades

	Soy de...	Soy...
la	Argentina	argentino,-a
	Bolivia	boliviano,-a
	Colombia	colombiano,-a
	Costa Rica	costarricense
	Cuba	cubano,-a
	Chile	chileno,-a
el	Ecuador	ecuatoriano,-a
	El Salvador	salvadoreño,-a
	España	español/española
los	Estados Unidos	estadounidense
	Guatemala	guatemalteco,-a
	Honduras	hondureño,-a
	México	mexicano,-a
	Nicaragua	nicaragüense
	Panamá	panameño,-a
el	Paraguay	paraguayo,-a
el	Perú	peruano,-a
	Puerto Rico	puertorriqueño,-a
la	República Dominicana	dominicano,-a
el	Uruguay	uruguayo,-a
	Venezuela	venezolano,-a

Somos salvadoreños.

Note: Singular masculine adjectives that end in *-o* have a feminine form that ends in *-a,* and most singular adjectives that end with an *-e* or with a consonant have only one singular form. However, for masculine adjectives of nationality that end with a consonant, add *-a* to make the feminine form: *español → española.*

Answers

23 Creative self-expression.

Notes

Point out the dieresis *(diéresis)* on the word *nicaragüense.* This linguistic point is explained for students in *Somos así ¡YA!* You may wish to note for interested students that for the letter combinations *gue* and *gui,* the *u* is never pronounced. The two dots, or dieresis, over the *u* indicate that the letter should be pronounced, as happens here with *nicaragüense.*

Many Uruguayans refer to themselves as *orientales.*

Activities

Connections. Give students a map of the Americas and have them fill in the countries where Spanish is spoken and the nationality of the people who live there.

Critical Thinking. Using a map (see the front of *Somos así LISTOS* or the transparency maps that accompany *Somos así EN SUS MARCAS),* practice the adjectives of nationality for the Spanish-speaking parts of the world. Say the following while pointing to one of the countries on the map: *Si* (name of person/people) *es de aquí, ¿qué es?;* students should answer with *Es* (nationality). You may choose to have various students direct the class to add variety.

Multiple Intelligences (intrapersonal/linguistic). Ask students to bring in some photographs that depict things they did or what they looked like when they were little. Then prepare a list of similarities and differences between then and now.

NATIONAL STANDARDS
C1.2, C1.3, C3.2, C4.1, C5.1

Answers

24
1. B
2. F
3. E
4. H
5. J
6. G
7. I
8. A
9. C
10. D

25 Answers will vary. Students in each group should speak Spanish and work cooperatively to prepare a single list of names and nationalities. Leaders of groups who have completed the activity successfully will be able to identify several students by name and nationality.

Activities

Expansion. Ask students if they can guess the nationality of people from Equatorial Guinea: *guineano,-a.*

Multiple Intelligences (bodily-kinesthetic/spatial). For additional writing practice, and in order to encourage visual learners with artistic skills, have students prepare maps of the Spanish-speaking world in Spanish, adding any details they wish to borrow from the color maps at the beginning of the textbook. Where students write the name of the country, have them add in parentheses the adjective of nationality that identifies someone from that country.

TPR. Offer appropriate Total Physical Response (TPR) support, where possible: Have students point to the places they say or hear, using the maps at the front of the book or a classroom wall map, if one is available.

LAS PALMERAS
COMIDA SALVADOREÑA
LATINA
MARISCOS Y POLLO

24 Las nacionalidades

Di de qué país eran algunas personas que te presentaron unos amigos la semana pasada, conectando lógicamente las oraciones de la columna B con las oraciones de la columna A.

Juan era colombiano.

Rubí era ecuatoriana.

A
1. Pilar y Raquel eran de Panamá.
2. Mercedes era de Guatemala.
3. Los amigos de Bernardo eran de Nicaragua.
4. La señorita Trujillo era de Puerto Rico.
5. La señora Paloma era de España.
6. Sara era del Perú.
7. Los señores Toro eran de España también.
8. Todos éramos de los Estados Unidos.
9. Marcos y Pablo eran de la República Dominicana.
10. Quique era de Chile.

B
A. Éramos estadounidenses.
B. Eran panameñas.
C. Eran dominicanos.
D. Era chileno.
E. Eran nicaragüenses.
F. Era guatemalteca.
G. Era peruana.
H. Era puertorriqueña.
I. Eran españoles.
J. Era española.

25 Tu nombre y tu nacionalidad

Trabajando en grupos pequeños, cada miembro del grupo debe ir a preguntar el nombre y la nacionalidad de otros seis estudiantes. (Todos deben contestar con una de las nacionalidades de cualquiera de los países de habla hispana.) Luego, regresa a tu grupo y comparte *(share)* la información con tus compañeros/as. Un miembro del grupo debe preparar un resumen *(summary)* de toda la información. Por último, otro miembro del grupo debe presentar la información a la clase, señalando a las personas y diciendo su nacionalidad.

A: ¿Cómo te llamas?
B: Me llamo Alicia.
A: ¿Cuál es tu nacionalidad?
B: Soy salvadoreña.

Somos dominicanos.

26 Muchas nacionalidades

Trabajando en parejas, alterna con tu compañero/a de clase en preguntar y en contestar de dónde eran las siguientes personas que Uds. conocieron *(met)* en la visita al zoológico. Sigue el modelo.

el señor Barrera/Lima
A: ¿De dónde era el señor Barrera?
B: Era del Perú.
A: Ah, ¿sí? No sabía que era peruano.
B: Claro. Es de Lima.

1. el señor y la señora Villegas/La Paz
2. las amigas de Esteban/Quito
3. Augusto/Tegucigalpa
4. don Raúl/Santa Fe de Bogotá
5. Luisa y Carlota/Buenos Aires
6. la señora Pastrana/La Habana
7. Eva y su hermana/Madrid
8. Antonio/Managua
9. Olman y su hermana/San José
10. Timoteo y su prima/Caracas

Repaso *rápido*

		albergue juvenil
↑		parque de atracciones
↑		Venta del Batán
↑		zoológico
teleférico		→

¿Dónde está el zoológico?

Ser vs. *estar*

You already have learned that *ser* and *estar* are each used for very different situations. How much of the following do you recall?

- *Ser* may express origin.
  Soy de El Salvador. — **I am** from El Salvador.
  Soy salvadoreño. — **I am** Salvadoran.

- Sometimes *ser* expresses a characteristic that distinguishes people or objects from one another.
  *El zoológico **era** fascinante.* — The zoo **was** fascinating.
  *¡Qué exigente **eres**!* — How demanding **you are**!

- *Estar* is used to express a temporary condition.
  ***Estamos** muy bien.* — **We are** very well.
  *¡Qué gordo **estaba** el elefante!* — How fat the elephant **was**!

- *Estar* also may refer to location.
  *¿Dónde **está** el zoológico?* — Where **is** the zoo?

Although *estar* generally is used to express location, note this exception: *Ser* can refer to the location of an event, in which case it is the equivalent of **to take place.**
*¿Dónde **son** los fuegos artificiales?* — Where do the fireworks **take place**?

Estamos perdidas.

¿Dónde son los fuegos artificiales?

27 ¿Ser o estar?

Completa las siguientes oraciones con la forma apropiada del presente o del imperfecto de *ser* o *estar*, según las situaciones.

 El zoológico de San Diego <u>es</u> uno de los zoológicos estadounidenses más grandes.
Cuando fuimos al jardín zoológico el día <u>estaba</u> nublado.

1. David <u>(1)</u> muy chistoso hoy. Ayer estaba muy triste.
2. Este zoológico <u>(2)</u> muy grande. Tiene más de tres mil animales.
3. ¡Las montañas que vimos en la América Central <u>(3)</u> fascinantes!
4. El hipopótamo <u>(4)</u> un animal muy gordo. No conozco ninguno delgado.
5. Las golosinas no <u>(5)</u> muy buenas para tu cuerpo. No debes comerlas.
6. Mi amiga panameña <u>(6)</u> en San Salvador de vacaciones el mes pasado cuando la llamé.
7. Las panteras americanas <u>(7)</u> salvajes y muy feroces. Nadie tiene una en su casa.
8. ¡La serpiente <u>(8)</u> sobre mi cámara cuando trataba de tomar una foto! ¡Qué miedo!
9. El desfile <u>(9)</u> ayer a las dos de la tarde en el parque.
10. ¿<u>(10)</u> enfermas las tortugas ecuatorianas anteayer?

El león era muy grande.

El gorila gritaba cuando estaba enojado.

28 Eras veterinario/a

 Imagina que eras veterinario/a y fuiste a un zoológico en El Salvador para hacer un estudio. Completa las observaciones que hiciste durante tu visita, usando las indicaciones que se dan. Sigue el modelo.

monos/hondureño/contento/de verme
Los monos hondureños estaban contentos de verme.

1. iguanas/mexicano/muy chistoso
2. camellos/nervioso/de ver a tanta gente
3. elefantes/africano/cansado/por no dormir bien
4. leones/africano/salvaje
5. serpientes/americano/enfermo/por comer plástico
6. panteras/negro/feroz
7. zoológico/salvadoreño/maravilloso

CLINICA VETERINARIA
BOUTIQUE ANIMAL
COLLOTO

CONSULTAS
VACUNACIONES
INSEMINACION
ARTIFICIAL
ANALISIS

"Toda la atención profesional para tus pequeños amigos"

PECES, PAJAROS
PERROS, GATOS
TORTUGAS
ALIMENTACION
COMPLEMENTOS
PELUQUERIA

C/. Camino Real, Esquina José Cima - COLLOTO - OVIEDO. Telf. 598 50 42

Cuando lo vi, el león estaba muy cansado.

Autoevaluación. Como repaso y autoevaluación, responde lo siguiente:

1. Name three different things in Spanish that you might see at an amusement park.
2. Imagine you went to an amusement park yesterday. Describe how the day was and what you did.
3. Name five animals in Spanish that you would expect to see at the zoo.
4. Describe something you did, where you went and what you saw when you were six years old.
5. How would you say there were more than one hundred animals in the zoo?
6. Give the nationality of a person from the following countries: El Salvador, México, Puerto Rico, España, Estados Unidos.
7. What do you know about El Salvador?

Activities

Cooperative Learning. As an alternative activity, have students work in small groups preparing their own surveys on topics of their choosing. Each student should participate in one or more aspects of the survey. Have students report their findings to the class.

Expansion. Dictate a letter of the alphabet to the class. Give students three minutes to write any words they can think of in Spanish that begin with that letter. After calling time, ask students to read their lists aloud. The student with the longest list of correct words wins.

Pronunciation. To ensure proper pronunciation, model each word or expression and have students repeat after you.

Students with Special Needs. Select several words and phrases for individual students to use orally in sentences.

¡La práctica hace al maestro!

Estoy preocupado.

A Comunicación

This activity has three parts. *Parte A:* Working in pairs, each student conducts a survey on the current emotional or physical condition of four different students in the class and then returns to his or her partner to compile the results. *Parte B:* One member of each pair reports the information to the class, while a student (or the teacher) makes a graph *(gráfica)* of the results on the chalkboard for the entire class. *Parte C:* Students then take turns asking one another questions in Spanish about the information on the graph.

Parte A:
A: ¿Cómo estás?
B: Estoy apurado/a.

Parte B:
En nuestra encuesta, tres estudiantes estaban contentos, uno estaba triste, tres estaban cansados y uno estaba apurado.

	contentos	apurados	cansados	enfermos	nerviosos	tristes
Pareja 1	III	I	III			I
Pareja 2	III	II	I	I		I
Pareja 3	II	III			II	I
Pareja 4	II	I	I	I		II
TOTAL	**10**	**7**	**5**	**2**	**3**	**5**

Parte C:
A: ¿Cuántos estudiantes en la clase estaban apurados?
B: Siete estudiantes estaban apurados.

B Conexión con la tecnología

Utilize a spreadsheet program to chart the results of the classroom survey in the form of a bar graph or a pie chart. Make it more interesting by including different colors and by importing graphics and clip art.

VOCABULARIO

Nacionalidades
africano,-a
argentino,-a
boliviano,-a
chileno,-a
colombiano,-a
costarricense
cubano,-a
dominicano,-a
ecuatoriano,-a
español, española
estadounidense
guatemalteco,-a
hondureño,-a
nicaragüense
panameño,-a
paraguayo,-a
peruano,-a
puertorriqueño,-a
salvadoreño,-a
uruguayo,-a
venezolano,-a

En el parque de atracciones
la atracción
el desfile
los fuegos artificiales
el globo
la golosina
la montaña rusa

En el zoológico
el animal
el camello
la cebra
el elefante
el flamenco
el gorila
el guía, la guía
el hipopótamo

la iguana
el (jardín) zoológico
la jirafa
el león
el mono
la pantera
la selva
la serpiente
el tigre
la tortuga

Para describir
antiguo,-a
chistoso,-a
fascinante
feroz
maravilloso,-a
salvaje

Verbos
gritar
había
imaginar(se)
molestar

Expresiones y otras palabras
el África
la América (Central/del
   Norte/del Sur)
bienvenido,-a
la cámara
como
más de
la montaña
el plástico
la visita

Soy salvadoreña.

¡La iguana es chistosa!

Content reviewed in *Lección 8*
- preterite tense
- describing
- diminutives
- showing possession

Notes

The word *Tegucigalpa* means **silver city** *(ciudad de plata)*.

Activities

Connections. Show students where Honduras is located using the maps in the front of the book or the transparencies from *Somos así LISTOS.*

Critical Listening. Play the audiocassette/audio compact disc recording of the dialog. Instruct students to cover the words as they listen to the conversation. Then ask several individuals to tell where the conversation takes place and what the people are talking about.

Prereading Strategy. Use transparencies 31 and 32 to introduce students to the vocabulary used in the dialog. Instruct students to cover up the dialog with one hand and look at the illustration and have them imagine where the conversation takes place and what the people are saying to one another. Finally, ask students to look through the dialog quickly to find cognates and other words or expressions they already know.

Lección 8

El Gran Circo de las Estrellas

DAVID: **Durante°** las vacaciones mi familia y yo fuimos a un **circo** grande y buenísimo que estaba en Tegucigalpa.

LUISA: ¿A cuál?

DAVID: Era el **Gran°** Circo de las **Estrellas.°** Había **acróbatas** con mucha **destreza,°** una **banda** de música y **osos** blancos y negros muy grandes.

LUISA: ¡Qué divertido!

DAVID: Los osos blancos parecían como **ositos de peluche.°**

LUISA: ¡Qué lindos! Y, ¿qué fue lo más **emocionante?°**

DAVID: Lo más emocionante fue cuando yo toqué a los leones que estaban en la **jaula.** Todo el mundo gritaba cuando ellos **rugían.**

LUISA: **¡Pobre°** muchacho! **¡Qué mentira tan°** grande! Nunca tocaste a los leones. ¡Ja, ja, ja!

Durante *during* **Gran** *great* **Estrellas** *Stars* **destreza** *skill, expertise* **ositos de peluche** *little teddy bears* **emocionante** *exciting* **Pobre** *Poor* **¡Qué (mentira) tan (grande)!** *What a (big lie)!*

1 ¿Qué comprendiste?

1. ¿Qué lugar visitaron David y su familia durante las vacaciones?
2. ¿Cómo era el lugar?
3. ¿Qué había allí?
4. ¿Quiénes tenían mucha destreza?
5. ¿Qué fue lo más emocionante?
6. ¿Cuándo gritaba todo el mundo?
7. ¿Piensa Luisa que David dice la verdad?

2 Charlando

1. ¿Te gusta ir al circo? Explica.
2. ¿Fuiste a algún circo en tus últimas vacaciones? ¿Cómo era?
3. ¿Qué viste allí? ¿Qué fue lo más emocionante?
4. ¿Te gusta hacer fila en una taquilla para comprar boletos? Explica.
5. ¿Tuviste un osito de peluche cuando eras niño/a?

3 ¿Qué vio Inés?

Inés fue al circo ayer y hoy está hablando con Nicolás sobre lo que ella vio. Completa el siguiente diálogo con las palabras de la lista para saber lo que dicen.

rugían   peluche   boletos   taquilla
banda   fila   destreza   emocionante

NICOLÁS: Oye, Inés, ¿qué había en el circo que viste ayer?
INÉS: Había acróbatas con gran (1), payasos chistosos, una (2) de música y unos osos blancos que parecían ositos de (3).
NICOLÁS: Y, ¿qué era lo más (4)?
INÉS: Lo más emocionante eran los leones. Ellos (5) mucho.
NICOLÁS: Y, ¿qué era lo más aburrido?
INÉS: Lo más aburrido era la (6) que había en la (7) para comprar los (8). Había mucha gente.

Las acróbatas tenían mucha destreza.

Fuimos al Circo Mundial. ¡Era muy emocionante!

Capítulo 4   **159**

Honduras

Quiz/Activity 2

Activity 2

Activities

Connections. Discuss the following questions with students: *¿En dónde está Honduras?; ¿Cuál es la lengua oficial de Honduras?; ¿Qué país está al oeste de Honduras?; ¿Cuál es la capital del país?; ¿Qué tienen en común Honduras, México y Guatemala?; ¿Qué ciudad maya era un importante centro cultural y religioso?; ¿En qué año consiguió Honduras su independencia de España?; ¿En qué está basada la economía de Honduras?; ¿Qué necesita Honduras para la reconstrucción después del huracán Mitch?*

Prereading Strategy. This *Conexión cultural* allows students to learn more about the Spanish-speaking world by reading about Honduras in Spanish. The vocabulary and structures have been controlled to enable individuals to read in the target language and enjoy the experience. Note for the class that it is not essential to understand every word in order to read Spanish; the meaning of important but unknown passive vocabulary has been provided to facilitate an enjoyable experience. Before beginning the *Conexión cultural*, consider asking some general preparation questions about the theme of the reading: What is the capital of Honduras? Where is Honduras located? What else do students know about Honduras? Then have students skim the *Conexión cultural* for cognates and any words or expressions they already know.

Conexión cultural

Honduras

Honduras es un país grande de la América Central. Está ubicado entre el Mar Caribe al noreste, Nicaragua al sureste, El Salvador al suroeste y Guatemala al oeste. Al sur tiene costas en el Océano Pacífico en el Golfo de Fonseca. La capital del país, y la ciudad más grande, es Tegucigalpa, con más de 700.000 habitantes.

Como México y Guatemala, Honduras tiene una larga historia y comparte *(shares)* la influencia del gran imperio maya. Los mayas fundaron la ciudad de Copán en el siglo V en la región que hoy es Honduras. Esta ciudad era un importante centro cultural y religioso. Cuando los españoles llegaron a Copán para empezar la colonización en el siglo XV, sólo encontraron ruinas del antiguo imperio maya. La colonización terminó cuando Honduras consiguió su independencia de España en 1821.

Las ruinas mayas de Copán son espectaculares.

Honduras no es un país rico. Tiene una economía basada *(based)* en el café y los plátanos. Adicionalmente, en 1998, el huracán Mitch pasó por el territorio hondureño causando daños *(damages)* increíbles a muchas ciudades, destruyendo casas, hospitales, escuelas, sistemas de transporte e industria. Sólo en la industria de plátanos, hubo pérdidas *(there were losses)* de más de $800 millones de dólares. Para la reconstrucción del país, Honduras necesita más de $2 billones de dólares y 30 años de trabajo.

La industria de plátanos es importante para la economía de Honduras.

CONEXIONES 4

Cruzando fronteras

Haz un mapa de Honduras, en relación a los Estados Unidos, incluyendo sus países vecinos (El Salvador, Guatemala y Nicaragua). Añade los nombres de las capitales de estos países y los principales cuerpos de agua.

IDIOMA

¡Buenísimo/a!

In situations where "very," "most" or "extremely" are used with an adjective in English, the ending *-ísimo* (and the variations *-ísima, -ísimos* and *-ísimas*) often can be added to an adjective in Spanish. For adjectives that end in a vowel, the appropriate *-ísimo* ending usually replaces the final vowel.

Ése es un oso grande.	That is a **big** bear.
Ése es un oso grandísimo.	That is a **very big** bear.

but:

La cebra estaba sucia.	The zebra was **dirty.**
La cebra estaba sucísima.	The zebra was **very dirty.**

For adjectives that end in *-ble,* change the *-ble* to *-bil* before adding the *-ísimo* ending.

Ese payaso era amable.	That clown was **nice.**
Ese payaso era amabilísimo.	That clown was **very nice.**

Adjectives with an accent mark lose the accent mark when an *-ísimo* ending is added.

Las panteras eran rápidas.	The panthers were **fast.**
Las panteras eran rapidísimas.	The panthers were **very fast.**

Attach the appropriate form of *-ísimo* directly to the end of adjectives that end in a consonant, but first remove any plural endings before attaching *-ísimo*.

Era fácil hablar con los acróbatas.	It was **easy** to talk to the acrobats.
Era facilísimo hablar con los acróbatas.	It was **very easy** to talk to the acrobats.

but:

Los acróbatas hacían cosas difíciles.	The acrobats did **difficult** things.
Los acróbatas hacían cosas dificilísimas.	The acrobats did **extremely difficult** things.

Los acróbatas eran buenísimos.

Adjectives that end in *-co/-ca, -go/-ga* or *-z* require a spelling change when a form of *-ísimo* is added.

c → qu:	cómico	→	comiquísimo
g → gu:	larga	→	larguísima
z → c:	feliz	→	felicísimo

Este payaso estaba tristísimo.

 Activities 3-4

 Quiz/Activity 1

Answers

4 Check maps for accuracy.

Notes

Explain that the accent mark for words with the *-ísimo* ending is invariable.

Introduce superlatives by having students listen to your example: *Hoy estoy cansadísimo/a; ¿Estás tú cansadísimo/a también?*

Point out that the superlative meaning may also be expressed in Spanish using the expression *sumamente* followed by an adjective: *Estoy sumamente cansado.*

Explain that *magnífico, fantástico, maravilloso, estupendo,* etc., already have a superlative meaning and are not modified with the suffix *–ísimo.*

Note that young people in any country often have favorite colloquial expressions. For example, a Spanish teenager might describe something as *buenísimo* or *super-bueno, rapidísimo* or *super-rápido.*

Activities

Connections. Have students prepare a detailed report about the Maya city of Copán.

Cooperative Learning. Students work in small groups in order to develop statements about their school using the ending *-ísimo.* (*La clase de español es interesantísima.*) As an alternative, students work in small groups in order to develop statements about their city using the ending *-ísimo.* The group's statements/opinions should then be shared with the class.

NATIONAL STANDARDS
C1.1, C3.1, C4.1

¿Qué piensas tú?

Imagina que alguien te está haciendo las siguientes descripciones sobre algunas cosas que había en el circo, pero tú piensas lo opuesto. Haz oraciones para decir qué piensas tú, usando una forma de *-ísimo/a*.

> La taquilla era grande.
> Te equivocas. La taquilla era pequeñísima.

1. Los osos eran pequeños.
2. El payaso era aburrido.
3. Los elefantes eran delgados.
4. Todos nosotros estábamos tristes.
5. La banda era buena.
6. Había muchos animales ese día.
7. Los acróbatas eran bajos.
8. Los monos eran lentos.

El elefante era amabilísimo.

¡El circo era buenísimo!

Imagina que el fin de semana pasado tú y tu familia fueron a un circo hondureño. Trabajando en parejas, alterna con tu compañero/a de clase en preguntar y en contestar cómo eran o estaban las siguientes cosas del circo, usando la forma apropiada de *-ísimo* y las indicaciones que se dan. Sigue el modelo.

> ser/los boletos muy baratos
> **A:** ¿Eran los boletos muy baratos?
> **B:** Sí. ¡Los boletos eran baratísimos!
>
> estar/los elefantes muy gordos
> **B:** ¿Estaban los elefantes muy gordos?
> **A:** Sí. ¡Los elefantes estaban gordísimos!

1. ser/el circo hondureño muy interesante
2. estar/los acróbatas muy nerviosos
3. estar/las jaulas muy sucias
4. ser/los osos muy feroces
5. estar/la fila muy larga
6. ser/los payasos muy chistosos
7. ser/los ositos de peluche muy lindos
8. ser/los rugidos muy feos
9. ser/la banda muy buena
10. estar/Uds. muy cansados al final del día

Los payasos eran comiquísimos.

7 Una carta de David

David tiene la tendencia de exagerar *(exaggerate)* todo. Cambia los adjetivos indicados en su carta a la forma apropiada de *-ísimo.*

Queridos padres:

Ahora estoy *ocupado,* pero también estoy *contento* de saludarlos. Esta va a ser una carta *corta.* ¿Cómo van las cosas en casa? Les cuento que ayer estuve en un circo *bueno.* Había unos osos *grandes* y unas panteras *feroces.* También había unos acróbatas hondureños, pero era *difícil* verlos pues ellos estaban muy alto. Todo lo que ellos hacían era *fácil.* Creo que yo puedo hacer todo lo que ellos hacían con los ojos cerrados. Fue una tarde *divertida.* Bueno, ya no les cuento más. Un saludo para todos.

Con *mucho* amor,

David

Repaso rápido

Las terminaciones *-ito* e *-ita*

To show affection or to indicate that someone or something is small, several different endings can be added to a noun. The most common of these endings is a form of *-ito (-ita, -itos, -itas),* which usually replaces the final vowel of a noun: *oso → osito.* However, there are many exceptions for this rule: *animal → animalito.* Other diminutive endings include *-cito (-cita, -citos, -citas), -illo (-illa, -illos, -illas), -uelo (-uela, -uelos, -uelas)* and *-ico (-ica, -icos, -icas).* Try to become familiar with as many variations as you can since the endings vary from person to person and from country to country.

"Los Ositos Cariñositos"

¿Cuánto cuestan los globitos?

Quiz/Activity 2

Answers

7 Queridísimos, ocupadísimo, contentísimo, cortísima, buenísimo, grandísimos, ferocísimas, dificilísimo, facilísimo, divertidísima, muchísimo

Notes

The diminutive is usually associated with an affective nuance: small is viewed as nice, charming or emotionally engaging.

Note that some words may require a spelling change: *poquito (poco).*

Point out that the word *hombre* retains the letter *e* before adding the ending *-cito.* In addition, be sure students understand why the *c* in *flamenco* changes to *qu.*

Activities

Expansion. Have students find examples of the diminutive forms in the clipping shown at the bottom of this page.

NATIONAL STANDARDS
C1.2, C4.1

Activity 9

Answers

8
1. una ventana
2. una casa
3. Gloria y Carmen
4. unos globos
5. unos pollos
6. unos flamencos
7. Humberto
8. unas flores
9. un papá
10. unos papeles

9
1. ...amiguitas...ositos.
2. ...amiguitos...caballitos.
3. ...bandita....
4. ...elefantitos...filita....
5. ...osito...jaulita.
6. ...payasitos....

Activities

Spanish for Spanish Speakers.
Ask students to read the clipping with the monkey and then ask them questions to determine how much they understood: *Según la descripción, ¿cómo es el animal de la ilustración?; ¿Cómo es la cola del animal?; ¿Cómo parecen ser los animales?*

NATIONAL STANDARDS
C1.2, C4.1

8 De pequeño a grande

Escribe la forma original de los siguientes diminutivos.

 un hombrecito
un hombre

1. una ventanilla
2. una casita
3. Glorita y Carmencita
4. unos globitos
5. unos polluelos
6. unos flamenquitos
7. Humbertico
8. unas florcitas
9. un papacito
10. unos papelitos

Son tan pequeños, tan pequeños, que su cola es más grande que ellos. Parecen bebés aun cuando son adultos.

¿Es un monito bonito?

9 ¡Qué exagerada!

Luisa es un poco exagerada como David, pero ella tiene la tendencia de usar las terminaciones *-ito* e *-ita*. Cambia las palabras en itálica a la forma apropiada de *-ito* o *-ita* para ver cómo Luisa diría *(would say)* las siguientes oraciones.

Veía muchos *leones* en el circo.
Veía muchos *leoncitos* en el circo.

1. Mis *amigas* veían unos *osos*.
2. A mis *amigos* no les gustaron los *caballos*.
3. La *banda* del circo tocaba buena música.
4. Los *elefantes* hacían una *fila* muy simpática.
5. Veíamos un *oso* muy bonito en una *jaula*.
6. Los *payasos* eran muy chistosos.

La bandita del circo tocaba música buenísima.

IDIOMA

Los adjetivos y su posición

In Spanish, adjectives are masculine or feminine and singular or plural and usually follow the nouns they modify.

Era un pájaro **hondureño***.*	It was a **Honduran** bird.
Los osos **blancos** *eran muy grandes.*	The **white** bears were very big.

Some exceptions to this rule are demonstrative adjectives *(este, ese, aquel)*, adjectives of quantity *(mucho, poco)*, cardinal numbers *(dos, tres)*, question-asking words *(¿qué?)* and indefinite adjectives *(otro)*. They precede the nouns they modify.

¿Conoces a **ese** *niño?*	Do you know **that** boy?
Vimos **pocos** *gorilas.*	We saw **few** gorillas.
Había **cuatro** *elefantes en el circo.*	There were **four** elephants in the circus.
*¿***Qué** *payaso preferías?*	**What** clown did you prefer?
El **otro** *payaso es guatemalteco.*	The **other** clown is Guatemalan.

Adjectives that describe a permanent characteristic often precede the noun they describe.

Las **feroces** *panteras rugían.*	The **ferocious** panthers roared.
La **blanca** *nieve caía.*	The **white** snow was falling.

Ordinal numbers usually precede a noun, although they may sometimes be used after a noun, especially in headings and for titles. **Note:** Cardinal numbers precede ordinal numbers when both are used in one sentence to refer to the same noun.

Éste es el **tercer** *circo del año.*	This is the **third** circus of the year.
Eran los **dos primeros** *hombres en la fila.*	They were the **first two** men in the line.

but:

Juan Carlos **I** *(Juan Carlos* **Primero***)*	Juan Carlos I (Juan Carlos **the First**)

Several common adjectives may be used before or after the nouns they describe. **Note:** Before a masculine singular noun, *bueno* changes to *buen* and *malo* changes to *mal*.

Era un animal **pequeño***.*	
Era un **pequeño** *animal.*	It was a **small** animal.
Era un **buen** *circo.*	
Era un circo **bueno***.*	It was a **good** circus.
Ella no era una **mala** *acróbata.*	
Ella no era una acróbata **mala***.*	She was not a **bad** acrobat.

Notes

Adjectives can be placed before the noun for emphasis and emotional effect. For example: *un extraordinario viaje, una maravillosa vista.*

Some adjectives, such as *bello, buen, gran, horrible, mal, mejor, nuevo, peor, pequeño* and *verdadero,* usually come before the noun and add a nuance of moral or esthetic appreciation: *el peor examen, la verdadera razón.*

Point out that Juan Carlos I has been king of Spain since 1975.

Remind students that the following adjectives drop the final *-o* when they precede a masculine singular noun: *alguno (algún), bueno (buen), malo (mal), ninguno (ningún), primero (primer)* and *tercero (tercer).*

Activities

Spanish for Spanish Speakers.
Have students find out how many Hispanic performers are part of a well-known circus (e.g., Barnum and Bailey Ringling Brothers Circus). What do they do? Where did they receive their training? What do they like best about the circus?

¿Conoces a ese payaso?

NATIONAL STANDARDS
C1.2, C4.1

Answers

10
1. ...cuatro payasos....
2. ...mucha destreza.
3. Todos nosotros....
4. ...música buena./...buena música.
5. ...leones africanos....
6. ...acróbata bueno./...buen acróbata.
7. ...gran circo....
8. ...circo nuevo....
9. ...osos blancos....

Activities

Critical Thinking. Have students explain their answers for activity 10.

Expansion. Ask the following personal questions: *¿Te gustan las clases fáciles o las difíciles?; ¿Te gusta la música clásica o la moderna?; ¿Te gustan las películas cómicas o las dramáticas?; ¿Te gustan los coches deportivos o los económicos?*

The meanings of some adjectives actually change according to their placement before or after a noun. For example, placed before a noun, *grande* may be the equivalent of **great**. (Before singular nouns, *grande* changes to *gran*.) Placed after a noun, a form of *grande* conveys that someone or something is **big**.

*Es un **gran** circo.*	It is a **great** circus.
*Es un circo **grande**.*	It is a **big** circus.

Here are some other adjectives that change their meanings depending upon their placement before or after a noun:

*un amigo **viejo***	an **old** (elderly) friend	*un **viejo** amigo*	an **old** (I have known him a long time) friend
*la chica **pobre***	the **poor** (without much money) girl	*la **pobre** chica*	the **poor** (pitiful) girl
*el **mismo** payaso*	the **same** clown	*el payaso **mismo***	the clown **himself**
*un coche **nuevo***	a (never-owned) **new** car	*un **nuevo** coche*	a **new** car (that is new to me, but that may have been previously owned)

If two or more adjectives describe a noun, they may be used as follows: place both (or all) after the noun, connecting the last two with the word *y;* or place one before and one (or more) after the noun, according to the preceding rules. (The shorter, more subjective adjective usually precedes the noun.)

*Era el **primer** circo **grande** y **bueno** del año.*	It was the **first good big** circus of the year.

10 En el circo

¿Cómo eran todos en el circo? Completa las siguientes oraciones con los adjetivos indicados, decidiendo la posición correcta para cada uno y haciendo los cambios necesarios.

 Había una ___ banda (grande). Tenía cincuenta personas. (grande)

1. Había (1) payasos (1) muy chistosos. (cuatro)
2. Los acróbatas tenían (2) destreza (2). (mucho)
3. (3) nosotros (3) fuimos al circo. (todo)
4. Tocaban (4) música (4). (bueno)
5. Los (5) leones (5) eran lo mejor del circo. (africano)
6. El muchacho más joven era un (6) acróbata (6). (bueno)
7. Era un (7) circo (7) porque era buenísimo. (grande)
8. Era un (8) circo (8) en la ciudad. (nuevo)
9. Los (9) osos (9) eran muy cariñosos. (blanco)

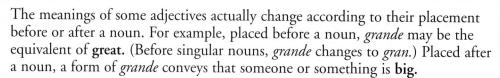

¡Era un buen acróbata!

El payaso era un viejo amigo de la familia.

11 ¿Qué había en el circo?

Di qué había en el circo, usando las pistas entre paréntesis y haciendo los cambios necesarios. Sigue el modelo.

 fila/largo (La fila no era corta.)
Había una fila larga.

1. banda/grande (La banda era pequeña pero fantástica.)
2. amigo/viejo (Vi a un amigo que conozco desde cuando yo era muy pequeño/a.)
3. acróbatas/hondureño (Los acróbatas eran de Honduras.)
4. payasos/malo (Los payasos no eran buenos.)
5. mujer/pobre (Una mujer con mucho dinero perdió su boleto y no podía entrar.)
6. ositos de peluche/mucho (Vi más de diez mil ositos de peluche.)
7. oso/blanco (El oso que vi no era negro.)

CIRCO GRAN FELE

12 Circo Internacional

Mira el siguiente dibujo y escribe ocho oraciones completas para describir las siguientes cosas, usando por lo menos dos adjetivos en cada descripción.

1. el circo
2. el elefante
3. los acróbatas
4. los osos
5. la banda
6. los leones
7. la jaula de los leones
8. el payaso

Los adjetivos como sustantivos
Sometimes an adjective can be used in combination with an article to take the place of a noun. The article and adjective that remain must be masculine or feminine and singular or plural, according to the noun they replace.

¿Te gustan los osos blancos o *los* (osos) *negros*?

Do you like the white bears or **the black ones**?

Me gusta el blanco.

Answers

11 Possible answers:
1. ...una gran banda.
2. ...un viejo amigo.
3. ...unos acróbatas hondureños.
4. ...unos malos payasos./...unos payasos malos.
5. ...una pobre mujer.
6. ...muchos ositos de peluche.
7. ...un oso blanco.

12 Creative writing practice. Check descriptions for adjective-noun agreement and position.

Activities

Critical Thinking. Prepare a group composition: Using transparency 33, call on individuals to describe what they see. Decide as a class whether the description is appropriate. Then have students write down each statement the class agrees adequately describes the illustration. As an alternative activity, have one student write the composition on the board. When you have completed the composition, call on individuals to read back what you wrote as a class. (To ensure that everyone participates, have everyone in class copy the composition and submit it to you.)

Language through Action. Using overhead transparency 33, ask students to come up and point to the people and items you name in Spanish.

Spanish for Spanish Speakers. Have students prepare a written description in Spanish of at least 100 words about what they see in the illustration of the Circo Internacional that accompanies activity 12.

Students with Special Needs. Provide another example for activity 11.

NATIONAL STANDARDS
C1.2, C4.1, C5.2

¿Qué pasó en la finca?

 Quiz/Activity 4

 Activities 34-35

 Activity 7

 Quiz/Activity 4

Answers

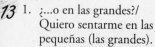

13 1. ¿...o en las grandes?/
Quiero sentarme en las pequeñas (las grandes).

2. ¿...o los baratos?/Compra los caros (los baratos).

3. ¿...o al bajo?/Pregunta los precios al alto (al bajo).

4. ¿...o unos rojos?/Tráeles a los niños unos amarillos (unos rojos).

5. ¿...o la hondureña?/ Prefiero comer la hondureña (la mexicana).

Notes

Other terms for *puerco* are *cochino*, *chancho* and *cerdo*. Another word for *rabo* is *cola*.

Activities

Cooperative Learning. After introducing the dialog (playing the audiocassette/audio compact disc, modeling words and phrases for student repetition, practicing the animal vocabulary, etc.), have students work in pairs practicing the dialog. Circulate and assist with pronunciation and intonation.

Prereading Strategy. Use transparencies 34 and 35 to introduce students to the vocabulary used in this dialog. Then instruct students to cover up the dialog with one hand and look at the illustration. Ask them to imagine where the conversation takes place and what the people are saying to one another. Finally, have students look through the dialog quickly to find cognates and other words or expressions they already know.

National STANDARDS
C1.1, C1.2, C4.1

---

13 **Haciendo fila**

 Trabajando en parejas, alterna con tu compañero/a de clase en hacer y contestar las siguientes preguntas. Usen los adjetivos entre paréntesis para completar las preguntas y contestarlas. Hagan los cambios necesarios.

> ¿Hago la fila larga o...? (corto)
> **A:** ¿Hago la fila larga o la corta?
> **B:** Haz la larga./Haz la corta.

1. ¿Quieres sentarte en las sillas pequeñas o en...? (grande)
2. ¿Compro los boletos caros o...? (barato)
3. ¿Le pregunto los precios al señor alto o...? (bajo)
4. ¿Les traigo a los niños unos globos amarillos o...? (rojo)
5. ¿Qué prefieres comer después del circo, la comida mexicana o...? (hondureño)

¿Qué pasó en la finca?

EN buen clima sin problemas de plagas, vendo finca de 7 caballerías. Tiene café, cardamomo, bosques, nacimientos, potreros. 560688 noches.
DC=0517542

23 caballerías: 12 bien empastadas, incluyo 350 vientres, 20 toros, total 500 reses, instalaciones ganaderas, localizado Poptún Petén. Ovigua 20563.
DC-0514567

8 **Quintas y chalets**

EN RIOBAMBA
VENDO HERMOSA PROPIEDAD DE 7 HECTÁREAS APROPIADA PARA HOSTERÍA: CASA 670 M2, BODEGAS. TELÉFONOS: 03-943314, 03-94255,02468669.

HUMBERTO: ¿Recuerdas lo chistoso que **ocurrió°** en la **finca°** ayer por la noche?
SILVIA: ¿Ayer? No recuerdo.
HUMBERTO: Cuando la tía Carmen estaba recogiendo las **gallinas,** una de ellas, la de **plumas°** rojas, se le **escapó°** cuando los perros empezaron a **ladrar.°**
SILVIA: ¡Ah, sí, lo recuerdo! Ella salió **detrás de°** la gallina, y como era de noche, no vio nuestros **puercos** y **fue a parar°** **encima de°** uno de ellos. Fue muy divertido, pero ¿qué hay con eso?

HUMBERTO: Dime algo que no sé. ¿Fue tu puerco o **el mío°** el que la tía cocinó hoy?
SILVIA: Fue **el tuyo.°**
HUMBERTO: Fue lo que pensé.

ocurrió *occurred* **finca** *ranch, farm* **plumas** *feathers* **escapó** *escaped* **ladrar** *to bark* **detrás de** *after, behind*
fue a parar *ended up* **encima de** *above, over, on top of* **el mío** *mine* **el tuyo** *yours*

14 ¿Qué comprendiste?

1. ¿Dónde ocurrió algo chistoso ayer?
2. ¿Qué gallina se le escapó a la tía Carmen?
3. ¿Cuándo se le escapó la gallina?
4. ¿Qué hizo la tía Carmen cuando la gallina se le escapó?
5. ¿Encima de qué fue a parar la tía Carmen?
6. ¿De quién era el puerco que preparó la tía?

15 Charlando

1. ¿Te gustaría tener una finca? Explica.
2. ¿Qué animales te gustaría tener en tu finca?
3. ¿Te gusta mirar las estrellas en el cielo? Explica.
4. ¿Hay bosques donde vives? ¿Te gusta ir a los bosques?

¿Son estos puercos los tuyos?

CONEXIONES

16 Cruzando fronteras

Estudia más sobre los animales de la finca que acabas de aprender. Di si son animales herbívoros o carnívoros; mamíferos u ovíparos; dónde viven comúnmente, qué comen y cualquier otra información que te interese. Busca información sobre estos animales en la biblioteca o en la Internet, si es necesario.

17 ¿Qué animal es?

Adivina qué animales son los siguientes, según las descripciones.

 Tiene cuatro patas y ladra.
Es un perro.

1. Es muy feroz y tiene una cabeza grande con mucho pelo.
2. Es blanca y tiene mucha lana.
3. Es gordo y come de todo.
4. Tiene orejas largas, es blanco y salta.
5. Tiene cuatro patas y da leche.
6. Es pequeñito y gris, tiene un rabo delgado y largo y le gusta mucho el queso.

un restaurante para perros

Perro rico, perro pobre

Mientras los gozques callejeros buscan restos de comida entre las canecas de basura y se mueren de hambre, los saneados y estilizados perros de familias pudientes ya tienen un nuevo lujo: un restaurante exclusivo. La italiana Anna Leonardi ha abierto un exquisito comedor para perros en la localidad de Novi Ligure, cerca de Génova. Croquetas, galletas, leche... forman parte del menú del Dog Bar, que sólo funciona los sábados y domingos. En pocas semanas, el local se ha convertido en centro de reunión de distinguidas italianas que, mientras sus canes se llenan el estómago con manjares especialmente preparados para ellos, charlan sobre este invento que les ha eliminado su problema de pensar en menúes caseros para sus mascotas.

Activities 14-15, 17

Answers

14 1. En la finca ocurrió algo chistoso ayer.
2. Se le escapó la (gallina) de plumas rojas.
3. Se le escapó cuando los perros empezaron a ladrar.
4. Salió detrás de ella.
5. Fue a parar encima de uno de los puercos.
6. El puerco era de Humberto.

15 Answers will vary.

16 Answers will vary.

17 1. Es un león.
2. Es una oveja.
3. Es un puerco.
4. Es un conejo.
5. Es una vaca.
6. Es un ratón.

Notes

Other words that are commonly used to refer to a farm are *la granja* and *la hacienda*.

Activities

Expansion. Additional questions (*¿Qué comprendiste?*): *¿Qué hacía Carmen con las gallinas?*; *¿Qué no vio la tía porque era de noche?*

Additional questions (*Charlando*): *¿Qué animales tienen cuernos?*; *¿Qué animales tienen rabo?*; *¿Qué animales tienen plumas?*; *¿Qué animales están en el establo?*; *¿En dónde hay muchos árboles?*; *¿Qué ves en el cielo?*; *¿Tiene tu familia una finca?*; *¿Tienes un perro? ¿Ladra mucho?*; *¿Qué es lo que más te gusta de una finca?*; *¿Prefieres la vida en una finca o la vida en una ciudad? ¿Por qué?*

Spanish for Spanish Speakers. Ask for volunteers to read the article *Perro rico, perro pobre*. Then have students tell the class what the clipping is about.

NATIONAL STANDARDS
C1.1, C1.2, C2.1, C3.1, C4.1

Lo que los animales dicen

Quiz/Activity 5

Answers

18 Answers will vary.

Notes

Note that certain animal sounds vary from Spanish to English.

Inform students that *vuelan* is the third-person plural present-tense form of the stem-changing verb *volar* (to fly) and requires the change *o → ue*.

Activities

Multiple Intelligences (linguistic/spatial). Have students draw a farm, including animals. Students then label the animals. Place the best drawings on the walls of the room.

REINO ANIMAL
USADO
Busque aquí
201-Perros.Cruces
202-Otros animales domésticos
203-Accesorios reino animal
204-Animales de ganadería
205-Animales perdidos y hallados
206-Demanda reino animal

18 **Los animales de la casa, la finca y el zoológico**

Prepara tres listas de animales, según dónde se pueden encontrar. Usa *la casa, la finca* y *el zoológico* para clasificarlos.

casa	finca	zoológico
el perro	la vaca	el hipopótamo

Lo que los animales dicen

Algo más

Lo que los animales hacen

You already know how to say in Spanish many things that people do: *caminamos, hablamos, comemos.* Do you know what some animals do?

Todos los animales **comen.**   *Los pájaros* **vuelan.**
Los caballos **corren.**   *Los perros* **ladran.**
Los conejos **saltan.**   *Los tigres y los leones* **rugen.**

¿Qué hace tu pájaro?

Las vacas
cruzan la calle.

¿Ruge el perro?

Tenía cuatro patas y decía miau, miau.

  En una finca

Imagina que tu sobrinito estuvo en una finca durante el fin de semana pasado. ¿Qué animales te está describiendo?

 Tenía cuatro patas y decía *jiii, jiii*. Era un caballo.

1. Decía *oinc, oinc.*
2. Decía *guau, guau.*
3. Decía *quiquiriquí.*
4. Decían *muuu, muuu.*
5. Decían *cua, cua* y volaban.
6. Decía *miau, miau.*
7. Tenía orejas largas y saltaba pero no decía nada.

PARAti

Proverbios y dichos

When a dog barks, many times it is for show, a bluff, and the dog most likely will not bite. If a dog does not immediately try to bite, it probably will not. The same can be said of a person who is all talk and no action. Their talk is like a bark that never leads to a bite because the person does not follow through. Do not let words or barks intimidate you. Judge people by what they do and not what they say because *Perro que ladra no muerde* (A barking dog does not bite).

 Adivina, adivinador

Trabajando en parejas, alterna con tu compañero/a de clase en describir ocho animales y en adivinar qué animal es.

A: Tiene cuatro patas, un rabo y ruge. ¿Puedes adivinar qué animal estoy describiendo?
B: Es un león.

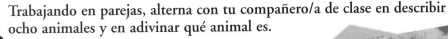
Tenemos mucha lana. ¿Qué somos?

Answers

19 1. Era un puerco.
2. Era un perro.
3. Era un gallo.
4. Eran unas vacas.
5. Eran unos patos.
6. Era un gato.
7. Era un conejo.

20 Creative self-expression.

Notes

Another way to say *Perro que ladra no muerde* is *Mucha espuma y poco chocolate*. (A lot of foam but very little chocolate.)

Activities

Expansion. For activity 20, ask students to draw the animal being described.

NATIONAL STANDARDS
C1.2, C3.1, C3.2

Notes

Review the simple possessive adjectives with students. For a quick warm-up exercise, have students change simple possessive adjectives to the stressed form.

Activities

Expansion. Practice possessive forms by borrowing several different items from students (for example, a book, pen, backpack, hat and keys). Ask questions such as *¿Es tu bolígrafo?; ¿Es el bolígrafo tuyo?* and *¿Es (el) tuyo?* until the owner is identified. Then ask follow-up questions *(¿De quién es el bolígrafo?)* so that the third-person forms are also practiced.

IDIOMA

Los adjetivos posesivos: formas largas

You already have learned to show possession by using *de* + a noun/pronoun *(el caballo de mis tíos/de ellos)*. You also have learned to show possession using the following short-form possessive adjectives, which are used before the noun they modify: *mi(s), tu(s), su(s), nuestro(s), nuestra(s), vuestro(s), vuestra(s)*. There are also long-form (or stressed) possessive adjectives.

mío(s), mía(s)	*my, (of) mine*	nuestro(s), nuestra(s)	*our, (of) ours*
tuyo(s), tuya(s)	*your, (of) yours*	vuestro(s), vuestra(s)	*your, (of) yours*
suyo(s), suya(s)	*your, (of) yours (Ud.), his, (of) his, her, (of) hers, its*	suyo(s), suya(s)	*your, (of) yours (Uds.), their, (of) theirs*

The long-form possessive adjectives agree with and usually follow the nouns they modify.

*Ésa es la vaca **mía**.*	That is **my** cow.
*¿Es ése el pato **tuyo**?*	Is that **your** duck?
*Éste es el toro **nuestro**.*	This is **our** bull.
*¿Son éstos los pavos **suyos**?*	Are these **your** turkeys?
*Todos ésos son animales **nuestros**.*	All of those are **our** animals.

The possessive adjectives also may be used immediately after a form of the verb *ser*.

*¿Son **suyos**?*	Are they **yours**?
*Sí, son **nuestros**.*	They are **ours**.

As you probably have noticed, the meaning of *suyo(s), suya(s)* is not always clear. To clarify the meaning of a sentence, it may sometimes be necessary to substitute a phrase that uses *de* followed by a prepositional pronoun.

*¿Son los animales **suyos**?* → *¿Son los animales **de Ud./de él/de ella/de Uds./de ellos/de ellas**?*
(Are the animals **yours/his/hers/yours/theirs**?)

¡Este gato es mío!

21 La fiesta de la tía Carmen

Carmen tiene una fiesta el viernes en su finca, y quiere saber cuántas personas van a ir. Di con quién van a la fiesta las siguientes personas, usando las indicaciones que se dan.

> María/unas primas
> María va a ir a la fiesta con unas primas suyas.

1. yo/una amiga
2. tú/unos compañeros
3. nosotros/unos parientes
4. tu amiga/una tía

5. tus padres/unos amigos
6. Uds./unos sobrinos
7. mi hermano/unas amigas
8. Ud./una compañera

22 Una invitación

Juan llama a Ana para invitarla a ver los animales de su finca. Completa su diálogo para saber lo que dicen, usando las siguientes palabras: *de él, de ellas, mi, mío, mis, nuestros, tu, tus, tuyo.* Cada palabra se usa sólo una vez.

JUAN: Aló, Ana. Te llamo para ver si quieres venir a la finca para ver *(1)* animales.

ANA: Sí. Me gustaría mucho. ¿Te importa si voy con Rogelio?

JUAN: ¿Rogelio? ¿Quién es? ¿Es *(2)* novio?

ANA: No. Es un primo *(3)* que está visitándome de Honduras.

JUAN: No, no hay problema.

ANA: ¿Puedo también ir con Elena y Paloma, las hermanas menores *(4)*, y Paquita, una amiguita *(5)*?

JUAN: Es mucha gente, ¿no?

ANA: Sí, pero a ellos les gustaría mucho ver *(6)* animales. Y ahora que lo pienso, a *(7)* padres también les gustaría verlos... y a Mateo también.

JUAN: ¿Quién es? ¿Otro primo *(8)*? ¿Un vecino?

ANA: ¡Claro que no! ¡Es *(9)* perro!

23 ¡Qué confusión!

Hoy en la finca hay una confusión con todos los animales. Trabajando en parejas, alterna con tu compañero/a de clase en hacer y en contestar preguntas para decir si los siguientes animales son o no son de las personas indicadas. Sigue el modelo.

> ellos/oveja
> A: ¿Es su oveja?
> B: Sí, (No, no) es la oveja suya.

1. nosotros/animales
2. tú/toro
3. Uds./puerco
4. ellas/pavos

5. tú/patos
6. él/vacas
7. ella/conejo
8. ellos/gallinas

¿Son sus ovejas?

Answers

21 1. Yo voy...con una amiga mía.
2. Tú vas...con unos compañeros tuyos.
3. Nosotros vamos...con unos parientes nuestros.
4. Tu amiga va...con una tía suya.
5. Tus padres van...con unos amigos suyos.
6. Uds. van...con unos sobrinos suyos.
7. Mi hermano va...con unas amigas suyas.
8. Ud. va...con una compañera suya.

22 1. nuestros (mis)
2. tu
3. mío
4. de él
5. de ellas
6. tus
7. mis
8. tuyo
9. mi

23 1. ¿Son nuestros animales?/...son los animales suyos (nuestros).
2. ¿Es tu toro?/...es el toro mío.
3. ¿Es su puerco?/...es el puerco nuestro.
4. ¿Son sus pavos?/...son los pavos suyos.
5. ¿Son tus patos?/...son los patos míos.
6. ¿Son sus vacas?/...son las vacas suyas.
7. ¿Es su conejo?/...es el conejo suyo.
8. ¿Son sus gallinas?/...son las gallinas suyas.

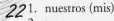

Activities

Students with Special Needs. Model one or two of the correct responses for activity 22.

NATIONAL STANDARDS
C1.1, C1.2, C4.1

Answers

24 1. ¿Son nuestros animales?/...son los animales de Uds.
3. ¿Es el puerco de Uds.?/...es el puerco nuestro.
4. ¿Son los pavos de ellas?/...son los pavos de ellas.
6. ¿Son las vacas de él?/...son las vacas de él.
7. ¿Es el conejo de ella?/...es el conejo de ella.
8. ¿Son las gallinas de ellos?/...son las gallinas de ellos.

25 1. ...tienes los tuyos.
2. ...tenemos el nuestro.
3. ...tiene los suyos.
4. ...tengo la mía.
5. ...tienen los suyos.
6. ...tiene las suyas.
7. ...tienen los suyos.
8. ...tienen el suyo.

Notes

Although possessive pronouns are generally used with the corresponding definite article, the article may be omitted after the verb *ser.*

Activities

Spanish for Spanish Speakers. Pair bilingual and nonbilingual students for activity 25.

Students with Special Needs. Model one or two of the correct responses for activity 25.

---

24 ¡De nuevo!

Haz otra vez las oraciones 1, 3, 4, 6, 7 y 8 de la actividad anterior, tratando de hacerlas más claras. Sigue el modelo.

   ellos/oveja
   A: ¿Es la oveja *de ellos?*
   B: Sí, (No, no) es la oveja *de ellos.*

Algo más

El pavo más curioso es el nuestro.

Los pronombres posesivos

Possessive pronouns frequently may be used in place of a possessive adjective and a noun. They are formed by placing a definite article in front of the long-form possessive adjectives.

Observe how possessive pronouns are used in the following sentences:

*Veo tu burro y **el mío** también.*
I see your donkey and **mine,** too.

*Mis vacas están delgadas y también lo están **las tuyas.***
My cows are thin and so are **yours.**

*¿Es ese conejo **el nuestro?***
Is that rabbit **ours?**

*Nuestros gallos son ésos y **los suyos** son éstos.*
Our roosters are (those ones) over there and **yours** are (these ones) over here.

25 Tres familias vecinas

Los Pinto, los Espinel y los Vargas tienen tres fincas vecinas. Sus animales se escaparon y se mezclaron *(became mixed)* ayer. Ahora el señor Pinto está haciendo un inventario *(inventory)* de los animales. Completa las siguientes oraciones para ver lo que dice durante el inventario.

1. Yo tengo mis animales y tú....
2. Uds. tienen su pavo y nosotros....
3. Álvaro tiene sus patos y Maruja....
4. Ud. tiene su oveja y yo....
5. Tú tienes tus pájaros y Uds.....
6. Patricia tiene sus gallinas y el señor Vargas....
7. Nosotros tenemos nuestros caballos y los Espinel y los Vargas....
8. Nosotros tenemos nuestro burro y el señor y la señora Espinel....

¡Eres mi puerco! Ven conmigo.

26 En la feria agrícola

En la feria agrícola *(4-H Fair)* de tu comunidad hay animales tuyos y animales de un amigo tuyo. Di de quién es y dónde está cada uno de los animales, usando las pistas que se dan. Sigue el modelo.

Activity 26

Activity 11

ese/burro/tú
Ese burro es el tuyo.

1. ese/toro/tú
2. aquellas/vacas/Paco
3. esas/gallinas/yo
4. aquel/pavo/nosotros
5. aquel/gallo/yo
6. estas/ovejas/Uds.
7. estos/puercos/Celia
8. ese/pájaro/él
9. este/conejo/ella

Answers

26 1. Ese toro es el tuyo.
2. Aquellas vacas son las suyas.
3. Esas gallinas son las mías.
4. Aquel pavo es el nuestro.
5. Aquel gallo es el mío.
6. Estas ovejas son las suyas.
7. Estos puercos son los suyos.
8. Ese pájaro es el suyo.
9. Este conejo es el suyo.

Notes

The construction *lo* followed by an adjective is used to describe a general characteristic or an abstract quality. Introduce the use of *lo* by asking students: *¿Qué es lo más fácil de esta clase?; ¿Qué es lo mejor de este colegio?;* etc.

Algo más

Lo con adjetivos/adverbios

You already know that the word *lo* can be used as a direct object pronoun meaning **him, it** or **you**. *Lo* can also be used with an adjective or adverb followed by the word *que* as an equivalent for **how** (+ **adjective/adverb**).

*¿Sabes **lo grande** que es el establo?*
*Uds. saben **lo mucho** que me gustan los bosques.*

Do you know **how big** the stable is?
You know **how much** I like the forest.

Note: Although the form of the adjective may change, the word *lo* remains the same in each example.

NATIONAL STANDARDS
C1.2, C4.1

Activity 27

Quiz/Activity 6

Activity 12

Answers

27 1. ¡No sabes lo bonitas que son!
2. ¡No sabes lo chistoso que es!
3. ¡No sabes lo interesante que era!
4. ¡No sabes lo emocionante que era!
5. ¡No sabes lo modernos que van a ser!
6. ¡No sabes lo lejos que está!

28 Creative self-expression.

Notes

You may wish to note that a variation of the pattern *¡Qué* (+ noun) *tan* (+adjective)!* is *¡Qué* (+ noun) *más* (+adjective)!*

Activities

Cooperative Learning. Have students do activities 27-28 in pairs or in small groups.

Students with Special Needs. Model an additional correct response for activities 27-28.

---

27 ¡No sabes lo mucho que sabemos!

Usa la palabra *lo* con un adjetivo o un adverbio para contestar las preguntas, siguiendo el modelo.

¿Son bonitos los pájaros guatemaltecos?
¡No sabes lo bonitos que son!

1. ¿Son bonitas esas flores?
2. ¿Es chistoso tu ratón?
3. ¿Era interesante tu visita a la finca?
4. ¿Era emocionante la música?
5. ¿Van a ser modernos los establos?
6. ¿Está lejos tu finca?

¿Son bonitos los pájaros guatemaltecos?

Algo más

¡Qué vaca tan grande!

You already know that the word *qué* can be combined with an adjective or a noun to express strong feelings about something you are experiencing: *¡Qué emocionante!* (How exciting!), *¡Qué destreza!* (What skill!). You can also express strong feelings using the following construction:

¡Qué	(+ *noun*)	tan	(+ *adjective*)!

¡Qué árbol tan alto!   What a tall tree!
¡Qué cuernos tan grandes!   What big horns!

28 ¿Cuál es tu opinión?

Di tu opinión sobre las siguientes situaciones, usando la construcción *¡Qué* (+ noun) *tan* (+ adjective)!

Es la medianoche y se ve la luna.
¡Qué luna tan bonita!

1. Ves un toro con cuernos muy grandes y un rabo muy corto.
2. Estás en un bosque grande con muchos árboles altos.
3. Unos pájaros de muchos colores vuelan sobre ti.
4. Ves unos patos que fueron a parar en el lago.
5. Hace buen tiempo y el cielo está muy azul.
6. Hay una estrella muy bonita en el cielo.
7. Un conejo está saltando por el bosque.

¿Qué hace el conejito?

¡Este elefante es grandísimo!

¿Es este gallo el suyo?

¡Qué perro tan cariñoso!

Autoevaluación. Como repaso y autoevaluación, responde lo siguiente:
  1. Name three different things in Spanish that you might see at the circus.
  2. Imagine you went to the circus. Describe your experience, including something that was extremely fun or interesting.
  3. Describe two people or animals using diminutives.
  4. In Spanish, name four animals and the sounds they make.
  5. Name two items that are yours and one that belongs to your friend.
  6. Ask a friend if she knows how big the sky is.
  7. Describe three objects and express strong feelings about each.
  8. What do you know about Honduras?

 Activity 13

Answers

A Creative self-expression.

B Creative self-expression.

Notes

www

Search Engines
Lycos
http://www.lycos.com/
Yahoo
http://www.yahoo.com/
Yahoo Español
http://espanol.yahoo.com/
Webcrawler
http://www.webcrawler.com/
Infoseek
http://www.infoseek.com/
Altavista
http://www.altavista.digital.com/

Remember, Web addresses are prone to change, so check out sites and search engines before students try to use them and experience problems.

Activities

Expansion. Ask students to describe animals that belong to their family, such as pets or farm animals. The descriptions should include photos and be shared with the class.

Students with Special Needs. Review the comparative and the superlative of adjectives before beginning activity A: *¿Es más grande que un ratón?*

Technology. Using the Internet, have students search for information about a circus or zoo. Using the information, students should then create an informative or promotional piece about the subject chosen. Students might include such things as location, schedules, cost, attractions that visitors can observe or programs in which visitors can participate. The piece may be created as an electronic file on the computer or as a flyer printed on paper.

¡La práctica hace al maestro!

A Comunicación

On your notebook, write the name in Spanish of an animal you have learned in this chapter. Then, working with a partner, play this game: Take turns asking no more than eight questions in order to identify the other person's animal. Questions must have either *sí* or *no* for an answer. The winner is the person who guesses the name of the other person's animal first.

A: ¿Es pequeñito y blanco?
B: No.

¿Es grande y feroz?

B Conexión con la tecnología

Visit a virtual zoo. Search the Internet for sites that allow you to visit a virtual zoo. Report back to the class about the Internet locations of the ones you liked the most. See how many animals you could name in Spanish.

¿Sabes qué soy?

VOCABULARIO

Activities

Expansion. Select several words and phrases for individual students to use orally in sentences.

Multiple Intelligences (bodily-kinesthetic/interpersonal/linguistic). Have students cut out pictures of the animals they learned in spanish or have artistically talented students draw some of them. Then have students work in cooperative pairs or in small groups asking about, describing and identifying these animals.

Pronunciation. To ensure proper pronunciation, model each word or expression and have students repeat after you.

El circo

el acróbata, la acróbata
la banda
el boleto
el circo
la destreza
la fila
la jaula
el oso (de peluche)
el payaso
el rugido
la taquilla

La finca

el árbol
el bosque
el burro
el cielo
el conejo
el cuerno
el establo
la estrella
la finca
la gallina
el gallo
la luna
la oveja
el pájaro

la pata
el pato
el pavo
la pluma
el puerco
el rabo
el ratón
el toro
la vaca

Verbos

escapar(se)
ladrar
ocurrir
rugir
saltar
volar (ue)

Expresiones y otras palabras

detrás de
durante
emocionante
encima de
gran
ir a parar
lo (+ *adjective/adverb*)
mío,-a
nuestro,-a

pobre
¡Qué (+ *noun*) tan
  (+ *adjective*)!
suyo,-a
tuyo,-a

Parece ser un oso, pero no lo es. ¿Qué es?

NATIONAL STANDARDS
C1.2, C4.1

Answers

Activities

Critical Listening. Play the *Somos así LISTOS* audiocassette/audio compact disc version of the reading. Tell students to listen for the main ideas the speaker is addressing. Finally, have several individuals state what they believe the main theme of the reading is.

Multiple Intelligences (intrapersonal/linguistic). Have students write a short composition in Spanish about a favorite pet or animal. In the composition, students should describe the animal and tell about any special characteristics or talents of the animal.

Prereading Strategy. Prepare students for the content of the reading by asking some general questions on the reading topic, such as the questions found in the *Preparación.* Next, play the first paragraph of the recording of the *A leer* section, using the corresponding audiocassette or compact disc that is part of the Audiocassette/Audio CD Program. As an alternative, you may choose to read the first paragraph yourself. Read the paragraph again with students following along in the book. Give students a moment to look over the paragraph silently on their own and then have them ask questions. Ask for a student to volunteer to read the paragraph aloud. Continue in this way for subsequent paragraphs.

Students with Special Needs. Read through the circus announcement as a class activity and answer questions to be certain all students understand the content before attempting the questions on page 181.

---

a leer

Estrategia

Preparación

Estrategia para leer: *guessing meaning from context*

When reading in another language, you will often encounter words you do not know. Before looking in a dictionary, gather clues from the context to help you identify what a word means. The context includes what is written before and after the unknown word. Looking for these contextual clues will help improve your reading skills and will also make reading more enjoyable because you spend less time looking up words in a dictionary.

Como preparación para la lectura, di qué quieren decir las palabras en negrilla según el contexto.

1. El año *pasado* el circo visitó Honduras por primera vez.
2. El circo va a hacer más de cincuenta *presentaciones* en la capital.
3. El público recibió a los artistas con grandes *aplausos*.
4. El circo tiene una *carpa* muy grande de muchos colores.

De México con cariño a
HONDURAS
EL CIRCO MAS GRANDE DE MEXICO
FUNDADO EN 1872
Circo Hnos
SUAREZ
LA MARAVILLA
HUMANA DEL SIGLO XX
Los únicos siameses vivos en
el mundo
RONNIE & DONNIE
Atención
Tegucigalpa
FUNCIONES:
LUNES A VIERNES: 7:30 P.M.
SABADO: 4:00 - 7:30 P.M.
DOMINGO: 11:30 A.M.-3:00 y 7:30 P.M.
DIAS FERIADOS:
4:00 P.M. y 7:30 P.M.
EN GIGANTESCAS
CARPAS TIPO ESTADIO AZTECA
Desde el 9 de febrero.
HOY
La gran parada del Circo
el día 9 de febrero
a las 11:00 A.M.
Venta de boletos desde
las 10:30 am en el Circo.

¡El gran Circo de los Hermanos Suárez!

El año pasado visitó Honduras por primera vez, en su **gira** por la América Central, el gran Circo de los Hermanos Suárez con un **éxito** total. La gente decía que era lo mejor que visitaba a Honduras en muchos años. Pues, bien, este año está otra vez aquí y ya está divirtiendo al público hondureño. Con más de cincuenta presentaciones, el circo hace su gira más larga por el país. Este maravilloso circo, el más grande de México, tiene fascinantes atracciones para personas de todas las edades.

Ayer mi familia y yo visitamos al circo en su primera presentación de este año en la ciudad. Todos estábamos muy **emocionados** y contentos. **Al principio** pensábamos que todo iba a ser un **dolor** de cabeza pues sabíamos que mucha gente iba para verlo, pero todo era diferente de lo que imaginábamos. La fila para comprar los boletos era corta y rápida. La gente entraba al circo en forma muy **organizada** y lo mejor de todo, el circo era excelente. En su gran **carpa** había acróbatas de gran destreza, payasos y muchos animales salvajes. Los feroces tigres y leones africanos hacían gritar a más de una persona. El desfile de los elefantes **sorprendía** a chicos y a grandes. Los payasos eran muy chistosos y hacían **morir de la risa** a todo el mundo. Los acróbatas nos hacían **poner los pelos de punta.** Al terminar la función todos **premiábamos** a los artistas con grandes aplausos.

Ud., si no tiene planes para la semana que viene, ya sabe adónde ir. El circo va a estar en la ciudad por diez semanas más. Hay funciones todos los días y los boletos no son caros. Vaya con su familia y diviértase.

gira *tour* **éxito** *success* **emocionados** *excited* **Al principio** *At the beginning* **dolor** *pain* **organizada** *organized* **carpa** *tent* **sorprendía** *surprised* **morir de la risa** *die laughing* **poner los pelos de punta** *our hair stand on end (with fear)* **premiábamos** *rewarded*

A ¿Qué comprendiste?

1. ¿Cómo se llama el circo que visitó Honduras el año pasado?
2. ¿Cuántas veces visitó el circo a Honduras el año pasado?
3. ¿De dónde es el circo?
4. ¿Qué decía la gente de este circo?
5. ¿Cuántas presentaciones va a hacer el circo?
6. ¿A qué hora son las funciones los sábados?
7. ¿Cómo era la fila para comprar los boletos?
8. ¿Qué animales había en este circo?

B Charlando

1. ¿Piensas que el Circo de los Hermanos Suárez es un circo bueno?
2. ¿Hay algún circo de visita en donde tú vives? ¿Cómo se llama?
3. ¿Por cuánto tiempo va a estar?
4. ¿Te gusta ir al circo?
5. ¿Buscas información en el periódico de los eventos que quieres ver o visitar? Explica.

Answers

A
1. Se llama el Circo de los Hermanos Suárez.
2. Una vez.
3. Es de México.
4. La gente decía que era lo mejor que visitaba a Honduras en muchos años.
5. El circo va a tener más de cincuenta presentaciones.
6. Las funciones de los sábados son a las cuatro y a las siete y media.
7. La fila era corta y rápida.
8. Había tigres y leones africanos.

 B Answers will vary.

Activities

Expansion. Additional questions (*¿Qué comprendiste?*): *¿Cuántos cognados hay en la lectura ¡El gran Circo de los Hermanos Suárez!? ¿Cuáles son?; ¿Es éste un circo pequeño o grande?; ¿Desde cuándo tiene presentaciones el circo?; ¿Por cuántas semanas va a estar el circo?*

Additional questions (*Charlando*): *¿Cuándo fue la última vez que fuiste al circo?; ¿Cómo era ese circo? ¿Era grande o pequeño?; ¿Qué animales había?; ¿Había animales salvajes?; ¿Qué es lo que más te gusta de un circo? Explica.; ¿Te gustaba ir al circo cuando eras niño/a?; ¿Con quién ibas al circo?*

Spanish for Spanish Speakers. Ask students to read the advertisement for the Suárez Brothers' Circus and then ask them questions to determine how much they understood: *¿De dónde es el circo?; ¿Cuándo fue fundado el circo?; ¿En qué días hay funciones?; ¿Dónde se va a presentar el circo?*

NATIONAL STANDARDS
C1.2, C2.1, C3.1, C4.1, C5.2

Creative writing practice.

Activities

Multiple Intelligences (linguistic). Have students write a poem on some aspect of El Salvador or Honduras.

Technology. Using a multimedia authoring program, students write and illustrate a story about a circus or zoo focusing on saving wildlife or eliminating animal abuse (i.e., animals that are abused at a poorly run circus or zoo). One such computer program that allows this type of work is Story Book Weaver Deluxe®, although others exist.

a escribir

Estrategia

Estrategia para escribir: *writing a cinquain poem*

A poem captures a part of your world in words, creating a picture that can be seen by the mind's eye. Some poems are serious and explore social issues, while others are creative descriptions which present something in a unique way. A cinquain is a five-line poem.

How to write a cinquain

Prewriting

Step 1: Choose an **object, person, place,** or **idea** that you would like to write about.

Step 2: Brainstorm and list as many descriptions and adjectives about your topic as you can think of. Be creative. Consult the Spanish/English dictionary if necessary.

Step 3: Read this example of a cinquain and observe how it is composed.

> La vida
> Contenta, triste
> Los años pasan
> Lenta, rápida
> Como una montaña rusa.

Composing

Line 1: Write the name of the **object, person, place** or **idea.**
Line 2: Write two descriptions or adjectives about the topic in line 1.
Line 3: Write a phrase comparing something with the topic.
Line 4: Write two descriptions or adjectives about line 3.
Line 5: Write a word or phrase that describes and ties together both lines one and three.

Now compose your own cinquain poem by following these guidelines.

Activities

Spanish for Spanish Speakers. Have students write a short description in Spanish of at least 100 words describing a trip they took to a circus that they saw or a farm or ranch that they visited. In the description, students should tell about what they saw and did, whom they went with and any other details they wish.

repaso

Now that I have completed this chapter, I can...
- ✓ seek and provide personal information.
- ✓ describe in the past.
- ✓ talk about activities at a special event.
- ✓ identify animals.
- ✓ express quantities.
- ✓ provide background information about the past.
- ✓ indicate past intentions.
- ✓ discuss nationality.
- ✓ add emphasis to a description.
- ✓ recognize and express size.
- ✓ state possession.
- ✓ identify sounds that animals make.

I can also...
- ✓ read in Spanish about life in El Salvador and Honduras.
- ✓ identify opportunities to use Spanish to find a career or be a volunteer.
- ✓ identify to what animal groups some animals belong.
- ✓ read and understand a zoo schedule in Spanish.

La ciudad maya de Copán está en Honduras.

Al oso le gustaba nadar.

Capítulo 4 183

NATIONAL STANDARDS
C1.1, C1.2, C1.3, C2.1, C2.2, C3.1, C3.2, C4.1, C4.2

Notes

Review the communicative functions for the chapter. A checkoff list of the functions appears at the end of *Capítulo 5* (see page 229), along with additional objectives that students can use as a self-check to evaluate their own progress.

Activities

Connections. Have students name some cities in the Caribbean. Then ask if anyone in class has visited or knows someone who has visited any Caribbean countries. Ask what students know about Puerto Rico, the Dominican Republic and Cuba.

Critical Thinking. The visuals that appear on pages 184-185 depict the functions, cultural setting and themes of the chapter ahead and serve to further student connections to the countries and people students are studying in this chapter. Use these supportive visuals as an introduction to the themes that students will be studying. Ask about any similarities and differences students observe, what words they are able to understand, what conclusions they can draw from the information, and so forth.

Multiple Intelligences (logical-mathematical). Ask if students know what currency is used in Puerto Rico. Then have students find out the value in dollars for the *peso dominicano*. Sources for currency exchange rates include various newspapers (i.e., the business section of the local paper and the *Wall Street Journal*) and the Internet. The school Media Specialist may be able to help students find others sources for exchange rates, as well.

¿Qué recuerdas?

In this chapter you will be able to:

- talk about what someone remembers
- seek and provide personal information
- describe clothing
- report past actions and events
- talk about everyday activities
- identify foods
- use metric weights and measurements
- read and order from a menu

- write about the past
- express opinions
- ask for advice
- state what was happening at a specific time
- describe how something was done
- express length of time
- discuss food preparation

Cuba
Nombre oficial: República de Cuba

Población: 11.050.000

Capital: La Habana

Ciudades importantes: Santiago de Cuba, Camagüey, Holguín, Santa Clara

Unidad monetaria: el peso

Fiesta nacional: 1° de enero, Día de la Liberación

Gente famosa: José Martí (escritor y político); Alicia Alonso (bailarina); Nicolás Guillén (poeta)

Puerto Rico
Nombre oficial: Estado Libre Asociado de Puerto Rico

Población: 3.685.000

Capital: San Juan

Ciudades importantes: Ponce, Mayagüez, Bayamón

Unidad monetaria: el dólar (EE.UU.)

Fiesta nacional: 4 de julio, Día de la Independencia de los EE.UU.

Gente famosa: Raúl Julia (actor); Miguel Pou (pintor); Roberto Clemente (beisbolista); Ricky Martin (cantante)

República Dominicana
Nombre oficial: República Dominicana

Población: 8.100.000

Capital: Santo Domingo

Ciudades importantes: Santiago de los Caballeros, Puerto Plata

Unidad monetaria: el peso dominicano (RD$)

Fiesta nacional: 27 de febrero, Día de la Independencia

Gente famosa: Juan Luis Guerra (cantante); Sammy Sosa (beisbolista)

185

NATIONAL STANDARDS
C1.2, C5.2

¿Dónde estuvieron Uds. anoche?

Quiz/Activity 1

Activity 36

Content reviewed in *Lección 9*
- seeking and providing personal information
- imperfect tense
- preterite tense
- everyday activities
- foods
- past tense

Notes

Inform students that as they travel they will hear some native speakers use *hubieron* as a plural form of the impersonal expression *hubo*.

The verb *acordar(se)* requires the stem change *o → ue* in the present tense.

Activities

Critical Listening. Play the audiocassette/audio compact disc recording of the dialog. Instruct students to cover the words as they listen to the conversation in order to develop good listening skills before concentrating on reading Spanish. Have students look at the illustration and imagine what the people are saying to one another. Ask several individuals to state what they believe is the main theme of the conversation.

Prereading Strategy. Instruct students to cover up the dialog with one hand and look at the illustration. Ask them to imagine where the conversation takes place and what the people are saying to one another. Finally, have students look through the dialog quickly to find cognates and other words and expressions they already know.

Lección 9

Contexto cultural
CUBA

¿Dónde estuvieron Uds. anoche?

Jaime y Raimundo, dos hermanos cubanos, hablan con sus novias, Sandra, de la República Dominicana, y Carmen, de Puerto Rico.

SANDRA: Chicos, ¿dónde estuvieron **anoche?**° Los llamamos a las siete y nadie contestó.

CARMEN: ¿Fueron a alguna **parte**° sin nosotras?

JAIME: Ay, perdón. **No nos acordábamos de**° que Uds. iban a llamar. Era **probable** que cuando llamaron nosotros estábamos en...

SANDRA: ...en una fiesta donde había música, baile y mucha gente... y me imagino que era en la casa de Javier.

RAIMUNDO: ¿Qué estás **describiendo?**° No **hubo**° ninguna fiesta en la casa de Javier. Estábamos en el supermercado.

CARMEN: ¿En el supermercado?

JAIME: Sí, comprábamos la comida **necesaria** para una cena **elegante** que les vamos a preparar el sábado.

SANDRA: ¡Qué lindos! Entonces vamos a comprar algo elegante para ponernos. Adiós.

anoche *last night* **parte** *place, part* **No nos acordábamos (de)** *We did not remember*
describiendo *describing* **hubo** *there was (were)*

NATIONAL STANDARDS
C1.2, C4.1

186 Lección 9

1 ¿Qué comprendiste?

1. ¿A qué hora llamaron las chicas a los chicos anoche?
2. ¿Sabían los chicos que las chicas iban a llamar?
3. ¿Qué era probable, según Sandra?
4. ¿Hubo una fiesta anoche?
5. ¿Dónde estaban los chicos cuando las chicas llamaron?
6. ¿Qué hacían los chicos allí?

Estábamos en el supermercado.

Estudiaba en mi cuarto anoche.

2 Charlando

1. ¿Te acuerdas siempre de lo que tienes que hacer?
2. ¿Dónde estuviste anoche a las siete?
3. ¿Qué hacías a esa hora?
4. ¿Fuiste a alguna parte especial el fin de semana pasado? Describe el lugar.

 Activities 1-2

Answers

1. 1. Ellas los llamaron a las siete.
   2. Sí, sabían, pero no se acordaban que iban a llamar.
   3. Era probable que los muchachos estaban en una fiesta en la casa de Javier.
   4. No, no hubo una fiesta anoche.
   5. Los chicos estaban en el supermercado cuando las chicas llamaron.
   6. Compraban la comida necesaria para preparar una cena elegante para las chicas.

2. Answers will vary.

Notes

When you review answers for the sections *¿Qué comprendiste?* and *Charlando,* have students call on one another to remove yourself from always being at the center of classroom discussions.

Note that the two girls in this photograph work in the deli section of a supermarket.

Activities

Expansion. Additional questions (*¿Qué comprendiste?*): *¿De dónde son los chicos?*; *¿De dónde es Sandra?*; *¿De dónde es Carmen?*; *¿Fueron Jaime y Raimundo a alguna parte sin las chicas?*; *¿Cómo era la fiesta que Sandra describe?*; *¿Son los chicos y las chicas hermanos?*; *¿Estaban en casa los chicos anoche?*; *¿Dónde dice Sandra que ellos estaban?*; *¿Adónde van las chicas?*

Additional questions (*Charlando*): *¿Preparas la cena para tus amigos/as?*; *¿Preparaste algo anoche para la cena?*; *¿Te gusta preparar la cena?*; *¿Quién te invitó la última vez a cenar?*; *¿Cuándo fue la última fiesta elegante a la que fuiste?*; *¿Dónde estabas la última vez que preparaste alguna comida?*

NATIONAL STANDARDS
C1.2, C2.1, C4.1, C4.2

Notes

As a cultural note, point out that many people believe Cuba produces some of the world's finest cigars. However, you also may wish to remind students of the hazards of smoking any kind of tobacco, regardless of the quality.

Baseball is extremely popular in Cuba and the Cuban national team has been very successful in international competition.

Activities

Connections. Show students where Cuba is located using the maps in the front of the book or the transparencies that are part of this program.

Prereading Strategy. This *Conexión cultural* provides an opportunity for students to increase what they know about the Spanish-speaking world by reading about Cuba in Spanish. Before beginning the *Conexión cultural*, consider asking some general preparation questions about the theme of the reading: Where is Cuba located? What is the name of Cuba's capital? What do students know about Cuba? Then have students skim the *Conexión cultural* for cognates and any words or expressions they already know.

Spanish for Spanish Speakers. Ask students general questions to determine how much they understood: *¿Dónde está Cuba?; ¿Cómo es?; ¿Qué puede uno ver o hacer en Cuba?; ¿Qué más sabes acerca de Cuba?*

Conexión *cultural*

Cuba: El Caribe a todo sol

Es la isla más grande del Caribe. Está situada a sólo 145 kilómetros (90 millas) al sur de la Florida, a la entrada *(entrance)* del Golfo de México. La isla tiene mucho que ofrecer, como magníficas playas de aguas azules y claras, clima tropical, bosques y ciudades coloniales.

La plaza de la Catedral en la Habana Vieja.

Su población y su cultura son una combinación de la herencia *(heritage)* española y africana. Su lengua oficial es el español. Su sistema económico es el socialismo, el cual existe desde la revolución cubana hecha por Fidel Castro en 1959.

La Habana, su capital, es la ciudad más grande. El sector antiguo, La Habana Vieja, conserva la arquitectura colonial española con calles estrechas *(narrow)* y viejas mansiones. Por el contrario, en La Habana Nueva, hay avenidas anchas *(wide)*, edificios modernos y grandes hoteles. Otras ciudades importantes de la isla son Santiago de Cuba, Cienfuegos, Camagüey y Guantánamo, donde hay una base naval militar de los Estados Unidos.

Las industrias más importantes de su economía son el azúcar, el tabaco y el turismo. De todas partes de Europa y Latinoamérica van turistas para bañarse en sus playas tropicales y escuchar la música cubana, que es una combinación de guitarra española y tambores *(drums)* africanos.

Desde 1960 ha existido en Cuba un embargo económico impuesto *(imposed)* por los Estados Unidos. Hoy la isla tiene problemas económicos que tiene que resolver.

así es **Cuba**
es historia · es caribe · es alegría · es su gente

Hay muchos autos clásicos en Cuba.

Vivo en La Habana, Cuba.

3 Cruzando fronteras

Lee las siguientes oraciones sobre Cuba. Luego, di si cada oración es verdad o falsa.

1. Cuba está en el Caribe.
2. Cuba es la isla más pequeña del Caribe.
3. Las lenguas oficiales de Cuba son el español y el inglés.
4. La capital de Cuba es La Habana.
5. Las calles de La Habana Vieja no son estrechas.
6. El café, el azúcar y el turismo son las industrias más importantes de la isla.
7. La población y la cultura cubana son una combinación de la herencia española y mexicana.

Compré muchas cosas en Cuba.

Repaso *rápido*

El pretérito

You have learned to recognize and use the preterite tense to express simple past actions in Spanish. Review the formation of regular verbs for this frequently used verb tense in the chart that follows.

	preparar:	comer:	vivir:
yo	preparé	comí	viví
tú	preparaste	comiste	viviste
Ud./él/ella	preparó	comió	vivió
nosotros/nosotras	preparamos	comimos	vivimos
vosotros/vosotras	preparasteis	comisteis	vivisteis
Uds./ellos/ellas	prepararon	comieron	vivieron

Do you recall the spelling changes that occur in the preterite tense?

explicar	c → qu	expliqué
pagar	g → gu	pagué
almorzar	z → c	almorcé

Do you remember that the verbs *conseguir (i, i), despedirse (i, i), divertirse (ie, i), dormir (ue, u), mentir (ie, i), pedir (i, i), preferir (ie, i), repetir (i, i), seguir (i, i), sentir (ie, i), sentirse (ie, i),* and *vestirse (i, i)* all require a stem change in the *Ud., él, ella, Uds., ellos* and *ellas* form of the preterite tense?

sentir (ie, i): sentí, sentiste, sintió, sentimos, sentisteis, sintieron
dormir (ue, u): dormí, dormiste, durmió, dormimos, dormisteis, durmieron
pedir (i, i): pedí, pediste, pidió, pedimos, pedisteis, pidieron

The following preterite-tense verbs have irregularities: *caer(se), dar, decir, estar, hacer, ir, leer, oír, ser, tener* and *ver.* If you have forgotten any of these forms, you may review them in the Appendices.

Answers

3
1. verdad
2. falsa
3. falsa
4. verdad
5. falsa
6. falsa
7. falsa

Notes

The Cuban revolution resulted in the arrival of many Cuban immigrants to the United States. A second wave of immigrants, referred to sometimes as *los marielitos,* arrived in 1980. Their presence is especially noticeable in the part of Miami known as **Little Havana.**

Although education and health care are available to all Cubans, most schools lack books and supplies. There is also a lack of medicines in hospitals, clinics and pharmacies.

La Habana Vieja has been named a world heritage site by UNESCO, which is providing funds to restore the area.

Remind students that they remove the endings *-ar, -er* and *-ir* before adding the endings shown in the chart reviewing the preterite tense.

Activities

Multiple Intelligences (linguistic). Ask students to tell you what Cuba is like, according to the clipping on page 188.

Spanish for Spanish Speakers. Select one or two of José Martí's *Versos sencillos* for students to read. Students must write a short critique of the poem(s).

Students with Special Needs. Remind students that they can improve their knowledge of and ability to express themselves in correct Spanish by reviewing previously learned structures and vocabulary on a regular basis.

NATIONAL STANDARDS
C1.2, C2.2, C3.1, C4.1

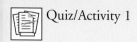
Answers

4 1. me levanté
2. buscó
3. fui/tuve
4. empecé
5. llegó
6. preparamos
7. vinieron
8. se vistieron (nos vestimos)
9. empezamos
10. oímos
11. Llovió/nos divertimos
12. se despidieron

5 1. salieron
2. toqué
3. leyó
4. te quedaste
5. comieron
6. visitamos
7. vio
8. estuvieron
9. compraron
10. consiguió

Notes

Give an example or two of how *conocer* is used in the preterite tense for **to meet:** *Conocí a la señora y al señor Blanco en la fiesta el sábado pasado* (I met Mr. and Mrs. Blanco at the party last Saturday).

Activities

Expansion. As a follow-up to activities 4 and 5, ask students to say what different family members and friends did last night or last weekend. They may choose from the verbs found in these activities or provide new information.

Students with Special Needs. Model the first sentence for activity 4.

4 Una cena elegante

Imagina que invitaste a unos amigos a cenar en tu casa el sábado pasado. Completa las siguientes oraciones con el pretérito del verbo indicado para decir lo que pasó ese día.

1. Yo *(levantarse)* a las siete y diez.
2. Mi madre *(buscar)* algunos de los ingredientes por la mañana en el mercado.
3. Yo no *(ir)* con ella porque *(tener)* que arreglar la casa.
4. Yo *(empezar)* a cocinar a las dos y media.
5. Mi amigo, Andrés, *(llegar)* para ayudarme a las tres.
6. Nosotros *(preparar)* una receta especial de arroz con pollo.
7. Unos amigos *(venir)* a las seis.
8. Todos *(vestirse)* con ropa elegante.
9. Nosotros *(empezar)* a comer a las siete.
10. Nosotros *(oír)* unos discos compactos de música clásica durante la cena.
11. *(Llover)* toda la noche pero nosotros *(divertirse)* mucho.
12. Todos mis amigos *(despedirse)* de mí a las diez.

5 Todos hicieron algo anoche

Completa las oraciones con la forma apropiada del pretérito de los verbos entre paréntesis para decir lo que hicieron anoche las siguientes personas.

 Sandra *(llamar)* a sus amigas.
Sandra *llamó* a sus amigas.

1. Ellas *(salir)* a correr.
2. Yo *(tocar)* la guitarra.
3. Miguel *(leer)* el periódico.
4. Tú *(quedarte)* en tu cuarto.
5. Uds. *(comer)* comida cubana.
6. Nosotros *(visitar)* a los abuelos.
7. Claudia *(ver)* una película sobre el Caribe.
8. Raimundo y Jaime *(estar)* en el supermercado.
9. Ellos *(comprar)* la comida necesaria para una cena elegante.
10. Ud. *(conseguir)* un regalo para llevar a una fiesta de quince años.

PARA ti

El pretérito de *conocer*
You have learned to use *conocer* to indicate who someone knows or to state what someone is familiar with. In the preterite tense, *conocer* is the equivalent of **to meet.**

*¿A quién **conociste** tú anoche?* — Whom **did you meet** last night?

***Conocí** a la familia de Raimundo.* — **I met** Raimundo's family.

Unos platos cubanos.

6 ## Durante la cena

Imagina que durante la cena tus padres te hacen algunas preguntas sobre la visita que hiciste al zoológico con tu amiga Natalia y tus amigos Paco y Alicia. Contesta sus preguntas, usando la información entre paréntesis y la forma apropiada del pretérito.

 ¿Con quién fuiste al zoológico? (ir con Paco, Alicia y Natalia)
Fui con Paco, Alicia y Natalia.

1. ¿Cómo fueron Uds.? (ir en metro)
2. ¿Dónde almorzaron Uds.? (almorzar en la cafetería del zoológico)
3. ¿Te acordaste de ver la exhibición especial de pájaros del Caribe? (sí/acordarme)
4. ¿Les gustó a tus amigas la visita al zoológico? (sí/divertirse mucho)
5. ¿Compró Natalia algo para su hermanito, Julio? (sí/conseguirle una serpiente de plástico)
6. ¿Qué más hicieron Uds.? (subir a un elefante)
7. ¿Te pasó otra cosa interesante? (sí/conocer/unos chicos del Caribe)
8. ¿Hasta qué hora se quedaron en el zoológico? (quedarse hasta las cinco)

El pretérito y el imperfecto

One sentence may contain various combinations of the two past tenses: *pretérito/pretérito, imperfecto/pretérito, pretérito/imperfecto, imperfecto/imperfecto.* For example, all verbs may be in the preterite tense if you are stating simple facts.

> *Fui a la tienda y compré algo de comida para la cena.*
>
> **I went** to the store and **bought** some food for supper.

In addition, a sentence may contain one verb that is in the imperfect tense and another that is in the preterite tense: Use the imperfect tense in a sentence to describe a repeated (habitual) past action or ongoing condition; use the preterite tense to state what happened during the repeated or ongoing action/condition.

> *Estaba en la cocina cuando tú llamaste.*
>
> **I was** in the kitchen when **you called.**

Finally, more than one verb may be in the imperfect tense when you are describing simultaneous ongoing actions or conditions.

> *Veíamos la televisión mientras esperábamos a Pilar.*
>
> **We were watching** television while **we were waiting** for Pilar.

Cuando los vi, ellos estaban tocando música en la playa de Varadero.

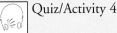 Activity 6

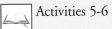 Quiz/Activity 4

Activities 5-6

Quiz/Activity 2

Answers

6
1. Fuimos en metro.
2. Almorzamos en la cafetería del zoológico.
3. Sí, me acordé de ver la exhibición especial de pájaros del Caribe.
4. Sí, se divirtieron mucho.
5. Sí, le consiguió una serpiente de plástico.
6. Subimos a un elefante.
7. Sí, conocí a unos chicos del Caribe.
8. Nos quedamos hasta las cinco.

Notes

Point out to students that the imperfect answers the question **What were the circumstances?**, while the preterite answers the question **What happened?**

Activities

Critical Listening. In order to reinforce the uses of the preterite and the imperfect, give several statements in English and ask students if they would use the preterite or the imperfect in Spanish. Then give statements in Spanish and ask the students to explain whether you used the preterite or the imperfect and why.

Multiple Intelligences (linguistic). Have students tell you what the sign says at the top of page 191.

 **NATIONAL STANDARDS**
C1.2, C4.1

7
1. fueron
2. estaba/llegaron
3. iba/tenía
4. llamaron
5. te bañabas/llamaron
6. Eran/pedimos
7. salimos
8. compró
9. Llovía/salimos
10. Era/eran

8
1. hiciste
2. ibas
3. fuimos
4. Se divirtieron
5. nos divertimos
6. llovió
7. podíamos/pudimos
8. hacía/hizo
9. Era/Fue
10. tuve

9 Possible answers:
1. vi
2. iba
3. conocí
4. dijo
5. encontraba (encontró)
6. buscaba
7. tenía
8. hablamos
9. dijo
10. tenían
11. dije
12. fui
13. estaba
14. salí
15. fui
16. entré
17. dijo
18. esperaba
19. íbamos
20. subí
21. me lavé
22. me preparé

Activities

Critical Thinking. Ask students to justify their responses for activity 7.

Spanish for Spanish Speakers. Ask students to summarize what they understand after reading the advertisement on page 192.

---

7 Anoche

Completa las siguientes oraciones lógicamente, escogiendo la palabra (o frase) apropiada para decir lo que las siguientes personas hacían o hicieron anoche.

1. Jaime y Raimundo también *(fueron/iban)* al supermercado anoche.
2. Yo *(estuve/estaba)* en el supermercado cuando Jaime y Raimundo *(llegaron/llegaban)* a hacer sus compras.
3. Raimundo *(fue/iba)* a comprar carne, pero no *(tuvo/tenía)* bastante dinero.
4. Algunas compañeras *(llamaron/llamaban)* a las siete.
5. Tú *(te bañaste/te bañabas)* cuando ellas *(llamaron/llamaban)*.
6. *(Fueron/Eran)* las siete cuando nosotros les *(pedimos/pedíamos)* prestado a mis padres el dinero necesario para comprar la comida.
7. Nosotros *(salimos/salíamos)* a las seis y media para ir al supermercado.
8. Una señora *(compró/compraba)* veinte libras de papas.
9. *(Llovió/Llovía)* cuando *(salimos/salíamos)* del supermercado.
10. *(Fue/Era)* probable que cuando llegamos a casa *(fueron/eran)* las diez.

8 El fin de semana

Pilar y Paz son buenas amigas. Completa su siguiente diálogo con el imperfecto o con el pretérito de los verbos indicados.

PILAR: Paz, ¿qué *1. (hacer)* tú durante el fin de semana? ¿No *2. (ir)* a ir al zoológico?

PAZ: El sábado Daniel y yo *3. (ir)* al parque de atracciones.

PILAR: ¿*4. (Divertirse)* Uds. mucho?

PAZ: Pues, sí y no. Por la mañana nosotros *5. (divertirse)* en las atracciones, pero *6. (llover)* casi toda la tarde y no *7. (poder)* hacer nada.

PILAR: ¡Pobrecitos! El domingo *8. (hacer)* buen tiempo todo el día.

PAZ: ¡Claro! *9. (Ser)* un día fantástico para ir al parque de atracciones, pero el domingo yo *10. (tener)* que ir con mi familia a visitar a los abuelos.

9 Ayer por la tarde

Di lo que te pasó ayer, completando el siguiente párrafo con el imperfecto o con el pretérito de los verbos indicados.

Ayer por la tarde yo *1. (ver)* a mi amiga, Amalia, en el centro comercial. Ella *2. (ir)* de compras con su mamá a quien yo *3. (conocer)* por primera vez ese día. Me *4. (decir)* que no *5. (encontrar)* lo que ella *6. (buscar)*. Yo no *7. (tener)* mucho tiempo, pero nosotros *8. (hablar)* un poco. Luego, su mamá *9. (decir)* que ellas *10. (tener)* que continuar con sus compras. Yo les *11. (decir)* "adiós" y me *12. (ir)* adonde *13. (estar)* mi carro. Yo *14. (salir)* del centro comercial y *15. (ir)* a mi casa. Cuando yo *16. (entrar)* a la casa, mi mamá me *17. (decir)* que la familia me *18. (esperar)* y que nosotros *19. (ir)* a cenar en media hora. Yo *20. (subir)* al baño donde *21. (lavarse)* las manos y *22. (prepararse)* para la cena.

SUPERMERCADOS
CAFAM
HOY 9 a.m. a 3 p.m.

■ Floresta y 20 de Julio hasta las 5 p.m.
■ Ciudad Roma, Soacha, Servitienda Chía y Kennedy 1 hasta las 4 p.m.

CERRADO ÚNICAMENTE
■ Colseguros

10 ¿Qué hiciste la semana pasada?

Di dos o tres cosas que hiciste cada día de la semana pasada.

 El lunes me vestí a las seis, me desayuné a las seis y media y fui al colegio a las siete.

11 Una cena en tu colegio

Di qué hacían estas personas para preparar una cena elegante que van a tener esta noche en tu colegio. Sigue el modelo.

 unos amigos (preparar la ensalada)/otros amigos (limpiar las mesas)
Unos amigos preparaban la ensalada mientras otros amigos limpiaban las mesas.

1. Raúl (limpiar los cubiertos)/Yolanda y Javier (lavar los platos)
2. Laura y Diego (poner flores en las mesas)/Andrés (poner los manteles y las servilletas)
3. tú (barrer el piso)/yo (arreglar las mesas)
4. ellos (comprar los refrescos necesarios)/Uds. (cocinar la comida necesaria)
5. Ud. (sacar la basura)/Sandra (ir a buscar más ayuda)
6. los profesores (dirigir el trabajo)/nosotros (hacer los quehaceres)

Este Año Nuevo cene en su casa atendido por:

RESTAURANT
PALACIO DANUBIO AZUL

Cena para seis:
$11.460
1 Wantan Cantonés
1 Kai Si Kim
1 Siu Mai
1 Pavo Danubio Especial
1 Filete Lyon Chung
1 Pollo Tamarindo
1 Chancho Perla
1 Diente Chaumin
1 Corvina Yee Sun
6 Arroz Chaufán

Cena Para:
2: $4.300   4: $7.980
3: $5.900   5: $9.480

Pedidos: 2331745 - 2313588 - 2333856
REYES LAVALLE 3240 (Detrás I. Municipalidad Las Condes)

Había muchas piñas en el mercado.

Algo más

Hay, había o hubo

The impersonal expressions *hay, había* and *hubo* are forms of the infinitive *haber* (to have). *Hay* is an irregular present-tense form of *haber* and is the equivalent of **there is/there are**. The imperfect tense of *haber, había,* and the irregular preterite-tense form of *haber, hubo,* are both equivalent to **there was/there were**.

 Quiz/Activity 5

 Activity 7

 Quiz/Activity 3

Answers

10 Creative self-expression. Each sentence should contain two preterite-tense verbs that indicate two actions students completed each day of the week.

11
1. Raúl limpiaba...Yolanda y Javier lavaban....
2. Laura y Diego ponían... Andrés ponía....
3. Tú barrías...yo arreglaba....
4. Ellos compraban...Uds. cocinaban....
5. Ud. sacaba...Sandra iba....
6. Los profesores dirigían... nosotros hacíamos....

Notes

Have students summarize their classmates' statements in order to practice third-person singular forms of the preterite tense for activity 10.

Activities

Cooperative Learning. After students have prepared answers to activity 10, have them work in cooperative pairs discussing each other's activities.

Critical Thinking. Ask groups of students to summarize several things they did yesterday and why they did them, for example, *Fui al restaurante porque tenía hambre.* As they develop their ideas, they should consider specific actions (preterite) and the states of being (imperfect) that caused them. Have several groups share their examples with the class.

NATIONAL STANDARDS
C1.2, C4.1, C5.2

Notes

Point out that Raimundo uses the metric measurement *kilogramos,* which is often shortened to *kilos.* The metric system is explained further on page 197.

Note for students that *anduvimos* is the preterite tense of *andar* and *cupo* is the preterite tense of *caber.*

Point out that *te ríes* is the present tense of the reflexive verb *reírse.* Other irregular present-tense forms and the irregular preterite tense of *reírse* and *freír* are presented later in this lesson.

The verb *caber* is regular in all forms of the present tense except *yo quepo.* You may wish to tell your students that even children who are native speakers of Spanish sometimes make the error of using *cabo.*

Activities

Cooperative Learning. After introducing the dialog (playing the audiocassette/audio compact disc, modeling words and phrases for student repetition, practicing the vocabulary for referring to foods, etc.), have students work in groups of three practicing the dialog. Circulate and assist with pronunciation and intonation.

TPR. Using overhead transparencies 37 and 38 (¿*Qué compraron?*), ask students to come up and point to the food items you name in Spanish.

12 ¿Hay, había o hubo?

Completa las siguientes oraciones con *hay, había* o *hubo,* según sea apropiado.

1. Mañana (1) una cena en la casa de un amigo, pero no es elegante.
2. El año pasado no (2) ninguna cena elegante en mi casa.
3. Anoche (3) una cena elegante en la casa de unos amigos, pero nadie podía ir.
4. Ayer (4) una cena elegante en mi casa cuando yo llegué de la biblioteca.
5. El año pasado (5) dos fiestas elegantes en mi colegio.
6. Hoy (6) una fiesta en la casa de Javier y voy a ir.

¿Qué compraron?

MADRE: ¿Adónde fueron Uds. anoche?
JAIME: **Anduvimos°** por el supermercado buscando la comida para la cena del sábado.
MADRE: ¿Pudieron conseguir **todo?°**
RAIMUNDO: Sí, todo. Compramos tanto que casi **no cupo°** en el baúl del carro.
MADRE: Jaime, ¿por qué **te ríes?°** ¿Cuál es el **chiste?°**
JAIME: No hay ningún chiste. Me estoy riendo porque pienso que compramos **demasiadas** cosas.
RAIMUNDO: Sí, tantas cosas que casi necesitamos alquilar un **camión.°**
MADRE: Pero, ¿qué compraron?
JAIME: ¡Mira! Compramos **duraznos,°** **papayas, melones°** y una **piña°** para la ensalada de frutas.
RAIMUNDO: Y para el plato **principal** compramos **carne de res,°** **costillas,°** tres libras de arroz y cinco **kilogramos°** de papas para **freír.°**

Anduvimos *we walked* **todo** *everything* **no cupo** *it didn't fit* **te ríes** *are you laughing* **chiste** *joke* **camión** *truck* **duraznos** *peaches* **melones** *melons, cantaloupes* **piña** *pineapple* **carne de res** *beef* **costillas** *ribs* **kilogramos (kilos)** *kilograms (1,000 grams or 2.205 pounds)* **freír** *fry*

13 ¿Qué comprendiste?

1. ¿Qué hicieron los chicos anoche?
2. ¿Qué dijo Raimundo que casi necesitaron alquilar?
3. ¿Qué frutas compraron para la ensalada?
4. ¿Qué comida compraron para el plato principal?
5. ¿Cuántos kilos de papas compraron?

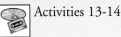

PIÑA EN RODAJAS
"Hoja Redonda"
1/. 1'250 000

790 MIL

ENSALADA DE FRUTAS
"Hoja Redonda"
1/. 1'250 000

790 MIL

14 Charlando

1. ¿A qué supermercado fuiste la última vez?
2. ¿Qué comida compraste?
3. ¿Compraste comida para toda la familia o sólo para ti?
4. ¿Te cupo todo lo que compraste en el baúl?

15 Una lista en la computadora

Imagina que cuando estabas haciendo una lista de compras para ir al supermercado, algo pasó con tu computadora. Pon las letras de cada comida en su orden correcto para reorganizar la lista antes de ir de compras.

```
  1.  2 sklio de caren de rse
  2.  1 kloi de cosstilla
  3.  5 klosi de paasp
  4.  moeid koli de chizroo
  5.  lchee
  6.  pna
  7.  3-4 dzsnoura
  8.  1 payapa
  9.  4 mneloes
 10.  1 pñia
 11.  1 klio de caseollb
 12.  2 asguteaca
 13.  lcheaug
 14.  3 tmsateo
 15.  1 ltaa de gsunteisa
 16.  2 pieimsnto
 17.  vgrinae
 18.  mdeio koli de mllaniatequ
 19.  hdelao de chateoloc
 20.  joug de nanaarj
```

Más comida en el supermercado

la aceituna	olive
la calabaza	pumpkin
la cereza	cherry
la chuleta de puerco	pork chop
el coco	coconut
la espinaca	spinach
el frijol	bean
el melocotón	peach
la sandía	watermelon

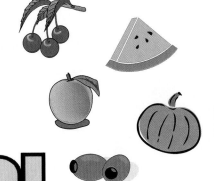

Answers

13 1. Anduvieron por el supermercado buscando la comida para la cena del sábado.
2. Dijo que casi necesitaron alquilar un camión.
3. Compraron duraznos, papayas, melones y una piña para la ensalada de frutas.
4. Para el plato principal compraron carne de res, costillas, arroz y papas.
5. Compraron cinco kilos de papas.

14 Answers will vary.

15 1. 2 kilos de carne de res
2. 1 kilo de costillas
3. 5 kilos de papas
4. medio kilo de chorizo
5. leche
6. pan
7. 3-4 duraznos
8. 1 papaya
9. 4 melones
10. 1 piña
11. 1 kilo de cebollas
12. 2 aguacates
13. lechuga
14. 3 tomates
15. 1 lata de guisantes
16. 2 pimientos
17. vinagre
18. medio kilo de mantequilla
19. helado de chocolate
20. jugo de naranja

Activities

Expansion. Additional questions (¿Qué comprendiste?): ¿Cuándo fueron los chicos al supermercado?; ¿Para qué fueron al supermercado?; ¿Consiguieron todo los chicos?; ¿Por qué a los chicos casi no les cupo en el baúl del carro todo lo que compraron?; ¿Qué van a hacer con las papas?

Additional questions (Charlando): ¿Cuándo fue la última vez que fuiste al supermercado?; ¿Comes más carne o verduras?; ¿Qué frutas te gustan?; ¿Te gusta la ensalada de frutas?

NATIONAL STANDARDS
C1.2, C2.1, C2.2, C4.1

¿Por qué se ríen ellos?

El presente de los verbos *reír* y *freír*

The verbs *reír(se)* and *freír* are irregular in the present tense. However, both verbs are formed following the same pattern, so learning the conjugation of one will help you learn the conjugation of the other.

reír(se)	
(me) río	(nos) reímos
(te) ríes	(os) reís
(se) ríe	(se) ríen
gerundio: riendo (riéndose)	

freír	
frío	freímos
fríes	freís
fríe	fríen
gerundio: friendo	

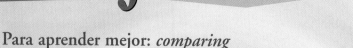

Estrategia

Para aprender mejor: *comparing*

You have already learned many words in Spanish. There are many more words in the language that you have not learned, but that does not mean you will not understand an unknown word when you see or hear it. Use your knowledge to make comparisons to new words. Does it look like something similar to what you have learned? Are the verb endings similar to another verb that you have used? Learning to compare new words to those you already know will help increase your understanding of new vocabulary.

16 ¿Por qué se ríen?

Haz las preguntas necesarias para saber por qué se ríen las siguientes personas.

Antonio
¿Por qué se ríe Antonio?

1. Uds.
2. tú
3. Dolores y Yolanda
4. ella
5. ellos
6. Héctor
7. yo
8. todos nosotros

¿Por qué se ríe Antonio?

17 Todos fríen

Hoy todos fríen algo. Haz oraciones completas, usando la forma apropiada del presente del verbo *freír* para decir lo que hacen las siguientes personas.

el señor Silva/arroz para una paella
El señor Silva fríe el arroz para una paella.

1. tú/huevos
2. Uds./papas
3. don Carlos/pollo
4. yo/tocino para ponerlo en un plato especial
5. la señora Castro y su esposo/cebollas y pimientos verdes
6. todos nosotros/algo para una cena elegante

PARA ti

Los grados centígrados
Do you remember how to convert degrees Fahrenheit to centigrade? Here is the formula:

$$\frac{C°}{5} \times 9 + 32 = F°$$

Conexión *Cultural*

El sistema métrico

How far is it from home to school? How much do you weigh? What is the temperature today? Most likely you would answer these questions using the terms **miles, pounds** and **degrees Fahrenheit**. However, if you were in one of the Spanish-speaking parts of the world, chances are you would use the metric system and express miles as kilometers, pounds as kilograms and degrees Fahrenheit as degrees Celsius (or centigrade).

The metric system is quickly becoming the worldwide standard for weights and measures due to its ease of use. Metric measurements are based upon multiples of ten.

10 millimeters	=	1 centimeter
10 centimeters	=	1 decimeter
10 decimeters	=	1 meter

Look at the following equivalents:

LENGTH/*LONGITUD*

1 centimeter/*centímetro*	= 0.3937 inches/*pulgadas*
1 meter/*metro*	= 1.094 yards/*yardas*
1 kilometer/*kilómetro*	= 0.621 miles/*millas*

WEIGHT/*PESO*

1 gram/*gramo*	= 0.035 ounces/*onzas*
1 kilogram/*kilogramo*	= 2.205 pounds/*libras*
1 metric ton/*tonelada métrica*	= 2,204.6 pounds/*libras*

AREA/*ÁREA*

1 hectare/*hectárea*	= 2.47 acres/*acres*

MOUSSE DE CIRUELAS

Ingredientes:
1 caja de ciruelas pasas (300 grs. aprox.)
1/2 taza de agua
3/4 taza de azúcar
5 claras batidas a la nieve
2 sobres de gelatina sin sabor
1 taza de crema de leche

El peso del bebé es de 7.5 kilogramos.

Answers

17 1. Fríes los huevos.
2. Fríen las papas.
3. Don Carlos fríe el pollo.
4. Frío el tocino para ponerlo en un plato especial.
5. La señora Castro y su esposo fríen las cebollas y los pimientos verdes.
6. Todos nosotros freímos algo para una cena elegante.

Notes

Connections. You may wish to teach how to find degrees centigrade using the formula:

$$C° = 5/9 \times (F° - 32).$$

Remind students that some food words may vary from country to country. For example, *papas* in Latin America are called *patatas* in Spain. Similarly, *chuletas de puerco* are also called *chuletas de cerdo*.

Activities

Multiple Intelligences (logical-mathematical). Have students convert several metric measurements as a class activity. (You may wish to obtain the help of a math or home economics teacher.) As an alternative, take student suggestions to prepare a list of several measurements that students will convert as a homework assignment.

Spanish for Spanish Speakers. After reading the recipe for *Mousse de ciruelas* on page 197, ask students questions to determine how much they understood: *¿Cuántos gramos de ciruelas requiere la receta?; ¿Cuáles son los ingredientes del Mousse de ciruelas?; ¿Qué son las claras?; ¿Qué quieren decir las letras "grs."?*

NATIONAL STANDARDS
C1.2, C3.2, C4.1, C4.2

Activity 18

Quiz/Activity 6

Activities 10-11

Quiz/Activity 6

Answers

18 1. Es (answers will vary) kilos.
2. Es (answers will vary) metro(s) con (answers will vary) centímetro(s).
3. Hay diez milímetros en un centímetro.
4. Hay (answers will vary) kilómetros de mi casa al colegio.
5. Compró (answers will vary) litros de leche la semana pasada.
6. Hace (answers will vary) grados.

Notes

Draw students' attention to similarities in the conjugations of the verbs *reír* and *freír* and the verbs *conducir* and *traducir*.

Point out that *caer* and *creer* follow the pattern of *leer*, adding accent marks and changing *i → y* for the third person: *leyó, leyeron; creyó, creyeron*.

Activities

Students with Special Needs. As a class activity, have students make up sentences using the preterite-tense verb forms shown on page 198.

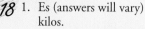

NATIONAL STANDARDS
C1.2, C2.2, C3.1, C4.1, C5.2

18 Cruzando fronteras

Contesta las siguientes preguntas en español, usando el sistema métrico.

1. ¿Cuál es tu peso?
2. ¿Cuál es tu estatura *(How tall are you)*?
3. ¿Cuántos milímetros hay en un centímetro?
4. ¿Cuántos kilómetros hay de tu casa al colegio?
5. ¿Cuántos litros de leche compró tu familia la semana pasada?
6. ¿Qué temperatura hace ahora?

Venimos en autobus.

IDIOMA

Más verbos irregulares en el pretérito

You have already learned how to use several irregular preterite-tense verbs in Spanish. The following chart provides some additional verbs that are irregular in the preterite tense. Learning them will improve your ability to talk about the past.

andar:	anduve, anduviste, anduvo, anduvimos, anduvisteis, anduvieron
caber:	cupe, cupiste, cupo, cupimos, cupisteis, cupieron
conducir:	conduje, condujiste, condujo, condujimos, condujisteis, condujeron
freír:	freí, freíste, frió, freímos, freísteis, frieron
leer:	leí, leíste, leyó, leímos, leísteis, leyeron
poder:	pude, pudiste, pudo, pudimos, pudisteis, pudieron
poner:	puse, pusiste, puso, pusimos, pusisteis, pusieron
querer:	quise, quisiste, quiso, quisimos, quisisteis, quisieron
reír:	reí, reíste, rió, reímos, reísteis, rieron
saber:	supe, supiste, supo, supimos, supisteis, supieron
traducir:	traduje, tradujiste, tradujo, tradujimos, tradujisteis, tradujeron
traer:	traje, trajiste, trajo, trajimos, trajisteis, trajeron
venir:	vine, viniste, vino, vinimos, vinisteis, vinieron

In the preterite tense, *saber* is the equivalent of **to find out.** *Querer* may mean **to try** when used affirmatively in the preterite tense or **to refuse** when used negatively.

*¿Qué **supiste** anoche?*
***Supe** que hubo una cena elegante en la casa de Raimundo.*
***Quise** ir, pero mis padres **no quisieron** darme permiso.*

What **did you find out** last night?
I **found out** there was an elegant supper at Raimundo's house.
I **tried** to go, but my parents **refused** to give me permission.

198   Lección 9

19 ¿Qué pasó?

Toma elementos de cada columna para formar ocho oraciones completas y lógicas. Haz los cambios que sean necesarios.

A	B	C
yo	andar	poner todo en el camión
tú	freír	un kilo de duraznos del mercado
Raimundo	poder	por el parque todo el día
Sandra y Carmen	poner	demasiadas papas en aceite
Jaime	querer	la fecha de la cena hace un mes
mi madre	saber	preparar una receta difícil
mis hermanos	traer	las costillas en el refrigerador
nosotros	venir	del supermercado hace dos horas

20 ¿Qué hacían?

Di lo que hacían las siguientes personas ayer por la tarde, de acuerdo con las ilustraciones.

 Cristina/andar
Cristina anduvo por el supermercado.

1. Guillermo y Manuel/ir   2. nosotros/conducir   3. los niños/andar

4. Gloria/poder ir   5. Uds./querer ir   6. tú/venir

7. yo/querer ir   8. la familia Torres/conducir

 Activity 20

Answers

19 Answers will vary.

20 Possible answers:
1. ...fueron al banco.
2. ...condujimos al parque.
3. ...anduvieron por el zoológico.
4. ...pudo ir al centro.
5. ...quisieron ir al centro comercial.
6. ...viniste a la biblioteca.
7. ...quise ir al cine.
8. ...condujo al parque de atracciones.

Activities

Expansion. Ask the following questions in order to practice irregular preterite verbs: *¿Qué ropa te pusiste esta mañana?; ¿A qué hora viniste al colegio?; ¿Viniste caminando o condujiste al colegio?; ¿Qué cosas trajiste al colegio?; ¿Qué cosas trajiste a la clase de español?* The questions may also be presented in the third-person plural *(Uds.)*.

Students with Special Needs. Model a sentence for activity 19.

 NATIONAL STANDARDS
C1.2, C4.1

Answers

21 1. ¿Quién tradujo el menú al español?/Yo traduje....
2. ¿Quién vino al restaurante ayer?/Muchas personas vinieron....
3. ¿Cuántas papas freíste?/Freí....
4. ¿Dónde puso Lorenzo la carne de res?/Lorenzo puso....
5. ¿Qué no cupo en el refrigerador?/Todo cupo....
6. ¿Quién trajo demasiadas frutas del mercado?/ Norberto y Mónica trajeron....

22 1. fueron
2. anduvieron
3. compraron
4. estaban
5. pudieron
6. Llevaron
7. trajeron
8. tenía
9. cupieron
10. quiso
11. encontró
12. vino
13. dijo
14. necesitaba
15. puso
16. supo
17. hizo
18. hizo

Activities

Prereading Strategy. Encourage students to find cognates and other words they are able to recognize and understand in the menu on page 201. Then ask students some questions to prepare them for reading in depth: What is the name of the restaurant? *(Restaurante Sazón Caribe)*; What can a customer order to drink? (juices, hot chocolate, coffee, tea); What seafood is available? (clams, shrimp, crab and octopus).

Students with Special Needs. Model a second sentence for activity 21 and conjugate the first verb *(ir)* for activity 22.

21 En el restaurante de tu tío

Imagina que tú trabajas en el restaurante de tu tío. Él estuvo enfermo ayer y ahora te hace algunas preguntas sobre lo que pasó ayer. Trabajando en parejas, alterna con tu compañero/a de clase en hacer y en contestar las preguntas que te hace tu tío. Sigue el modelo.

quién/no poder trabajar (Ricardo)
A: ¿Quién no pudo trabajar ayer?
B: Ricardo no pudo trabajar ayer.

1. quién/traducir el menú al español (yo)
2. quién/venir al restaurante (muchas personas)
3. cuántas papas/freír/tú (5 kilogramos)
4. dónde/poner/Lorenzo/la carne de res (el refrigerador)
5. qué/no caber en el refrigerador (todo)
6. quién/traer demasiadas frutas del mercado (Norberto y Mónica)

Ricardo no pudo trabajar ayer, pero hoy sí trabaja.

22 Anoche en el supermercado

Jaime y Raimundo estuvieron anoche en el supermercado. Completa el siguiente párrafo o con el imperfecto o con el pretérito de los verbos indicados para saber lo que hicieron.

Jaime y Raimundo 1. *(ir)* anoche al supermercado. Ellos 2. *(andar)* por el supermercado por casi dos horas y 3. *(comprar)* muchas cosas para la cena del sábado. Ellos 4. *(estar)* muy felices porque 5. *(poder)* conseguirlo todo. 6. *(Llevar)* el carro sin nada y lo 7. *(traer)* con demasiada comida. El carro 8. *(tener)* tantas cosas que los muchachos casi no 9. *(caber)*. Raimundo 10. *(querer)* conseguir un camión, pero no 11. *(encontrar)* ninguno. Un muchacho del supermercado 12. *(venir)* para ayudarlos, pero Jaime 13. *(decir)* que no 14. *(necesitar)* ayuda ni tampoco un camión. Él 15. *(poner)* todo en el carro. Raimundo nunca 16. *(saber)* cómo Jaime lo 17. *(hacer)*, pero él cree que lo 18. *(hacer)* muy bien.

Esta muchacha nos dijo cuánto costaba.

23 Una entrevista

Trabajando en parejas, hazle una entrevista de cinco a diez minutos a tu compañero/a, preguntándole sobre la última vez que fue de compras. Usa el pretérito y el imperfecto en tus preguntas. Luego, tu compañero/a te hace una entrevista a ti.

A: ¿Por dónde anduviste de compras la última vez?
B: Anduve de compras por las tiendas del barrio.
A: ¿Querías comprar algo para ti o para otra persona?
B: Quería comprar algo para mi mamá.

El menú

Restaurante
SAZÓN CARIBE

MENÚ

El desayuno - ¡Buenos días!

* Jugo de frutas
  naranja
  toronja
  piña
  papaya

* Chocolate
* Café con leche
* Té
* Cereal

* Huevos
  con tocino
  con salchicha
  con cebolla y tomate

El almuerzo - ¡Buenas tardes!

* Carnes
  carne de res
  costillas
  filete
  ternera *veal*

* Aves
  pollo
  pavo
  pato

* Mariscos
  almejas *clam*
  camarones *shrimp*
  cangrejo *crab*
  pulpo

* Cremas
  de tomate
  de cebolla
  de camarón *seafood*

* Arroces
  con pollo
  con mariscos

* Postres
  flan de limón
  flan de ciruela *cherry*
  flan de pera

La cena - ¡Buenas noches!

* Sandwiches
  de queso
  de jamón
  de pollo

* Sopas
  de verduras
  del día

* Helados
  de fresa
  de vainilla
  de chocolate

 Quiz/Activity 7

 Activity 39

 Activities 12-13

 Quiz/Activity 7

Answers
23 Creative self-expression.

Notes
Another way to say *el menú* is *la carta*.

Remind students that in the Spanish-speaking world, lunch (*el almuerzo* or *la comida*) is often larger than dinner (*la cena*). This fact is reflected in the menu at the *Restaurante Sazón Caribe*.

Activities
Cooperative Learning. Working in pairs, have students take turns asking one another what foods they like on the menu for the restaurant *Sazón Caribe*.

Language through Action. In groups of three, have students write a dialog between a server and two customers in which the customers are not sure what they want to order (they should use the menu on this page to place their order). The server must make recommendations and give reasons for each suggestion. Ask for volunteers or select students to present their dialogs to the class.

Multiple Intelligences (bodily-kinesthetic/spatial). Have students ask for a copy of the menu from a favorite local restaurant. Then have them use the items listed to prepare the equivalent menu in Spanish, adding a design of their own. Have students work in pairs, asking and answering questions in Spanish about each other's menus.

NATIONAL STANDARDS
C1.1, C1.2, C4.1, C5.1

Answers

24
1. Hay almejas, camarones, cangrejo y pulpo.
2. No, no ofrecen cremas para la cena. Ofrecen sopas.
3. Puedo ordenar chocolate, café con leche, té o cereal.
4. No, no es un ave. Es una carne.
5. Para el almuerzo tienen flanes de limón, de ciruela y de pera.
6. Tiene jugos de naranja, toronja, piña y papaya.
7. Preparan los huevos con tocino, con salchicha y con cebolla y tomate.

25 Possible answers:
1. ¿...ordenaron...?/ ...ordenaron carne de res y papas.
2. ¿...ordenó...?/...ordenó almejas.
3. ¿...ordenaste...?/...ordené camarones.
4. ¿...ordenó...?/...ordenó cangrejo.
5. ¿...ordenaron...?/ ...ordenamos costillas.
6. ¿...ordenamos...?/ ...ordenamos papaya y piña.
7. ¿...ordenaron...?/ ...ordenaron salchichas y huevos.
8. ¿...ordené...?/...ordenaste pulpo.

Notes

The term *plancha* refers to a **grill**, where students may have seen eggs cooked in a diner, restaurant or café, so *a la plancha* is literally **on the grill**. Point out the word *vapor* refers to **vapor** or **steam**. Although they may recognize the term *huevos*, students will not necessarily know *revueltos,* for **scrambled**, or *fritos,* for **fried**.

24 ¿Qué comprendiste?

Contesta las siguientes preguntas sobre el menú del Restaurante Sazón Caribe.

1. ¿Qué mariscos hay?
2. ¿Ofrecen cremas para la cena? ¿Qué ofrecen?
3. ¿Qué puedes ordenar para desayunar diferente de jugos y huevos?
4. ¿Es la ternera un ave? ¿Qué es?
5. ¿Qué postres tienen para el almuerzo?
6. ¿Qué jugos tiene este restaurante para el desayuno?
7. ¿Cómo preparan los huevos?

25 En el restaurante Sazón Caribe

Trabajando en parejas, alterna con tu compañero/a de clase en hacer y contestar preguntas para decir lo que ordenaron las siguientes personas cuando fueron al restaurante.

PARA ti

Más palabras en el menú

a la plancha	*grilled*
al vapor	*steamed*
asado/a	*roasted*
el cordero	*lamb*
los huevos revueltos	*scrambled eggs*
los huevos fritos	*fried eggs*
la langosta	*lobster*

Amalia
A: ¿Qué ordenó Amalia?
B: Amalia ordenó ternera.

1. Sara e Ignacio   2. Susana   3. tú   4. Jairo Alfonso

5. Uds.   6. todos nosotros   7. Esteban y Jesús   8. yo

Oportunidades

El menú

Is there a Latin-American or Spanish restaurant in your community? If so, the next time you go there, try ordering your meal in Spanish. This will not only give you an opportunity to practice what you have learned in this lesson about food, but the occasion also will give you a chance to test your ability to communicate in Spanish. In addition, practicing your Spanish with native speakers is a fun way to improve your pronunciation and listening comprehension skills.

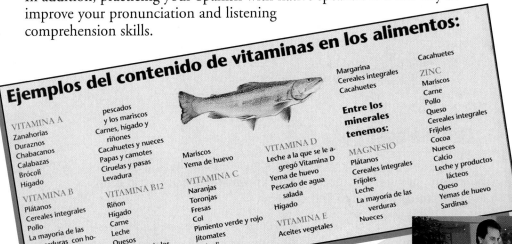

Ejemplos del contenido de vitaminas en los alimentos:

VITAMINA A
Zanahorias
Duraznos
Chabacanos
Calabazas
Brócoli
Hígado

VITAMINA B
Plátanos
Cereales integrales
Pollo
La mayoría de las verduras con hojas (como puede ser la lechuga)
La mayoría de los

pescados y los mariscos
Carnes, hígado y riñones
Cacahuetes y nueces
Papas y camotes
Ciruelas y pasas
Levadura

VITAMINA B12
Riñon
Hígado
Carne
Leche
Quesos
La mayoría de los pescados

Mariscos
Yema de huevo

VITAMINA C
Naranjas
Toronjas
Fresas
Col
Pimiento verde y rojo
Jitomates
Brócoli

VITAMINA D
Leche a la que se le agregó Vitamina D
Yema de huevo
Pescado de agua salada
Hígado

VITAMINA E
Aceites vegetales

Margarina
Cereales integrales
Cacahuetes

Entre los minerales tenemos:

MAGNESIO
Plátanos
Cereales integrales
Frijoles
Leche
La mayoría de las verduras
Nueces

Cacahuetes

ZINC
Mariscos
Carne
Pollo
Queso
Cereales integrales
Frijoles
Cocoa
Nueces
Calcio
Leche y productos lácteos
Queso
Yemas de huevo
Sardinas

¿Qué van a ordenar esta noche? Tenemos una langosta al vapor muy especial.

 **26 Quiero...**

 Trabajando en grupos de tres, un estudiante hace el papel de camarero/a, otro el de cocinero/a *(cook)* y otro el de cliente que va a comer a un restaurante. El camarero debe escribir y repetir lo que el cliente pide del menú (usen el menú del Restaurante Sazón Caribe). Luego, el camarero debe reportar al cocinero lo que el cliente pidió. El cocinero debe repetir lo que el camarero dice. Al terminar deben cambiar papeles *(change roles)*.

CAMARERO:	¿Qué va a ordenar?
CLIENTE:	Quiero una crema de cebolla y unas costillas.
CAMARERO:	*(Write down the order while saying it aloud in Spanish.)* Una crema de cebolla y unas costillas.
COCINERO:	¿Qué ordenó el señor?
CAMARERO:	El señor ordenó una crema de cebolla y unas costillas.
COCINERO:	Muy bien, una crema de cebolla y unas costillas.

Answers
26 Creative self-expression.

Notes
This *Oportunidades* recognizes the importance of using Spanish as an enjoyable and worthwhile tool in real life for authentic communication in another person's first language.

Activities
Connections. Encourage students to find cognates and other words they are able to recognize and understand in the realia that accompanies the section *Oportunidades* on this page. Then begin a discussion about the nutritional value of the foods listed (i.e., what foods are high in vitamin C?; what foods have magnesium?).

Multiple Intelligences (intrapersonal/linguistic). Additional questions (*¿Qué comprendiste?*): *¿Cuáles son tres de tus comidas favoritas?; Describe tu plato principal favorito.*

NATIONAL STANDARDS
C1.1, C1.2, C1.3, C2.1, C2.2, C4.1, C5.1, C5.2

Answers

27
1. camarón (El camarón no es un lugar.)
2. carne de res (La carne de res no es un marisco.)
3. camión (El camión no es una comida.)
4. sandwich (El sandwich no se puede tomar.)
5. camarón (El camarón no viene del puerco.)
6. crema (La crema no es una fruta.)
7. melón (El melón no es un animal.)
8. costilla (La costilla no es un ave.)
9. chiste (El chiste no se come.)
10. vainilla (La vainilla no es una carne.)

28
1. ...leíamos...vino....
2. ...sabía...preguntó...quería.
3. ...pudieron...eran....
4. ...quería...tenía....
5. ...cabía...comió....
6. ...trajiste...podías....

Notes

Remind students that in many Spanish-speaking countries, telephone numbers are given two numbers at a time, as shown in the advertisement on this page for the *Restaurante El Marinero.*

Activities

Critical Thinking. Have students justify their answers for activity 28.

Students with Special Needs. Help students get started with activity 27 by giving the answers to the first one or two sets of words.

27 ¿Cuál no corresponde?

Trabajando en parejas, alterna con tu compañero/a de clase en decir la palabra de cada grupo que no corresponde lógicamente. Luego, explica por qué no corresponde.

1. aeropuerto — camarón — tienda — lechería
2. almejas — cangrejo — carne de res — pulpo
3. carne — camión — ave — marisco
4. té — café — chocolate — sandwich
5. tocino — salchicha — camarón — puerco
6. toronja — crema — piña — pera
7. melón — camello — pantera — ratón
8. costilla — pato — pavo — pollo
9. galleta — ciruela — chiste — durazno
10. filete — vainilla — ternera — costillas

28 ¿Qué les pasó?

Di lo que les pasó a las siguientes personas cuando fueron a un restaurante la semana pasada, usando la forma apropiada del pretérito o del imperfecto de los verbos indicados.

Cuando la gente *(llegar),* los camareros *(poner)* las mesas.
Cuando la gente <u>llegó</u>, los camareros <u>ponían</u> las mesas.

1. Cuando nosotros *(leer)* el menú, el camarero *(venir)* a la mesa.
2. Yo no *(saber)* qué pedir cuando el camarero me *(preguntar)* lo que yo *(querer).*
3. Rodrigo y Carlota no *(poder)* pedir los camarones porque *(ser)* muy caros.
4. Yo *(querer)* comer comida cubana, pero el restaurante no *(tener)* nada de Cuba.
5. A la hora de comer el postre, a Armando no le *(caber)* nada porque *(comer)* mucha ternera.
6. Tú no *(traer)* dinero y no *(poder)* pagar tu comida.

El Bosque Encantado

*Comida Criolla
(Todo Hecho al Momento)

*Tacos de:
Pollo
Carne
Jueyes
Langosta
Camarones
Y Mucho Más
*Alcapurrias
*Bacalaitos
*Piononos
*Rellenos

Batidas Piña Colada,
Jugos Naturales, y Más.

PLÁTANO
CHIAPAS CALIDAD
DE EXPORTACION   A SOLO N $ 1.26 KG.

MANGO
PARAISO SELECTO   A SOLO N $ 0.94 KG.

LIMÓN
AGRIO COLIMA   A SOLO N $ 1.24 KG.

SANDÍA
ROJA DULCE   A SOLO N $ 0.38 KG.

TUNA
BLANCA SIN ESPINAS   A SOLO N $ 1.64 KG.

ZANAHORIA
FRESCA   A SOLO N $ 0.82 KG.

Autoevaluación. Como repaso y autoevaluación, responde lo siguiente:
1. Write three sentences telling what you did yesterday.
2. How would you say in Spanish that you met the president yesterday?
3. In four sentences, describe the last time you were invited somewhere for dinner.
4. Tell a friend in Spanish that there was an elegant dinner at the Cuban restaurant in your neighborhood last year.
5. Name three food items you learned in this lesson.
6. In complete sentences, write three different foods that people you know fry.
7. In the metric system, how tall are you? How much do you weigh? How far is it from your home to your school?
8. How would you say in Spanish that you found out the food server from the restaurant speaks Spanish?
9. What do you know about Cuba?

Answers

Autoevaluación
Possible answers:
1. Answers will vary.
2. Ayer conocí al presidente.
3. Answers will vary.
4. El año pasado hubo una cena elegante en el restaurante cubano de mi barrio.
5. el durazno, la papaya, el melón, la piña, la carne de res, la costilla
6. Yo frío los huevos. Mis padres fríen las papas. Mi hermana fríe el pollo. La vecina fríe las cebollas y los pimientos verdes.
7. Answers will vary.
8. Supe que el camarero del restaurante habla español.
9. Answers will vary.

Notes
The sign that appears in the upper-left-hand side of the page shows several foods that are typically served at a roadside restaurant stand in Puerto Rico.

Activities
Multiple Intelligences (intrapersonal/linguistic). As an additional activity, have students tell about the last time they ate at a formal restaurant. They should tell whom they went with, what foods they ate, what they had to drink and any other details they wish.

Spanish for Spanish Speakers.
Ask students some questions in order to determine how well they understand the advertisements on pages 204-205: ¿Son los tres anuncios de restaurantes?; ¿Para qué son los anuncios?; ¿Qué tipo de comida ofrecen en los dos restaurantes?; ¿Cómo se llaman los restaurantes de los anuncios?; ¿Cuál es el número de teléfono del Restaurante El Marinero?

NATIONAL STANDARDS
C1.1, C2.2, C3.1, C4.1, C4.2

Activity 14

Answers

A Creative self-expression.

B Creative writing practice.

Notes
www

Search Engines
Lycos
http://www.lycos.com/
Yahoo
http://www.yahoo.com/
Yahoo Español
http://espanol.yahoo.com/
Webcrawler
http://www.webcrawler.com/
Infoseek
http://www.infoseek.com/
Altavista
http://www.altavista.digital.com/

Since Internet addresses change, be sure to check out all Web sites and search engines before students try to use them and experience problems.

Hold a Hispanic food-tasting day for which each student makes a Hispanic dish to share with others in the class.

As part of your classroom management, set a time limit for activity A. Then hold students accountable for their work by selecting several pairs of students to summarize the information for the class.

NATIONAL STANDARDS
C1.1, C1.3, C3.1, C4.1, C5.1

¡La práctica hace al maestro!

A Comunicación

Working with a partner, take notes as you talk about what each of you did during the past week. Make up any of the information you wish. As you talk, list one thing your partner did each day. Be sure to add any possible details, based upon your partner's description. Finally, present the information to another pair of students.

A: ¿Qué hiciste el lunes de la semana pasada?

B: Comí en la Casa Blanca.

A: Y, ¿cómo era la cena?

B: Era muy elegante y había mucha comida y muchos camareros.

A: ¿Qué comieron?

B: Crema de cebolla, pulpo y de postre comimos flan de limón.

Anoche comimos hamburguesas en el restaurante.

B Conexión con la tecnología

Utilizing one of the search engines, carry out an Internet search for Latin-American or Spanish recipes. Print out several that you would like to try. You may wish to make one or more of the recipes to share with others in the class. Bring a copy of the recipe to share with the class as well. Finally, discuss the system of measurements used in the recipe(s).

206   Lección 9

VOCABULARIO

¿Cuántos kilos quiere Ud.?

La comida

la almeja
el ave
el camarón
el cangrejo
la carne de res
el cereal
la ciruela
la costilla
la crema
el durazno
el filete
el flan
el limón
el marisco
el melón
la papaya
la pera
la piña
el pulpo
la salchicha
el sandwich
el té
la ternera
el tocino
la toronja
la vainilla

Verbos

acordar(se) (de) (ue)
andar
caber
describir
freír (i, i)
hubo
reír(se) (i, i)

Expresiones y otras palabras

anoche
el camión
el chiste
demasiado,-a
elegante
el kilo(gramo)
el menú
necesario,-a
la parte
principal
probable
todo

¿Qué frutas vendían en el mercado?

Me acordé de comprar cereal para el desayuno.

Testing/Assessment
Test Booklet
Oral Proficiency
   Evaluation Manual
Portfolio Assessment

Activities

Cooperative Learning. Have students say a word they have learned in Spanish and then select someone else to spell the word. Have them check their spelling and then switch roles.

Multiple Intelligences (linguistic). Dictate a letter of the alphabet to the class. Give students three minutes to write any words they can think of in Spanish that begin with that letter. After calling time, ask students to read their lists aloud. The student with the longest list of correct words wins.

Pronunciation. To ensure proper pronunciation, model each word or expression and have students repeat after you.

NATIONAL STANDARDS
C1.2, C4.1

Content reviewed in *Lección 10*
- clothing
- foods
- describing how something was done
- expressing length of time

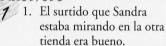
Answers

1
1. El surtido que Sandra estaba mirando en la otra tienda era bueno.
2. No le gusta.
3. Es de seda.
4. Sí, hay uno.

2 Answers will vary.

Notes
The verb *probar(se)* requires the stem change $o \rightarrow ua$ in the present tense.

Activities
Critical Listening. Play the audiocassette/audio compact disc recording of the dialog as students look at the illustration and imagine what the people are saying to one another.

Expansion. Additional questions (*¿Qué comprendiste?*): *¿A quién le debe pedir Sandra un consejo, según Carmen?*; *¿Qué está buscando Sandra?*; *¿Qué le aconseja el dependiente a Sandra?*; *¿En qué mano tiene el dependiente el vestido a cuadros?*; *¿De qué color es el vestido a rayas?*

Additional questions (*Charlando*): *¿Qué tienda tiene un buen surtido de ropa donde vives?*; *¿Cuál es tu tela favorita?*; *¿Pides ayuda a un dependiente cuando necesitas consejo?*

Contexto cultural
EL CARIBE

Lección 10
Buscando un vestido

SANDRA: El **surtido**° de vestidos que estaba mirando en la otra tienda era bueno.
CARMEN: Sí, pero aquí también hay buena **variedad** de vestidos.
SANDRA: Bueno, el problema es que no puedo **decidir** cuál comprar.
CARMEN: Entonces, pídele un **consejo**° al **dependiente.**°
SANDRA: Señor, busco un vestido elegante para una cena. ¿Qué me **aconseja?**
DEPENDIENTE: A ver. **¿Qué le parece**° este azul **a rayas?**°
SANDRA: No me gusta y, **además,**° parece **desteñido.**°
DEPENDIENTE: ¿Y este negro **a cuadros**° blancos? La **tela**° es de seda. ¿Quiere **probárselo?**° Allí está el **vestidor.**

surtido *assortment, supply, selection* **consejo** *advice* **dependiente** *clerk* **¿Qué le parece...?** *What do you think...?* **a rayas** *striped* **además** *besides, furthermore* **desteñido** *faded* **a cuadros** *plaid, checkered* **tela** *fabric, cloth* **probárselo** *to try it (on)*

¿Qué comprendiste?
1. ¿Cómo era el surtido de vestidos en la otra tienda?
2. ¿Cómo le parece a Sandra el vestido a rayas?
3. ¿De qué tela es el vestido negro a cuadros?
4. ¿Hay un vestidor en la tienda?

Charlando
1. ¿Te gusta llevar ropa desteñida? Explica.
2. ¿Pides consejo cuando vas a comprar ropa? ¿A quién se lo pides?
3. ¿Aconsejas a tus amigos/as cuando vas de compras con ellos?
4. ¿Te pruebas la ropa que vas a comprar?

PARA ti

Expresiones adicionales

color claro	light color
color oscuro	dark color
color entero	solid color
estampado/a	printed
hacer juego	to match
la talla	size
vestido largo	full-length evening dress

Conexión cultural

El Caribe

Puerto Rico, la República Dominicana y Cuba son los países de habla hispana que están en el Caribe. Todos ellos tienen playas muy bonitas y clima tropical todo el año. ¿Te acuerdas por qué están unidos históricamente? Cristóbal Colón los visitó durante sus viajes al continente americano en el siglo XV.

Estas tres naciones tienen, además, una gran influencia en el mundo por sus contribuciones en los deportes, la música y la

REPÚBLICA DOMINICANA

literatura. A nivel internacional, se destacan en deportes como el béisbol, el boxeo y el básquetbol. En la música, ritmos como el merengue, la salsa y el mambo se bailan en todo el mundo. La literatura caribeña tiene un gran representante en el autor cubano, José Martí. Su libro de poemas, *Versos sencillos,* es muy famoso. La canción *Guantanamera,* que es muy conocida, está basada en uno de los versos de este libro.

Como ves, hay mucho para ver y conocer en el Caribe. ¿No te gustaría ir para explorarlo?

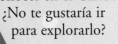

Los ritmos del Caribe se bailan en todo el mundo.

C U B A
LA ISLA GRANDE

Estatua de Cristóbal Colón en la República Dominicana.

Quiz/Activity 2

Activity 2

Notes

Inform students that *José Martí* is a national hero in Cuba, having been a leader in the battle for independence.

Students may need help with the meaning of the following words: *históricamente* (historically), *se destacan* (stand out), *nivel* (level).

Activities

Communities. Assign each student to return to the next class session with the name of a well-known person from each of these three Spanish-speaking Caribbean countries.

Critical Thinking. Ask students if they can name the capital cities of Puerto Rico, the Dominican Republic and Cuba. In turn, name other Spanish-speaking countries and ask the students to recall the capitals.

Prereading Strategy. This *Conexión cultural* provides an opportunity for students to increase their knowledge about the Spanish-speaking world by reading about the Caribbean in Spanish. Before beginning the *Conexión cultural,* consider asking some general preparation questions about the theme of the reading: What are some Spanish-speaking Caribbean countries? What do students know about these places? Then have students skim the *Conexión cultural* for cognates and any words or expressions they already know.

NATIONAL STANDARDS
C1.2, C3.2, C4.1, C4.2

Answers

3 Check maps for accuracy.

Notes

Note that the Dominican Republic shares the island of *Hispaniola* with Haiti.

Point out that the official status of Puerto Rico is that of a U.S. Commonwealth (*Estado Libre Asociado*).

Activities

Critical Thinking. Have students prepare a list comparing Cuba, Puerto Rico and the Dominican Republic. Their list can include both similarities and differences.

Expansion. Ask students if they have visited any islands of the Caribbean. If so, ask for volunteers to give a presentation in which they describe one or more islands.

Multiple Intelligences (linguistic/spatial). In groups of four, have students imagine they are preparing a marketing campaign for the tourist office of Puerto Rico or the Dominican Republic. Have them create a poster and a pamphlet that include the places a tourist might want to visit and the things they can do there.

Students with Special Needs. Review the formation of regular present participles with students: For *-ar* verbs, drop the *-ar* and add *-ando*; for *-er* and *-ir* verbs, drop the *-er/-ir* ending and add *-iendo*. In addition, remind students that verbs in the imperfect progressive tense have the same spelling and stem changes as the present progressive tense, which students already have learned.

CONEXIONES
3 Cruzando fronteras

Dibuja un mapa del Caribe, en relación a los Estados Unidos, con Puerto Rico, la República Dominicana, Cuba y otros países del área. Añade los nombres de las capitales de estos países, las montañas, los lagos, los ríos (*rivers*) y otros puntos geográficos, si puedes. Busca información en la biblioteca o la Internet si es necesario.

Una playa hermosa de Cuba.

Oportunidades

Viajando al Caribe

Travel to the Spanish-speaking islands of the Caribbean is very popular among Americans, especially during a long, cold winter. Many companies offer reduced rates and reasonable travel packages. If you travel to the Caribbean, speaking Spanish will enable you to find unique areas and experience activities that are off the beaten path of other tourists.

IDIOMA

El imperfecto progresivo

Just as the present progressive tense describes something that is occurring right now, the imperfect progressive tense tells what was going on at a specific time in the past, often when something else happened. It is formed by combining the imperfect tense of *estar* with the present participle of a verb.

*Yo **estaba pensando** en comprar una camisa a rayas.*	I was **thinking** about buying a striped shirt.
*Cuando los vi ayer **estaban comprando** un vestido a cuadros.*	When I saw them yesterday, **they were buying** a plaid dress.

Object pronouns may precede the form of *estar* or may follow and be attached to the present participle, which may require a written accent mark in order to maintain the original stress of the present participle without the pronoun.

***Lo** estaba comprando.*	→	*Estaba comprándo**lo**.*
***Nos** estábamos probando unos zapatos.*	→	*Estábamos probándo**nos** unos zapatos.*

4 ¿Qué estaban haciendo?

Di lo que estaban haciendo las siguientes personas cuando las viste ayer, de acuerdo con las ilustraciones.

 Andrés

Cuando lo vi, Andrés estaba comiendo costillas.

1. tú   2. Mario   3. Margarita y Carlota   4. David y Paloma

5. tú y yo   6. Sandra   7. Luis e Isabel   8. mi hermano

5 El día de Enrique

Completa el diálogo entre Enrique y su amigo Daniel, usando la forma apropiada del imperfecto progresivo de los verbos indicados para saber lo que dicen.

DANIEL: Hola, Enrique. ¿Qué tal?

ENRIQUE: No muy bien.

DANIEL: ¿Por qué? ¿Qué pasó?

ENRIQUE: Bueno, todo empezó esta mañana muy temprano. Cuando yo 1. *(dormir),* un camión pasó por mi cuadra y su claxon me despertó. Después, cuando 2. *(ducharse),* el agua caliente se acabó, y cuando 3. *(afeitarse),* la luz se fue. Luego, cuando 4. *(desayunarse),* se me cayó el chocolate caliente en el pantalón nuevo.

DANIEL: ¡Qué día!

ENRIQUE: Espera, eso no es todo. Cuando la profesora 5. *(leer)* los poemas de José Martí en la clase, me dormí. Después, cuando mis amigos y yo 6. *(jugar)* al béisbol, empezó a llover muy fuerte. Cuando 7. *(volver)* a casa, vi que no tenía todos los libros para hacer mis tareas. ¿Y sabes qué pasó ahora cuando 8. *(ver)* mi programa de televisión favorito?

DANIEL: No, ¿qué?

ENRIQUE: ¡Llamaste tú!

 Activity 4

Answers

4 Possible answers:
1. ...te vi, tú estabas friendo huevos con tocino.
2. ...lo vi, Mario estaba probándose (se estaba probando) un nuevo suéter.
3. ...las vi, Margarita y Carlota estaban patinando en el parque.
4. ...los vi, David y Paloma estaban pescando.
5. ...nos vimos, nosotros estábamos leyendo en la biblioteca.
6. ...la vi, Sandra estaba describiendo una tela a cuadros.
7. ...los vi, Luis e Isabel estaban escuchando la radio.
8. ...lo vi, mi hermano estaba durmiendo.

5
1. estaba durmiendo
2. me estaba duchando
3. me estaba afeitando
4. me estaba desayunando
5. estaba leyendo
6. estábamos jugando
7. estaba volviendo
8. estaba viendo

Notes

Note that it is often possible to convey the same meaning with either the imperfect or the imperfect progressive tense. For example, **I was eating in the restaurant** could be expressed as *Comía en el restaurante* or *Estaba comiendo en el restaurante.*

Point out that activity 5 includes many examples of how a preterite action interrupts or cuts off an ongoing action.

NATIONAL STANDARDS
C1.2, C4.1

Answers

6
1. ¿...estaban haciendo...?/ Estaban leyendo el periódico.
2. ¿...estaba haciendo...?/ Estaba preparando la comida.
3. ¿...estaba haciendo...?/ Estaba pasando la aspiradora.
4. ¿...estaba haciendo...?/ Estaba durmiendo.
5. ¿...estabas haciendo...?/ Estaba friendo papas en la cocina.
6. ¿...estaban haciendo Uds.?/Estábamos haciendo muchas cosas.

Notes

Note for students that some verbs are rarely used in the progressive tenses in Spanish. The most common are: *ser, estar* and *llevar* (to wear).

Activities

Students with Special Needs. Model a second sentence for activity 6.

6 Nadie contestó

Imagina que anoche llamaste a un(a) amigo/a a las siete de la noche, pero nadie contestó el teléfono. Trabajando en parejas, alterna con tu compañero/a de clase en hacer preguntas y contestarlas para saber qué estaban haciendo todos en ese momento.

    tus hermanos menores/andar por el parque
    A: ¿Qué estaban haciendo tus hermanos?
    B: Estaban andando por el parque.

1. tu madre y tu padre/leer el periódico
2. tu hermana mayor/preparar la comida
3. tu hermano mayor/pasar la aspiradora
4. tu abuela/dormir
5. tú/freír papas en la cocina
6. Uds./hacer muchas cosas

Algo más

El progresivo: un poco más

The two most commonly used progressive tenses are the present and the imperfect progressive, which usually consist of a form of the verb *estar* plus a present participle. In addition to *estar*, several other verbs can be used to form the progressive tenses. The most common of these are *seguir*, which you already have learned to use, *andar, continuar* and *venir*.

*María y Jorge **siguen** leyendo.*	María and Jorge **keep on** reading.
*Juana **andaba** por la calle pensando.*	Juana **was walking** down the street thinking.
*Yo **continuaba** estudiando.*	I **kept on** (**continued**) studying.
Venían manejando.	**They came** driving.

Seguíamos charlando en el parque.

IDIOMA

Verbos irregulares en el subjuntivo

The following verbs are irregular in the present-tense subjunctive. They do not have a present-tense indicative *yo* form that ends in *-o*.

	dar	estar	ir	saber	ser
yo	dé	esté	vaya	sepa	sea
tú	des	estés	vayas	sepas	seas
Ud./él/ella	dé	esté	vaya	sepa	sea
nosotros/nosotras	demos	estemos	vayamos	sepamos	seamos
vosotros/vosotras	deis	estéis	vayáis	sepáis	seáis
Uds./ellos/ellas	den	estén	vayan	sepan	sean

Quiero que vayan al otro lado de la piscina.

15 La familia de Felipe

Haz oraciones en el subjuntivo, escogiendo elementos de cada columna para saber lo que dicen los siguientes familiares de Felipe.

 Su mamá dice que nosotros estemos más tiempo en casa.

A	B	C	D
su mamá	tú	dar	de comer a los gatos
sus tíos	ellos	ser	a arreglar el armario
su bisabuelo	yo	estar	más tiempo en casa
sus padres	nosotros	ir	buenos estudiantes
sus abuelos	ella		en casa a las cinco
su madrastra	él		al zoológico
su hermanastro	Uds.		dinero para la fiesta

16 ¿A qué hora?

Tú tienes que decir la hora en que algunas personas de la familia deben estar en la casa para la reunión con todos los parientes. Trabajando en parejas, alterna con tu compañero/a de clase en hacer preguntas y contestarlas, usando las indicaciones que se dan.

 el marido de Blanca/ocho de la mañana
A: ¿A qué hora debe estar el marido de Blanca?
B: Digo que el marido de Blanca esté a las ocho de la mañana.

1. la mujer de Roberto/ocho y media de la noche
2. yo/veinte para las siete de la noche
3. mi hermanastro/seis de la tarde
4. mis tíos/ocho de la noche
5. mi madrastra/ocho y cuarto de la mañana
6. mis hermanastras/ocho de la noche
7. nosotros/siete de la noche
8. mi abuelo/cuatro de la tarde

Decimos que Conchita esté a las dos de la tarde.

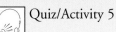

Answers

15 Answers will vary.

16
1. ¿...debe estar...?/...esté....
2. ¿...debo estar...?/...estés....
3. ¿...debe estar...?/...esté....
4. ¿...deben estar...?/...estén....
5. ¿...debe estar...?/...esté....
6. ¿...deben estar...?/...estén....
7. ¿...debemos estar...?/...estemos....
8. ¿...debe estar...?/...esté....

Activities

Expansion. As a follow-up to activity 15, ask students to develop statements consisting of advice commonly given in their families. For example: *Mi padre dice que estudiemos más; Mi hermana quiere que yo arregle la casa.*

Students with Special Needs. Review telling time with students before completing activity 16.

NATIONAL STANDARDS
C1.1, C1.2, C4.1, C5.1

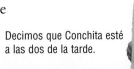

Activity 17

Answers

17 Possible answers:
1. Mi bisabuelo dice que mi hermano y yo vayamos al parque de atracciones.
2. Mi hermanastra dice que tú vayas a la playa.
3. Mi madrastra dice que nosotros vayamos al centro.
4. Mi padrastro dice que yo vaya al parque.
5. Mis tías dicen que Uds. vayan al colegio.
6. Mi abuela dice que mi hermanastro vaya al zoológico.

Notes

Comparisons. Although common in the United States, the terms *padrastro, madrastra, hermanastro* and *hermanastra* are used sparingly in Spanish-speaking countries. Instead, Spanish-speaking natives often use *el esposo de mi madre (mamá)* for **stepfather**, *la esposa de mi padre* for **stepmother**, *el hijo del esposo de mi padre/madre (papá/mamá)* for **stepbrother**, *la hija del esposo de mi padre/madre (papá/mamá)* for **stepsister,** and so forth.

17 ¿Adónde?

Di adónde dicen las siguientes personas que vayan diferentes miembros de la familia, según las ilustraciones.

 mis tíos/mis hermanas
Mis tíos dicen que mis hermanas vayan al museo.

1. mi bisabuelo/mi hermano y yo

2. mi hermanastra/tú

3. mi madrastra/ nosotros

4. mi padrastro/yo

5. mis tías/Uds.

6. mi abuela/mi hermanastro

Mi madre dice que demos un paseo en bote. (Lago Titicaca, Bolivia.)

NATIONAL STANDARDS
C1.2, C4.1

244   Lección 11

Trabajando en casa

 Trabajando en casa
Activity 18

 Quiz/Activity 6

 Activity 44

Activity 8

Answers

18 1. Insiste en que Ramón vaya afuera y corte el césped y que luego pinte la cerca y el muro del jardín porque están rayados.
2. Porque afuera está haciendo mucho calor y él quiere hacer algo adentro donde está el aire acondicionado.
3. Ramón debe tener cuidado.
4. Hay un sótano.
5. Quiere que él lo espere afuera.

Notes

Remind students that accent marks sometimes are omitted from newspaper and magazine advertisements due to typesetting restrictions (as in the case of *céspedes* in the advertisement in the lower right-hand corner of this page). This is changing as computer-generated type becomes more common.

Activities

Expansion. Additional questions (*¿Qué comprendiste?*): *¿Cómo están el muro y la cerca?; ¿Con qué palabra de cariño llama Puala a Ramón?; ¿Quién puede ayudarle a Ramón?; ¿Qué quiere arreglar Ramón adentro de la casa?; ¿Adónde va Ramón para conseguir todo lo que necesita?*

Spanish for Spanish Speakers. Have students read and summarize the content of the advertisement on this page.

PAULA: Amor, **insisto en** que vayas **afuera°** y **cortes°** el césped. Luego, quiero que pintes la **cerca** y el **muro** del **jardín** porque están **rayados.°**

RAMÓN: Pero, corazón, está haciendo mucho calor afuera y el **aire acondicionado** está aquí **adentro.°**

PAULA: Sí, amor, pero trabajar **al aire libre°** y tomar **aire puro** es mejor. Felipe te ayuda.

RAMÓN: Ah, me acabo de acordar que hay un **mueble°** en la sala que puedo arreglar y....

PAULA: No te preocupes, Juana y yo **nos encargamos de°** ese mueble. Ve afuera y **ten cuidado.°**

RAMÓN: **Tú ganas.°** Que Felipe me espere afuera. Voy **abajo,°** al **sótano,°** a sacar lo que necesito.

afuera *outside* **cortes** *cut, mow* **rayados** *scratched, striped* **adentro** *inside* **al aire libre** *outdoors* **mueble** *piece of furniture* **nos encargamos de** *we are taking cave of* **ten cuidado** *be careful* **Tú ganas** *you win* **abajo** *downstairs, down* **sótano** *basement*

18 ¿Qué comprendiste?

1. ¿En qué insiste Paula?
2. ¿Por qué Ramón quiere hacer algo adentro?
3. ¿Quién debe tener cuidado?
4. ¿Qué hay abajo?
5. ¿Qué quiere Ramón que haga Felipe?

NATIONAL STANDARDS
C1.2, C2.1, C5.2

Activity 19

 Activity 9

Quiz/Activity 5

Answers

19 Answers will vary.

20
1. sepa
2. estudie
3. sea
4. estudiar
5. la ayude
6. pase
7. haga
8. cuelgue
9. salga
10. tenga
11. esté

Notes

When speaking, people often drop the main clause of a sentence as they try to hurry their speech. You may choose to note this point for your students, using some commonly heard examples in Spanish: *Que descanses,* for example, is common instead of "(I would like for you to) rest," and *Que duermas bien* is used in many households in place of "(I would like for you to) sleep well."

Activities

Expansion. Additional questions *(Charlando): ¿Te gusta cortar el césped de tu casa?; ¿Te gusta hacer algo afuera cuando hace mucho calor? Explica; ¿Qué prefieres hacer?; ¿Qué quehaceres de la casa te gusta de hacer?*

NATIONAL STANDARDS
C1.1, C1.2, C2.2, C4.1, C4.2

19 Charlando

1. ¿Te gusta hacer actividades al aire libre? ¿Cuáles?
2. ¿Por qué crees que es bueno tomar aire puro?
3. ¿Hay una cerca en tu casa? ¿De qué color es?
4. ¿Crees que en la vida es importante ganar? Explica.
5. ¿Quién se encarga de pintar los muros o muebles rayados en tu casa?

Algo más

Más sobre el subjuntivo con mandatos indirectos

You already have learned to use the subjunctive after the causal verbs *querer* and *decir*. Some other verbs that indicate that one person is indirectly trying to influence another include the following: *aconsejar, decidir, insistir (en), necesitar, ordenar, pedir, permitir* and *preferir*. These and other causal verbs follow the pattern of *querer* and *decir* and are followed by the subjunctive when there is a change of subject in the part of the sentence (clause) introduced by *que*.

Paula insiste en que Ramón pinte la cerca.	Paula **insists that Ramón paint** the fence.
Ramón prefiere que Felipe lo haga.	Ramón **prefers that Felipe do** it.

20 Las memorias de Felipe

Completa el siguiente párrafo que Felipe escribió en su diario con las formas apropiadas de los verbos entre paréntesis.

> Mis padres quieren que yo 1. (saber) hablar español muy bien porque va a ser muy importante para mi futuro. Mi papito siempre me pide que 2. (estudiar) mucho. Él insiste en que yo 3. (ser) un buen estudiante. A veces prefiero no 4. (estudiar). Entonces, mi mamita me ordena que yo 5. (ayudarla) con los quehaceres del hogar. A veces ella necesita que yo 6. (pasar) la aspiradora, que 7. (hacer) la cama y que 8. (colgar) la ropa. Otras veces ella permite que yo 9. (salir) para estar con mis amigos. Me aconseja que 10. (tener) cuidado cuando salgo, pero siempre prefiere que yo 11. (estar) en casa con la familia.

246   **Lección 11**

21 ¡Todos preguntan!

Contesta las siguientes preguntas, usando las indicaciones que se dan. Sigue el modelo.

¿Qué decide tu mamá? (mi hermano/ayudar afuera a su padrastro)
Mi mamá decide que mi hermano ayude afuera a su padrastro.

1. ¿Qué permites tú? (Uds./estar adentro en el sótano donde hay aire acondicionado)
2. ¿Qué necesitan Uds.? (alguien/arreglar el muro y los muebles)
3. ¿Qué aconsejan ellos? (nosotros/ser buenos estudiantes)
4. ¿En qué insiste tu tío? (su mujer/darle permiso para jugar al tenis)
5. ¿Qué ordena Carlos? (los niños/no exagerar tanto)
6. ¿Qué pide la tía Graciela? (su sobrino/darle un beso)
7. ¿Qué quiere tu padrastro? (yo/ir abajo y limpiar el sótano)
8. ¿Qué prefiere Felipe? (ellos/cortar el césped del jardín y arreglar la cerca)
9. ¿Qué quieren tus padres? (nosotros/saber español)
10. ¿Qué necesita tu bisabuela? (yo/ir a cortar el césped)

Sus padres insisten en que Rodolfo limpie el jardín.

22 En tu familia

Escribe una oración usando cada uno de los siguientes verbos para tratar de influenciar a ocho personas diferentes de tu familia: *aconsejar, decidir, insistir en, necesitar, ordenar, pedir, permitir* y *preferir*. Sé creativo/a.

Yo insisto en que mi hermanastra arregle su armario porque está muy sucio.

Insisto en que mi hermanastra arregle su armario.

247

NATIONAL STANDARDS
C1.2, C4.1

Answers

21
1. Yo permito que Uds. estén....
2. Uds. necesitan que alguien arregle....
3. Ellos aconsejan que (nosotros) seamos....
4. Mi tío insiste en que su mujer le dé....
5. Carlos ordena que los niños no exageren....
6. La tía Graciela pide que su sobrino le dé....
7. Mi padrastro quiere que (yo) vaya...que limpie....
8. Felipe prefiere que ellos corten...que arreglen....
9. Mis padres quieren que (nosotros) sepamos....
10. Mi bisabuela necesita que (yo) vaya....

22 Creative self-expression.

Trabajando en casa (continuación)
Activity 23
Activity 10

Quiz/Activity 6

Answers

23 1. Felipe está arriba.
2. Le manda que lo ayude afuera.
3. No deja salir de la casa a Felipe.
4. Se refiere a que no salga con sus amigos.
5. Answers will vary.
6. Answers will vary.

Notes

The word *broma* may also refers to a practical joke. Students will find it interesting to note that December 28 *(el Día de los Inocentes)* is a traditional day for such jokes in many Spanish-speaking countries. The equivalent in the United States is April Fool's Day (April 1).

Activities

Critical Listening. Play the audiocassette/audio compact disc recording of the dialog as students listen to the conversation. Have them look at the illustration and imagine what the people are saying to one another. Finally, ask several individuals to state what they believe the main theme of the conversation is.

Expansion. Additional questions *(¿Qué comprendiste?): ¿Qué está haciendo Felipe?; ¿Quién hace una broma?; ¿Te gusta hacer bromas como Felipe?*

Prereading Strategy. Note for students that this dialog is a continuation of the dialog that began on page 245. Then have students look through the dialog quickly to find cognates and other words or expressions they already know.

Trabajando en casa (continuación)

PAULA: ¡Felipe!
FELIPE: Estoy aquí **arriba,**° mamá.
PAULA: Tu papá **te manda**° que lo ayudes afuera.
FELIPE: Afuera no puedo. Tú no me **dejas**° salir de la casa.
PAULA: ¿A qué **te refieres?**°
FELIPE: Tú quieres que yo esté hoy todo el día en la casa, ¿verdad?
PAULA: Sí, pero no me refiero a que estés adentro de la casa. Claro que sí te permito salir a ayudar a tu padrastro.
FELIPE: Era una **broma,**° mamá.

arriba *upstairs, up, above* **te manda** *orders you* **dejas** *you let* **te refieres** *do you refer* **broma** *chiste*

¡Felipe!

23 **¿Qué comprendiste?**

1. ¿Dónde está Felipe?
2. ¿Qué le manda a Felipe su papá?
3. ¿A quién no deja Paula salir de la casa?
4. ¿A qué se refiere Paula cuando dice que no deja salir de la casa a Felipe?
5. ¿Te permiten tus padres salir de casa todos los fines de semana con tus amigos/as? ¿Por cuánto tiempo?
6. ¿Te gusta hacer bromas? Explica.

Algo más

Verbos de causa sin el subjuntivo

You have learned that causal verbs are followed by the subjunctive when there is a change of subject. However, the causal verbs *dejar, hacer, invitar, mandar* and *permitir* may be followed by an infinitive instead of the subjunctive, even when there is a change of subject. In such instances, the sentence requires an indirect object.

*Mi padre **me manda que haga** la cama.*
*Yo no **permito que** el **niño** juegue en la sala.*
*Mi madre **hace que** nosotros **comamos** todo.*

*Mi padre **me manda hacer** la cama.*
*Yo no **le permito jugar** en la sala.*

*Mi madre **nos hace comer** todo.*

NATIONAL STANDARDS
C1.2, C2.1, C4.1, C4.2

24 De todos los días

Las siguientes oraciones describen situaciones que pasan todos los días en un hogar. Dilas en forma diferente sin usar el subjuntivo.

Mi papá me pide limpiar las ventanas.

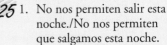

El padre deja que sus hijos salgan a tomar aire puro al parque.
El padre los deja salir a tomar aire puro al parque.

1. Mandas a tu hermano que arregle su cuarto.
2. No dejamos que Uds. manejen nuestro carro.
3. Dejo que mis hermanitos vean televisión.
4. La mamá manda a sus hijos que corten el césped del jardín.
5. La tía permite que su sobrina juegue afuera, al aire libre.
6. Los abuelos hacen que sus nietos tomen toda la sopa.

25 De dos formas diferentes

Las siguientes parejas de oraciones se pueden combinar de dos formas diferentes. Haz la primera combinación sin usar el subjuntivo y la segunda usándolo.

Su mamá le manda cortar el césped.

Mis padres no me permiten que salga antes de hacer la tarea.

Queremos viajar. No nos dejan hacerlo.
No nos dejan viajar./No nos dejan que viajemos.

1. Queremos salir esta noche. No nos permiten hacerlo.
2. Voy arriba. Mi madrastra me manda hacerlo.
3. Juega con sus amigos. Dejo a Timoteo hacerlo.
4. Inés y Elisa limpian el cuarto. Su mamá les manda hacerlo.
5. Ganas el partido de tenis. Te permito hacerlo.
6. Vienes a mi casa a almorzar. Te invito a hacerlo.
7. Estudio mucho. Mi papá me pide hacerlo.

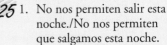
Activity 24

Answers

24
1. Le mandas arreglar su cuarto.
2. No les dejamos manejar nuestro carro.
3. Les dejo ver televisión.
4. La mamá les manda cortar el césped del jardín.
5. La tía le permite jugar afuera, al aire libre.
6. Los abuelos les hacen tomar toda la sopa.

25
1. No nos permiten salir esta noche./No nos permiten que salgamos esta noche.
2. Mi madrastra me manda ir arriba./Mi madrastra me manda que vaya arriba.
3. Le dejo jugar con sus amigos./Le dejo que juegue con sus amigos.
4. Su mamá les manda limpiar el cuarto./Su mamá les manda que limpien el cuarto.
5. Te permito ganar el partido de tenis./Te permito que ganes el partido de tenis.
6. Te invito venir a mi casa a almorzar./Te invito que vengas a mi casa a almorzar.
7. Mi papá me pide estudiar mucho./Mi papá me pide que estudie mucho.

NATIONAL STANDARDS
C1.2, C4.1

En la casa

Quiz/Activity 7

Activities 45-46

Activity 11

Quiz/Activity 7

Answers
26 1. Es una reja.
2. Es una escoba.
3. Es una chimenea.
4. Es una bombilla.
5. Es un tocador.
6. Es un ventilador.
7. Es un sillón.
8. Es una cortina.

Notes
Point out that the word *madera* really refers to **wood**; the word for **firewood** is *leña*.

Point out that *chimenea* refers to either the **chimney** or the **fireplace**.

Activities
Prereading Strategy. Using transparency 46, introduce students to the vocabulary used in this dialog. Pronounce each of the words in the illustration and have students repeat them. Next, point to words and call on students to spell them. Finally, point to some of the objects included in the illustration and ask students to tell you in Spanish what they are.

TPR. Using overhead transparencies 45 and 46 (*En la casa*), ask students to come up and point to the items you name in Spanish.

En la casa

26 Cosas de la casa

Di qué son las siguientes cosas que se pueden encontrar en una casa.

Es un ladrillo.

 1.
 2.
 3.
 4.
 5.
 6.
 7.
 8.

NATIONAL STANDARDS
C1.2, C4.1

250 Lección 11

27 Todo yo

Di lo que los miembros de tu familia quieren que tú hagas, usando las indicaciones que se dan.

 tía/insistir en/lavar las cortinas de mi cuarto
Mi tía insiste en que lave las cortinas de mi cuarto.

1. bisabuelo/insistir en/encargarme de arreglar el techo y las rejas de la casa
2. hermanos/querer/comprar una alarma nueva para despertarme
3. padre/querer/poner una bombilla nueva en la sala
4. madre/preferir/limpiar su tocador
5. abuelos/pedir/comprar unos cuadros para la casa
6. tío/decir/conseguir algunos ladrillos para arreglar los muros del patio
7. el marido de mi tía/querer/traerle el sillón de la sala
8. hermanastro/querer/barrer la azotea
9. hermanastra/necesitar/ayudarla a poner madera en la chimenea

La arquitectura hispana
In the Spanish-speaking areas of the world, you will find old homes that display the stately features of Spanish colonial architecture. You will find many modern houses and apartments as well. However, whether old or new, two interesting architectural features that you may see on a home are *la azotea*, a flat roof that is used as an extension or replacement for a patio, and *las rejas*, wrought iron window grills or fences that serve for protection and decoration.

28 En casa

Escribe cuatro oraciones originales, usando el subjuntivo para describir las circunstancias que se muestran *(are shown)* en las ilustraciones.

1.

2.

3.

4.

Autoevaluación. Como repaso y autoevaluación, responde lo siguiente:
1 Name two chores you do at home.
2. What do you know about Bolivia?
3. Suggest or request in Spanish that your little brother help you clean the garage.
4. Imagine your Spanish class is preparing an end-of-the-year dance. Say what tasks your teacher wants each of you to do to prepare for the dance.
5. Who are the members of your family?
6. List two bits of advice for a friend who is about to take a trip to a Spanish-speaking country.
7. Name three things that your parents do not permit you to do.
8. Name three objects in your house that you have learned in this lesson.

 Activity 27

 Activity 47

Answers
27 1. Mi bisabuelo insiste en que me encargue....
2. Mis hermanos quieren que compre....
3. Mi padre quiere que ponga....
4. Mi madre prefiere que limpie....
5. Mis abuelos me piden que compre....
6. Mi tío dice que consiga....
7. El marido de mi tía quiere que le traiga....
8. Mi hermanastro quiere que barra....
9. Mi hermanastra necesita que la ayude....

28 Creative self-expression.

Autoevaluación
Possible answers:
1. Paso la aspiradora. Limpio mi cuarto.
2. Answers will vary.
3. Quiero que me ayudes a limpiar el garaje.
4. La profesora quiere que Laura y yo hagamos las invitaciones. Dice que David ponga las sillas al lado de la pared.
5. Answers will vary.
6. Answers will vary.
7. Mis padres no me permiten que yo salga de casa a las once de la noche. Ellos no me permiten que yo fume. Mamá y papá no me permiten que yo use su tarjeta de crédito.
8. el ventilador, la cortina, la bombilla, la escoba

Activities
Students with Special Needs.
Offer a model for activity 28: *La mamá quiere que Jairo ponga una bombilla nueva.*

NATIONAL STANDARDS
C1.1, C1.2, C2.1, C2.2, C3.1, C3.2, C4.1, C4.2, C5.1

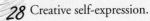

 Activity 12

Notes

For all oral activities, listen for the correct pronunciation and determine if students appear to understand what they are saying and hearing. Also, be sure students personalize information so that it is meaningful to them.

Activities

Technology. As a variation of the activity *Conexión con la tecnología*, ask students to take pictures of a house and then create an electronic photograph album of their ideal or dream home (using a scanner or a digital camera). Once that is done, students write a description of both the house in general and of the individual rooms. (**Note:** Since the house is a dream house, students will need to use the subjunctive in their descriptions.) If students have key pals, have them send their descriptions followed by the digitized photographs via e-mail. Then ask if the recipient(s) can match the descriptions with the corresponding digital album. Finally, if the school has a Web page, try to arrange to put the electronic dream homes and descriptions on the Web page for other schools, key pals and interested parties to visit.

¡La práctica hace al maestro!

A Comunicación

Working in groups of six, first decide who will play the role of various family members. Then form two concentric circles of three, with students who are playing the part of adults in one circle and students who are playing the part of children in the other circle. Now do the following: 1) The adults use one of the causal verbs to ask the children to perform a household chore or to help with an errand; 2) the children must answer by saying someone else should do the requested task; 3) the adults rotate one person to the left and begin the activity again, making a different request. Switch roles after each person has had an opportunity to make three requests or to respond three times.

A: Mercedes, quiero que pases la aspiradora por la sala, por favor.

B: Ay, no, papá. Que lo haga mi hermanastra.

B Conexión con la tecnología

Use a camera or a camcorder to photograph or film the different parts of your house. Then prepare a script in Spanish to identify the rooms and objects being seen, and to tell which family members you advise to do particular household chores. Be creative! Share your presentation with the rest of the class.

El cuarto de mis padres.

El comedor de mi casa.

Testing/Assessment
Test Booklet
Oral Proficiency
  Evaluation Manual
Portfolio Assessment

Notes

Another expression for *cortar el césped* is *podar el césped* or *podar el pasto*.

Activities

Cooperative Learning. Ask students to say a word they have learned in Spanish and then select someone else to spell the word. Have them check their spelling and then switch roles.

Critical Thinking. *El verdugo*. The idea of the game is to guess a word. One student goes to the board and writes one blank for each letter of any word. The other students then begin to guess letters of the alphabet that might be in that word. Each correct letter is inserted into the proper blank. If the correct letter is not guessed, the student at the board draws in a part of a hanged person. The game continues until the word had been guessed or the complete hanged person has been drawn. You may want to make the game more challenging by drawing in a part of the hanged person for every vowel guessed, since the vowels first would probably make the entire word much easier to figure out. This game may be played with the class divided into two teams or with the entire class guessing the letters.

Expansion. Select several words and phrases for individual students to use orally in sentences.

Pronunciation. To ensure proper pronunciation, model each word or expression and have students repeat after you.

La casa

- el aire (acondicionado)
- la alarma
- la alfombra
- el armario – closet,
- el ático
- la azotea
- la bombilla – light bulb
- la cerca – rec
- la chimenea
- la cortina
- el cuadro
- la escoba
- el hogar
- el jardín
- — el ladrillo
- el lavadero – laundry room
- la madera
- el mueble
- el muro – exterior wall
- la reja – fence
- el sillón – arm chair
- el sótano
- el techo
- el tocador – dresser
- el ventilador – fan

Indrde limpiar lavar

La familia

- el bisabuelo, la bisabuela
- ✓ el hermanastro,
- ✓ la hermanastra
- ✓ la madrastra
- la mamá
- el marido
- ✓ el miembro
- la mujer
- ✓ el padrastro
- el papá

Verbos

- cortar
- dejar
- encargar(se) (de)
- exagerar
- ganar
- insistir (en)
- invitar
- mandar
- referir(se) (ie, i)

Expresiones y otras palabras

- abajo
- adentro
- afuera
- al aire libre
- arriba
- el beso
- la broma
- el cuidado
- tener cuidado
- puro,-a
- rayado,-a

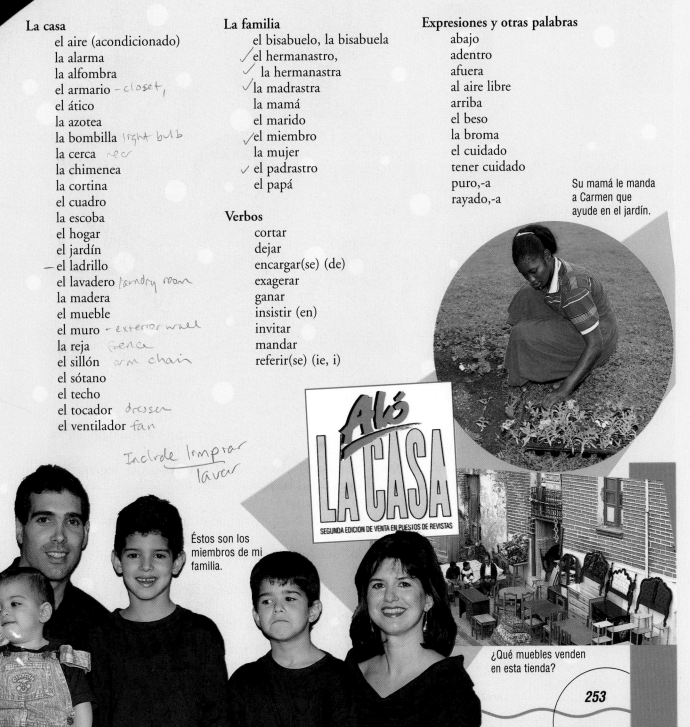

Su mamá le manda a Carmen que ayude en el jardín.

Éstos son los miembros de mi familia.

Aló LA CASA
SEGUNDA EDICION DE VENTA EN PUESTOS DE REVISTAS

¿Qué muebles venden en esta tienda?

253

Content reviewed in *Lección 12*
- describing a household
- expressing emotions
- family

Notes

Inform your students that *Los Tiempos* is a newspaper from Cochabamba, Bolivia.

ʷʷʷ

Los Tiempos:
http://www.lostiempos.com

Activities

Critical Listening. Play the audiocassette/audio compact disc recording of the dialog. Instruct students to cover the words as they listen to the conversation in order to develop good listening skills before concentrating on reading Spanish. Have students look at the illustration and imagine what the people are saying to each other. Ask several individuals to state what they believe the main theme of the conversation is.

Prereading Strategy. Ask students to think about the last time they asked their parents for permission to go out to do something with friends that required them to be out late at night. Then have them cover the dialog and look at the illustration. Ask them to imagine who the individuals are, where the conversation takes place and what the people are saying to one another. Finally, have students look through the dialog quickly to find cognates and other words or expressions they already know.

Contexto cultural
LOS PAÍSES BOLIVARIANOS

Lección 12

Las reglas de la casa

la cerradura   la llave

JUANA: Papito, ¿es posible que esta noche Sergio y yo vayamos a una fiesta en el **club**?

RAMÓN: Está bien, pero si sales, **espero°** que recuerdes que tienes que **regresar°** a la medianoche, y no olvides llevar las **llaves.**

JUANA: Ay, papá, ¿por qué tan temprano?

RAMÓN: Ésas son las **reglas°** de la casa. No quieres que tu mamá y yo nos preocupemos por ti toda la noche, ¿verdad?

JUANA: No, papito, pero **dudo°** que Sergio me quiera traer tan temprano. Además, no deben **temer°** nada.

RAMÓN: Es mejor que te traiga temprano si él no quiere tener problemas con tu papito.

JUANA: Sí, papá. ¡**Estoy segura de°** que vamos a llegar **a tiempo!°**

espero *I hope* **regresar** *volver* **reglas** *rules* **dudo** *I doubt* **temer** *fear* **Estoy segura de** *I am sure* (of) **a tiempo** *on time*

1 ¿Qué comprendiste?

1. ¿Adónde es posible que Sergio y Juana vayan por la noche?
2. ¿A qué hora tiene que regresar Juana si va a la fiesta?
3. ¿Qué duda Juana?
4. ¿De qué está segura Juana?
5. ¿En qué lugar se pone la llave para abrir la puerta?

2 Charlando

1. ¿A qué lugares vas con tus amigos?
2. ¿Tienen reglas en tu casa que debes seguir? ¿Cuáles?
3. ¿Tienes que regresar temprano cuando sales por la noche? Explica.
4. ¿Se preocupan mucho tus padres cuando sales por la noche? Explica.

¿A qué lugares vas con tus amigos?

Estrategia

Para leer mejor: *observing contextual cues*

Read for ideas rather than look up every word you do not recognize. You can become a better reader by observing contextual cues and by becoming better at discerning the meaning of words. With this in mind, remember that the ending *-dad* is approximately the English equivalent for **-ty.** You have already seen many words that end in *-dad*, such as *variedad, calidad* and *actividad*.

Some words that do not follow this pattern are *edad* (age), *verdad* (truth) and *Navidad* (Christmas).

 CERRAJERIA

"EL RAPIDO"

SE HACEN LLAVES PARA
AUTOMOVILES
CHAPAS, CANDADOS, ETC.
DUPLICADO DE LLAVES
PARA ALARMAS
LLAVES PARA AUTOS
CODIFICADOS
SERVICIO A DOMICILIO

83-93-89

Av. Américas Local 45 en
el exterior del Mercado Hidalgo,
Col. B. Juárez

Los países bolivarianos

 Quiz/Activity 2

 Activity 1

Notes

Some words that may cause problems for some students include the following: *nació* (was born), *lucha* (battle), *sueño* (dream), *bajo* (under), *poder ver realizado* (being able to see fulfilled), *gobiernos* (governments), *objetivo* (objective), *sobrepasar* (overcome).

Activities

Critical Thinking. Remind students that they have seen many words that end in *-dad*, such as *variedad*, *calidad* and *actividad*. Based upon these examples, ask if students can give an approximate English equivalent for the ending *-dad*: -ty. Some words that do not follow this pattern are *edad* (age), *verdad* (truth) and *Navidad* (Christmas). Ask if students can find examples of words that follow this pattern in this *Conexión cultural (unidad, realidad)*.

Prereading Strategy. This *Conexión cultural* provides an opportunity for students to increase what they know about the Spanish-speaking world by reading about the countries which Simón Bolívar helped gain their independence from Spain. The vocabulary and structures have been controlled to enable individuals to read in the target language and enjoy the experience. Note for the class that it is not essential to understand every word in order to read Spanish; the meaning of important but unknown passive vocabulary has been provided to facilitate an enjoyable experience. Before beginning the *Conexión cultural,* have students skim the content in order to find the names of the countries that make up the *países bolivarianos.* Then have students skim the *Conexión cultural* for cognates and any words or expressions they already know.

NATIONAL STANDARDS
C1.2, C4.1, C5.2

Conexión cultural

Los países bolivarianos

La Plaza Bolívar en Mérida, Venezuela.

Se da el nombre de países bolivarianos a las repúblicas que Simón Bolívar ayudó a libertar *(liberate)* de los españoles. Estos países fueron Bolivia, Colombia, Ecuador, Perú y Venezuela. En estas naciones Simón Bolívar es conocido como el Libertador y el héroe nacional.

El Libertador Simón Bolívar.

Bolívar nació en Caracas, Venezuela, en 1783. La mayor parte de su vida la dedicó a la lucha por la independencia de estos países. Su sueño era el de unir *(unite)* a todas las repúblicas que libertó para formar una sola nación bajo el nombre de la Gran Colombia. El Libertador murió *(died)* el 17 de diciembre de 1830 en Santa Marta, Colombia, sin poder ver realizado este gran sueño.

El sueño de unidad de Bolívar sigue siendo el ideal de los gobiernos de estos cinco países. En principio, el objetivo es el de buscar la unidad de sus mercados y así fortalecer *(strengthen)* la economía del área. Su meta *(goal)* final es poder conseguir la unidad total de estas naciones, y de esta manera formar una sola república. El camino para llegar a esta meta es largo y difícil. Todavía son muchos los obstáculos que hay que sobrepasar, pero posiblemente, algún día este sueño sea realidad.

VENEZUELA
COLOMBIA
ECUADOR
PERÚ
BOLIVIA
PAÍSES BOLIVARIANOS DE AMÉRICA LATINA

Simón Bolívar
POCAS FIGURAS EN LA HISTORIA han desempeñado un papel tan decisivo en un continente entero como lo hizo Bolívar. Como líder político y militar durante las guerras de independencia de Colombia, Venezuela, Bolivia, Perú y Ecuador, su presencia y su acción fueron decisivos. La labor inagotable del Libertador para financiar las guerras de liberación hicieron posible la independencia de la corona española. Algunos historiadores sostienen que la influencia del Libertador fue más importante que la que tuvieron Julio César o Carlomagno, pues los cambios que surgieron después de su intervención resultaron más permanentes y porque las regiones que afectó son más extensas. Pero es innegable que Bolívar moldeó la historia de una gran región del mundo.

3 Cruzando fronteras

Haz un mapa de la América del Sur y colorea los países bolivarianos. Luego, añade los nombres de las capitales de estos países, las montañas, los lagos, los ríos y otros puntos geográficos que puedas. Busca información en la biblioteca o en la Internet si es necesario.

IDIOMA

El subjuntivo con verbos de emoción y duda

The subjunctive is used in Spanish after verbs that express emotions (such as anger, annoyance, fear, happiness, regret, sadness or surprise) or doubt when there is a change of subject in the clause that is introduced by *que*. Some verbs of emotion that you have already seen include *agradar* (to please), *divertir* (to amuse, to have fun), *esperar* (to hope), *gustar* (to like, to be pleasing), *importar* (to be important, to matter), *molestar* (to bother), *parecer bien/mal* (to seem right/wrong), *preocupar* (to worry), *sentir* (to be sorry, to feel sorry, to regret) *temer* (to fear) and *tener miedo de* (to be afraid).

Si sales con tus amigas, quiero que regreses temprano.

Espero que regreses temprano.	**I hope you return** early.
Me agrada que estés bien.	**I'm glad (It pleases me) that you're** well.

The principal verb of doubt is *dudar* (to doubt). The verbs *creer* and *pensar* and the expression *estar seguro/a (de)* imply doubt when they are negative.

Dudo que Felipe vaya a ayudar.	**I doubt (that) Felipe is going** to help.
No creo que él ayude mucho.	**I don't think (that) he helps** much.
No pienso que a Felipe le guste pasar la aspiradora.	**I don't think Felipe likes** to vacuum.
No estoy seguro de que vaya a ayudar.	**I'm not sure he is** going to help.

¡Me agrada mucho que estés aquí!

Capítulo 6   257

Activities 2-3

Quiz/Activity 1

Answers

3 Check maps for accuracy.

Notes

Quickly review what students have learned about the subjunctive before beginning to talk about using the subjunctive with verbs of emotion and doubt. Be sure students know the conjugation of verbs in the subjunctive.

Comparisons. Compare the use of **that/***que* in English and in Spanish: The word **that** is not always necessary in English, as indicated by the parentheses in the example **I doubt (that) Felipe is going to help.** The word **that** is not really necessary in the example **I'm glad that you're well.**

Connections. Make a geographical connection for students by encouraging them to include a variety of geographical features in the maps they create for activity 3.

NATIONAL STANDARDS
C1.2, C1.3, C3.1, C4.1

Answers

4
1. Ud. espera que nosotros vayamos....
2. A Ramón le molesta que yo traiga....
3. Yo tengo miedo de que ellos no vayan....
4. Paula teme que Juana no tenga....
5. Juana espera que su hermano ayude....
6. A Ramón le gusta que Juana regrese....
7. A sus padres les agrada que Juana y Felipe ayuden....
8. A sus tíos no les importa que tú seas....
9. A nosotros nos preocupa que Juana y Felipe coman....
10. La novia de Felipe siente que él tenga....

5
1. Temo que la abuela venga mañana.
2. Es importante que almorcemos hoy.
3. No esperamos que llueva hoy.
4. Dudo que regresen temprano.
5. Me parece mal que no tengan las llaves.
6. Espero que empieces a limpiar pronto.
7. Siento que nieve mucho aquí.

Activities

Students with Special Needs. Model a second sentence for activity 4.

4 ¿Qué piensan?

Haz oraciones completas para decir lo que piensan o sienten las siguientes personas, usando las indicaciones que se dan.

> a Felipe/parecerle bien/su hermana/seguir las reglas
> A Felipe le parece bien que su hermana siga las reglas.

1. Ud./esperar/nosotros/ir a la fiesta del club con Juana
2. a Ramón/molestar/yo/traer a Juana después de la medianoche
3. yo/tener miedo de/ellos/no ir a la fiesta
4. Paula/temer/Juana/no tener las llaves de la casa
5. Juana/esperar/su hermano/ayudar a su padre
6. a Ramón/gustar/Juana/regresar a tiempo
7. a sus padres/agradar/Juana y Felipe/ayudar en la casa
8. a sus tíos/no importar/tú/ser amigo de Felipe
9. a nosotros/preocupar/Juana y Felipe/comer poco
10. la novia de Felipe/sentir/él/tener que estar en la casa todo el día

5 Preguntas y más preguntas

Todos preguntan algo en casa. Combina las dos oraciones en una sola oración.

> ¿Ayudas en el hogar? (Sí, creo).
> Creo que ayudo en el hogar.

1. ¿Viene la abuela mañana? (Temo que sí).
2. ¿Almorzamos hoy? (Sí, es importante).
3. ¿Llueve hoy? (No, no esperamos).
4. ¿Regresan tus padres temprano? (Lo dudo).
5. ¿Te parece bien que no tengan las llaves? (Me parece mal).
6. ¿Cuándo empiezas a limpiar? (Pronto, espero).
7. ¿Nieva mucho aquí? (Sí, lo siento).

Es claro que ayudo en el hogar.

6 Toda la familia tiene dudas

Haz oraciones completas para expresar las dudas que tienen hoy algunos miembros de tu familia, usando *dudar, no creer, no estar seguro/a de o no pensar,* y las indicaciones que se dan.

> La cerradura de la casa es buena. (mi abuela)
> Mi abuela duda (no cree/no está segura de/no piensa) que la cerradura de la casa sea buena.

1. La tía invita a sus amigas a jugar a las cartas. (Uds.)
2. El aire acondicionado está trabajando bien. (tú)
3. Mis padres compran más cuadros para la sala. (mi hermanastro)
4. Nosotros siempre tenemos mucho cuidado cuando lavamos los platos. (ellos)
5. Le gustan las bromas a mi abuelo. (mi tía)
6. La fiesta va a ser en el club. (nosotros)
7. Mis hermanas se encargan de arreglar la cocina hoy. (yo)
8. Mis hermanos tienen las llaves de la casa. (mi madre)

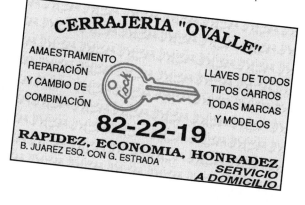

¡Su hermana duda que el bebé pueda caminar solo!

CERRAJERIA "OVALLE"

AMAESTRAMIENTO
REPARACIÓN
Y CAMBIO DE
COMBINACIÓN

LLAVES DE TODOS
TIPOS CARROS
TODAS MARCAS
Y MODELOS

82-22-19

RAPIDEZ, ECONOMIA, HONRADEZ
B. JUAREZ ESQ. CON G. ESTRADA

SERVICIO
A DOMICILIO

7 ¿Qué dudas?

Trabajando en parejas, alterna con tu compañero/a de clase en decir cinco oraciones y, luego, ponerlas en duda. Usen *dudar, no creer, no estar seguro/a o no pensar* en cada oración y traten de ser tan creativos/as como sea posible.

> A: Pienso que la gente va a ser más inteligente en el año dos mil diez.
> B: Dudo (No creo/No estoy seguro,-a /No pienso) que la gente vaya a ser más inteligente en el año dos mil diez.

Capítulo 6  259

Activity 8

Activities 4-5

Quiz/Activity 2

Answers

8 1. Nos complace que Gabriel tenga....
2. ¿Le encanta a Lupe que Uds. jueguen...?
3. Me fascina que tú siempre cortes....
4. A ellos les interesa que Ud. sea....
5. ¿Temen mis padres que nosotros no lleguemos...?
6. ¿Tiene Gloria miedo de que nadie venga...?
7. Me alegra que la fiesta empiece....
8. ¿Te molesta que Julio no use...?
9. ¿Espera Javier que nos sentemos...?
10. A mi padrastro le interesa que (yo) estudie....

Notes

Briefly review *gustar* and other similarly formed verbs before introducing the *Algo más* on this page.

Although the verb *complacer* usually is conjugated and used following the pattern of *gustar*, it may also be conjugated for use with the first- and second-person subjects. In such cases, it is conjugated following the pattern of *conducir (conduzco)* and *traducir (traduzco): complazco.*

Algo más

Otros verbos de emoción

Other verbs that express emotion are usually conjugated following the pattern of gustar:

alegrar (de)	to make happy
complacer	to please
encantar	to enchant, to delight
fascinar	to fascinate
interesar	to interest

When the verb *alegrar* becomes reflexive it is followed by the word *de* and no longer follows the pattern of *gustar*. Compare these two sentences:

Me alegra que ayudes en casa.
Me alegro de que ayudes en casa.

Me alegra que seas mi amiga.

I am glad you help at home.

8 Algunas emociones

¿Cómo cambian las siguientes oraciones si se ponen las frases entre paréntesis primero? Sigue los modelos.

 La comida es muy mala. (Me molesta....)
Me molesta que la comida sea muy mala.

Nosotros vamos al club. (Natalia se alegra de....)
Natalia se alegra de que nosotros vayamos al club.

1. Gabriel tiene un hogar excelente. (Nos complace....)
2. Uds. juegan al aire libre. (¿Le encanta a Lupe...?)
3. Tú siempre cortas el césped. (Me fascina....)
4. Ud. es una persona inteligente. (A ellos les interesa....)
5. No llegamos a tiempo. (¿Temen mis padres...?)
6. Nadie viene a la fiesta. (¿Tiene Gloria miedo de...?)
7. La fiesta empieza a tiempo. (Me alegra....)
8. Julio no usa el ventilador cuando hace calor. (¿Te molesta...?)
9. Nos sentamos en el jardín. (¿Espera Javier...?)
10. Estudio español. (A mi padrastro le interesa....)

9 Emociones de tu familia

Completa las siguientes oraciones con ideas que sean verdad para tu familia. Puedes inventar las ideas, si prefieres.

> A mi madre le complace que....
> A mi madre le complace que yo ayude con los quehaceres.

1. A mi hermano le preocupa que....
2. A mis hermanas les gusta que....
3. A mis padres les alegra que....
4. A mi abuela le fascina que....
5. A mis tíos les complace que....
6. A mi abuelo le interesa que....
7. A mi padre le agrada que....
8. A mi madre le molesta que....

ÉL hijo ÚNICO

10 Expresando tus emociones personales

Completa las siguientes oraciones de una manera original para expresar emociones personales, usando el subjuntivo.

> Me fascina....
> Me fascina que mi hermana me ayude a arreglar mi cuarto.

1. Temo....
2. Me alegro....
3. Me encanta....
4. Espero....
5. Me interesa....
6. Me complace....
7. Siento....
8. Me molesta....

A todos nos alegra que estemos juntos.

Temo que mis padres estén enojados conmigo.

Answers
9 Creative self-expression.
10 Creative self-expression.

Notes
Review. Review family vocabulary with students.

Activities
Cooperative Learning. Have students work in pairs or small groups asking and answering questions that require students to answer using the expressions in activity 10: *¿Qué te fascina?/Me fascina que haga un día bonito hoy.*

Students with Special Needs. Model a second sentence for activities 9-10.

NATIONAL STANDARDS
C1.1, C1.2, C4.1, C5.2

Notes

Note that the word *que* is not used when the impersonal expression is followed by an infinitive instead of a conjugated verb.

Activities

Expansion. Ask students if they can think of other expressions to add to the list of *expresiones impersonales*.

Multiple Intelligences (intrapersonal/linguistic). Have students write five rules to live by, using five different impersonal expressions and the present tense of the subjunctive: *Es importante que yo siga las reglas de la casa.*

Algo más

El subjuntivo con expresiones impersonales

Several impersonal expressions in Spanish are followed by *que* and the subjunctive when they express doubt or state an opinion and when the verb that

¡Es importante que ayudes en casa!

follows has its own subject. Compare the following sentences:

Es importante que limpies tu cuarto.

It is important **for you to clean** (that you clean) your room.

but:

Es importante limpiar la casa hoy.

It is important **to clean** the house today.

Some of the more common impersonal expressions include the following:

es difícil (que)	it is unlikely (that)
es dudoso (que)	it is doubtful (that)
es fácil (que)	it is likely (that)
es importante (que)	it is important (that)
es imposible (que)	it is impossible (that)
es mejor (que)	it is better (that)
es necesario (que)	it is necessary (that)
es posible (que)	it is possible (that)
es preciso (que)	it is necessary (that)
es probable (que)	it is probable (that)
es una lástima (que)	it is a pity (that)
es urgente (que)	it is urgent (that)
más vale (que)	it is better (that)
conviene (que)	it is fitting (that)

Es importante que ella limpie su cuarto antes de salir.

The impersonal expressions *es claro* (it is clear), *es evidente* (it is evident), *es obvio* (it is obvious), *es seguro* (it is sure) and *es verdad* (it is true) are followed by the indicative. However, when these expressions are negative, they express doubt and, therefore, they require the subjunctive.

Es evidente que quieres ayudar.
No es evidente que quieras ayudar.

It is clear that you want to help.
It is not clear that you want to help.

11 ¿Cuál es tu opinión?

Completa las siguientes oraciones con la forma apropiada de los verbos indicados para dar tu opinión.

 Es dudoso que Carlos (compre) unas cortinas nuevas para su casa. (comprar)

1. Es necesario que tú (1) de comer tanto. (dejar)
2. Es difícil que ellos (2) de su hogar. (irse)
3. Es evidente que Uds. (3) mucho a sus padres. (querer)
4. Es probable que nosotros (4) a Venezuela y Colombia. (viajar)
5. No es seguro que sus amigos (5) al club también. (ir)
6. Es claro que Hernán (6) arreglar el aire acondicionado. (saber)
7. Es imposible que nosotros (7) dos casas. (tener)
8. Es fácil que mi padrastro y mi mamá (8) pronto. (llegar)
9. Es preciso que yo (9) más tiempo en casa. (estar)
10. Es obvio que Uds. (10) los dientes todos los días. (cepillarse)

12 ¿Qué opinas?

Da una opinión para cada una de las situaciones que se muestran en las siguientes ilustraciones, usando las indicaciones que se dan.

 es necesario/Rogelio
Es necesario que Rogelio haga la cama.

1. más vale/Isabel

2. es importante/ellos

3. es urgente/él

4. conviene/Antonio y Elisa

5. es preciso/tú

6. es una lástima/yo

Proverbios y dichos
It is important to finish a task, even if you complete it much later than you would have liked. Following through with what you begin is an important quality. It demonstrates responsibility and your commitment to reach your goal. As the saying goes: *Más vale tarde que nunca* (Better late than never).

 Activity 12

Answers

11
1. dejes
2. se vayan
3. quieren
4. viajemos
5. vayan
6. sabe
7. tengamos
8. lleguen
9. esté
10. se cepillan

12 Possible answers:
1. Más vale que Isabel lleve las llaves.
2. Es importante que ellos laven la ropa.
3. Es urgente que él vaya al médico.
4. Conviene que Antonio y Elisa pasen la aspiradora por la alfombra.
5. Es preciso que tú arregles el techo.
6. Es una lástima que yo no pueda salir a jugar al béisbol.

Notes

Most impersonal expressions are formed with the verb *ser.*

Activities

Cooperative Learning. Ask small groups of students to brainstorm and then develop a list of five logical pieces of advice for a student who will be visiting a Spanish-speaking country. Each piece of advice should begin with an impersonal expression or a verb of influence/emotion.

NATIONAL STANDARDS
C1.1, C1.2, C3.2

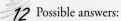

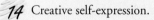
 ## 13 Permiso para un camping

Imagina que tus padres te dan permiso para ir de camping con unos amigos, pero primero expresan sus opiniones. Haz oraciones completas para saber lo que ellos dicen, usando las indicaciones que se dan.

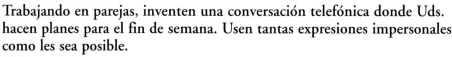
    conviene/Carlos y Clara/llevar/sus chaquetas
    Conviene que Carlos y Clara lleven sus chaquetas.

1. posible/hacer/mucho frío
2. mejor/Sandra/llevar/más agua
3. fácil/Uds./perderse/en las montañas
4. preciso/nadie/estar solo
5. importante/tú/divertirte/en este camping
6. más vale/tú/llamarnos/cuando regresen
7. lástima/nosotros/no ir
8. probable/tío Jairo/recogerlos

14 En el teléfono

Trabajando en parejas, inventen una conversación telefónica donde Uds. hacen planes para el fin de semana. Usen tantas expresiones impersonales como les sea posible.

    A: ¡Aló! ¿Margarita?
    B: Hola, Luz. ¿Qué vamos a hacer el fin de semana?
    A: Vamos al parque a jugar volibol.
    B: Es mejor que naveguemos en la Internet. Es posible que llueva el sábado.
    A: Es una lástima que llueva el sábado.

¡Aló! ¿Margarita?

Hola, Luz.

La abuela cumple años

el pastel

RAMÓN: El sábado vamos a ir a visitar a la abuela porque cumple años. Más vale que no tengan otro **plan**.

JUANA: Sí, es preciso que todos vayamos. Ella va a estar muy feliz de ver a toda la familia.

PAULA: ¿Por qué **te sonríes**,° Felipe? ¿Tienes otros planes? Si tienes planes, debes **cambiarlos**.°

FELIPE: Sí, mamá, tengo otro plan, pero mi abuela está primero.

JUANA: Debemos llevarle algo de regalo. ¿Qué les parece un **pastel**, unas galletas y algo para la casa?

FELIPE: ¿Por qué no le llevamos un refrigerador?

JUANA: Es mejor que no hables. Siempre te gusta exagerar.

PAULA: Bueno, no **comiencen**° a **discutir**.° **Cualquiera** de Uds. debe prepararle un pastel hoy mismo. ¿A qué hora vamos a ir el sábado, Ramón?

RAMÓN: Conviene que estemos temprano. Vamos a las nueve de la mañana.

te sonríes *you smile* **cambiarlos** *change them* **comiencen** *empiecen* **discutir** *to argue, to discuss*

Notes

Students may find it amusing that the noun *cumpleaños* comes from the expression *cumplir años,* as can be noted in the dialog title *La abuela cumple años.*

Point out that the verb *sonreírse* is conjugated following the pattern of *reírse.*

Let students know that *comenzar* is conjugated following the pattern of *empezar.*

Remind students that the word *cumpleaños* is normally a singular noun although it ends in *-s: mi cumpleaños* (my birthday); *mis cumpleaños* (my birthdays).

Activities

Critical Listening. Play the audiocassette/audio compact disc recording of the dialog as students look at the illustration and imagine what the people are saying to one another. Then ask students to state what they believe the main theme of the conversation is.

Prereading Strategy. Ask students to think about the last time they planned a birthday celebration. Then instruct students to cover the dialog with their hands and look at the illustration. Ask them to imagine who the individuals are, where the conversation takes place and what the people are saying to one another. Finally, have students look through the dialog quickly to find cognates and other words or expressions they already know.

NATIONAL STANDARDS
C1.2, C4.1

Algunos aparatos de la casa
Activities 15-16

Quiz/Activity 5

Activities 48-49

Activities 8-9

Quiz/Activity 4

Answers

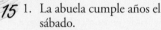

15 1. La abuela cumple años el sábado.
2. Porque ella va a estar muy feliz de ver a toda la familia.
3. Felipe se sonríe.
4. Ella piensa que deben llevarle de regalo un pastel, unas galletas y algo para la casa.
5. Cualquiera de los chicos debe prepararle el pastel.
6. Deben prepararlo hoy mismo.

16 Answers will vary.

17 Creative self-expression.

Notes

Review. This would be a good time to review some of the vocabulary students have learned pertaining to the house: rooms of the house, items in various rooms, etc.

Activities

Expansion. Additional questions (*¿Qué comprendiste?*): *¿Qué dice Felipe que ellos pueden regalarle a la abuela?; ¿Quiénes comienzan a discutir?; ¿A quién siempre le gusta exagerar?; ¿A qué hora van a ir a visitar a la abuela?*

Additional questions (*Charlando*): *¿Haces planes con tu familia? ¿De qué tipo?; ¿Sabes preparar pasteles o galletas?; ¿Cuál fue la última sorpresa que tuviste?*

TPR. Using overhead transparencies 48 and 49 (*Algunos aparatos de la casa*), ask students to come up and point to the people and items you name in Spanish.

NATIONAL STANDARDS
C1.1, C1.2, C2.1, C4.2, C5.2

---

15 **¿Qué comprendiste?**

1. ¿Quién cumple años el sábado?
2. ¿Por qué es preciso que todos vayan a visitarla?
3. ¿Quién se sonríe?
4. ¿Qué piensa Juana que deben llevarle de regalo a la abuela?
5. ¿Quién debe prepararle el pastel a la abuela?
6. ¿Cuándo deben preparar el pastel?

Es el cumpleaños de la abuela.

16 **Charlando**

1. ¿Discutes con tus hermanos/as? ¿Con quién discutes? Explica.
2. ¿Qué tipo de regalos te gusta recibir para tu cumpleaños?
3. ¿Cómo celebran los cumpleaños en tu familia?
4. Cuando tu familia quiere hacer planes contigo, ¿cambias tus planes si ya tienes otros planes con tus amigos/as? Explica.

17 **Un evento importante**

Expresa tus opiniones o dudas acerca del próximo evento importante que hay en tu familia o en tu colegio, usando una de las siguientes expresiones: *Es dudoso, es fácil, es una lástima, es imposible, es necesario, es posible, es importante, es preciso, es probable, es mejor, es urgente, más vale, conviene.* Puedes inventar la información si quieres. Sé creativo/a.

 Es difícil que mis tías vengan a la fiesta de cumpleaños de mi abuelo.

Algunos aparatos de la casa

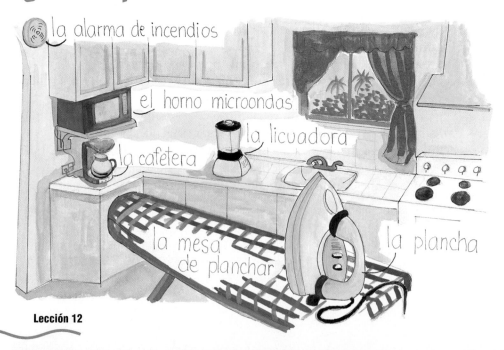
la alarma de incendios
el horno microondas
la licuadora
la cafetera
la mesa de planchar
la plancha

18 Los aparatos de la casa

Di qué aparatos son, de acuerdo con las siguientes pistas.

> Es fácil que Ud. haga el café con este aparato. La cafetera.

1. Es poco probable que Ud. pueda cocinar rápidamente la comida sin este aparato.
2. Es seguro que Ud. puede hacer muchos jugos con este aparato.
3. Conviene que Ud. tenga este aparato para tener fresca y fría la comida.
4. Es una lástima que Ud. no tenga este aparato cuando es verano y hace mucho calor.
5. Es importante que Ud. tenga este aparato para saber cuándo hay un incendio en la casa.
6. Es claro que Ud. puede lavar fácilmente los platos y los cubiertos con este aparato.
7. Es posible que Ud. use este aparato para limpiar las alfombras.
8. Es imposible que Ud. planche la ropa sin este aparato.
9. Es difícil que Ud. pueda cocinar la comida sin este aparato.

¿Qué es?

Otros aparatos de la casa

el abrelatas	can opener
la batidora	beater
el calentador de agua	water heater
el procesador de alimentos	food processor
la secadora	dryer
la tostadora	toaster
la videocasetera	videocassette recorder

¿Qué aparatos de la cocina puedes identificar?

Oportunidades

Carreras que usan el español

You already are aware that the ability to communicate in another language can enhance your career *(carrera)* opportunities. By now you have accumulated many skills in Spanish that will allow you to work in various fields some day. One possibility might be a career in advertising. Would you like to use your creativity and work in an advertising agency to promote products for people who speak Spanish? Marketing is a career that also offers many opportunities to use a second language and communicate ideas to other people. Consider these jobs as a unique way for you to practice your Spanish and use your imagination without limits.

Mucho gusto. Soy directora de publicidad.

Activity 18

Quiz/Activity 5

Answers

18
1. El horno microondas.
2. La licuadora.
3. El refrigerador.
4. El aire acondicionado./El ventilador.
5. La alarma de incendios.
6. El lavaplatos.
7. La aspiradora.
8. La plancha.
9. La estufa.

Notes

If you know some people in marketing positions, ask them to come to your class and talk about opportunities they are aware of that allow students to use Spanish in a marketing career.

Activities

Communities. Discuss careers in marketing as they pertain to your community. Encourage students to investigate doing some volunteer work with a local organization as a way of learning about how local companies market their products.

Cooperative Learning. Ask small groups of students to develop and then share with the class five logical pieces of advice for a student who will be interviewing for a job. The advice should begin with impersonal expressions or verbs of influence/emotion.

Critical Thinking. Ask students to rank the different household items in order of importance. Students should then share their lists in small groups and justify the order given.

Expansion. Ask students to look for examples of Spanish or bilingual advertising. Examples should be shared with the class.

Multiple Intelligences (linguistic). Have students prepare a television advertisement for one of the small appliances they have learned.

NATIONAL STANDARDS
C1.2, C4.2, C5.1

19 Trabajando en una agencia de publicidad

Imagina que trabajas para una agencia de publicidad *(advertising agency)* y estás prepararando los textos para algunos avisos *(advertisements)*. Completa los siguientes textos con una expresión y el subjuntivo del verbo apropiado.

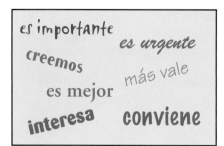

es importante   es urgente
creemos   más vale
es mejor
interesa   conviene

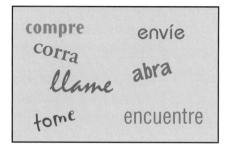

compre   envíe
corra
llame   abra
tome   encuentre

> *Es mejor que Ud. compre nuestra alarma de incendios Alerta. Su familia va a vivir más tranquila.*

1.
   (1) que Ud. nos (1) su dirección hoy mismo. Vamos a enviarle información importante sobre lo mejor en aparatos eléctricos *Icasa.*

2.
   Le (2) que Ud. (2) a nuestros Almacenes Azúcar ahora mismo. Hoy tenemos los mejores precios en lámparas para su casa.

   Almacenes Azúcar

3.
   Nos (3) que Ud. (3) el mejor café. Compre nuestra cafetera Café ya.

4.
   (4) que Ud. (4) esta carta ahora mismo. Su vida va a ser mejor.

5.
   No (5) que Ud. (5) mejores escobas que las nuestras. Escobas Superior barren mejor.

6.
   (6) que nos (6) hoy. Aquí en la revista *Semana* tenemos una linda plancha de regalo para Ud.

20 Es preciso que...

Haz oraciones completas para decir qué es preciso que las siguientes personas hagan, añadiendo las palabras que sean necesarias.

> mi papá/comprar/horno microondas
> Es preciso que mi papá compre un horno microondas.

1. Uds./encontrar/muebles pequeños
2. tú/preparar/pastel ahora mismo
3. mi bisabuela/conseguir/mesa de planchar
4. los padres de mi amigo/tener/perro/cuidar la casa
5. yo/tener/armario grande
6. nosotros/buscar/cafetera nueva
7. mis tíos/tener/buenos vecinos
8. mi hermana y su marido/comprar/sillones baratos

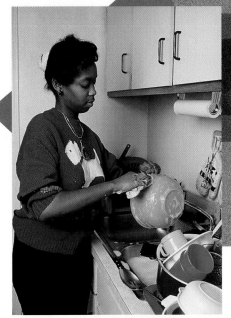
¡Es preciso que mis padres compren un lavaplatos!

21 Todo te complace

Todos tienen algo ahora que no tenían ayer. Di que te complace que las siguientes personas tengan esas cosas, usando las indicaciones que se dan. Haz los cambios que sean necesarios.

> Mis vecinos tenían una alarma de incendios vieja. (nuevo)
> Me complace que los vecinos tengan ahora una alarma de incendios nueva.

1. Mi hermano tenía una escoba muy mala. (bueno)
2. Los abuelos tenían un horno antiguo. (microondas)
3. Mi hermanastra tenía un lavadero muy feo. (bonito)
4. La mujer de mi hermano tenía un lavaplatos eléctrico viejo. (nuevo)
5. Mis tíos tenían unas bombillas de poca luz. (mucho)
6. Yo tenía en mi jardín una cerca amarilla. (negro)
7. Mi mamá tenía un tocador pequeño. (grande)

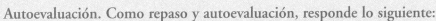

Autoevaluación. Como repaso y autoevaluación, responde lo siguiente:
1. What are two of the rules of your house?
2. What do you know about Simón Bolívar?
3. Name three things that either are important to you, bother you or worry you.
4. Use two impersonal expressions to give your opinion about the chores you do at home.
5. Explain how your family celebrates birthdays.
6. Name four household appliances in Spanish.

Answers

20
1. ...Uds. encuentren unos muebles pequeños.
2. ...tú prepares el pastel ahora mismo.
3. ...mi bisabuela consiga una mesa de planchar.
4. ...los padres de mi amigo tengan un perro para cuidar la casa.
5. ...yo tenga un armario grande.
6. ...nosotros busquemos una cafetera nueva.
7. ...mis tíos tengan buenos vecinos.
8. ...mi hermana y su marido compren unos sillones baratos.

21
1. ...tenga ahora...buena.
2. ...tengan ahora...microondas.
3. ...tenga ahora...bonito.
4. ...tenga ahora...nuevo.
5. ...tengan ahora...mucha....
6. ...tengas ahora en tu...negra.
7. ...tenga ahora...grande.

Autoevaluación
Possible answers:
1. Dos reglas de mi casa son: que yo no salga de casa después de las once de la noche y que nadie fume en casa.
2. Answers will vary.
3. Answers will vary.
4. Es una lástima que yo tenga que limpiar la cocina en vez de salir. Es necesario que yo haga la comida los lunes.
5. Answers will vary.
6. el horno microondas, la licuadora, el refrigerador, el aire acondicionado, el ventilador, la alarma de incendios, el lavaplatos, la aspiradora, la plancha, la estufa

Activities
Students with Special Needs.
Model a second sentence for activities 20-21.

NATIONAL STANDARDS
C1.2, C4.1, C5.2

Activity 10

Answers

A Creative self-expression.

B Creative writing practice.

Notes

Students will find it fun to play the roles of family members in activity A.

Encourage creativity as students prepare activity B. Tell them they are writing about a future dream home, so they may include any technological innovation they wish. Give an example or two of some possibilities to get things started: Billionaire founder of Microsoft, Bill Gates, has computer screens embedded in walls throughout his family's home that display scenes (artwork, beautiful geographic locations, etc.) as a person enters a room.

Brainstorm some technology terms that students might include in their sentences before assigning activity B.

For all oral activities, listen for the correct pronunciation and determine if students appear to understand what they are saying and hearing. Also, be sure students personalize information so that it is meaningful to them.

Activities

Expansion. You may wish to have some groups present their dialogs in front of the class after adequate practice.

¡La práctica hace al maestro!

A Comunicación

Working in groups of four, pretend that you are a family and prepare a dialog like *La abuela cumple años* in which you discuss plans to visit a relative. Include new expressions and vocabulary from this lesson and be sure to use the subjunctive where appropriate.

B Conexión con la tecnología

Technology is an integral part of our lives. We depend upon it to run our homes as well as our offices. Write sentences to tell about the technology you want your own home to have. Remember to use the subjunctive after impersonal expressions and verbs of emotion.

Es importante que mi casa tenga una computadora en todos los cuartos.
Espero que la puerta de mi garaje sea automática.

¿Quieres que tu casa tenga un televisor tan grande como éste?

CONJUNTO RESIDENCIAL *alameda de suba*

En Suba con fabuloso parque privado casas desde 90 Mts.2 con tres alcobas, cuarto de servicio y patio de ropas.

Compare antes de decidir

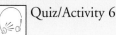

Testing/Assessment
Test Booklet
Oral Proficiency
    Evaluation Manual
Portfolio Assessment

VOCABULARIO

Aparatos de la casa
la alarma de incendios
el aparato
la cafetera
la cerradura
el horno (microondas)
la licuadora
la llave
la mesa de planchar
la plancha

Para describir
claro,-a
dudoso,-a
evidente
imposible
obvio,-a
preciso,-a
seguro,-a
urgente

Verbos
alegrar(se) (de)
cambiar
comenzar (ie)
complacer
convenir
discutir
dudar
encantar
esperar
fascinar
interesar
planchar
regresar
sonreír(se) (i, i)
temer
valer

Expresiones y otras palabras
a tiempo
el club
cualquiera
el incendio
la lástima
más vale que
el pastel
el plan
la regla
ser difícil que
ser fácil que

Activities

Expansion. Dictate a letter of the alphabet to the class. Give students three minutes to write any words they can think of in Spanish that begin with that letter. After calling time, ask students to read their lists aloud. The student with the longest list of correct words wins.

Pronunciation. To ensure proper pronunciation, model each word or expression and have students repeat after you.

Students with Special Needs. Students should review the vocabulary and determine how many of the expressions they recognize and know how to use. Have students find unknown words in previously studied lessons, or have them find expressions they might have forgotten in the vocabulary section at the end of the book.

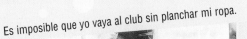
Es imposible que yo vaya al club sin planchar mi ropa.

¡Es mejor que nosotros nos comamos este pastel!

Capítulo 6 271

NATIONAL STANDARDS
C1.2, C4.1

Quiz/Activity 7

Answers

Preparación
1. The reading is about the Hispanic family.
2. A, C, D, F and G

Notes

The *A leer* is intended to provide a formal opportunity for students to improve their ability to read in Spanish. Remind students they do not need to understand every word in order to read in Spanish. Equivalents for difficult words have been provided to help students enjoy the contents of the readings without having to look up important but passive vocabulary.

Be sure to cover the *Preparación* activity prior to beginning the *A leer*.

Activities

Critical Listening. Play the audiocassette/audio compact disc version of the reading. Tell students to listen for the main ideas each speaker is addressing. Finally, have several individuals state what they believe the main theme of the reading is.

a leer

Estrategia

Preparación

Estrategia para leer: *skim for the main idea and anticipate related vocabulary*
Skimming is looking over a reading quickly to get a general ideal of what it is about. This allows you to predict what will be in the reading. Skimming also helps you to anticipate related vocabulary that will probably be found in the reading.

Contesta las siguientes preguntas como preparación para la lectura.
1. Skim the following passage by looking at the title, the subtitles, pictures, and the first sentence of each paragraph. What do you predict this reading is about?
2. After skimming the reading, which of the following words and expressions do you think will be found in it?

   A. tradicional   E. rebelde
   B. independiente   F. el respeto
   C. la autoridad   G. la unidad familiar
   D. los valores morales

La familia hispana

Irene (Venezuela): En mi país nos gusta hacer muchas actividades en familia, como salir a comer, ir a fiestas, ir de compras, por ejemplo. El respeto a los padres es muy importante. Si mi mamá o mi papá me dicen que regrese temprano, tengo que regresar temprano. Muchas veces pedimos la **bendición** a nuestros padres o **seres queridos** adultos, **ya sea** como saludo o despedida. Los fines de semana son los días para salir con la familia. Los sábados vamos generalmente a la playa a comer pescado y los

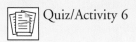

domingos vamos a la casa de los abuelos donde nos divertimos con los primos hablando de lo que pasó en la semana. Durante la semana, siempre se cena con toda la familia, porque para el almuerzo es difícil que nos reunamos todos.

Paloma (España): Las familias españolas de hoy son muy diferentes de las familias españolas de hace unos años. Las familias de hoy son más pequeñas; las chicas y los chicos **se casan** cuando son mayores, a los veintisiete o a los veintiocho años, generalmente; hay muchas mujeres que trabajan fuera de su casa; y en general, la gente pasa más su tiempo haciendo cosas personales más que antes, especialmente navegando en la Internet. **Aun** así, todavía se cena en familia, y en los fines de semana se va a visitar a los parientes o amigos. Los hijos normalmente viven con sus padres hasta que se casan. El respeto a los adultos es también muy importante en mi país. No se discute lo que dicen los padres. Mamá generalmente se encarga del cuidado de la casa. Cada hijo se encarga de su cuarto y, a veces, ayudamos a lavar los platos.

Rosario (Guatemala): Al igual que en otros países, la vida familiar está cambiando **de acuerdo** con el ritmo de vida de la **época** y el lugar. En Guatemala hay muchas familias pobres. A veces los hijos de estas familias tienen que trabajar en la calle desde muy pequeños. Los hijos mayores **incluso** llegan a ser los que llevan la comida a la casa y dan el dinero para la educación de sus hermanos menores. Pero también hay familias de clase **media** y alta muy ricas en las que los padres

son los que dan todo a los hijos. En muchas de estas casas hay **empleadas** de servicio que ayudan con los quehaceres de la casa. Los hijos usualmente se dedican a estudiar y a jugar con sus amigos o amigas.

Notes

Use maps to discuss where the people on pages 272-274 live.

Activities

Prereading Strategy. Prepare students for the content of the reading by asking some general questions on the reading topic, such as the questions found in the *Preparación*. Next, play the first paragraph of the recording of *A leer*, using the corresponding audiocassette or compact disc that is part of the Audiocassette/Audio CD Program. As an alternative, you may choose to read the first paragraph yourself. Read the paragraph again with students following along in the book. Give students a moment to look over the paragraph silently on their own and then have them ask questions. Ask for a student to volunteer to read the paragraph aloud. Continue in this way for subsequent paragraphs.

NATIONAL STANDARDS
C1.2, C3.2, C4.1

Comparisons. Point out that it is not uncommon for Spanish speakers to use both their first and middle names on an everyday basis (the student from Costa Rica is *Juan Carlos*). Other examples include *Ana María* and *José Luis*.

Activities

Multiple Intelligences (interpersonal/intrapersonal). Conduct a discussion about family life beginning with the following questions: *¿Qué haces los fines de semana con tu familia?; ¿Cenas durante la semana con tu familia? Explica.; ¿Es pequeña o grande tu familia? ¿Cuántas personas hay en tu familia?; En tu casa, ¿quién consigue el dinero para la comida?; ¿Cuántos cognados hay en la lectura La familia hispana? ¿Cuáles son?*

Juan Carlos (Costa Rica): En mi país los padres ponen mucha atención al **comportamiento** de sus hijos, a las relaciones con los amigos, para así **evitar** problemas tales como la drogadicción o el alcoholismo. Al igual que en otros países, los hijos se quedan en la casa de los padres hasta que salgan de la universidad o se casen. Antes, las familias eran bastante grandes, pero esto está cambiando. Hoy en día una familia **promedio** consiste de cuatro miembros, los papás y dos hijos. Es bonito escuchar las conversaciones de nuestros familiares sobre viejos tiempos, especialmente en visitas o en fiestas en las que todos nos reunimos.

Jairo (Colombia): En mi país todavía **mantenemos** la **unidad** familiar, lo que quiere decir que nos gusta mucho estar juntos y vivir en el mismo hogar. Es en el hogar donde aprendemos a querer y donde los padres nos **educan** y nos transmiten los **valores** morales. La casa es el lugar donde **compartimos** lo bueno y lo malo de la vida. Los hijos podemos quedarnos en la casa de nuestros padres toda la vida si queremos. En la casa tenemos mucha libertad, lo que nos permite hacer lo que nos guste. Pero claro, debemos respetar las reglas de la casa. También podemos traer nuestros amigos para estudiar o hacer fiestas. Muchas veces a nuestros padres les gusta estar en las fiestas porque así pueden conocer a nuestros amigos, hablar con ellos y, lo más importante, bailar con ellos.

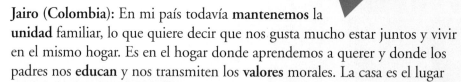

bendición *blessing* **seres queridos** *loved ones* **ya sea** *whether* **se casan** *they get married* **Aun** *Even then* **Al igual que** *Just as* **de acuerdo** *according to* **época** *era* **incluso** *even* **media** *middle* **empleadas** *maids* **comportamiento** *behavior* **evitar** *to avoid* **permanecen** *they stay* **promedio** *average* **mantenemos** *keep* **unidad** *unity* **educan** *they teach* **valores** *values* **compartimos** *we share*

A ¿Qué comprendiste?

1. ¿En qué país piden los chicos y las chicas la bendición de los padres?
2. ¿Adónde va Irene los sábados?
3. ¿En qué pasa más su tiempo hoy la gente en España?
4. ¿Dónde hay muchas familias pobres, según la lectura?
5. ¿Quiénes tienen que trabajar en la calle para conseguir dinero?
6. ¿Qué problemas dice Juan Carlos que pueden tener en su país los jóvenes?
7. ¿Hasta cuándo se quedan los hijos en la casa, según Juan Carlos?
8. ¿Qué debe respetar Jairo en su casa?

B Charlando

1. En qué son diferentes las familias hispanas de tu familia?
2. ¿Crees que los problemas de la drogadicción y el alcoholismo se pueden acabar? ¿Cómo?
3. ¿Qué piensas de quedarte en casa con tus padres hasta los treinta años? ¿Te gustaría? Explica.
4. ¿Qué fue lo más interesante de la lectura para ti?

Para nosotros, la familia es importante.

Activities A-B

Answers

A
1. En Venezuela, los chicos y las chicas piden la bendición de los padres.
2. Irene va a la playa.
3. Pasa más su tiempo navegando en la Internet.
4. En Guatemala hay muchas familias pobres.
5. Algunos de los hijos de las familias pobres tienen que trabajar en la calle para conseguir dinero.
6. Los jóvenes pueden tener problemas de drogadicción y alcoholismo.
7. Están en la familia hasta que salen de la universidad o se casan.
8. Debe respetar las reglas de la casa.

B Answers will vary.

Activities

Communities. Discuss student conclusions about culture based upon the *A leer* titled *La familia hispana*. Ask how students feel about what Irene, Paloma, Rosario, Juan Carlos and Jairo say about their families and life in their respective countries. Finally, discuss how family life in the United States compares to family life in the countries where these five people live.

NATIONAL STANDARDS
C1.2, C2.1, C3.1

a escribir

Estrategia

Estrategia para escribir: *comparing and contrasting*

To give your reader a clear mental picture of what you are describing, it is sometimes useful to compare and contrast aspects of a topic. Use a Venn diagram (overlapping circles, each containing one aspect of a topic) to help you visualize your comparisons and your contrasts.

MI HOGAR

AHORA   LAS DOS FAMILIAS   EN EL FUTURO

casa tradicional   2 hijos   casa moderna, una piscina, más baños

Write a composition of eight to ten lines in which you compare and contrast your home and family life now with what you envision when you have your own home and family in ten or fifteen years. Tell about your likes and dislikes, and how you would like things to be in the future. Be sure to use the subjunctive after verbs of wanting and emotion. Add artwork or graphics to your composition when you are finished to enhance the descriptions.

Mi familia y yo vivimos en una casa antigua. En el futuro, quiero que mi casa sea moderna con una piscina muy grande. También quiero que mi casa tenga muchos baños. No me gusta que mi hermana y yo usemos el mismo baño. Cuando tenga familia espero tener dos hijos y también quiero que cada uno tenga su baño.

repaso

¡Me encanta que mi marido sea tan chistoso!

Now that I have completed this chapter, I can...
- ✓ tell someone what to do.
- ✓ report what others say.
- ✓ state wishes and preferences.
- ✓ talk about everyday activities.
- ✓ talk about family.
- ✓ make a request.
- ✓ advise and suggest.
- ✓ describe a household.
- ✓ express uncertainty.
- ✓ express doubt.
- ✓ express emotion.
- ✓ state hopes.
- ✓ state an opinion.
- ✓ discuss time.

I can also...
- ✓ read in Spanish about life in Bolivia and other countries that Simón Bolívar helped liberate.
- ✓ talk about my responsibilities at home.
- ✓ read a newspaper advertisement in Spanish.
- ✓ read for ideas and cues in context.
- ✓ recognize opportunities for employment in advertising and marketing.

Los Andes, al pie de los cuales está La Paz, Bolivia.

Activities

Communities. Find out if there is a nursing home in your locality that has Spanish-speaking residents, a club or a church with Spanish-speaking elders. Plan a visit to the home, club or church and bring a cake *(torta)* for all to share. Have your students interview the residents/members to find out their date and country of birth, when they came to the United States, how many children they have and whether or not their children helped at home with the household chores.

Multiple Intelligences (linguistic). Assign small groups the task of developing and presenting an advertisement for a given product. The advertisement should include both the subjunctive and commands in an effort to persuade consumers to buy the product. Have students present their advertisements to the entire class.

NATIONAL STANDARDS
C1.1, C1.2, C1.3, C2.1, C2.2, C3.1, C3.2, C4.1, C4.2, C5.1, C5.2

Las noticias

CAPÍTULO 7

Uruguay
Nombre oficial: República Oriental del Uruguay

Población: 3.300.000

Capital: Montevideo

Ciudades importantes: Salto, Paysandú, Las Piedras

Unidad monetaria: el peso uruguayo

Fiesta nacional: 25 de agosto, Día de la Independencia

Gente famosa: Eduardo Galeano (ensayista); Juana de Ibarbourou (poetisa); Juan Carlos Onetti (escritor)

Paraguay
Nombre oficial: República del Paraguay

Población: 5.300.000

Capital: Asunción

Ciudades importantes: Ciudad del Este, San Lorenzo, Concepción

Unidad monetaria: el guaraní

Fiesta nacional: 14 de mayo, Día de la Independencia

Gente famosa: Augusto Roa Bastos (escritor)

Notes

The communicative functions appear here with accompanying supportive visuals depicting what students will be studying in the chapter. A checkoff list of the functions appears at the end of *Capítulo 7* (see page 321), along with additional objectives that students can use as a self-check to evaluate their own progress.

In this chapter you will be able to:

- express events in the past
- talk about the news
- discuss what has happened
- discuss a television broadcast
- talk about everyday activities
- describe people and objects
- write about what someone has done
- identify sections of newspapers and magazines
- relate two events in the past
- discuss a radio broadcast
- talk about soccer
- add emphasis to a description
- express wishes

279

Content reviewed in *Lección 13*
- everyday activities
- reflexive verbs
- describing

Answers

1 1. Está cubierto de cereal.
2. Hay un plato roto.
3. Se cayó.
4. No, no se ha lastimado.
5. Answers will vary.
6. Answers will vary.

Activities

Critical Listening. Play the audiocassette/audio compact disc recording of the dialog as students listen to the conversation. Ask students what Silvia was doing before she was interrupted by Javier. Then have students look at the illustration and imagine what the people are saying to each other. Finally, ask several individuals to state what they believe the main theme of the conversation is.

Expansion. Additional questions (*¿Qué comprendiste?*): *¿En qué país está Punta del Este?; ¿Qué ha ocurrido en la carretera que va a Punta del Este?; ¿Qué está haciendo Silvia?; ¿Cómo está el piso, según Silvia?; ¿Qué le pasó a Silvia en la cocina?; ¿Quiere Javier oír a la reportera?; ¿Qué quiere ver Silvia?*

Students with Special Needs. The formation and use of the present perfect tense is explained later in this lesson. For this reason, difficult constructions that students may have trouble understanding are noted in the glossed section that follows this and the next dialog. Encourage students to try to discern meaning from contextual cues and these glossed notes.

Lección 13

Contexto cultural
URUGUAY

Las noticias

JAVIER: Oye, Silvia, ¿sabes qué **ha pasado?**° El piso está **cubierto**° de cereal y hay un plato **roto.**° ¿Qué **has hecho?**°
SILVIA: Me caí. El piso está muy **resbaloso.**°
JAVIER: **¿Te has lastimado?**°
SILVIA: No. Déjame ver las noticias. La **reportera** está hablando de un accidente.
JAVIER: ¡Sí, cómo no!

ha pasado *has happened (present perfect tense of* pasar) **cubierto** *covered (past participle of* cubrir) **roto** *broken (past participle of* romper) **has hecho** *have you done (present perfect tense of* hacer) **resbaloso** *slippery* **¿Te has lastimado?** *Have you injured (hurt) yourself? (present perfect tense of* lastimarse)*

¿Qué comprendiste?

1. ¿De qué está cubierto el piso de la cocina?
2. ¿Qué más hay en el piso?
3. ¿Qué le pasó a Silvia?
4. ¿Se ha lastimado Silvia?
5. ¿Ha ocurrido algún accidente en la ciudad donde vives? ¿De qué tipo?
6. ¿Te ha ocurrido algún accidente en tu casa en el último mes? ¿Qué te pasó?

Conexión cultural

El Uruguay

La República Oriental del Uruguay, su nombre oficial, es el país más pequeño de la América del Sur después de Surinam. Como los otros países que has estudiado, el español es su lengua oficial. Está ubicado entre el Brasil al norte y al este, la Argentina al oeste, el Océano Atlántico al sureste y el Río de la Plata al suroeste.

La capital del país, y la ciudad más grande, es Montevideo, con una población de más de un millón de habitantes. Otras ciudades importantes del Uruguay son Salto y Punta del Este.

Los españoles llegaron en el siglo XVI cuando Juan Díaz de Solís fue a parar a lo que hoy es el Río de la Plata. Un grupo de españoles de la Compañía de Jesús estableció la ciudad de Santo Domingo de Soriano en 1624. Durante los años siguientes otra gente de Europa continuó la colonización de la región. Doscientos años más tarde, el día 25 de agosto de 1825, Uruguay declaró su independencia de España.

Hoy el Uruguay es un país cosmopolita. Su población, que en su mayoría vive en las ciudades, muestra una variedad de herencias. El ochenta y cinco por ciento de su gente es de origen europeo, la mayor parte de la cual es de origen español o italiano.

Punta del Este, Uruguay.

Montevideo, la capital del Uruguay.

 El Uruguay

 Quiz/Activity 2

 Activity 1

Notes

www

> Uruguay
> General Information
> http://uruguay.org.uy/
> Travel Information
> http://www.turismo.gub.uy/

Nearly half of Uruguay's citizens live in the capital, Montevideo.

The currency of Uruguay is the *peso uruguayo*.

Activities

Connections. Talk with students about Uruguay in preparation for assigning this reading. Begin with the country's location in the world and in South America with respect to surrounding geographical features, using the maps in the front of the book or the transparencies that are part of this program.

Prereading Strategy. This *Conexión cultural* provides an opportunity for students to increase what they know about the Spanish-speaking world by reading about Uruguay in Spanish. The vocabulary and structures have been controlled to enable individuals to read in the target language and enjoy the experience. Note for the class that it is not essential to understand every word in order to read Spanish; unknown passive vocabulary has been limited to facilitate an enjoyable reading experience. Before beginning the *Conexión cultural*, consider asking some general preparation questions about the theme of the reading: What is the capital of Uruguay? Where is Uruguay located? What else do students know about Uruguay? Then have students skim the *Conexión cultural* for cognates and any words or expressions they already know.

NATIONAL STANDARDS
C1.2, C3.2, C4.1, C5.2

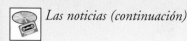

Las noticias (continuación)

Answers

2
1. El nombre oficial del país es la República Oriental del Uruguay.
2. No. Es un país pequeño.
3. Está en la América del Sur, entre el Brasil al norte y al este, la Argentina al oeste, el Océano Atlántico al sureste y el Río de la Plata al suroeste.
4. Se habla español.
5. Sus países vecinos son el Brasil y la Argentina.
6. El Río de la Plata y el Océano Atlántico tocan el país al sur.
7. La capital es Montevideo.
8. Tiene una población de más de un millón de habitantes.
9. Declaró su independencia el 25 de agosto de 1825.
10. Hoy el Uruguay es un país cosmopolita; la mayor parte de su población es de origen español o italiano.

Notes

After reading the dialog, explain to the students that the situation presented in the dialog is intended to be funny and in no way pretends to show that it is okay for dogs or animals to bite one another. If students question the drawings, explain that they are intended only to illustrate the irony of the situation and are intended to be humorous.

Activities

Prereading Strategy. Ask students to talk about some event they have experienced in which what actually happened was the opposite of what they expected. Then instruct students to cover the dialog with their hands and look at the illustration. Ask them to imagine what funny reversal of events has occurred and what the people are saying to each other.

Cruzando fronteras

¿Qué sabes sobre el Uruguay? Contesta las siguientes preguntas.

1. ¿Cuál es el nombre oficial del país?
2. ¿Es el Uruguay un país grande? Explica.
3. ¿Dónde está el Uruguay?
4. ¿Qué lengua se habla en el Uruguay?
5. ¿Cuáles son los países vecinos del Uruguay?
6. ¿Qué cuerpos de agua tocan el país al sur?
7. ¿Cuál es la capital del país?
8. ¿Cuántas personas viven en la capital?
9. ¿Cuándo declaró el Uruguay su independencia de España?
10. ¿Cómo es el Uruguay hoy? Explica.

Las noticias (continuación)

¡Ja, ja, ja!

JAVIER: Silvia, ¿por qué **no has limpiado**° el piso?
SILVIA: ¡Ay, perdón! He estado viendo las noticias.
JAVIER: ¿Qué **acontecimiento**° especial ha pasado?
SILVIA: Nada, pero hoy **me he muerto de la risa**° con una noticia muy chistosa.
JAVIER: Pero, si las noticias son siempre **serias**, ¿qué **han mostrado**° de chistoso?
SILVIA: Mostraron a un hombre y a su perro en Montevideo.
JAVIER: Y, ¿qué pasó?
SILVIA: Bueno, lo **normal** es que los perros **muerdan**° a las personas. Y esta vez fue un hombre **quien** mordió a su perro. ¡Ja, ja, ja!

no has limpiado *haven't you cleaned* **acontecimiento** *event, happening* **me he muerto de la risa** *I died laughing* **han mostrado** *have they shown* **muerdan** *bite*

3 ¿Qué comprendiste?

1. ¿Por qué Silvia no ha limpiado el piso?
2. ¿Hubo algún acontecimiento especial en las noticias?
3. ¿Cómo son siempre las noticias, según Javier?
4. ¿Qué ha pasado que no es normal?

Activities 3-4

Quiz/Activity 3

Activity 2

Quiz/Activity 1

Nombres y **N**oticias

■ PEDRO ALMODÓVAR recibió ayer un premio César (semejante a un Oscar) honorífico por su carrera artística, un galardón equivalente a los Goya españoles, que le concedió la Academia de las Artes y de las Ciencias Cinematográficas francesa en París. La actriz española **Rossy de Palma** presentó al homenajeado, al que definió como su "padre cinematográfico" y otra de sus habituales colaboradoras, **Victoria Abril**, le entregó el galardón.

Almodóvar

Algo más

Para hablar de las noticias

un accidente	*accident*
una actividad	*activity*
una catástrofe	*catastrophe*
una celebración	*celebration*
un huracán	*hurricane*
un misterio	*mystery*
una ocasión	*occasion*
una protesta	*protest*
una reunión	*meeting, reunion*
un robo	*robbery*
un suceso	*event, happening*
un temblor	*tremor*

Hubo una protesta hoy en la ciudad.

Answers

3
1. No ha limpiado el piso porque ha estado viendo las noticias.
2. No, no ha pasado nada especial.
3. Según Javier, las noticias son siempre serias.
4. Un hombre mordió a un perro.

4 Answers will vary.

Notes

The word *suceso* is synonymous with *acontecimiento*.

Activities

Communities. Have students investigate who the person in the clipping next to activity 3 is.

Expansion. Additional questions (*¿Qué comprendiste?*): *¿Cómo era una de las noticias de hoy?; ¿En qué país está Montevideo?; ¿Qué es lo normal, según Silvia?; ¿Quién se ríe?; ¿Qué han mostrado de chistoso en las noticias, según Silvia?*

Additional questions (*Charlando*): *¿Piensas que las noticias deben ser siempre serias? ¿Por qué?; ¿Ves las noticias en la televisión todos los días? ¿A qué hora?; ¿Te gusta comer cuando ves la televisión? ¿Qué comes?; ¿Piensas que ver las noticias es importante? ¿Por qué?; ¿Te gustaría ser reportero o reportera de televisión? Explica.*

4 Charlando

1. ¿Te gusta ver las noticias? Explica.
2. ¿Qué noticia importante o seria ha pasado donde tú vives?
3. ¿Hubo algún suceso o acontecimiento importante esta semana en el país? ¿Cuál?
4. ¿Crees que una noticia chistosa puede ser especial o importante? Explica.

Más sobre las noticias

la huelga	*strike*
el choque	*collision*
el crimen	*crime*
la explosión	*explosion*
la guerra	*war*
herido,-a	*wounded*
la tormenta	*storm*
el terremoto	*earthquake*

NATIONAL STANDARDS
C1.1, C1.2, C2.1, C4.2, C5.2

Oportunidades

El español y la televisión

If you have access to one of the Spanish channels on television, be sure to tune in to news programs to test how much you are able to understand. Begin a habit of listening to or watching programs and news in Spanish, even if you do not understand everything at first, because it will help you become accustomed to the sounds of spoken Spanish. Not only that, it will also keep you informed.

Es divertido ver programas en español.

5 Resumen de noticias

Aquí tienes un artículo que describe varios acontecimientos que han ocurrido durante el año. Completa el siguiente párrafo, usando una de las palabras de la lista. Cada palabra se usa una vez.

accidente	catástrofe	huracán	ocasión	reunión
acontecimientos	celebraciones	misterio	protesta	robos

Resumen de noticias del año

Lo siguiente es un resumen de los (1) más importantes que han ocurrido durante el año: En enero hubo una gran (2) en el país, cuando los vientos del (3) Estela barrieron con varias ciudades pequeñas de la costa este. En febrero hubo una (4) nacional de padres de familia para hablar sobre los problemas entre padres e hijos. En marzo un avión tuvo un (5) fatal en su viaje de Montevideo a Nueva York. En abril hubo una (6) de más de cien mil personas amigas de la ecología en favor de los bosques del país.

En mayo, en medio de un gran (7), el Banco de la República tuvo uno de los (8) más grandes de su historia sin que hasta hoy la policía sepa quién lo hizo. Finalmente, el mes pasado con (9) del día del padre se hicieron muchas (10) para los papás de todo el país.

Un huracán muy fuerte.

Accidente

Un muerto y tres heridos fue el resultado de un accidente de tránsito, ocurrido en la Ruta 5 Sur, a la altura del paso bajo nivel Salesianos, en Santiago.

En ese lugar, el conductor Waldo Zambrano Arellano, quien guiaba el auto patente HJ-6134, perdió el control del vehículo y chocó con un poste del alumbrado público. A raíz del impacto, falleció en el mismo lugar su esposa, identificada como María Troncoso González.

Con lesiones graves resultó el hijo del matrimonio, Arnaldo Zambrano Troncoso, de 14 años, y con heridas leves, otra pasajera, de nombre Elena Ponce Troncoso. Estos últimos -como también el chofer, quien quedó lesionado- fueron atendidos en el hospital Barros Luco.

6 Las noticias de tu comunidad

Haz un reporte de las noticias o sucesos más importantes que han pasado durante la semana en tu comunidad. Da toda la información que puedas.

 El lunes hubo un accidente entre dos camiones en la carretera número noventa y cuatro. El martes hubo una celebración por el Día de la Raza.

IDIOMA

El pretérito perfecto y el participio

Use the *pretérito perfecto,* or present perfect tense, to refer to the past in a general sense or to talk about something specific that **has happened** recently. This compound verb tense is formed from the present tense of the helping verb *haber* (to have) and the past participle *(participio)* of a verb.

he	hemos
has	habéis
ha	han

+ past participle

The past participle of a verb in Spanish is often equal to English words ending in *-ed.* Form the past participle of regular *-ar* verbs by changing the *-ar* of the infinitive to *-ado.* For regular *-er* and *-ir* verbs, change the infinitive ending *-er* or *-ir* to *-ido.*

pasar	→	*pasado* (happened)
comer	→	*comido* (eaten)
vivir	→	*vivido* (lived)
ir	→	*ido* (gone)

Nosotras hemos vivido en Montevideo.

Look at these examples:

*¿Qué **ha pasado** en las noticias?*
*Ya **he comido** la cena.*
***Nosotras hemos vivido** en Montevideo.*
*¿**Han ido** Uds. a Montevideo alguna vez?*

What **has happened** in the news?
I have already **eaten** dinner.
We have lived in Montevideo.
Have you ever **gone** to Montevideo?

Object pronouns precede the conjugated form of *haber.* However, when an expression uses the infinitive of *haber,* attach object pronouns directly to the end of the infinitive form of *haber.*

*¿Qué **les ha pasado** aquí?*
*Siento **no haberte contado.***

What **happened to them** here?
I am sorry **I did not tell you.**

Answers

6 Creative self-expression.

Notes

Explain to students that the past participle always ends in *-o* in the perfect tenses: it does not change to agree with changes in subjects.

The past participles are invariable in form when they are part of a perfect construction but they change their endings when they function as adjectives.

Comparisons. Point out that in English the regular past participle ends in **-ed.**

Activities

Critical Listening. Ask students to prepare four sentences using the present perfect tense to say things they and other family members have done. Three of the statements should be true while one must be an innocent lie. Then have individual students present their sentences while the others listen and identify the statement that is false.

Critical Thinking. Have students find and bring to class two copies each of two or three newspaper or magazine clippings that contain examples of the present perfect tense. As a homework assignment, have students circle the present perfect-tense verb forms on one of the copies of each article to use as an answer sheet. In class, pair students and ask for partners to find and circle examples of the present perfect tense in each other's articles. Then have students compare the verbs they circled with the student's answer sheet.

NATIONAL STANDARDS
C1.1, C1.2, C1.3, C3.1, C4.1, C5.1

7 Noticias en la red

Lee las siguientes noticias de una página de información de la Internet y, luego, encuentra seis participios.

Netscape Netcenter

El País

Montevideo 15°C

JUEVES, 25 de MARZO   9:11 A.M.

NOTICIAS BREVES

Internacional
Nacional
Política
Tecnología
Deportes
El tiempo
Arte
Automóviles
Libros
Empleos
Viajes

Muchos accidentes han ocurrido recientemente en la carretera entre Montevideo y Punta del Este. Los vecinos del lugar dicen que todo se debe a la gran actividad de camiones que pasan por esta ruta.

•••

Con ocasión de la posesión del nuevo presidente de la república, se han reunido en la capital uruguaya presidentes de muchos países del mundo.

•••

Algo diferente ocurrió ayer cuando un hombre mordió a su perro, diciendo que su perro trató de morderlo a él primero. Éste es el primer suceso de este tipo que ha pasado en la ciudad.

•••

Un temblor de poca intensidad ocurrió ayer en la capital. Con éste han sido ya tres los temblores de tierra que han ocurrido en Montevideo esta semana.

•••

Una importante reunión de miembros de la comunidad del barrio La Carolina con miembros de la policía se realizó esta mañana para estudiar la situación de los robos que han venido pasando en el sector.

8 En el zoológico

Completa las siguientes oraciones, usando el pretérito perfecto y las indicaciones que se dan para saber lo que Silvia y sus amigos dicen en su visita al zoológico.

   Nosotros no <u>hemos terminado</u> la visita al zoológico todavía. (terminar)

1. Nosotras <u>(1)</u> de comer a las tortugas. (dar)
2. Unos señores <u>(2)</u> a la jaula de las panteras. (entrar)
3. El gorila <u>(3)</u> al árbol. (subir)
4. Mis amigos y yo <u>(4)</u> por el zoológico. (correr)
5. Yo <u>(5)</u> todo tipo de pájaros. (ver)
6. Mis amigos <u>(6)</u> la exhibición de los leones. (visitar)
7. Los leones <u>(7)</u> mucho. (rugir)
8. Alicia <u>(8)</u> con los monos. (jugar)
9. Los monos <u>(9)</u> plátanos todo el día. (comer)

9 Varias veces al mes

Haz oraciones completas para decir el número de veces que ha ocurrido lo siguiente, usando las indicaciones que se dan.

Verónica/comprar el periódico/15
Verónica ha comprado el periódico quince veces este mes.

1. los niños/salir a patinar/6
2. Ud./limpiar la chimenea/1
3. tú/barrer el garaje/7
4. ellos/discutir con sus amigas/2
5. yo/alquilar la misma película/2
6. don Juan/ir de compras/4
7. Francisco y Mónica/almorzar juntos/10

¿Cuántas veces han ganado esta semana?

10 ¿Cuántas veces?

Haz oraciones con el pretérito perfecto para decir cuántas veces has hecho las actividades indicadas esta semana.

ir al colegio
He ido al colegio cinco veces esta semana.

1. llegar tarde al colegio
2. comer el almuerzo
3. mentir
4. conducir el carro de mis padres
5. hablar español con mi profesor/a de español
6. dar un paseo
7. conocer a una persona nueva

¿QUÉ HAS HECHO MUCHO ESTA SEMANA?
lunes
domingo
jueves
martes
miércoles
viernes
sábado

 Activity 10

Answers

9 1. Los niños han salido...seis veces....
   2. Ud. ha limpiado...una vez....
   3. Tú has barrido...siete veces....
   4. Ellos han discutido...dos veces....
   5. Yo he alquilado...dos veces....
   6. Don Juan ha ido...cuatro veces....
   7. Francisco y Mónica han almorzado...diez veces....

10 Answers will vary. Past participles should be as follows: llegado, comido, mentido, conducido, hablado, dado, conocido

Notes

The proverb offers an enjoyable opportunity to learn about the subtleties of speaking Spanish like a native. Learning proverbs extends students' understanding of the language and culture of people throughout the world who speak Spanish.

Activities

Students with Special Needs. Provide a second example for activities 9-10.

PARА ti

Proverbios y dichos
To a person who pays attention, only a few words of explanation are necessary. When something is not understood, often the problem does not lie with the message, but rather with the person who receives it. Paying close attention and listening carefully the first time will save you time in the end. As the saying goes: *A buen entendedor pocas palabras bastan* (A word to the wise is sufficient).

¿Qué dicen? No entiendo.

Entiendo.

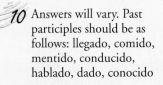
NATIONAL STANDARDS
C1.2, C3.2, C4.1, C4.2

Answers

11
1. ha ocurrido
2. ha hablado
3. Han mostrado
4. he mirado
5. ha trabajado
6. han escapado
7. has tenido
8. he dormido

Notes

Explain that the accent mark on *caído, creído,* and so forth, prevents a diphthong and, therefore, changes the pronunciation. The Appendices for *Somos así LISTOS* provide an explanation of the syllabification and accentuation rules.

Activities

Spanish for Spanish Speakers. Ask students to read the article that accompanies activity 11 and summarize what it is about.

11 ## En las noticias

Completa el siguiente diálogo entre Pilar y David, usando el pretérito perfecto de los verbos indicados para saber lo que dicen sobre el robo en el Banco de la República.

■ **500 millones de sucres en robos** • Ése es el monto aproximado de pérdidas por cuatro robos ocurridos este fin de semana en un almacén y tres viviendas, en Guayaquil. El mayor fue a la compañía EICA, en la avenida Juan Tanca Marengo. A las 08h50, según la denuncia de Carlos Silver, seis personas llegaron a bordo de un auto Nissan color plomo y un furgón verde, ambos sin placas y se llevaron 8 motores fuera de borda, una cámara fotográfica, dos cajas de herramientas. La pérdida superaría los trescientos millones de sucres. Mientras tanto, más de cien millones fueron las pérdidas por el asalto a una vivienda en la ciudadela Bellavista. De ella se llevaron un lote de joyas valorado en 20 mil dólares y varios electrodomésticos.

PILAR: David, ¿qué *1. (ocurrir)* hoy en las noticias?

DAVID: Un reportero *2. (hablar)* sobre un robo en el Banco de la República.

PILAR: ¿Cómo? ¿Un robo? ¿*3. (mostrar)* ellos las personas que estaban en el banco?

DAVID: Todavía no.

PILAR: ¿Estás seguro?

DAVID: Sí, claro. Yo *4. (mirar)* las noticias todo el día. Pero, ¿por qué te preocupas tanto?

PILAR: Bueno, tengo un amigo que *5. (trabajar)* por muchos años en ese banco.

DAVID: No te preocupes. Todas las personas *6. (escapar)* de allí, según dijo la policía.

PILAR: ¡Qué bueno! ¿Y nadie se lastimó cuando escapaban?

DAVID: No, nadie. Mira, Pilar, creo que tú *7. (tener)* un día muy largo. Ve a descansar un poco.

PILAR: Sí, está bien. No *8. (dormir)* lo suficiente. Hasta mañana, David.

Algo más

Daniel ha escrito en su diario muchas veces esta semana.

Participios irregulares

The following verbs have irregular past participles:

abrir	**abierto** (opened)	morir	**muerto** (died)
cubrir	**cubierto** (covered)	poner	**puesto** (put)
decir	**dicho** (said, told)	romper	**roto** (broken, torn)
escribir	**escrito** (written)	ver	**visto** (seen)
hacer	**hecho** (done, made)	volver	**vuelto** (returned)

Although they are regular, the past participles of some verbs require a written accent mark:

caer	**caído** (fallen)	oír	**oído** (heard, listened to)
creer	**creído** (believed)	reír	**reído** (laughed)
leer	**leído** (read)	traer	**traído** (brought)

Variations of verbs in combination with prefixes and suffixes reflect the same irregularities of the original verb.

reír (to laugh)	**reído**
sonreír (to smile)	**sonreído**

¿Qué ha hecho el elefante?

288   Lección 13

12 Exageraciones

Di algo exagerado, usando el pretérito perfecto de los verbos indicados.

He escrito más de 5.000 libros de misterio.

    escribir
    He escrito más de cinco mil libros de misterio.

1. escribir
2. decir
3. traer a la clase
4. romper
5. correr
6. oír
7. hacer
8. leer
9. ver
10. poner

13 Muchas preguntas

Tu padre ha llegado a casa después de trabajar y ahora él te hace muchas preguntas. Trabajando en parejas, alterna con tu compañero/a de clase en hacer preguntas y contestarlas, usando el pretérito perfecto y las indicaciones que se dan. Sigue el modelo.

    traer este ventilador para el comedor/tú
    A: ¿Quién ha traído este ventilador para el comedor?
    B: Tú lo has traído.

1. poner la televisión en mi cuarto/yo
2. ver las noticias hoy/mi tío
3. morder el pan/un ratón
4. hacer estas galletas/mi tía
5. decir que el piso está resbaloso/mi mamá
6. escribir estos números de teléfono en mi libro/Rogelio
7. leer el periódico/todos nosotros
8. romper este vaso/Josefina
9. cubrir el piso con papeles/mi hermanastro
10. abrir todas las ventanas/los abuelos

En la televisión

Quiz/Activity 5

Answers

14 Answers will vary.

15 Creative self-expression.

Notes

In informal language use, Spanish speakers may refer to *la televisión* as *la tele*.

Note that the verbs *abrir, cubrir, escribir* and *romper* have no forms that are irregular other than the past participle.

Activities

Critical Listening. Play the audiocassette/audio compact disc recording of the dialog on page 291. Instruct students to cover the words as they listen to the conversation in order to develop good listening skills before concentrating on their ability to read Spanish. Ask students what the four friends are doing. Then have students look at the illustration on page 290 and imagine what the people are saying to one another. Finally, ask several individuals to state what they believe the main theme of the conversation is.

Prereading Strategy. Instruct students to cover up the dialog on page 291 with one hand and to look at the illustration on page 290. Then ask them to imagine what the theme of the conversation is and what the people are saying to one another.

14 Javier y su familia

Combinando elementos de cada columna, haz oraciones completas para decir lo que han hecho esta mañana algunos miembros de la familia de Javier.

 Sus tíos han traído la leche y el pan.

A	B	C
sus abuelos	leer	sus cosas en su lugar
su sobrina	escribir	una revista muy interesante
su papá	oír	una ventana jugando al fútbol
sus tíos	romper	un pastel con frutas
sus hermanas	abrir	la leche y el pan
su hermanastro	poner	una noticia sobre un temblor
su mamá	traer	una carta a su amiga del Uruguay
su prima	cubrir	todas las cortinas de la casa

15 Esta semana

Todos han hecho diferentes actividades durante esta semana. Trabajando en parejas, alterna con tu compañero/a de clase en hacer preguntas y en contestarlas para decir lo que han hecho durante la semana varias personas que Uds. conocen. Usen el pretérito perfecto en cada pregunta y respuesta.

A: ¿Qué han hecho tus hermanos esta semana?
B: Mis hermanos han visto las noticias en la televisión.

B: ¿Qué ha hecho la profesora de matemáticas?
A: La profesora de matemáticas ha dado mucha tarea a su clase.

En la televisión

ESTEBAN: En este **canal**° hay una **comedia** muy buena. Siempre me he reído viéndola.

MARISOL: Yo prefiero los programas de música. Me gusta ver a mis **cantantes**° favoritos.

SUSANA: A mí me gustan los de **concurso.**° Siempre he querido **participar** en uno para ganar **premios.**°

IGNACIO: Mis preferidos son los de noticias. He aprendido mucho viéndolos.

MARISOL: Sí, pero los **periodistas**° a veces **opinan** demasiado y no **informan** nada.

ESTEBAN: Miren, va a empezar un programa buenísimo....

canal *channel* **cantantes** *singers* (**programa de**) **concurso** *(game show) contest, competition* **premios** *prizes* **periodistas** *journalists*

16 ¿Qué comprendiste?

1. ¿Qué tipo de programa hay en el canal que los chicos están viendo?
2. ¿Qué tipo de programas prefiere Marisol?
3. ¿Quién ha querido participar en un programa de concurso?
4. ¿Quiénes opinan demasiado, según Marisol?

17 Charlando

1. ¿Quién es tu cantante favorito?
2. ¿Qué tipo de programa es tu favorito?
3. ¿Te gustaría participar en un programa de concurso y ganar premios? Explica.
4. ¿Crees que informar es algo fácil o difícil? ¿Por qué?

Ricky Martin

Shakira

Juan Luis Guerra

¿Se ha lastimado alguien?

Algo más

El pretérito perfecto: los verbos reflexivos

The present perfect tense of reflexive verbs is formed using a reflexive pronoun in combination with the present tense of *haber* and the past participle of a verb. Reflexive pronouns precede the conjugated form of *haber*. However, when an expression uses the infinitive *haber*, attach the reflexive pronouns directly to the end of the infinitive.

¿Se ha lastimado ella? Did she hurt herself?
Siento haberme olvidado. I am sorry I forgot.

Answers

16
1. Hay una comedia.
2. Marisol prefiere los programas de música.
3. Susana siempre ha querido participar en un programa de concurso.
4. Los periodistas opinan demasiado, según Marisol.

17 Answers will vary.

Notes

Point out that *programa(s)* is a masculine noun. Many other nouns that end in *-ma* are also masculine (*sistema, problema*, etc.).

Review. Review some of the reflexive verbs before discussing the contents of the *Algo más*.

Communities. Music is popular in Latin America, as well as throughout the rest of the world. The three names that accompany activity 17 are all pop superstars in the Spanish-speaking world. Ricky Martin is from Puerto Rico, Shakira is from Colombia, and Juan Luis Guerra is from the Dominican Republic.

Activities

Communities. Ask if students can name any well-known Hispanic singers. Ask if the performers sing in Spanish, in English or in both languages.

Expansion. Additional questions (*¿Qué comprendiste?*): *¿Qué están haciendo los chicos?*; *¿Qué programas son los favoritos de Ignacio? ¿Por qué?*

Additional questions (*Charlando*): *¿Qué canales ves mucho?*; *¿Te gustaría trabajar en la televsión? ¿Por qué?*

NATIONAL STANDARDS
C1.1, C1.2, C2.1, C4.1, C4.2, C5.2

Answers

18
1. se ha lastimado
2. se han equivocado
3. se ha bañado
4. se han muerto
5. se ha caído
6. habernos apurado
7. me he desayunado

19
1. ha dolido
2. has perdido
3. has tenido
4. se ha sentido
5. se han sentido
6. se ha caído
7. se ha roto
8. se ha lastimado
9. he visto
10. han traído
11. hemos tratado
12. han tenido
13. han dado

Activities

Spanish for Spanish Speakers.
Ask students to read the article about Dr. Michels's veterinary practice and then ask them questions to determine how much they understood: *¿A quién no puede ver la Dra. Michels?; ¿A quién puede ver? ¿Cuándo?; ¿Cómo se sienten los pacientes después de ir al consultorio de la doctora?*

CENTRO VETERINARIO
DRA. MICHELS
VACUNAS
RABIA, MOQUILLO
PARVO-VIRUS
DESPARASITACION
CIRUGIA
SERVICIO MEDICO

SERVICIO TECNICO
A DOMICILIO
J. CARRASCO Y 16 DE SEPT.
85-14-71

 18 ¿Qué ha pasado hoy?

Completa las siguientes oraciones para decir qué han hecho o qué les ha pasado a estas personas.

 Mi madrastra <u>se ha levantado</u> temprano para oír las noticias. (levantarse)

1. Paloma <u>(1)</u> subiendo el televisor al cuarto. (lastimarse)
2. Uds. <u>(2)</u> con la información que me dijeron sobre los huracanes. (equivocarse)
3. Mi hermana <u>(3)</u> mientras escuchaba las noticias. (bañarse)
4. Clara e Ignacio <u>(4)</u> de la risa viendo una comedia en el canal siete. (morirse)
5. Un hombre <u>(5)</u> cuando estaba haciendo un robo porque el piso de la tienda estaba resbaloso. (caerse)
6. Nosotros tuvimos un accidente por <u>(6)</u> mucho esta mañana. (apurarse)
7. Yo <u>(7)</u> mientras veía a mi cantante favorita en la televisión. (desayunarse)

19 La Dra. Michels

Completa el siguiente aviso lógicamente, usando el pretérito perfecto de los verbos indicados.

Dra. Michels

Soy la Dra. Michels. Si te *1. (doler)* el estómago en los últimos días, o si tú *2. (perder)* el apetito y no *3. (tener)* mucha hambre, no te puedo examinar. Si tu madre *4. (sentirse)* cansada, o si tus abuelos *5. (sentirse)* enfermos durante los últimos días, a ellos, ni mis colegas ni yo los podemos ayudar. Pero si tu gato *6. (caerse)* de un árbol y *7. (romperse)* una pata, o si *8. (lastimarse)* de alguna manera, ¡tráemelo! Soy veterinaria y *9. (ver)* que los problemas de los animales domésticos no son muy diferentes de los problemas de las personas. Por ejemplo, unos chicos me *10. (traer)* un perro que tenía dificultades para andar. ¡Sufría de artritis! También, mis colegas y yo *11. (tratar)* a gatos que *12. (tener)* apendicitis. ¡Sí! ¡Gatos! Mis pacientes nunca me *13. (dar)* las gracias, pero sé que se sienten mucho mejor después de venir a mi consultorio.

¡Qué lindo gatito!

 292   Lección 13

20 Preguntas personales

Contesta las siguientes preguntas con información sobre tu vida personal. Usa el pretérito perfecto en tus respuestas.

1. ¿A qué hora te has despertado hoy?
2. ¿Qué ropa te has puesto hoy?
3. ¿Cómo se llama el último periódico que has leído?
4. ¿Has escrito una noticia alguna vez?
5. ¿Siempre les has dicho la verdad a tus padres?
6. ¿Has ido a ver grabar un programa de televisión?
7. ¿Cuánto tiempo has tardado en contestar estas preguntas?

¿Cómo se llama la última revista que has leído?

En la televisión (continuación)

MARISOL: Ignacio, ¿prefieres los programas **nacionales** o los **extranjeros?°**

IGNACIO: Me gustan más los programas nacionales.

MARISOL: Oye, Susana, ¿qué **actor** o **actriz** te gusta más?

SUSANA: Bueno, a mí me gusta Jennifer López. Es una actriz **famosísima.** Ella **ha tenido** mucho **éxito,°** y estoy casi segura de que nunca ha **fracasado°** en nada.

IGNACIO: Sí, **estoy de acuerdo.°** Ella ha hecho muchos **personajes°** y ha **filmado** y **grabado°** muchas películas. El **público** la quiere mucho.

SUSANA: Me gustaría pedirle un **autógrafo...** Oye, ¿está Esteban dormido?

MARISOL: Sí, creo que se ha dormido. Lo vi **bostezando°** hace un minuto. Tantos **anuncios comerciales°** lo **aburren.**

extranjeros *foreign* **ha tenido éxito** *has been successful (has had success)* **fracasado** *failed* **estoy de acuerdo** *I agree* **personajes** *characters* **grabado** *videotaped* **bostezando** *yawning* **anuncios comerciales** *commercial announcements, commercials, advertisements*

En la televisión (continuación)
Activity 20

Quiz/Activity 6

Activity 9

Answers
20 Answers will vary.

Notes
The term *grabado* changes meaning according to the context (i.e., it can mean **recorded, tape-recorded** or **video-recorded**).

Activities
Cooperative Learning. For additional oral practice after students have completed activity 20, pair students and ask them to take turns asking and answering questions 1-7 in Spanish.

Multiple Intelligences (intrapersonal). Ask students to keep a log of personal activities and interesting events over a twenty-four-hour period. The log is then the starting point for a paragraph in which the students use the present perfect tense to discuss things they have recently done and events that have occurred in their lives.

Prereading Strategy. Note for students that this dialog is a continuation of the dialog that began on pages 290-291. Then have students look through the dialog quickly to find cognates and other words or expressions they already know.

NATIONAL STANDARDS
C1.1, C1.2, C1.3, C4.1

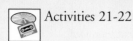

Activities 21–22

Answers

21 1. A Susana le gusta Jennifer López.
2. Ignacio está de acuerdo con ella.
3. Ha hecho muchos personajes. También ha filmado y ha grabado muchas películas.
4. El público la quiere mucho.
5. Marisol vio a Esteban bostezando.

22 Answers will vary.

Activities

Communities. In groups of four, have students investigate Spanish-speaking television networks in the United States. They should identify the name of each network, approximately how many different programs they offer, who some of the stars of programs are (e.g., Jaime Bayly) and any other details they may find. At least one of the students in each group should try to watch a program and then share details about the show with others in the group. Finally, one member of each group must share the results of the research with the class.

Expansion. Additional questions (*¿Qué comprendiste?*): *¿Qué tipo de programas prefiere Ignacio?; ¿Qué ha tenido Jennifer López?; ¿De qué está casi segura Susana que nunca ha hecho Jennifer López?; ¿Qué le gustaría pedirle Susana a Jennifer López?; ¿Dice Ignacio que él ha filmado y ha grabado muchos programas de televisión?*

Additional questions (*Charlando*): *¿Cuál es tu canal de televisión favorito? ¿Por qué?; ¿Qué personaje hace tu actor o actriz favorito/a?; ¿Cuál es tu cantante favorito/a?; ¿Crees que es fácil tener éxito trabajando en la televisión? Explica.; ¿Sabes quién es Salma Hayeck Alonso?; ¿Has visto alguna de sus películas? ¿Cuál?; ¿La has oído cantar? ¿Qué canción?*

NATIONAL STANDARDS
C1.1, C1.2, C2.1, C4.1, C4.2, C5.2

TELEVISIÓN

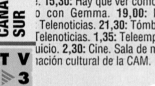

CANAL+ **JUEVES** **27** **VIERNES** **28** **SABADO**

CANAL PLUS
Cine. «El hijo de la pantera rosa». 11,30: «Adiós, tiburón». 13,05: Detrás de la cá- 13,30: Los 40 principales. 14,00: Más de- 14,55: Redacción. 15,00: National Geo- c en Canal +. 15,54: Cine. «Alma gitana». : Cine. «Un fin de semana con mamá». : Programa más o menos multiplicado o lo. 20,00: Redacción. 20,05: Especial Ca- Especial Oscars 96. Recta final. 20,30: Lo 21,53: Contrarreloj. 22,00: Estreno Ca- guardián de las palabras». 23,14: D lo mereces. 23,33: Cine. «An . 1,10: Cine. «Semillas «My family». 5,16: Cine. Documental naturaleza. «C ón».

10,00: Cine. «La isla de las cabezas 12,00: Deporte. Copa del Mund 13,30: Los 40 principales 14,55: Noticias. 15,00 «La invasión de l per» 17 04

10,00: On music. 10,30: Bal 40 al 1. 13,15: Magacin 14,55: Noticias. 15,0 . 16,36: Cine. Cine. «Hola, dacción. 2

TELE MADRID

CANAL SUR
Pasacalle. 8,20: La banda de... 10,0 s. 10,30: La banda de... 12,00: La 4,00: Vidas cruzadas. 14,30: La tard . 15,30: Hay que ver cómo son. 17,45: o con Gemma. 19,00: Madrid direct Telenoticias. 21,30: Tómbola. 23,30: Cine. Telenoticias. 1,35: Teleempleo. 1,50: En te uicio. 2,30: Cine. Sala de madrugada. 4,00: ación cultural de la CAM.

TV 3

TV-3

TV GALICIA

CANAL 9

ETB 1

¿Has visto una película de la actriz Jennifer López?

21 ## ¿Qué comprendiste?

1. ¿Qué actriz famosa le gusta a Susana?
2. ¿Quién está de acuerdo con Susana?
3. ¿Qué ha hecho Jennifer López?
4. Además de Susana, ¿quién quiere mucho a Jennifer López?
5. ¿A quién vio Marisol bostezando?

22 ## Charlando

1. ¿En qué actividad has tenido mucho éxito durante tu vida?
2. ¿Tienes miedo de fracasar? Explica.
3. ¿Te aburren los anuncios comerciales de la televisión? Explica.
4. ¿Prefieres los programas extranjeros o los nacionales? ¿Por qué?
5. ¿Quién es tu actor o actriz favorito/a?
6. ¿Le has pedido un autógrafo a un personaje famoso? ¿A quién?

294 Lección 13

Algo más

El participio como adjetivo

In Spanish, a past participle may be used as an adjective following a verb (such as *ser* or *estar*), or alone with a noun. As is the case with other adjectives you have learned, past participles that are used as adjectives must agree in number and gender with the noun they modify.

Toda la familia estaba sentada para ver la película.

La sala estaba **cubierta** *de periódicos.*	The living room was **covered** with newspapers.
También había una taza **rota** *en el piso.*	There was also a **broken** cup on the floor.
Los programas de música son **aburridos.**	Music shows are **boring.**

23 En la casa de Carlitos

Imagina que anoche en hubo un temblor la casa de Carlitos cuando tú estabas con él. Completa las siguientes oraciones con el participio de los verbos entre paréntesis para describir cómo estaba todo en ese momento.

> Las niñas estaban *(dormir)*.
> Las niñas estaban dormidas.

1. La mesa estaba *(poner)*.
2. Dos vasos estaban *(romper)*.
3. Yo estaba *(sentar)* en la sala.
4. Carlitos estaba muy *(aburrir)*.
5. El radio estaba *(apagar)*.
6. La comida estaba *(hacer)*.
7. Nosotros estábamos *(sentar)* en el comedor.
8. Las hermanas de Carlitos estaban *(preparar)* para salir.

GEOLOGIA
Temblores en febrero

Por EDUARDO CIFUENTES
DE EL NUEVO DIA

SI NO hubiera sido por el aumento en la actividad apreciado en los últimos cinco días del mes, febrero habría aparecido como uno de bajo ritmo y de mediocre potencial, sin, hasta entonces, temblores de magnitud 4.0 o más.

Pero los 16 sismos -una tercera parte del total mensual- registrados durante los días 24 al 28 voltearon las tornas, y han sido referido febrero como un

Estos datos, basados en la información que remite la Red Sísmica de Puerto Rico (Departamento de Geología; Universidad de Puerto Rico; Recinto de Mayagüez), suponen que, a lo largo de los últimos doce meses, se han sumado un total de 582 temblores en la región en la que nos ubicamos -cuyos límites corres... básicamente, con el m...

24 ¿Qué dijeron?

Completa las siguientes oraciones, usando la forma del adjetivo de los verbos indicados para saber lo que algunas personas dijeron en una reunión de amigos.

MA: He leído que hay un canal de comedia que es muy <u>(divertido)</u>. (divertir)

1. ELENA: Algunas personas han opinado que los libros de José Enrique Rodó son muy <u>(1)</u>. (leer)

2. NATALIA: Algunas veces me ha parecido que las noticias están llenas de personas <u>(2)</u>. (morir)

3. JULIA: He oído que *Sábado Gigante* es tu programa de televisión <u>(3)</u>. (preferir)

4. MATEO: Siempre he creído que las películas <u>(4)</u> en Hollywood son muy buenas. (filmar)

5. DAVID: Mi abuelo me ha dicho muchas veces que la gente bien <u>(5)</u> puede llegar a tener mucho éxito en la vida. (informar)

6. SUSANA: He sabido que Jennifer López tiene algunas canciones <u>(6)</u> en español. (grabar)

7. RODRIGO: He visto que algunos programas de concurso dan unos premios <u>(7)</u>. (exagerar)

8. TERESA: Siempre he pensado que los programas de noticias sólo presentan información <u>(8)</u>. (aburrir)

25 En la televisión

A Lorenzo y a Sara les gusta mucho ver la televisión juntos. Completa el siguiente párrafo, usando la forma del adjetivo de los verbos indicados para saber lo que veían Lorenzo y Sara ayer en la televisión.

En la mañana, Lorenzo y Sara estaban 1. *(sentar)* en la cocina, con los ojos muy 2. *(abrir)* viendo todo lo que pasaba en la televisión. En un programa 3. *(filmar)* en los Estados Unidos, mostraban actores y actrices de mucho éxito que recibían premios. Luego, los mostraban dando autógrafos al público que estaba 4. *(aburrir)* por haberlos esperado mucho tiempo. Más tarde, en las noticias nacionales los muchachos veían a algunos hombres 5. *(lastimar)* que participaban en una protesta, y que dos edificios 6. *(quemar)*

en un incendio hace cinco años eran hoy dos bonitos edificios para oficinas. Después, en los anuncios comerciales, veían una galleta 7. *(morder)* por un lado que cantaba y que bailaba para unos niños mientras ellos desayunaban. Por la noche, los muchachos casi 8. *(dormir)* y con los ojos casi 9. *(cerrar)* bostezaban mientras veían una comedia poco 10. *(divertir)* que los puso a dormir.

¿Qué revistas has leído tú?

Han caído tres centímetros de lluvia en Montevideo.

¿Has visitado las playas de Punta del Este?

Notes

Students should use the *Autoevaluación* to measure their own progress in learning the main elements of the lesson. The section also serves to prepare students for the lesson test.

Activities

Critical Listening. Have the groups working on the cooperative learning activity on page 296 develop a series of listening comprehension questions corresponding to the news reports. The questions should be distributed before the reports are given. Answers can be reviewed afterwards in class or submitted to the instructor.

Autoevaluación. Como repaso y autoevaluación, responde lo siguiente:
1. Name two things that have occurred recently in the news.
2. Name two things that have happened to you in the last week.
3. In Spanish, say that you have seen or heard three different people, places or things.
4. What is your favorite type of television program?
5. How would you say someone "has died of laughter" in Spanish?
6. What clothing items have you put on today?
7. Imagine you are a police detective and yesterday you walked into a home that had been burglarized. Describe what you saw in the room for the police report.
8. What do you know about Uruguay?

NATIONAL STANDARDS
C1.1, C2.1, C2.2, C3.1,
C4.1, C4.2, C5.1, C5.2

Answers

A Creative self-expression.

B Creative self-expression.

Notes

Select several students to share with the class the information they found out in activity A.

Activities

Spanish for Spanish Speakers. Reinforce students' speaking skills by asking your bilingual students to write a short composition summarizing their feelings about television. Offer some guidance by having them answer some of the following questions in their composition: *¿Cuál es tu canal de televisión favorito? ¿Por qué?; ¿Has visto programas de televisión extranjeros? ¿De dónde? ¿De qué tipo?; ¿Cuál es tu tipo de programa favorito? ¿Por qué?; ¿Cuál es tu actor o actriz favorito/a de la televisión?; ¿Qué personaje hace tu actor o actriz favorito/a?; ¿Te aburren o te gustan los anuncios comerciales de la televisión? ¿Por qué?*

Technology. Using a video camera, have students prepare a news report using news from your school. Talk about sports, dances and any special event(s). Include a weather report and any other important local news. If you work with a cooperating class abroad, propose an exchange of locally produced news reports.

¡La práctica hace al maestro!

A Comunicación

Find out some of the interesting things your classmates have done during their lives. First, prepare six questions in which you inquire whether someone has done several different activities during his or her life. Then, working in pairs, compare the questions and agree upon four that seem the most interesting. Next, each of you must ask a member of another pair the questions you have chosen. Return to your partner to share what each of you has learned about your classmates. Finally, one of you must summarize the information for the class.

A: ¿Has estado en algún programa de concurso?
B: No, nunca he estado en ningún programa de concurso./Sí, he estado en algunos programas de concurso. Por ejemplo, en California estuve en....

B Conexión con la tecnología

Find someone in your class or school who has cable or satellite access to the Spanish television networks, *Univisión*. Have them tape excerpts of several types of programs such as the news, the weather, a sitcom, a soap opera, a variety show, commercials, etc. View them in class and try to identify what type of program it is. Then discuss the differences between the programming shown on these networks and the programming on other networks that broadcast in the United States.

NOTICIAS 41

VOCABULARIO

Activities

Cooperative Learning. Ask students to say a word they have learned in Spanish and then select someone else to spell the word. Have them check their spelling and then switch roles.

Critical Thinking. Dictate a letter of the alphabet to the class. Give students three minutes to write any words they can think of in Spanish that begin with that letter. After calling time, ask students to read their lists aloud. The student with the longest list of correct words wins.

Expansion. Select several words and phrases for individual students to use orally in sentences.

Pronunciation. To ensure proper pronunciation, model each word or expression and have students repeat after you.

¿Qué catástrofe ha pasado aquí?

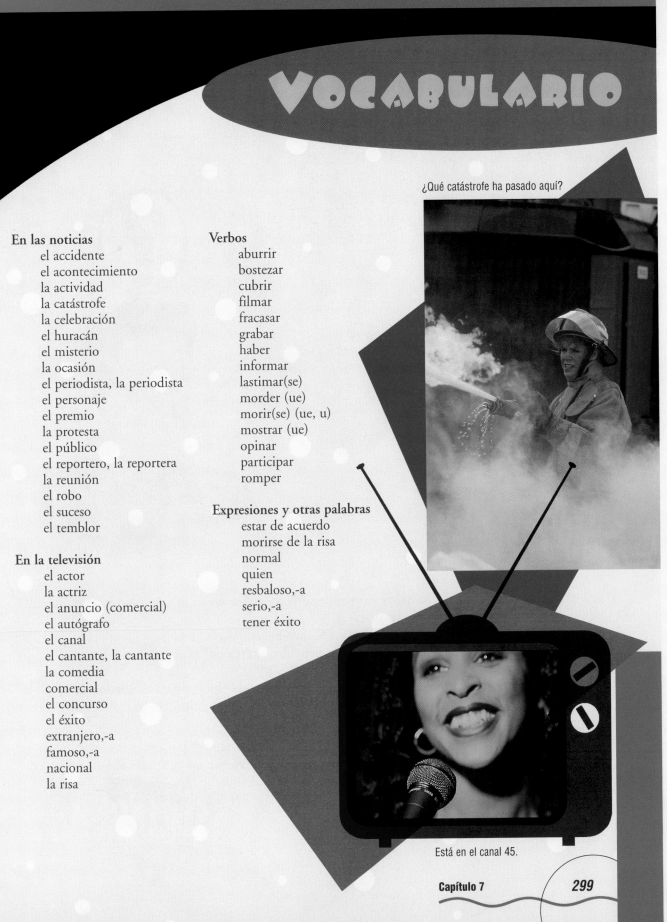

En las noticias
el accidente
el acontecimiento
la actividad
la catástrofe
la celebración
el huracán
el misterio
la ocasión
el periodista, la periodista
el personaje
el premio
la protesta
el público
el reportero, la reportera
la reunión
el robo
el suceso
el temblor

En la televisión
el actor
la actriz
el anuncio (comercial)
el autógrafo
el canal
el cantante, la cantante
la comedia
comercial
el concurso
el éxito
extranjero,-a
famoso,-a
nacional
la risa

Verbos
aburrir
bostezar
cubrir
filmar
fracasar
grabar
haber
informar
lastimar(se)
morder (ue)
morir(se) (ue, u)
mostrar (ue)
opinar
participar
romper

Expresiones y otras palabras
estar de acuerdo
morirse de la risa
normal
quien
resbaloso,-a
serio,-a
tener éxito

Está en el canal 45.

Capítulo 7

299

Content reviewed in *Lección 14*
- everyday activities
- sports
- weather
- describing
- passive voice

Notes

Technology. Tell your students that *La Nación* is one of the most influential newspapers in Asunción, Paraguay. They can find it on the Internet at the following address: *infonet.com.py/lanacion*

Other words for *periódico* are *prensa* and *diario*.

Activities

Cooperative Learning. After introducing the dialog (playing the audiocassette/audio compact disc, modeling words and phrases for student repetition, practicing newspaper vocabulary, etc.), have students work in pairs practicing the dialog. Circulate and assist with pronunciation and intonation.

Critical Listening. Play the audiocassette/audio compact disc recording of the dialog. Instruct students to cover the words as they listen to the conversation in order to develop good listening skills before concentrating on their ability to read Spanish. Have students look at the illustration and imagine what the people are saying to each other. Finally, ask several individuals to state what they believe the main theme of the conversation is.

Contexto cultural
PARAGUAY

Lección 14
En el periódico

SARA: Juan, yo había visto el periódico *La Nación* en la sala, pero **ya**° no está allí. ¿Tú lo has visto?

JUAN: Sí, lo vi en la cocina. ¿Qué vas a leer?

SARA: Bueno, quiero leer unos **artículos acerca de**° la **economía** del país.

JUAN: ¿Y por qué te interesa eso?

SARA: Porque es muy importante **enterarse de**° lo que pasa **alrededor de**° uno. Es parte de la **cultura**° de una persona. Si eres **culto,**° es probable que tengas más y mejores **oportunidades** en la vida.

JUAN: ¡Qué culta eres!

ya *ahora* **acerca de** *sobre* **enterarse de** *to find out, to become aware, to learn about* **alrededor de** *around* **cultura** *culture, knowledge* **culto** *cultured, well-read*

NATIONAL STANDARDS
C1.2, C4.1

1 ¿Qué comprendiste?

1. ¿En dónde había visto Sara el periódico esta mañana?
2. ¿Está el periódico allí todavía?
3. ¿Qué quiere leer Sara?
4. ¿Quién dice que es importante para las personas enterarse de lo que pasa alrededor de ellas?

Le gusta leer la sección de noticias nacionales.

Algo más

¿Qué hay en los periódicos y las revistas?

el artículo	*article*	la sección...	*section*
el aviso	*printed advertisement*	...de cultura y pasatiempos	*culture and leisure*
la columna	*column*	...de deportes	*sports*
la encuesta	*survey, poll*	...del hogar	*home*
la entrevista	*interview*	...económica	*economics*
la tabla	*chart*	...editorial	*editorial*
el titular	*headline*	...internacional	*international*
		...nacional	*national*

Voleibol: Brasil se llevó todos los honores. Pág. 3

D Deportes

Automovilismo
Pedro José Paladines ganó el domingo en Riobamba y es el líder absoluto de la Monomarca Mazda. Pág. 4

A4 *Editorial* **EL COMERCIO**

2 Charlando

1. ¿Qué es para ti una persona culta?
2. ¿Por qué crees que es bueno ser culto/a?
3. ¿Qué tipo de oportunidades crees que una persona pueda tener si es culta?
4. ¿Lees el periódico todos los días? ¿Qué secciones lees?
5. ¿Crees que enterarse de las noticias que pasan alrededor de uno es importante?

3 En el periódico

Trabajando en parejas, haz el papel de una de las personas del diálogo anterior.

Edición digital de NOTICIAS · AÑO XV
Asunción, Paraguay

PARAti

Más palabras de los periódicos

los anuncios clasificados	*classified ads*
el crucigrama	*crossword puzzle*
la política	*politics*
el pronóstico del tiempo	*weather forecast*
el reportaje	*report*
la vida social	*society pages*

Capítulo 7   **301**

Oportunidades

Los periódicos en español

There are many newspapers from Spanish-speaking countries that you can download from the Internet. Print one out and try to read several articles, underlining unfamiliar words and phrases. This is a good opportunity to challenge yourself and strengthen your reading comprehension in Spanish. Establish a habit of reading a newspaper every day; it will help you increase your vocabulary and keeps you informed about what is happening in the world.

4 Periódicos y revistas

Escoge la palabra que no pertenece en cada uno de los siguientes grupos de cuatro palabras.

1. televisión — pasatiempos — películas — resbaloso
2. actor — cantante — temblor — actriz
3. periodista — información — ya — reportero
4. tabla — cubierto — encuesta — entrevista
5. editorial — deportes — hogar — premio
6. internacional — económica — morder — nacional
7. alrededor — artículo — titular — columna

5 ¿En qué sección?

Di en qué sección de un periódico o una revista puedes encontrar lo que estás buscando, según la información que se da.

¿En qué sección hay noticias sobre el partido de fútbol?

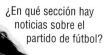

¿Dónde buscas para...

1. encontrar una columna donde tu periodista favorito/a ha dado su opinión acerca de una protesta sobre la destrucción de los bosques tropicales?
2. leer una entrevista que le han hecho a tu actor/actriz favorito/a?
3. ver si tu equipo favorito ha ganado un partido de fútbol?
4. informarte sobre alguna catástrofe que ha ocurrido en los Estados Unidos?
5. enterarte del precio del oro o de la plata en el mercado internacional?
6. leer un artículo sobre algún acontecimiento que ha ocurrido en el Uruguay?
7. encontrar el precio de unos pantalones de algodón que están en oferta en el centro comercial?
8. mirar una encuesta sobre el número de niños que hay en cada casa de un barrio nuevo?

Lo busco en...

A. la sección económica.
B. la sección de deportes.
C. la sección editorial.
D. la sección de avisos comerciales.
E. la sección de cultura y pasatiempos.
F. la sección del hogar.
G. la sección nacional.
H. la sección internacional.

Conexión cultural

EL CORAZÓN DE SUDAMÉRICA

Paraguay

Si eres una persona que amas la naturaleza, la cultura, el paisaje y las tradiciones, ven con nosotros.

El Paraguay

El Paraguay, con más de cuatro millones y medio de habitantes, se encuentra en el corazón de la América del Sur, rodeado por la Argentina (al sur, al este y al oeste), el Brasil (al norte y al este) y Bolivia (al norte y al oeste). La capital del país es la ciudad de Asunción. La lengua oficial es el español, aunque hay otra lengua nacional, el guaraní, que la hablan y la entienden la mayoría de los paraguayos.

El río Paraguay divide al país en dos regiones naturales, la región Oriental y la Occidental (o el Chaco). El país también está dividido en diecinueve departamentos; cinco de ellos están en la región del Chaco. En esta región no hay grandes ciudades. Es uno de los últimos lugares del mundo donde todavía se encuentran grandes extensiones de tierra virgen, con sus ecosistemas casi intactos.

El Paraguay no tiene costas sobre el mar, pero sus dos ríos principales, el Paraguay y el Paraná, comunican al país con el Océano Atlántico. En el Paraná, que está entre el Brasil y el Paraguay, se encuentra la central hidroeléctrica de Itaipú, la más grande del mundo.

El clima del Paraguay es cálido. La temperatura promedio al año es de veintidós grados centígrados, y el promedio anual de días de sol es de trescientos diez. Los meses del verano, que va desde octubre hasta marzo, son calientes y la temperatura promedio es de treinta y un grados centígrados. El invierno es corto, y su temperatura promedio es de catorce grados.

[Dirección General de Turismo, Ministerio de Obras Públicas y Comunicaciones, Asunción.]

Una protesta de maestros en Asunción, Paraguay.

Yo hablo guaraní.

PARAGUAY

TIERRA DE SOL Y DE AVENTURAS

Artesanía

Notes

~www~

Paraguay
General Information
http://www.yagua.com/
http://www.presidencia.gov.pyl

The currency of Paraguay is the *guaraní*. *Guaraní* also refers to an indigenous population and the language people speak.

Remind students that they have learned that the names of some countries in Spanish are preceded by a definite article. *El Paraguay* is one such country. In actual usage, however, many native speakers of Spanish drop the article.

Students may need help with the meaning of the following words: *rodeado* (surrounded), *entienden* (understand), *departamentos* (political division similar to states), *tierra* (land), *central hidroeléctrica* (hydroelectric plant), *cálido* (warm), *promedio* (average).

NATIONAL STANDARDS
C1.2, C3.2, C4.1, C4.2, C5.2

Answers

6
1. El Paraguay está en el corazón de la América del Sur.
2. La capital del Paraguay es Asunción.
3. La Argentina, el Brasil y Bolivia están alrededor del Paraguay.
4. En el Paraguay se hablan el español y el guaraní.
5. El país está dividido en dos regiones naturales por el río Paraguay.
6. El Paraguay no tiene costas sobre ningún océano.
7. La central hidroeléctrica de Itaipú está entre el Paraguay y el Brasil.
8. El verano en el Paraguay es desde el mes de octubre hasta el mes de marzo.

7
1. ...habías leído....
2. ...había leído....
3. ...había leído....
4. ...habíamos leído....
5. ...había leído....
6. ...habían leído....
7. ...habían leído....
8. ...había leído....

Notes

You may wish to review the formation of regular and irregular past participles before introducing the past perfect.

Activities

Students with Special Needs.
Model a second sentence for activity 7.

Cultura

Con dos paneles y una muestra retrospectiva se inician los homenajes al pintor Eduardo Kingman.

 CONEXIONES

6 Cruzando fronteras

¿Qué sabes sobre el Paraguay? Contesta las siguientes preguntas.

1. ¿Dónde está el Paraguay?
2. ¿Cuál es la capital del Paraguay?
3. ¿Qué países están alrededor del Paraguay?
4. ¿Qué lenguas se hablan en el Paraguay?
5. ¿Qué río divide el país en dos regiones naturales?
6. ¿Sobre qué océano tiene el Paraguay costa?
7. ¿Dónde está la central hidroeléctrica de Itaipú?
8. ¿Desde qué mes y hasta qué mes es verano en el Paraguay?

 **IDIOMA**

El pretérito pluscuamperfecto

The past perfect tense *(el pretérito pluscuamperfecto)* describes an event in the past that had happened prior to another past event. It consists of the imperfect tense of *haber* and a past participle.

*Juan **había leído** el periódico cuando Sara llegó.*	**Juan had read** the newspaper when Sara arrived.
*Ellos ya **se habían** bañado cuando empezó el temblor.*	**They had** already **bathed** when the tremor started.

Object and reflexive pronouns precede the conjugated form of *haber* in the past perfect tense. However, when an expression uses the infinitive of *haber,* attach object pronouns directly to the end of the infinitive form of *haber.*

*Ya **me había** vestido.*	I had already gotten dressed.
*Comieron sin **haberme esperado**.*	They ate without waiting for me.

7 Todos leían el periódico

Durante el viaje a la escuela tú y otros estudiantes leían el periódico en el autobús. Di qué habían leído en el periódico las siguientes personas cuando el autobús llegó al colegio.

 Rodolfo/un artículo sobre un museo en la sección de cultura y pasatiempos
Rodolfo había leído un artículo sobre un museo en la sección de cultura y pasatiempos cuando el autobús llegó al colegio.

1. tú/un artículo acerca de la economía del país
2. Rafael/un artículo en la sección del hogar
3. Antonio/los titulares de la sección internacional
4. todos nosotros/una parte del periódico
5. Eliana/la columna de un periodista famoso en la sección editorial
6. Rodrigo e Isabel/la sección económica
7. Laura y Mónica/una entrevista al cantante Juan Luis Guerra
8. yo/una encuesta acerca del número de personas que ya no fuman

8 ¿Qué les había ocurrido?

Algunas personas querían hacer ciertas *(certain)* actividades que no podían hacer porque les había ocurrido algo. Di lo que las siguientes personas no podían hacer y por qué, según las indicaciones.

Bernardo quería ver las noticias. (nosotros/llevarnos el televisor)
Bernardo quería ver las noticias pero no podía porque nosotros nos habíamos llevado el televisor.

1. Mis amigos querían leer la entrevista sobre su actor favorito. (alguien/quemar el periódico en la chimenea)
2. Yo quería esquiar. (yo/lastimarme una pierna)
3. Alicia quería ir a pescar. (ella/pescar un resfriado)
4. Uds. querían llevar la sección editorial. (alguien/tomarla)
5. Querías llegar a tiempo a la celebración. (tú/tener un accidente)
6. Queríamos pedir el autógrafo a nuestras cantantes favoritas. (ellas/salir)

9 La carta de Santiago

Santiago escribió una carta a su amiga Natalia desde el Paraguay. Completa la carta, usando el pluscuamperfecto de los verbos indicados para saber lo que Santiago dice en su carta.

Asunción, 24 de febrero

Querida Natalia:

Yo 1. (pensar) escribirte antes, pero no 2. (tener) el tiempo para hacerlo. Como yo tampoco 3. (recibir) una carta tuya, decidí escribirte ya.

Quería contarte lo que 4. (hacer) mis amigos y yo aquí en Asunción desde que llegamos. Nosotros visitamos la central hidroeléctrica de Itaipú la semana pasada. Yo nunca 5. (ver) algo tan interesante. Creo que cuando regrese al colegio, voy a escribir un artículo para el periódico. En Asunción fuimos a un museo, pero no pudimos entrar porque ellos 6. (cerrar) temprano. Parece que hubo una protesta, pero nosotros no 7. (enterarnos).

Como no pudimos visitar el museo, pensamos ir a nadar, pues la temperatura era como de treinta grados centígrados. No me lo vas a creer, pero cuando llegamos a la piscina, 8. (empezar) a llover.

No te cuento más por ahora. Voy a dejar algo más para contarte cuando regrese.

Con cariño,

Santiago

PD. ¿Me 9. (escribir) tú antes? Espero que sí. Chao.

Answers

8
1. ...no podían porque alguien había quemado el periódico en la chimenea.
2. ...no podía porque me había lastimado una pierna.
3. ...no podía porque había pescado un resfriado.
4. ...no podían porque alguien la había tomado.
5. ...no podías porque habías tenido un accidente.
6. ...no podíamos porque ellas habían salido.

9
1. había pensado
2. había tenido
3. había recibido
4. habíamos hecho
5. había visto
6. habían cerrado
7. nos habíamos enterado
8. había empezado
9. habías escrito

Notes

Comparisons. Explain that when two past actions are presented in the same sentence, the pluperfect indicates which action happened first. In general, the uses of the pluperfect are similar in Spanish and in English.

The letters *PD* at the end of Santiago's correspondence are the equivalent of the English **PS**.

Review. Review weather expressions with students before assigning activity 9.

Answers

10
1. había llamado
2. habían comprado
3. había escrito
4. había traducido
5. se había ido
6. haberse enterado
7. habían leído
8. habías llegado
9. habían encontrado
10. había preparado
11. había visto
12. había hecho

11
1. ¿Habían jugado Manuel y Pedrito al fútbol...?/ ...habían jugado.
2. ¿Había roto la tía un vaso...?/...lo había roto.
3. ¿Había visto la abuela la televisión...?/...la había visto.
4. ¿Habías preparado (tú) un pollo...?/...lo había preparado.
5. ¿Me había comprado (yo) un cepillo...?/...te lo habías comprado.
6. ¿Había ido papá de compras?/...había ido.
7. ¿Había leído el abuelo el periódico...?/...lo había leído.
8. ¿Había arreglado (yo) el armario...?/...lo habías arreglado.

Activities

Critical Thinking. Say the present perfect tense of several verbs and call on students to give the past perfect tense of each.

10 Ayer antes de las seis

Fernando está contando lo que varias personas habían hecho ayer antes de las seis cuando vio por primera vez el artículo que había escrito para una revista paraguaya. Completa el párrafo, usando el tiempo apropiado de los verbos indicados.

Mis padres y yo <u>habíamos decidido</u> invitar a la casa a unos parientes a una celebración. Yo ya *1. (llamar)* a algunos amigos para invitarlos a la casa. Los amigos ya *2. (comprar)* la revista en una librería internacional cuando llegaron. Yo *3. (escribir)* el artículo para una columna en la sección Arte y Cultura. El artículo se llamaba *La gente guaraní: lengua y cultura.* Mi amiga, Claudia, ya lo *4. (traducir)* al inglés para algunos amigos en el carro. Mi hermano ya *5. (irse)* sin *6. (enterarse)* de nuestra pequeña celebración. Uds. ya *7. (leer)* la revista pero tú todavía no *8. (llegar)* a esa sección. Mis parientes ya *9. (encontrar)* la tabla que iba con el artículo que yo *10. (preparar)*, pero no la podían entender. Claro, yo *11. (ver)* lo que yo *12. (hacer)*, pero verlo en forma final era ¡fantástico!

11 No recuerdo

Imagina que tú no puedes recordar algunas cosas que hiciste o que algunas personas hicieron ayer en tu casa, y ahora le haces preguntas a tu hermano/a para tratar de recordar. Trabajando en parejas, alterna con tu compañero/a de clase en hacer preguntas y contestarlas, usando las indicaciones que se dan. Sigue el modelo.

Paloma/lavar
A: ¿Había lavado Paloma los platos ayer?
B: Sí, (No, no) los había lavado.

1. Manuel y Pedrito/jugar   2. la tía/romper   3. la abuela/ver   4. tú/preparar

5. yo/comprarse   6. papá/ir de compras   7. el abuelo/leer   8. yo/arreglar

12 Antes de acostarse

Escribe en una hoja de papel una lista de diez cosas que tú y otros miembros de tu familia habían hecho ayer antes de acostarse. Puedes inventar la información si quieres.

Yo me había puesto el pijama.
Mi madre había recogido la mesa.

Las noticias se escuchan por Radio Ñandutí

la camiseta

VOZ: En el Paraguay las noticias y los deportes **se escuchan°** por Radio Ñandutí, la gran **emisora°** paraguaya. Ahora sigue **narrando°** en los **micrófonos** de Ñandutí Rigoberto Osa, su **comentarista°** estrella.

RIGOBERTO: Hola, **aficionados°** del fútbol, hoy desde Asunción estamos **llevándoles°** **en vivo°** el partido entre los equipos del Paraguay y la Argentina. Estamos ahora en la **transmisión** del segundo **tiempo°** de este superinteresante partido. El **marcador°** del partido es dos a uno **a favor del** equipo del Paraguay. El **gol** fue **marcado°** por Leonidas, con la **camiseta** número quince.

se escuchan *are heard, listened to* **emisora** *radio station* **narrando** *announcing, narrating* **comentarista** *commentator* **aficionados** *fans* **llevándoles** *bringing to you* **en vivo** *live* **tiempo** *period, half* **marcador** *score* **marcado** *scored*

Las noticias se escuchan por Radio Ñandutí

Quiz/Activity 4

Activity 5

Answers

12 Creative self-expression.

Notes

Note for students that the verb *marcar* requires the spelling change *c → qu* in the *Ud./Uds.* commands and in the subjunctive.

Another word for *partido* (game) is *encuentro* (match). An *emisora* also may be called an *estación de radio*.

Review. Review some everyday activities that students have already learned before assigning activity 12.

Tell your students that Radio Ñandutí is one of the most important stations in Paraguay. It was founded in 1962. Students can listen to Radio Ñandutí on the Internet.

www
Radio Ñandutí
http://www.holding.com.py/nanduti/

Remind students that *fútbol* is extremely popular in the Spanish-speaking world. A game such as the one presented in the dialog (Paraguay-Argentina) would be followed with great interest and enthusiasm.

Activities

Cooperative Learning. After introducing the dialog (playing the audiocassette/audio compact disc and modeling words and phrases for student repetition), have students work in pairs practicing the dialog. Circulate and assist with pronunciation and intonation.

Expansion. Extend activity 12 by having students organize the sentences logically in paragraphs to create a short composition. You may decide to have students hand in what they wrote.

NATIONAL STANDARDS
C1.1, C1.2, C1.3, C3.2, C4.1

Answers

13 1. Las noticias y los deportes se escuchan por Radio Ñandutí en el Paraguay.
2. Está narrando un partido de fútbol.
3. Los aficionados al fútbol están escuchando la transmisión.
4. Se juega el segundo tiempo.
5. Sí, está muy interesante. El comentarista dice que está superinteresante.
6. El marcador es dos a uno a favor del equipo del Paraguay.
7. El jugador que marcó el gol tiene la camiseta con el número quince.

14 Answers will vary.

Notes

Communities. Soccer *(fútbol)* is the most watched sport in the Spanish-speaking world. During *el Mundial de Fútbol* (World Cup), which is held every four years, *la fiebre del gol* is at its peak. Ask if students are able to name recent World Cup winners or host countries.

Ask if students recognize the name of the radio station in the advertisement that accompanies activity 14.

Activities

Critical Listening. Ask small groups of students to identify five well-known personalities in sports, politics or entertainment. They should then describe each one by using the verb *ser* and an adjective with a logical prefix. Ask each group to present its descriptions to the class.

13 **¿Qué comprendiste?**

1. ¿En qué país se escuchan las noticias y los deportes por Radio Ñandutí?
2. ¿Qué está narrando Rigoberto Osa?
3. ¿Quiénes están escuchando la transmisión?
4. ¿Qué tiempo se juega del partido?
5. ¿Está interesante el partido, según el comentarista? Explica.
6. ¿Cuál es el marcador? ¿A favor de quién?
7. ¿Qué número tiene en la camiseta el jugador que marcó el gol?

¿Están escuchando la transmisión?

14 **Charlando**

1. ¿Cuál es tu emisora favorita? ¿Qué tipo de programas tienen?
2. ¿Cómo se llama tu comentarista de radio o televisión favorito/a?
3. ¿Se juega al fútbol en tu colegio? ¿Qué se juega?
4. ¿Escuchas noticias deportivas por la radio? Explica.
5. ¿Escuchas transmisiones en vivo de deportes por la radio? ¿Qué transmisiones escuchas?
6. ¿Has escuchado alguna transmisión de radio de un partido de fútbol? ¿Dónde? ¿Qué equipos jugaban?

RADIO
ñandutí 14
LA GRAN EMISORA PARAGUAYA

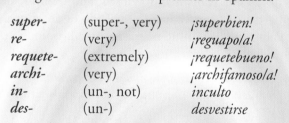
¿Son superprecios?

Estrategia

Para hablar mejor: *applying prefixes*

You may have wondered about the word *superinteresante* in the preceding dialog. The expression consists of the prefix *super-* and the adjective *interesante,* and is equivalent to someone saying "superinteresting" or "incredibly interesting" in English. Prefixes are common in Spanish and learning them will help improve your ability to express yourself correctly in Spanish. They may be used, much as they are in English, to make a new word, or simply to add emphasis to what the speaker is saying. The following are some common prefixes in Spanish:

super-	(super-, very)	¡superbien!	very well!
re-	(very)	¡reguapo/a!	very handsome/pretty!
requete-	(extremely)	¡requetebueno!	extremely good!
archi-	(very)	¡archifamoso/a!	very famous!
in-	(un-, not)	inculto	uncultured, not well-read
des-	(un-)	desvestirse	to get undressed

15 ¡Tus nietos!

Imagina que ya eres abuelo/a y les cuentas a tus nietos cosas de cuando eras joven. Di lo mismo, usando los prefijos *super-, re-, requete-, archi-, in-* o *des-*.

 Yo había sido un comentarista de radio *muy famoso*.
Yo había sido un comentarista de radio *archifamoso*.

1. Cuando jugaba al fútbol, siempre llevaba una camiseta que era *muy bonita*.
2. A los treinta años, había leído mucho y ya no era una persona de *poca cultura*.
3. Mis amigos y yo habíamos sido *muy aficionados* al fútbol.
4. Cuando tenía veinte años, sólo había narrado partidos *muy malos*.
5. Mi madre no me dejaba salir a jugar fútbol si mi cuarto estaba *sin arreglar*.
6. Yo había trabajado en una emisora *muy buena*.

Repaso *rápido*

Este artículo se había leído mucho.

La voz pasiva

You already have learned to combine *se* with the *él/ella/Ud.* form of a verb or with the *ellos/ellas/Uds.* form of a verb when the performer of an action is indefinite or unknown (where speakers of English often use "one," "people" or "they"). When the subject (which may precede or follow the verb) is singular, the verb is singular. Similarly, if the subject is plural, so is the verb.

*Esa entrevista **se había leído** mucho.*

That interview **had been read** a lot. (**Many people had read** that interview.)

*El español y el guaraní **se hablan** en el Paraguay.*

Spanish and Guarani **are spoken/They speak** Spanish and Guarani in Paraguay.

16 La Copa Mundial

Las siguientes oraciones describen lo que hacen los miembros de la familia Rubín para prepararse para una superfiesta el día de la final de la Copa Mundial de Fútbol. Cámbialas, usando una construcción con *se*.

 Primero, arreglan la sala.
Primero, se arregla la sala.

1. Luego, lavan las ventanas.
2. Más tarde, limpian el piso de la cocina.
3. Cubren la mesa con un mantel.
4. Preparan la comida.
5. Cepillan al perro y al gato.
6. Ponen la mesa.
7. Después, traen los refrescos.
8. Finalmente, hacen unas galletas de perlas de chocolate.

Activities 15-16

Quiz/Activity 4

Answers

15 Possible answers:
1. ...rebonita.
2. ...inculta.
3. ...superaficionados....
4. ...requetemalos.
5. ...desarreglado.
6. ...requetebuena.

16 Possible answers:
1. ...se lavan....
2. ...se limpia....
3. Se cubre....
4. Se prepara....
5. Se cepilla....
6. Se pone....
7. ...se traen....
8. ...se hacen....

Notes

Remind students that when *se* is used in this impersonal reflexive construction, the subject may precede or follow the verb.

Activities

Multiple Intelligences (logical-mathematical/linguistic). Ask students to imagine they are going to have a party at their house that is similar to the one at the Rubín home. What would the event be? How should students prepare? Have students write a short composition about their preparations, using the *se* construction.

Students with Special Needs. Have students divide the following words into two parts, prefix and stem word: *archifantástico, desarreglar, inactivo, reinteligente, requetebién, superexcelente*. You may then wish to ask students to tell you what each word means.

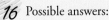

NATIONAL STANDARDS
C1.2, C2.1, C4.1, C4.2

Activity 17

 Quiz/Activity 6

 Activities 7-8

 Quiz/Activity 5

Answers

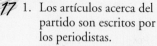

1. Los artículos acerca del partido son escritos por los periodistas.
2. Muchas oportunidades para marcar un gol son dadas por el jugador número diez.
3. El partido es narrado por los comentaristas de la radio.
4. Los goles son marcados por los jugadores estrella.
5. Las calles cerca del estadio son cerradas por la policía.
6. Los perros calientes son vendidos por los muchachos.

Notes

Spanish has a true passive construction that uses a form of the verb *ser* with a past participle: *Los muchachos fueron presentados por sus padres.* However, the passive construction that is most commonly used is that expressed by *se* followed by a third-person verb.

Activities

Students with Special Needs. Model an additional sentence for activity 17.

IDIOMA

La voz pasiva: un poco más

In most sentences, the subject of the sentence performs an action. These sentences are said to be in the active voice.

Leonidas marcó el gol. Leonidas scored the goal.
Andrés Cantor narró Andrés Cantor announced
el partido. the game.

However, where the subject is not the doer of an action but instead receives an action, the sentence is said to be in the passive voice. In the passive-voice examples that follow, note the use of a form of the verb *ser* plus a past participle, which is treated like an adjective and, therefore, must agree with the subject in gender and number. The word *por* usually follows and is used to tell by whom the action was performed.

La Copa Mundial fue narrada por Andrés Cantor.

*El gol **fue marcado** por Leonidas.* The goal **was scored** by Leonidas.
*El partido **fue narrado** por* The game **was announced** by
Andrés Cantor. Andrés Cantor.

17 Muchas cosas pasan

Durante un partido de fútbol muchas cosas pasan. Di las siguientes oraciones, usando la voz pasiva.

 Los aficionados compran camisetas.
Las camisetas son compradas por los aficionados.

1. Los periodistas escriben artículos acerca del partido.
2. El jugador número diez da muchas oportunidades para marcar un gol.
3. Los comentaristas de la radio narran el partido.
4. Los jugadores estrella marcan los goles.
5. La policía cierra las calles cerca del estadio.
6. Los muchachos venden perros calientes.

La pelota fue pasada por la delantera.

310   Lección 14

18 Lorenzo tiene mala memoria

Hay muchos datos *(facts)* culturales que Lorenzo no puede recordar. Ayúdalo a recordar, escribiendo otra vez las siguientes oraciones en la voz pasiva y completándolas con la información correcta.

> Shakespeare escribió el libro *El viejo y el mar*.
> No, ese libro <u>fue escrito por Hemingway</u>.

1. Cristobal Colón ayudó a cinco países de la América del Sur a conseguir su libertad *(freedom)* de los españoles.
   No, estos cinco países....
2. Abraham Lincoln dijo *"I have a dream..."* ("Tengo un sueño...")
   No, esto....
3. Australia vendió el estado de Alaska a los Estados Unidos.
   No, este estado....
4. Gabriel García Márquez escribió los *Versos Sencillos*.
   No, estos versos....
5. Cantinflas visitó la luna por primera vez.
   No, la luna....
6. El Sur ganó la Guerra *(war)* Civil estadounidense.
   No, la Guerra Civil estadounidense....

Estos libros fueron escritos por Isabel Allende.

19 Un partido de fútbol

Trabajando en parejas, alterna con tu compañero/a de clase en hacer preguntas y contestarlas, usando la voz pasiva para decir quiénes hicieron las cosas indicadas. Sigue el modelo.

> dar camisetas a los aficionados (los jugadores del equipo)
> **A:** ¿Quién dio camisetas a los aficionados?
> **B:** Las camisetas fueron dadas a los aficionados por los jugadores del equipo.

1. cambiar el marcador en el segundo tiempo (el jugador con la camiseta número tres)
2. sacar las fotos para los periódicos (los reporteros de la sección deportiva)
3. narrar el partido (Edgar)
4. llevar en vivo el partido a los hogares (la emisora Radio Ñandutí)
5. describir el partido en la televisión (dos comentaristas superfamosos)
6. marcar los goles (el jugador con la camiseta número trece)

Answers

18
1. ...fueron ayudados por Simón Bolívar.
2. ...fue dicho por Martin Luther King, Jr.
3. ...fue vendido por Rusia.
4. ...fueron escritos por José Martí.
5. ...fue visitada por primera vez por Neil Armstrong.
6. ...fue ganada por el Norte.

19
1. ¿...cambió...?/El marcador fue cambiado en el segundo tiempo por....
2. ¿...sacó...?/Las fotos para los periódicos fueron sacadas por....
3. ¿...narró...?/El partido fue narrado por....
4. ¿...llevó...?/El partido fue llevado en vivo a los hogares por....
5. ¿...describió...?/El partido fue descrito en la televisión por....
6. ¿...marcó...?/Los goles fueron marcados por....

NATIONAL STANDARDS
C1.1, C1.2, C2.1, C4.2, C5.2

El fútbol
Activity 20

Activities 52-53

Answers

 20 1. ...habían sido cepillados por....
2. ...había sido puesta por....
3. ...habían sido traídos por....
4. ...habían sido hechas por....
5. ...había sido arreglada por....
6. ...habían sido lavadas por....
7. ...había sido limpiado por....
8. ...había sido preparada por....

Notes

Other words for *portero* are *arquero* and *guardavalla*. The word for **tie (score)** is *el empate.*

Activities

Prereading Strategy. Ask students to name some of the player positions on a soccer team. Then, using transparency 53, preteach the vocabulary: Pronounce each of the words in the illustration and have students repeat them; then use transparency 52 to point to some of the people included in the illustration and ask students to identify what position they play or who they are.

TPR. Using overhead transparencies 52 and 53 *(El fútbol)*, ask students to come up and point to the people you name in Spanish.

20 Una fiesta requetebuena

Imagina que fuiste a la fiesta que la familia Rubín había organizado para la final de la Copa Mundial de Fútbol. Di quién había hecho cada actividad cuando llegaste, según las indicaciones. Sigue el modelo, y usa el pluscuamperfecto en cada oración.

 Jorge había comprado las flores.
Las flores habían sido compradas por Jorge.

1. Los niños habían cepillado al perro y al gato.
2. Jorge había puesto la mesa.
3. Doña Elena y su nuevo esposo habían traído los refrescos.
4. El papá había hecho unas galletas de perlas de chocolate.
5. La mamá había arreglado la sala.
6. Elisa había lavado las ventanas.
7. Jorge había limpiado el piso de la cocina.
8. El papá había preparado la comida.

El fútbol

Mundial

La FIFA pidió a los jueces sancionar todo intento de violencia. Los 34 árbitros pasaron los exámenes.

Algo más

Para hablar del fútbol

el campeonato	*championship*	la pena máxima	*penalty*
el defensor	*defender*	el tiro	*shot*
el delantero	*forward*	el portero	*goaltender*
el mediocampista	*midfielder*	empatar	*to tie*

21 El último partido

Todos van para ver sus equipos favoritos en el último partido de fútbol. Di lo que todos quieren que pase, usando las indicaciones que se dan y el subjuntivo.

> Pilar/el árbitro/cantar una pena máxima
> Pilar quiere que el árbitro cante una pena máxima.

1. Uds./los delanteros/hacer otro tiro para empatar el partido
2. todos nosotros/el campeonato/terminar bien
3. Jaime y Enrique/los defensores/no dejar hacer más goles
4. Ernesto/su equipo/ganar el campeonato
5. Diego y Susana/los espectadores/gritar más
6. yo/el portero/no irse detrás de la pelota
7. tú/el delantero/hacer más goles

¿Cantó una pena máxima?

22 Nos gusta el fútbol

Trabajando en grupos, habla del fútbol con tus compañeros/as. Puedes hablar de la última vez que fuiste a un partido o de tus equipos y tus jugadores favoritos y la posición en que juegan.

> Mi equipo favorito es.... La última vez que lo vi jugar, fue en un estadio en Miami. Ese día había hecho sol por la mañana. Pero cuando llegamos al estadio, empezó a llover.

Autoevaluación. Como repaso y autoevaluación, responde lo siguiente:

1. What sections of a newspaper do you enjoy reading?
2. Imagine your friend arrived late to a school dance. Tell three things that had happened before your friend arrived.
3. Describe three things you did or saw prior to arriving at school today.
4. Imagine you are a radio announcer providing commentaries for a soccer match. What would you say to your audience?
5. Name three things that were done, said or written by someone you know.
6. What do you know about Paraguay?

 Activity 21

 Activity 9

 Quiz/Activity 6

Answers

21
1. ...quieren que los delanteros hagan....
2. ...queremos que el campeonato termine....
3. ...quieren que los defensores no dejen....
4. ...quiere que su equipo gane....
5. ...quieren que los espectadores griten....
6. ...quiero que el portero no se vaya....
7. ...quieres que el delantero haga....

22 Creative self-expression.

Autoevaluación
Possible answers:
1. Me gusta leer los titulares y la sección de deportes.
2. La profesora Fernández había cantado una canción en español. Carlos había tomado un refresco. Yo había escrito en mi cuaderno.
3. Yo había tomado el desayuno, me había cepillado los dientes y me había puesto la chaqueta para salir. También vi que mi madre había hecho un sandwich para el almuerzo.
4. Answers will vary.
5. Answers will vary.
6. Answers will vary.

NATIONAL STANDARDS
C1.1, C1.2, C1.3, C2.1, C2.2, C3.1, C4.1, C4.2, C5.1

Activity 10

Answers

A Creative self-expression.

B Creative self-expression.

Notes

In this era of expanding choices, technological advances and an increasingly diverse society require highly skilled individuals to meet the workforce needs of a global economy. The process of learning has become a lifelong journey that combines rigorous academic study with community and workplace experiences. Young people require relevance and the opportunity to apply academic skills in the community and in realistic workplace conditions. Activities like this *Conexión con la tecnología* offer realistic opportunities for students to combine Spanish with new skills in a simulated workplace experience. Encourage students to investigate related community volunteer/workplace opportunities that fit with their own plans for the future.

Activities

Multiple Intelligences (bodily-kinesthetic/linguistic/spatial). Students present their newscast orally in pairs, in small groups or to the entire class. Encourage creativity by having students prepare appropriate visual reinforcement of their presentation.

¡La práctica hace al maestro!

A Comunicación

Make a list of eight activities you did the past week and note what you did to prepare for each activity listed. Then, working in pairs, take turns asking questions about what each of you did.

A: ¿Qué hiciste esta semana?

B: Jugué un partido de fútbol.

A: ¿Qué habías hecho para jugar el partido?

B: Pues, había hecho muchos tiros de práctica para poder marcar goles en el partido.

jugar un partido de fútbol
(Tuve que hacer muchos tiros de práctica.)

comprar una pelota de fútbol
(Trabajé ocho horas.)

B Conexión con la tecnología

Imagine you have been asked to audition to report your school's news on a local Hispanic radio station. Make a three- to five-minute tape recording in Spanish to submit as your audition. Start your report by identifying yourself and telling the name and call letters for the radio station. Include the weather for today, the results of the most recent sports events, the traffic report, and any other newsworthy information happening in your school at the present time. In order to get the job you will need to be creative, so incorporate any special effects you can.

NATIONAL STANDARDS
C1.1, C1.2, C1.3, C4.1, C4.2, C5.1

VOCABULARIO

Testing/Assessment
Test Booklet
Oral Proficiency
Evaluation Manual
Portfolio Assessment

Activities

Expansion. Select several words and phrases for individual students to use orally in sentences.

Pronunciation. To ensure proper pronunciation, model each word or expression and have students repeat after you.

Students with Special Needs. Have students label and bring to class examples from the local newspaper of the vocabulary shown in the *Algo más* on page 301. For example, students might write on a piece of cardboard or on a piece of construction paper the words *la sección de deportes*. Encourage creativity. Students can practice the vocabulary working in pairs or small groups, asking and answering questions about one another's work: *¿Qué es?/Es la sección de deportes.*

El fútbol
el aficionado, la aficionada
el árbitro, la árbitra
la camiseta
el campeonato
el defensor, la defensora
el delantero, la delantera
el espectador, la espectadora
el gol
el marcador
el mediocampista,
    la mediocampista
la pelota
la pena (máxima)
el portero, la portera
el tiempo
el tiro

El periódico
el artículo
el aviso
la columna
la cultura
la economía
editorial
la encuesta
la entrevista
internacional
la sección
la tabla
el titular

La radio
el comentarista, la
    comentarista
la emisora
en vivo
el micrófono
la transmisión

Verbos
empatar
enterar(se) de
escuchar
llevar
marcar
narrar

Expresiones y otras palabras
acerca de
a favor (de)
alrededor de
culto,-a
económico,-a
máximo,-a
la oportunidad
ya

Una transmisión en vivo desde una escuela en Asunción.

¿Qué ha hecho el delantero de la camiseta número 5?

NATIONAL STANDARDS
C1.2, C4.1

Quiz/Activity 7

Quiz/Activity 7

Answers

Preparación

1. Statement 3 best describes the main theme of the reading.
2. Statements 1, 2 and 4 are the supporting information of the reading.

Notes

www

El Nuevo Herald
http://www.elherald.com/
Radio Stations
http://www.caracol.com.co/
http://www.rcn.com.co/

a leer

Estrategia

Preparación

Estrategia para leer: *distinguish the main theme from the supporting information*

When you are reading an informative text, such as a news article, first skim the text to identify the main idea and distinguish it from any supporting information. The main idea is the central theme around which the article is built. The supporting details form the body of the paragraphs and serve to develop the main topic. Knowing which part of the reading is the main idea and which is the supporting information will help you better understand the reading.

Como preparación para la lectura, primero lee rápidamente *(skim)* el artículo. Luego decide cuál de las siguientes ideas representa el tema principal y cuáles representan las ideas de apoyo *(support)* de lo que vas a leer.

1. Radio Caracol-WSUA 1260 AM da información desde Colombia sobre las condiciones actuales en la zona del terremoto.
2. Un violento terremoto sacudió a diecisiete poblaciones de Colombia.
3. Las comunidades colombianas en el sur de la Florida organizan la ayuda para los damnificados del terremoto de Colombia.
4. Dos aviones salieron con 25.000 libras de medicamentos y comida desde Miami para Colombia.

CARACOL COLOMBIA

MÁS COMPAÑÍA

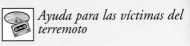

Ayuda para las víctimas del terremoto

MIAMI – En una rápida reacción ayer, las comunidades colombianas del sur de la Florida comenzaron a organizar la ayuda para los **damnificados** del violento terremoto que **sacudió** a diecisiete poblaciones de Colombia.

Según las **cifras** oficiales colombianas, el martes por la tarde el número de muertos era de por lo menos 900, con más de 1.500 **heridos**. El terremoto fue de una magnitud de 6.0 grados en la escala de Richter.

En menos de veinticuatro horas, dos aviones salieron con 25.000 libras de medicamentos y comida desde Miami para las zonas afectadas. Carmenza Jaramillo, cónsul general de Colombia en Miami, anunció que se abrieron dos **cuentas bancarias** para recolectar dinero en efectivo para las víctimas de Colombia. También se establecieron varios puntos de recolección para que los residentes del sur de la Florida puedan participar en la ayuda humanitaria.

Los voluntarios ayudan a las víctimas del terremoto en Colombia.

Notes

Glossed words are defined at the end of the reading on page 319.

Activities

Critical Listening. Play the audiocassette/audio compact disc version of the reading one paragraph at a time. Tell students to listen for the main ideas the speaker is addressing. Finally, have several individuals state what they believe the main theme of each paragraph is.

Prereading Strategy. Prepare students for the content of the reading by asking some general questions on the reading topic, such as the questions found in the *Preparación*. Next, play the first paragraph of the recording of the *A leer* section, using the corresponding audiocassette or compact disc that is part of the Audiocassette/Audio CD Program. As an alternative, you may choose to read the first paragraph yourself. Read the paragraph again with students following along in the book. Give students a moment to look over the paragraph silently on their own and then have them ask questions. Ask for a student to volunteer to read the paragraph aloud. Continue in this way for subsequent paragraphs.

NATIONAL STANDARDS
C1.2, C3.2, C4.1

Activities

Critical Thinking. Ask small groups of students to compare a popular local or national newspaper from the United States with a popular newspaper from a Spanish-speaking country. They should describe both papers and look for similarities and differences in terms of format, content, photos, style, etc. The information should then be shared with the class.

Multiple Intelligences (linguistic). As a quick additional activity that will inspire creativity, ask students to select an important date in the history of the state and write a headline about that event. Tell students that the event may be cultural, an economic or financial news item, a sports result, a tragedy, or any other event they wish. Students may wish to consult a book on the history of the state, an encyclopedia, newspapers from the past, etc. Then extend the activity by having students write an imaginary headline for some imaginary past or future event.

Un equipo de voluntarios de Miami ayuda a buscar damnificados del terremoto. (Armenia, Colombia).

"Estamos sorprendidos con la solidaridad de la gente en Miami", expresó Jaramillo. "Espero que esta generosidad continúe, porque sólo con la ayuda de todos podemos empezar a reconstruir el país".

Durante todo el día de ayer, los colombianos utilizaron las emisoras Radio Caracol-WSUA 1260 AM y RCN-Miami 1360 AM, para pedir la ayuda de los residentes del sur de la Florida y para dar información desde Colombia sobre las condiciones **actuales** en la zona del terremoto.

"Estoy muy preocupada por la situación en mi país", dijo Alba Lucía López, quien ha vivido en una de las ciudades más afectadas por el terremoto. "Estoy tratando de comunicarme con mis familiares desde ayer, pero no he tenido éxito".

Mientras tanto, en el almacén de Intel América, cerca del Aeropuerto Internacional de Miami, un **ejército** de voluntarios trabaja como **hormigas** preparando **cajas** con ayuda para las víctimas de Colombia. Entre los artículos más necesarios para los damnificados están: agua **potable**, comida **enlatada**, medicamentos, leche **en polvo**, linternas, pilas y **tiendas de campaña**.

damnificados *víctimas* **sacudió** *shook* **cifras** *numbers* **heridos** *wounded* **cuentas bancarias** *bank accounts* **actuales** *current* **ejército** *army* **hormigas** *ants* **cajas** *boxes* **potable** *drinkable* **enlatada** *canned* **en polvo** *powdered* **tiendas de campaña** *tents*

[Sacado del artículo *Los colombianos de la Florida ayudan a las víctimas del terremoto* del periódico *El Miami Herald*; Miami, Florida; enero 27 de 1999.]

 ¿Qué comprendiste?

1. ¿Dónde ocurrió el terremoto?
2. ¿Quiénes organizan la ayuda para las víctimas del terremoto?
3. ¿Cuál fue la magnitud del terremoto?
4. ¿Adónde les pueden donar dinero a las víctimas?
5. ¿Quién trabaja en la preparación de cajas con ayuda para las víctimas?
6. ¿Cuáles son los artículos más necesarios para los damnificados?

 Charlando

1. ¿Ha ocurrido un terremoto donde tú vives?
2. ¿Cómo te comunicas cuando hay una crisis natural en donde vives?
3. ¿Qué artículos tiene tu familia en caso de una emergencia?
4. ¿Qué grupos ayudan en tu comunidad cuando hay un desastre?

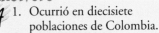

Answers

A 1. Ocurrió en diecisiete poblaciones de Colombia.
2. Las comunidades colombianas del sur de la Florida organizan la ayuda para las víctimas del terremoto.
3. Fue de una magnitud de 6.0 grados en la escala de Richter.
4. Pueden donarles dinero en dos cuentas bancarias.
5. Un ejército de voluntarios trabaja en la preparación de las cajas.
6. Los más necesarios son agua potable, comida enlatada, medicamentos, leche en polvo, linternas, pilas y tiendas de campaña.

B Answers will vary.

Activities

Connections. Using the Internet, newspapers, magazines, and so forth, have students prepare a detailed report about the destruction and aftermath of Hurricane Mitch. Then have students prepare a newscast that they must videotape and share with the class.

Multiple Intelligences (linguistic/spatial). As a follow-up to this writing assignment, combine the news articles to make a newspaper. Students should submit the final copy on disk so that a student can work on the layout and design of the paper.

Spanish for Spanish Speakers. Consider having students write a short summary of the article about the earthquake and its effects.

NATIONAL STANDARDS
C1.1, C1.2, C2.1, C3.2, C4.1

Answers

Creative writing practice.

Notes

Review. Review some of the writing strategies students have learned over the course of the year. Encourage students to apply as many of these strategies as possible in the article.

This *A escribir* provides a formal opportunity for students to improve their ability to write in Spanish, modeling their news articles after similar professionally written articles.

Point out that students should imitate other professionally written articles, but they should not plagiarize another person's work.

The section *A escribir* is not required content. You may choose to skip the section based upon your professional observation about how well students' writing skills are progressing, and as your school's curriculum dictates.

a **escribir**

Estrategia

Estrategia para escribir: *modeling a style of writing*

When you write an article about a news event, first find a few examples of similar news articles to use as models. Notice the formal style of writing that is used and the kind of information that is presented. If you imitate the writing style and include the same kind of information, your article will be perceived by the reader as a factual account of important news about a person, place or event.

Write a news article reporting about a person, an event, a tragedy, a discovery, etc., that you consider interesting. Make sure your writing models the following pattern for reporting the news:

> 13 de marzo
>
> Noticias de la semana:
> Esta semana han ocurrido
> cinco acontecimientos
> importantes en nuestra
> ciudad.

1. Provide a **title** that summarizes the theme of the article.
2. State the **dateline** to indicate where the report takes place.
3. Begin with the **who?, what?, when?, where?** or **why?** information to catch the readers' attention and make them want to continue reading the rest of the article.
4. Include supporting details in the paragraphs in order to develop the main theme.

Portfolio Assessment
Select an activity from *Capítulo 7* to include in the *Somos así* Portfolio Assessment.

repaso

Now that I have completed this chapter, I can...

✓ express events in the past.
✓ talk about the news.
✓ discuss what has happened.
✓ discuss a television broadcast.
✓ talk about everyday activities.
✓ describe people and objects.
✓ write about what someone has done.
✓ identify sections of newspapers and magazines.
✓ relate two events in the past.
✓ discuss a radio broadcast.
✓ talk about soccer.
✓ add emphasis to a description.
✓ express wishes.

I can also...
✓ read in Spanish about life in Uruguay and Paraguay.
✓ identify opportunities to read and listen to authentic Spanish in the newspaper and on television.
✓ use prefixes in Spanish to add emphasis.

¿Cuál de ellos es el portero?

Activities

Language through Action. Use a wall map of South America or an overhead transparency of the map in the front of this book to review Uruguay and Paraguay. Have individual students go to the map. *(Ve al mapa.)* Have students touch *(toca)* or point to *(señala)* the items mentioned in activity 6: *su capital es Asunción, el río Paraguay divide al país en dos regiones naturales,* and so forth.

Spanish for Spanish Speakers. Have students read a section from the book *Ariel* or *La vida nueva* by the Uruguayan writer José Enrique Rodó. They should then write a short summary describing the work or their feelings about the work.

Technology. In groups of four, students download a newspaper published in Uruguay or Paraguay. Have each group prepare a summary of the contents of the front page.

NATIONAL STANDARDS
C1.1, C1.2, C1.3, C2.1, C2.2, C3.1, C3.2, C4.1, C4.2, C5.1, C5.2

Chapters 8-10 of *Somos así LISTOS* are intended as a bridge to ease the transition for students who are continuing with Spanish and who will be using *Somos así ¡YA!* With this in mind, students will be required to gather and provide increasingly more challenging information in Spanish (e.g., the longer *A leer* in *Capítulos* 8-9; more challenging activities and projects with instructions in Spanish). The philosophy of gradually increasing the amount of Spanish in a carefully articulated program of study without overwhelming students culminates in *Capítulo 10* of *Somos así LISTOS* in which the sections *Oportunidades, Estrategia* and *Autoevaluación* appear entirely in Spanish as part of the goal. *Somos así ¡YA!* requires students to gather and provide all information (except grammar explanations) in Spanish.

Activities

Critical Thinking. Have students look at the illustration and photos on pages 322 and 323. Ask where students think the chapter takes place. Then have students guess what they think they will be learning in the chapter.

Multiple Intelligences (musical). Play music from Spain to make an auditory connection as you talk with the class about the country and its geography.

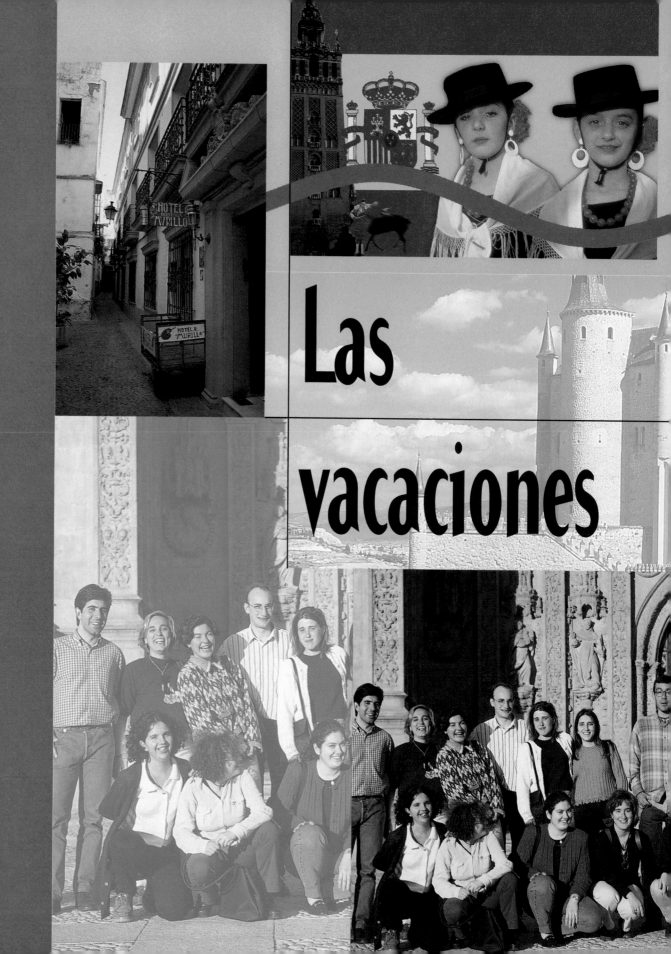

Las vacaciones

CAPÍTULO 8

España
Nombre oficial: Reino de España

Población: 39.193.000

Capital: Madrid

Ciudades importantes: Barcelona, Granada, Sevilla

Unidad monetaria: la peseta

Fiesta nacional: 12 de octubre, Día de la Hispanidad

Gente famosa: Antonio Banderas (actor), Pablo Picasso (pintor), Enrique Iglesias (cantante), Arantxa Sánchez Vicario (tenista)

Notes

Discuss the communicative functions students will be learning in *Capítulo 8*. A checkoff list of the functions appears at the end of the chapter (see page 371), along with additional objectives that students can use as a self-check to evaluate their own progress.

In this chapter you will be able to:

- seek and provide personal information
- plan vacations
- talk about the future
- express emotion
- talk about everyday activities
- express uncertainty or probability
- make travel and lodging arrangements
- identify people and items associated with travel
- state wishes and preferences
- talk about schedules
- use the twenty-four-hour clock
- express logical conclusions
- write about hopes and dreams

323

NATIONAL STANDARDS
C1.2, C5.2

Content reviewed in *Lección 15*
- seeking and providing personal information
- planning a vacation
- foods
- the future with *ir a*
- schedules
- places in a city
- reflexive verbs

Notes

Depending upon circumstances and individual differences, some people use the words *boleto*, *billete* or *tiquete* used in place of *pasaje*.

Activities

Critical Listening. Play the audiocassette/audio compact disc recording of the dialog. Instruct students to cover the words as they listen to the conversation in order to develop good listening skills before concentrating on their ability to read Spanish. Have students look at the illustration and imagine what the people are saying to one another. Ask several individuals to state what they believe the main theme of the conversation is.

Prereading Strategy. Talk to students about where they would like to travel. Ask about such things as what they would like to do there, whether there are any particular foods they would like to eat during their trip, and how they might go about making travel arrangements.

Spanish for Spanish Speakers. Ask students to read the recipe on page 325 and then ask them questions to determine how much they understood: *¿Cuáles son los ingredientes de la tortilla española?*; *¿Cómo se prepara?*

Lección 15

Contexto cultural

ESPAÑA

Las próximas vacaciones

¿Tortilla?

la maleta

GRACIELA: ¿Adónde irás las próximas vacaciones?

CAMILA: Vamos a ir a España. Quiero **saborear**° unas tortillas e ir a una **corrida**° de toros.

GRACIELA: Pero las tortillas son mexicanas.

CAMILA: No todas. En España llaman tortilla a lo que en México llaman **omelet**.

GRACIELA: ¡Ah, comprendo! Y, ¿ya han hecho los planes para el viaje?

CAMILA: Sí. La otra semana vamos a ir a la **agencia de viajes** para comprar los **pasajes.**° Estoy tan **emocionada**° que ya estoy haciendo las **maletas**.

GRACIELA: ¡Olé, amiga! ¡Qué **dicha**° la tuya!

saborear *to taste, to savor* **corrida** *bullfight* **pasajes** *tickets* **emocionada** *excited* **dicha** *happiness*

1 ¿Qué comprendiste?

1. ¿Adónde va a ir Camila en las próximas vacaciones?
2. ¿Qué quiere saborear Camila?
3. ¿A qué llaman tortilla en España?
4. ¿Adónde van a ir Camila y su familia la otra semana?
5. ¿Qué van a comprar allí?
6. ¿Está Graciela muy emocionada?
7. ¿Qué está haciendo Camila ya?

MAGAZINE
TOROS

Enrique Ponce, matador español.

¡Matador!

La corrida de toros

If you are in Spain on a Sunday afternoon, you may choose to go to the *plaza de toros* to see a *corrida de toros* (bullfight). There you will experience an event that has been a part of Spanish culture for centuries. You are probably already familiar with the role of the *matador,* who challenges the *toro* while holding nothing more than a *capa* (cape). When the passes please the crowd, the shout of *¡Olé!* fills the arena. However, when the matador's work is poorly done, the crowd whistles and shows its disapproval.

Spaniards do not consider the *corrida* a sport. It is considered to be more of a ritualistic struggle between human and animal that some people cherish and that others dislike.

Conexión Cultural

La tortilla española

Has visto que muchas veces las palabras cambian de significado, según dónde se usan en el mundo. Saber las diferencias de significado cuando viajas te puede ayudar a expresarte correctamente. La palabra *tortilla* es un buen ejemplo de este fenómeno. En México, las *tortillas* se hacen de masa de maíz o de masa de trigo. Frecuentemente, con ellas se envuelven carne y verduras, como se hace con un pan para hacer un sandwich. En cambio, en España, la palabra *tortilla* se refiere a un omelet. Aquí tienes una receta para hacer una tortilla tradicional que es muy popular en España.

pelada *cut* **pedazos** *pieces* **cucharadas** *tablespoonfuls* **batidos** *beaten* **Caliente** *Heat* **sartén** *frying pan* **vaya endureciendo** *begins to thicken* **debajo** *underneath* **fondo** *bottom* **dorado** *golden*

LA TORTILLA ESPAÑOLA

(ingredientes para cuatro personas)
1 patata grande **pelada** y cortada en **pedazos**
1 cebolla grande cortada en pedazos

4 **cucharadas** de aceite de oliva
5 huevos **batidos**
un poco de sal

Preparación
1. **Caliente** el aceite en una **sartén**.
2. Añada la patata y la cebolla y cocínelas hasta que estén suaves.
3. Ponga la sal.
4. Añada los huevos batidos lentamente, 1/3 a la vez; levante la tortilla tan pronto como **vaya endureciendo** para permitir que más huevos vayan **debajo**.
5. Cocine hasta que el **fondo** esté firme.
6. Para cocinar la parte de encima, invierta un plato sobre la tortilla y voltee la sartén. Luego, ponga la tortilla en la sartén otra vez.
7. Cocine hasta que el fondo esté **dorado**.
8. Se puede comer fría o caliente.

 La tortilla española
Activity 1

 Quiz/Activity 2

 Activity 1

Answers

1.
1. Va a ir a España.
2. Quiere saborear unas tortillas.
3. En España llaman tortilla al omelet.
4. La otra semana van a ir a la agencia de viajes.
5. Van a comprar los pasajes.
6. No. Camila está muy emocionada.
7. Camila ya está haciendo las maletas.

Notes

Several countries in the Spanish-speaking world have bullfights. In addition to Spain, there are bullfights in Mexico, in parts of Central America and in the northern countries of South America. In Portugal, another variation of bullfighting consists of a rider on horseback in the ring with a bull.

Another term for *matador* is *torero.*

Students may have difficulty understanding the following words: *significado* (meaning), *masa de maíz* (cornmeal), *masa de trigo* (wheat flour) and *se envuelven* (are wrapped).

Point out that the equivalent of *papa* (potato) in Spain is *patata.*

Activities

Communities. Have students prepare a report about bullfighting.

Connections. Divide the class into groups of four. Have each group prepare a *tortilla española* and share it with the class.

Expansion. Additional questions *¿Qué comprendiste?*: ¿Va a ir sola Camila a España?; ¿Con quién va a ir?; ¿Ya han hecho Camila y su familia los planes para el viaje?

NATIONAL STANDARDS
C1.2, C2.1, C3.1, C3.2, C4.1, C4.2

Cruzando fronteras

¿Qué sabes sobre la tortilla española? Di si cada una de las siguientes oraciones es *verdad* o *falsa*.

1. Las palabras no cambian nunca de significado de un país a otro.
2. Las tortillas en México se hacen de arroz y de frutas.
3. En las tortillas mexicanas se envuelven carne y verduras.
4. En España, la palabra *tortilla* quiere decir *omelet*.
5. La tortilla española se hace de patata (papa), cebolla, pollo, carne y aceite.
6. La tortilla española se puede comer fría o caliente.

Las próximas vacaciones (continuación)

el príncipe   la reina   el rey   la princesa

GRACIELA: Un viaje a España debe tener muchos **gastos,°** ¿verdad?
CAMILA: Sí, tiene demasiados gastos, pero mis padres me van a ayudar.
GRACIELA: Qué **suerte°** tienes. Espero que **goces°** mucho.
CAMILA: **A lo mejor°** no regresamos y decidimos vivir allá.
GRACIELA: Sí, no me digas, y vivirás con un **príncipe** español y tú serás su **princesa.**
CAMILA: **Puede ser.°** Luego, seremos el **rey** y la **reina.**
GRACIELA: ¡Estás **soñando!°**
CAMILA: Soñar no cuesta nada. Anoche soñé que yo iba a volver a **nacer°** en España y....
GRACIELA: ¡Qué dices! Creo que mejor me voy. Chao.

gastos *expenses* **suerte** *luck* **goces** *you enjoy* **a lo mejor** *maybe* **Puede ser** A lo mejor **soñando** *dreaming* **nacer** *to be born*

3 ¿Qué comprendiste?

1. ¿Quién tiene la suerte de viajar?
2. ¿Qué espera Graciela?
3. ¿Qué piensa Camila que a lo mejor va a pasar?
4. ¿Con quién dice Graciela que Camila va a vivir?
5. ¿Qué cree Camila que ella va a ser después de ser una princesa?
6. ¿Qué soñó anoche Camila?

4 Charlando

1. ¿Adónde irás en tus próximas vacaciones?
2. ¿Te gusta soñar? Explica.
3. ¿Has visto una corrida de toros? ¿Dónde?
4. ¿Cuál ha sido tu dicha más grande?
5. ¿Qué gastos tienes cuando vas de viaje?
6. ¿Has oído hablar de algún rey o de alguna reina? ¿De dónde?

Repaso rápido

El futuro con *ir a*

Do you recall how to state what is going to happen using the present tense of *ir* followed by *a* and an infinitive? Look at the following:

¿A qué hora va a salir el avión?

Nosotros vamos a comprar los pasajes el viernes.
El avión va a llegar en una hora.

We **are going to buy the tickets** on Friday.
The plane **is going to arrive** in one hour.

5 En Madrid

Imagina que estás en el Aeropuerto Internacional de Barajas, en Madrid. Di adónde van a ir de vacaciones las siguientes personas y a qué hora van a salir de España, combinando palabras y expresiones de las tres columnas. Añade las palabras que sean necesarias.

 Tú vas a ir a Panamá y vas a salir a las siete de la mañana.

A	B	C
la familia Guerra	Puerto Rico	7:00 A.M.
Leonor y Miguel	Argentina	8:40 A.M.
don Rubén	México	10:20 P.M.
nosotros	Costa Rica	2:15 P.M.
la señorita Torres	Paraguay	3:50 P.M.
tú	Panamá	4:30 P.M.
los señores Robleda	Venezuela	9:45 P.M.

Activities 3-5

Quiz/Activity 2

Answers

3 1. Camila tiene la suerte de viajar.
2. Graciela espera que Camila goce mucho.
3. Camila piensa que a lo mejor no van a regresar y decidan vivir en España.
4. Graciela dice que Camila va a vivir con un príncipe español.
5. Ella cree que va a ser una reina.
6. Soñó que iba a volver a nacer en España.

4 Answers will vary.

5 Answers will vary.

Notes

The construction *ir a* followed by an infinitive is the most common way to express the future in Spanish, especially in spoken Spanish.

Review. Review asking for and telling time as they relate to the schedules on this page, reminding students that they should use the expression *¿A qué hora (verb)?* when talking about when a plane departs or arrives.

Activities

Expansion. Additional questions (*¿Qué comprendiste?*): *¿Qué no cuesta nada, según Camila?*; *¿Soñó Graciela que ella iba a ser una reina?*

Additional questions (*Charlando*): *¿Con quién vas a ir en tu próximo viaje?*; *¿Qué planes tienes para tu próximo viaje?*; *¿Quién hace las maletas cuando van de viaje en tu familia?*; *¿Te gustaría ser un rey o una reina? ¿Por qué?*; *¿Qué soñaste anoche?*

NATIONAL STANDARDS
C1.1, C1.2, C2.2, C4.1

Answers

6 Creative self-expression.

Notes

Select several pairs of students to perform their dialog in front of the class.

Cultures. Valencia is the third largest city in Spain. The region of Valencia is an industrial and agricultural center known for its oranges and its *paella valenciana*.

Point out that the future-tense endings are always preceded by the letter *r* whether the verb is formed regularly or not.

Activities

Cooperative Learning. Encourage students to ask a variety of different questions for activity 6. Then have students switch partners for additional practice.

Critical Thinking. Ask students to give you the subjects of the following forms: *irán, tomaré, hablarás, comeremos, llevaré, leerá, viajarán, beberé,* etc.

Students with Special Needs. After discussing the *Idioma* on the future tense, practice the formation of the future tense of several verbs not shown on page 328.

---

6 Haciendo planes

Trabajando en parejas, alterna con tu compañero/a de clase en preguntarse los planes para las próximas vacaciones (adónde van a ir, cuándo van a ir, con quién, qué van a hacer, qué lugares van a visitar, etc.). Puedes inventar los planes si quieres. Trata de usar las expresiones que has aprendido en esta lección.

Viajaré a Sevilla.

A: ¿Adónde vas a ir de vacaciones?
B: Voy a ir a Barcelona, España.
A: ¿Qué vas a hacer allá?
B: Voy a ir a comer tortillas.
A: ¿Cuándo vas a ir?
B: Voy a ir el seis de septiembre.

IDIOMA

El futuro

As you have seen, the present tense of a verb is often used in conversation in order to refer to the future.

Vamos a Málaga mañana.   **We're going** to Málaga tomorrow.

You also have learned to talk about the future using the construction *ir + a + infinitive.*

¿Van a ir en avión?   **Are you going to go** by plane?

Spanish also has a true future tense *(el futuro)* that may be used to tell what will happen. It is usually formed by adding the endings *-é, -ás, -á, -emos, -éis* and *-án* to the infinitive form of the verb.

viajar		comer		abrir	
viajaré	viajaremos	comeré	comeremos	abriré	abriremos
viajarás	viajaréis	comerás	comeréis	abrirás	abriréis
viajará	viajarán	comerá	comerán	abrirá	abrirán

Look at these examples:

Yo viajaré a Valencia mañana.   **I'll travel** to Valencia tomorrow.
Nosotros iremos en tren.   **We'll go** by train.
El avión llegará a las tres.   The plane **will arrive** at three o'clock.

7 ¿Qué harán?

Di estas oraciones de otra manera para ver qué van a hacer las siguientes personas.

> Rodrigo va a comer un omelet en el almuerzo.
> Rodrigo comerá un omelet en el almuerzo.

1. Luz y Liliana, muy emocionadas, van a preparar su viaje a España.
2. Yo voy a subir las maletas que están en el sótano.
3. Mauricio e Isabel van a saborear unas ricas tortillas españolas.
4. Carolina va a ir al aeropuerto.
5. Tú vas a recoger unos pasajes en la agencia de viajes.
6. Nosotros vamos a ver al rey, a la reina y a los príncipes de España por la televisión.

8 Los planes de Camila

Completa el siguiente párrafo con el futuro de los verbos indicados para saber cuáles son los planes de Camila para mañana.

Mañana yo 1. *(ir)* temprano a la agencia de viajes y 2. *(comprar)* el pasaje para mi viaje a España. Luego, 3. *(regresar)* a casa y 4. *(preparar)* un omelet para el almuerzo. Después del almuerzo, mi hermano y yo 5. *(conducir)* hasta una tienda en el centro de la ciudad donde él 6. *(mirar)* una maleta que quiere comprar. En la tarde, mis padres y yo 7. *(hablar)* de los gastos de mi viaje. Van a ser muchos, pero por suerte mi padre los 8. *(cubrir)* casi todos. Finalmente en la noche, yo 9. *(ver)* mi programa favorito de televisión, "Nacer y vivir", y 10. *(comer)* una tortilla antes de ir a dormir.

9 Las próximas vacaciones

Imagina que tú y tus amigos hacen planes para las próximas vacaciones. Completa las siguientes oraciones con la forma del futuro de los verbos indicados.

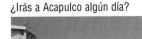
¿Irás a Acapulco algún día?

> Claudia *(conocer)* la América del Sur.
> Claudia *conocerá* la América del Sur.

1. Uds. *(escribir)* cartas para sus amigos.
2. Mi familia y yo *(ir)* a Acapulco, México.
3. Juan Manuel y Fernando *(trabajar)* en una agencia de viajes.
4. Tú *(esquiar)* en Chile.
5. Yo *(viajar)* a la casa de mis tíos en Acapulco.
6. Álvaro y Patricia *(visitar)* el parque de atracciones.
7. Norberto *(ir)* a las corridas de toros en España.
8. Nosotros *(comer)* omelets en el D.F.

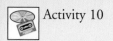

Answers

1. Nosotros estaremos en....
2. Mi hermano saboreará....
3. Mis padres irán a una corrida de toros y gritarán....
4. La dicha no será... volveremos a....
5. Mi papá cubrirá....

11 1. ¿...iremos...?/...irán al Museo del Prado.
2. ¿...irá...?/...irá a la Oficina Municipal de Turismo.
3. ¿...irán...?/...irán al Teatro Real.
4. ¿...irá...?/...irá al Monumento a Cervantes.
5. ¿...irán...?/...irán al Banco de España.
6. ¿...irás...?/...iré a la Iglesia Pontificia de San Miguel.
7. ¿...iré...?/...irás al Teatro de la Zarzuela.
8. ¿...irán...?/...iremos a la Torre de los Lujanes.

Activities

Cooperative Learning. Ask students to imagine that they have the unique ability to predict the future. Working in pairs, they should become palm readers and make five predictions for their partner. (This can be a fun activity to share with the rest of the class.)

Expansion. Have students prepare a list of people they know. (They may make up any names or relationships they wish.) Then have students indicate where each of the people on the list will be going during the next month, and on what day, using the future tense.

---

10 ¿Qué pasará?

Imagina que tú y tu familia van a hacer un viaje a España en una semana. Haz oraciones completas para decir qué pasará en los próximos días, usando las indicaciones que se dan. Añade las palabras que sean necesarias.

1. nosotros/estar/Madrid por un mes
2. mi hermano/saborear unas tortillas
3. mis padres/ir/una corrida de toros y/gritar olé
4. la dicha/no ser muy grande en un mes porque nosotros/volver/casa
5. mi papá/cubrir todos los gastos

11 ¿Adónde irán en Madrid?

Trabajando en parejas, alterna con tu compañero/a de clase en preguntar y contestar a qué lugares irán cada una de las siguientes personas, según el mapa y las indicaciones que se dan.

Natalia y sus tíos/52
A: ¿Adónde irán Natalia y sus tíos?
B: Natalia y sus tíos irán al Edificio España.

1. Lorenzo y yo/30
2. don Joaquín/20
3. Martín y su hermana/12
4. Gloria/55
5. Adriana y su esposo/40
6. tú/18
7. yo/39
8. Uds./16

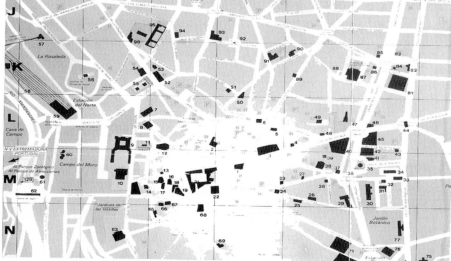

CORRESPONDENCIA CON LA ENUMERACION EN EL PLANO DE MADRID
MONUMENTOS, MUSEOS Y LUGARES DE INTERES GENERAL

1. Sede de la Comunidad de Madrid
2. Convento de las Descalzas Reales
3. Real Casa de la Aduana y Real Academia de Bellas Artes
4. Las Calatravas
5. Oratorio del Caballero de Gracia
6. Telefónica
7. Palacio del Senado y Museo del Pueblo Español
8. Convento de la Encarnación
9. Palacio Real
10. Nuestra Sra. de la Almudena
11. Estatua de Felipe IV
12. Teatro Real
13. Patronato Municipal de Turismo
14. Santísimo Sacramento y Capitanía General
15. Ayuntamiento
16. Torre de los Lujanes
17. Casa de Cisneros
18. Iglesia Pontificia de San Miguel
19. San Justo

20. Oficina Municipal de Turismo
21. Conjunto de la Plaza Mayor
22. Ministerio de Asuntos Exteriores
23. Teatro Español
24. Cámara de Comercio
25. Real Academia de la Historia
26. Convento de las Trinitarias
27. Ateneo de Madrid
28. Dirección Gral. de Turismo Comunidad de Madrid (Oficina de Turismo)
29. Ministerio de Sanidad y Seguridad Social
30. Museo del Prado
31. San Jerónimo el Real
32. Real Academia de la Lengua Española
33. Casón del Buen Retiro (Arte Moderno – "Guernica")
34. Museo del Ejército
35. Obelisco al Dos de Mayo
36. Fuente de Neptuno
37. Palacio de Villahermosa (Museo de Pinturas)

38. Congreso de los Diputados
39. Teatro de la Zarzuela
40. Banco de España
41. Bolsa de Madrid
42. Ministerio de la Marina
43. Museo de Artes Decorativas
44. Puerta de Alcalá
45. Palacio de Comunicaciones
46. Palacio de Linares
47. Fuente de Cibeles y Palacio de Buenavista
48. San José
49. Casa de las Siete Chimeneas
50. San Antonio de los Alemanes
51. San Plácido
52. Edificio España
53. San Marcos
54. Torre de Madrid y Oficina de Turismo
55. Monumento a Cervantes

Algo más

El futuro de probabilidad

The future tense also may be used in Spanish to express uncertainty in questions and probability in answers that refer to the present. Compare the following:

¿A qué hora llegará?	**I wonder** what time it will arrive.
Él saldrá en el próximo tren.	**He is probably (He must be) leaving** on the next train.
Comerán tortillas ahora.	**I imagine they are eating** tortillas.
Ellos estarán en la playa.	**They probably are (must be)** at the beach.

Ellos estarán en la playa. (Mallorca, España.)

12 Una opinión

Expresa una opinión sobre cada una de las siguientes situaciones, usando el futuro de probabilidad.

Javier está en una agencia de viajes.
Comprará un pasaje.

1. Son las once y Eliana todavía está durmiendo.
2. Esteban y Miguel están en una piscina.
3. Jorge y su mujer están en el aeropuerto con maletas.
4. Tú estás viendo a un matador y a un toro.
5. Ana y su esposo están en la cocina y tienen los ingredientes para preparar tortillas.
6. A Camila le gustan los huevos, las patatas (las papas) y las cebollas, y está en un restaurante en Madrid.

 Activity 12

 Quiz/Activity 4

 Activity 6

Answers

12 Possible answers:
1. Estará muy cansada.
2. Nadarán.
3. Viajarán.
4. Estarás en una corrida.
5. Prepararán unas tortillas.
6. Comerá una tortilla española.

Notes

The future tense is most often used for distant projects and possibilities. The present tense can also be used for a future meaning when there is a certainty: *¿Estás en tu casa esta tarde?*

Activities

Critical Thinking. As an additional activity to practice the future tense of probability, have students list the names of several people, including both close friends and family as well as celebrities. Students should then say where each person probably is right now: *¿El Presidente? Estará en la Casa Blanca.*

Students with Special Needs. To practice the future of probability, have students say the following in Spanish: 1) What time do you think it is?/It's probably five o'clock.; 2) I wonder where Lucy is./She's probably at school.; 3) I suppose she is coming./She'll probably be here soon.

NATIONAL STANDARDS
C1.2, C4.1

Activity 13

Answers

13
1. Estará en la cocina.
2. Estarán en el banco.
3. Estarán en un (el) restaurante español.
4. Estará en la plaza de toros.
5. Estará en el almacén.
6. Estará en la agencia de viajes.
7. Estarán en Madrid.

14
1. ¿Dónde estarán...?
2. ¿Qué llevaré...?
3. ¿Cuál será...?
4. ¿Quién cubrirá...?
5. ¿Cómo preparará...?
6. ¿Dónde estarán...?
7. ¿Quién viajará...?

Notes

Spain is the only Spanish-speaking country with a monarchy. The current king is Juan Carlos I de Borbón, and the future king is his son Felipe (*Príncipe de Asturias*).

Activities

Language through Action.
Prepare cards that state feelings or conditions that can be easily dramatized (for example, *tener sueño* or *estar triste*). Distribute the cards and ask students to take turns acting out the different feelings. After each action, the class must use the future of probability to say how the student is probably feeling. (*Tendrá sueño.*; *Estará triste.*)

13 Ahora mismo

Di dónde piensas que estarán las siguientes personas ahora mismo, según lo que hacen y las indicaciones que se dan.

  Camila está durmiendo y soñando con su viaje a España. (cuarto)
Estará en el cuarto.

1. La tía de Camila está preparando omelets. (cocina)
2. Wilson y Daniel están consiguiendo dinero para pagar los gastos del viaje. (banco)
3. Graciela y su hermano están saboreando unas tortillas. (restaurante español)
4. La familia Perdomo está viendo una corrida de toros. (plaza de toros)
5. Teresa está comprando unas maletas. (almacén)
6. Camila está comprando los pasajes. (agencia de viajes)
7. Elena y su prima están viendo al Rey Juan Carlos y a la Reina Sofía. (Madrid)

Si están en el Palacio Real de Madrid, estarán viendo al Rey Juan Carlos y a la Reina Sofía.

14 ¿Qué te preguntas?

Expresa las siguientes ideas con una pregunta, usando el futuro de probabilidad. Sigue el modelo.

  Me pregunto cuánto cuestan los pasajes.
¿Cuánto costarán los pasajes?

1. Me pregunto dónde están los príncipes de España ahora.
2. Me pregunto qué llevo de ropa para mi viaje.
3. Me pregunto cuál es la temperatura en Madrid.
4. Me pregunto quién cubre nuestra visita a Madrid para el periódico.
5. Me pregunto cómo prepara mi tía las tortillas.
6. Me pregunto dónde están los pasajes.
7. Me pregunto quién viaja también a España.

¿Dónde estará el Príncipe Felipe de España?

Las reservaciones

Notes

Point out that there is a significant time change between the United States and Spain. (During most of the year, Spanish time is seven hours ahead of central standard time in the United States.)

Activities

Critical Listening. Play the audiocassette/audio compact disc version of the dialog. Instruct students to cover the words with one hand and to concentrate on listening carefully to what the speakers are saying while they look at the illustration and imagine what the people are saying to one another. Have several individuals state what they believe the main theme of the conversation is.

Prereading Strategy. Instruct students to cover up the dialog with one hand and to look at the illustration. Ask them to imagine where the conversation takes place and what the people are saying to one another. Finally, have students look through the dialog quickly to find cognates and other words or expressions they already know.

AGENTE: Buenos días, ¿en qué las puedo ayudar?

YOLANDA: Hace dos semanas hice unas **reservaciones**, y quiero comprar los pasajes ahora.

AGENTE: Permítame, miro en la **pantalla.** ¿Cuál es su **nombre° completo?**

YOLANDA: Es Yolanda Giraldo de Hernández.

AGENTE: Sí, aquí está. ¿Son cuatro pasajes para un viaje **sencillo...?°**

YOLANDA: No, señor. Son cuatro **de ida y vuelta.°** ¡Queremos regresar!

CAMILA: ¡Ay, mamá, yo no! Yo **me mudaré°** para allá.

AGENTE: Sí, señora, con **destino** a Madrid, en **tarifa°** económica. La **salida°** es el 15 de junio y la **llegada°** a Madrid es al día siguiente. El regreso es el 17 de julio.

CAMILA: ¿Saldremos temprano el quince?

AGENTE: No, el **vuelo°** saldrá a las cinco de la tarde. Es el último que hará esa **compañía aérea** ese día. ¿Pagan a crédito o con **cheque?°**

YOLANDA: A crédito. **Cargue°** todo en esta tarjeta, por favor.

nombre *name* **sencillo** *one-way* **de ida y vuelta** *round-trip* **me mudaré** *I will move* **tarifa** *fare* **salida** *departure* **llegada** *arrival* **vuelo** *flight* **cheque** *check* **cargue** *charge*

Capítulo 8   **333**

NATIONAL STANDARDS
C2.1, C4.1

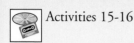

Answers

15
1. Hizo unas reservaciones.
2. El agente mira la información en la pantalla.
3. Es Yolanda Giraldo de Hernández.
4. Son para un viaje de ida y vuelta.
5. El destino es Madrid.
6. La tarifa de los pasajes es económica.
7. La salida es el 15 de junio y la llegada a España es al día siguiente.
8. Viajan en el último vuelo.

16 Answers will vary.

Activities

Expansion. Additional questions (*¿Qué comprendiste?*): *¿En dónde están Yolanda y Camila?*; *¿Cuál es el nombre completo del agente?*; *¿Van a viajar Yolanda y Camila solas?*; *¿A qué hora saldrá el vuelo?*; *¿Cómo va Yolanda a pagar los pasajes?*

Additional questions (*Charlando*): *¿Quién hace las reservaciones de los pasajes cuando tu familia va de viaje?*; *¿Tienes una compañía aérea favorita? ¿Cuál?*; *¿Tiene buenas tarifas?*; *¿Pagas algo con cheque? ¿Qué?*

Ask students where they think Toledo is located. Then use a map of Spain to ask *¿Dónde está Toledo en este mapa?* A possible answer might be *Está en España, al suroeste de Madrid.*

---

15 ¿Qué comprendiste?

1. ¿Qué hizo Yolanda hace dos semanas?
2. ¿En dónde mira el agente la información?
3. ¿Cuál es el nombre completo de Yolanda?
4. ¿Los pasajes que van a comprar son para un viaje sencillo o para un viaje de ida y vuelta?
5. ¿Cuál es el destino del viaje?
6. ¿Cuál es la tarifa de los pasajes?
7. ¿Cuándo es la salida y cuándo es la llegada a España?
8. ¿En qué vuelo de la compañía aérea viajan Yolanda y Camila?

Aquí puedes hacer reservaciones y comprar pas...

EUROVIA TRAVEL
AGENCIA DE VIAJES

71 N.° BD 348681   BILLETE + RESERVA   EL

RENFE
C. I. F.: G-28016749

DE	→	A	CLASE	FECHA	HORA SALIDA	TIPO DE TREN	COCHE	N.º PLAZA	DEPART
M.ATCH.AVE		SEVILLA SJ 1	21.09	16.00	TALGO	0011	005V	NO P
		HORA DE LLEGADA-->: 19.40				CLIMATIZ.		

Tarifa   002 RESERVA DE PLAZAS
Forma de pago   METALICO   Pesetas   ***2330...

16 Charlando

1. ¿Cuál es tu nombre completo?
2. ¿Has hecho algún viaje sencillo? ¿Adónde?
3. ¿Cuál fue tu destino en tu último viaje? ¿Fue a algún lugar donde se habla español?
4. ¿Te gustaría mudarte de donde vives? ¿A qué lugar te gustaría mudarte?
5. ¿Crees que cargar gastos en una tarjeta de crédito es mejor que pagar en efectivo? ¿Por qué?

PARAti

Otras palabras y expresiones

el asiento	seat
el billete	ticket
la cancelación	cancellation
la clase económica	coach class
la confirmación	confirmation
el cupo	space available
el pase a bordo	boarding pass
la primera clase	first class
la ventanilla	window

¿A qué hora sale el tren con destino a Toledo?

Próximas Salidas

...adas   ...orrido

Cercanías			Regionales y L. Recorrido			
Vía	Hora	Destino	Vía	Hora	Destino	Vía	Tren
2		FUENLABRADA	9	13:50	ALBACETE	5	R EXP
5		MOSTOL/SOTO	8	14:03	SEGOVIA	2	REGIO
5	13:48	PARLA	6	14:15	ALICANTE	5	TALGO
5	13:52	GUADALAJARA	3	14:25	TOLEDO	4	REGIO
4	13:53	CHAMAR/P PI	2	15:20	BILBO/HENDA	5	TALGO
5	13:55	ARANJUEZ	4	15:30	CACE/BADAJO	5	TALGO
5	13:55	P PIO/ROZAS	7	15:58	SANTANDER	5	TALGO
	13:57	TRES CANTOS	2	16:03	SEGOVIA	2	REGIO
	14:01	ALCALA	3				

NATIONAL STANDARDS
C1.1, C1.2, C2.1, C4.1

Algo más

El futuro: los verbos reflexivos

Form the future tense of reflexive verbs in the same way you have learned to form the present tense of nonreflexive verbs. The reflexive pronoun must agree with the subject and must precede the verb.

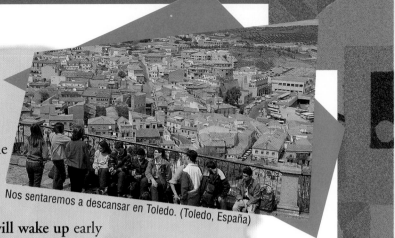
Nos sentaremos a descansar en Toledo. (Toledo, España)

Me despertaré tempranο para llegar a tiempo al aeropuerto.
Ellos se bañarán antes de salir para el aeropuerto.

I will wake up early to arrive at the airport on time.
They will take a bath before going to the airport.

17 En un programa para estudiantes extranjeros

Mañana vas a ir a España para estudiar en un programa para estudiantes extranjeros. Trabajando en parejas, alterna con tu compañero/a de clase en preguntar y en contestar a qué hora harás *(you will do)* las siguientes actividades para prepararte.

acostarte
A: ¿A qué hora te acostarás?
B: Me acostaré a las nueve.

1. despertarte
2. levantarte
3. bañarte
4. desayunarte
5. peinarte
6. despedirte de todos nosotros

18 ¿Cuándo?

Trabajando en parejas, alterna con tu compañero/a de clase en hacer preguntas y contestarlas para saber cuándo las siguientes personas harán *(will do)* las cosas indicadas.

mi mamá/maquillarse (cuando tú salgas del baño)
A: ¿Cuándo se maquillará mi mamá?
B: Se maquillará cuando tú salgas del baño.

1. Ud./vestirse (cuando termine de planchar el pantalón)
2. yo/cepillarse el pelo (cuando consigas el cepillo)
3. ellos/afeitarse (cuando lleguen a Madrid)
4. los tíos/levantarse (cuando estemos listos para salir)
5. nosotros/irnos para el aeropuerto (cuando pongamos las maletas en el carro)
6. la familia/mudarse para España (cuando nos aburramos de vivir aquí)
7. Camila/desayunarse (cuando todos estén listos)
8. tú/bañarse (cuando mi hermana salga del baño)

¿A qué hora se peinará Julieta?

Answers

17
1. ¿...te despertarás?/Me despertaré....
2. ¿...te levantarás?/Me levantaré....
3. ¿...te bañarás?/Me bañaré....
4. ¿...te desayunarás?/Me desayunaré....
5. ¿...te peinarás?/Me peinaré....
6. ¿...te despedirás...?/Me despediré....

18
1. ¿...se vestirá...?/Me vestiré....
2. ¿...me cepillaré...?/Te cepillarás....
3. ¿...se afeitarán...?/Se afeitarán....
4. ¿...se levantarán...?/Se levantarán....
5. ¿...nos iremos...?/Nos iremos....
6. ¿...se mudará...?/Se mudará....
7. ¿...se desayunará...?/Se desayunará....
8. ¿...te bañarás?/Me bañaré....

Notes

Review. Review some reflexive verbs with students before discussing the *Algo más* on page 335.

Encourage students to study and/or travel abroad during or after high school. Consider organizing a student trip to Spain or another Spanish-speaking country through a student-oriented travel agency.

NATIONAL STANDARDS
C1.1, C1.2, C4.1

Notes

Remind students that in Spain (especially in the south) people use the subject pronoun *vosotros,-as.*

Point out the similarities among irregular stems: 1) loss of a vowel (*e* of the infinitive ending) for *poder, querer, saber* and *caber;* 2) a special stem *(decir, hacer);* 3) loss of a vowel *(e* of the infinitive ending) and the addition of the letter *d (poner, salir, tener, venir).*

Activities

Students with Special Needs. After discussing the *Idioma* titled *El futuro de los verbos irregulares,* have students close their books and then practice the formation of the future tense of the verbs shown on this page.

TPR. Check students' understanding of verb tenses by making several travel statements that have either already occurred or that will occur: *Fui a España el año pasado./Mi familia y yo iremos a la América del Sur el año que viene.* Have students raise their left hand if the sentence is in the past tense; have them raise their right hand if the sentence is in the future tense.

IDIOMA

El futuro de los verbos irregulares

Some verbs use a modified form of the infinitive in the future tense. However, their endings remain the same as for regular verbs. The following verbs drop the letter *e* from the infinitive ending:

caber	poder	querer	saber
cabré	podré	querré	sabré
cabrás	podrás	querrás	sabrás
cabrá	podrá	querrá	sabrá
cabremos	podremos	querremos	sabremos
cabréis	podréis	querréis	sabréis
cabrán	podrán	querrán	sabrán

The vowel of the infinitive endings *-er* and *-ir* changes to *d* in these verbs:

poner	salir	tener	venir
pondré	saldré	tendré	vendré
pondrás	saldrás	tendrás	vendrás
pondrá	saldrá	tendrá	vendrá
pondremos	saldremos	tendremos	vendremos
pondréis	saldréis	tendréis	vendréis
pondrán	saldrán	tendrán	vendrán

The letters *e* and *c* are dropped from the infinitives *decir* and *hacer* before adding the future-tense endings.

decir	hacer
diré	haré
dirás	harás
dirá	hará
diremos	haremos
diréis	haréis
dirán	harán

Haremos nuestra tarea juntas.

19 Hablando del viaje

Completa las siguientes oraciones con la forma apropiada del futuro de los verbos indicados.

 Las tías (podrán) cargar todos sus gastos en sus tarjetas de crédito. (poder)

1. Alejandro y Santiago (1) que pagar los pasajes con cheque. (tener)
2. Cuando regresemos de España, (2) en una compañía aérea diferente. (venir)
3. Yo (3) que Uds. me traigan algo de España. (querer)
4. Tanta ropa no (4) en una maleta. (caber)
5. ¿(5) tú toda tu ropa en dos maletas? (poner)
6. El viernes, a lo mejor nosotros (6) a las nueve de la mañana. (salir)
7. Javier (7) las reservaciones del hotel mañana. (hacer)
8. El agente no (8) si hay vuelos sin mirar en la pantalla. (saber)
9. ¿Cuándo (9) Mauricio su nombre completo y la otra información que necesitan a los señores de la agencia? (decirles)

Podremos ir al Parque del Buen Retiro. (Madrid, España.)

20 ¡A España!

Imagina que viajas mañana a España con algunos miembros de tu familia. Haz oraciones completas, tomando elementos de cada columna, usando el futuro. Puedes inventar la información que quieras.

 Mis hermanos pondrán sus cosas en sus maletas.

A	B	C
mis hermanos	venir	pagar los pasajes con cheque
todos nosotros	tener	cargar todo en su tarjeta
el vuelo	saber	un vuelo con destino a Madrid
mis abuelos	salir	la hora de salida
yo	poner	a tiempo
mi papá	poder	reservaciones de ida y vuelta
mis tíos	hacer	sus cosas en sus maletas
mi mamá	querer	de Miami en el primer vuelo

Activity 20

Answers

19 1. tendrán
2. vendremos
3. querré
4. cabrá
5. Pondrás
6. saldremos
7. hará
8. sabrá
9. les dirá

20 Answers will vary.

Activities

Critical Thinking. Have students use any ten verbs of their choosing to write ten different statements that use the future tense and that tell about the future of your city or state. The statements can be serious or funny. Then have students work in pairs or in small groups to correct the statements and to choose each student's best statement. Finally, as a class activity, call on individuals to share their best sentences.

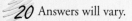
NATIONAL STANDARDS
C1.1, C1.2, C4.1

21 El adivino

Ramón fue a ver a un adivino *(fortune-teller)* ayer. Haz oraciones completas para saber lo que el adivino le dice a Ramón que va a pasar, usando las indicaciones que se dan. Añade las palabras que sean necesarias.

 tu vuelo/salir/muy tarde/martes
Tu vuelo saldrá muy tarde el martes.

1. tu hermanita/no querer ir/viaje a última hora
2. tus tías/poder conseguir/sólo un pasaje de ida/vuelta
3. tú/no tener/reservaciones listas
4. tú y tu familia/decir/sus nombres completos cuando lleguen/hotel
5. a tu hermano/no caberle/toda la ropa/una maleta
6. tus padres/tener/mucha paz/sus vacaciones
7. tus abuelos/venir/día antes/viaje
8. el agente/no saber/tarifas para un viaje/Madrid

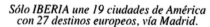

Sólo IBERIA une 19 ciudades de América con 27 destinos europeos, vía Madrid.

Asunción. Bogotá. Buenos Aires. Cancún. Caracas. Guatemala. La Habana. Lima. Managua. México. Montevideo. Panamá. Quito. Río de Janeiro. San José. San Juan. Santiago de Chile. Santo Domingo. Sao Paulo.

22 Las vacaciones del señor Gómez

Cuando el señor Gómez está pensando en voz alta *(aloud)* acerca de lo que hará durante las vacaciones, su secretaria entra a su oficina. Completa el siguiente párrafo con el futuro del verbo indicado para saber lo que pasa.

SR. GÓMEZ: Mañana es mi primer día de vacaciones. ¡Por fin, *1. (poder)* descansar! *2. (Levantarse)* al mediodía. *3. (Ponerse)* un pantalón y una camisa requetecómodos, ¡nada de trajes!, y unos zapatos deportivos. *4. (Desayunarse)* sin tener que mirar el reloj cada dos segundos. *5. (Leer)* ese libro que hace meses está en mi cuarto. Y, lo mejor de todo ¡no *6. (tener)* que ir a reuniones a ninguna parte! *7. (Hacer)* exactamente lo que quiera todos los días.

SECRETARIA: Buenos días, Sr. Gómez. Su mujer está al teléfono.

SR. GÓMEZ: Gracias.... Hola, Pilar, ¿pasa algo?

PILAR: No, te llamo para decirte que no hagas planes para mañana. A las ocho y media, nosotros *8. (llevar)* a Robertico al médico. Luego, *9. (ir)* al zoológico. Se lo prometí a los niños. A la una, *10. (comer)* en casa de tus padres. Y a las cinco, mi hermana y sus hijos *11. (venir)* a ver una película.

SR. GÓMEZ: ¡Oh, no! Pero amor, ¿y mis vacaciones?

Oportunidades

En la agencia de viajes

If you are traveling within a Spanish-speaking country, you may have to go to a travel agency to confirm your reservations for the airplane and hotels scheduled in your itinerary. Perhaps you also will need to make new arrangements to include additional interesting sites you want to visit. Take that opportunity to practice all you have learned in Spanish and see if you can acquire new words that you did not know.

iiLLÁMENOS HOY MISMO!!
RESERVE SU PLAZA EN
VIAJES OVIEDO, S.L.
C/. Cervantes, 4 • 33004 OVIEDO
De Lunes a Viernes de 9.30 a 13.30 y de 16.30 a 19.30
Tels.(98) 523 12 77 - 527 18 82
iiBUEN VIAJE!!
VEFA
MAS CERCA DE VD.
LAS RESERVAS SON OBLIGATORIAS

23 Haciendo reservaciones

¿Cómo llegamos a la plaza de toros?

Imagina que estás en una agencia de viajes, hablando con el agente para arreglar todos los detalles de tu viaje. Trabajando en parejas, alterna con tu compañero/a de clase en hacer preguntas y en contestarlas. Usa el futuro y las indicaciones que se dan.

> cuál/ser/su destino final (Granada)
> **A:** ¿Cuál será su destino final?
> **B:** Mi destino final será Granada.

1. cuándo/tener Ud./listas mis reservaciones (en cinco minutos)
2. cuándo/saber Ud./si hay más vuelos para Granada el viernes (tan pronto como tenga la información en la pantalla)
3. qué compañía aérea/poder/darnos tarifas más económicas (ninguna otra compañía aérea)
4. cuándo/salir el vuelo (tarde en la noche)
5. a qué hora/ser/la llegada a Granada (a las seis de la mañana)
6. cómo/poder yo/conseguir el nombre completo del hotel al que vamos (si habla con aquella señorita)

Su destino final será Barcelona, ¿verdad?

Activity 11

Answers

24 1. Le pide unos folletos de las ciudades por las que va su itinerario.
2. No, no tiene. Tiene una guía turística.
3. No, él no necesita una visa.
4. El pasaporte de Blanca se vence en tres años.
5. Answers will vary.
6. Answers will vary.
7. Answers will vary.

Activities

Multiple Intelligences (logical-mathematical). Ask individual students or small groups to develop an itinerary for a two-week trip to Spain. The itinerary should include travel information and information on the cities and places of interest to be visited. Possible resources include library materials, the Internet and travel brochures.

Prereading Strategy. Instruct students to skim the illustration's contents for any words or expressions they already know. Then ask them to imagine where the conversation takes place and what the people are saying to one another. Finally, ask several individuals to state what they believe the main theme of the conversation is.

En la agencia de viajes

vence *expire* folletos *brochures*

24 En la agencia de viajes

Contesta las siguientes preguntas.

1. ¿Qué le pide don Augusto a la agente?
2. ¿Tiene la agente lo que don Augusto le pide? ¿Qué tiene ella?
3. ¿Necesita Alberto una visa para el país adonde va a viajar?
4. ¿Cuándo se vence el pasaporte de Blanca?
5. ¿Tienes un pasaporte? ¿Cuándo se vence?
6. ¿Cómo sabes si se necesita una visa?
7. Si hicieras un viaje a España, ¿qué itinerario te gustaría hacer?

¿Cuál folleto quieres ver?

25 Los preparativos

Haz oraciones en el futuro, para saber lo que las siguientes personas dicen acerca de los preparativos de su viaje.

 Luz/hacer/reservaciones para un viaje de ida y vuelta
Luz hará reservaciones para un viaje de ida y vuelta.

1. José y Carmen/necesitar/una guía turística de Barcelona
2. nosotros/tener/suerte si podemos viajar esta semana
3. mi pasaporte/vencerse/en dos años
4. ellas/tener/que conseguir una visa
5. yo/poder/conseguir mañana folletos de Toledo
6. el agente/saber/el mejor itinerario para visitar España
7. tú/querer/hacer un viaje sencillo
8. Graciela/venir/mañana para hablar del viaje

 ## 26 Preparaciones de un viaje

Imagina que harás un viaje por varios países con un miembro de tu familia y ahora están hablando de lo que será importante recordar para el viaje. Trabajando en parejas, hablen del viaje y de lo que tendrán que hacer para prepararse.

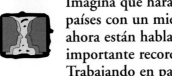

A: ¿Tienes folletos de España?
B: No. Tendré que conseguir algunos.
A: Bueno, yo tengo unas guías turísticas pero son viejas.
B: Entonces tendremos que ir a la agencia de viajes.

España

BARCELONA

Autoevaluación. Como repaso y autoevaluación, responde lo siguiente:
1. What ingredients does a Spanish tortilla have?
2. Where are you going for your next vacation? Describe what you will do and see.
3. Where do you dream going?
4. Name three things that you will do in the future.
5. Imagine that you have a job interview (entrevista) tomorrow. Name three things that you will do to prepare yourself for the interview.
6. List three things that you will have or do in ten years.
7. What do you know about Spain?

Answers

25 1. ...necesitarán....
2. Tendremos....
3. ...se vencerá....
4. ...tendrán....
5. Podré....
6. ...sabrá....
7. Querrás....
8. ...vendrá....

26 Creative self-expression.

Autoevaluación
Possible answers:
1. patata, cebolla, huevo, aceite, sal
2. Answers will vary.
3. Sueño que....
4. Trabajaré en una oficina importante. Viviré en una casa muy grande. Ganaré la lotería.
5. Me peinaré. Me vestiré con ropa cómoda pero elegante. Me iré de casa temprano para no llegar tarde.
6. Tendré mi trabajo ideal.
7. Answers will vary.

Notes
Cultures. Although many people associate bullfighting with Spain, not everyone condones the bullfight. Whereas it is considered an unchanging tradition for many people in the Spanish-speaking countries where bullfights take place, a number of people in these countries as well as throughout the world protest the cruelty the bullfighting inflicts upon the animal.

Activities
Multiple Intelligences (bodily-kinesthetic). Talk with your colleagues in home economics or with the staff of your school cafeteria to see if arrangements can be made for your class to make the recipe for *tortilla española* during school hours. As an alternative, have several students make the recipe at home. Students can either bring in the *tortilla española* for everyone to sample or prepare the dish for a family meal.

NATIONAL STANDARDS
C1.2, C1.3, C2.1, C2.2, C4.1, C5.1, C5.2

Answers

A Creative self-expression.

B Creative self-expression.

Notes

~WWW~ Iberia
http://www.iberia.com/
Travel Information
http://www.lycos.com/travel
City Net (General Information)
http://www.city.net
Subway Navigator (Worldwide)
*http://metro.ratp.fr:10001/bin/
cities/english*

Select several students to share with the class the information they found out in activities A and B.

Activities

Technology. Have students search the Internet for a hotel in Madrid. Determine the subway stop nearest the hotel. (You can find information about subways on the Subway Navigator® home page.) Students must plan a visit to the Prado Museum using the subway: They must determine what line(s) to take from the hotel to the museum. Finally, have students print out a hard copy of the route to use when discussing their trip.

¡La práctica hace al maestro!

A Comunicación

Working with a partner, pretend you are in a travel agency and play the parts of a travel agent and a client planning a vacation. Discuss such things as departure time *(hora de salida),* arrival time *(hora de llegada),* destination *(destino),* schedule *(horario),* what you will see and so forth. Make reservations (you may wish to call an airline or a travel agent to obtain the actual information). Add any other details you wish.

¿Quiere Ud. hacer reservaciones para un viaje a la República Dominicana?

B Conexión con la tecnología

Imagine you are going to Spain for your next vacation. You will fly with *Iberia Airlines* and will depart from Miami, Florida. Search the Internet for the web page for *Iberia* and find flight information in Spanish. Make sure to have the dates you plan to travel, the time you would like to depart and the type of seats you want. Print out the information you get and report to the class on what you found. What are the expenses for your trip?

NATIONAL STANDARDS
C1.1, C1.3, C3.1, C4.1,
C5.1, C5.2

VOCABULARIO

Las vacaciones
aéreo,-a
la agencia de viajes
el agente, la agente
la compañía
de ida y vuelta
el destino
el folleto
el gasto
la guía
el itinerario
la llegada
la maleta
el pasaje
el pasaporte
la reservación
la salida
sencillo,-a
la tarifa
turístico,-a
la visa
el vuelo

La familia real
la princesa
el príncipe
la reina
el rey

Verbos
cargar
gozar
mudar(se)
nacer
saborear
soñar
vencer

Expresiones y otras palabras
a lo mejor
adonde
el cheque
completo,-a
la corrida
la dicha
emocionado,-a
el nombre
el omelet
la pantalla
puede ser
la suerte

¿Dónde estará la oficina de turismo?

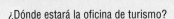

Soñé que volví a nacer y vivía en este
edificio. (Plaza de Cibeles, Madrid.)

Notes
Another word for *maleta* is *valija*.

Review with students how to use
this reference list of words and
expressions as a self-test of the
new active vocabulary for a lesson:
Select two or three words that
students do not know; return to
where the word was first
introduced to see how it was used;
encourage students to try to
determine what the word means.

Activities
Cooperative Learning. Ask
students to say a word they have
learned in Spanish and then select
someone else to spell the word.
Have them check their spelling
and then switch roles.

Critical Thinking. Dictate a letter
of the alphabet to the class. Give
students three minutes to write as
many words as they can think of
in Spanish that begin with that
letter. After calling time, ask
students to read their lists aloud.
The student with the longest list
of correct words wins.

Pronunciation. To ensure proper
pronunciation, model each word
or expression and have students
repeat after you.

NATIONAL STANDARDS
C1.2, C4.1, C5.2

Content reviewed in *Lección 16*
• planning a vacation
• telling time
• schedules

Answers

1. Van al mostrador de la aerolínea.
2. Son cuatro los pasajeros de la familia de Rodrigo.
3. No quieren viajar en la sección de fumar.
4. Llevan cinco maletas y dos maletines como equipaje de mano.
5. El avión sale a las dieciséis horas.
6. Deben abordar por el muelle internacional.
7. Tendrán que pasar primero por emigración.

Notes

Another term for *aerolínea* is *línea aérea* or *compañía aérea*.

Point out that the airline employee uses the twenty-four-hour clock when giving the departure time. *Las dieciséis horas* is equivalent to 4:00 P.M.

Activities

Critical Listening. Play the audiocassette/audio compact disc recording of the dialog as students look at the illustration and imagine what the people are saying to one another. Ask several individuals to state what they believe the main theme of the conversation is. Finally, ask if students know where the conversation takes place (at an airport).

Lección 16

Contexto cultural
ESPAÑA

En el mostrador de la aerolínea

el maletín IBERIA
el pasajero
la pasajera

CAMILA: Allí está el **mostrador°** de la **aerolínea**.

RODRIGO: Ah, sí. Esperen aquí mientras yo voy con Sergio a **registrar°** y **entregar°** el **equipaje.°**

SEÑOR: Buenas tardes. ¿Cuántos **pasajeros** son?

RODRIGO: Somos cuatro.

SEÑOR: Me permiten ver sus pasaportes.

RODRIGO: Sí, señor, aquí están. Preferiríamos estar en la **sección** de no fumar.

SEÑOR: No hay problema. ¿Cuántas **piezas°** de equipaje llevan?

RODRIGO: Llevamos cinco maletas y dos **maletines** como **equipaje de mano.°**

SERGIO: ¿A qué hora sale el avión?

SEÑOR: Su avión saldrá a las dieciséis horas. Deben **abordar°** por el **muelle°** internacional, puerta de salida número ocho, pero tendrán que pasar primero por **emigración**. Feliz viaje.

mostrador *counter* **registrar** *to check in* **entregar** *to hand in* **equipaje** *luggage* **piezas** *pieces* **equipaje de mano** *carry-on luggage* **abordar** *board* **muelle** *concourse, pier*

¿Qué comprendiste?

1. ¿Adónde van Rodrigo y Sergio a registrar y entregar el equipaje?
2. ¿Cuántos son los pasajeros en la familia de Rodrigo?
3. ¿En qué sección del avión no quieren viajar Rodrigo y su familia?
4. ¿Cuántas piezas de equipaje llevan ellos?
5. ¿A qué hora sale el avión de ellos?
6. ¿Por cuál muelle deben abordar el avión?
7. ¿Por dónde tendrán ellos que pasar primero?

2 Charlando

1. ¿En qué sección del avión te gusta viajar?
2. ¿Cuántas maletas llevas cuando vas de viaje?
3. ¿Cuántas piezas de equipaje de mano llevas cuando vas de viaje?
4. ¿Has pasado por emigración alguna vez? ¿Qué hiciste allí?

¿Dónde se entrega el equipaje?

Algo más

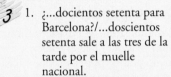

La hora de veinticuatro horas

Schedules sometimes are written using a twenty-four-hour clock. As you travel in the Spanish-speaking parts of the world, you will often encounter schedules for trains, planes, ships, movies and television programs that appear unrecognizable to someone who is not familiar with this cultural point. Actually, the twenty-four-hour clock is quite simple and can be helpful in determining if an event occurs during the daytime or at night. Look at the following and compare the times as they would be stated using a twenty-four-hour clock:

9:15   *Son las nueve y cuarto de la mañana.*
15:30   *Son las tres y media de la tarde.* (15:30 - 12:00 = 3:30)
22:55   *Son las once menos cinco de la noche.* (22:55 - 12:00 = 10:55)

¿Qué hora es?

3 Trabajando en el mostrador de una aerolínea

Imagina que trabajas en el mostrador de una aerolínea en el aeropuerto Barajas de Madrid, contestando el teléfono de información sobre salidas de vuelos. Trabajando en parejas, alterna con tu compañero/a de clase en preguntar la hora de salida de los vuelos y en contestar, diciendo la hora y el muelle de donde salen. Sigue el modelo.

A: ¿A qué hora sale el vuelo ciento cincuenta y cinco para Sevilla?
B: El vuelo ciento cincuenta y cinco sale a las dos y media de la tarde por el muelle nacional.

SALIDAS

Ciudad	Vuelos	Hora	Muelle
Sevilla	155	14:30	Nacional
Barcelona	270	15:00	Nacional
Buenos Aires	015	16:45	Internacional
Nueva York	310	17:15	Internacional
Granada	068	20:00	Nacional

Capítulo 8   345

Answers

2 Answers will vary.

3
1. ¿...docientos setenta para Barcelona?/...doscientos setenta sale a las tres de la tarde por el muelle nacional.
2. ¿...cero quince para Buenos Aires?/...cero quince sale a las cuatro y cuarenta y cinco de la tarde por el muelle internacional.
3. ¿...trescientos diez para Nueva York?/...trescientos diez sale a las cinco y cuarto de la tarde por el muelle internacional.
4. ¿...cero sesenta y ocho para Granada?/...cero sesenta y ocho sale a las ocho de la noche por el muelle nacional.

Activities

Cooperative Learning. After introducing and practicing the dialog on page 344 (playing the audiocassette/audio compact disc, modeling words and phrases for student repetition, practicing travel vocabulary, etc.), have students work in small groups practicing the dialog. Circulate and assist with pronunciation and intonation.

Expansion. Additional questions (*¿Qué comprendiste?*): *¿Con quién va Rodrigo al mostrador?*; *¿Qué le pide el señor del mostrador a Rodrigo?*; *¿A qué puerta de salida deben ir Rodrigo y su familia?*; *¿Qué les desea el señor de la aerolínea a Rodrigo y a su familia?*

NATIONAL STANDARDS
C1.1, C1.2, C1.3, C4.1, C5.1

Notes

Renfe is an acronym that stands for *Red nacional de ferrocarriles españoles.*

Activities

Connections. Show students where the places named in the *Conexión cultural* on page 347 are located, using the maps in the front of the book or the transparencies that are part of this program.

Pronunciation. A typical Spanish tongue twister makes reference to trains and helps practice the trilled *-rr*: *Erre con erre cigarro, erre con erre barril, rápido corren los carros por la línea del ferrocarril.*

TPR. Using the train schedule on page 346, make several statements about departure times as students point to the correct time: *El tren sale para Zaragoza a las cuatro y cuarto de la tarde.* (Students should point to 16:15 on the line for Zaragoza.)

4 Trenes Renfe

¿A qué hora saldrán los trenes de Madrid para estas ciudades? Trabajando en parejas, alterna con tu compañero/a de clase en hacer y contestar preguntas, según las horas de salida.

La estación de trenes Atocha en Madrid, España.

Horario de trenes Renfe De Madrid a:

Ciudad	Horas de salida						
La Coruña	06:15	21:50					
Salamanca	00:15	04:45	08:00	11:15	17:45	21:00	
Murcia	06:10	22:55					
Toledo	06:00	08:30	11:00	16:00	21:00	23:30	
Córdoba	06:05	08:50	11:35	18:50	21:35		
San Sebastián	00:15	04:45	08:00	11:15	17:45	21:00	23:30
Zaragoza	01:15	04:15	16:15	23:15			
Granada	05:55	08:50	11:45	14:40	17:35	20:30	
Sevilla	06:05	21:35	24:00				

Oportunidades

En el aeropuerto

Airports can be excellent places to practice a world language since many people from different parts of the world travel through them. If you are traveling to or from a Spanish-speaking city or country, it is possible that you will meet people who speak Spanish. Test your skills and chat with someone. When you are checking in at an airport where Spanish is spoken, chances are that the airline agent will speak to you in Spanish as well.

¿Me permite ver su pasaporte?

Conexión *cultural*

España

La historia de España es muy rica y fascinante. La geografía española ha contribuido a la diversidad de la nación. La España de hoy y sus cuarenta millones de habitantes son como un espejo que reflejan la historia y la geografía del país.

Madrid, la capital, es la ciudad más grande del país y es el centro del gobierno. También allí está la corona española, representada por los reyes de España. La ciudad está ubicada aproximadamente en el centro del país. La ciudad ofrece algunas de las muestras más importantes de arte del mundo en el Museo del Prado. La cosmopolita ciudad de Barcelona, el puerto más grande del país, está situada en la costa este de España en la región más rica y poblada del país. La arquitectura de Antonio Gaudí se ve en varios lugares de esta ciudad. La tercera ciudad en población de España, Valencia, está ubicada en la costa mediterránea, al sur de Barcelona. Esta área es famosa tanto por su producción industrial como por sus productos agrícolas. En contraste directo con estas ciudades grandes y cosmopolitas, España también tiene numerosas ciudades pequeñas y pueblos donde la vida tiene un ritmo más lento.

El Museo del Prado.

Al sur de Madrid, en la región de Castilla-La Mancha, los veranos son muy calientes y los inviernos muy fríos. El clima es muy diferente en la región pesquera y agrícola de Galicia, que está en la parte noroeste del país. Aunque esta región sólo representa un séptimo del tamaño del país, recibe un tercio de la lluvia anual de España.

Una calle de Madrid, España.

Algunas personas creen que el corazón y el alma de España están representados por la región de Andalucía, al sur del país. Allí uno puede ver la arquitectura mora que quedó de la ocupación musulmana de la ciudad de Sevilla. Otras ciudades de la región de Andalucía donde se ve reflejada la historia musulmana de España son Málaga, Córdoba y Granada.

Ella baila flamenco, un baile típico español.

España

Quiz/Activity 3

Activity 2

Notes

España
General Information
http://www.sispain.org/spanish/

When reading the *Conexión cultural* on Spain, some students may have difficulty with the following words: *contribuido* (contributed), *reflejan* (reflect), *gobierno* (government), *corona* (crown), *muestras* (specimens), *situada* (situated), *poblada* (populated), *agrícolas* (agricultural), *pueblos* (towns), *un tercio* (one-third), *alma* (soul), *mora* (Moorish) and *musulmana* (Moslem).

The most famous work of Antonio Gaudí is the unfinished church *La Sagrada Familia*, which has become a symbol of Barcelona.

Activities

Prereading Strategy. This *Conexión cultural* provides an opportunity for students to increase what they know about the Spanish-speaking world by reading about Spain in Spanish. The vocabulary and structures have been controlled to enable individuals to read in the target language and enjoy the experience. Note for the class that it is not essential to understand every word in order to read Spanish. The meaning of important but unknown passive vocabulary has been provided to facilitate an enjoyable experience. Before beginning the *Conexión cultural*, consider asking some general preparation questions about the theme of the reading: What is Spain's capital? Where is Spain located? What else do students know about Spain? Then have students skim the *Conexión cultural* for cognates and any words or expressions they already know.

NATIONAL STANDARDS
C1.2, C3.2, C4.1, C5.2

Quiz/Activity 4

Activities 3-4

Quizzes/Activities 2-3

Answers

5
1. La capital de España es Madrid.
2. El Museo del Prado está en la capital de España.
3. Es de Antonio Gaudí.
4. Los veranos son muy calientes y los inviernos muy fríos en la región de Castilla-La Mancha.
5. Creen que está representado en la región de Andalucía.

Notes

The conditional-tense endings are the same as the *-er* and *-ir* endings for the imperfect tense. Before beginning the conditional, review the imperfect with students. Then have students change verbs from the imperfect tense to the conditional.

Point out that all conditional forms take a written accent.

Activities

Connections. Have students prepare a report explaining the contributions of the Arabs to Spain.

Critical Thinking. Say the future tense of several verbs and call on students to give the conditional tense of each.

XIONES

5 Cruzando fronteras

¿Qué sabes sobre España? Contesta las siguientes preguntas.

1. ¿Cuál es la capital de España?
2. ¿Qué museo importante está en la capital de España?
3. ¿De quién es la arquitectura que se ve en varios lugares de Barcelona?
4. ¿En qué región española los veranos son muy calientes y los inviernos muy fríos?
5. ¿En dónde creen algunas personas que está representado el corazón y el alma de España?

La Casa Batlló fue diseñada por Antonio Gaudí. (Barcelona, España.)

IDIOMA

El condicional

Just as the future tense in Spanish is used to tell what will happen, the conditional tense *(el condicional)* tells what would happen or what someone would do (under certain conditions). It is usually formed by adding the endings *-ía, -ías, -ía, -íamos, -íais* and *-ían* to the infinitive form of the verb.

viajar	
viajaría	viajaríamos
viajarías	viajaríais
viajaría	viajarían

comer	
comería	comeríamos
comerías	comeríais
comería	comerían

abrir	
abriría	abriríamos
abrirías	abriríais
abriría	abrirían

Look at the following examples:

Me gustaría ir a la ciudad de Toledo.
¿Viajarías allí pronto?
¡Sería maravilloso!
¿Irías tú en tren o en avión?

I would like to go to the city of Toledo.
Would you **travel** there soon?
That **would be** marvellous!
Would you **go** by train or by plane?

¿Te gustaría viajar a Segovia?

6 ¿Qué dijeron todos?

Completa las siguientes oraciones con la forma del condicional de los verbos indicados, para saber lo que dijeron en el mostrador de la aerolínea las siguientes personas.

 Rodrigo dijo que él <u>preferiría</u> llevar sólo un maletín como equipaje de mano. (preferir)

1. La señorita nos dijo que sólo <u>(1)</u> dos piezas de equipaje por cada pasajero. (registrar)
2. Un señor nos dijo que nosotros <u>(2)</u> abordar el avión en quince minutos. (deber)
3. Unas mujeres dijeron que <u>(3)</u> a alguien que las ayude con sus maletas. (necesitar)
4. Camila y Yolanda dijeron que <u>(4)</u> en la cafetería mientras Rodrigo hace el registro. (estar)
5. Dije que yo <u>(5)</u> ir primero a emigración. (preferir)
6. Camila dijo que le <u>(6)</u> sentarse en el corredor. (gustar)
7. Rodrigo y Yolanda dijeron que <u>(7)</u> viajar en la sección de no fumar. (preferir)

7 Volver a nacer

Di lo que a las siguientes personas les gustaría hacer si volvieran a nacer, usando el condicional. Añade las palabras que sean necesarias.

 Graciela y su hermano/ser/príncipes
Graciela y su hermano serían principes.

1. tú/aprender/volar un avión
2. yo/escribir/libro sobre cómo ser feliz
3. Camila/nacer/España
4. Sergio/trabajar/agencia de viajes
5. Yolanda/vivir/reyes de España
6. nosotros/conocer/más gente interesante
7. Rodrigo/viajar/todo el mundo
8. Mónica e Inés/gustarles/trabajar como agente de viajes

¿AGENCIA DE VIAJES?

Si volvieran a nacer, serían princesa y príncipe.

 Activity 7

Answers

6 1. registraría
   2. deberíamos
   3. necesitarían
   4. estarían
   5. preferiría
   6. gustaría
   7. preferirían

7 1. ...aprenderías a volar un avión.
   2. ...escribiría un libro sobre cómo ser feliz.
   3. ...nacería en España.
   4. ...trabajaría en una agencia de viajes.
   5. ...viviría con los reyes de España.
   6. ...conoceríamos a más gente interesante.
   7. ...viajaría por todo el mundo.
   8. A Mónica e Inés les gustaría trabajar como agente de viajes.

Notes

Explain that the conditional tense is usually paired with a verb in the past tense, whereas the future tense is usually paired with a verb in the present tense.

Activities

Students with Special Needs. Ask if students can figure out the meaning of *si volvieran a nacer* (if they were born again) in activity 7. The formation of the imperfect subjunctive *(volvieran)* will be presented in *Somos así ¡YA!*

Answers

8 1. Correrías....
2. Iría....
3. Esperaríamos....
4. Dejarían....
5. Pondría....
6. Pediría....

9 1. ¿...llevarías?/Llevaría....
2. ¿...viajarías?/Viajaría....
3. ¿...irías?/No iría....
4. ¿...volarías?/Volaría....
5. ¿...estarías...?/Estaría....
6. ¿...visitarías?/Visitaría....

Notes

The conditional tense is commonly used with the verbs *deber, gustar* and *poder,* as well as with other verbs, to reflect courtesy or to politely suggest something. Note, however, that the conditional tense is not used to express **would** in the sense of past habitual action, for which the imperfect is used: *De niña, yo pasaba los inviernos en las montañas.* (As a child, I would spend every winter in the mountains.)

Activities

Expansion. Ask students to consider what they would be if they were not human: *¿Qué animal serías?; ¿Qué color serías?; ¿Qué estación del año serías?; ¿Qué día de la semana serías?;* etc.

NATIONAL STANDARDS
C1.1, C1.2, C1.3, C4.1, C4.2, C5.1

 8 ## ¿Qué harían?

Di lo que harían las siguientes personas en cada una de las siguientes situaciones, usando las indicaciones que se dan.

 Paloma olvidó su equipaje de mano en la casa. (viajar en otro vuelo)
Viajaría en otro vuelo.

1. Tienes que abordar en cinco minutos por el muelle nacional, pero estás en el muelle internacional. (correr al muelle nacional)
2. Tengo un problema para salir del país y estoy en el aeropuerto. (ir a la oficina de emigración)
3. No llegamos a tiempo al aeropuerto y perdemos nuestro avión a Toledo. (esperar para tomar el siguiente vuelo)
4. Los chicos no pueden registrar todo su equipaje. (dejar una maleta con sus padres)
5. Felipe tiene mucha ropa para llevar. (poner todo en dos maletas)
6. Doña Isabel tiene que llevar cinco maletas. (pedir ayuda a alguien)

 9 ## Dando consejos

Imagina que tú eres una persona con experiencia en viajar a España y todos te hacen preguntas para pedirte consejos. Trabajando en parejas, alterna con tu compañero/a de clase en hacer preguntas y en contestarlas, usando el condicional y la información que sea apropiada.

Iría a Segovia para ver el Alcázar.

dónde/comprar los pasajes
A: ¿Dónde comprarías los pasajes?
B: Compraría los pasajes en la agencia de viajes.

1. cuántas piezas de equipaje/llevar
2. en qué sección del avión/viajar
3. adónde/no ir
4. en qué aerolínea/volar
5. a qué hora/estar en el aeropuerto
6. qué ciudades/visitar

Proverbios y dichos
Plan ahead and do things when you are able to because you never can be certain there will be enough time tomorrow. Try to complete what you can today and do not postpone tasks. Do not procrastinate. As the saying goes: *No dejes para mañana lo que puedas hacer hoy* (Do not put off for tomorrow what can be done today).

10 ¡No dejes para mañana lo que puedas hacer hoy!

Lorenzo siempre promete muchas cosas pero nunca las cumple porque es perezoso. Completa el siguiente párrafo con la forma apropiada del condicional para ver lo que no hizo.

Lorenzo les prometió a sus padres y a su novia que haría muchas cosas durante el verano. Le dijo a su padre que *1. (buscar)* un trabajo, *2. (cortar)* el césped y *3. (lavar)* el carro cada semana. No lo hizo. Le dijo a su madre que *4. (levantarse)* temprano y la *5. (ayudar)* en el jardín. Tampoco lo hizo. Le prometió a su novia que los dos *6. (ir)* a la playa, *7. (ver)* buenas películas y *8. (jugar)* al tenis. No hicieron ninguna de estas cosas. ¡Ahora, parece que nadie quiere ayudarlo a él! Ayer, le pidió dinero a su padre, y su padre le contestó: "Mañana". Le preguntó a su madre si le *9. (comprar)* ropa nueva y ella respondió: "Un día de éstos". Cuando le dijo a su novia que le *10. (gustar)* invitarla a cenar, ella le contestó: "¡Nunca más!". Ahora Lorenzo entiende por qué se dice: *¡No dejes para mañana lo que puedas hacer hoy!*

Bienvenidos a su vuelo número 108

La tripulación les da la bienvenida a su vuelo número 108, sin escalas.

Por favor, podrían abrocharse los cinturones de seguridad y colocar sus respaldares en posición vertical.

el compartimiento

la auxiliar de vuelo

el auxiliar de vuelo

No, mijita. Va a despegar.

el piloto

¿El avión va a aterrizar?

la mesita

tripulación *crew* **bienvenida** *welcome* **escalas** *stopover* **aterrizar** *to land* **despegar** *to take off* **abrocharse** *to fasten* **colocar** poner **respaldares** *seat-back*

Answers

10 1. buscaría
    2. cortaría
    3. lavaría
    4. se levantaría
    5. ayudaría
    6. irían
    7. verían
    8. jugarían
    9. compraría
   10. gustaría

Notes

Point out that the word for **welcome** (*bienvenido*) acts as an adjective and therefore can have four different forms. In this case the plural *bienvenidos* is used for male and female passengers.

Another word for *el respaldar* is *el respaldo.*

Other ways of referring to the *auxiliar de vuelo* include *azafata, aeromozo (aeromoza)* and *sobrecargo.*

Activities

Critical Listening. Play the audiocassette/audio compact disc recording of the dialog. Instruct students to cover the words as they listen to the conversation in order to develop good listening skills before concentrating on their ability to read Spanish. Have students look at the illustration and imagine what the people are saying to one another. Ask several individuals to state what they believe the main theme of the conversation is. Finally, ask if students know where the conversation takes place (on an airplane).

NATIONAL STANDARDS
C1.2, C4.1

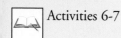

Notes

The conditional stems are highlighted in bold in this *Algo más*. All endings are first- or third-person singular for consistency.

Go over the list of verbs with a modified future stem and have students contrast their future form with their conditional form.

Activities

Students with Special Needs. For additional practice, give different subjects for the listed verbs and ask students to give the corresponding conditional forms of each. For example, you say *poder/tú;* the student must say *podrías.*

---

11 **Viajando en avión**

Contesta las siguientes preguntas.

1. ¿Has viajado en avión alguna vez? ¿Cuándo?
2. ¿Hizo el avión alguna escala? ¿Dónde?
3. ¿Te gustaría ser miembro de la tripulación de un avión? ¿Qué te gustaría ser?
4. ¿Te gusta más cuando un avión despega o cuando aterriza? ¿Por qué?
5. ¿Crees que las medidas de seguridad que se toman en un avión son buenas? Explica.

IBERIA B
LINEAS AEREAS DE ESPAÑA
GRUPO

Algo más

El condicional de los verbos irregulares

Verbs that are irregular in the future tense have identical irregular stems in the conditional. However, their endings remain the same as for regular verbs.

- Verbs that drop the letter *e* from the infinitive ending:

  caber → **cabría**   *poder* → **podría**   *querer* → **querría**   *saber* → **sabría**

- Verbs that change the vowel of the infinitive endings *-er* and *-ir* to *d:*

  poner → **pondría**   *salir* → **saldría**   *tener* → **tendría**   *venir* → **vendría**

- Drop the letters *e* and *c* from the infinitives of *decir* and *hacer* before adding the future-tense endings.

  decir → **diría**   *hacer* → **haría**

Podrías visitar al rey y a la reina aquí en su palacio. (Madrid, España.)

12 ¿Qué cosas harías en el avión?

Haz oraciones completas, usando el condicional. Añade las palabras que sean necesarias.

> poder/dormir durante todo/vuelo
> Podría dormir durante todo el vuelo.

1. jugar/ajedrez sobre/mesita de la silla
2. hablar/con toda/tripulación
3. colocar/el respaldar/posición vertical
4. poner/el equipaje de mano/compartimiento
5. tener/un poco de miedo/aterrizar
6. abrocharme/el cinturón de seguridad/despegar
7. querer/volar en al avión con el piloto
8. decirle/al piloto que me deje volar/avión

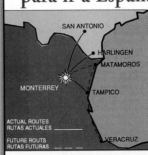

EN SU VIAJE DE NEGOCIOS O DE PLACER ...
Somos su mejor compañía para ir a España

Siendo la primera línea aérea alimentadora en México que cubre Rutas Internacionales y en conjunto con Mexicana de Aviación, Aeromonterrey responde a las necesidades del demandante mercado de la región noreste de México y el Estado de Texas en Los Estados Unidos, con Servicios Aéreos de Excelente Calidad. Al volar con nosotros confirmará que Aeromonterrey es su mejor compañía!

SAN ANTONIO
HARLINGEN
MATAMOROS
MONTERREY
TAMPICO
ACTUAL ROUTES RUTAS ACTUALES _____
FUTURE ROUTS RUTAS FUTURAS _____
VERACRUZ

Yo le contaría chistes al auxiliar de vuelo.

13 ¿Qué no harían?

Di lo que no harían (would not do) nunca las siguientes personas, usando el condicional. Luego, di lo que preferirían hacer.

> yo
> (Yo) Nunca entregaría todo mi equipaje en el mostrador. Preferiría siempre llevar conmigo un equipaje de mano con algunas cosas personales.

1. el profesor/la profesora
2. mis amigos/amigas y yo
3. el cantante Enrique Iglesias
4. el presidente de los Estados Unidos
5. la actriz Jennifer López
6. mis padres
7. mi mejor amigo/amiga
8. tú

NATIONAL STANDARDS
C1.2, C4.1, C5.2

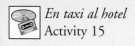

En taxi al hotel
Activity 15

Answers

14 Creative self-expression.

15 1. No, van a alojarse en un hotel.
2. Van en taxi.
3. Llegaron a las seis de la mañana, hora de Madrid.
4. Lo bueno fue que revisaron rápido las maletas en la aduana.
5. Se pregunta si Graciela iría ayer a la casa para darle de comer a su perro.

Notes

The taxi driver makes reference to *paradores,* which are government-run inns that tend to be located in historical buildings and out-of-the-way places.

Taxi procedures may vary from one country to another. In Spain's larger cities it is easy to hail a cab on the street. The charge is determined by the amount indicated on the *taxímetro* (meter) upon reaching the destination.

Activities

Critical Listening. Play the audiocassette/audio compact disc recording of the dialog. Instruct students to cover the words as they listen to the conversation in order to develop good listening skills before concentrating on their ability to read Spanish. Have students look at the illustration and imagine what the people are saying to one another. Ask several individuals to state what they believe the main theme of the conversation is. Finally, ask if students know where the conversation takes place (in a taxi on the way to a hotel).

NATIONAL STANDARDS
C1.2, C2.1, C3.1, C4.1, C5.1

354   **Lección 16**

14 Con cinco millones de dólares...

Imagina que has ganado cinco millones de dólares. Trabajando en parejas, alterna con tu compañero/a de clase en hacer preguntas y en contestarlas para saber seis cosas que cada uno/a haría con ese dinero.

A: ¿Qué sería lo primero que tú harías con cinco millones de dólares?
B: Haría un viaje por todo el mundo.

En taxi al hotel

SEÑOR: ¿Van a **alojarse°** en algún **parador?°**
RODRIGO: No, señor. Por favor, llévenos al **hotel** *Novotel.*
SEÑOR: Con gusto.
YOLANDA: ¡Fue un viaje muy largo! ¿A qué hora llegamos?
RODRIGO: Llegamos a las seis de la mañana, hora de Madrid y ya son las siete y media.
SERGIO: Lo bueno fue que nos **revisaron°** rápido las maletas en la **aduana.°**
YOLANDA: Sí, tuvimos suerte. ¿En qué piensas, Camila?
CAMILA: Pienso si Graciela iría ayer a la casa para darle de comer a mi perro.
YOLANDA: ¡Claro! No te preocupes. Tu perro estará bien.

alojarse *to stay, to lodge* **parador** *inn* **revisaron** *checked* **aduana** *customs*

15 ¿Qué comprendiste?

1. ¿Van Rodrigo y su familia a alojarse en un parador?
2. ¿Cómo van ellos al hotel?
3. ¿A qué hora llegaron a su destino?
4. ¿Qué fue lo bueno, según Sergio?
5. ¿Qué se pregunta Camila?

Por favor, llévenos al hotel.

16 En el aeropuerto

Todos en el aeropuerto hacen preguntas. Trabajando en parejas, alterna con tu compañero/a de clase en preguntar y en contestar a qué hora ocurrirán las siguientes cosas. Usa las pistas que se dan.

aterrizar/el próximo avión (1:30 P.M.)
A: ¿A qué hora aterrizará el próximo avión?
B: Aterrizará a la una y media de la tarde.

1. llegar/Pedro y Lucía a Madrid (10:30 A.M.)
2. servir el desayuno/ellos (6:30 A.M.)
3. alojarse/tus amigos en el hotel (8:00 P.M.)
4. despegar/tu avión (2:00 P.M.)
5. estar/Graciela en la aduana (4:15 P.M.)
6. salir/el piloto (1:50 P.M.)
7. ser/la bienvenida en el hotel (8:30 P.M.)

En la recepción del hotel

Si dudas, pregunta.

Ajuntament de Barcelona

RODRIGO: Buenos días. Tenemos una reservación.
SEÑOR: Sus **apellidos,**° por favor.
RODRIGO: Hernández Rojas.
SEÑOR: Señor Hernández, Ud. tiene una reservación para una **habitación**° con una cama **doble** y dos **sencillas,**° por cinco noches, ¿verdad?
RODRIGO: Sí, y preferiríamos una habitación donde no escuchemos el **ruido**° de la calle.
SEÑOR: ¡Cómo no! Señor Hernández, ¿podría **firmar**° aquí?
RODRIGO: Sí, claro.
YOLANDA: Perdón, señor, ¿tiene la habitación agua **potable**° y **servicio al cuarto?**
SEÑOR: Sí, señora. Aquí esta su llave. **En seguida**° el **botones** los llevará a su habitación. ¡Bienvenidos al hotel! Es un **placer**° tenerlos aquí.

apellidos *last names, surnames* **habitación** *room* **sencillas** *single* **ruido** *noise* **firmar** *to sign*
potable *drinkable* **En seguida** *Immediately* **placer** *pleasure*

¿A qué hora?
Remember to ask when something is going to occur (or has already occurred) using the question *¿A qué hora...?* Answer using *a la/las* followed by the time.

| ¿A qué hora llegaron a Madrid? | Llegamos **a las** seis. |
| ¿A qué hora estarán en el hotel? | Vamos a estar en el hotel en una hora, **a las** siete. |

En la recepción del hotel
Activity 16

Quiz/Activity 6

Activity 8

Answers

16
1. ¿...llegarán...?/Llegarán a las diez y media de la mañana.
2. ¿...servirán...?/Servirán el desayuno a las seis y media de la mañana.
3. ¿...se alojarán...?/Se alojarán a las ocho de la noche.
4. ¿...despegará...?/Despegará a las dos de la tarde.
5. ¿...estará...?/Estará a las cuatro y cuarto de la tarde.
6. ¿...saldrá...?/Saldrá a las dos menos diez de la tarde.
7. ¿...será...?/Será a las ocho y media de la noche.

Notes

It is interesting to note that the hotel employees called *botones* get their name from the large buttons found on their traditional uniforms.

Activities

Cooperative Learning. Divide the class into groups of two. Each group prepares a conversation in Spanish between a hotel clerk and a tourist who wants a room.

Prereading Strategy. Ask students to describe what it was like at the last hotel where they stayed overnight with their parents. Find out what the check-in procedure was like and any other circumstances or amenities they remember. Then, instruct students to cover the dialog with one hand and to look at the illustration. Ask them to imagine where the conversation takes place and what the people are saying to one another. Finally, have students look through the dialog quickly to find cognates and any words or expressions they already know.

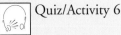
NATIONAL STANDARDS
C1.1, C1.2, C4.1, C4.2, C5.2

Answers

17 1. Está en la recepción del hotel.
2. Los apellidos de Rodrigo son Hernández Rojas.
3. La reservación es para una habitación con cama doble y dos camas sencillas por cinco noches.
4. Preferirían una habitación en donde no escuchen el ruido de la calle.
5. Tiene agua potable.
6. El botones los llevará en seguida a la habitación.
7. Es un placer tenerlos a ellos en el hotel.

18 Answers will vary.

Notes

The currency of Spain has been the *peseta*. However, the European Community is phasing out the currencies of member nations and replacing them with a common currency called the *euro*.

Activities

Critical Thinking. Ask students to explain why Rodrigo gives two last names: *Hernández Rojas*. Remind students that they have already learned that in Spanish-speaking countries people have two last names, the first being their father's and the second being their mother's.

Expansion. Additional questions (*¿Qué comprendiste?*): *¿Cómo es el hotel?*; *¿Para cuántas personas es la reservación?*

Additional questions (*Charlando*): *¿Te molesta el ruido para dormir?*; *¿Es importante para ti que una habitación de un hotel tenga servicio al cuarto?*

Technology. In groups of three have students find a list of *paradores* in the Madrid area. They must choose two where they would like to stay and then write down why they want to stay there.

17 ¿Qué comprendiste?

1. ¿En qué parte del hotel está la familia Hernández?
2. ¿Cuáles son los apellidos de Rodrigo?
3. ¿Cómo es la reservación de la familia Hernández?
4. ¿Cómo preferirían la habitación?
5. Además de servicio al cuarto, ¿qué más tiene la habitación?
6. ¿Quién los llevará a la habitación?
7. ¿Qué es un placer para el recepcionista?

¿En qué parte del hotel están ellos?

Algo más

¿Dónde nos alojamos?

As you travel, you will find a wide range of places to lodge. For example, you may wish to stay in a government-run *parador*, a *pensión* (which offers both lodging and meals for one price) or you may instead decide to stay at any of a wide selection of private hotels.

El parador de Alarcón es un antiguo castillo. (Cuenca, España.)

Hotels often are rated according to their cleanliness, amenities offered, price range and so forth. In some Spanish-speaking countries, hotels may be classified as follows: *de lujo* (luxury), *de primera clase* (first-class), *de segunda clase* (second-class) and *de tercera clase* (third-class). Elsewhere, hotels may be ranked in categories according to the number of stars (*estrellas*) they are awarded. For example, *cinco estrellas* (five stars) is an expensive hotel that has very strict standards and offers many amenities to guests.

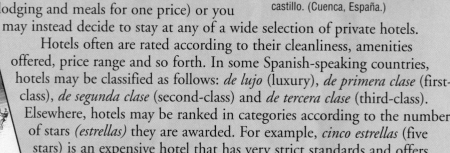
Con muchas alternativas
Hotel Vejo
REINOSA · CANTABRIA

18 Charlando

1. ¿Cuál es tu apellido?
2. ¿Es tu cama doble o sencilla?
3. Cuando viajas, ¿en qué clase de hoteles te gusta alojarte?
4. ¿Cómo era el último hotel donde estuviste? ¿Dónde estaba?

Oportunidades

Los hoteles

Traveling to Spanish-speaking countries is a great opportunity to practice your skills in the language. A hotel may be one of the first places you will have the chance to speak in Spanish. Do not be shy and miss that opportunity. Encourage yourself to see how much you can understand and what you can say. You probably will find out that many employees at large hotels speak English, but do not let that stop you from practicing your Spanish. Give it your best effort and do not worry about making mistakes.

19 En Novotel

Imagina cómo sería la vida en el hotel Novotel. Lee el aviso del hotel, y luego contesta las preguntas que siguen.

1. ¿Qué tendrías en la habitación?
2. ¿Cuántos canales tendrías en la televisión?
3. ¿Cómo sería el desayuno, además de variado?
4. ¿Hasta qué hora tendrías tiempo para ir a comer al restaurante Le Grill?
5. ¿En cuántos hoteles de la misma compañía podrías alojarte en España?

En Novotel
no tenemos habitaciones con número.
Tenemos clientes con nombre.

La sonrisa es la mejor forma de expresar la calidad del servicio. Ningún cliente se siente extraño en NOVOTEL.

La comodidad es nuestro éxito.
Habitaciones con todas las comodidades, TV (6 canales), radio-despertador, minibar... para que su estancia sea más confortable.

El más variado y completo desayuno buffet para iniciar su jornada.

Restaurante "LE GRILL" abierto desde las 6.00 h. hasta las 24.00 h. ininterrumpidamente para degustar desde el plato más simple hasta la más elaborada recomendación del chef.

En NOVOTEL cuidamos los detalles.

novotel
Novotel. Para vivirlo

NOVOTEL MADRID	NOVOTEL GERONA	NOVOTEL COSTA DEL SOL-MIJAS
Albacete,1. 28027 MADRID	Autopista A-7, salida 8	Ctra. Mijas a Fuengirola, Km. 4.
Tel.(91) 405 46 00. Telex 41862 NOVMD	Riudellots de la Selva- GERONA	29650 Mijas. (MALAGA)
TELEFAX (91) 404 11 05	Tel. (972) 47 71 00 Telex 57238	Tel. (952) 48 64 00. Telex 79696
	Telefax (972) 47 72 96	

Whereas *catalán* (Catalan) is a Romance language like Spanish, Portuguese, French, Romanian and Italian, the origin of the Basque language, *eusquera*, is unknown and remains a mystery.

Activities

Connections. Have students find out all the languages that are spoken in Spain and in what region.

Critical Thinking. Given that Spanish (*español, castellano*), *catalán* and *gallego* are Romance languages, there are certain similarities among the three. Ask interested students to obtain an example of *catalán* or *gallego* from the Internet and see which words are similar to Spanish.

Conexión *cultural*

Ella es española y rubia.

La diversidad cultural española

Spain is a country of contrasts. Many Spaniards are fair and blond because their ancestors were Celts. Other people have dark complexions because their ancestors were Moors. Spain's diversity is reflected in the languages spoken by Spaniards in different parts of the country, as well.

Although Spanish (which sometimes is referred to as *castellano)* is the nation's official language, a significant number of people speak other languages as well. For example, many of the Basque people who live in the northern region of *el País Vasco* speak *eusquera*. Likewise, people who live in the northeastern region of *Cataluña* speak *catalán*.

Soy del País Vasco y hablo eusquera.

DICIONARIU CASTELLAN-ASTURIANU

CASTELLAN - ASTURIANU
DICIONARIU

PRINCIPAU D'ASTURIES
CONSEYERÍA D'EDUCACIÓN,
CULTURA Y DEPORTE

La Voz de Asturias

ALIMENTACIÓ - FORÉS

26

Se habla catalán en Barcelona.

Soy de Andalucía, al sur de España.

20 Cruzando fronteras

Haz un mapa de España y añade el nombre de la capital del país, las ciudades principales, las montañas, los lagos, los ríos y otros puntos geográficos que puedas. Luego, colorea los lugares donde se habla eusquera y catalán. Puedes consultar el mapa de España que está en este libro, o un atlas, si lo deseas.

21 Organizando un viaje

Imagina que irás de viaje a España. ¿En qué orden *(order)* ocurrirían las siguientes situaciones?

1. Revisarían el equipaje en la aduana.
2. Abordaría el avión en el muelle internacional.
3. Entregaría el equipaje.
4. Conseguiría un pasaporte.
5. Me abrocharía el cinturón.
6. Me alojaría en un parador.
7. Haría la reservación de una habitación con una cama sencilla.
8. El botones me llevaría a la habitación.
9. Compraría un pasaje de ida y vuelta.
10. Iría a una agencia de viajes.
11. El avión aterrizaría.
12. Iría al mostrador de la aerolínea.
13. Querría ir a España.
14. El avión despegaría.
15. Pondría mi ropa en una maleta.

VIAJES

C O P A L A S.A. de C.V.

- ASESORES DE VIAJES
- VENTA DE BOLETOS Y EXCURSIONES
  NACIONALES E INTERNACIONALES
- RENTA DE AUTOMOVILES
- RESERVACIONES DE HOTELES

SERVICIO A DOMICILIO GRATUITO

TELS. 82-83-26 * 82-82-37
81-32-89 * 81-32-98 * 81-32-79
FAX: 82-80-20

BELISARIO DOMINGUEZ No. 2313-1 ALTOS

Activity 9

Quiz/Activity 6

Answers

20 Check maps for accuracy.

21 Possible order:
13, 10, 9, 7, 4, 15, 12, 3, 2, 5, 14, 11, 1, 6, 8

Activities

Expansion. Discuss with the class the meaning of the advertisement on this page: What kind of company is this? What do they do? What is their phone numbers?

NATIONAL STANDARDS
C1.2, C4.1, C5.1

Algo más

El condicional de probabilidad

Just as the future tense is used in Spanish to express uncertainty or probability in the present, the conditional tense expresses what was uncertain or probable in the past. Compare the following:

Serían las seis cuando salieron.	**It must have been (probably was)** six when they left.
Sergio hablaría a su novia.	**Sergio was probably talking** to his girlfriend.
Irían solos.	**They probably went (must have gone)** alone.

22 ¿Qué fue probable?

Catalina no está segura de que muchas cosas pasaron. Usa el condicional de probabilidad para indicar lo que fue probable, según Catalina, de acuerdo con la información que se da.

 Mi hermano me dijo que iba a salir temprano para el aeropuerto.
Mi hermano me dijo que saldría temprano para el aeropuerto.

1. Mis padres me dijeron que iban a salir para Madrid a las tres.
2. Dijo que iba a tener las habitaciones listas.
3. Una persona me dijo que el vuelo de mis tías iba a salir a tiempo.
4. El recepcionista me dijo que las habitaciones de mis parientes iban a tener agua potable.
5. El botones dijo que iba a llevar todas las maletas a la habitación.
6. Mi papá dijo que iba a firmar algún papel en la recepción del hotel.

23 No contestan

Cuando Graciela llamó a su amiga Camila al hotel a diferentes horas durante el día, ni ella ni su familia contestaban el teléfono de la habitación. Haz oraciones completas, usando las indicaciones que se dan para saber lo que piensa Graciela.

 Camila no estaba a las 8:30 A.M. (desayunarse en el restaurante)
Camila se desayunaría en el restaurante.

1. Su papá no estaba a las 10:00 A.M. (hablar con el botones en la recepción)
2. Su mamá no estaba a las 10:30 A.M. (tomar agua potable en la cocina del hotel)
3. Sus padres no estaban a las 11:00 A.M. (broncearse en la playa)
4. Todos no estaban a las 12:00 P.M. (almorzar en el restaurante porque no había servicio al cuarto)
5. Su hermano no estaba a las 3:00 P.M. (nadar en la piscina)
6. Sus padres no estaban a las 4:45 P.M. (dar un paseo por la ciudad)
7. Camila no estaba a las 9:45 P.M. (salir con sus nuevos amigos)

La Plaza Mayor de Salamanca, España.

¿Te gustaría visitar el Museo del Prado?

Esta catedral, La Sagrada Familia, fue diseñada por Antonio Gaudí.
¿En qué ciudad crees que está?

Autoevaluación. Como repaso y autoevaluación, responde lo siguiente:
1. Describe your last experience in an airport.
2. List what time you do the following activities using the twenty-four-hour clock: wake up in the morning, go to school, eat lunch, return home, eat dinner, study.
3. Describe what you would do if you won a large sum of money.
4. How would you ask an airline agent what time the plane will arrive?
5. If you could build a hotel, what would it be like? What kind of people would stay there?
6. How would you say in Spanish that it probably was five o'clock when the flight attendant brought the food?
7. What do you know about Spain?

Answers

A Creative self-expression.

B Creative self-expression.

Notes

Travel Information
http://www.salidas.com/

Select several students to share with the class the information they found out in activities A and B.

Activities

Expansion. As an alternative to activity B, ask students to make a list of several places in your community or state where there is a significant Spanish-speaking population or where there is a marked Hispanic influence that can be seen and described. Then have students write about one or more of the places, telling why they would like to go there, when and with whom they would like to go and any other details they wish.

¡La práctica hace al maestro!

A Comunicación

Working in pairs, plan the ideal trip to Spain. Discuss where and when you would like to go, where you would like to stay, what you would like to do and anything else that would make the trip perfect!

A: ¿Adónde te gustaría ir en España?
B: Primero, querría visitar Andalucía porque quiero ver la Alhambra. ¿Adónde te alojarías tú?
A: Preferiría alojarme en un parador.

B Conexión con la tecnología

Part of planning a trip to Spain is choosing the hotel in which you will stay. Using the Internet, find information about at least five hotels in one of the cities you plan to visit. Find out the rates of each hotel, including the rates for different types of rooms, and note any special offers and amenities. Print out the information and share it with the class. Describe all of the hotel options you found. Then tell the class which hotel you would prefer to stay in, and why.

JUNTA DE ANDALUCIA
Consejeria de Cultura y Medio Ambiente
Patronato de la Alhambra y Generalife

Alcazaba
Palacios Nazaries
Baño de Comares y Lindaraja
Partal y Torres
Generalife

Billete individual para visita diurna, por una sola vez en el día que se expende y el siguiente para continuarla en los Recintos no visitados.

Precio: 525 pts.

Consérvese hasta la salida.   Nº 798146

Granada,
El Patronato tiene la facultad de modificar itinerarios o suprimir espacios visitables por razones organizativas y/o de conservación.

NATIONAL STANDARDS
C1.1, C1.2, C1.3, C3.2,
C4.1, C5.1, C5.2

El parador de Granada tiene un restaurante excelente.

VOCABULARIO

En el aeropuerto
la aduana
la aerolínea
la emigración
el equipaje
el equipaje de mano
la escala
el maletín
el mostrador
el muelle

En el avión
el auxiliar de vuelo,
  la auxiliar de vuelo
el compartimiento
la mesita
el pasajero
el piloto
el respaldar
la tripulación

En el hotel
el botones
la habitación
el hotel
el lujo
el parador
la recepción
el recepcionista,
  la recepcionista
servicio al cuarto

Verbos
abordar
abrochar(se)
alojar(se)
aterrizar
colocar
despegar
entregar
firmar
registrar
revisar

Expresiones y otras palabras
el apellido
la bienvenida
la clase
doble
en seguida
la pieza
el placer
la posición
potable
el ruido
sencillo,-a
el servicio
vertical

Activities

Critical Thinking. Dictate a letter of the alphabet to the class. Give students three minutes to write as many words as they can think of in Spanish that begin with that letter. After calling time, ask students to read their lists aloud. The student with the longest list of correct words wins.

Expansion. Select several words and phrases for individual students to use orally in sentences.

Pronunciation. To ensure proper pronunciation, model each word or expression and have students repeat after you.

Están abordando el avión.

Le presento al piloto de su vuelo.

¿Podríamos ayudarlo con su equipaje?

NATIONAL STANDARDS
C1.2, C4.1

Answers

Preparación
1. verdadera
2. falsa
3. verdadera
4. falsa
5. falsa

Notes

Glossed words are defined at the end of the reading on pages 368-369.

Be sure to cover the *Preparación* activity prior to beginning the *A leer*.

Activities

Critical Listening. Play the audiocassette/audio compact disc version of the reading one paragraph at a time. Tell students to listen for the main ideas the speaker is addressing. Finally, have several individuals state what they believe the main theme of each paragraph is.

Prereading Strategy. Prepare students for the content of the reading by asking some general questions on the reading topic, such as the questions found in the *Preparación*. Next, play the first paragraph of the recording of the *A leer* section, using the corresponding audiocassette or compact disc that is part of the Audiocassette/Audio CD Program. As an alternative, you may choose to read the first paragraph yourself. Read the paragraph again with students following along in the book. Give students a moment to look over the paragraph silently on their own and then have them ask questions. Ask for a student to volunteer to read the paragraph aloud. Continue in this way for subsequent paragraphs.

a leer

Estrategia

Preparación

Estrategia para leer: *utilize a combination of reading strategies*

When you read in Spanish, it is not necessary to translate word for word. Instead, combine several reading strategies you have already learned. First, scan the passage for clues about its probable content. Then, skim the paragraphs looking for the main ideas and for cognates to aid your comprehension. Also, when you encounter new words, use the context to guess their possible meanings. Try these reading strategies as you begin the following passage taken from Spanish literature.

Como preparación para la lectura, primero lee rápidamente *(skim)* la historia de Lázaro. Luego di si las siguientes oraciones son verdaderas o falsas.

1. El personaje principal es un niño que se llama Lázaro.
2. Toda la acción ocurre en el sur de España.
3. La acción tiene lugar en el pasado.
4. Lázaro es de una familia rica.
5. Lázaro tiene una vida muy feliz.

Lázaro cuenta su vida y de quién fue hijo

Pues sepa vuestra **merced** que a mí me llaman Lázaro de Tormes, hijo de Tomé González y de Antona Pérez, naturales de Tejares, **aldea** de Salamanca. Mi **nacimiento** fue **dentro del** río Tormes por la cual causa tomé el **sobrenombre,** y fue de esta manera.

Mi padre, a quien **Dios** perdone, tenía como trabajo el **proveer** una *aceña* que está a la **orilla** de aquel río, en el cual fue **molinero** más de quince años; estando mi madre una noche en el **molino** le llegó la hora y me **parió** a mí allí; de manera que con verdad me puedo decir nacido en el río.

aceña

Pues siendo yo niño de ocho años mi padre fue **preso.** En este tiempo **se hizo cierta armada contra** los **moros** en la cual fue mi padre, que en este tiempo ya estaba **fuera** de la **cárcel,** y sirviendo a su señor perdió la vida. Espero en Dios que esté en la gloria.

Mi **viuda madre** como **se viese** sola y sin marido, decidió acercarse a los buenos e irse a vivir a la ciudad. Allí hacía la comida a ciertos estudiantes y lavaba la ropa a ciertos **mozos de caballos** del Comendador de la Magdalena. Allí conoció a un hombre moreno, este hombre venía algunas veces a nuestra casa, y se iba por la mañana; otras veces llegaba de día a comprar *huevos* y entraba en casa. Yo al principio tenía miedo de él viéndole el color y el **mal gesto** que siempre tenía, pero cuando vi que con su **venida** era mejor el comer, empecé a quererlo bien porque siempre traía pan, pedazos de carne y en el invierno *leños* a los que **nos calentábamos.**

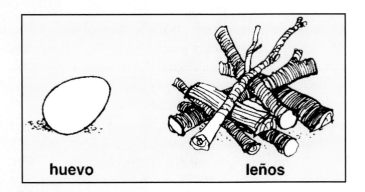

huevo   leños

Notes

Review. Review some of the reading strategies students have learned over the course of the year. Encourage students to apply as many of these strategies as possible in the article.

Students may need help with the following: *naturales* (natives), *acercarse a los buenos* (join the good people), *pedazos* (pieces), *debe de haber* (must there be), *llegara a saberse* (came to know), *aun* (even), *crió* (raised), *guiarle* (guide him), *duró* (lasted) and *saber* (knowledge).

Activities

Spanish for Spanish Speakers. Have students write a short composition in which they discuss the importance of the *pícaro* in Spanish literature and society.

NATIONAL STANDARDS
C1.2, C3.2, C4.1

Sucedió todo de manera que mi madre vino a darme un hermano, un negrito muy bonito, con el que yo jugaba. Y me acuerdo que estando el negro de mi padrastro jugando con el niño, como éste veía a mi madre y a mí blancos, y a él no, **huía** de él con miedo y se iba a donde estaba mi madre y señalándole con el dedo decía: «Madre, **coco**».

Yo, aunque era pequeño todavía, **noté** aquella palabra de mi hermanito y dije para mí: «¡Cuántos de éstos debe de haber en el mundo que **huyen** de otros porque no se ven a sí mismos!».

Quiso nuestra mala fortuna que llegara a saberse que mi padrastro se llevaba la **mitad** de la *cebada* que le daban para los caballos a casa de mi madre para después venderla y que también hacía perdidas las **mantas** de los caballos. Con todo esto ayudaba a mi madre para **criar** a mi hermanito. **Se probó** todo esto que digo y aún más, porque a mí me preguntaban, **amenazándome,** y como niño que era respondía y descubría, con el mucho miedo que tenía, todo cuanto sabía. Mi padrastro fue preso y a mi madre le dijeron que no **entrase** más en la casa de **dicho** Comendador. Entonces ella se fue a servir a los que vivían en el **Mesón** de la Solana y allí, pasando muchos trabajos, crió a mi hermanito hasta que supo andar y a mí hasta ser buen **mozuelo** que iba a buscar **vino** y **todo lo demás** que me mandaban los que vivían en el mesón.

cebada

En este tiempo llegó al mesón un viejo, era un **ciego,** el cual pensando que yo sería bueno para guiarle, le pidió a mi madre que me **dejase** ir con él. Mi madre lo hizo diciéndole cómo yo era hijo de un buen hombre el cual había muerto en la **batalla** de los Gelves por defender la **fe** y que ella esperaba en Dios que yo no sería peor hombre que mi padre y que le **rogaba** que me **tratase** bien, pues era **huérfano.**

El ciego respondió que lo haría así y que me recibía no como mozo sino como hijo. Y así empecé a servir y a guiar a mi nuevo y viejo **amo.**

Estuvimos en Salamanca algunos días, pero a mi amo la **ganancia** le pareció poca y decidió irse de allí. Cuando íbamos a **partir** yo fui a ver a mi madre, y, **ambos llorando,** me dio su **bendición** y me dijo:

—Hijo, ya sé que no te veré más; sé bueno, y Dios te guíe; yo te he criado y te he puesto con buen amo, así que **válete por ti solo.** Y me fui hacia donde estaba mi amo, que me estaba esperando.

Notes

This reading passage is taken from the Spanish picaresque novel *Lazarillo de Tormes*.

Salimos de Salamanca y llegando al puente hay a la **entrada** de él un animal de **piedra,** que tiene forma de toro, el ciego me mandó que me **llegase** cerca del animal y puesto allí me dijo:

—Lázaro, **acerca** el oído a ese toro y oirás un gran ruido dentro de él.

Yo lo hice creyendo que sería así; cuando el ciego sintió que tenía la cabeza junto a la piedra me dio tal **golpe** con su mano contra el toro que el dolor me duró más de tres días, y me dijo:

—Aprende que el mozo de ciego un punto ha de saber más que el **diablo.**

Y se rió mucho.

Me pareció que en ese momento desperté de la **simpleza** en que como niño dormido estaba. Y dije para mí: «Verdad dice éste, pues soy solo, tengo que ver y pensar cómo me sepa valer».

Empezamos nuestro camino y en muy pocos días me enseñó **jerigonza** y como viese que yo tenía buen **ingenio** estaba muy contento y me decía: «Yo no te puedo dar oro ni plata, pero te mostraré muchos consejos para vivir». Y fue así, que después de Dios, éste me dio la vida y, siendo ciego, me **alumbró** y guió en la **carrera** de vivir. Le cuento a vuestra merced estas cosas para mostrar cuánta **virtud** es que los hombres pobres y bajos sepan subir y cuánto **vicio** es el que los hombres siendo ricos y altos se dejen bajar.

Activities

Multiple Intelligences (intrapersonal/linguistic). *¿Dónde naciste tú?; ¿Tienes algún hermanastro/a? ¿Cómo es?; ¿Conoces a alguna persona que sea ciega?; ¿Qué crees que es lo más importante que has aprendido en la vida hasta hoy?*

águila

Mi amo en su **oficio** era un *águila:* sabía de memoria más de cien **oraciones,** tenía un tono bajo y tranquilo que hacía **resonar** la iglesia donde **rezaba** y cuando rezaba ponía un **rostro devoto.**

Además de esto tenía otras mil formas de sacarle el dinero a la gente. Sabía oraciones para todo, a las mujeres que iban a parir les decía si iba a ser hijo o hija y decía que **Galeno** no supo la mitad de lo que él sabía para curar toda clase de **enfermedades.**

A todo el que le decía que sufría de algún mal, le decía mi amo: «Haced esto, haréis lo otro». Con todo esto la gente andaba siempre detrás de él, especialmente las mujeres que creían todo cuanto les decía. De las mujeres sacaba mucho dinero y ganaba más en un mes que cien ciegos en un año.

Pero también quiero que sepa vuestra merced que con todo lo que tenía jamás vi un hombre tan **avariento,** tanto que me **mataba** de hambre y no me daba **ni siquiera** lo necesario. Digo verdad: si **yo no hubiera sabido** valerme por mí mismo, muchas veces **hubiera muerto** de hambre; pero con todo su saber, las más de las veces yo llevaba lo mejor. Para esto le hacía **burlas,** de las cuales contaré algunas.

(continuará)

merced *grace* **aldea** *village* **nacimiento** *birth* **dentro del** *in* **sobrenombre** *surname* **Dios** *God* **proveer** *taking care of* **orilla** *shore* **molinero** *miller* **molino** *mill* **parió** *gave birth to* **preso** *jailed* **se hizo cierta armada contra** *raised a certain navy against* **moros** *Moors* **fuera** *outside* **cárcel** *jail* **viuda madre** *widowed mother* **se viese** *found herself* **mozos de caballos** *stableboys* **mal gesto** *poor appearance* **venida** *arrival* **nos calentábamos** *warmed ourselves* **Sucedió todo** *Everything happened* **huía** *fled* **coco** *boogeyman* **noté** *I noticed* **huyen** *flee* **mitad** *half* **mantas** *blankets* **criar** *to raise* **Se probó** *was proven* **amenazándome** *threatening me* **no entrase** *he not enter* **dicho** *said* **Mesón** *Inn* **mozuelo** *youngster* **vino** *wine* **todo lo demás** *everything else* **ciego** *blind (man)* **dejase** *let* **batalla** *battle* **fe** *faith* **rogaba** *she begged* **tratase** *treat* **huérfano** *orphan* **amo** *master* **ganancia** *earnings* **partir** *leave* **ambos llorando** *both crying*

bendición *blessing* **válete por ti solo** *take care of yourself* **entrada** *entrance* **piedra** *stone* **llegase** *got* **acerca** *put close* **golpe** *blow* **diablo** *devil* **simpleza** *innocence* **jerigonza** *a slang (of thieves)* **ingenio** *intelligence* **alumbró** *enlightened* **carrera** *road* **virtud** *virtue* **vicio** *vice* **oficio** *work* **oraciones** *prayers* **resonar** *resonate* **rezaba** *prayed* **rostro devoto** *devout face* **Galeno** *famous Greek doctor (131-201 B.C.)* **enfermedades** *illnesses* **avariento** *greedy* **mataba** *killed* **ni siquiera** *not even* **si yo no hubiera sabido** *if I had not known* **hubiera muerto** *I would have died* **burlas** *tricks*

Excerpt from:
Lazarillo de Tormes; author unknown. Copyright Grafisk Forlag A/S, Copenhagen.
The *Easy Reader* (a B-level book) with the same title is published by EMC/Paradigm Publishing.

¿Qué comprendiste?

1. ¿Dónde nació Lazarillo?
2. ¿Qué hacía la mamá de Lazarillo en la ciudad después de que su esposo murió?
3. ¿Cómo era el hombre para el cual Lazarillo servía de guía?
4. ¿Qué forma tenía el animal que Lazarillo encontró en un puente cuando salía de Salamanca?
5. ¿Qué le dijo el ciego a Lazarillo que no le podía dar?
6. ¿Qué le dijo el ciego a Lazarillo que sí le podía dar?
7. ¿Qué ganaba el ciego diciendo mentiras?

Charlando

1. ¿Has servido alguna vez de guía para alguien? ¿Para quién y por qué?
2. ¿Qué crees que es lo más importante que alguien te puede dar en la vida?
3. ¿Quién es la persona que te ha dado más consejos en la vida?
4. ¿Has ganado algún dinero en la vida? ¿Cómo lo has ganado?
5. ¿Qué piensas de las personas que dicen muchas mentiras?

a escribir

Estrategia

Estrategia para escribir: *arranging an itinerary in chronological order*

When you are writing the itinerary for a trip, it is a good idea to arrange the text in a chronological sequence. That is, you should present the events in the order they will occur, using words like: *primero, segundo, entonces, después* and *por último*. To make clear divisions in the sequence of events, use numbers, bullets or bold print.

It is a tradition at your high school for seniors to take a trip after graduation (*el viaje de graduación*). List the itinerary for your ideal graduation trip or cruise. State when the trip will occur and where you will go. Then describe what you will see, and name some of the things you will do. Conclude the composition by discussing your feelings about the upcoming trip.

Primero, iremos a Toledo.

Luego, visitaremos la Plaza Mayor de Madrid.

Portfolio Assessment
Select an activity from
Capítulo 8 to include in the
Somos así Portfolio
Assessment.

repaso

Now that I have completed this chapter, I can...
✓ seek and provide personal information.
✓ plan vacations.
✓ talk about the future.
✓ express emotion.
✓ talk about everyday activities.
✓ express uncertainty or probability.
✓ make travel and lodging arrangements.
✓ identify people and items associated with travel.
✓ state wishes and preferences.
✓ talk about schedules.
✓ use the twenty-four-hour clock.
✓ express logical conclusions.
✓ write about hopes and dreams.

I can also...
✓ identify the ingredients in a Spanish
  tortilla.
✓ read in Spanish about life in Spain.
✓ identify opportunities to use Spanish
  while traveling.
✓ read about various classes of hotels
  in Spain.

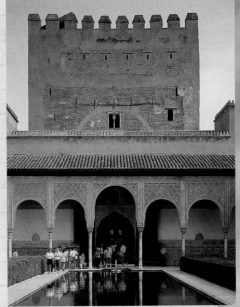

Para las próximas vacaciones, me gustaría
visitar la Alhambra.(Granada, España.)

NATIONAL STANDARDS
C1.1, C1.2, C2.1, C2.2,
C3.1, C4.1, C4.2, C5.2

Notes

Discuss the communicative functions students will be learning in *Capítulo 9*. A checkoff list of the functions appears at the end of the chapter (see page 419), along with additional objectives that students can use as a self-check to evaluate their own progress.

Activities

Critical Thinking. Use the visuals that appear on pages 372-373 to discuss the functions, cultural setting and themes of the chapter ahead. For example, ask students to answer the following: 1) What are the people in these photographs doing?; 2) What do students think they will be studying in the chapter?; 3) What is the piece of realia on page 373?

Hablando del futuro

CAPÍTULO 9

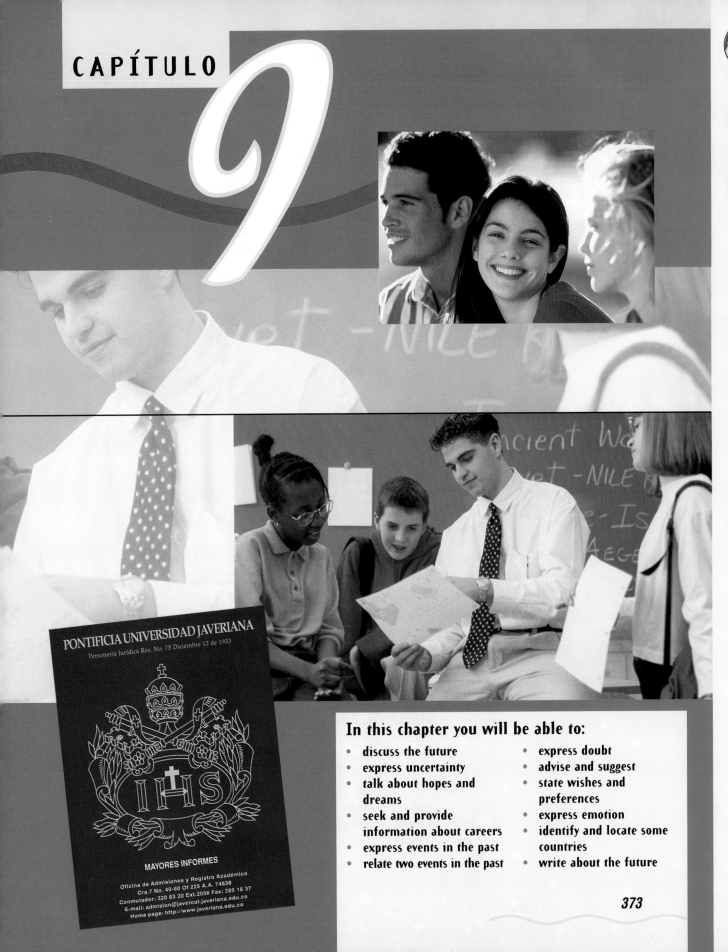

Activities

Critical Thinking. Give students blank maps of the world (or have students prepare the maps). They must then identify the countries where Spanish is spoken by writing the names of the countries and capitals they know in their correct location on the maps. Extend the activity by having students add the names of some non-Spanish-speaking countries and their capitals. Keep the maps in order to compare student work after studying about other countries of the world in this chapter.

PONTIFICIA UNIVERSIDAD JAVERIANA
Personería Jurídica Res. No. 73 Diciembre 12 de 1933

IHS

MAYORES INFORMES

Oficina de Admisiones y Registro Académico
Cra. 7 No. 40-90 Of 225 A.A. 74838
Conmutador: 320 83 20 Ext.2056 Fax: 285 16 37
E-mail: admision@javercol.javeriana.edu.co
Home page: http://www.javeriana.edu.co

In this chapter you will be able to:

- discuss the future
- express uncertainty
- talk about hopes and dreams
- seek and provide information about careers
- express events in the past
- relate two events in the past
- express doubt
- advise and suggest
- state wishes and preferences
- express emotion
- identify and locate some countries
- write about the future

373

NATIONAL STANDARDS
C1.2, C5.2

Asistir a la universidad

Quiz/Activity 1

Content reviewed in *Lección 17*
- jobs and careers
- the verb *haber*
- everyday activities
- subjunctive
- expressing opinions

Notes

This would be a good time to remind students about the difference between cognates and false cognates: *asistir a* is a false cognate (since it means **to attend** and not **to assist**, as it may seem it would mean).

The terms *refresco* and *gaseosa* are just two of many different ways people refer to soft drinks shown in the illustration. In addition, fruit beverages are common throughout the Spanish-speaking world, much as in the United States.

Activities

Cooperative Learning. Review the advice that Verónica receives from her parents in the dialog. Then ask students to work in small groups to discuss other advice they receive from relatives. Each group should present a summary to the class.

Critical Listening. Play the audiocassette/audio compact disc recording of the dialog as students listen to the conversation. Ask several individuals to state what they believe the main theme of the conversation is. Finally, ask if students know where the conversation takes place (at the dinner table in a home in New York City).

Prereading Strategy. Talk with students about what they plan to do in their future. Discuss whether they intend to go to a college, to a university or to some other school for additional training after high school.

NATIONAL STANDARDS
C2.1, C3.2, C4.1

Lección 17

Asistir a la universidad

Contexto cultural
EL MUNDO

*Verónica, una chica de Nueva York, habla con sus padres sobre su **futuro**.*

PABLO:	Es importante que, al terminar el colegio, hayas decidido qué **carrera°** estudiar en la **universidad.**
VERÓNICA:	Ya lo he pensado, pero no sé si quiero **asistir a°** una universidad después de terminar el colegio. Creo que tengo otras **aspiraciones.**
SILVIA:	¡Cómo! No vas a asistir a la universidad? Hoy en cualquier parte del mundo es necesario tener una carrera.
VERÓNICA:	No, no mamá. Sí, quiero ir a la universidad, pero me gustaría primero trabajar para poder ganar algún dinero y **experiencia** en la vida **real.** Mi **sueño°** es ser una **mujer de negocios°** y viajar por todo el mundo.
SILVIA:	Eso está muy bien, pero tu papá y yo queremos que, al terminar el colegio, tú empieces una carrera en la universidad.
PABLO:	Sí, amor. Te aconsejo que busques un **empleo°** para el verano y, luego, en el otoño empiezas la universidad.
VERÓNICA:	Eso es una buena idea. Entonces, empezaré a buscar un trabajo de verano en alguna **empresa°** de negocios. Así, espero que, al terminar el colegio, ya haya sido **aceptada°** y pueda mostrar que soy una buena **empleada.°**

carrera *career* **asistir a** *to attend* **sueño** *dream* **mujer de negocios** *businesswoman* **empleo** *job*
empresa *business* **aceptada** *accepted* **empleada** *employee*

1 ¿Qué comprendiste?

1. ¿Qué es importante que Verónica haya decidido al terminar el colegio?
2. ¿Qué no sabe Verónica?
3. ¿Qué le gustaría hacer primero a Verónica?
4. ¿Cuál es el sueño de Verónica?
5. ¿Qué quieren los padres de Verónica que ella haga al terminar el colegio?
6. ¿Qué le aconseja Pablo a Verónica?
7. ¿Dónde empezará Verónica a buscar un trabajo de verano?
8. ¿En qué espera que ya haya sido aceptada Verónica al terminar el colegio?

2 Charlando

1. ¿Cuáles son tus aspiraciones después de terminar el colegio?
2. ¿Crees que estudiar una carrera es importante para tener un mejor futuro? Explica.
3. ¿Tienes algún sueño especial? ¿Cuál?
4. ¿Tienes algún empleo? ¿Cuál? ¿En qué empresa?
5. ¿Crees que la experiencia es importante para conseguir un empleo? ¿Por qué?

Oportunidades

Las carreras

Many careers can be expanded to the international market if you are bilingual. In addition, speaking a second language can enhance your salary and reduce the field of candidates competing in the same job market. If you are interested in a particular career, you may want to investigate the job opportunities for that career in the global market.

Trabajan en negocios internacionales.

Sólo Llegan los que tienen una Buena Formación

DIFUSORA
Internacional
DEUSTO

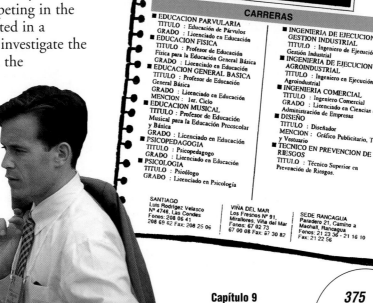

UNIVERSIDAD EDUCARES

CARRERAS

■ EDUCACION PARVULARIA
TITULO : Educación de Párvulos
GRADO : Licenciado en Educación
■ EDUCACION FISICA
TITULO : Profesor de Educación
Física para la Educación General Básica
GRADO : Licenciado en Educación
■ EDUCACION GENERAL BASICA
TITULO : Profesor de Educación
General Básica
GRADO : Licenciado en Educación
MENCION : 1er. Ciclo
■ EDUCACION MUSICAL
TITULO : Profesor de Educación
Musical para la Educación Preescolar
y Básica
GRADO : Licenciado en Educación
■ PSICOPEDAGOGIA
TITULO : Psicopedagogo
GRADO : Licenciado en Educación
■ PSICOLOGIA
TITULO : Psicólogo
GRADO : Licenciado en Psicología

■ INGENIERIA DE EJECUCION EN
GESTION INDUSTRIAL
TITULO : Ingeniero de Ejecución en
Gestión Industrial
■ INGENIERIA DE EJECUCION
AGROINDUSTRIAL
TITULO : Ingeniero en Ejecución
Agroindustrial
■ INGENIERIA COMERCIAL
TITULO : Ingeniero Comercial
GRADO : Licenciado en Ciencias de la
Administración de Empresas
■ DISEÑO
TITULO : Diseñador
MENCION : Gráfico Publicitario, Textil
y Vestuario
■ TECNICO EN PREVENCION DE
RIESGOS
TITULO : Técnico Superior en
Prevención de Riesgos

SANTIAGO
Luis Rodríguez Velasco
Nº 4746, Las Condes
Fonos: 208 06 41
208 69 62 Fax: 208 25 06

VIÑA DEL MAR
Los Fresnos Nº 91,
Miraflores, Viña del Mar
Fonos: 67 02 73
67 00 08 Fax: 67 30 82

SEDE RANCAGUA
Paradero 21, Camino a
Machalí, Rancagua
Fonos: 21 23 36 - 21 16 10
Fax: 21 22 56

Answers

1
1. Es importante que haya decidido qué carrera estudiar en la universidad.
2. No sabe si quiere asistir a la universidad después de terminar el colegio.
3. Primero le gustaría trabajar para poder ganar algún dinero y experiencia en la vida real.
4. El sueño de Verónica es ser una mujer de negocios y viajar por todo el mundo.
5. Ellos quieren que ella empiece una carrera en la universidad.
6. Le aconseja que busque un empleo para el verano y, luego, que en el otoño empiece la universidad.
7. Empezará a buscar un trabajo de verano en alguna empresa de negocios.
8. Espera que ya haya sido aceptada en algún empleo.

2 Answers will vary.

Activities

Expansion. Additional questions (*¿Qué comprendiste?*): *¿De dónde es Verónica?; ¿Quién es Silvia?; ¿Quién es Pablo?; ¿Qué es muy importante para Silvia?*

Additional questions (*Charlando*): *¿Con quién has hablado acerca de tus aspiraciones para después de terminar el colegio? ¿Te ayudó hablar con esa persona?; ¿Es importante para ti empezar a ganar dinero desde temprano? Explica.*

Students with Special Needs. Ask students to identify any cognates they can find in the dialog on page 374.

 NATIONAL STANDARDS
C1.1, C1.2, C2.1, C3.2, C4.1, C4.2, C5.2

www

Ecology
http://www.amarillas.com/verdes/index.htm

Remind students that the problems shown in the photographs on this page are not unique to the Spanish-speaking world, but rather are an issue that every nation faces.

Activities

Critical Thinking. Verónica (from the dialog on page 374) decided to obtain valuable work experience with a company before beginning her studies at a university. Students have many choices to make about their future. Some may attend a university, some may go to technical institutes and others may begin work immediately. You may decide to develop this topic as a classroom conversation with the help of a school counselor.

Conexión Cultural

Nuestros sueños para el planeta

Soñar con nuestro futuro tiene relación directa con los sueños para nuestro planeta y su población. Es seguro que siempre queremos lo mejor para el mundo pero, a veces, es difícil evitar *(avoid)* problemas como la guerra, la pobreza y los desastres naturales. En estos casos, será importante que nosotros, y toda la comunidad mundial, ayudemos a las víctimas de estas tragedias en la reconstrucción de sus vidas.

Sin embargo, hay problemas que sí podemos evitar o tratar de controlar mejor. Pero primero será preciso que respetemos más nuestro planeta, conservando nuestros recursos naturales *(natural resources)*, reduciendo la contaminación del agua y del aire y buscando otras formas de energía. También sería buena idea participar en una organización que beneficie a la comunidad y al mundo. ¿Qué más puede uno hacer para que nuestro futuro y el del mundo sean lo mejor posible?

La pobreza...

la contaminación...

y la guerra...

...son problemas internacionales.

Cruzando fronteras

Haz una lista de algunos de los problemas que existen en el mundo. Selecciona uno y lee sobre su origen y su evolución, y lo que se está haciendo hoy para solucionarlo. Busca información en la biblioteca o en la Internet, si es necesario. Luego, presenta la información a la clase.

Oportunidades

Ayudando a solucionar los problemas del mundo

If you are interested in devoting a period of time in your future to assist people in the world community who need help, there are many organizations you could contact. Local community service groups and churches often need volunteers. In addition, many national organizations need Spanish-speaking volunteers. Friends of the Americas (*www.amigoslink.org*) is one such charitable organization, dedicated to providing medical, spiritual, educational and disaster relief assistance to Hispanic countries. Other nonprofit volunteer organizations include International Volunteer Opportunities (*www.interaction.org*), the United Nations Volunteer Program (*www.un.org*) and the Peace Corps (*www.peacecorps.gov*). When you have experienced a disaster, you understand the importance of giving back to the world community.

Ayudamos a las víctimas del huracán en Honduras.

Answers

3 Answers will vary.

Notes

WWW

Service Learning
www.amigoslink.org
www.interaction.org
www.un.org
www.peacecorps.gov

Encourage students to talk with their parents/guardians, the school counselor, coaches and other interested parties regarding the possibility of learning while volunteering their services with a community organization. Explain that service learning volunteer activities offer students opportunities to learn the principles of giving back to their communities, getting involved and becoming responsible citizens, while at the same time developing the necessary skills and competencies for their eventual immersion into the real world.

Point out the missing accents in the clippings for the words *día* and *acción*. Remind students that many Spanish magazines and newspapers drop the accent marks from words with capital letters due to space restrictions in setting the type.

NATIONAL STANDARDS
C1.2, C1.3, C3.1, C3.2, C4.1, C4.2, C5.2

Los empleos

 Quizzes/Activities 2-3

 Activities 57-58

 Activities 1-2

 Quizzes/Activities 1-2

Notes

Check to be certain that students understand what these people do.

Activities

Language through Action. Ask students to look at this illustration of various people's jobs. Inform students that you will be saying several words in Spanish. Have students raise their right hand if the item they hear appears in the illustration; have them raise their left hand if the word does not appear in the illustration.

Students with Special Needs. Talk with students about some possible careers. Using transparency 58, review the vocabulary: Pronounce each of the words in the illustration and have students repeat them. Then use transparency 57 to point to some of the people included in the illustration and ask students what the person is.

Los empleos

la bombera

el carpintero

el chofer

el fotógrafo

la mecánica

la peluquera

el programador

el secretario

la veterinaria

Algo más

Más sobre los empleos

el abogado, la abogada	*lawyer*
el agricultor, la agricultora	*farmer*
el artista, la artista	*artist*
el bibliotecario, la bibliotecaria	*librarian*
el escritor, la escritora	*writer*
el gerente, la gerente	*manager*
el ingeniero, la ingeniera	*engineer*
el obrero, la obrera	*worker*
el profesor, la profesora	*teacher*
el taxista, la taxista	*taxi driver*
el vendedor, la vendedora	*salesperson*

Soy ingeniera ambiental.

SE HACEN REFORMAS COMPLETAS
- ALBAÑILERIA
- FONTANERIA
- ELECTRICIDAD
- PINTURA
- CARPINTERIA

PARA ti

Más empleos

el biólogo marino/la bióloga marina	*marine biologist*
el contador/la contadora	*accountant*
el corredor/la corredora de bolsa	*stock broker*
el director/la directora de mercadeo	*marketing director*
el diseñador/la diseñadora de páginas web	*web page designer*
el economista/la economista	*economist*
el ingeniero/la ingeniera ambiental	*environmental engineer*
el ingeniero/la ingeniera de sistemas	*systems engineer*
el sicólogo/la sicóloga	*psychologist*
el técnico/la técnica de computación	*computer technician*

4 Los empleos

Di la palabra que no es un empleo en cada uno de los siguientes grupos de cuatro palabras.

1. recepcionista — bibliotecario — empresa — escritor
2. mecánico — hablado — secretario — veterinaria
3. aceptada — obrero — agricultor — vendedora
4. artista — piloto — carrera — gerente
5. taxista — agente — universidad — fotógrafa
6. bombero — carpintero — peluquera — experiencia
7. abogado — asistir — ingeniero — programador

5 Las profesiones

Di lo que les gustaría ser a las siguientes personas, combinando palabras de las tres columnas. Haz los cambios y añade las palabras que sean necesarias.

 A Yolanda le gustaría ser artista.

A	B	C
Alberto	gustar	ingeniero
Yolanda		profesor
Elena y Verónica		agricultor
Sofía		fotógrafo
tú		abogado
ellos		bombero
Nicolás y Ricardo		deportista
Diego		carpintero
Ud.		artista
nosotros		veterinario
Silvia y Ernesto		programador
yo		escritor

A Yolanda le gustaría ser artista.

Answers

4 1. empresa
   2. hablado
   3. aceptada
   4. carrera
   5. universidad
   6. experiencia
   7. asistir

5 Answers will vary.

Notes

Remind students that the indefinite article is not usually used with careers after forms of the verb *ser*.

Activities

Communities. Invite a professional who uses Spanish in his or her work to talk to the class.

Cooperative Learning. Have students prepare a list of five or six occupations they find appealing, and tell why. Then, working in cooperative pairs or small groups, ask students to discuss what they wrote. Finally, have one student summarize for the class what each pair or group discussed.

NATIONAL STANDARDS
C1.2, C4.1

BENEMERITO
CUERPO
VOLUNTARIO
DE BOMBEROS
DE GUATEMALA

BENEMERITO C.V.B. GUATEMALA

¿SABE USTED CUANTOS RECURSOS NECESITAN LOS BOMBEROS PARA COMBATIR UN INCENDIO?

Los Bomberos Voluntarios solicitan su colaboración económica para adquirir unidades y equipo para su servicio.

HAGA SU APORTE HOY MISMO A LA CUENTA ESPECIAL EN EL BANCO PROMOTOR Y AYUDENOS PARA AYUDAR

AGOSTO, MES DEL BOMBERO VOLUNTARIO

6 Todos tienen carreras diferentes

Di lo que las siguientes personas son, según las ilustraciones.

 Raquel
Ella es abogada.

1. Armando y Susana

6. Eduardo y Juan

2. Silvia

7. Paula

3. Enrique y Benjamín

8. Pablo

4. Susana

9. Miguel y Rafael

5. Sergio

10. María

7 ¿Qué empleo tienen?

Di qué empleo tienen las siguientes personas, de acuerdo con las descripciones de lo que cada uno de ellos hace.

Don Alfonso enseña historia en una universidad.
Don Alfonso es profesor.

1. Victoria trabaja en un banco y hace muchos negocios.
2. María dirige el trabajo de muchas personas en una empresa grande.
3. Virginia maneja un carro y lleva a personas de un lugar a otro.
4. Hernán prepara comidas en un restaurante argentino.
5. Carlos arregla carros.
6. Diego hace casas de ladrillo.
7. Doña Mercedes arregla los dientes de las personas.
8. Martín entrega y recibe libros en la biblioteca.
9. Antonio corta el pelo.
10. Lucía recoge verduras y frutas en una finca.

¿Qué empleo tienen ellos?

8 ¿Qué les gustaría ser?

Trabajando en grupos pequeños, hagan una lista de lo que a cada uno le gustaría ser en la vida. Un estudiante debe dar un resumen a la clase.

A Felipe le gustaría ser futbolista, a Marcela le gustaría ser médica, a Camila le gustaría ser abogada, a Andrés le gustaría ser veterinario y a mí me gustaría ser escritor.

¿Les gustaría ser futbolistas?

9 ¿Quién es?

Trabajando en parejas, alterna con tu compañero/a de clase en describir a alguien, diciendo lo que hace en su empleo. Luego, tu compañero/a debe adivinar quién es.

A: Esta persona es un deportista dominicano. Corre y juega al béisbol muy bien. ¿Quién es?
B: Es Sammy Sosa.

10 ¿Qué hacen tus parientes?

Trabajando en parejas, alterna con tu compañero/a de clase en preguntar y contestar sobre los empleos de diferentes miembros de sus familias.

A: ¿Cuál es el empleo de tu papá?
B: Mi papá es escritor. ¿Cuál es el empleo de tu papá?
A: Mi papá es abogado.

Sammy Sosa es beisbolista.

Rigoberta Menchú es una escritora y activista guatemalteca.

Answers

8 Answers will vary.

9 Creative self-expression.

10 Answers will vary.

Notes

In 1998, Sammy Sosa and Mark McGwire engaged in a memorable home run race and both ultimately broke the long-standing record for the most home runs in a single season.

Many major league baseball players are from Latin American nations. Baseball is especially popular in the Dominican Republic, Cuba, Puerto Rico, Mexico and Venezuela.

Activities

Expansion. As a follow-up to activity 8, ask students to further investigate the career(s) that they would like to pursue. For example, what are the academic requirements? What experience beyond the classroom would be helpful in pursuing this goal? What does a person in this profession do during a typical day/week?

Multiple Intelligences (linguistic). Ask students to identify other famous athletes from the Spanish-speaking world. In the case of a favorite athlete, encourage them to write a fan letter in Spanish.

NATIONAL STANDARDS
C1.1, C1.2, C4.1, C5.1, C5.2

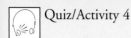

Answers

11 1. hemos asistido
2. han decidido
3. he decidido
4. ha decidido
5. han pensado
6. ha pensado
7. ha visitado
8. ha oído
9. has trabajado
10. Has pensado

Activities

Expansion. The preterite perfect, the future perfect and the conditional perfect tenses have been included in Appendix B should you wish to teach them along with this review of the uses of *haber*.

Spanish for Spanish Speakers. Ask students to read the advertisements on pages 382-383 and then ask them questions to determine how much they understood: *¿Dónde está la universidad del anuncio de la página 382?; ¿Qué es una veterinaria?; ¿Cómo se llama la veterinaria del anuncio de la página 383?*

Students with Special Needs. Model the first sentence for activity 11 and a second sentence for activity 12 on page 383.

Repaso *rápido*

Repaso rápido: usos de *haber*

The verb *haber* is used in various tenses as an impersonal expression: *hay* (there is, there are), *había* (there was, there were), *hubo* (there was, there were). Compare the following:

*¿**Hay** una universidad donde vives?* — **Is there** a university where you live?
***Había** mucho que aprender.* — **There was** a lot to learn.
*Oí que **hubo** una cena elegante en la universidad la semana pasada.* — I heard **there was** an elegant dinner at the university last week.

The present tense of *haber* may be combined with a past participle to form the present perfect tense *(el pretérito perfecto),* which often is used to describe something that has happened recently or to describe something that has occurred over a period of time and that continues today.

***He pensado** ser ingeniero.* — **I have thought** about becoming an engineer.
*¿A qué universidad **has decidido** asistir?* — Which university **have you decided** to attend?

The imperfect tense of *haber* may be combined with a past pasticiple to form the past perfect tense *(el pluscuamperfecto),* which is used to describe an event in the past that had happened prior to another event.

***Había terminado** de comer cuando llamaste.* — **I had finished** eating when you called.
*Ya **habían comido** cuando sus amigas llegaron.* — **They had** already **eaten** when their friends arrived.

11 La composición de Guillermo

Guillermo escribió una composición corta sobre lo que él y sus amigos piensan hacer después de terminar el colegio. Completa el siguiente párrafo con la forma apropiada del pretérito perfecto de los verbos entre paréntesis.

> En mi clase somos veinte estudiantes. Todos nosotros 1. (asistir) al mismo colegio por dos años. Algunos de mis compañeros ya 2. (decidir) qué hacer después de terminar el colegio. Yo todavía no 3. (decidir) si quiero estudiar o trabajar. La idea de estudiar una carrera en la universidad me parece una aspiración muy importante. Alberto 4. (decidir) estudiar para ser cocinero. A él le gusta mucho la comida. Claudia y Mónica 5. (pensar) estudiar una carrera, pero no saben cuál. Juanita 6. (pensar) trabajar para ganar algo de experiencia antes de asistir a una universidad. Ella ya 7. (visitar) algunas empresas para buscar un empleo, pero todavía no 8. (oír) nada de ellas. Y tú, ¿9. (trabajar) alguna vez? ¿10. (pensar) qué hacer después de terminar el colegio? ¿Qué te gustaría hacer en el futuro?

12 ¿Qué empleo tienen hoy?

Imagina que las siguientes personas tienen hoy un empleo en algo diferente de la carrera que habían estudiado. Di la carrera que habían estudiado y el empleo que tienen hoy, usando las pistas que se dan. Sigue el modelo.

Julia/veterinario/profesor
Julia había estudiado una carrera para ser veterinaria, pero hoy tiene un empleo como profesora.

1. Marcela/peluquero/secretario
2. Enrique/abogado/vendedor
3. Santiago y Carolina/ programador/escritor
4. tú/fotógrafo/carpintero
5. Luis y su amigo/mecánico/bombero
6. Marta/ingeniero/artista

VETERINARIA DEL PACIFICO

CLINICA-CIRUGIA-RAYOS X HOSPITALIZACION-PENSION FARMACIA-PELUQUERIA VENTA DE MASCOTAS Y ACCESORIOS

82-67-27

Río Baluarte 1034, Col. Palos Prietos a Espaldas de C. Camionera

IDIOMA

El pretérito perfecto del subjuntivo

You have learned several circumstances that require the subjunctive. When the *pretérito perfecto* is in the subjunctive, its formation is quite simple: Combine the present subjunctive forms of *haber* with the past participle of a verb.

Julia había estudiado para ser veterinaria, pero hoy es profesora.

hablar	hacer	vestirse (i, i)
haya hablado	haya hecho	me haya vestido
hayas hablado	hayas hecho	te hayas vestido
haya hablado	haya hecho	se haya vestido
hayamos hablado	hayamos hecho	nos hayamos vestido
hayáis hablado	hayáis hecho	os hayáis vestido
hayan hablado	hayan hecho	se hayan vestido

Look at the following examples:

*Espero que él ya **haya decidido** qué hacer al terminar el colegio.*

I hope he **has** already **decided** what to do after finishing school.

*No creo que ella **haya empezado** a estudiar en la universidad.*

I doubt that she **has begun** to study at the university.

Capítulo 9   383

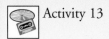

Activity 13

Answers

13 1. ...ha decidido....
2. ...han decidido....
3. ...ha decidido....
4. ...hayan decidido....
5. ...haya decidido....
6. ...haya decidido....
7. ...hayan decidido....
8. ...hayas decidido....

14 Possible answers:
1. ...ellos hayan estudiado para ser escritores.
2. ...Uds. hayan estudiado para ser veterinarios.
3. ...ellos hayan estudiado para ser cocineros.
4. ...ella haya estudiado para ser peluquera.
5. ...Ud. haya estudiado para ser agricultor(a).
6. ...tú hayas estudiado para ser artista.
7. ...ella haya estudiado para ser mecánica.
8. ...ellas hayan estudiado para ser ingenieras.

Activities

Students with Special Needs.
Quiz students on the following words, which they already have learned: *el actor/la actriz, el agente de viajes/la agente de viajes, el auxiliar de vuelo/la auxiliar de vuelo, el cajero/la cajera, el camarero/la camarera, el cantante/la cantante, el cocinero/la cocinera, el comentarista/la comentarista, el dentista/la dentista, el deportista (el basquetbolista, el tenista, etc.)/la deportista (la basquetbolista, la tenista, etc.), el enfermero/la enfermera, el médico/la médica, el mesero/la mesera, el periodista/la periodista, el policía/la policía, el profesor/la profesora, el recepcionista/la recepcionista* and *el reportero/la reportera.*

---

 13 ¿Qué crees?

Haz oraciones completas para decir si crees o no que las siguientes personas han decidido qué estudiar, según las indicaciones. Sigue el modelo.

 Armando/sí
Creo que Armando ya ha decidido qué estudiar en la universidad.

Gabriela/no
No creo que Gabriela haya decidido todavía qué estudiar en la universidad.

1. ella/sí
2. Manuel y Cristina/sí
3. Lorenzo/sí
4. Francisco y David/no
5. Paloma/no
6. Sara/no
7. Dolores y Margarita/no
8. tú/no

Universidad San Francisco de Quito

14 Todo es posible

Muchas veces puedes decir lo que una persona es, de acuerdo con las cosas que hace. Mira las ilustraciones y di lo que es posible que las siguientes personas hayan estudiado, según lo que hacen.

Rogelio
Es posible que él haya estudiado para ser carpintero.

1. Inés y Juan   2. Uds.   3. Ernesto y Rodolfo   4. Elisa

5. Ud.   6. tú   7. Marta   8. Rosa y María

15 Cuando el tiempo pasa

Cambia las siguientes oraciones al pretérito perfecto del subjuntivo.

 Es probable que Guillermo consiga el empleo.
Es probable que Guillermo haya conseguido el empleo.

1. Es probable que Ud. no piense mucho acerca del futuro.
2. Espero que Verónica vaya a la universidad.
3. Espero que tú decidas qué carrera estudiar en la universidad.
4. No creo que ellos tengan mucha experiencia como mecánicos.
5. Es posible que mis amigos y yo busquemos trabajo en una empresa de negocios.
6. Es posible que Raquel y Luis estudien para ser abogados.
7. No creo que Jairo se cambie de camisa para ir a buscar empleo.

Es posible que hayan pensado estudiar en la Universidad de Salamanca.

16 Hablando con papá

Juan habla con su papá acerca del futuro. Completa el siguiente diálogo con la forma apropiada del pretérito perfecto del subjuntivo de los verbos entre paréntesis.

PAPÁ: Espero que ya 1. *(pensar)* muy bien qué estudiar en la universidad.
JUAN: Bueno, no creo que yo 2. *(tener)* mucho tiempo para hacerlo.
PAPÁ: Pero, mijito, ¿por qué?
JUAN: Siempre he estado muy ocupado haciendo mis tareas.
PAPÁ: No creo yo que siempre te 3. *(ver)* haciendo tareas. Muchos días te he visto perdiendo el tiempo con tus amigos en la Internet.
JUAN: Ay, papá, no perdemos el tiempo en la Internet.
PAPÁ: No creo que Uds. alguna vez 4. *(buscar)* algo importante en la Internet.
JUAN: Qué exagerado eres, papá. Es una lástima que tú no 5. *(ver)* lo que buscamos mis amigos y yo la semana pasada.
PAPÁ: ¿Qué buscaron?
JUAN: Buscamos artículos sobre los problemas del país y del mundo.
PAPÁ: ¡Qué bueno! Eso es importante. Pero creo que deben empezar a buscar universidades. En la Internet hay mucha información.
JUAN: Bueno, creo que empezaré a buscar algo de eso.
PAPÁ: Me alegro de que 6. *(entender)* lo que te he dicho.

17 1. Dudo que Uds. se hayan registrado....
2. No pienso que Andrés haya nacido....
3. Es importante que (nosotros) hayamos pasado....
4. Espero que María haya conseguido....
5. Es importante que (tú) hayas decidido....
6. Es una lástima que (yo) no me haya preguntado....
7. Es posible que Pedro y Marisol hayan ganado....

18 1. ha
2. hubo
3. había
4. hay
5. han
6. haya
7. hayamos
8. ha

Notes

Before beginning activity 18, point out that students will have to choose from the past perfect, present perfect and present perfect subjunctive.

17 En la cafetería

Tú y tus amigos hablan en la cafetería. Haz oraciones completas para decir lo que las siguientes personas dicen. Sigue el modelo.

 Carmenza/tener la oportunidad de estudiar una carrera (no creo)
No creo que Carmenza haya tenido la oportunidad de estudiar una carrera.

1. Uds./registrarse para tomar la clase de historia (dudo)
2. Andrés/nacer para ser artista (no pienso)
3. nosotros/pasar el examen de historia (es importante)
4. María/conseguir un empleo (espero)
5. tú/decidir ir a la universidad (es importante)
6. yo/no preguntarme antes qué hacer en el futuro (es una lástima)
7. Pedro y Marisol/ganar alguna experiencia después de su viaje a la América del Sur (es posible)

18 Todos opinan algo

Es posible que ellos hayan pensado qué van a hacer en el futuro.

Espero que vayamos a la misma universidad.

Escoge la forma apropiada del verbo *haber* para completar lógicamente las siguientes oraciones.

 No creo que ella (ha/haya) ido a la empresa ayer.
No creo que ella haya ido a la empresa ayer.

1. Josefina cree que su hermanastro (había/ha) sido aceptado en la universidad donde él quiere estudiar.
2. El año pasado no (hubo/habíamos) muchos estudiantes que querían ser abogados.
3. En el sueño que tuve anoche yo (he/había) terminado mi carrera como ingeniero con mucho éxito.
4. En esta empresa (hay/haya) más de cinco empleados con aspiraciones para ser gerentes.
5. Esteban y Fernando (hayan/han) decidido trabajar por un tiempo primero.
6. Espero que él (ha/haya) conseguido el empleo que estaba buscando.
7. No creo que todos nosotros (hemos/hayamos) estudiado en el mismo colegio en los últimos cuatro años.
8. Alicia no (ha/habías) decidido todavía a qué universidad quiere asistir.

Amigos por correspondencia

Santo Domingo, 15 de abril

Estimada° Elena:

Vi tu carta en una revista. Siempre he querido tener amigos por **correspondencia. Ojalá**° que podamos tener una buena **amistad.**°

　　Te cuento que me llamo Santiago García Robleda, vivo en Santo Domingo, República Dominicana, y soy estudiante del Colegio Colón. Me gustan los deportes **acuáticos. Practico** el **buceo,** el **esquí** y la **pesca.** También me gusta mucho la música y el **baile.** Tengo una gran **colección** de CDs de merengue. Mi padre siempre quiere que escuche la música bien **suave.**° El próximo año es mi último año en el colegio. Al terminar quizás **lo extrañe**° mucho. Todavía no sé lo que voy a hacer después de terminar el colegio. Mi sueño es tener una familia, **fuerte**° y **unida,**° y poder ser un padre estupendo. Me gustaría tener dos hijos. Quizás ellos sean como yo. Creo que ser padre será lo más **hermoso**° de esta vida. ¿Qué crees tú?

　　Bueno, ojalá escribas pronto. Puedes hacerlo a mi e-mail. Mi dirección es santiago@caribe.satel.com. Me gustaría saber cuáles son tus aspiraciones, lo que te gusta y lo que piensas hacer al terminar el colegio.

　　Atentamente,°
　　　　Santiago

Estimada *Dear* **Ojalá** *Would that, If only, I hope* **amistad** *friendship* **suave** *soft* **lo extrañe** *I'll miss it* **fuerte** *strong* **unida** *united, connected* **hermoso** *beautiful, lovely* **Atentamente** *Respectfully, Yours truly*

Notes

Be sure that students understand that an *amigo/amiga por correspondencia* is a pen pal.

Santiago uses *Estimada* as a salutation and *Atentamente* as a closing in his initial letter to Elena. Note that the two young people may change to the less formal *Querida* and *Abrazos* once a friendship is established.

The verb *practicar* is regular in the present tense. Note for students, however, that the *Ud./Uds.* commands (*practique Ud./ practiquen Uds.*) and the preterite tense (*yo practiqué*) follow the pattern of *buscar* and require the spelling change $c \rightarrow qu$.

Activities

Multiple Intelligences (linguistic). Using Santiago's letter as a model, ask students to write a letter of introduction to a pen pal or key pal. If possible, share the correspondence with students at another school and encourage them to reply.

Prereading Strategy. Talk with students about their favorite pastimes. Ask students if they have ever had a key pal or pen pal. Then instruct students to cover the reading with one hand and look at the illustrations. Finally, have students look through the reading quickly to find cognates and words or expressions they have already learned.

Capítulo 9　　387

NATIONAL STANDARDS
C1.2

Answers

19 1. Santiago siempre ha querido tener amigos por correspondencia.
2. Santiago desea poder tener una buena amistad con Elena.
3. Santiago practica el buceo, el esquí y la pesca.
4. Le gusta mucho la música y el baile.
5. Quiere que la escuche muy suave.
6. Va a ser probable que él extrañe mucho el colegio.
7. Santiago quiere que su familia sea fuerte y unida.
8. Santiago dice que ser padre es lo más hermoso de esta vida.

20 Answers will vary.

Notes

The section on the subjunctive can be skipped if you feel your students have a good grasp of how to use it.

Activities

Expansion. Additional questions (*¿Qué comprendiste?*): *¿A quién le escribe Santiago?; ¿Por qué le escribe Santiago a ella?; ¿Cuáles son los apellidos de Santiago?; ¿Qué quiere saber Santiago de Elena?*

Additional questions (*Charlando*): *¿En qué año del bachillerato estás?; ¿Qué deportes practicas?; ¿Te gustaría tener muchos niños/as?; ¿Qué opinas de tener muchos niños/as?; ¿Crees que ser padre o madre es importante? ¿Por qué?*

---

19 ¿Qué comprendiste?

1. ¿Qué ha querido tener siempre Santiago?
2. ¿Qué desea Santiago al escribir la carta?
3. ¿Qué deportes acuáticos practica Santiago?
4. ¿Qué le gusta mucho a Santiago?
5. ¿Cómo quiere el padre de Santiago que él escuche la música?
6. ¿Qué va a ser probable que Santiago extrañe mucho?
7. ¿Cómo quiere Santiago que sea su familia?
8. ¿Qué dice Santiago acerca de ser padre?

20 Charlando

1. ¿Tienes amigos por correspondencia? ¿Por e-mail? ¿De dónde?
2. ¿Crees que tener una buena amistad es fácil o difícil? ¿Por qué?
3. ¿Practicas deportes acuáticos? ¿Cuáles?
4. ¿Tienes alguna colección? ¿De qué?
5. ¿Crees que es importante que una familia sea fuerte y unida? Explica.

¿Crees que es importante que una familia sea fuerte y unida?

IDIOMA

Más sobre el subjuntivo

You have learned to use the subjunctive mood in many different situations: indirect commands, after verbs of emotion, after certain impersonal expressions, etc. In addition, some words and expressions must be followed by the subjunctive when they suggest an element of doubt, indefiniteness or hope.

- **como**

  *Va a hacerlo **como quiera**.*   He/She is going to do it **however he/she wants.**

- **cualquiera**

  ***Cualquiera que escojas** está bien conmigo.*   **Whichever one you choose** is okay with me.

- **dondequiera**

  ***Dondequiera que estudies**, vas a tener que estudiar mucho.*   **Wherever you study,** you are going to have to study a lot.

- **lo que**

  *Uds. pueden estudiar **lo que quieran**.*   You can study **whatever you want.**

- **ojalá (que)**
  ¡Ojalá (que) estudies en la universidad!

  I hope you study at the university!

- **quienquiera**
  Quienquiera que trabaje mucho puede trabajar aquí.

  Whoever works a lot can work here.

- **quizás (quizá)**
  Quizás él esté estudiando ingeniería.

  Perhaps he is studying engineering.

Un amigo por correspondencia

Silvia tiene un amigo por correspondencia en España. Completa su carta con la forma apropiada del subjuntivo de los verbos indicados para saber lo que ella le cuenta.

Quizás él esté estudiando química.

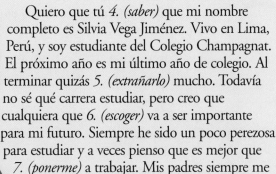

Lima, 6 de mayo

Estimado Antonio:

Hola, ¿cómo estás? Espero que tú *1. (estar)* muy bien. Ésta es la primera carta que yo le escribo a alguien de España. Espero que no *2. (ser)* la última. Ojalá que *3. (poder)* conocerte pronto.

Quiero que tú *4. (saber)* que mi nombre completo es Silvia Vega Jiménez. Vivo en Lima, Perú, y soy estudiante del Colegio Champagnat. El próximo año es mi último año de colegio. Al terminar quizás *5. (extrañarlo)* mucho. Todavía no sé qué carrera estudiar, pero creo que cualquiera que *6. (escoger)* va a ser importante para mi futuro. Siempre he sido un poco perezosa para estudiar y a veces pienso que es mejor que *7. (ponerme)* a trabajar. Mis padres siempre me dicen que debo estudiar como *8. (ser)* y que también puedo estudiar lo que *9. (querer)*.

De mi familia te cuento que tengo un hermano que siempre me toma el pelo, pero él es muy simpático. Espero que quienquiera que *10. (vivir)* contigo no te tome mucho el pelo.

Bueno, ojalá *11. (escribir)* pronto. Quisiera saber de ti y de lo que quieres hacer en el futuro.

Atentamente,

Silvia

Todavía no sé qué carrera estudiar.

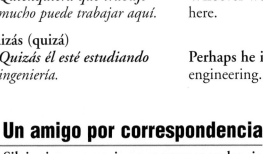

Answers

21
1. estés
2. sea
3. pueda
4. sepas
5. lo extrañe
6. escoja
7. me ponga
8. sea
9. quiera
10. viva
11. escribas

Notes

Point out that the word *ojalá* comes from Arabic. In fact, approximately 25 percent of Spanish words come from Arabic due to the Moorish presence in Spain from 711 until 1492.

Activities

TPR. (Use variations of this TPR activity to teach or review any vocabulary topic.) Choose a theme, "**jobs**," for example. Inform students they are to raise their right hand if the item names a job, and their left hand if the item does not name a job. (This part of the activity will vary depending upon the vocabulary topic.) Then say several words in Spanish to teach and test students' comprehension of vocabulary: *el mesero* (right hand), *la zanahoria* (left hand), *la mujer de negocios* (right hand), *el cuchillo* (left hand), *el avión* (left hand), and so forth.

NATIONAL STANDARDS
C1.2, C4.1

22 Una reunión mañana

Completa las siguientes oraciones con la forma apropiada de los verbos indicados.

 Quizás (yo) te <u>vea</u> mañana. (ver)

1. Ven a la empresa como tú <u>(1)</u>. (preferir)
2. Te encontraré dondequiera que <u>(2)</u>. (estar)
3. Ojalá que nosotros <u>(3)</u> a tiempo. (llegar)
4. Pablo, Diana y Mercedes pueden hacer lo que ellos <u>(4)</u> mientras estamos asistiendo a la reunión mañana. (querer)
5. Quizás nosotros no <u>(5)</u> que estar allí todo el día. (tener)
6. Puedes volver conmigo o quedarte, como te <u>(6)</u> mejor. (convenir)
7. Quienquiera que <u>(7)</u> el empleo está bien conmigo. (conseguir)

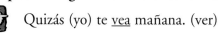

Quizás yo las vea el sábado.

23 Información personal

Completa las siguientes oraciones con información que sea posible para tu futuro.

 Como <u>sea, asistiré a la universidad.</u>

1. Ojalá que....
2. Quienquiera que....
3. Quizás mi familia....
4. Espero que....
5. Voy a hacer lo que....
6. Dondequiera que yo y mi familia....
7. Es probable que....
8. Cualquiera....

UNIVERSIDAD NACIONAL AUTONOMA DE MEXICO

24 ¿Qué dicen?

Haz oraciones completas, usando las pistas que se dan para saber lo que algunas personas dicen.

> quizás/ellas/practicar/el esquí y el buceo
> Quizás ellas practiquen el esquí y el buceo.

1. ojalá/tú/tener/amistades para toda la vida
2. lo que/tú/hacer/hazlo bien
3. dondequiera/tú/ir/debes de ser siempre el mismo
4. cualquiera/ser/la música que tú/escuchar/debes escucharla bien suave
5. ojalá/tú/poder/escribirme pronto
6. cualquiera/saber/dónde es el baile debe decírnolo ahora
7. quienquiera/despertarse/primero mañana debe despertarnos a todos

Quizás ella practique el esquí acuático.

25 Sueños y aspiraciones

Trabajando en parejas, hablen de sus sueños o aspiraciones, usando las siguientes palabras: *como, dondequiera, lo que, ojalá (que)* y *quizás.*

> A: Ojalá sea un abogado famoso.
> B: Quizás pueda ayudar con los problemas del mundo.

Ojalá que yo sea entrenador de un equipo.

DAVID GUTIERREZ ZERECERO
ABOGADO

ASESORIA JURIDICA EN JUICIOS DE:

CONTRATOS DE ARRENDAMIENTO TESTAMENTARIOS E INTESTAMENTARIOS DIVORCIOS, MERCANTILES Y AMPAROS

TEL. 82-04-11

Heriberto Frías No. 1509
Despacho 16, Centro

Autoevaluación. Como repaso y autoevaluación, responde lo siguiente:

1. What are some of your plans after graduation?
2. Name two problems you see in the world.
3. What careers have you considered for your future? Could you use Spanish in your career choice?
4. Name two things that you have done to help your parents this week.
5. Name something you hope people have learned from one of the problems in the world.
6. What three things would you write about yourself in a letter to a pen pal?
7. Imagine that your friend is going on vacation to a place where you have been before. Advise your friend of several things to do or see there.

Activity 10

Notes

-www-

Job Search
http://www.cmjobscareers.com/busquedas.htm

Technology. Make certain to explain any Web-use policies your school may have before assigning this project. The ATE Teacher's Introduction offers tips and guidelines for using technology in the classroom.

Before assigning activity A, have students brainstorm and prepare for the activity by writing down their goals and aspirations.

Students should share with the class the information they found on the Internet about jobs.

¡La práctica hace al maestro!

A Comunicación

Working with a partner, talk about your goals and aspirations. Tell what you plan to do after high school. Discuss whether you would like to continue your education at a university, whether you would like to begin to work immediately after receiving your diploma, or if you would prefer to study and work at the same time. Continue by discussing any future plans you may have.

B Conexión con la tecnología

Use the Internet to contact the web site for a company or corporation where you might like to work. Then follow their prompts to see what employment opportunities they offer that use Spanish. Find out what the prerequisites are, where the openings are and what the salary range is. Print out the results of your job search to share with the rest of the class.

Hemos encontrado mucha información sobre las carreras.

VOCABULARIO

Notes

The *Vocabulario* is intended as a resource for reviewing the active vocabulary for the lesson. As a self-test, have students determine how many of the words and expressions they recognize and know how to use.

Activities

Pronunciation. To ensure proper pronunciation, model each word or expression and have students repeat after you.

Los empleos

el abogado, la abogada
el agricultor, la agricultora
el artista, la artista
el bibliotecario, la bibliotecaria
el bombero, la bombera
el carpintero, la carpintera
el chofer, la chofer
el empleado, la empleada
el empleo
el escritor, la escritora
el fotógrafo, la fotógrafa
el gerente, la gerente
el hombre de negocios
el ingeniero, la ingeniera
el mecánico, la mecánica
la mujer de negocios
el obrero, la obrera
el peluquero, la peluquera
el programador, la programadora
el secretario, la secretaria
el taxista, la taxista
el vendedor, la vendedora
el veterinario, la veterinaria

Verbos

asistir a
extrañar
practicar

Expresiones y otras palabras

aceptado,-a
acuático,-a
la amistad
la aspiración
atentamente
el baile
el buceo
la carrera

la colección
la correspondencia
dondequiera
la empresa
estimado,-a
el esquí
la experiencia
fuerte
el futuro
hermoso,-a
el negocio
ojalá
la pesca
quienquiera
real
suave
el sueño
unido,-a
la universidad

G.C. ASESORES GERENCIALES

SOLICITA

2 Contadores(as)
Lic. en Contaduría, experiencia mínima 8 años, sueldo Bs. 40/50.000

1 Gerente de Tienda
Caballeros. Exp. indispensable en electrodomésticos, electrónica. Suel-do Bs. 25/30.000, más bonos

2 Jefes de Reaseguro y Coaseguros
Caballeros, experiencia mínima de 3 años. Bs. 35/40.000

1 Supervisor de Producción
Exp. empresas avícolas, manejo de personal, control de calidad, empaque. Bs. 35/40.000

4 Analistas en Ramo de Personas
Exp. en H.C.M., cálculos, emisiones y reclamos. Bs. 18/20.000

6 Representantes de Ventas
Caballeros. Exp. en ventas de pinturas, con vehículo. Bs. 25.000 más comisiones de 3% y gastos de vehículo

5 Promotores de Ventas
T.S.U. en Mercadeo y Publicidad, con experiencia, y vehículo, para impor tante empresa de Servicio Automotor. Bs. 27.000, más comisión

3 Asistentes Administrativos
... diantes de Administración, damas y caballeros. Exp. ... ... manejo micros, ventas. Bs. 25/30.000

... ... rensable experiencia bancaria. Bs. 18/22.000

... de Cobranzas
... eriencia mínima de 2 años. Bs. 18/20.000

... res Contables
... costos. Bs. 15/18.000

... scriptoras de Datos
... 8.000

... cretarias Ejecutivas
... ira. Bs. 22/25.000

... Secretarias Dpto. Ventas
... Exp. cargo similar, atención vendedores, clientes. Bs. 18/20.000

1 Secretaria Contable
Exp. llevar libros banco, conciliaciones, retenciones. Bs. 20.000

2 Secretarias Dpto. Computación
Manejo de Wordstar, Lotus, paquetes contables, micros o Macintosh. Bs. 20/22.000

5 Secretarias Mecanógrafas
Con conocimientos generales de oficinas, buena mecanógrafa. Bs. 15/18.000

2 Oficinistas Aduaneros
Conocimientos básicos de aranceles, manejo de cargas y embarques de guías aéreas. Bs. 15/17.000

5 Recepcionistas o Centralistas
Mecanógrafas con experiencia, de excelente presencia, mínimo 3er año, edad 18/25, zonas. Macaracuay, C.C.C.T. Chacao, Los Ruices, Centro Bs. 12/14.000

Presentarse con currículum y foto a la avenida Casanova, Centro Comercial Cediaz, Torre Este, P. 3, Ofc. E-23, Sabana Grande. De lunes a viernes, en horario de 8 am. 12 m y 1 pm a 5 pm. Información teléfonos: 761.3520 - 761.3810.

Se Necesita el Siguiente Personal

Mecánico
Técnico Mecánico, 2 años de experiencia (mínimo), sólidos conocimientos de bombas, equipos industriales y de la utilización de los equipos inherentes al cargo.

Electricista
Técnico Electricista, 2 años de experiencia (mínimo), conocimientos en tableros de control, detección de fallas y lectura de planos.

Auxiliar Técnico 1
Egresado INCE en mecánica industrial, conocimientos generales de plome-ría y aire acondicionado.

Auxiliar Técnico 2
Egresado INCE en Electricidad Industrial, conocimientos en motores eléctri-cos y tableros.

Chofer
Licencia de 4a., con experiencia en la zona metropolitana, en cuanto a compra de repuestos y equipos industriales.

Mantenimiento
Sexo masculino, mayor de 30 años, experiencia como aseador preferible-mente en el Área de Hoteles y/o clínicas.
Los interesados pueden enviar su curriculum vitae o información al Apartado Nº 60039 de Chacao, Atención Sr. César Reyes.

¿Puedes identificar qué empleo tiene cada uno de ellos?

¡Qué suerte tienes!

Quiz/Activity 1

Activity 59

Activity 1

Content reviewed in *Lección 18*
- future tense
- subjunctive
- expressing doubt
- expressing emotion
- describing

Notes
Note that the verb *organizar* requires the spelling change z → c: *organicemos*.

Activities
Critical Listening. Play the audiocassette/audio compact disc recording of the dialog. Instruct students to cover the words as they listen to the conversation in order to develop good listening skills before concentrating on reading Spanish. Have students look at the illustration and imagine what the people are saying to one another. Ask several individuals to state what they believe the main theme of the conversation is.

Prereading Strategy. Instruct students to cover up the dialog with one hand and look at the illustration. Ask them to imagine what the people are saying to one another. Finally, have students look through the dialog quickly to find cognates and other words or expressions they already know.

Contexto cultural
EL MUNDO

Lección 18
¡Qué suerte tienes!

TERESA: En un mes visitaré **Francia** e **Inglaterra** y todavía no lo puedo creer. Ése ha sido uno de mis sueños más grandes y, **por fin,**° será **realidad.**

LAURA: ¡Qué suerte tienes! Mi gran sueño es o vivir en una **isla en medio del**° **océano** donde pueda ver todas las mañanas el **mar**° o tener una casita a la **orilla**° de un **río. Sin embargo,**° parece que nunca será realidad ninguno de estos sueños.

TERESA: Algún día tu sueño será realidad. Debes **mantener**° una **actitud** positiva. **A propósito,**° ¿sabías que Mateo estudiará en una universidad en **Italia?**

LAURA: **¡No me digas!**°

TERESA: Sí, asistirá a la **Facultad**° de Economía y quizás se quede a vivir allá.

LAURA: ¡Qué bueno! **Siempre se sale con la suya.**°

TERESA: Conviene que le **organicemos**° una fiesta de **despedida.**°

LAURA: ¡Qué **magnífica** idea! Bueno, yo te llamo mañana para organizarla.

TERESA: Sí, llámame.

por fin *finally* **en medio del** *in the middle (center) of* **mar** *sea* **orilla** *shore* **Sin embargo** *Nevertheless* **mantener** *to keep, to maintain* **A propósito** *By the way* **¡No me digas!** *You don't say!* **Facultad** *School (of a university)* **Siempre se sale con la suya.** *He always gets his way.* **organicemos** *we should organize* **despedida** *farewell, good-bye*

1 ¿Qué comprendiste?

1. ¿Cuál es el sueño que por fin será realidad para Teresa?
2. ¿Cuál es el gran sueño de Laura?
3. ¿Qué debe mantener Laura para hacer su sueño realidad, según Teresa?
4. ¿Quién se sale siempre con la suya?
5. ¿Qué quieren organizarle Teresa y Laura a Mateo?
6. ¿Cuál es una magnífica idea, según Laura?
7. ¿Qué le dice con la mano Laura a Teresa que ella va a hacer mañana?

2 Charlando

1. ¿Por qué crees que es bueno mantener una buena actitud?
2. ¿Has organizado alguna fiesta de despedida para algún amigo/a? ¿Para quién? ¿Adónde iba tu amigo/a?
3. ¿Has tenido algún sueño que se te haya hecho realidad? Explica.
4. ¿Usas las manos para hablar? Explica.

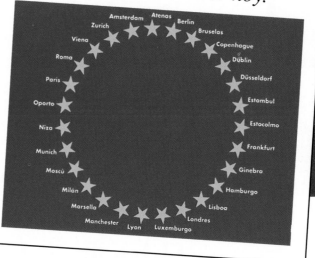

IBERIA: Nº 1 en Iberoamérica

Piense qué ciudad de Europa le gustaría conocer hoy.

Answers

1
1. El sueño que por fin será realidad para Teresa es visitar Francia e Inglaterra.
2. El gran sueño de Laura es o vivir en una isla en medio del océano donde pueda ver todas las mañanas el mar, o tener una casita a la orilla de un río.
3. Según Teresa, Laura debe mantener una actitud positiva.
4. Mateo se sale siempre con la suya.
5. Quieren organizarle una fiesta de despedida.
6. Es una magnífica idea organizarle una fiesta de despedida a Mateo.
7. Laura le dice a Teresa que la va a llamar.

2 Answers will vary.

Notes
As you discuss gestures, remind students that certain body contact is typical of Spanish speakers. For example, two women or a male and female will often greet or say good bye with a kiss on the cheek (two kisses in Spain) while two men will shake hands or share an *abrazo* (hug).

Activities
Expansion. Additional questions (*¿Qué comprendiste?*): *¿Dónde estudiará Mateo?; ¿A qué escuela asistirá Mateo?*

 Estrategia

Para hablar mejor: *using body language*

How much can you say without speaking? Think about it, when you are talking with someone in English your facial expressions, gestures and even your posture or proximity to a person communicate a lot. For example, your friends and family can probably tell immediately when you are angry simply by looking at you. In addition, you can describe something that is very small just by putting your thumb and forefinger together to signal how small the object is.

Learning body language is an important part of improving your fluency in Spanish, as well. Observe native Spanish speakers as they talk and begin to imitate the gestures they use. Watch a speaker's face and learn to interpret non-spoken cues that tell what the person is thinking or feeling. Then begin to use body language to speak Spanish without saying a word.

¿Qué está diciendo ella?

NATIONAL STANDARDS
C1.1, C1.2, C2.1, C3.2, C4.1, C4.2, C5.2

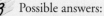

Answers

 3 Possible answers:
1. Marisol dice que escuche.
2. Paula dice que piense.
3. Héctor dice que va a llamar.
4. Yolanda dice que está cansada.
5. Joaquín dice que hay problemas.

Notes

Show students what the hand gestures look like in person. Then add others you know.

Activities

Communities. After studying gestures commonly used by Spanish speakers, ask students to consider their own body language: What gestures do they use and what messages do they convey? Are their gestures similar to or different from those of Spanish speakers?

Critical Thinking. Using transparency 60, ask students to guess what the people in the illustration are communicating with gestures.

 PARAti

Proverbios y dichos
Do not be afraid to dream or set big goals for yourself even though you think they might seem impossible to attain. You have nothing to lose by dreaming. After all, as the Spanish saying goes, *Soñar no cuesta nada* (To dream is free).

El lenguaje del cuerpo

Martín

Marisol

Paula

Héctor

Yolanda

Joaquín

 3 **¿Qué dicen?**

Di lo que crees que cada una de las personas de la ilustración está diciendo con su cuerpo.

 Martín dice que tenga cuidado.

Repaso *rápido*

El futuro

Use the future tense to tell what will happen. The endings are the same for all verbs.

é	emos
ás	éis
á	án

Look at the following:

Él viajará mañana a Francia. **He will travel** tomorrow to France.
Yo estudiaré en Inglaterra. **I'll study** in England.

The future tense also can be used in Spanish to indicate what is probable at the present time.

Estarán en Ecuador ahora. **I imagine they are** in Ecuador now.
Ella llegará ahora mismo. **She is probably arriving** right now.

The following verbs have irregular stems:

caber: **cabr**	poder: **podr**	querer: **querr**	saber: **sabr**	decir: **dir**
poner: **pondr**	salir: **saldr**	tener: **tendr**	venir: **vendr**	hacer: **har**

Estarán en Ecuador.

4 La despedida para Mateo

Laura y Teresa organizan la fiesta de despedida para Mateo. Completa las siguientes oraciones con la forma del futuro de los verbos indicados.

 Mi hermano *(encargarse)* de mantener ocupado a Mateo.
Mi hermano se encargará de mantener ocupado a Mateo.

1. Teresa *(preparar)* la lista de invitados.
2. Yo *(tener)* que ir al supermercado para comprar algunos refrescos y comida.
3. Juanita *(conseguir)* la música para el baile.
4. Fernando *(venir)* con Mateo el viernes a las nueve para empezar la fiesta.
5. Laura *(llamar)* a todos los invitados.
6. Tú *(hacer)* un pastel bien grande.
7. Carlos y Sara *(escribir)* una señal que diga: ¡Buena suerte!
8. Nosotros *(poner)* todos los muebles en su lugar después de la fiesta.

 Quiz/Activity 3

 Activities 3-4

 Quiz/Activity 1

Answers

4
1. preparará
2. tendré
3. conseguirá
4. vendrá
5. llamará
6. harás
7. escribirán
8. pondremos

Notes

Skip the *Repaso rápido* and activities 4 and 5 if you are comfortable with your students' understanding of how to form and use the future tense in Spanish.

Activities

Cooperative Learning. As indicated in the dialog and readings found in this chapter, students are making plans for the summer and for the future. Ask small groups of students to discuss their plans and then present them to the class.

Critical Listening. Say aloud several verbs that are in either the past or the future tense. Ask students to raise their left hand if the verb is in the past tense, and their right hand if the verb is in the future tense.

Students with Special Needs. Model a second sentence for activity 4.

NATIONAL STANDARDS
C1.2, C4.1

Answers

5 1. ¿...pasarás...?/Pasaré....
2. ¿...mantendrás...?/
Mantendré....
3. ¿...harás...?/Haré....
4. ¿...extrañarás...?/
Extrañaré....
5. ¿...vivirás?/Viviré en....
6. ¿...tendrás...?/Tendré....
7. ¿...será...?/Será....

Notes

The *Universidad de Salamanca*, founded in 1218, is one of the oldest and most prestigious universities in Europe.

Remind students that there must be a change of subject in order to use the subjunctive.

The section on the subjunctive and accompanying activities can be skipped if you feel your students have a good grasp of how to use the subjunctive.

Activities

Critical Thinking. Have students prepare a list of advice they would offer their own children (or another younger family member). Then ask students to justify each suggestion.

Spanish for Spanish Speakers. Talk with students about the newspaper clipping on page 398. Then ask questions to determine how much students understood: *¿Dónde está la Universidad del Valle?; ¿Qué están ofreciendo el veintiuno de septiembre? ¿A qué hora?; ¿Qué carreras ofrecen?; ¿Dónde puede uno conseguir más información?*

---

5 Tu vida en el futuro

Imagina cómo será tu vida en el futuro. Trabajando en parejas, alterna con tu compañero/a de clase en hacer preguntas y en contestarlas para saber algunas cosas del futuro.

en qué/trabajar (en una oficina como programador)
A: ¿En qué trabajarás?
B: Trabajaré en una oficina como programador.

1. dónde/pasar vacaciones en un año (en una isla en medio del océano)
2. qué/mantener siempre (una buena actitud)
3. cuánto dinero/hacer (mucho dinero)
4. qué/extrañar en veinte años (jugar al fútbol con mis amigos)
5. dónde/vivir (en Francia)
6. qué/tener en diez años (una casa magnífica a la orilla de un río)
7. cómo/ser tu familia (grande y unida)

IDIOMA

El subjuntivo: un resumen

Remember to use the subjunctive mood in the following circumstances:

- as an indirect/implied command
  ¡Que lo haga Teresa! — Let Teresa do it!
  ¡Quiero que Paula lo haga! — I want Paula to do it!

- after causal verbs if there is a change of subject
  Te aconsejo que estudies en España. — I advise you to study in Spain.
  Prefiero que tu hermanastra vaya a Francia. — I prefer that your stepsister go to France.

- after verbs that indicate emotion or doubt
  Nos alegra de que pienses asistir a la universidad. — It pleases us that you are thinking about attending the university.
  Dudo que ella haya llegado a Italia todavía. — I doubt she has arrived in Italy yet.

Te aconsejo que estudies en España.

VNIVERSIDAD DE SALAMANCA

- after impersonal expressions that imply doubt, emotion or uncertainty

  Es probable que (ella) compre una casa a la orilla del mar. It's probable that she will buy a house on the seashore.

  Es importante que empieces a pensar en tu futuro. It is important that you begin to think about your future.

- after the expressions *como, cualquiera, dondequiera, lo que, ojalá (que), quienquiera* and *quizá(s)* when they suggest an element of doubt, indefiniteness or hope

  Quizás (yo) estudie en la Facultad de Economía. Perhaps I'll study in the School of Economics.

  Ojalá que ella se salga con la suya. I hope she gets her way.

6 Todos dicen algo

Haz oraciones completas, usando el subjuntivo para saber lo que dicen los siguientes miembros de la familia de Eva.

  JUAN: (querer/que Eva/estudiar/en Inglaterra)
  JUAN: Quiero que Eva estudie en Inglaterra.

1. SUSANA: (preferir/que todos nosotros/asistir/a una universidad de aquí)
2. RICARDO: (ser/probable que yo/decidir/estudiar en la Facultad de Química)
3. ARMANDO: (ojalá que tú/no cambiar/de opinión)
4. GABRIELA: (convenir/que/nosotros/organizarle/una fiesta de despedida a Eva)
5. EVA: (mamá, que mi hermanita/no decir/nada)
6. PEDRO: (dudar/que ella/querer/ir tan lejos)
7. CLARA: (no creer/que ella/tener/nada que hacer allá)

Quiero que estudies en Inglaterra.

Answers

6
1. Prefiero que todos nosotros asistamos a una universidad de aquí.
2. Es probable que yo decida estudiar en la Facultad de Química.
3. Ojalá que no cambies de opinión.
4. Conviene que nosotros le organicemos una fiesta de despedida a Eva.
5. Mamá, que mi hermanita no diga nada.
6. Dudo que ella quiera ir tan lejos.
7. No creo que ella tenga nada que hacer allá.

NATIONAL STANDARDS
C1.2, C4.1

7 ¿Se necesita o no?

Decide si se necesita o no el subjuntivo en cada una de las siguientes
oraciones. Si se necesita, di la forma apropiada.

 Es importante que tú *(mantener)* una buena actitud.
Es importante que tú <u>mantengas</u> una buena actitud.

Es necesario *(organizarle)* una fiesta de despedida a Mateo.
No se necesita.

1. Por fin, mis sueños van a
   (ser) realidad.
2. Mi padre me permite que yo *(ir)* a
   Inglaterra este verano.
3. Creo que *(pescar)* a la orilla de un río es
   mi pasatiempo favorito.
4. Los dejo *(trabajar)* todo el tiempo
   que quieran.
5. Mis padres quieren que yo *(pensar)* en
   el futuro.
6. Lo que ellos quieren *(hacer)* es jugar al fútbol.
7. Quiero *(tener)* una casa en una isla en
   medio del océano.
8. Quizás ellos *(salirse)* con la suya.
9. Mi padre dice que yo *(asistir)* a la Facultad de
   Economía de la Universidad Nacional.

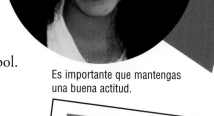

Es importante que mantengas
una buena actitud.

8 ¡Hablando con tus hijos!

Imagina que ya eres padre o madre y hablas con
tus hijos para darles consejos o decirles lo que
piensas. Haz oraciones completas, usando el
subjuntivo para saber lo que les dices a tus hijos.

querer/ir/a la universidad
Quiero que vayan a la universidad.

1. aconsejarles/mantener/una buena actitud en
   la vida
2. querer/siempre decir/la verdad
3. insistir en/siempre buscar/buenas amistades
4. esperar/no tratar/de salirse siempre con
   la suya
5. esperar/siempre ser/buenos estudiantes
6. pedirles/siempre organizar/su cuarto antes
   de salir
7. prefiero/practicar/deportes como la pesca
   o el buceo

9 En camino al volcán

José es el guía de un grupo de turistas que van a caminar por una selva en Costa Rica para llegar a un volcán. Completa el siguiente diálogo, usando la forma apropiada del subjuntivo, el indicativo o el infinitivo de los verbos indicados.

JOSÉ: Bueno, aquí empieza el camino que va hasta el volcán apagado. Antes de comenzar a caminar, quiero *1. (decirles)* unas cuantas cosas. Primero, es muy probable que *2. (llover)* muy pronto. Así que conviene que Uds. *3. (ponerse)* las botas y que *4. (llevar)* un impermeable de plástico en las mochilas *(backpacks)*. Segundo, no creo que nosotros *5. (tardar)* más de dos horas en llegar al volcán. Allí, podemos hacer lo que *6. (querer)*: bañarnos en el laguito, tomar una siesta, comer, etc. Recuerden, es importantísimo que todos nosotros *7. (quedarse)* con el grupo para no perdernos. ¿Tienen alguna pregunta?

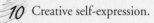
Quiero que me sigan para que no se pierdan.

NIÑA: Señor, ¿hay aquí leones salvajes que *8. (comer)* a la gente?

JOSÉ: *(riéndose)* No, no te preocupes. Aquí no hay nada que te *9. (poder)* hacer daño.

SEÑOR: ¿Cree Ud. que nosotros *10. (ir)* a ver algunos animales?

JOSÉ: Es casi seguro que nosotros *11. (ver)* serpientes, monos y pájaros de muchos colores diferentes. Bueno, si no hay más preguntas, ¡adelante! ¡Ojalá que todos Uds. *12. (divertirse)* y que *13. (sacar)* muy buenas fotos!

Ojalá que haya pájaros de muchos colores.

10 De tu vida personal

Completa las siguientes oraciones lógicamente para hablar de tu futuro. Usa el subjuntivo, el indicativo o el infinitivo, según sea necesario.

    Espero que....
Espero que pueda viajar por todo el mundo.

1. Estoy seguro de que....
2. Quizás....
3. Ojalá que....
4. No creo que....
5. Mi aspiración más grande es....
6. Mi gran sueño es....
7. Será importante que....
8. Creo que me gustaría....

Espero que lleguemos a lo más alto.

Capítulo 9   401

Notes

Point out that many Spanish speakers learn as children that *América* is one continent as opposed to two (*América del Norte* and *América del Sur*).

Communities. The choices for obtaining information in Spanish about the rest of the world are growing greater every year. Television stations that broadcast in Spanish across the world include cable stations such as *Univisión, CBS Telenoticias, CNN En Español,* and so forth. The countries shown on this map also receive broadcasts of the same or similar content as the world becomes smaller every year.

Activities

Expansion. Teach the Spanish names for other countries shown on the world map on pages 402-403.

Prereading Strategy. Using transparency 62, pronounce each of the words in the illustration and have students repeat them. Then use transparency 61 to point to some of the sites included in the illustration and ask students to name the country.

TPR. Read aloud the names of several sites shown on the map on pages 402-403. Have students locate and point to each place you name.

Conexión *Cultural*

El mundo

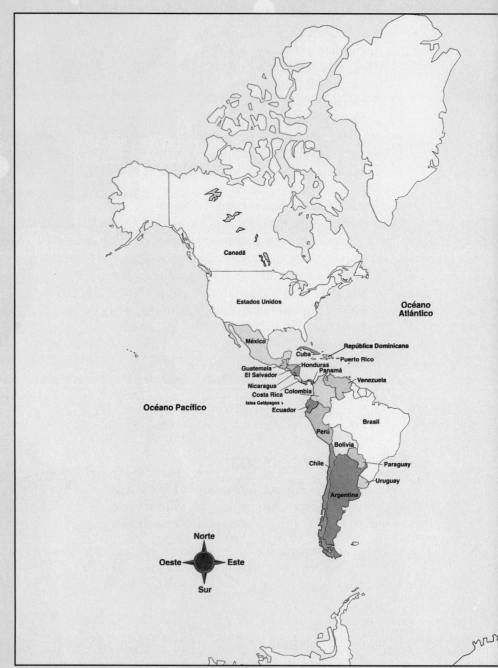

El mundo
http://www.lonelyplanet.com/dest
/index1.htm

Remind students that Spanish is widely spoken in the central African country of *Guinea Ecuatorial*.

Activities

Connections. As an additional activity, ask students to give the capitals of the countries indicated on the map.

Critical Listening. Try using the directions *norte, sur, este* and *oeste* to discuss the location of the sites shown on the map.

Multiple Intelligences (bodily-kinesthetic). In order to practice countries and nationalities, toss a beach ball to a student while saying the name of a country and ask him/her to say the corresponding nationality. In turn, the student should toss the ball to another classmate while naming a different country. The game continues and involves all students. As a variation, toss the beach ball while saying a country and the recipient must respond with the capital city.

NATIONAL STANDARDS
C1.2, C5.2

Notes

The Spanish word *americano* can refer to anyone from the American continent(s). For this reason, it is best for U.S. citizens to identify themselves as *estadounidenses* or *de los Estados Unidos*.

Activities

Connections. Extend the information provided in this *Algo más* by having students identify various places on a wall map of the world.

Multiple Intelligences (spatial). For additional writing practice, and in order to encourage visual learners with artistic skills, have students prepare maps of the world in Spanish, adding any details they wish.

TPR. Offer appropriate TPR support, where possible: Have students point to the places they hear, using the maps at the front of the book or a classroom wall map, if one is available.

Algo más

¿Adónde te gustaría viajar?

el África	africano,-a
la América	americano,-a
la América Central	centroamericano,-a
la América del Norte	norteamericano,-a
la América del Sur	suramericano,-a
el Asia	asiático,-a
Australia	australiano, -a
Europa	europeo,-a

Algunos países del mundo

Alemania	alemán, alemana
Arabia Saudita	saudita
el Brasil	brasileño,-a
el Canadá	canadiense
la China	chino,-a
Francia	francés, francesa
Inglaterra	inglés, inglesa
Italia	italiano,-a
el Japón	japonés, japonesa
Kenya	kenyano,-a
Marruecos	marroquí
Portugal	portugués, portuguesa
Rusia	ruso,-a

Me gustaría ir a la Patagonia, una región de la América del Sur.

Cada vez más gente está descubriendo el mapa del tesoro.

Un espectacular crecimiento del producto nacional bruto. Los costes más competitivos. Los elevados índices de productividad y rentabilidad han convertido a Portugal en el camino más corto hacia los mercados europeos y de otros continentes.

Por eso hay cada vez más gente que no viene a Portugal a tomar el sol. Aunque, de paso, lo toma. Disfrutando de una calidad de vida mayor de la que se imaginaba.

Ven a Portugal. Descubre el turismo de negocios. Recorre el MAPA DEL TESORO.

Empieza a imaginar Portugal, llamando al (91) 571 59 68.

Portugal.
Más de lo que te imaginas.

PARAti

Más países del mundo

Camboya	*Cambodia*
Croacia	*Croatia*
Egipto	*Egypt*
Iraq	*Iraq*
Irán	*Iran*
Irlanda	*Ireland*
Israel	*Israel*
Jordania	*Jordan*
Libia	*Libya*
Siria	*Syria*
Turquía	*Turkey*
Vietnam	*Vietnam*

¿Te gustaría ir a Alemania?

11 Cruzando fronteras

Identifica en español los lugares indicados, según los números.

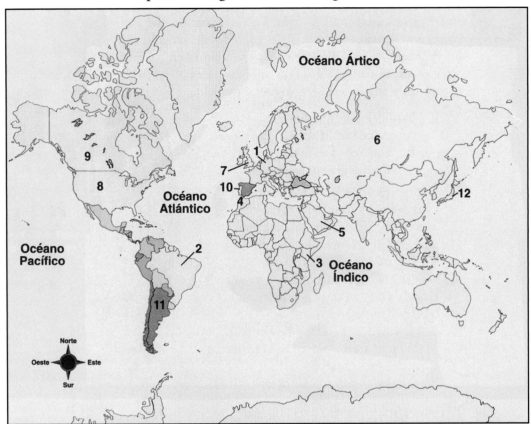

12 Las nacionalidades

Di de qué nacionalidad son las siguientes personas, según el país donde nacieron.

 Roberto/Italia
Es italiano.

1. João/el Portugal
2. Carolyn/Australia
3. Boris/Rusia
4. Hassan/Marruecos
5. Alí/Arabia Saudita
6. Marcelo y Mario/Chile
7. Hua/la China
8. Pablo/México
9. Hiroshi/el Japón
10. Jomo/Kenya
11. Sophie y Marie/Francia
12. Charles/Inglaterra
13. Raquel/el Brasil
14. Thom/el Canadá
15. Markus/Alemania

Roberto es italiano.

Activity 12

Answers

11
1. Alemania
2. Brasil
3. Kenya
4. Marruecos
5. Arabia Saudita
6. Rusia
7. Inglaterra
8. Estados Unidos
9. Canadá
10. Portugal
11. Argentina
12. Japón

12
1. Es portugués.
2. Es australiana.
3. Es ruso.
4. Es marroquí.
5. Es saudita.
6. Son chilenos.
7. Es chino.
8. Es mexicano.
9. Es japonés.
10. Es kenyano.
11. Son francesas.
12. Es inglés.
13. Es brasileña.
14. Es canadiense.
15. Es alemán.

Activities

Language through Action. Read aloud the name of several sites shown on the map on pages 402-403. Have students locate and point to each place you name.

NATIONAL STANDARDS
C1.1, C1.2, C3.1, C4.1

13 De todo el mundo

Imagina que estudiantes de diferentes partes del mundo visitarán tu ciudad para una reunión internacional. Tú y tu amigo/a leen una lista y tratan de adivinar de qué países son y cuáles son sus nacionalidades de acuerdo con los nombres de cada uno de ellos. Trabajando en parejas, alterna con tu compañero/a de clase en hacer preguntas y en contestarlas. Sigue el modelo.

Yamid/Japón (Arabia Saudita)
A: ¿Será Yamid del Japón?
B: No creo que Yamid sea japonés. Creo qué él es saudita.

1. George/Estados Unidos (Inglaterra)
2. Claudette y Laure/Italia (Francia)
3. Vasco dos Santos/Brasil (Portugal)
4. Mijael y Boris/Australia (Rusia)
5. Michiko/China (Japón)
6. Mogo/Marruecos (Kenya)
7. Beatrix y Hans/Francia (Alemania)
8. Michael/Inglaterra (Canadá)
9. Frank y Sydney/Canadá (Australia)
10. Mohamed/Arabia Saudita (Marruecos)
11. Raquel/Chile (Brasil)
12. Franchesco y Giovanni/Portugal (Italia)

No creo que Mike sea brasileño. Creo que él es australiano.

14 Dicen que...

Las siguientes personas han viajado por varios países del mundo. Trabajando en parejas, alterna con tu compañero/a de clase en decir que has oído que estas personas han visitado los siguientes países y en decir que dudas que los hayan visitado. Usen cualquiera de las expresiones de duda que conocen, escogiendo una de las siguientes: *dudar, no creer, no pensar, no estar seguro/a de, es difícil, es dudoso, no es probable, no es claro, no es evidente, no es seguro* y *no es verdad*.

el señor y la señora Torres/Italia
A: El señor y la señora Torres dicen que han visitado Italia.
B: Dudo que hayan visitado Italia.

1. los abuelos de Santiago/Australia
2. Miguel y Carlos/China
3. el padre de Diana y Carolina/Portugal
4. el presidente de la empresa/Arabia Saudita
5. los tíos de Susana/Rusia
6. Graciela/Marruecos
7. Felipe/Rusia
8. Esteban/Alemania

¿Dudas que hayan visitado Italia?

15 Preguntas personales

Contesta las siguientes preguntas en español.

1. ¿Cuáles son los tres países del mundo que más te gustaría visitar?
2. ¿En qué país del mundo diferente del tuyo te gustaría vivir?
3. ¿Te gustaría estudiar en una universidad de otro país? Explica.
4. ¿Tienes amigos o amigas por correspondencia de otros países del mundo? ¿De dónde?
5. ¿Conoces a alguna persona que sea de otro país y que viva en donde tú vives? ¿De dónde es? ¿Cómo se llama?
6. ¿Has estado en algún país europeo, africano o asiático? ¿En cuál?
7. ¿Has estado en la América Central o en la América del Sur? ¿En dónde?

16 Tu futuro

Contesta las siguientes preguntas, usando el tiempo futuro o el subjuntivo.

1. ¿Dónde vivirás en el año 2005?
2. ¿Qué países visitarás en los próximos diez años?
3. ¿Cuándo comprarás tu primera casa?
4. ¿Qué clase será de más ayuda para ti en el futuro?
5. ¿Irás a una universidad después de terminar tus estudios en el colegio? Explica.
6. ¿Dónde estarás en cinco años?
7. ¿Qué empleo tendrás en diez años?

17 Encuesta sobre el futuro

Haz una encuesta a cuatro compañeros/as de tu clase para saber lo que contestaron a las preguntas de la actividad anterior. Luego, trabajando en parejas preparen un informe con la información obtenida *(collected)* y preséntenlo a la clase.

Cinco estudiantes piensan que vivirán en el mismo lugar en el año 2005.

En el año 2005 viviré en el sur de Francia.

Autoevaluación. Como repaso y autoevaluación, responde lo siguiente:

1. Sketch two uses of body language you could use in a Spanish-speaking city to communicate with someone.
2. List three things to describe how your life will be in five years.
3. Use three suggestions your parents gave you to advise a friend.
4. Imagine you are a travel agent creating a travel brochure. Write what activities and sites will be featured on the tour to three countries.

Activity 10

Answers

A Creative self-expression.

B Creative self-expression.

Notes

www

Travel Information
http://www.lycos.com/travel/
http://www.itn.net
http://www.travelzoo.com
Search Engines
Lycos
http://www.lycos.com/
Yahoo
http://www.yahoo.com/
Yahoo Español
http://espanol.yahoo.com/
Webcrawler
http://www.webcrawler.com/
Infoseek
http://www.infoseek.com/
Altavista
http://www.altavista.digital.com/

Technology. Suggest that students use one of the many available Internet search engines to do their search for summer-abroad programs mentioned in activity B.

For all oral activities, listen for the correct pronunciation and determine if students appear to understand what they are saying and hearing. Also, be sure students personalize information so that it is meaningful to them.

Encourage creativity as students prepare activity B. Tell them they are writing about travel to another country, so they may actually be able to use the information to begin to make plans for a trip they would like to take some day.

NATIONAL STANDARDS
C1.1, C1.2, C1.3, C3.2,
C4.1, C4.2, C5.1

¡La práctica hace al maestro!

A Comunicación

Working in groups of four students, talk about what the world will be like in the future. You may wish to include some of the following in your discussion: possible problems and their solutions; your hopes and dreams for the future and how they can be accomplished; how the world will change.

B Conexión con la tecnología

Plan a vacation to another country this summer, selecting from any of the places you have learned in this lesson. Search the Internet for information about the country you have chosen and possible travel packages to that place or to some site in a part of the world you have always wanted to see. Print out the information on the packages that interest you the most and that offer the best prices. Share your findings with the rest of the class. Tell which trip you would choose, how much it would cost and what is included in the price. Illustrate your presentation with information you downloaded and printed out.

SEMANA SANTA en...
RIO DE JANEIRO Y BUZIOS
3 al 10 ABRIL
DESDE USD **1.065***
INCLUYE: Pasaje Aéreo Santiago/Rio/Santiago vía VARIG.
Alojamiento en **Rio**, HOTEL LEME PALACE. En **Buzios**, Hotel 5 estrellas COLONNA PARK. Desayunos brasileros, 5 cenas en diferentes restaurants de Buzios. Traslados.

PAULO •BUENOS AIRES •PUNTA DEL ESTE •MONTEVIDEO

Plan Revista Suramericana
El plan ideal para Navidad y año Nuevo !
INCLUYE: Cena Especial de Navidad en Rio, Cena y Fiesta de Año Nuevo en Buenos Aires.
OPCIONAL: Lima y Cuzco.

CREDITO:
Con o sin cuota inicial
Hasta 24 meses de plazo
SALIDA: Diciembre 20

Informes e inscripciones:

mayatur s.a.
Av. 19 No. 6-68 Int. 5 B
Tel: 2819800 Bogotá

OPERADOR TERRESTRE
mel-inter

Viajes Melka
Colombia
Calle 100 No. 20-10 Tel: 2181155
Bogotá. Colombia

Avianca
Las Aerolíneas de Colombia

•BARILOCHE •PUERTO MONTT •SANTIAGO •VIÑA DEL MAR

408   Lección 18

VOCABULARIO

Países y regiones
Alemania
Arabia Saudita
el Asia
Australia
el Brasil
el Canadá
la China
Europa
Francia
Inglaterra
Italia
el Japón
Kenya
Marruecos
Portugal
Rusia

Nacionalidades
alemán, alemana
asiático,-a
australiano,-a
brasileño,-a
canadiense
centroamericano,-a
chino,-a
europeo,-a
francés, francesa
inglés, inglesa
italiano,-a
japonés, japonesa
kenyano,-a
marroquí
norteamericano,-a
portugués, portuguesa
ruso,-a
saudita
suramericano,-a

Verbos
mantener
organizar

Expresiones y otras palabras
la actitud
a propósito
la despedida
en medio de
la facultad
la isla
magnífico,-a
el mar
el medio
¡no me digas!
el océano
la orilla
por fin
la realidad
el río
siempre salirse con
 la suya
sin embargo

Ling es china.

Omondi es de Kenya. Es kenyano.

¿Te gustaría viajar a Rusia? (Moscú, Rusia.)

Quiz/Activity 6

Testing/Assessment
Test Booklet
Oral Proficiency
 Evaluation Manual
Portfolio Assessment

Notes
Review. This would be a good time to review adjective-noun agreement, using the adjectives of nationality listed on this page.

Activities
Cooperative Learning. Ask students to say a word they have learned in Spanish and then select someone else to spell the word. Have them check their spelling and then switch roles.

Expansion. Select several words and phrases for individual students to use orally in sentences.

Pronunciation. To ensure proper pronunciation, model each word or expression and have students repeat after you.

Students with Special Needs. Develop creative thinking, writing and public speaking skills by asking students to imagine they have just been elected to the position of governor of your state. What would they say in a speech about the future of your state? Assign students to write an inaugural address that discusses items mentioned in activity A on page 408.

Technology. Using the Internet, find information about at least five hotels in one of the cities you plan to visit in activity B on page 408. Find out the rates of each hotel, including the rates for different types of rooms, and note any special offers and amenities. Print out the information and share it with the class. Describe all of the hotel options you found. Then tell the class which hotel you would prefer to stay in and why.

NATIONAL STANDARDS
C1.2, C4.1

Lázaro cuenta su vida y de quién fue hijo (continuación)

Quiz/Activity 7

Quiz/Activity 7

Answers

Preparación

1. Las pone en un fardel.
2. Utiliza una argolla y un candado.
3. Lo pone en un jarrillo (o jarro).
4. Usa una paja.

Notes

Be sure to cover the *Preparación* activity prior to beginning the *A leer*.

Activities

Critical Listening. Play the audiocassette/audio compact disc version of the reading one paragraph at a time. Tell students to listen for the main ideas the speaker is addressing. Finally, have several individuals state what they believe the main theme of each paragraph is.

Prereading Strategy. Prepare students for the content of the reading by asking some general questions on the reading topic, such as the questions found in the *Preparación*. Next, play the first paragraph of the recording of *A leer*, using the corresponding audiocassette or compact disc that is part of the Audiocassette/Audio CD Program. As an alternative, you may choose to read the first paragraph yourself. Read the paragraph again with students following along in the book. Give students a moment to look over the paragraph silently on their own and then have them ask questions. Ask for a student to volunteer to read the paragraph aloud. Continue in this way for subsequent paragraphs.

a leer

Estrategia

Preparación

Estrategia para leer: *using accompanying visuals to predict content*

Illustrations do more than just attract the reader's attention. Visuals that accompany a reading often depict what takes place in the selected text and can enhance your comprehension.

Mira las ilustraciones de la lectura y, luego, contesta las siguientes preguntas como preparación para la lectura.

1. ¿En dónde pone el ciego su comida y sus cosas?
2. ¿Qué utiliza el ciego para cerrar el fardel?
3. ¿En dónde pone el ciego el vino?
4. ¿Qué usa Lázaro para tomar vino en secreto?

Lázaro cuenta su vida y de quién fue hijo (continuación)

El ciego llevaba el pan y todas las otras cosas que le daban en un *fardel* de tela que por la boca se cerraba con una *argolla* con su *candado* y llave. **Metía** las cosas y las sacaba con tanto cuidado que no era posible quitarle una **migaja**. Pero yo tomaba lo poco que me daba y lo comía en dos **bocados**. Después que cerraba el fardel con el candado se quedaba tranquilo pensando que yo estaba haciendo otras cosas, pero yo por un lado del fardel que muchas veces **descosía** y volvía a **coser** le sacaba el pan y la *longaniza*.

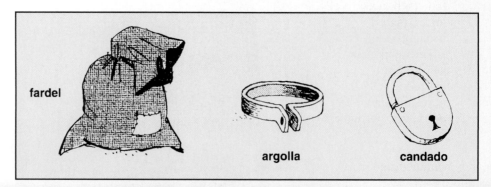

fardel / argolla / candado

Solía poner junto a sí un *jarrillo* de **vino** cuando comíamos. Yo lo **cogía** y **bebía** de él sin hacer ruido y lo volvía a poner en su lugar. Pero esto me **duró** poco, porque al ir a beber el ciego conocía la **falta** del vino y así por guardar el vino, nunca **soltaba** el *jarro* y lo tenía siempre **cogido** por el *asa.* Pero yo con una *paja,* que para ello tenía hecha, metiéndola por la *boca* del jarro, dejaba al viejo sin nada. Pero pienso que me sintió y desde entonces ponía el jarro entre las piernas y le **tapaba** con la mano y de esta manera bebía seguro.

longaniza

Yo, como me gustaba el vino, moría por él; y viendo que la paja ya **no me aprovechaba** ni valía, decidí hacer en el **fondo** del jarro un **agujero** y taparlo con un poco de **cera**. Al tiempo de comer, me ponía entre las piernas del ciego, como si **tuviera** frío, para **calentarme** en la pobre *lumbre* que teníamos; al calor de la lumbre se deshacía la cera y comenzaba el vino a caerme en la boca y yo la ponía de tal manera que no se perdía ni una **gota.**

asa • jarrillo (jarro) • paja • boca • lumbre

Notes

Review. Remind students to draw upon the strategies they have learned for reading: skimming, scanning, looking for visual cues, etc.

Activities

Students with Special Needs. Have students quickly scan the content for cognates and known vocabulary before reading for in-depth understanding. Remind students to draw upon skills they have learned in order to recognize these cognates.

Cuando el pobre ciego iba a beber no encontraba nada. **Se desesperaba** no sabiendo qué podía ser.

—No diréis, tío, que os lo bebo yo—decía—pues no soltáis el jarro de la mano.

Tantas **vueltas** le dio al jarro que encontró el agujero, al poner el dedo en él, comprendió el **engaño**, pero aunque él supo lo que era, hizo como si **no hubiera visto** nada. Y al otro día, me puse como **de costumbre**, sin pensar lo que el ciego me estaba preparando, y creyendo que el mal ciego no me sentía. Y estando recibiendo aquellas dulces gotas, mi cara puesta hacia el cielo, un poco cerrados los ojos para mejor gustar del vino, el **desesperado** ciego, levantando con toda la **fuerza** de sus manos el jarro, le dejó caer sobre mi boca, ayudándose como digo con todo su poder, de manera que yo, pobre Lázaro, que nada de esto esperaba, sentí como si el cielo con todo lo que hay en él, me **hubiese caído** encima.

Fue tal el **golpe** que me hizo perder el **sentido** y el **jarrazo** tan fuerte que los **pedazos** del jarro se me metieron en la cara rompiéndomela en muchos lugares y rompiéndome también los dientes, sin los cuales hasta hoy me quedé.

Desde aquella hora quise mal al ciego, y aunque él me quería y me cuidaba bien, bien vi que se había alegrado mucho con el cruel **castigo.** Me lavó con vino las **heridas** que me había hecho con los pedazos del jarro y riéndose decía:

—¿Qué te parece, Lázaro? Lo que te **enfermó** te pone **sano** y te da la **salud.**

Cuando estuve bueno de los golpes, aunque yo quería perdonarle lo del jarrazo, no podía por el mal **trato** que desde entonces me hizo el mal ciego: me **castigaba** sin causa ni razón y cuando alguno le decía que por qué me **trataba** tan mal contaba lo del jarro, diciendo:

—¿Pensáis que este mi mozo es bueno? Pues oíd.

Y los que le oían decían:

—¡Mirad! ¿Y quién pensaría que un muchacho tan pequeño era tan malo? **Castigadlo,** castigadlo.

Y él al oír lo que la gente le decía otra cosa no hacía.

Yo por hacerle mal y **daño** siempre le llevaba por los peores caminos; si había piedras le llevaba por ellas. Con estas cosas mi amo me **tentaba** la cabeza

Activities
Students with Special Needs.
Check with students regularly to
see what problems they are having
with the reading.

con la parte alta de su **palo** de ciego que siempre llevaba con él. Yo tenía la cabeza llena de las **señales** de sus manos y aunque yo le **juraba** que no lo hacía por causarle mal sino por encontrar mejor camino, él no me lo creía: tal era el grandísimo entender de aquel mal ciego.

Y porque vea vuestra merced hasta dónde llegaba el **ingenio** de este hombre le contaré un **caso** de los muchos que con él me **sucedieron.**

Cuando salimos de Salamanca su idea fue venir a **tierras** de Toledo porque decía que la gente era más rica, aunque no era amiga de dar muchas **limosnas.** Fuimos por los mejores pueblos, si encontraba mucha **ganancia** nos quedábamos, si no la encontrábamos al tercer día nos íbamos.

Sucedió que llegando a un lugar que llaman Almorox, en el tiempo de las *uvas* le dieron un gran *racimo* de ellas. Como el racimo se le **deshacía** en las manos, decidió comerlo, por contentarme, pues aquel día me había dado muchos golpes. Nos sentamos y me dijo:

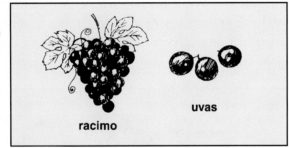

uvas

racimo

—Lázaro, ahora quiero que los dos comamos este racimo de uvas y que tengas de él tanta parte como yo. Será de esta manera: tú **cogerás** una uva y yo otra, pero sólo una, hasta que lo acabemos.

Dicho esto, comenzamos a comer, pero a la segunda vez el mal ciego cambió de idea y comenzó a coger de dos en dos pensando que yo estaba haciendo lo mismo. Como vi que él hacía esto, yo hacía más: comía de dos en dos o de tres en tres.

Cuando acabamos de comer las uvas me dijo:

—Lázaro, me has **engañado.** Tú has comido las uvas de tres en tres.

—No comí—dije yo—pero, ¿por qué lo piensa así vuestra merced?

—¿Sabes en qué veo que comiste las uvas de tres en tres?—respondió él. En que yo las comía de dos en dos y tú **callabas.**

Yo me reía, y aunque muchacho bien comprendí que mi **amo** era hombre que conocía el mundo.

Pero por no ser **prolijo,** dejo de contar aquí muchas cosas que me sucedieron con este mi primer amo y quiero decir cómo me despedí de él.

Estábamos en el mesón de Escalona y me dio un pedazo de longaniza para que se la **asase,** después me dio dinero y me **mandó** a buscar vino. **Mas** el demonio quiso que cuando salía a buscar el vino **viese** en el suelo un *nabo* pequeño, largo y malo, que alguien había dejado en el suelo por ser tan malo y como **estuviésemos** solos el ciego y yo, teniendo yo dentro el **olor** de la longaniza y sabiendo que había de **gozar** sólo del olor, no mirando lo que me podía suceder, mientras el ciego me daba el dinero para comprar el vino, saqué la longaniza del *asador* y metí en él el nabo. Mi amo tomó el asador y empezó a darle vueltas al fuego, queriendo **asar** al que por malo nadie había querido comer.

Yo fui a buscar el vino con el cual no tardé en comer la longaniza y cuando volví vi que mi amo tenía el nabo entre dos *rebanadas* de pan, el cual no había conocido porque no había tocado con la mano. Al morder en las rebanadas de pan, pensando morder también la longaniza, se encontró con el nabo frío y dijo:

Activities

Students with Special Needs. Break the reading into sections so students do not become discouraged.

—¿Qué es esto, Lazarillo?

—¡Pobre de mí!—dije yo—Yo ¿no vengo de comprar el vino? Alguno que estaba aquí ha hecho esta **burla.**

—No, no,—dijo él—que yo no he dejado de la mano el asador ni un solo momento; no es posible.

Yo juraba y volvía a jurar que estaba libre de aquello, pero poco me aprovechó pues al **maldito** ciego nada **se le escondía.**

Se levantó, me cogió la cabeza con sus manos, me abrió la boca y metió en ella su larga *nariz.* Con esto, como la longaniza no había hecho asiento aún en el estómago, salió de él por mi boca al mismo tiempo que su nariz, dándole en ella.

—¡Oh gran Dios, quién **estuviera** en aquella hora de muerto! Fue tal su **coraje** que si **no acudiera** gente al ruido y me **sacara** de sus manos, que estaban llenas de los pocos *pelos* que yo tenía, pienso que **hubiera dejado** allí la vida.

Contaba el maldito ciego a todos los que allí llegaban lo del jarro y lo del racimo. La **risa** de todos era tan grande que la gente que pasaba por la calle entraba a ver la fiesta.

La **mesonera** y los demás que allí estaban nos hicieron amigos y con el vino que había ido a comprar para beber, me lavaron la cara. El ciego se reía y decía:

—De verdad este **mozo** me **gasta** en lavarle más vino en un año que el que yo bebo en dos.

Y volviéndose a mí me decía:

—En verdad, Lázaro, más le debes al vino que a tu padre, porque aquél una vez te dio la vida, mas el vino mil veces te la ha dado. Y contaba, riendo, cuántas veces me había **herido** la cara y me la había **curado** con vino.

Y los que me estaban lavando la cara reían mucho. Sin embargo yo muchas veces me acuerdo de aquel hombre y **me pesa de** las burlas que le hice, aunque también es verdad que bien lo pagué.

Visto todo esto y el mal trato que me daba yo había decidido dejarle, como lo hice. Y fue así, que luego otro día anduvimos por la calle pidiendo limosna. Era un día en que llovía mucho y como la noche iba llegando me dijo:

—Lázaro, esta agua no deja de caer, y cuando sea más de noche, la *lluvia* será más fuerte. Vámonos a la posada con tiempo.

Para ir a la posada había que pasar un *arroyo* que con la mucha lluvia era bastante grande entonces.

Yo le dije:

—Tío, el arroyo va muy **ancho,** pero si así lo queréis, veo un **sitio** por donde podremos pasar más pronto sin **mojarnos** porque allí el arroyo es más estrecho y saltando no nos mojaremos.

Le pareció bien y dijo:

—Piensas bien, por eso te quiero. Llévame a ese lugar por donde el arroyo **se estrecha**

lluvia

POSADA

poste   arroyo

que ahora es invierno y **sabe** mal el agua, y peor sabe llevar los pies mojados.

Yo lo llevé derecho a un *poste* de **piedra** que había en la plaza y le dije:

—Tío, éste es el **paso** más estrecho que hay en el arroyo.

Como llovía mucho y él se mojaba, con la prisa que llevábamos por salir del agua que nos caía encima y, lo más principal, porque Dios le **cegó** el **entendimiento** y creyó en mí dijo:

—Ponme bien derecho y salta tú el arroyo.

Yo le puse bien derecho **enfrente** del poste, di un salto y me puse detrás del poste. Desde allí le dije:

—Salte vuestra merced todo lo que pueda.

Apenas lo había acabado de decir cuando el pobre ciego saltó con tal fuerza que dio con la cabeza en el poste y cayó luego **para atrás medio** muerto y con la cabeza rota.

Yo le dije:

—¿Cómo **olió** vuestra merced la longaniza y no el poste? ¡**Oled**! ¡Oled!

Y le dejé con mucha gente que había ido a ayudarle. Antes de que la noche **llegase**, llegué yo a Torrijos. No supe nunca lo que hizo Dios con el ciego, ni me ocupé nunca de saberlo.

Metía *He put (inside);* **migaja** *crumb;* **bocados** *mouthfuls;* **descosía** *unraveled;* **coser** *sew;* **vino** *wine;* **cogía** *took;* **bebía** *drank;* **duró** *lasted;* **falta** *lack;* **soltaba** *let go of;* **cogido** *held;* **tapaba** *covered;* **no me aprovechaba** *was of no use to me;* **fondo** *bottom;* **agujero** *hole;* **cera** *wax;* **tuviera** *I were;* **calentarme** *warm myself;* **gota** *drop;* **Se desesperaba** *He got upset;* **vueltas** *turns;* **engaño** *trick;* **no hubiera visto** *he had not seen;* **de costumbre** *as usual;* **desesperado** *exasperated;* **fuerza** *strength;* **hubiese caído** *would have fallen;* **golpe** *hit;* **sentido** *consciousness;* **jarrazo** *blow (from a pitcher);* **pedazos** *pieces;* **castigo** *punishment;* **heridas** *wounds;* **enfermó** *made you sick;* **sano** *well;* **salud** *health;* **trato** *treatment;* **castigaba** *he punished;* **trataba** *he treated;* **Castigadlo** *Punish him;* **daño** *harm;* **tentaba** *hit;* **palo** *stick;* **señales** *signs;* **juraba** *swore;* **ingenio** *ingenuity;* **caso** *case;* **sucedieron** *happened;* **tierras** *lands;* **limosnas** *alms;* **ganancia** *earnings;* **deshacía** *came apart;* **cogerás** *will take;* **engañado** *tricked;* **callabas** *kept quiet;* **amo** *master;* **prolijo** *wordy;* **asase** *roast;* **mandó** *sent;* **Mas** *But;* **viese** *I would see;* **estuviésemos** *we were;* **olor** *smell;* **gozar** *to enjoy;* **asar** *roast;* **burla** *trick;* **maldito** *evil;* **se le escondía** *could be kept from him;* **estuviera** *was;* **coraje** *rage;* **no acudiera** *hadn't come;* **sacara** *to take (out);* **hubiera dejado** *would have left;* **risa** *laughter;* **mesonera** *innkeeper's wife;* **mozo** *boy;* **gasta** *costs;* **herido** *wounded;* **curado** *cured;* **me pesa de** *I regret;* **ancho** *wide;* **sitio** *place;* **mojarnos** *getting ourselves wet;* **se estrecha** *becomes narrow;* **sabe** *tastes;* **piedra** *stone;* **paso** *strait;* **cegó** *blinded;* **entendimiento** *understanding;* **enfrente** *in front of;* **Apenas** *Hardly;* **para atrás** *backwards;* **medio** *half;* **olió** *smelled;* **¡Oled!** *Sniff, Smell!;* **llegase** *arrived*

> Excerpt from:
> *Lazarillo de Tormes;* author unknown. Copyright Grafisk Forlag A/S, Copenhagen. The *Easy Reader* (a B-level book) with the same title is published by EMC/Paradigm Publishing.

A ¿Qué comprendiste?

1. ¿A quién trataba mal el ciego?
2. ¿Qué le quitaba Lazarillo al ciego todo el tiempo de su jarro?
3. ¿Qué le rompió el ciego a Lazarillo con el jarro?
4. ¿Qué fruta comieron el ciego y Lazarillo en Almorox?
5. ¿Cómo se llamaba el lugar donde el ciego quería comer longaniza?
6. ¿Cómo estaba el tiempo el último día que Lazarillo estuvo con el ciego?

B Charlando

1. ¿Qué piensas de la forma en que el ciego trataba a Lazarillo?
2. ¿Crees que el ciego era una persona buena o mala? Explica.
3. ¿Piensas que Lazarillo era un niño feliz? ¿Por qué?
4. ¿Cómo crees que será la vida de Lazarillo en el futuro? Explica.

Activities A-B

Answers

A
1. El ciego trataba mal a Lazarillo.
2. Le quitaba el vino.
3. Le rompió la cara y los dientes.
4. Comieron uvas.
5. El lugar se llamaba Escalona.
6. El tiempo estaba malo porque llovía.

B Creative self-expression.

Notes
Remind students that the *A leer* offers a formal opportunity for students to improve their ability to read in Spanish. They do not need to understand every word in order to read in Spanish. Equivalents for difficult words have been provided to help students enjoy the contents of the readings without having to look up important but passive vocabulary.

Activities
Expansion. *¿Qué piensas de las personas que tratan (treat) mal a otras? Explica.; ¿Crees que tomar bebidas alcohólicas es bueno o malo para una persona de cualquier edad? Explica.; ¿Cómo crees que una persona ciega puede saber lo que está ocurriendo? Explica.; ¿Le has hecho alguna vez una burla (trick) a alguien? ¿Cuándo y por qué?; ¿Cuáles son los cognados en la lectura* **Lázaro cuenta su vida y de quién fue hijo?**

Multiple Intelligences (linguistic). Have students write a one-page composition about Lazarillo de Tormes. They may wish to select a particular aspect of *A leer* to discuss, or they may decide to write a simple essay summarizing the story.

NATIONAL STANDARDS
C1.1, C1.2, C2.1, C2.2, C3.2, C4.1, C4.2

Activities

Communities. Suggest to students that they talk to their parents about ways they may use Spanish and communication skills they are developing in order to volunteer in the community. For example, students may wish to volunteer with a local ecology organization. Discuss with the class how this might affect both the students' and the community's future.

Multiple Intelligences (intrapersonal/linguistic). Have students write a 150- to 200-word composition about their future. In the composition, have them describe their life, including where they will live and what they will be doing. Tell about their dreams and personal aspirations and discuss some of the things they will do to attain them.

a escribir

Estrategia

Estrategia para escribir: *using graphic organizers*

When you begin the writing process, one way to get started is to brainstorm ideas about your topic. Then to make sure your ideas flow in a logical sequence, it is helpful to use a graphic organizer. Venn diagrams, concept maps and time lines can help you visualize different aspects of your theme.

Cuando tenga veinte años, estudiaré en Inglaterra.

Draw a time line that shows how you think your life will evolve over the next twenty years. Then write a composition based on the time line of your life. Be sure to tell where you will live and what you will be doing. Include your personal goals and tell some of the things you will do to attain them. Remember to use connecting words to make your sentences flow together smoothly. To make your composition more visually appealing, illustrate your time line and include it at the bottom of your paper.

Portfolio Assessment
Select an activity from *Capítulo 9* to include in the *Somos así* Portfolio Assessment.

repaso

Now that I have completed this chapter, I can...

✓ discuss the future.
✓ express uncertainty.
✓ talk about hopes and dreams.
✓ seek and provide information about careers.
✓ express events in the past.
✓ relate two events in the past.
✓ express doubt.
✓ advise and suggest.
✓ state wishes and preferences.
✓ express emotion.
✓ identify and locate some countries.
✓ write about the future.

I can also...

✓ read about world problems in Spanish.
✓ talk about pastimes.
✓ use body language to communicate.
✓ talk about my life in Spanish.
✓ use technology to find information.

Espero que pueda ayudar a solucionar algunos de los problemas del mundo.

Activities

Cooperative Learning. The end of the school year is full of farewells and mixed emotions. Ask small groups of students to prepare statements using the subjunctive that summarize their hopes, wishes and feelings. Summaries are then presented to the class.

Critical Thinking. Provide students with blank map outlines of the world (or have students prepare the maps) on which they can write the names of the countries and capitals they know. Have students compare the maps with the maps they did before starting the chapter (see page 373).

Multiple Intelligences (intrapersonal). Have students contact a local college or university and a local vocational/technical college (or have students talk with a school counselor) to obtain information about career opportunities. Then have students make a list in Spanish of possible career choices that appeal to them.

NATIONAL STANDARDS
C1.1, C1.2, C1.3, C2.1, C2.2, C3.1, C3.2, C4.2, C5.1, C5.2

Talk with the class about the communicative functions students will be learning in *Capítulo 10*. A checkoff list of the functions appears at the end of the chapter (see page 447), along with additional objectives that students can use as a self-check to evaluate their own progress.

The Portfolio Assessment Program provides a checklist of all the communicative functions for *Somos así LISTOS*. Review the list with individuals to see how thoroughly students have mastered the content of the textbook.

Capítulo 10 provides a simple review of the contents of *Somos así LISTOS*. It includes no new vocabulary or grammar, so you have the choice of whether or not you would like to teach the contents, depending upon time constraints and your own particular curricular needs. Pick and choose specific content you would like to review (e.g., the present perfect, expressions and vocabulary). You may skip activities or add to the review according to the time you have available and according to students' needs.

Activities

Critical Thinking. The visuals that appear on pages 420-421 symbolize the new world that students have ahead of them. Using the photographs, the identification card and the clipping from a brochure for the *Universidad Complutense*, discuss the functions and themes of the chapter ahead. For example, ask students to answer the following: 1) Who is the person in the photograph in the upper-left-hand corner of page 420?; 2) What is the object in the photograph in the upper-right-hand corner of page 420?; 3) What appears in the realia on page 421?; 4) What do students think they will be studying in the chapter?

NATIONAL STANDARDS
C1.2, C5.2

Un nuevo mundo

CAPÍTULO 10

OFICINA UNIVERSITARIA
UNIVERSIDAD COMPLUTENSE
Central Hispano 20

UNIVERSIDAD AUTONOMA DE YUCATAN
FACULTAD DE CIENCIAS ANTROPOLOGICAS
AÑO ESCOLAR

ALUMNO JENNIFER ANDERSON
CARRERA LIC. EN CIENCIAS ANTROPOLOGICAS
CURSO 3er. AÑO GRUPO B
MATRICULA ESTUDIANTE ESPECIAL
DIRECCION 23 No.180-A x 8 y 10 G. GINERES

In this chapter you will be able to:
- express past actions and events
- discuss everyday activities
- write about everyday life
- talk about contemporary Hispanic culture
- talk about the future
- express emotion
- state wishes and preferences

421

El mundo
The chapter *Un nuevo mundo* deals with some of the opportunities that students have been afforded because they know Spanish. Skills and knowledge acquired in Spanish class using *Somos así* enable students to communicate with people, travel, study, work and live just about anywhere they desire throughout the world wherever Spanish is spoken.

Notes
By choosing to teach from *Capítulo 10* your students will have an opportunity to talk about what they have done during the past year (activities, what they have learned, etc.). They will also have an opportunity to discuss their future (opportunities to study, careers, future travel and other topics that are challenging and enjoyable).

Activities
Multiple Intelligences (musical). Play music from one of the Spanish-speaking countries or by one of the Spanish-speaking musicians students have studied in *Somos así LISTOS*. Then ask students to offer insights about the music, such as where the music is from or who performs the piece.

NATIONAL STANDARDS
C1.2, C5.2

Un amigo por e-mail
Activity 1

 Quiz/Activity 1

 Activity 63

Activity 1

Content reviewed in *Lección 19*
- talking about everyday activities
- expressing past actions and events
- present perfect tense
- technology
- writing about the past and everyday life

Answers

1 1. Conoció a su amiga Catalina.
2. Vive en el mismo barrio.
3. Estuvo un poco enferma, pescó un resfriado.
4. Porque ha estado más tiempo con su familia.
5. Visitó a sus tías de Miami.
6. Navegó en la Internet.
7. Busca universidades para estudiar en otro país.

Activities

Critical Listening. Play the audiocassette/audio compact disc recording of the e-mail. Instruct students to cover the words and listen carefully. Finally, ask several individuals to state what they believe the main theme of the e-mail is.

Multiple Intelligences (linguistic). Ask students to take the role of Francisco and to compose a logical response to the e-mail from Teresa.

Students with Special Needs. Ask students several leading questions: Who wrote the e-mail?; To whom is the e-mail addressed?; What do the words in the address field mean (*A, De, Asunto, Copias a, Anexos*)?

NATIONAL STANDARDS
C1.1, C1.2, C2.1, C2.2, C3.2, C4.1, C4.2

Lección 19

Contexto cultural
EL MUNDO

Un amigo por e-mail

Teresa, una chica de Chicago, le escribe un e-mail a su amigo Francisco de Buenos Aires, Argentina.

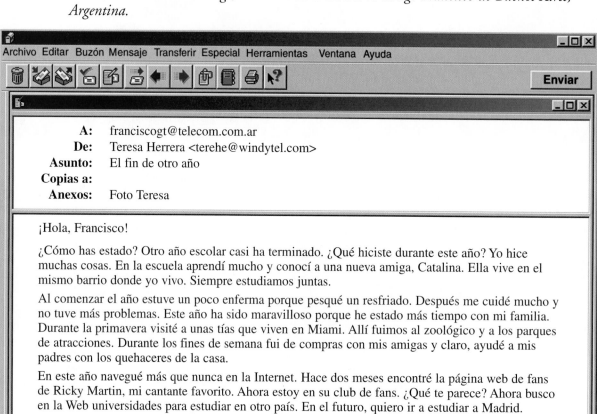

Archivo Editar Buzón Mensaje Transferir Especial Herramientas Ventana Ayuda

Enviar

A:	franciscogt@telecom.com.ar
De:	Teresa Herrera <terehe@windytel.com>
Asunto:	El fin de otro año
Copias a:	
Anexos:	Foto Teresa

¡Hola, Francisco!

¿Cómo has estado? Otro año escolar casi ha terminado. ¿Qué hiciste durante este año? Yo hice muchas cosas. En la escuela aprendí mucho y conocí a una nueva amiga, Catalina. Ella vive en el mismo barrio donde yo vivo. Siempre estudiamos juntas.

Al comenzar el año estuve un poco enferma porque pesqué un resfriado. Después me cuidé mucho y no tuve más problemas. Este año ha sido maravilloso porque he estado más tiempo con mi familia. Durante la primavera visité a unas tías que viven en Miami. Allí fuimos al zoológico y a los parques de atracciones. Durante los fines de semana fui de compras con mis amigas y claro, ayudé a mis padres con los quehaceres de la casa.

En este año navegué más que nunca en la Internet. Hace dos meses encontré la página web de fans de Ricky Martin, mi cantante favorito. Ahora estoy en su club de fans. ¿Qué te parece? Ahora busco en la Web universidades para estudiar en otro país. En el futuro, quiero ir a estudiar a Madrid.

Bueno, ya te conté sobre mi año, ahora cuéntame sobre el tuyo. ¿Te gustaría estudiar aquí en los Estados Unidos o piensas estudiar en Buenos Aires? Recuerda, mi casa es tu casa.

Cuídate mucho,

Teresa

 ## ¿Qué comprendiste?

1. ¿A quién conoció Teresa en su escuela?
2. ¿Dónde vive Catalina?
3. ¿Cómo estuvo Teresa al comenzar el año?
4. ¿Por qué ha sido un año maravilloso para Teresa?
5. ¿A quién visitó en la primavera?
6. ¿Qué hizo Teresa este año más que nunca?
7. ¿Qué busca Teresa ahora en la red?

2 Charlando

1. ¿Tienes amigos por e-mail? ¿De dónde son?
2. ¿Conociste a nuevos amigos en la escuela este año? ¿A quiénes?
3. ¿Cuál fue la clase que más te gustó?
4. ¿Perteneces a algún club de fans? ¿A cuál?
5. ¿Te gusta navegar por la Internet?
6. ¿Piensas estudiar en otro país en el futuro?

3 ¿Qué hiciste este año?

Trabajando en parejas, alterna con tu compañero/a de clase en hacer preguntas y contestarlas sobre lo que hicieron o lo que pasó durante el año.

A: ¿Estuviste enfermo/a este año?
B: Sí, (No, no) estuve enfermo/a.

Conexión cultural

E-mail, la aplicación más popular del mundo

Hasta hace poco tiempo, mucha gente perdía amigos que vivían en otros lugares muy lejos, pero con la llegada del e-mail enviar mensajes se volvió algo muy fácil y hasta divertido.

Algunos datos *(facts)* que confirman la importancia del correo electrónico son los siguientes: hay casi doscientos sesenta y tres millones de direcciones de correo electrónico en el mundo, y cada usuario recibe al día un promedio *(average)* de 30 mensajes diarios, según la compañía Yankee Group; lo primero que hace el 70 por ciento de los usuarios al conectarse a la Internet es consultar su correo, según Jupiter Communications; el 69 por ciento de los usuarios considera que el correo es la aplicación más importante de la Internet, según Cyberatlas.

Eso quiere decir que el correo electrónico se convirtió en algo indispensable para la vida social y de trabajo de los internautas. Sin embargo, no

El correo electrónico es indispensable para la vida social.

todos esos mensajes son de interés para el destinatario *(addressee)*. Algunas compañías que conocen el potencial del correo electrónico han convertido a los usuarios en destinatarios de muchos mensajes publicitarios de todo tipo.

[Tomado del artículo *Correo electrónico, la aplicación más popular* de la revista *Enter*; Santa Fe de Bogotá, Colombia.]

Answers

2 Answers will vary.

3 Answers will vary.

Notes

www

E-mail
http://www.iecc.org/
http://www.latinmail.com/
http://espana.youpy.com/index.jsp
http://www.buzon.com/

Note that beginning with this chapter, the sections *Conexión cultural, Oportunidades, Estrategia* and *Autoevaluación* are entirely in Spanish. This keeps with the goal of providing an ever-increasing amount of content in the target language, but in a controlled and planned effort to avoid overburdening students' abilities and in order to make learning Spanish a worthwhile and enjoyable experience.

Activities

Prereading Strategy. This *Conexión cultural* provides an opportunity for students to improve their ability to acquire information in Spanish. Note for the class that it is not essential to understand every word in order to read Spanish; the meaning of important but unknown passive vocabulary has been provided to facilitate an enjoyable experience. Before beginning the *Conexión cultural,* consider asking some general preparation questions about the theme of the reading: Can students name any geographic locations that have Spanish names? Then have students skim the reading for cognates and any words or expressions they already know.

NATIONAL STANDARDS
C1.1, C1.2, C2.1, C2.2, C3.2, C4.1, C4.2

Activity 3

Answers

4 Possible answers include: la luz, el teléfono, la radio, la televisión, el carro, la computadora, la Internet.

5 Creative self-expression.

Notes

You may opt to use all the contents of lessons 19-20 with the entire class, or you may want to offer parts of the chapter to select students who are capable or who have a particular need to study a portion of the content. For example, seniors who will not be returning may benefit from some of the topics covered; gifted and highly motivated students may enjoy doing portions of the chapter independent of the rest of the class.

Activities

Multiple Intelligences (interpersonal/linguistic). Plan an e-mail exchange in which students describe their families and ask for information about the families of their key pals. Allow students to use imaginary families if they prefer. To do the activity, students should include the following: personal biographical information (name, date of birth, age, etc.); information about family (names, descriptions, where people live); questions asking for similar information about the key pal.

CONEXIONES

4 Cruzando fronteras

Haz una lista de cinco inventos *(invention)* tecnológicos que tú piensas han sido indispensables para la vida del ser humano en el último siglo y explica por qué. Busca información en tu libro de ciencias, en la biblioteca o en la Internet si es necesario. Luego, comparte la información con la clase.

¿Es indispensable el teléfono?

5 Un nuevo mundo

Trabajando en grupos pequeños hablen sobre nuevos inventos tecnológicos que piensan van a haber en veinte años. Luego, una persona del grupo debe presentar las conclusiones a la clase.

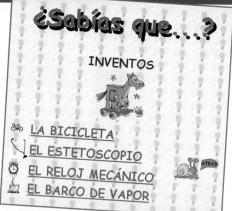

¿Sabías que...?

INVENTOS

- LA BICICLETA
- EL ESTETOSCOPIO
- EL RELOJ MECÁNICO
- EL BARCO DE VAPOR

ATRÁS

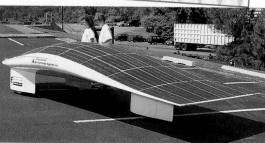

En el futuro, todos los carros usarán energía solar.

Oportunidades

Amigos en el cyberespacio

La tecnología del e-mail ha hecho posible que hoy en día podamos hacer amigos en todo el mundo. Nuevos amigos, especialmente de otros países, pueden ampliar tu conocimiento de otras culturas y enriquecer la percepción del planeta que todos compartimos. Aún mas, tener y mantenerse en contacto con amigos de otros países, especialmente de habla hispana, te ayudará a mejorar tus habilidades para expresarte en español, así como también a tener buenas amistades.

El e-mail nos permite hacer nuevos amigos en todas partes del mundo.

6 Buscando amigos

Usando un motor de búsqueda, encuentra una página web en donde puedas contactar chicos y chicas por e-mail de algún país de habla hispana. Selecciona a alguien que te interese y escríbele un e-mail diciéndole quién eres, de dónde eres y contándole que te gustaría ser su amigo/a por correo electrónico.

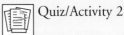

Repaso *rápido*

El pretérito perfecto y el participio

Remember to use the present perfect tense to refer to the past in a general sense or to talk about something specific that **has happened** recently. It is formed from the present tense of the helping verb *haber* (to have) and the past participle *(participio)* of a verb.

he	hemos		
has	habéis	**+**	past participle
ha	han		

Form the past participle of regular *-ar* verbs by changing the *-ar* of the infinitive to *-ado*. For regular *-er* and *-ir* verbs, change the infinitive ending *-er* or *-ir* to *-ido*.

organizar	→	*organizado* (organized)
conocer	→	*conocido* (known)
asistir	→	*asistido* (attended)
ir	→	*ido* (gone)

Look at these examples:

¿Has organizado un club de fans?
He conocido a mucha gente.
Nosotros hemos asistido a la misma escuela.
¿Han ido Uds. a Chile alguna vez?

Have you organized a fan club?
I have known a lot people.
We have attended the same school.

Have you ever **gone** to Chile?

(Santiago, Chile.)

¿Has ido a Chile alguna vez?

Hemos asistido a la misma escuela.

(Isla de Pascua, Chile.)

Activities 4-5

Quiz/Activity 2

Answers

6 Creative writing practice.

Notes

Remind students that the *pretérito perfecto* is used similarly in Spanish and in English: It expresses a past action that the speaker sees as related to the present in some way.

Remember to check Web site addresses since they change frequently.

www

Intercultural E-Mail Connections
http://www.stolaf.edu/network/iecc

Activities

Cooperative Learning. Practice the present perfect tense by asking students to discuss things they have done and things that have happened during the past school year. They should work in pairs or small groups and then present a summary to the class.

NATIONAL STANDARDS
C1.2, C4.1, C5.1, C5.2

 Activity 7

NATIONAL STANDARDS
C1.1, C1.2, C3.2, C4.1, C4.2, C5.1, C5.2

 7 ## ¿Qué han aprendido este año?

Todos han estudiado y aprendido mucho este año. Di lo que las siguientes personas han aprendido, usando las indicaciones que se dan.

 Gabriel/muchos proverbios
Gabriel ha aprendido muchos proverbios.

1. Sandra y David/sobre los animales salvajes
2. Clara/mucho sobre los países de habla hispana
3. tú/mucho sobre tecnología
4. Pablo/sobre los problemas del mundo
5. Ud./a hacer tortillas españolas
6. nosotros/mucho español

PARAti

Proverbios y dichos
Once you learn something thoroughly it remains in your memory beyond any test you will take in school. There are many things in life that you will learn, such as a second language that will be with you for a long time to come. As the saying goes, *Lo que bien se aprende nunca se olvida.* (Something well-learned is not easily forgotten).

 8 ## Tus actividades favoritas

Navegar en la Internet ha sido una de las actividades favoritas de Teresa durante el año. Trabajando en parejas, alterna con tu compañero/a de clase en hacer preguntas y contestarlas para decir si las siguientes actividades han sido sus favoritas durante este año.

navegar en la Internet
A: ¿Ha sido navegar en la Internet una de tus actividades favoritas este año?
B: Sí, (No, no) ha sido una de mis actividades favoritas este año.

los partidos de fútbol
A: ¿Han sido los partidos de fútbol una de tus actividades favoritas este año?
B: Sí, (No, no) han sido una de mis actividades favoritas este año.

Montar en bicicleta ha sido una de nuestras actividades favoritas.

1. los viajes
2. escribir e-mails
3. los picnics
4. el básquetbol
5. ir al cine
6. las fiestas
7. el camping
8. ver televisión
9. estudiar español
10. el tenis

Maestros del Web
Maestros del Web
Webmasters Hispanos
La comunidad de Webmasters hispanos

Quiz/Activity 3

Activities 6-7

9 El club de fans de Ricky Martin

Lee esta información que Teresa consiguió en la página web de Ricky Martin. Luego, contesta las preguntas que siguen.

1. ¿De dónde es Ricky Martin?
2. ¿Cuándo cumplió años Ricky Martin?
3. A los veintiocho años, ¿cuál ha sido su comida favorita?
4. ¿Quién es su actor favorito?
5. ¿Has escuchado alguna canción de Fito Páez?
6. ¿Has visto un concierto de Charly García?
7. ¿Has pensado estudiar para ser cantante o actor/actriz?
8. ¿Te gustaría estar en el club de fans de Ricky Martin?

Ricky **Ontro**

Nació en... **Hato Rey, Puerto Rico.**
Cumple... **24 de diciembre.**
Edad... **28 años.**
Signo... **Capricornio.**
Comida favorita... **puertorriqueña, cubana e italiana.**
Mejor actor... **Robert de Niro.**
Músicos que admira... **Fito Páez, Charly García.**

10 ¡A escribir!

Escribe un e-mail de dos párrafos en español al amigo/la amiga que conseguiste en la actividad 6, contándole algunas de las cosas que hiciste o que han pasado durante el año. Sé creativo/a.

Estrategia

Para hablar mejor: usando proverbios y dichos

Las personas nativas de habla hispana escuchan proverbios y dichos a lo largo de sus vidas y los usan en sus conversaciones diarias como parte del ambiente que los rodea (*surrounds them*). Tú has aprendido algunos de estos proverbios y dichos en *Somos así LISTOS*, ¿cuántos de estos recuerdas? ¿Los usas? ¿Puedes adivinar el significado de los que aparecen abajo? El uso de los proverbios y dichos añadirá carácter y fluidez a tu español.

Siempre se sale con la suya.

Te está tomando el pelo.

Más vale tarde que nunca.

Me costó un ojo de la cara.

No lo tome a pecho.

¡Habla hasta por los codos!

¡Si lo sabré yo!

Eso es chino para mí.

Answers

9
1. Es de Hato Rey, Puerto Rico.
2. Cumplió años el 24 de diciembre.
3. Su comida favorita ha sido la puertorriqueña, la cubana y la italiana.
4. Su actor favorito es Robert de Niro.
5. Sí, (No, no) he escuchado alguna (ninguna) canción de Fito Páez.
6. Sí, (No, no) he visto un concierto de Charly García.
7. Sí, (No, no) lo he pensado.
8. Sí, (No, no) me gustaría.

10 Creative writing practice.

Notes

You may wish to help students with the meaning of some of these expressions: *Siempre se sale con la suya.* (He/She always gets his/her way.); *Te está tomando el pelo.* (He/She is pulling your leg.); *Más vale tarde que nunca.* (Better late than never.); *Me costó un ojo de la cara.* (It cost me an arm and a leg.); *No lo tome a pecho.* (Don't take it too personally/to heart.); *¡Si lo sabré yo!* (You don't need to tell me!); *¡Habla hasta por los codos!* (He/She talks a lot!); *Eso es chino para mí.* (It's Greek to me.)

Activities

Multiple Intelligences (linguistic). Have students summarize the information provided on this page in a short composition about Ricky Martin.

Spanish for Spanish Speakers. Have students write a seventy-five-word composition about a favorite musician.

NATIONAL STANDARDS
C1.2, C4.1, C5.1, C5.2

Notes

When the National Standards in Foreign Language Education Project established a new national framework of standards for language education in the United States, the resulting document, titled *Standards for Foreign Language Learning: Preparing for the 21st Century,* summarized the needs and concerns of language learners and language teachers. *Somos así LISTOS* reflects professional concern for addressing the five Cs of communication, culture, connections, comparisons and communities. Like *Capítulos 1-9, Capítulo 10* blends the five Cs with pedagogically sound content, fun activities and an ongoing discussion of the wealth of opportunities that learning a world language opens up for students, empowering them to become successful learners and users of world languages.

Activities

Multiple Intelligences (spatial). As a variation on activity 12, have students develop collages including photos that document important activities/events of the past year.

Students with Special Needs. Have students tell you the verb tense or mood of the verbs in the expressions in activity 11. If appropriate, use the expressions as a starting point for a comprehensive review of the verb tenses and moods.

11 ¿Qué dirías?

Conecta lógicamente las situaciones de la columna *A* con las expresiones de la columna *B* para saber lo que dirías en cada caso.

A

1. Bromeando, Juan le dice a Rosario que su casa salió volando por el cielo.
2. Tu papá te pidió lavar la ropa por la mañana, pero lo olvidaste y lo hiciste por la tarde.
3. Después de insistir mucho, Teresa consiguió el empleo que quería.
4. Carolina fue a una tienda a comprar una blusa que le costó muchísimo dinero.
5. César le hizo una broma a su amiga, pero a ella no le gustó mucho.
6. Tú y tu familia están visitando Arabia Saudita y tus padres te piden que les traduzcas unas señales que están en árabe.
7. Tienes algunos problemas con la computadora y tu amigo te viene a contar lo difícil que son las computadoras para él.
8. Conoces a una persona que habla muchísimo.

B

A. No lo tome a pecho.
B. Más vale tarde que nunca.
C. ¡Habla hasta por los codos!
D. Eso es chino para mí.
E. Le está tomando el pelo.
F. ¡Si lo sabré yo!
G. Le costó un ojo de la cara.
H. Siempre se sale con la suya.

Me costó un ojo de la cara.

12 ¡Una obra de arte!

Crea una pintura *(painting)* o un dibujo que represente una actividad o un evento, de la familia o del colegio, que haya sido importante para ti durante el año. Usa la técnica que quieras.

Mis pinturas representan mis experiencias de la vida.

¿Crees que algún día todos tendremos un teléfono con video?

¡Nuestra actividad favorita este año ha sido el volibol!

Este año he tomado muchos exámenes.

Autoevaluación. Como repaso y autoevaluación, responde lo siguiente:
1. Di cinco cosas que hiciste este año en el colegio.
2. ¿Qué información sabes sobre el e-mail?
3. Di dos inventos tecnológicos que existen hoy y un invento que piensas va a haber en el futuro.
4. ¿Qué información acerca de ti puedes escribirle en español a tu amigo/a de correo electrónico?
5. Di tres cosas que has aprendido este año.
6. ¿Cuál ha sido tu actividad favorita este año?
7. Di un proverbio que hayas leído en español este año y escribe una corta explicación acerca de él.

Answers

Autoevaluación
Possible answers:
1. Answers will vary.
2. Hay 263 millones de direcciones de correo electrónico en el mundo. Cada usuario recibe al día un promedio de 30 mensajes.
3. La computadora. El fax. En el futuro será posible que exista una cámara de video en todos los teléfonos.
4. Answers will vary.
5. Answers will vary.
6. Mi actividad favorita este año ha sido estudiar el español.
7. Answers will vary.

Activities

TPR. (Use variations of this TPR activity to teach or review any vocabulary topic.) Choose a theme, "countries in the Spanish-speaking world," for example. Inform students they are to raise their right hand if the item names a country where Spanish is the official language, and their left hand if the item does not name one of the Spanish-speaking countries. (This part of the activity will vary depending upon the vocabulary topic.) Then say several words in Spanish to teach and test student comprehension of vocabulary: *España* (right hand), *la silla* (left hand), *México* (right hand), *el cuchillo* (left hand), *el ratón* (left hand), and so forth.

NATIONAL STANDARDS
C3.1, C4.1, C4.2, C5.2

Activity 8

Quizzes/Activities 3-4

Answers

A Creative self-expression.

B Creative self-expression.

Notes

www

Search Engines:
Altavista
http://www.altavista.com/
MSN
http://search.msn.com/allinone.asp
Infoseek
http://infoseek.go.com/
Webcrawler
http://webcrawler.com

Culture. Explain who these well-known people are: *Daisy Fuentes,* television personality; *Shakira, Enrique Iglesias, Juan Luis Guerra, Gloria Estefan,* singers; *Plácido Domingo,* opera singer; *Celia Cruz,* singer of popular traditional music; *Rubén Blades,* actor and singer; *Antonio Banderas, Salma Hayek, María Conchita Alonso, Rosie Pérez, Jimmy Smits,* actors; *Edward James Olmos,* actor and director; *Isabel Allende, Sandra Cisneros,* authors; *Gabriel García Márquez, Octavio Paz,* Nobel Prize-winning authors; *Alex Rodríguez, Pedro Martínez, Sammy Sosa, Edgar Rentería,* baseball players. Draw upon your students' interests and reinforce their knowledge of Spanish-speaking people in your community.

Activities

Expansion. Have students write a short summary about what they discussed for the *Comunicación* activity.

NATIONAL STANDARDS
C1.1, C1.3, C4.1, C4.2, C5.1, C5.2

¡La práctica hace al maestro!

A Comunicación

Working with a partner, take turns interviewing one another about your lives during the year. The information may be about classes this year, family activities, favorite activities you have done with friends, daily lives, etc. Be imaginative! Take notes about what is being said and prepare a written report about your interview.

B Conexión con la tecnología

Search the World Wide Web to find a home page that provides information about clubs for any Hispanic actor, singer or athlete. Write an e-mail to one of its members and tell him/her about you and your life. Finally, tell the person why you like that particular actor, singer or athlete and ask for some interesting background information that you would like to know about the celebrity.

El beisbolista Alex Rodríguez.

■ **Antonio Banderas**

El actor Antonio Banderas quiere dedicarse a las grandes regatas. Se va a comprar un velero que cuesta 25 millones de pesetas y ya está enrolando a una tripulación perfectamente preparada para las competiciones. Se trata de un barco galardonado en varias ocasiones en concursos de vela. En la compra, realizada por el hermano del actor, no hubo problemas de dinero.

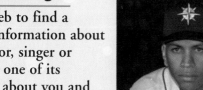

¿Qué recuerdas?

Answers

¿Qué recuerdas?

1. Hay influencia hispana en los EE.UU. (Mural en el "Mission District", San Francisco, CA.)
2. Simón Bolívar es el héroe nacional en Bolivia, Colombia, Ecuador, Perú y Venezuela. (Estátua de Simón Bolívar en La Paz, Bolivia.)
3. El D.F., o Distrito Federal, es la capital de México.
4. Punta del Este, Uruguay.
5. Las ruinas mayas de Copán están en Honduras.
6. Sevilla, España.

Activities

Multiple Intelligences (intrapersonal/linguistic/spatial). Ask students about the pictures they see on this page. What do they know about each place? Where would they like to go? Use the opportunity to talk about what students have learned during the year and to gauge your success preparing them to take what they are learning in class out into the community to be lifelong learners and users of Spanish.

Content reviewed in *Lección 19*
- opportunities to use Spanish in careers and for study
- future tense
- Spanish-speaking countries
- express wishes and preferences

Activities

Critical Listening. Explain to students that they will hear Spanish speakers who have been recorded on audiocassette tape or on audio compact disc. They are not expected to understand everything they hear. However, students should listen carefully to the sounds, tone and rhythm of the language while trying to guess what topics are being discussed.

Expansion. Invite exchange students in your school to visit your classes in order to discuss their experiences in the United States and the benefits of study in another country.

Technology. Have students plan a vacation to Spain this summer. They should search the Internet for possible travel packages to sites in Spain and the Canary Islands. Ask them to print out the information on the plans that interest them the most and have the best prices, and share their findings with the rest of the class. Have them tell which trip they would choose, how much it would cost, and what is included in the price. Suggest that students illustrate their presentation with information they downloaded and printed out.

NATIONAL STANDARDS
C1.2, C4.1

Contexto cultural
EL MUNDO

Lección 20

Un nuevo mundo

Los siguientes chicos de los Estados Unidos dicen en qué ciudad y país de habla hispana les gustaría estudiar una carrera o trabajar.

Me gustaría estudiar veterinaria en Madrid, España.

Yo quiero trabajar en negocios internacionales en Buenos Aires, Argentina.

Mary Parker, Miami

Quisiera estudiar ingeniería en Caracas, Venezuela.

Julie Stilp, Minneapolis

Paul Morales, Chicago

Me gustaría estudiar para ser diseñadora de páginas web en Santiago, Chile.

Yo quiero trabajar como profesor en San José, Costa Rica.

Nancy Martínez, Nueva York

Antonio Herrera, Los Ángeles

Quisiera trabajar como médico en Santo Domingo, República Dominicana.

Scott Peterson, Dallas

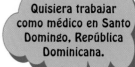

¿Qué comprendiste?

1. ¿En dónde quiere estudiar Mary?
2. ¿Qué quiere estudiar Julie en España?
3. ¿En qué quiere trabajar Paul?
4. ¿Quién quiere estudiar para ser diseñador de páginas web en Chile?
5. ¿En dónde quiere Antonio trabajar como médico?
6. ¿En qué quiere trabajar Scott?

Charlando

1. ¿En que país de habla hispana te gustaría estudiar después de terminar el colegio?
2. ¿Te gustaría trabajar en otro país? ¿En cuál?
3. ¿Piensas que estudiar o trabajar en otro país es algo bueno para tu futuro? Explica.

Conexión Cultural

¿Dónde puedo seguir estudiando?

Una vez que hayas decidido qué estudiar o qué tipo de trabajo quieres hacer, debes buscar las instituciones o compañías donde quieres estudiar o trabajar, ya sea en los Estados Unidos o en el extranjero. Si es fuera del país, debes decidir en qué país de habla hispana quieres estudiar o trabajar y conseguir información para saber cómo es la vida allí. Hoy existen muchas universidades y muchas compañías multinacionales que ofrecen programas de intercambio (exchange) o trabajos internacionales en todo el mundo.

Para estudiar, puedes escoger entre hacer la carrera que quieres seguir en una universidad del país o del extranjero, o hacer un programa de intercambio para estudiar en otro país por un período corto de tiempo y luego regresar. Para trabajar, puedes escoger entre hacer una práctica de trabajo en una compañía de otro país mientras eres estudiante, o buscar un trabajo permanente con una compañía aquí o en el extranjero.

Para recibir más información puedes consultar con tu consejero o consejera (counselor) en el colegio al que asistes, la consejería de educación de la embajada del país que te interese o en la Web.

¿Quisieras estudiar en la UNAM, en México, D.F.?

¿Te gustaría estudiar en Santiago, Chile?

Answers

1. 1. Mary quiere estudiar en Caracas, Venezuela.
   2. Julie quiere estudiar veterinaria en España.
   3. Paul quiere trabajar en negocios internacionales.
   4. Nancy quiere estudiar para ser diseñadora de páginas web en Chile.
   5. Antonio quiere trabajar como médico en Santo Domingo, República Dominicana.
   6. Scott quiere trabajar como profesor.

2. Answers will vary.

Activities

Expansion. Point out that the imperfect subjunctive form of *querer, quisiera,* in the *Para ti* is roughly equivalent to **would like.** The actual formation of the imperfect subjunctive is taught in *Somos así ¡YA!* However, the imperfect subjunctive forms of the verbs *hablar, comer* and *escribir* have been included in the Appendices of *Somos así LISTOS* if you wish to include an introductory explanation of the imperfect subjunctive in conjunction with this use of *quisiera.*

433

NATIONAL STANDARDS
C1.1, C1.2, C3.2, C4.1, C5.2

CONEXIONES

 ## 3 Cruzando fronteras

Haz una lista de tres países hispanos donde te gustaría estudiar o trabajar. Luego di dos cosas que sabes de cada país. Presenta la información a la clase.

¿Quisieras estudiar en Buenos Aires, Argentina?

 ## 4 Conexión con la tecnología

Escoge un país de la lista que hiciste en la actividad anterior. Busca información sobre ese lugar en la Internet. Averigua cómo es la vida en ese país para saber si es similar o diferente a la vida en tu comunidad. Luego, busca datos de interés, como festivales, fiestas, sitios turísticos y restaurantes. Finalmente, busca mapas de la ciudad donde quieres vivir e imprímelos *(print them)*. Presenta la información a la clase.

 ## 5 Estudiar en otro país

Trabajando en grupos pequeños, hablen de las ventajas y desventajas de estudiar en otro país. Escriban las conclusiones, y luego, una persona del grupo debe presentar un resumen a la clase.

Oportunidades

Sin límites

Si alguna vez le has dicho a alguien que estás aprendiendo español y la respuesta ha sido "¿por qué?", es probable que esa persona no sepa de la gran cantidad de oportunidades de trabajo disponibles (*available*) para las personas bilingües. No importa si eres bombero o abogado, saber español te ayudará a mejorar tus probabilidades de tener éxito en el futuro. Además, tus habilidades para comunicarte en español te abrirán muchas puertas y te ayudarán a hacer cualquier trabajo que escojas.

6 Trabajos internacionales

Lee el siguiente aviso de una página web, y luego, contesta las preguntas que siguen.

Podrías usar tu español trabajando como médico.

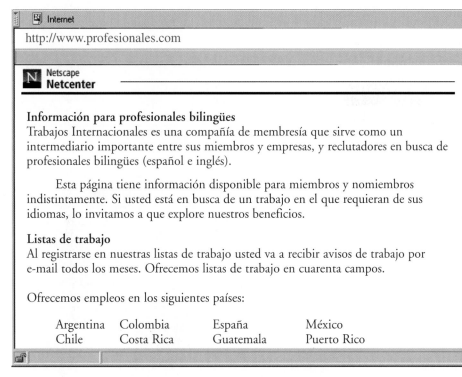

http://www.profesionales.com

Netscape Netcenter

Información para profesionales bilingües
Trabajos Internacionales es una compañía de membresía que sirve como un intermediario importante entre sus miembros y empresas, y reclutadores en busca de profesionales bilingües (español e inglés).

Esta página tiene información disponible para miembros y nomiembros indistintamente. Si usted está en busca de un trabajo en el que requieran de sus idiomas, lo invitamos a que explore nuestros beneficios.

Listas de trabajo
Al registrarse en nuestras listas de trabajo usted va a recibir avisos de trabajo por e-mail todos los meses. Ofrecemos listas de trabajo en cuarenta campos.

Ofrecemos empleos en los siguientes países:

Argentina	Colombia	España	México
Chile	Costa Rica	Guatemala	Puerto Rico

1. ¿Qué tipo de profesionales pueden estar interesados en esta página web?
2. ¿Se necesita ser miembro para usar los servicios de esta compañía?
3. Si te registras en sus listas de trabajo, ¿qué vas a recibir?
4. ¿En cuántos tipos de trabajo ofrecen listas?
5. ¿En cuántos países de habla hispana ofrecen trabajos?

 Activities 3-4

 Quiz/Activity 2

Answers

6
1. Profesionales bilingües que hablen español e inglés y que busquen trabajo.
2. No se necesita ser miembro.
3. Voy a recibir avisos de trabajo por e-mail todos los meses.
4. Ofrecen listas en cuarenta tipos de trabajo.
5. Ofrecen trabajos en ocho países de habla hispana.

Notes

Ask students if they can recognize the words they do not know by reading in context. Words that they might not recognize are: *membresía* (the word is derived from the word *miembro*), *reclutadores* (recruiters), *disponibles* (available), *requieran* (require), *campos* (fields).

Activities

Communities. Have students choose a Spanish-speaking country where they would like to work and find out how they need to prepare and what they need to do to work there. Ask students to share the information they found with the class.

Technology. Using the Internet, have students find out the types of jobs a bilingual person would find in the countries listed on the Web page shown on this page.

NATIONAL STANDARDS
C1.2, C4.1, C5.1

7 Una entrevista

Trabajando en parejas, pregúntale a tu compañero/a de clase la siguiente información para saber sobre sus planes para el futuro. Averigua cualquier otra información que necesites. Después de la entrevista, escribe un párrafo sobre los planes que tiene para el futuro tu compañero/a.

 lo que piensa estudiar al terminar el colegio
A: ¿Qué piensas estudiar al terminar el colegio?
B: Pienso estudiar para ser artista.

1. lugar donde quiere estudiar
2. si le gustaría estudiar en otro país
3. trabajo que le gustaría tener
4. lugar donde preferiría tener su trabajo
5. si le gustaría trabajar en otro país

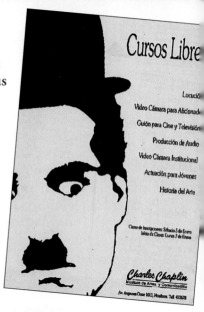

Oportunidades

Estudiando en un país de habla hispana

Hasta este momento tu has aprendido mucho sobre otras culturas y has mejorado tus habilidades para hablar español a través de diferentes medios como la televisión internacional, el e-mail, la Internet, etc. Pero ninguna de estas formas se puede comparar con la oportunidad de estudiar en el exterior y poder estar inmerso completamente en un ambiente auténtico de habla hispana. Estudiando en un país de habla hispana a través de un programa de intercambio, por ejemplo, te da la oportunidad de seguir estudiando, mientras aprendes en un ambiente en el que a la vez puedes experimentar la cultura y la lengua de primera mano.

Universidad Autónoma de Centro América

Unos estudiantes en la Universidad Católica, Quito, Ecuador.

8 Cruzando fronteras

Lee el siguiente aviso sobre un programa de intercambio. Después, contesta las preguntas.

CAMPUS COLIMA MÉXICO

Vivimos en un mundo de gran variedad cultural, en el cual el tener una visión internacional es cada vez más indispensable para el éxito profesional. El Programa de Intercambio Internacional es una inversión que puedes hacer durante tu vida de estudiante, la cual podrá llegar a ser un factor importante para abrirte muchas puertas en el aspecto profesional.

Estudiar en el extranjero es culturalmente enriquecedor y profesionalmente una gran recompensa.

¿Quiénes pueden participar?
Todos los estudiantes que reúnan las siguientes condiciones:

- Estar en 3°, 4°, 5°, 6° o 7° semestre de su carrera al momento de entregar la solicitud. Es importante aclarar que la recepción de solicitudes es únicamente al inicio de cada semestre, por lo que se deberá considerar esto al momento de entregar la solicitud.
- Tener un promedio global en la carrera igual o superior a 83 o su equivalente.
- Hablar español, francés o alemán según el país al que se viaje.

1. ¿Qué es importante para tener éxito en el mundo de hoy, según el aviso?
2. ¿Cómo se llama el programa que ofrecen?
3. ¿Por qué participar en este programa puede ser un factor importante?
4. ¿Qué es muy enriquecedor, según el artículo?
5. ¿Cuáles son las condiciones que se deben tener para participar?

9 Buscando universidad

¿Qué buscarías en una universidad donde quieres estudiar en el futuro? Haz una lista de las características más importantes que buscarías en ese lugar.

 Que tenga estudiantes de todo el mundo.

UNIVERSIDAD GABRIELA MISTRAL

ADMISIÓN

CARRERAS:
- DERECHO
- INGENIERIA COMERCIAL
- PSICOLOGIA
- EDUCACION: BASICA Y PARVULARIA
- CONTADOR AUDITOR (PROGRAMA DE LA TARDE)
- BACHILLERATO EN CIENCIAS SOCIALES
- PERIODISMO

Capítulo 10   437

Answers

8
1. Es importante tener una visión internacional.
2. Se llama Programa de Intercambio Internacional.
3. Porque puede abrir muchas puertas en el aspecto profesional.
4. Estudiar en el extranjero es muy enriquecedor.
5. Se debe estar en tercero, cuarto, quinto, sexto o séptimo semestre de una carrera, tener un promedio de notas superior a ochenta y tres o su equivalente, hablar español, francés o alemán según el país al que se viaje.

9 Answers will vary.

Notes

Ask students if they can recognize the words they do not know by reading in context. Words that they might not recognize are: *inversión* (investment), *enriquecedor* (enriching), *solicitud* (application), *recepción* (receiving), *inicio* (beginning), *promedio* (average).

Activities

Pronunciation. As a quick review, remind students that words that begin with the letters *k* and *w* are foreign; no words in Spanish begin with *rr,* but *r* is pronounced with a trill *(erre)* when it appears at the beginning of a word. In addition, the letter *x* may be pronounced quite differently in Spanish, as can be seen in the word *México* (where the pronunciation is like the *wh* in the English word **who**), the name *Xiomara* (where the pronunciation is like the sound of *s* in the English word **sing**) and the word *contexto* (where the sound is like the *x* in the English word **context**).

NATIONAL STANDARDS
C1.2, C3.2, C4.1, C5.2

Quiz/Activity 3

Quiz/Activity 3

Answers

10 Creative self-expression.

11
1. Lo más difícil es la elección de la carrera.
2. Sí, el prestigio y la seriedad son factores importantes al escoger una universidad.
3. Se debe hacer una lista con todos los formularios, cartas, fotografías y certificados que se necesitan.
4. Cuando se va a estudiar en el extranjero.
5. Es importante escoger una compañía de correos seria.

Notes

Encourage students to read for recognition by looking first at unknown words in their context. Students may need help with the following words: *desarrollo* (development), *puesto* (place), *salón* (room), *seriedad* (seriousness), *perfil* (profile), *personal docente* (teaching staff), *convenios* (partnership), *inscripción* (registration), *papeleo* (paper work), *formularios* (applications), *recoléctalos* (gather them), *comprueba* (check).

Activities

Critical Thinking. Write several words on the board or on an overhead transparency (e.g., *e-mail, España, universidad*). Ask students to write or say words that are related to the words you wrote down (they should be ready to justify their answers): *e-mail-Internet* (both require a computer); *España-paella* (*paella* is a saffron-flavored rice dish that is very popular in Spain); *universidad-estudiar* (you have to study if you are accepted at a university). As an alternative, have students do the activity in pairs.

 NATIONAL STANDARDS
C1.2, C1.3, C3.2, C4.1, C4.2, C5.1

10 Un trabajo

 Trabajando en parejas, hablen de las características más importantes que buscarían en un trabajo. Escriban sus conclusiones y, luego, compártanlas con otra pareja de estudiantes de la clase.

 Queremos un trabajo que sea en español.

11 Consejos para ingresar a una universidad

El siguiente artículo te da algunos consejos que debes seguir una vez que hayas decidido qué carrera estudiar en la universidad. Léelo y, luego, contesta las preguntas que siguen.

Consejos para un proceso de admisión con éxito

Ya pasaste lo más difícil: la elección de la carrera con la que inicias tu formación profesional. Ahora sigue el proceso de admisión. De su buen plan y desarrollo dependerán tu tranquilidad y tu puesto en el nuevo salón de clase.

Elección de la universidad. Al escoger una universidad es muy importante tener en cuenta los siguientes factores: prestigio y seriedad de la institución, registros oficiales correspondientes, perfil de la carrera, orientación ideológica de la institución, características del personal docente, existencia de convenios con instituciones del país y/o el extranjero. Ojo con: los costos, las condiciones para pagar y las fechas de inscripción.

Papeleo. Para no tener que dar vueltas y no tener dolores de cabeza, haz una lista de todos los formularios, cartas, fotografías y certificados requeridos. Recoléctalos con tiempo, teniendo en cuenta la fecha de entrega. Antes de salir de tu casa comprueba, lista en mano, si llevas todo lo necesario. Si vas a estudiar en el extranjero, sé doblemente cuidadoso con todo lo que te piden. En lo que respecta al envío de documentos, escoge una compañía seria y ten en cuenta los tiempos de entrega del correo.

 **¡Ojo!**
As you know, the word *ojo* means **eye**, but not in all circumstances. *Ojo* can be used in Spanish as an expression to say **watch out** or **stay alert**.

1. ¿Qué es lo más difícil, según el artículo?
2. ¿Son el prestigio y la seriedad factores importantes al escoger una universidad, según el artículo?
3. ¿Qué se debe hacer para no tener dolores de cabeza?
4. ¿Cuándo se debe tener mucho cuidado con lo que piden?
5. ¿Qué es importante tener en cuenta al enviar documentos?

438 Lección 20

12 En resumen

Escribe una composición de dos párrafos sobre tus planes para el futuro. Describe si piensas ir a la universidad o buscar un trabajo, o cualquier otro plan que tengas después de terminar el colegio.

Colegio Hispánico
MIGUEL DE UNAMUNO
SALAMANCA – SANTANDER
ESPAÑOL PARA EXTRANJEROS

13 ¿Eres cantante?

Escribe una canción en español sobre algún tema que describa tu futuro. Después, puedes leer o cantar tu canción para la clase.

Canto una canción sobre mi futuro.

En el futuro, pienso asistir a la universidad.

Autoevaluación. Como repaso y autoevaluación, responde lo siguiente:

1. Si pudieras escoger un país de habla hispana donde podrías seguir estudiando o trabajando, ¿cuál escogerías?
2. Escribe un aviso de trabajo corto para algún puesto donde se busca a alguien que sea bilingüe.
3. ¿Cuáles son tus planes para el futuro?
4. Di tres cosas que son importantes para ti al escoger una universidad.
5. Imagina que has estado buscando por diez años una carrera para estudiar después de terminar el colegio. ¿Qué consejo le darías a un estudiante que esté buscando una carrera para estudiar después del colegio?
6. Haz una lista de dos universidades que ofrezcan programas de estudios en el exterior a las cuales te gustaría asistir.

En el futuro, podrías jugar al fútbol en España.

Activity 7

Quizzes/Activities 4-5

Answers

A Creative self-expression.

B Creative self-expression.

Activities

Expansion. Have students write a short summary about what they discussed for the *Comunicación* activity.

Multiple Intelligences (linguistic). Talk with students about what they plan to do in their future. Discuss whether they intend to go to a college, to a university or to some other school for additional training after high school. Ask students what they aspire to. Find out whether they have specific career or life goals.

¡La práctica hace al maestro!

Comunicación

Working in groups of three, talk in Spanish about how you think your life is going to be in ten years. Consider any decisions you may have made recently or plan to make in the near future and discuss how they might affect your life in the future years.

¿Cómo va a ser tu vida en diez años?

Conexión con la tecnología

Complete an Internet search for on-line information about study abroad programs in Spanish-speaking countries. Select a university or an institution in a country you would like to study and live in. Print out all the information concerning requirements for enrollment in that place and share them with the rest of the class. Make a bulletin board to display your findings.

Ellas están viendo la página web de una universidad.

NATIONAL STANDARDS
C1.1, C1.3, C3.1, C4.1,

¿Qué recuerdas?

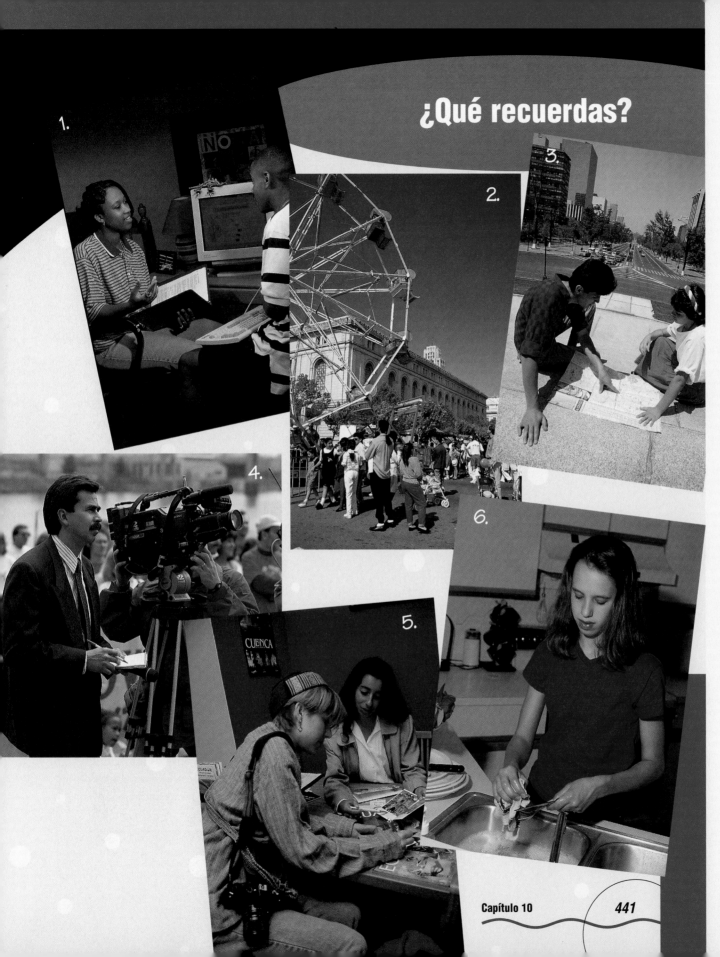

1.

2.

3.

4.

5.

6.

Testing/Assessment
Test Booklet
Oral Proficiency
   Evaluation Manual
Portfolio Assessment

Answers

¿Qué recuerdas?
1. Están usando la Internet.
2. Un parque de atracciones.
3. ¿En qué dirección está...?
4. Es un reportero de la televisión.
5. Una agencia de viajes.
6. Ella está lavando los platos.

Activities

Communities. Suggest to students that they talk to their parents about ways they may use Spanish and communication skills they have developed during the year in order to volunteer in the community. Over the summer, students may decide they wish to volunteer at the local library, using Spanish with Spanish-speaking customers. Start a class discussion of other ways students may be able participate in community service.

Multiple Intelligences (intrapersonal/linguistic/spatial). Ask students about the pictures they see on this page. What do they know about each place? Where would they like to go? Use the opportunity to talk about what students have learned during the year and to gauge your success in preparing them to take what they are learning in class out into the community to be lifelong learners and users of Spanish.

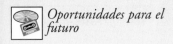 *Oportunidades para el futuro*

a leer

Estrategia

Preparación

Estrategia para leer: *recognize related words*
Many words are similar in meaning and spelling because they are related to a base word such as a verb or a noun. When you are reading an unfamiliar text, you can figure out the meaning of new words by combining what you already know about a base word with clues you gather from the context of the related word.

Como preparación para la lectura, lee la siguiente lista de palabras y sus palabras relacionadas. Luego, di qué crees que significan en inglés las palabras relacionadas.

1. cambiar → el intercambio
2. participar → el/la participante
3. preferir → la preferencia
4. vender → la venta
5. encargar → el/la encargado/a

Oportunidades para el futuro

¡Bienvenido a Worldwide Classroom!
Durante los últimos 28 años hemos trabajado para incrementar la educación e intercambios culturales para jóvenes y adultos. Worldwide Classroom es hoy la mayor fuente de información para estudiantes que están buscando un programa internacional.

   ¿Tiene problemas para encontrar su programa internacional? Díganos lo que busca y podemos ayudarle a usted. Aquí, usted puede encontrar más de 10.000 instituciones participantes en más de 92 países. Estas instituciones participantes incluyen universidades, institutos técnicos, centros culturales, etc. Estamos seguros que usted puede encontrar el programa perfecto en el país de su preferencia y en la ciudad que usted desee. Consulte ya nuestra página web: worldwideclass.com

Estudiantes Internacionales

La Universidad San Francisco de Quito considera que el intercambio cultural es excelente para el desarrollo intelectual de las personas.

Los estudiantes internacionales cuyo idioma natal no sea el español y que deseen estudiar en la USFQ deben haber estudiado como mínimo un año de español en la universidad de origen.

Se puede aplicar a la USFQ por medio de los programas de intercambio establecidos entre nuestra universidad y otras instituciones en el exterior.

Todos los estudiantes internacionales al llegar a Quito toman un examen de español para ser ubicados en el curso correspondiente del idioma. Aquellos estudiantes internacionales que no pertenezcan a un programa establecido por la USFQ y otra universidad extranjera, deberán solicitar el paquete de admisiones a la Oficina de Programas Internacionales.

La Oficina de Programas Internacionales facilita la información necesaria con respecto al tipo de visa que requieran los estudiantes internacionales quienes tienen los mismos deberes y derechos que los estudiantes regulares de la USFQ. Todos los estudiantes internacionales tienen un tutor asignado por el Director de Programas Internacionales, que es el encargado de guiar al estudiante en asuntos académicos durante su estadía en el USFQ.

Fechas de aplicación: para tramitar las visas de estudiante, la Oficina de Programas Internacionales aceptará las solicitudes de admisión hasta estas fechas:

Primer semestre: hasta el 15 de julio.

Segundo semestre: hasta el 15 de noviembre.

Orientación para estudiantes internacionales

En la semana anterior al inicio de clases se realiza la Semana de Orientación, en la cual los estudiantes internacionales, en grupos pequeños, participan con estudiantes nacionales y miembros de la facultad, en un seminario para familiarizarse con la USFQ y la cultura ecuatoriana. Durante esta semana se les hará el examen de español para saber su ubicación apropiada en el nivel correspondiente.

Vivienda para estudiantes internacionales

Los estudiantes internacionales viven con familias ecuatorianas. Este programa está diseñado para que los estudiantes se sientan parte activa de la comunidad durante su estadía en el Ecuador. El vivir con una familia ecuatoriana le da al estudiante la oportunidad de compartir la cultura, intercambiar ideas y establecer lazos de amistad internacional.

Notes

Words that students might not recognize include the following: *fuente* (source), *desarrollo* (development), *pertenezcan* (belong), *paquete* (package), *deberes* (duties), *derechos* (rights), *encargardo* (person in charge), *asuntos* (matters), *estadía* (stay), *vivienda* (housing), *diseñado* (designed), *lazos* (bonds), *detalles* (details), *inscripciones* (registrations), *relacionadas* (related), *aprendizaje* (learning), *campo* (field), *dirigida* (addressed), *seguro* (insurance).

NATIONAL STANDARDS
C1.2, C4.1

Activities

Communities. Ask students to search the Internet for a newspaper from a Spanish-speaking country that contains an article about the United States. Then have them compare the coverage of that news story with the coverage of the same story by a newspaper published in the United States. Have them tell the class how the coverage is the same or different.

YAHOO en español

Busca personas bilingües (español-inglés) para trabajar como navegantes de red. Las funciones principales son revisar páginas web para incluirlas en bases de datos, ordenarlas de acuerdo con las categorías que ya existen y ayudar a controlar la evolución de esas categorías. El/la candidato/a debe ser una persona muy motivada, que demuestre capacidad en la toma de decisiones, habilidad para trabajar en equipo y orientación de servicio al cliente. Es importante que el/la candidato/a conozca las culturas de Latinoamérica y España, sea fluido en español escrito y oral y hable inglés. Otras calificaciones adicionales son: experiencia en trabajo con la Internet, atención a los detalles, abundancia de sentido común y excelentes habilidades de organización. Se prefieren personas con BS o BA. Al aplicar incluir carta de presentación.

FUNDACIÓN UNIVERSIDAD DE BOGOTÁ
JORGE TADEO LOZANO

Arquitectura

Comunicación Social

Publicidad

Derecho

Mercadeo

Biología marina

Ingeniería

Técnico agrícola

Técnico electricista

Inscripciones abiertas hasta el 15 de noviembre
Informes e inscripciones:
Carrera 8 No. 23-68, Of. 305
Santa Fe de Bogotá
Teléfono: 3341515

PONTIFICIA UNIVERSIDAD CATÓLICA DEL ECUADOR

La PUCE ofrece a la comunidad estudiantil internacional una sesión de verano de junio 15 a agosto 6.

Este curso consiste de tres áreas relacionadas:

1. Aprendizaje del español
   De lunes a jueves, de 9 A.M. a 12 P.M.
   (junio 15 - julio 22)
2. Ecología
   De lunes a jueves, 3 P.M. a 7 P.M.
   (junio 15 - julio 22)
3. Trabajo de campo
   Viernes, de 9 A.M. a 7 P.M.
   (junio 15 - julio 22)

Costo: $1900 dólares

Para mayor información, escribir e-mail a:
puce@edu.ec

REP de Ventas

Compañía clasificada 4A1 por Dun & Bradstreet busca vendedor(a) para expander su territorio. Gran oportunidad para ascender en la compañía. Líneas de productos incluyen: regalos, accesorios para mujer, productos importados, flores artificiales, productos de cuidado personal, relojes, etc. Bilingüe, inglés/español preferible. Necesita experiencia en ventas. Salario basado en comisiones e incluye gastos para viajar y un plan de seguro. Es necesario tener vehículo. Fax hoja de vida a:

The Gerson Company.

Activities A-B

CODATEL

Se busca Programador Bilingüe.
Lugar del trabajo: Ciudad de México, México
Requisitos: Profesional en sistemas, que hable español e inglés y tenga un año de experiencia en programación.
Excelente presentación.
Buena organización.
Salario: Competente.
Enviar hoja de vida a:
codatel@recurhum.mex

Agencia de Publicidad Internacional

Importante agencia internacional de publicidad necesita:
Cargo: Asistente de Márketing bilingüe para trabajar en Miami en el diseño de publicidad dirigida a la población hispana.
Requisitos: Tener título en Publicidad o Márketing, ser fluido en español e inglés y tener conocimiento en el manejo de computadoras.
Experiencia: No se requiere.
Enviar hoja de vida con carta de presentación y salario deseado a: 2080 Coralview Av., Miami, FL 33035.

 ¿Qué comprendiste?

1. ¿Qué clase de institutos hay en el programa de Worldwide Classroom?
2. ¿Qué tipo de empleado/a busca Gerson Company?
3. ¿Hasta qué fecha se pueden presentar solicitudes para estudiar durante el segundo semestre en la Universidad San Francisco de Quito?
4. ¿A qué universidad debe aplicar una persona si quiere estudiar durante el verano en Ecuador?
5. ¿A qué aviso debe responder una persona que le guste mucho la Internet?
6. ¿En qué universidad se puede estudiar para ser técnico electricista?
7. ¿En qué ciudad se ofrece un trabajo como programador?
8. ¿En qué trabajo no se necesita experiencia?

 Charlando

1. ¿Te gustaría participar en un programa internacional? Explica.
2. ¿Qué buscas en una universidad a la que quieres asistir?
3. ¿A qué programa de los anteriores te gustaría ir?
4. ¿Has buscado empleos en la Internet? ¿De qué tipo?
5. ¿Hay una feria de empleos o de universidades en tu ciudad?
6. ¿En qué tipo de trabajo tienes experiencia?

Answers

 A

1. Hay universidades, institutos técnicos, centros culturales, etc.
2. Busca un(a) vendedor(a).
3. Se pueden presentar hasta el 15 de noviembre.
4. Debe aplicar a la Pontificia Universidad Católica de Ecuador.
5. Debe responder al aviso de Yahoo en español.
6. Se puede estudiar para ser técnico electricista en la Universidad Jorge Tadeo Lozano.
7. En la Ciudad de México se ofrece un trabajo como programador.
8. En el trabajo de asistente de marketing no se necesita experiencia.

B Answers will vary.

Activities

Expansion. Additional questions (*¿Qué comprendiste?): ¿Cuántos años de experiencia tiene Worldwide Classroom?; ¿En cuántos países hay escuelas participantes?; ¿Qué productos vende The Gerson Company?; ¿Cuáles son los requisitos* (requirements) *para el trabajo de representante de ventas?*

Notes

Use the poem on this page as a model for students to write a poem about how they used to be. Be certain students follow all six steps.

Encourage students to try to recognize unknown words in context. Some words students may not recognize include the following: *arco iris* (rainbow), *brillante* (sparkling), *conocimiento* (knowledge), *vencer* (conquer), *tempestad* (storm).

Review some of the writing strategies students have learned over the course of the year. Encourage students to apply as many of these strategies as possible in the composition.

Activities

Expansion. Read another poem for students and ask follow-up questions about the content.

La suela
Una vez yo era
parte de un zapato nuevo.
Limpio, fresco,
sin arrugas.
El mundo era
sólo el interior
de mi caja de cartón.

Un día voy a ser
parte de un zapato viejo.
Sucio, cansado.
Voy a experimentar
las calles largas,
las playas tibias,
los parques verdes,
y... otros suelos.

(Margarita)

Multiple Intelligences (linguistic). Have students enter their "I used to be" poem in their writer's journal. How to create a writer's journal was addressed in the *A escribir* section at the end of *Capítulo 2* in *Somos así EN SUS MARCAS.*

Estrategia para escribir: *using similes, metaphors and symbols*

Poems use words to paint scenes from your world. To create an image with only a few words, you can make use of symbols, metaphors and similes. Some words can represent more than one idea when they are used in a symbolic way. You can compare things with fewer words when you employ similes, which are comparisons that use *como* (like, as), or metaphors, which are comparisons that do not use *como*.

Write an *I used to be* poem. Choose two objects to symbolize yourself. One object symbolizes how you used to see, hear, feel, live, think, etc., and the other one represents how you are going to see, hear, feel, live, think, etc. Once you have chosen your symbols, study the sample below, then follow the steps to complete your poem.

El arco iris
Antes me sentía
como un rayo de luz.
Pasaba por la vida
sin una percepción clara.
Perdido en un mundo
brillante.

Pero, por fin pasé
por el prisma del
conocimiento.
Ahora voy a ser un arco iris,
ilustrado por mis experiencias.
Preparado para vencer
la tempestad de la vida.
        (Pepa)

Step 1: For the first line of your poem, form a verb in the imperfect tense to express how you "used to" be, see, hear, feel, live, think, etc.

Step 2: For the second line, name the object that symbolizes what you used to be or do.

Step 3: Use the next several lines to describe something about the object you just named that caused it to represent you.

Step 4: Start the next line with "*Un día voy a* (+ infinitive)" or "*Pronto voy a* (+ infinitive)."

Step 5: For the next line, name the object you chose to represent how you are going to be or what you are going to do.

Step 6: Use the next several lines to describe something about the object you just mentioned that makes it symbolize how you are going to be or what you are going to do.

repaso

Now that I have completed this chapter, I can...
- ✓ express past actions and events.
- ✓ discuss everyday ctivities.
- ✓ write about everyday life.
- ✓ talk about contemporary Hispanic culture.
- ✓ talk about the future.
- ✓ express emotion.
- ✓ state wishes and preferences.

I can also...
- ✓ use e-mail to communicate in Spanish.
- ✓ read web pages in Spanish.
- ✓ talk about technology.
- ✓ use proverbs and sayings to flavor speech.
- ✓ do a Web search.
- ✓ discuss various career opportunities.
- ✓ read about exchange programs in Spanish.

¿Adónde irá tu camino?

Portfolio Assessment
Select an activity from *Capítulo 10* to include in the *Somos así* Portfolio Assessment.

Notes

Remind students that time changes throughout the world from one geographic region to another. For example, if it is 7:00 A.M. in Chicago, it is 2:00 P.M. in Barcelona, Spain.

Activities

Communities. Begin a discussion about how students intend to use Spanish in the future. Ask questions and let them express thoughts about places they would like to visit, careers they are now considering and contributions they will be able to make to their community because they know Spanish.

Critical Thinking. Have students complete a culture project in which they look back on the countries already studied this year and make a collage that reflects what they have learned about that country. Remind students to keep in mind the theme for their collage: *Mirando hacia el pasado.*

Multiple Intelligences (intrapersonal/linguistic). Have students write a 150- to 200-word composition about their future. In the composition, they must describe their life, including where they will live and what they will be doing. They should tell about their dreams and personal aspirations and discuss some of the things they will do to attain them. Have students exchange papers and correct each other's spelling, underlining any errors, subject/verb agreement, content and make any suggestions in the margins. When they have received their papers back, students should make the necessary corrections and turn them in to you.

NATIONAL STANDARDS
C1.1, C1.2, C1.3, C2.1, C2.2, C3.1, C3.2, C4.1, C4.2, C5.1, C5.2

Appendices

Appendix A

Grammar Review

Definite articles

	Singular	Plural
Masculine	el	los
Feminine	la	las

Indefinite articles

	Singular	Plural
Masculine	un	unos
Feminine	una	unas

Adjective/noun agreement

	Singular	Plural
Masculine	El chico es alto.	Los chicos son altos.
Feminine	La chica es alta.	Las chicas son altas.

Pronouns

Singular	Subject	Direct object	Indirect object	Object of preposition	Reflexive
1st person	yo	me	me	mí	me
2nd person	tú	te	te	ti	te
3rd person	Ud.	lo/la	le	Ud.	se
	él	lo	le	él	se
	ella	la	le	ella	se
Plural					
1st person	nosotros	nos	nos	nosotros	nos
	nosotras	nos	nos	nosotras	nos
2nd person	vosotros	os	os	vosotros	os
	vosotras	os	os	vosotras	os
3rd person	Uds.	los/las	les	Uds.	se
	ellos	los	les	ellos	se
	ellas	las	les	ellas	se

Demonstrative pronouns

Singular		Plural		
Masculine	**Feminine**	**Masculine**	**Feminine**	**Neuter forms**
éste	ésta	éstos	éstas	esto
ése	ésa	ésos	ésas	eso
aquél	aquélla	aquéllos	aquéllas	aquello

Possessive pronouns

Singular	Singular form	Plural form
1st person	el mío la mía	los míos las mías
2nd person	el tuyo la tuya	los tuyos las tuyas
3rd person	el suyo la suya	los suyos las suyas

Plural	Singular form	Plural form
1st person	el nuestro la nuestra	los nuestros las nuestras
2nd person	el vuestro la vuestra	los vuestros las vuestras
3rd person	el suyo la suya	los suyos las suyas

Interrogatives

qué	*what*
cómo	*how*
dónde	*where*
cuándo	*when*
cuánto, -a, -os, -as	*how much, how many*
cuál/cuáles	*which (one)*
quién/quiénes	*who, whom*
por qué	*why*
para qué	*why, what for*

Demonstrative adjectives

Singular		Plural	
Masculine	**Feminine**	**Masculine**	**Feminine**
este	esta	estos	estas
ese	esa	esos	esas
aquel	aquella	aquellos	aquellas

Possessive adjectives: short form

Singular	Singular nouns	Plural nouns
1st person	mi hermano mi hermana	mis hermanos mis hermanas
2nd person	tu hermano tu hermana	tus hermanos tus hermanas
3rd person	su hermano su hermana	sus hermanos sus hermanas
Plural	**Singular nouns**	**Plural nouns**
1st person	nuestro hermano nuestra hermana	nuestros hermanos nuestras hermanas
2nd person	vuestro hermano vuestra hermana	vuestros hermanos vuestras hermanas
3rd person	su hermano su hermana	sus hermanos sus hermanas

Possessive adjectives: long form

Singular	Singular nouns	Plural nouns
1st person	un amigo mío una amiga mía	unos amigos míos unas amigas mías
2nd person	un amigo tuyo una amiga tuya	unos amigos tuyos unas amigas tuyas
3rd person	un amigo suyo una amiga suya	unos amigos suyos unos amigas suyas
Plural	**Singular nouns**	**Plural nouns**
1st person	un amigo nuestro una amiga nuestra	unos amigos nuestros unas amigas nuestras
2nd person	un amigo vuestro una amiga vuestra	unos amigos vuestros unas amigas vuestras
3rd person	un amigo suyo una amiga suya	unos amigos suyos unas amigas suyas

Appendix B

Verbs

Present tense (indicative)

Regular present tense		
hablar *(to speak)*	hablo hablas habla	hablamos habláis hablan
comer *(to eat)*	como comes come	comemos coméis comen
escribir *(to write)*	escribo escribes escribe	escribimos escribís escriben

Present tense of reflexive verbs (indicative)

lavarse *(to wash oneself)*	me lavo te lavas se lava	nos lavamos os laváis se lavan

Present tense of stem-changing verbs (indicative)

Stem-changing verbs are identified in this book by the presence of vowels in parentheses after the infinitive. If these verbs end in *-ar* or *-er,* they have only one change. If they end in *-ir,* they have two changes. The stem change of *-ar* and *-er* verbs and the first stem change of *-ir* verbs occur in all forms of the present tense, except *nosotros* and *vosotros.*

cerrar *(ie)* *(to close)*	e → ie	cierro cierras cierra	cerramos cerráis cierran

Verbs like **cerrar:** apretar *(to tighten),* atravesar *(to cross),* calentar *(to heat),* comenzar *(to begin),* despertar *(to wake up),* despertarse *(to awaken),* empezar *(to begin),* encerrar *(to lock up),* negar *(to deny),* nevar *(to snow),* pensar *(to think),* quebrar *(to break),* recomendar *(to recommend),* regar *(to water),* sentarse *(to sit down),* temblar *(to tremble),* tropezar *(to trip)*

contar *(ue)* *(to tell)*	o → ue	cuento cuentas cuenta	contamos contáis cuentan

Verbs like **contar:** acordar *(to agree),* acordarse *(to remember),* acostar *(to put to bed),* acostarse *(to lie down),* almorzar *(to have lunch),* colgar *(to hang),* costar *(to cost),* demostrar *(to demonstrate),* encontrar *(to find, to meet someone),* mostrar *(to show),* probar *(to taste, to try),* recordar *(to remember),* rogar *(to beg),* soltar *(to loosen),* sonar *(to ring, to sound),* soñar *(to dream),* volar *(to fly),* volcar *(to spill, to turn upside down)*

jugar *(ue)*	u → ue	juego	jugamos
(to play)		juegas	jugáis
		juega	juegan

perder *(ie)*	e → ie	pierdo	perdemos
(to lose)		pierdes	perdéis
		pierde	pierden

Verbs like **perder:** defender *(to defend)*, descender *(to descend, to go down)*, encender *(to light, to turn on)*, entender *(to understand)*, extender *(to extend)*, tender *(to spread out)*

volver *(ue)*	o → ue	vuelvo	volvemos
(to return)		vuelves	volvéis
		vuelve	vuelven

Verbs like **volver:** devolver *(to return something)*, doler *(to hurt)*, llover *(to rain)*, morder *(to bite)*, mover *(to move)*, resolver *(to resolve)*, soler *(to be in the habit of)*, torcer *(to twist)*

pedir *(i, i)*	e → i	pido	pedimos
(to ask for)		pides	pedís
		pide	piden

Verbs like **pedir:** conseguir *(to obtain, to attain, to get)*, despedirse *(to say good-bye)*, elegir *(to choose, to elect)*, medir *(to measure)*, perseguir *(to pursue)*, repetir *(to repeat)*, seguir *(to follow, to continue)*, vestirse *(to get dressed)*

sentir *(ie, i)*	e → ie	siento	sentimos
(to feel)		sientes	sentís
		siente	sienten

Verbs like **sentir:** advertir *(to warn)*, arrepentirse *(to regret)*, convertir *(to convert)*, convertirse *(to become)*, divertirse *(to have fun)*, herir *(to wound)*, invertir *(to invest)*, mentir *(to lie)*, preferir *(to prefer)*, requerir *(to require)*, sugerir *(to suggest)*

dormir *(ue, u)*	o → ue	duermo	dormimos
(to sleep)		duermes	dormís
		duerme	duermen

Another verb like **dormir:** morir *(to die)*

Present participle of regular verbs

The present participle of regular verbs is formed by replacing the *-ar* of the infinitive with *-ando* and the *-er* or *-ir* with *-iendo*.

Present participle of stem-changing verbs

Stem-changing verbs that end in *-ir* use the second stem change in the present participle.

dormir *(ue, u)*	durmiendo
seguir *(i, i)*	siguiendo
sentir *(ie, i)*	sintiendo

Progressive tenses

The present participle is used with the verbs *estar, continuar, seguir, andar* and some other motion verbs to produce the progressive tenses. They are reserved for recounting actions that are or were in progress at the time in question.

Regular command forms

	Affirmative		Negative
***-ar* verbs**	habla	(tú)	no hables
	hablad	(vosotros)	no habléis
	hable Ud.	(Ud.)	no hable Ud.
	hablen Uds.	(Uds.)	no hablen Uds.
	hablemos	(nosotros)	no hablemos
***-er* verbs**	come	(tú)	no comas
	comed	(vosotros)	no comáis
	coma Ud.	(Ud.)	no coma Ud.
	coman Uds.	(Uds.)	no coman Uds.
	comamos	(nosotros)	no comamos
***-ir* verbs**	escribe	(tú)	no escribas
	escribid	(vosotros)	no escribáis
	escriba Ud.	(Ud.)	no escriba Ud.
	escriban Uds.	(Uds.)	no escriban Uds.
	escribamos	(nosotros)	no escribamos

Commands of stem-changing verbs (indicative)

The stem change also occurs in *tú, Ud.* and *Uds.* commands, and the second change of *-ir* stem-changing verbs occurs in the *nosotros* command and in the negative *vosotros* command, as well.

cerrar *(to close)*	cierra	(tú)	no cierres
	cerrad	(vosotros)	no cerréis
	cierre Ud	(Ud.)	no cierre Ud.
	cierren Uds.	(Uds.)	no cierren Uds.
	cerremos	(nosotros)	no cerremos
volver *(to return)*	vuelve	(tú)	no vuelvas
	volved	(vosotros)	no volváis
	vuelva Ud.	(Ud.)	no vuelva Ud.
	vuelvan Uds.	(Uds.)	no vuelvan Uds.
	volvamos	(nosotros)	no volvamos
dormir *(to sleep)*	duerme	(tú)	no duermas
	dormid	(vosotros)	no durmáis
	duerma Ud.	(Ud.)	no duerma Ud.
	duerman Uds.	(Uds.)	no duerman Uds.
	durmamos	(nosotros)	no durmamos

Preterite tense (indicative)

hablar (to speak)	hablé	hablamos
	hablaste	hablasteis
	habló	hablaron
comer (to eat)	comí	comimos
	comiste	comisteis
	comió	comieron
escribir (to write)	escribí	escribimos
	escribiste	escribisteis
	escribió	escribieron

Preterite tense of stem-changing verbs (indicative)

Stem-changing verbs that end in -ar and -er are regular in the preterite tense. That is, they do not require a spelling change, and they use the regular preterite endings.

pensar *(ie)*	
pensé	pensamos
pensaste	pensasteis
pensó	pensaron

volver *(ue)*	
volví	volvimos
volviste	volvisteis
volvió	volvieron

Stem-changing verbs ending in -ir change their third-person forms in the preterite tense, but they still require the regular preterite endings.

sentir *(ie, i)*	
sentí	sentimos
sentiste	sentisteis
sintió	sintieron

dormirse *(ue, u)*	
me dormí	nos dormimos
te dormiste	os dormisteis
se durmió	se durmieron

Imperfect tense (indicative)

hablar (to speak)	hablaba	hablábamos
	hablabas	hablabais
	hablaba	hablaban
comer (to eat)	comía	comíamos
	comías	comíais
	comía	comían
escribir (to write)	escribía	escribíamos
	escribías	escribíais
	escribía	escribían

Future tense (indicative)

hablar (to speak)	hablaré	hablaremos
	hablarás	hablaréis
	hablará	hablarán
comer (to eat)	comeré	comeremos
	comerás	comeréis
	comerá	comerán
escribir (to write)	escribiré	escribiremos
	escribirás	escribiréis
	escribirá	escribirán

Conditional tense (indicative)

hablar (to speak)	hablaría	hablaríamos
	hablarías	hablaríais
	hablaría	hablarían
comer (to eat)	comería	comeríamos
	comerías	comeríais
	comería	comerían
escribir (to write)	escribiría	escribiríamos
	escribirías	escribirías
	escribiría	escribirían

Past participle

The past participle is formed by replacing the *-ar* of the infinitive with *-ado* and the *-er* or *-ir* with *-ido*.

hablar	hablado
comer	comido
vivir	vivido

Irregular past participles

abrir	abierto
cubrir	cubierto
decir	dicho
escribir	escrito
hacer	hecho
morir	muerto
poner	puesto
romper	roto
volver	vuelto
ver	visto

Present perfect tense (indicative)

The present perfect tense is formed by combining the present tense of *haber* and the past participle of a verb.

hablar *(to speak)*	he hablado	hemos hablado
	has hablado	habéis hablado
	ha hablado	han hablado
comer *(to eat)*	he comido	hemos comido
	has comido	habéis comido
	ha comido	han comido
vivir *(to live)*	he vivido	hemos vivido
	has vivido	habéis vivido
	ha vivido	han vivido

Pluperfect tense (indicative)

hablar *(to speak)*	había hablado	habíamos hablado
	habías hablado	habíais hablado
	había hablado	habían hablado

Preterite perfect tense (indicative)

hablar *(to speak)*	hube hablado	hubimos hablado
	hubiste hablado	hubisteis hablado
	hubo hablado	hubieron hablado

Future perfect tense (indicative)

hablar *(to speak)*	habré hablado	habremos hablado
	habrás hablado	habréis hablado
	habrá hablado	habrán hablado

Conditional perfect tense (indicative)

hablar *(to speak)*	habría hablado	habríamos hablado
	habrías hablado	habríais hablado
	habría hablado	habrían hablado

Present tense (subjunctive)

hablar *(to speak)*	hable	hablemos
	hables	habléis
	hable	hablen
comer *(to eat)*	coma	comamos
	comas	comáis
	coma	coman
escribir *(to write)*	escriba	escribamos
	escribas	escribáis
	escriba	escriban

Imperfect tense (subjunctive)

hablar *(to speak)*	hablara (hablase) hablaras (hablases) hablara (hablase)	habláramos (hablásemos) hablarais (hablaseis) hablaran (hablasen)
comer *(to eat)*	comiera (comiese) comieras (comieses) comiera (comiese)	comiéramos (comiésemos) comierais (comieseis) comieran (comiesen)
escribir *(to write)*	escribiera (escribiese) escribieras (escribieses) escribiera (escribiese)	escribiéramos (escribiésemos) escribierais (escribieseis) escribieran (escribiesen)

Present perfect tense (subjunctive)

hablar *(to speak)*	haya hablado hayas hablado haya hablado	hayamos hablado hayáis hablado hayan hablado

Pluperfect tense (subjunctive)

hablar *(to speak)*	hubiera (hubiese) hablado hubieras (hubieses) hablado hubiera (hubiese) hablado	hubiéramos (hubiésemos)) hablado hubieramos (hubieseis) hablado hubieran (hubiesen) hablado

Verbs with irregularities

The following charts provide some frequently used Spanish verbs with irregularities.

abrir *(to open)*	
past participle	abierto
Similar to:	cubrir *(to cover)*

andar *(to walk, to ride)*	
preterite	anduve, anduviste, anduvo, anduvimos, anduvisteis, anduvieron

buscar *(to look for)*	
preterite	busqué, buscaste, buscó, buscamos, buscasteis, buscaron
present subjunctive	busque, busques, busque, busquemos, busquéis, busquen
Similar to:	acercarse *(to get close, to approach)*, arrancar *(to start a motor)*, colocar *(to place)*, criticar *(to criticize)*, chocar *(to crash)*, equivocarse *(to make a mistake)*, explicar *(to explain)*, marcar *(to score a point)*, pescar *(to fish)*, platicar *(to chat)*, practicar *(to practice)*, sacar *(to take out)*, tocar *(to touch, to play an instrument)*

caber *(to fit into, to have room for)*

present	quepo, cabes, cabe, cabemos, cabéis, caben
preterite	cupe, cupiste, cupo, cupimos, cupisteis, cupieron
future	cabré, cabrás, cabrá, cabremos, cabréis, cabrán
present subjunctive	quepa, quepas, quepa, quepamos, quepáis, quepan

caer *(to fall)*

present	caigo, caes, cae, caemos, caéis, caen
preterite	caí, caíste, cayó, caímos, caísteis, cayeron
present participle	cayendo
present subjunctive	caiga, caigas, caiga, caigamos, caigáis, caigan
past participle	caído

conducir *(to drive, to conduct)*

present	conduzco, conduces, conduce, conducimos, conducís, conducen
preterite	conduje, condujiste, condujo, condujimos, condujisteis, condujeron
present subjunctive	conduzca, conduzcas, conduzca, conduzcamos, conduzcáis, conduzcan
Similar to:	traducir *(to translate)*

conocer *(to know)*

present	conozco, conoces, conoce, conocemos, conocéis, conocen
present subjunctive	conozca, conozcas, conozca, conozcamos, conozcáis, conozcan
Similar to:	complacer *(to please)*, crecer *(to grow, to increase)*, desaparecer *(to disappear)*, nacer *(to be born)*, ofrecer *(to offer)*

construir *(to build)*

present	construyo, construyes, construye, construimos, construís, construyen
preterite	construí, construiste, construyó, construimos, construisteis, construyeron
present participle	construyendo
present subjunctive	construya, construyas, construya, construyamos, construyáis, construyan

continuar *(to continue)*

present	continúo, continúas, continúa, continuamos, continuáis, continúan

convencer *(to convince)*

present	convenzo, convences, convence, convencemos, convencéis, convencen
present subjunctive	convenza, convenzas, convenza, convenzamos, convenzáis, convenzan
Similar to:	vencer *(to win, to expire)*

cubrir *(to cover)*

past participle	cubierto
Similar to:	abrir *(to open)*, descubrir *(to discover)*

dar *(to give)*

present	doy, das, da, damos, dais, dan
preterite	di, diste, dio, dimos, disteis, dieron
present subjunctive	dé, des, dé, demos, deis, den

decir *(to say, to tell)*

present	digo, dices, dice, decimos, decís, dicen
preterite	dije, dijiste, dijo, dijimos, dijisteis, dijeron
present participle	diciendo
command	di (tú)
future	diré, dirás, dirá, diremos, diréis, dirán
present subjunctive	diga, digas, diga, digamos, digáis, digan
past participle	dicho

dirigir *(to direct)*

present	dirijo, diriges, dirige, dirigimos, dirigís, dirigen
present subjunctive	dirija, dirijas, dirija, dirijamos, dirijáis, dirijan

empezar *(to begin, to start)*

present	empiezo, empiezas, empieza, empezamos, empezáis, empiezan
present subjunctive	empiece, empieces, empiece, empecemos, empecéis, empiecen
Similar to:	almorzar *(to eat lunch)*, aterrizar *(to land)*, comenzar *(to begin)*, gozar *(to enjoy)*, realizar *(to attain, to bring about)*

enviar *(to send)*

present	envío, envías, envía, enviamos, enviáis, envían
present subjunctive	envíe, envíes, envíe, enviemos, enviéis, envíen
Similar to:	esquiar *(to ski)*

escribir *(to write)*

past participle	escrito
Similar to:	describir *(to describe)*

escoger *(to choose)*

present	escojo, escoges, escoge, escogemos, escogéis, escogen
Similar to:	coger *(to pick),* recoger *(to pick up)*

estar *(to be)*

present	estoy, estás, está, estamos, estáis, están
preterite	estuve, estuviste, estuvo, estuvimos, estuvisteis, estuvieron
present subjunctive	esté, estés, esté, estemos, estéis, estén

haber *(to have)*

present	he, has, ha, hemos, habéis, han
preterite	hube, hubiste, hubo, hubimos, hubisteis, hubieron
future	habré, habrás, habrá, habremos, habréis, habrán
present subjunctive	haya, hayas, haya, hayamos, hayáis, hayan

hacer *(to do, to make)*

present	hago, haces, hace, hacemos, hacéis, hacen
preterite	hice, hiciste, hizo, hicimos, hicisteis, hicieron
command	haz (tú)
future	haré, harás, hará, haremos, haréis, harán
present subjunctive	haga, hagas, haga, hagamos, hagáis, hagan
past participle	hecho
Similar to:	deshacer *(to undo)*

ir *(to go)*

present	voy, vas, va, vamos, vais, van
preterite	fui, fuiste, fue, fuimos, fuisteis, fueron
imperfect	iba, ibas, iba, íbamos, ibais, iban
present participle	yendo
command	ve (tú)
present subjunctive	vaya, vayas, vaya, vayamos, vayáis, vayan

leer *(to read)*

preterite	leí, leíste, leyó, leímos, leísteis, leyeron
present participle	leyendo
past participle	leído
Similar to:	creer *(to believe)*

llegar *(to arrive)*

preterite	llegué, llegaste, llegó, llegamos, llegasteis, llegaron
present subjunctive	llegue, llegues, llegue, lleguemos, lleguéis, lleguen
Similar to:	agregar *(to add),* apagar *(to turn off),* colgar *(to hang up),* despegar *(to take off),* entregar *(to hand in),* jugar *(to play),* pagar *(to pay for)*

morir *(to die)*

past participle	muerto

oír *(to hear, to listen)*

present	oigo, oyes, oye, oímos, oís, oyen
preterite	oí, oíste, oyó, oímos, oísteis, oyeron
present participle	oyendo
present subjunctive	oiga, oigas, oiga, oigamos, oigáis, oigan
past participle	oído

poder *(to be able)*

present	puedo, puedes, puede, podemos, podéis, pueden
preterite	pude, pudiste, pudo, pudimos, pudisteis, pudieron
present participle	pudiendo
future	podré, podrás, podrá, podremos, podréis, podrán
present subjunctive	pueda, puedas, pueda, podamos, podáis, puedan

poner *(to put, to place, to set)*

present	pongo, pones, pone, ponemos, ponéis, ponen
preterite	puse, pusiste, puso, pusimos, pusisteis, pusieron
command	pon (tú)
future	pondré, pondrás, pondrá, pondremos, pondréis, pondrán
present subjunctive	ponga, pongas, ponga, pongamos, pongáis, pongan
past participle	puesto

proteger *(to protect)*

present	protejo, proteges, protege, protegemos, protegéis, protegen
present subjunctive	proteja, protejas, proteja, protejamos, protejáis, protejan

querer *(to wish, to want, to love)*

present	quiero, quieres, quiere, queremos, queréis, quieren
preterite	quise, quisiste, quiso, quisimos, quisisteis, quisieron
future	querré, querrás, querrá, querremos, querréis, querrán
present subjunctive	quiera, quieras, quiera, querramos, querráis, quieran

reír *(to laugh)*

present	río, ríes, ríe, reímos, reís, ríen
preterite	reí, reíste, rió, reímos, reísteis, rieron
present participle	riendo
present subjunctive	ría, rías, ría, ríamos, riáis, rían
Similar to:	freír *(to fry),* sonreír *(to smile)*

romper *(to break)*

past participle	roto

saber *(to know, to know how)*

present	sé, sabes, sabe, sabemos, sabéis, saben
preterite	supe, supiste, supo, supimos, supisteis, supieron
future	sabré, sabrás, sabrá, sabremos, sabréis, sabrán
present subjunctive	sepa, sepas, sepa, sepamos, sepáis, sepan

salir *(to leave)*

present	salgo, sales, sale, salimos, salís, salen
command	sal (tú)
future	saldré, saldrás, saldrá, saldremos, saldréis, saldrán
present subjunctive	salga, salgas, salga, salgamos, salgáis, salgan

seguir *(to follow, to continue)*

present	sigo, sigues, sigue, seguimos, seguís, siguen
present participle	siguiendo
present subjunctive	siga, sigas, siga, sigamos, sigáis, sigan
Similar to:	conseguir *(to obtain, to attain, to get)*

ser *(to be)*

present	soy, eres, es, somos, sois, son
preterite	fui, fuiste, fue, fuimos, fuisteis, fueron
imperfect	era, eras, era, éramos, erais, eran
command	sé (tú)
present subjunctive	sea, seas, sea, seamos, seáis, sean

tener *(to have)*

present	tengo, tienes, tiene, tenemos, tenéis, tienen
preterite	tuve, tuviste, tuvo, tuvimos, tuvisteis, tuvieron
command	ten (tú)
future	tendré, tendrás, tendrá, tendremos, tendréis, tendrán
present subjunctive	tenga, tengas, tenga, tengamos, tengáis, tengan
Similar to:	contener *(to contain),* detener *(to stop),* mantener *(to maintain),* obtener *(to obtain)*

torcer *(to twist)*

present	tuerzo, tuerces, tuerce, torcemos, torcéis, tuercen
present subjunctive	tuerza, tuerzas, tuerza, torzamos, torzáis, tuerzan

traer *(to bring)*

present	traigo, traes, trae, traemos, traéis, traen
preterite	traje, trajiste, trajo, trajimos, trajisteis, trajeron
present participle	trayendo
present subjunctive	traiga, traigas, traiga, traigamos, traigáis, traigan
past participle	traído
Similar to:	atraer *(to attract)*

valer *(to be worth)*

present	valgo, vales, vale, valemos, valéis, valen
preterite	valí, valiste, valió, valimos, valisteis, valieron
future	valdré, valdrás, valdrá, valdremos, valdréis, valdrán
present subjunctive	valga, valgas, valga, valgamos, valgáis, valgan

venir *(to come)*	
present	vengo, vienes, viene, venimos, venís, vienen
preterite	vine, viniste, vino, vinimos, vinisteis, vinieron
present participle	viniendo
command	ven (tú)
future	vendré, vendrás, vendrá, vendremos, vendréis, vendrán
present subjunctive	venga, vengas, venga, vengamos, vengáis, vengan
Similar to:	convenir *(to suit, to agree)*

ver *(to see)*	
present	veo, ves, ve, vemos, veis, ven
preterite	vi, viste, vio, vimos, visteis, vieron
imperfect	veía, veías, veía, veíamos, veíais, veían
present subjunctive	vea, veas, vea, veamos, veáis, vean
past participle	visto

volver *(to return)*	
past participle	vuelto
Similar to:	resolver *(to solve)*

Appendix C

Numbers

Ordinal numbers

1—primero,-a (primer)	6—sexto,-a
2—segundo,-a	7—séptimo,-a
3—tercero,-a (tercer)	8—octavo,-a
4—cuarto,-a	9—noveno,-a
5—quinto,-a	10—décimo,-a

Cardinal numbers 0-1.000

0—cero	13—trece	26—veintiséis	90—noventa
1—uno	14—catorce	27—veintisiete	100—cien/ciento
2—dos	15—quince	28—veintiocho	200—doscientos,-as
3—tres	16—dieciséis	29—veintinueve	300—trescientos,-as
4—cuatro	17—diecisiete	30—treinta	400—cuatrocientos,-as
5—cinco	18—dieciocho	31—treinta y uno	500—quinientos,-as
6—seis	19—diecinueve	32—treinta y dos	600—seiscientos,-as
7—siete	20—veinte	33—treinta y tres, etc.	700—setecientos,-as
8—ocho	21—veintiuno	40—cuarenta	800—ochocientos,-as
9—nueve	22—veintidós	50—cincuenta	900—novecientos,-as
10—diez	23—veintitrés	60—sesenta	1.000—mil
11—once	24—veinticuatro	70—setenta	
12—doce	25—veinticinco	80—ochenta	

Appendix D

Syllabification

Spanish vowels may be weak or strong. The vowels *a*, *e* and *o* are strong, whereas *i* (and sometimes *y*) and *u* are weak. The combination of one weak and one strong vowel or of two weak vowels produces a diphthong, two vowels pronounced as one.

A word in Spanish has as many syllables as it has vowels or diphthongs.

    al gu nas   lue go   pa la bra

A single consonant (including *ch*, *ll*, *rr*) between two vowels accompanies the second vowel and begins a syllable.

    a mi ga   fa vo ri to   mu cho

Two consonants are divided, the first going with the previous vowel and the second going with the following vowel.

    an tes   quin ce   ter mi nar

A consonant plus *l* or *r* is inseparable except for *rl*, *sl* and *sr*.

    ma dre   pa la bra   com ple tar   Car los   is la

If three consonants occur together, the last, or any inseparable combination, accompanies the following vowel to begin another syllable.

    es cri bir   som bre ro   trans por te

Prefixes should remain intact.

    re es cri bir

Appendix E

Accentuation

Words that end in *a, e, i, o, u, n* or *s* are pronounced with the major stress on the next-to-the-last syllable. No accent mark is needed to show this emphasis.

    octubre   refresco   señora

Words that end in any consonant except *n* or *s* are pronounced with the major stress on the last syllable. No accent mark is needed to show this emphasis.

    escribir   papel   reloj

Words that are not pronounced according to the above two rules need a written accent mark.

    lógico   canción   después   lápiz

An accent mark may be necessary to distinguish identical words with different meanings.

    dé/de   qué/que   sí/si   sólo/solo

An accent mark is often used to divide a diphthong into two separate syllables.

    día   frío   Raúl

Vocabulary Spanish/English

This section provides a summary of the vocabulary for *Somos así EN SUS MARCAS* and *Somos así LISTOS*. The number following an entry indicates the lesson in which an item is first actively used in *Somos así LISTOS*. The vocabulary from *Somos así EN SUS MARCAS* and additional words and expressions are included for reference and have no number. Obvious cognates and expressions that occur as passive vocabulary for recognition only have been excluded from this end vocabulary.

Abbreviations:

d.o. direct object	*i.o.* indirect object	*pl.* plural
f. feminine	*m.* masculine	*s.* singular

A

a to, at, in; *a caballo* on horseback; *a causa de* because of, due to; *a crédito* on credit; *a cuadros* plaid, checkered *10*; *a favor (de)* in favor (of) *14*; *a fin de que* so that; *a la derecha* to the right *5*; *a la izquierda* to the left *5*; *a la(s)...* at... o'clock; *a lo mejor* maybe *15*; *a pie* on foot; *a propósito* by the way *18*; *¿a qué hora?* at what time?; *a rayas* striped *10*; *a tiempo* on time *12*; *a veces* sometimes, at times; *a ver* let's see, hello (telephone greeting)

abajo downstairs, down *11*

abierto,-a open; *vocales abiertas* open vowels

el **abogado, la abogada** lawyer *17*

abordar to board *16*

abran: see *abrir*

el **abrazo** hug

abre: see *abrir*

la **abreviatura** abbreviation

el **abrigo** coat

abril April

abrir to open; *abran (Uds.* command) open; *abre (tú* command) open *4*

abrochar(se) to fasten *16*

la **abuela** grandmother

el **abuelo** grandfather

aburrido,-a bored, boring

aburrir to bore *13*

acabar to finish, to complete, to terminate; *acabar de* (+ infinitive) to have just

el **accidente** accident *13*

el **aceite** oil

la **aceituna** olive

el **acento** accent

la **acentuación** accentuation

aceptado,-a accepted *17*

la **acera** sidewalk *6*

acerca de about *14*

aclarar to make clear, to explain

aconsejar to advise, to suggest *10*

el **acontecimiento** event, happening *13*

acordar(se) (de) (ue) to remember *9*

acostar (ue) to put (someone) in bed *3*; *acostarse* to go to bed, to lie down *3*

acostumbrar(se) to get used to *4*

el **acróbata, la acróbata** acrobat *8*

la **actitud** attitude *18*

la **actividad** activity *13*

el **actor** actor (male) *13*

la **actriz** actor (female), actress *13*

acuático,-a aquatic, pertaining to water *17*

el **acuerdo** accord; *de acuerdo* agreed, okay; *estar de acuerdo* to agree *13*

adelante ahead, farther on *5*

además besides, furthermore *10*

adentro inside *11*

el **aderezo** seasoning, flavoring, dressing *10*

adiós good-bye

adivinar to guess

el **adjetivo** adjective; *adjetivo posesivo* possessive adjective

adonde where *15*

¿adónde? (to) where?

adornar to decorate

la **aduana** customs *16*

el **adverbio** adverb

aéreo,-a air, pertaining to air *15*

los **aeróbicos** aerobics; *hacer aeróbicos* to do aerobics

la **aerolínea** airline *16*

el **aeropuerto** airport *5*

afeitar(se) to shave *3*; *crema de afeitar* shaving cream *3*

el **aficionado, la aficionada** fan *14*

el **África** Africa *7*

africano,-a African *7*

afuera outside *11*

la **agencia** agency; *agencia de viajes* travel agency *15*

el **agente, la agente** agent *15*

agosto August

agradable nice, pleasing, agreeable *10*

agradar to please *10*

agregar to add *10*

el **agricultor, la agricultora** farmer *17*

el **agua** *(f.)* water; *agua mineral* mineral water

el **aguacate** avocado

ahora now; *ahora mismo* right now

ahorrar to save

el **aire** air *11*; *aire acondicionado* air conditioning *11*; *al aire libre* outdoors *11*

el **ajedrez** chess

el **ajo** garlic

al to the; *al aire libre* outdoors *11*; *al lado de* next to, beside

la **alarma** alarm *6*, alarm clock *11*; *alarma de incendios* fire alarm, smoke alarm *12*

el **álgebra** algebra

alegrar (de) to make happy *12*; *alegrarse (de)* to be glad *12*

alegre happy, merry, lively

alemán, alemana German *18*

Alemania Germany *18*

el **alfabeto** alphabet

la **alfombra** carpet, rug *11*

el **álgebra** algebra

algo something, anything

el **algodón** cotton

alguien someone, anyone, somebody, anybody

algún, alguna some, any

alguno,-a some, any

allá over there

allí there

el **almacén** department store, grocery store *5*; warehouse

la **almeja** clam *9*

almorzar (ue) to have lunch, to eat lunch *3*

el **almuerzo** lunch

aló hello (telephone greeting)

alojar(se) to lodge *16*; *alojarse* to stay *16*

alquilar to rent

alrededor de around *14*

alterna (*tú* command) alternate

el **alto** stop *6*

alto,-a tall, high

amable kind, nice

amarillo,-a yellow

ambiguo,-a ambiguous

la **América** America *7*; *América Central* Central America *7*; *América del Norte* North America *7*; *América del Sur* South America *7*

americano,-a American; *fútbol americano* football

el **amigo, la amiga** friend; *amigo/a por correspondencia* pen pal

la **amistad** friendship *17*

el **amor** love

anaranjado,-a orange (color)

andar to walk, to go *9*; to be *9*

andino,-a Andean, of the Andes Mountains

el **anillo** ring

el **animal** animal *7*

anoche last night *9*

anochecer to get dark, to turn to dusk *10*

anteayer the day before yesterday

anterior preceding

antes de before

antiguo,-a antique, ancient, old *7*

el **anuncio** announcement, advertisement *13*; *anuncio comercial* commercial announcement, commercial, advertisement *13*

añade: see *añadir*

añadir to add; *añade* (*tú* command) add

el **año** year; *Año Nuevo* New Year's (Day); *¿Cuántos años tienes?* How old are you?; *cumplir años* to have a birthday; *tener* (+ number) *años* to be (+ number) years old

apagar to turn off

el **aparato** appliance, apparatus *12*

el **apartamento** apartment *5*

el **apellido** last name, surname *16*

el **apodo** nickname

aprender to learn

apropiado,-a appropriate

apunta: see *apuntar*

apuntar to point; *apunta* (*tú* command) point (at); *apunten* (*Uds.* command) point (at)

apunten: see *apuntar*

apurado,-a in a hurry

apurar(se) to hurry up *10*

aquel, aquella that (far away)

aquél, aquélla that (one) *3*

aquello that *3*

aquellos, aquellas those (far away)

aquéllos, aquéllas those (ones) *11*

aquí here; *Aquí se habla español.* Spanish is spoken here.

árabe Arab

Arabia Saudita Saudi Arabia *18*

el **árbitro, la árbitro** referee, umpire *14*

el **árbol** tree *8*; *árbol genealógico* family tree

la **arena** sand

el **arete** earring

la **Argentina** Argentina

argentino,-a Argentinean *7*

el **armario** closet, wardrobe *11*; cupboard

el **arte** art

el **artículo** article *14*

el **artista, la artista** artist *17*

arreglar to arrange, to straighten, to fix

arriba upstairs, up, above *11*

la **arroba** at (the symbol @ used for e-mail addresses) *1*

el **arroz** rice

el **ascensor** elevator

así thus, that way *3*

el **Asia** Asia *18*

asiático,-a Asian *18*

la **asignatura** subject *1*

asistir a to attend *17*

la **aspiración** aspiration, hope *17*

la **aspiradora** vacuum; *pasar la aspiradora* to vacuum

atentamente respectfully, yours truly *17*

aterrizar to land *16*

el **ático** attic *11*

el **Atlántico** Atlantic Ocean

la **atracción** attraction *7*; (amusement) ride *7*; *parque de atracciones* amusement park

atravesado,-a crossed

el **aumento** increase

aun even

aunque although *12*

Australia Australia *18*

australiano,-a Australian *18*

el **autobús** bus; *estación de autobuses* bus station *11*

el **autógrafo** autograph *13*

automático,-a automatic; *escalera automática* escalator

el **auxiliar de vuelo, la auxiliar de vuelo** flight attendant *16*

el **ave** fowl, bird *9*

la **avenida** avenue

el **avión** airplane

el **aviso** printed advertisement *14*

¡ay! oh!

ayer yesterday

la **ayuda** help

ayudar to help

el **azafrán** saffron

la **azotea** flat roof *11*

los **aztecas** Aztecs

el **azúcar** sugar

la **azucarera** sugar bowl *10*

azul blue

B

bailar to dance

el **baile** dance, dancing *17*

bajar (un programa) to download (a software program) *1*

bajo under

bajo,-a short (not tall), low; *planta baja* ground floor; *zapato bajo* low-heel shoe

balanceado,-a balanced

el **baloncesto** basketball

el **banco** bank

la **banda** band *8*

bañar(se) to bathe *3*

el **baño** bathroom; *baño de los caballeros* men's restroom; *cuarto de baño* bathroom; *traje de baño* swimsuit

barato,-a cheap

el **barco** boat, ship

barrer to sweep

el **barril** barrel

el **barrio** neighborhood *6*

basado,-a based

el **básquetbol** basketball

el **basquetbolista, la basquetbolista** basketball player

bastante rather, fairly, sufficiently; enough, sufficient

la **basura** garbage

el **baúl** trunk *6*

la **bebida** drink

el **béisbol** baseball

las **bermudas** bermuda shorts *2*

el **beso** kiss *11*

la **biblioteca** library

el **bibliotecario, la bibliotecaria** librarian *17*

la **bicicleta** bicycle, bike

bien well; *quedarle bien a uno* to fit, to be becoming

la **bienvenida** welcome *16*

bienvenido,-a welcome *7*

la **billetera** wallet

la **biología** biology

la **bisabuela** great-grandmother *11*

el **bisabuelo** great-grandfather *11*

blanco,-a white

la **blusa** blouse

la **boca** mouth *4*

la **boda** wedding

el **boleto** ticket *8*

el **bolígrafo** pen

Bolivia Bolivia

boliviano,-a Bolivian *7*

el **bolso** handbag, purse

el **bombero, la bombera** fire fighter *17*

la **bombilla** light bulb *11*

bonito,-a pretty, good-looking, attractive

borra: see *borrar*

el **borrador** eraser

borrar to erase; *borra* (*tú* command) erase; *borren* (*Uds.* command) erase

borren: see *borrar*

el **bosque** forest *8*

bostezar to yawn *13*

la **bota** boot

el **bote** boat *2*

el **botones** bellhop *16*

el **Brasil** Brazil *18*

brasileño,-a Brazilian *18*

el **brazo** arm

la **broma** joke *11*

broncear(se) to tan *4*

el **buceo** scuba diving *17*

buen good (form of *bueno* before a *m., s.* noun); *hace buen tiempo* the weather is nice

bueno well, okay (pause in speech); hello (telephone greeting)

bueno,-a good; *buena suerte* good luck; *buenas noches* good night; *buenas tardes* good afternoon; *buenos días* good morning

la **bufanda** scarf

el **burro** burro, donkey *8*

buscar to look for

C

el **caballero** gentleman *5; baño de los caballeros* men's restroom

el **caballo** horse; *a caballo* on horseback

caber to fit (into) *9*

la **cabeza** head

cada each, every

la **cadena** chain

caer(se) to fall (down) *4*

café brown (color)

el **café** coffee

la **cafetera** coffee pot, coffee maker *12*

la **cafetería** cafeteria

la **caja** cashier's desk

el **cajero, la cajera** cashier *10*

el **calcetín** sock

el **calendario** calendar

la **calidad** quality

caliente hot

la **calle** street

calmar(se) to calm down *3*

el **calor** heat; *hace calor* it is hot; *tener calor* to be hot

calvo,-a bald

la **cama** bed

la **cámara** camera *7*

el **camarero, la camarera** food server *5*

el **camarón** shrimp *9*

cambiar to change *12*

el **cambio** change; *en cambio* on the other hand

el **camello** camel *7*

caminar to walk

el **camino** road, path

el **camión** truck *9*

la **camisa** shirt

la **camiseta** t-shirt *2*; jersey, polo shirt, undershirt *14*

el **campeonato** championship *14*

el **camping** camping *2*

el **Canadá** Canada *18*

canadiense Canadian *18*

el **canal** channel *13*

la **canción** song

el **cangrejo** crab *9*

canoso,-a white-haired

cansado,-a tired

el **cantante, la cantante** singer *13*

cantar to sing

la **cantidad** quantity

la **capital** capital

el **capitán** captain

el **capítulo** chapter

el **capó** hood *6*

la **cara** face *4*

la **característica** characteristic, trait; *características de personalidad* personality traits; *características físicas* physical traits

¡caramba! wow!

cargar to charge *15*

el **Caribe** Caribbean

cariñoso,-a affectionate

el **carnaval** carnival

la **carne** meat; *carne de res* beef *9*

la **carnicería** meat market, butcher shop *5*

caro,-a expensive

el **carpintero, la carpintera** carpenter *17*

la **carta** letter; playing card

la **carrera** career *17*

la **carretera** highway *5*

el **carro** car; *en carro* by car

la **casa** home, house; *en casa* at home

el **casete** cassette

casi almost

la **catarata** waterfall

la **catástrofe** catastrophe *13*

la **catedral** cathedral *5*

catorce fourteen

la **cebolla** onion

la **cebra** zebra *7*

la **celebración** celebration *13*

celebrar to celebrate

el **celular** cellular phone *1*

la **cena** dinner, supper *3*

cenar to have dinner, to have supper *3*

el **centavo** cent

el **centro** downtown, center; *centro comercial* shopping center, mall

centroamericano,-a Central American *18*

cepillar(se) to brush *3*

el **cepillo** brush *3*

la **cerca** fence *11*

cerca (de) near

el **cereal** cereal *9*

cero zero

cerrado,-a closed; *vocales cerradas* closed vowels

la **cerradura** lock *12*

cerrar (ie) to close; *cierra (tú command)* close; *cierren (Uds. command)* close

el **césped** lawn, grass *6*

el **cesto de papeles** wastebasket, wastepaper basket

el **champú** shampoo *3*

chao good-bye

la **chaqueta** jacket

charlando talking, chatting

el **cheque** check *15*

la **chica** girl

el **chico** boy, man, buddy

Chile Chile

chileno,-a Chilean *7*

la **chimenea** chimney, fireplace *11*

la **China** China *18*

chino,-a Chinese *18*

el **chisme** gossip *2*

el **chiste** joke *9*

chistoso,-a funny *7*

el **chocolate** chocolate

el **chofer, la chofer** chauffeur, driver *17*

el **chorizo** sausage (seasoned with red peppers)

el **cielo** sky *8*

cien one hundred

la **ciencia** science

ciento one hundred (when followed by another number)

cierra: see *cerrar*

cierren: see *cerrar*

el **cigarrillo** cigarette *4*

cinco five

cincuenta fifty

el **cine** movie theater

el **cinturón** belt; *cinturón de seguridad* seat belt, safety belt *6*

el **circo** circus *8*

la **ciruela** plum *9*

la **cita** appointment, date *4*

la **ciudad** city

la **civilización** civilization

claro,-a clear *12*

¡claro! of course!

la **clase** class *16*

clasificar to classify

el **claxon** horn *6*

el **clima** climate

el **club** club *12*

la **cocina** kitchen

cocinar to cook

el **cocinero, la cocinera** cook *10*

el **coche** car *6*; *en coche* by car

el **codo** elbow *4*

el **cognado** cognate

la **colección** collection *17*

el **colegio** school

colgar (ue) to hang

la **colina** hill

el **collar** necklace

colocar to put, to place *16*

Colombia Colombia

colombiano,-a Colombian *7*

la **colonia** colony

el **color** color

la **columna** column *14*

combinar to combine

la **comedia** comedy, play *13*

el **comedor** dining room

el **comentarista, la comentarista** commentator *14*

comenzar (ie) to begin, to start *12*

comer to eat; *dar de comer* to feed

comercial commercial *13*; *anuncio comercial* commercial announcement, commercial, advertisement *13*; *centro comercial* shopping center, mall

comerse to eat up, to eat completely *4*

cómico,-a comical, funny

la **comida** food; dinner *3*

como like, since; such as *7*

¿cómo? how?, what?; *¿Cómo?* What (did you say)?; *¿Cómo está (Ud.)?* How are you (formal)?; *¿Cómo están (Uds.)?* How are you (pl.)?; *¿Cómo estás (tú)?* How are you (informal)?; *¡Cómo no!* Of course!; *¿Cómo se dice...?* How do you say...?; *¿Cómo se escribe...?* How do you write (spell)...?; *¿Cómo se llama (Ud./él/ella)?* What is (your/his/her) name?; *¿Cómo te llamas?* What is your name?

cómodo,-a comfortable

el **compañero, la compañera** classmate, partner

la **compañía** company *15*

comparando comparing

el **compartimiento** compartment *16*

compartir to share

la **competencia** competition

complacer to please *12*

completa: see *completar*

completar to complete; *completa (tú command)* complete

completo,-a complete *15*

la **compra** purchase; *ir de compras* to go shopping

comprar to buy

comprender to understand; *comprendo* I understand

comprendo: see *comprender*

la **computadora** computer (machine)

la **comunicación** communication *1*

con with; *con (mucho) gusto* I would be (very) glad to; *con permiso* excuse me (with your permission), may I; *siempre salirse con la suya* to always get one's way *18*

el **concierto** concert

el **concurso** contest, competition *13*; *programa de concurso* game show

conducir to drive, to conduct, to direct *6*

conectado,-a connected *1*

el **conejo** rabbit *8*

la **conjunción** conjunction

conmigo with me

conocer to know, to be acquainted with, to be familiar with *6*; to meet

conocido,-a known, famous

conseguir (i, i) to obtain, to attain, to get *1*

el **consejo** advice *10*

el **consultorio** doctor's office

la **contaminación** contamination, pollution *1*; *contaminación*

ambiental environmental
pollution *1*

contar (ue) to tell (a story);
cuenta (*tú* command)
tell; *cuenten* (*Uds.*
command) tell

contener to contain *1*

contento,-a happy, glad; *estar
contento,-a (con)* to be
satisfied (with)

contesta: see *contestar*

contestar to answer; *contesta*
(*tú* command) answer;
contesten (*Uds.*
command) answer

contesten: see *contestar*

el **contexto** context

contigo with you (*tú*)

continúa: see *continuar*

continuar to continue;
continúa (*tú* command)
continue; *continúen* (*Uds.*
command) continue

continúen: see *continuar*

la **contracción** contraction

el **control remoto** remote control

convenir to be fitting, to
agree *12*

copiar to copy

el **corazón** heart *4*; honey (term
of endearment)

la **corbata** tie

cortar to cut, to mow *11*

la **cortesía** courtesy

la **cortina** curtain *11*

corto,-a short (not long)

correcto,-a right, correct

el **corredor** corridor, hallway *11*

el **corredor, la corredora** runner

el **correo** mail; *correo electrónico*
electronic mail *1; oficina
de correos* post office *11*

correr to run

la **correspondencia**
correspondence *17*

la **corrida** bullfight *15*

la **cosa** thing

la **costa** coast

Costa Rica Costa Rica

costar (ue) to cost

costarricense Costa Rican *7*

la **costilla** rib *9*

la **costura** sewing

crear to create

crecer to grow

el **crédito** credit; *a crédito* on
credit; *tarjeta de crédito*
credit card

creer to believe *2*

la **crema** cream *9; crema de
afeitar* shaving cream *3*

el **crucero** cruise ship *2*

cruzar to cross

el **cuaderno** notebook

la **cuadra** city block *5*

el **cuadro** square *10*; picture,
painting *11; a cuadros*
plaid, checkered *10*

¿cuál? which?, what?, which
one?; *(pl. ¿cuáles?)* which
ones?

la **cualidad** quality

cualquier, cualquiera any *10*

cualquiera any at all *12*

cuando when

¿cuándo? when?

¿cuánto,-a? how much?; *(pl.
¿cuántos,-as?)* how many?;
¿Cuánto (+ time
expression) *hace que* (+
present tense of verb)...?
How long...?; *¿Cuántos
años tienes?* How old are
you?

cuarenta forty

el **cuarto** quarter; room,
bedroom; *cuarto de baño*
bathroom; *cuarto de
charla* chat room *1;
menos cuarto* a quarter to,
a quarter before; *servicio
al cuarto* room service *16;
y cuarto* a quarter after, a
quarter past

cuarto,-a fourth

cuatro four

cuatrocientos,-as four
hundred

Cuba Cuba

cubano,-a Cuban *7*

los **cubiertos** silverware

cubrir to cover *13*

la **cuchara** tablespoon

la **cucharita** teaspoon

el **cuchillo** knife

el **cuello** neck *4*

la **cuenta** bill, check *10*

cuenta: see *contar*

el **cuerno** horn *8*

el **cuero** leather

el **cuerpo** body

el **cuidado** care *11; tener
cuidado* to be careful *11*

cuidar(se) to take care of *4*

culto,-a cultured,
well-read *14*

la **cultura** culture,
knowledge *14*

el **cumpleaños** birthday; *¡Feliz
cumpleaños!* Happy
birthday!

cumplir to become, to
become (+ number) years

old, to reach; *cumplir
años* to have a birthday

la **curva** curve *6*

cuyo,-a of which, whose

D

la **dama** lady

las **damas** checkers; *baño de las
damas* women's restroom

dar to give; *dar de comer* to
feed; *dar un paseo* to take
a walk; *dé* (*Ud.*
command) give

de from, of; *de acuerdo*
agreed, okay; *de cerca*
close up, from a short
distance *6; ¿de dónde?*
from where?; *¿De dónde
eres?* Where are you
from?; *¿De dónde es
(Ud./él/ella)?* Where are
you (formal) from?,
Where is (he/she/it)
from?; *de habla hispana*
Spanish-speaking; *de ida
y vuelta* round-trip *15; de
la mañana* in the
morning, A.M.; *de la
noche* at night, P.M.; *de la
tarde* in the afternoon,
P.M.; *de nada* you are
welcome, not at all; *de
todos los días* everyday; *¿de
veras?* really?; *¿Eres (tú)
de...?* Are you from...?

dé: see *dar*

deber should, to have to,
must, ought (expressing a
moral duty)

decidir to decide *10*

décimo,-a tenth

decir to tell, to say; *¿Cómo se
dice...?* How do you
say...?; *di* (*tú* command)
tell, say *4; díganme* (*Uds.*
command) tell me; *dime*
(*tú* command) tell me;
¡no me digas! you don't
say! *18; ¿Qué quiere
decir...?* What is the
meaning (of)...?; *querer
decir* to mean; *quiere decir*
it means; *se dice* one says

el **dedo** finger, toe

el **defensor, la defensora**
defender *14*

dejar (de) to leave; to stop, to
quit *4*; to let, to allow *11*

del of the, from the

el **delantero, la delantera**
forward *14*

delgado,-a thin
delicioso,-a delicious *10*
demasiado too (much)
demasiado,-a too many, too
    much *9*
la democracia democracy
la demora delay *6*
el dentista, la dentista dentist
el departamento department
el dependiente, la dependiente
    clerk *10*
el deporte sport
el deportista, la deportista
    athlete
    deportivo,-a sporty *6*
la derecha right *5*; *a la derecha*
    to the right *5*
    derecho straight ahead *5*
    derecho,-a right *4*
    desaparecido,-a missing
el desastre disaster
    desayunar(se) to have
    breakfast *3*
el desayuno breakfast *3*
    descansar to rest, to relax *4*
    describe: see *describir*
    describir to describe *9*;
    describe (*tú* command)
    describe
    desde since, from; *desde luego*
    of course *3*
    desear to wish
el deseo wish
el desfile parade *7*
el desierto desert
el desodorante deodorant *3*
la despedida farewell, good-bye *18*
    despedir(se) (i, i) to say
    good-bye *4*
    despegar to take off *16*
    despertar(se) (ie) to wake up *3*
    después afterwards, later,
    then; *después de* after
    destacar(se) to stand out
    desteñido,-a faded *10*
el destino destination *15*;
    destiny, fate
la destreza skill, expertise *8*
    desvestir(se) to undress
    detrás de behind, after *8*
    di: see *decir*
el día day; *buenos días* good
    morning; *de todos los días*
    everyday; *todos los días*
    every day
el diálogo dialog
    diario,-a daily
    dibuja: see *dibujar*
    dibujar to draw, to sketch;
    dibuja (*tú* command)

draw; *dibujen* (*Uds.*
    command) draw
    dibujen: see *dibujar*
el dibujo drawing, sketch
    diciembre December
el dictado dictation
la dicha happiness *15*
    diecinueve nineteen
    dieciocho eighteen
    dieciséis sixteen
    diecisiete seventeen
el diente tooth *4*
    diez ten
la diferencia difference
    diferente different *10*
    difícil difficult, hard; *ser*
    difícil que to be unlikely
    that *12*
    diga hello (telephone
    greeting)
    dígame tell me, hello
    (telephone greeting)
    díganme: see *decir*
    dime: see *decir*
el dinero money
la dirección instruction,
    guidance *5*; address *6*;
    direction *6*
el director, la directora director
    dirigir to direct
el disco record, disc; *disco*
    compacto compact disc,
    CD-ROM
    discutir to argue, to discuss *12*
el diskette diskette
    divertido,-a fun
    divertir (ie, i) to amuse *4*;
    divertirse to have fun *4*
    doblar to turn (a corner) *6*
    doble double *16*
    doce twelve
el doctor, la doctora doctor
    (abbreviation: *Dr., Dra.*) *4*
el dólar dollar
    doler (ue) to hurt *4*
    domingo Sunday; *el domingo*
    on Sunday
    dominicano,-a Dominican *7*
    don title of respect used
    before a man's first name
    donde where
    ¿dónde? where?; *¿de dónde?*
    from where?; *¿De dónde*
    eres? Where are you
    from?; *¿Dónde está...?*
    Where are you
    (formal)...?, Where is...?
    dondequiera wherever *17*
    doña title of respect used before
    a woman's first name

    dormir (ue, u) to sleep;
    dormirse to fall asleep *4*
    dos two
    doscientos,-as two hundred
    Dr. abbreviation for *doctor*
    Dra. abbreviation for *doctora*
la ducha shower *3*
    duchar(se) to shower *3*
    dudar to doubt *12*
    dudoso,-a doubtful *12*
    dulce sweet
el dulce candy *5*
la dulcería candy store *5*
    durante during *8*
el durazno peach *9*

E

    e and (used before a word
    beginning with *i* or *hi*)
la ecología ecology *1*
la economía economy *14*
    económico,-a economic *14*
el Ecuador Ecuador
    ecuatoriano,-a Ecuadorian *7*
la edad age
el edificio building *5*
el editorial editorial *14*
la educación física physical
    education
el efectivo cash; *en efectivo* in cash
    egoísta selfish
el ejemplo example; *por ejemplo*
    for example
el ejercicio exercise *4*
    el the *(m., s.)*
    él he; him (after a
    preposition); *Él se*
    llama.... His name is....
    El Salvador El Salvador
    eléctrico,-a electric
el elefante elephant *7*
    elegante elegant *9*
    ella she; her (after a
    preposition); *Ella se*
    llama.... Her name is....
    ello it, that (neuter form)
    ellos,-as they; them (after a
    preposition)
el e-mail e-mail *1*
la emigración emigration *16*
la emisora radio station *14*
    emocionado,-a excited *15*
    emocionante exciting *8*
    empatados: see *empate*
    empatar to tie (the score of a
    game) *14*
el empate tie; *partidos*
    empatados games tied
    empezar (ie) to begin, to start

el **empleado, la empleada**
employee *17*

el **empleo** job *17*

la **empresa** business *17*

en in, on, at; *en* (+ vehicle)
by (+ vehicle); *en cambio*
on the other hand; *en
carro* by car; *en casa* at
home; *en coche* by car; *en
cuanto* as soon as *12*; *en
efectivo* in cash; *en medio
de* in the middle of, in
the center of *18*; *en
resumen* in short; *en
seguida* immediately *16*;
en vivo live *14*

encantado,-a delighted, the
pleasure is mine

encantar to enchant, to
delight *12*

encargar (de) to make
responsible (for), to put
in charge (of) *11*;
encargarse (de) to take
care of, to take charge
(of) *11*

encender (ie) to light, to
turn on (a light)

la **enchilada** enchilada *5*

encima de above, over, on
top of *8*

encontrar (ue) to find *1*

la **encuesta** survey, poll *14*

enero January

el **énfasis** emphasis

el **enfermero, la enfermera**
nurse *4*

enfermo,-a sick

engordar to make fat *10*;
engordarse to get fat *10*

la **ensalada** salad

enseñar to teach, to show

enterar(se) de to find out, to
become aware, to learn
about *14*

entonces then

entrar to go in, to come in

entre between, among

entregar to hand in *16*

la **entrevista** interview *14*

enviar to send

el **equipaje** luggage *16*; *equipaje
de mano* carry-on
luggage *16*

el **equipo** team

equivocar(se) to make a
mistake *4*

eres: see *ser*

es: see *ser*

la **escala** stopover *16*

la **escalera** stairway, stairs;
escalera automática
escalator

escapar(se) to escape *8*

la **escena** scene

la **escoba** broom *11*

escoger to choose; *escogiendo*
choosing

escogiendo: see *escoger*

escriban: see *escribir*

escribe: see *escribir*

escribir to write; *¿Cómo se
escribe...?* How do you
write (spell)...?; *escriban*
(*Uds.* command) write;
escribe (*tú* command)
write; *se escribe* it is
written

el **escritor, la escritora** writer *17*

el **escritorio** desk

escucha: see *escuchar*

escuchar to hear, to listen
(to) *14*; *escucha* (*tú*
command) listen; *escuchen*
(*Uds.* command) listen

escuchen: see *escuchar*

la **escuela** school

ese, esa that

ése, ésa that (one) *3*

eso that (neuter form) *3*

esos, esas those

ésos, ésas those (ones) *3*

el **espacio** space

la **espalda** back *4*

España Spain

el **español** Spanish (language);
Aquí se habla español.
Spanish is spoken here.;
Se habla español. Spanish
is spoken.

español, española Spanish *7*

especial special

especializado,-a specialized

el **espectáculo** show

el **espectador, la espectadora**
spectator *14*

el **espejo** mirror *3*

esperar to wait (for) *3*; to
hope *12*

la **esposa** wife, spouse

el **esposo** husband, spouse

el **esquí** skiing *17*

el **esquiador, la esquiadora** skier

esquiar to ski

la **esquina** corner *5*

está: see *estar*

el **establo** stable *8*

la **estación** season; station *5*;
estación de autobuses bus
station *5*; *estación del*

metro subway station *5*;
estación del tren train
station *5*

el **estadio** stadium

el **Estado Libre Asociado**
Commonwealth

los **Estados Unidos** United
States of America

estadounidense something or
someone from the
United States *7*

están: see *estar*

estar to be; *¿Cómo está (Ud.)?*
How are you (formal)?;
¿Cómo están (Uds.)? How
are you *(pl.)*?; *¿Cómo estás
(tú)?* How are you
(informal)?; *¿Dónde
está...?* Where are you
(formal)...?, Where is...?;
está you (formal) are,
he/she/it is; *está
nublado,-a* it is cloudy;
está soleado,-a it is sunny;
están they are; *estar
contento,-a (con)* to be
satisfied (with); *estar de
acuerdo* to agree *13*; *estar
en oferta* to be on sale;
estar listo,-a to be ready;
estás you (informal) are;
estoy I am

estás: see *estar*

este well, so (pause in speech)

el **este** east *6*

este, esta this; *esta noche*
tonight

éste, ésta this (one) *3*

el **estéreo** stereo

estimado,-a dear *17*

esto this *3*

el **estómago** stomach *4*

estos, estas these

éstos, éstas these (ones) *3*

estoy: see *estar*

estrecho,-a narrow

la **estrella** star *8*

la **estructura** structure

estudia: see *estudiar*

el **estudiante, la estudiante**
student

estudiar to study; *estudia* (*tú*
command) study;
estudien (*Uds.* command)
study

estudien: see *estudiar*

el **estudio** study

la **estufa** stove

estupendo,-a wonderful,
marvellous

Europa Europe *18*
europeo,-a European *18*
evidente evident *12*
exagerar to exaggerate *11*
el examen exam, test
excelente excellent
el excusado toilet *3*
la exhibición exhibition *6*
exigente demanding *6*
el éxito success *13; tener éxito* to be successful, to be a success *13*
la experiencia experience *17*
explica: see *explicar*
la explicación explanation, reason
explicar to explain; *explica (tú* command) explain
el explorador, la exploradora explorer
la exportación exportation
exportador, exportadora exporting
expresar to express
la expresión expression
la extensión extension
extranjero,-a foreign *13*
extrañar to miss *17*

F

fácil easy; *ser fácil que* to be likely that *12*
la facultad school (of a university) *18*
la falda skirt
falso,-a false
la familia family
famoso,-a famous *13*
fantástico,-a fantastic, great
el faro headlight *6;* lighthouse
fascinante fascinating *7*
fascinar to fascinate *12*
el favor favor; *por favor* please
favorito,-a favorite
el fax fax *1*
febrero February
la fecha date
felicitaciones congratulations
feliz happy *(pl. felices); ¡Feliz cumpleaños!* Happy birthday!
femenino,-a feminine
feo,-a ugly
feroz fierce, ferocious *(pl. feroces) 7*
el ferrocarril railway, railroad
la fiesta party
la fila line, row *8*
el filete fillet, boneless cut of beef or fish *9*

filmar to film *13*
la filosofía philosophy
el fin end; *a fin de que* so that *12; fin de semana* weekend; *por fin* finally *18*
la finca ranch, farm *8*
firmar to sign *16*
la física physics
el flamenco flamingo *7;* type of dance
el flan custard *9*
la flauta flute
la flor flower
la florcita small flower
la florería flower shop *5*
el folleto brochure *15*
la forma form
la foto(grafía) photo
el fotógrafo, la fotógrafa photographer *17*
fracasar to fail *13*
francés, francesa French *18*
Francia France *18*
la frase phrase, sentence
el fregadero sink
freír (i, i) to fry *9*
el freno brake *6*
la fresa strawberry
el fresco cool; *hace fresco* it is cool
fresco,-a fresh, chilly
el frío cold; *hace frío* it is cold; *tener frío* to be cold
frío,-a cold
la fruta fruit
la frutería fruit store *5*
fue: see *ser*
el fuego fire; *fuegos artificiales* fireworks *7*
fueron: see *ser*
fuerte strong *17*
fumar to smoke *4*
fundar to found
el fútbol soccer; *fútbol americano* football
el futbolista, la futbolista soccer player
el futuro future *17*

G

las gafas de sol sunglasses *2*
la galleta cookie, biscuit *6*
la gallina hen *8*
el gallo rooster *8*
la gana desire; *tener ganas de* to feel like
ganados: see *ganar*
ganar to win, to earn *11; los partidos ganados* games won
el garaje garage
la garganta throat *4*

el gasto expense *15*
el gato, la gata cat
el género gender
generoso,-a generous
la gente people
la geografía geography
la geometría geometry
el gerente, la gerente manager *17*
el gerundio present participle
el gesto gesture
el gimnasio gym
el globo balloon *7;* globe *7*
el gobernador, la gobernadora governor
el gobierno government
el gol goal *14*
la golosina sweets *7*
gordo,-a fat
el gorila gorilla *7*
la gorra cap (baseball) *2*
gozar to enjoy *15*
la grabadora tape recorder (machine)
grabar to record *13*
gracias thanks; *muchas gracias* thank you very much
el grado degree
gran big (form of *grande* before a *m., s.* noun); great *8*
grande big
el grifo faucet *3*
la gripe flu *4*
gris gray
gritar to shout *7*
el grupo group; *grupo musical* musical group
el guante glove
guapo,-a good-looking, attractive, handsome, pretty
el guardabarros fender *6*
Guatemala Guatemala
guatemalteco,-a Guatemalan *7*
la guía guidebook *15*
el guía, la guía guide *7*
el guisante pea
la guitarra guitar
gustar to like, to be pleasing to; *me/te/le/nos/os/les gustaría...* I/you/he/she/it/we/they would like...
gustaría: see *gustar*
el gusto pleasure; *con (mucho) gusto* I would be (very) glad to; *el gusto es mío* the pleasure is mine; *¡Mucho gusto!* Glad to meet you!; *Tanto gusto.* So glad to meet you.

H

haber to have (auxiliary verb) *13*

había there was, there were *7*

la **habichuela** green bean

la **habitación** room *16*; bedroom

el **habitante, la habitante** inhabitant

habla: see *hablar*

el **habla** *(f.)* speech, speaking; *de habla hispana* Spanish-speaking

hablar to speak; *Aquí se habla español.* Spanish is spoken here.; *habla (tú* command) speak; *hablen* (*Uds.* command) speak; *Se habla español.* Spanish is spoken.

hablen: see *hablar*

hace: see *hacer*

hacer to do, to make; *¿Cuánto* (+ time expression) *hace que* (+ present tense of verb)...? How long...?; *hace buen (mal) tiempo* the weather is nice (bad); *hace fresco* it is cool; *hace frío (calor)* it is cold (hot); *hace* (+ time expression) *que* ago; *hace sol* it is sunny; *hace viento* it is windy; *hacer aeróbicos* to do aerobics; *hacer falta* to be necessary, to be lacking; *hacer una pregunta* to ask a question; *hagan* (*Uds.* command) do, make; *haz* (*tú* command) do, make; *haz el papel* play the part; *hecha* made; *La práctica hace al maestro.* Practice makes perfect.; *¿Qué temperatura hace?* What is the temperature?; *¿Qué tiempo hace?* How is the weather?

hacia toward *6*

hagan: see *hacer*

el **hambre** *(f.)* hunger; *tener hambre* to be hungry

hasta until, up to, down to; *hasta la vista* so long, see you later; *hasta luego* so long, see you later; *hasta mañana* see you tomorrow; *hasta pronto* see you soon

hay there is, there are; *hay neblina* it is *misty; hay sol* it is sunny

haz: see *hacer*

hecha: see *hacer*

la **heladería** ice cream parlor *5*

el **helado** ice cream

la **herencia** heritage; inheritance

la **hermana** sister

la **hermanastra** stepsister *11*

el **hermanastro** stepbrother *11*

el **hermano** brother

hermoso,-a beautiful, lovely *17*

el **hielo** ice; *patinar sobre hielo* to ice-skate

la **hija** daughter

el **hijo** son

el **hipopótamo** hippopotamus *7*

hispano,-a Hispanic; *de habla hispana* Spanish-speaking

la **historia** history

el **hogar** home *11*

la **hoja** sheet; *hoja de papel* sheet of paper

hola hi, hello

el **hombre** man; *hombre de negocios* businessman *17*

el **hombro** shoulder *4*

Honduras Honduras

hondureño,-a Honduran *7*

la **hora** hour; *¿a qué hora?* at what time?; *¿Qué hora es?* What time is it?

el **horario** schedule

el **horno** oven *12*; *horno microondas* microwave oven *12*

horrible horrible

el **hotel** hotel *16*

hoy today

hubo there was, there were *9*

el **huevo** egg

el **huracán** hurricane *13*

I

la **idea** idea

ideal ideal

la **iglesia** church *5*

ignorar to not know

la **iguana** iguana *7*

imagina: see *imaginar(se)*

la **imaginación** imagination

imaginar(se) to imagine *7*; *imagina (tú* command) imagine

el **imperio** empire

el **impermeable** raincoat

implicar to imply

importante important

importar to be important, to matter

imposible impossible *12*

los **incas** Incas

el **incendio** fire *12*; *alarma de incendios* fire alarm, smoke alarm *12*

indefinido,-a indefinite

la **independencia** independence

indica: see *indicar*

la **indicación** cue

indicado,-a indicated

indicar to indicate; *indica (tú* command) indicate

indígena native

la **información** information *1*

informar to inform *13*

el **informe** report

el **ingeniero, la ingeniera** engineer *17*

Inglaterra England *18*

el **inglés** English (language)

inglés, inglesa English *18*

el **ingrediente** ingredient

inicial initial

inmenso,-a immense

insistir (en) to insist (on) *11*

la **inspiración** inspiration

instalar to install *2*

inteligente intelligent

interesante interesting

interesar to interest *12*

internacional international *14*

la **Internet** Internet *1*

interrogativo,-a interrogative

el **invierno** winter

la **invitación** invitation

invitar to invite *11*

ir to go; *ir a* (+ infinitive) to be going to (do something); *ir a parar* to end up *8*; *ir de compras* to go shopping; *irse* to leave, to go away *4*; *irse de viaje* to go away on a trip *4*; *¡vamos!* let's go!; *¡vamos a* (+ infinitive)!* let's (+ infinitive)!; *vayan* (*Uds.* command) go to; *ve (tú* command) go to

la **isla** island *18*

Italia Italy *18*

italiano,-a Italian *18*

el **itinerario** itinerary *15*

la **izquierda** left *5*; *a la izquierda* to the left *5*

izquierdo,-a left *4*

J

el **jabón** soap *3*
el **jamón** ham
el **Japón** Japan *18*
japonés, japonesa Japanese *18*
el **jardín** garden *7*; *jardín zoológico* zoo, zoological garden *7*
la **jaula** cage *8*
la **jirafa** giraffe *7*
joven young
la **joya** jewel *10*
la **joyería** jewelry store *10*
el **juego** game
jueves Thursday; *el jueves* on Thursday
el **jugador, la jugadora** player
jugar (ue) to play; *jugar a* (+ sport/game) to play (+ sport/game)
el **jugo** juice *5*
julio July
junio June
junto,-a together

K

Kenya Kenya *18*
kenyano,-a Kenyan *18*
el **kilo(gramo)** kilo(gram) *9*

L

la **the** *(f., s.)*; her, it, you *(d.o.)*; *a la una* at one o'clock
el **lado** side; *al lado de* next to, beside; *por todos lados* everywhere
ladrar to bark *8*
el **ladrillo** brick *11*
el **lago** lake *4*
la **lámpara** lamp
la **lana** wool
la **langosta** lobster
el **lápiz** pencil *(pl. lápices)*
largo,-a long
las the *(f., pl.)*; them, you *(d.o.)*; *a las...* at...o'clock
la **lástima** shame, pity *12*; *¡Qué lástima!* What a shame!, Too bad!
lastimar(se) to injure, to hurt *13*
la **lata** can
el **lavabo** bathroom sink *3*
el **lavadero** laundry room *11*
el **lavaplatos eléctrico** dishwasher (machine)
lavar(se) to wash *3*
le (to, for) him, (to, for) her, (to, for) it, (to, for) you (formal) *(i.o.)*

lean: see *leer*
la **lección** lesson
la **lectura** reading
la **leche** milk
la **lechería** milk store, dairy (store) *5*
la **lechuga** lettuce
lee: see *leer*
leer to read; *lean (Uds. command)* read; *lee (tú command)* read
lejos (de) far (from)
la **lengua** tongue *4*; language
lento,-a slow
el **león** lion *7*
les (to, for) them, (to, for) you *(i.o.)*
la **letra** letter
levantar to raise, to lift *3*; *levantarse* to get up *3*; *levántate (tú command)* get up; *levántense (Uds. command)* get up
levántate: see *levantarse*
levántense: see *levantarse*
la **libertad** liberty, freedom
la **libra** pound
libre free; *al aire libre* outdoors *11*
la **librería** bookstore
el **libro** book
la **licuadora** blender *12*
el **líder** leader
limitar to limit
el **limón** lemon, lime *9*
el **limpiaparabrisas** windshield wiper *6*
limpiar to clean
limpio,-a clean
lindo,-a pretty
la **lista** list
listo,-a ready; smart; *estar listo,-a* to be ready; *ser listo,-a* to be smart
la **literatura** literature
llama: see *llamar*
llamar to call, to telephone; *¿Cómo se llama (Ud./él/ella)?* What is (your/his/her) name?; *¿Cómo te llamas?* What is your name?; *llamaron* they called (preterite of *llamar*); *llamarse* to be called *3*; *me llamo* my name is; *se llaman* their names are; *te llamas* your name is; *(Ud./Él/Ella) se llama....* (Your [formal]/His/Her) name is....

llamaron: see *llamar*
llamas: see *llamar*
llamo: see *llamar*
la **llanta** tire *6*
la **llave** key *12*
la **llegada** arrival *15*
llegar to arrive; *llegó* arrived (preterite of *llegar*)
llegó: see *llegar*
lleno,-a full *10*
llevar to take, to carry; to wear; to bring *14*; *llevarse* to take away, to get along *4*
llover (ue) to rain
la **lluvia** rain
lo him, it, you *(d.o.)*; *a lo mejor* maybe *15*; *lo (+ adjective/adverb)* how (+ adjective/adverb) *8*; *lo más (+ adverb) posible* as (+ adverb) as possible; *lo menos (+ adverb) posible* as (+ adverb) as possible; *lo que* what, that which; *lo siento* I am sorry; *lo siguiente* the following; *por lo menos* at least
loco,-a crazy
lógicamente logically
lógico,-a logical
los the *(m., pl.)*; them, you *(d.o.)*
luego then, later, soon; *desde luego* of course *11*; *hasta luego* so long, see you later; *luego que* as soon as *12*
el **lugar** place
el **lujo** luxury *16*
la **luna** moon *8*
lunes Monday; *el lunes* on Monday
la **luz** light *(pl. luces)*

M

la **madera** wood *11*
la **madrastra** stepmother *11*
la **madre** mother
maduro,-a ripe
el **maestro, la maestra** teacher, master; *La práctica hace al maestro.* Practice makes perfect.
magnífico,-a magnificent *18*
el **maíz** corn
mal badly; bad; *hace mal tiempo* the weather is bad
la **maleta** suitcase *15*
el **maletín** overnight bag, handbag, small suitcase, briefcase *16*
malo,-a bad

la **mamá** mother, mom *11*
mandar to order *11*
manejar to drive *6*
la **manera** manner, way
la **mano** hand; *equipaje de mano* carry-on luggage *16*
el **mantel** tablecloth
mantener to keep, to maintain *18*
la **mantequilla** butter
la **manzana** apple
mañana tomorrow; *hasta mañana* see you tomorrow; *pasado mañana* the day after tomorrow
la **mañana** morning; *de la mañana* A.M., in the morning; *por la mañana* in the morning
el **mapa** map
el **maquillaje** makeup *3*
maquillar to put makeup on (someone) *3*; *maquillarse* to put on makeup *3*
la **maquinita** little machine, video game
el **mar** sea *18*
maravilloso,-a marvellous, fantastic *7*
el **marcador** score *14*
marcar to score *14*
mariachi popular Mexican music and orchestra
el **marido** husband *11*
el **marisco** seafood *9*
martes Tuesday; *el martes* on Tuesday
marzo March
marroquí Moroccan *18*
Marruecos Morocco *18*
más more, else; *el/la/los/las* (+ noun) *más* (+ adjective) the most (+ adjective); *lo más* (+ adverb) *posible* as (+ adverb) as possible; *más de* more than *7*; *más* (+ noun/adjective/adverb) *que* more (+ noun/adjective/adverb) than; *más vale que* it is better that *12*
masculino,-a masculine
las **matemáticas** mathematics
el **material** material
máximo,-a maximum *14*; *pena máxima* penalty *14*
maya Mayan
los **mayas** Mayans
mayo May

la **mayonesa** mayonnaise *10*
mayor older, oldest; greater, greatest
la **mayoría** majority
la **mayúscula** capital letter
me (to, for) me *(i.o.)*; me *(d.o.)*; *me llaman* they call me; *me llamo* my name is
el **mecánico, la mecánica** mechanic *17*
la **medianoche** midnight; *Es medianoche.* It is midnight.
la **medicina** medicine *4*
el **médico, la médica** doctor
el **medio** means; middle, center *18*; *en medio de* in the middle of, in the center of *18*
medio,-a half; *y media* half past
el **mediocampista, la mediocampista** midfielder *14*
el **mediodía** noon; *Es mediodía.* It is noon.
mejor better; *a lo mejor* maybe *15*; *el/la/los/las mejor/mejores* (+ noun) the best (+ noun)
mejorar to improve
el **melón** melon, cantaloupe *9*
menor younger, youngest; lesser, least
menos minus, until, before, to (to express time); less; *el/la/los/las* (+ noun) *menos* (+ adjective) the least (+ adjective + noun); *lo menos* (+ adverb) *posible* as (+ adverb) as possible; *menos* (+ noun/adjective/adverb) *que* less (+ noun/adjective/adverb) than; *menos cuarto* a quarter to, a quarter before; *por lo menos* at least
mentir (ie, i) to lie
la **mentira** lie
el **menú** menu *9*
el **mercado** market
el **merengue** merengue (dance music)
el **mes** month
la **mesa** table; *mesa de planchar* ironing board *12*; *poner la mesa* to set the table; *recoger la mesa* to clear the table
el **mesero, la mesera** food server *10*

la **mesita** tray table *16*
el **metro** subway; *estación del metro* subway station *11*
mexicano,-a Mexican *5*
México Mexico
mi my; *(pl. mis)* my
mí me (after a preposition)
el **micrófono** microphone *14*
el **miedo** fear; *tener miedo de* to be afraid of
el **miembro** member *11*
mientras (que) while *6*
miércoles Wednesday; *el miércoles* on Wednesday
mil thousand
mínimo,-a minimum
la **minúscula** lowercase
el **minuto** minute
mío,-a my, (of) mine *8*; *el gusto es mío* the pleasure is mine
mira: see *mirar*
mirar to look (at); *mira (tú* command) look; *mira* hey, look (pause in speech); *miren (Uds.* command) look; *miren* hey, look (pause in speech)
miren: see *mirar*
mismo right (in the very moment, place, etc.); *ahora mismo* right now
mismo,-a same
el **misterio** mystery *13*
el **modelo** model
moderno,-a modern *6*
molestar to bother *7*
la **moneda** coin, money *5*
el **mono** monkey *7*
la **montaña** mountain *7*; *montaña rusa* roller coaster *7*
montar to ride
el **monumento** monument *5*
morder (ue) to bite *13*
moreno,-a brunet, brunette, dark-haired, dark-skinned
morir(se) (ue, u) to die *13*; *morirse de la risa* to die laughing *13*
la **mostaza** mustard *10*
el **mostrador** counter *16*
mostrar (ue) to show *13*
la **moto(cicleta)** motorcycle
el **motor** motor, engine *6*; *motor de búsqueda* search engine *1*
la **muchacha** girl, young woman
el **muchacho** boy, guy

muchísimo very much, a lot

mucho much, a lot, very, very much

mucho,-a much, a lot of, very; *(pl. muchos,-as)* many; *con (mucho) gusto* I would be (very) glad to; *muchas gracias* thank you very much; *¡Mucho gusto!* Glad to meet you!

mudar(se) to move *15*

el **mueble** piece of furniture *11*

el **muelle** concourse, pier *16*

la **mujer** woman; wife *11*; *mujer de negocios* businesswoman *17*

el **mundo** world *1*; *todo el mundo* everyone, everybody *2*

la **muralla** wall

el **muro** (exterior) wall *11*

el **museo** museum

la **música** music

muy very

N

nacer to be born *15*

la **nación** nation

nacional national *13*

nada nothing; *de nada* you are welcome, not at all

nadar to swim

nadie nobody

la **naranja** orange

la **nariz** nose *4*

narrar to announce, to narrate *14*

navegar to surf *1*

la **Navidad** Christmas

la **neblina** mist; *hay neblina* it is misty

necesario,-a necessary *9*

necesitar to need

negativo,-a negative

los **negocios** business *17*; *hombre de negocios* businessman *17*; *mujer de negocios* businesswoman *17*

negro,-a black

nervioso,-a nervous

nevar (ie) to snow

ni not even; *ni...ni* neither...nor

Nicaragua Nicaragua

nicaragüense Nicaraguan *7*

la **nieta** granddaughter

el **nieto** grandson

la **nieve** snow

ningún, ninguna none, not any

ninguno,-a none, not any

el **niño, la niña** child *4*

el **nivel** level

no no; *¡Cómo no!* Of course!; *No lo/la veo.* I do not see him (it)/her (it).; *¡no me digas!* you don't say! *18*; *No sé.* I do not know.

la **noche** night; *buenas noches* good night; *de la noche* *P.M.,* at night; *esta noche* tonight; *por la noche* at night

el **nombre** name *15*

el **noreste** northeast *6*

normal normal *13*

el **noroeste** northwest *6*

el **norte** north *6*; *América del Norte* North America *11*

norteamericano,-a North American *18*

nos (to, for) us *(i.o.)*; us *(d.o.)*

nosotros,-as we; us (after a preposition)

la **noticia** news *2*

novecientos,-as nine hundred

noveno,-a ninth

noventa ninety

la **novia** girlfriend *2*

noviembre November

el **novio** boyfriend *2*

nublado,-a cloudy; *está nublado* it is cloudy

nuestro,-a our, (of) ours *8*

nueve nine

nuevo,-a new; *Año Nuevo* New Year's (Day)

el **número** number; *número de teléfono* telephone number

nunca never

O

o or; *o...o* either...or

la **obra** work, play

el **obrero, la obrera** worker *17*

obvio,-a obvious *12*

la **ocasión** occasion *13*

el **océano** ocean *18*

octavo,-a eighth

octubre October

ocupado,-a busy, occupied

ocupar to occupy

ocurrir to occur *8*

ochenta eighty

ocho eight

ochocientos,-as eight hundred

la **odisea** odyssey

el **oeste** west *6*

la **oferta** sale; *estar en oferta* to be on sale

oficial official

la **oficina** office; *oficina de correos* post office *5*

ofrecer to offer *6*

el **oído** (inner) ear *4*; sense of hearing

oigan hey, listen (pause in speech)

oigo hello (telephone greeting)

oír to hear, to listen (to); *oigan* hey, listen (pause in speech); *oigo* hello (telephone greeting); *oye* hey, listen (pause in speech)

ojalá would that, if only, I hope *17*

el **ojo** eye *4*

olé bravo

la **olla** pot, saucepan

olvidar(se) to forget *4*

el **omelet** omelet *15*

la **omisión** omission

once eleven

opinar to give an opinion *13*; to form an opinion *13*

la **oportunidad** opportunity *14*

el **opuesto** opposite

la **oración** sentence

el **orden** order

ordenar to order *5*

la **oreja** (outer) ear *4*

la **organización** organization

organizar to organize *18*

el **órgano** organ

la **orilla** shore *18*

el **oro** gold

os (to, for) you (Spain, informal, *pl., i.o.*), you (Spain, informal, *pl., d.o.*)

el **oso** bear *8*; *oso de peluche* teddy bear *8*

el **otoño** autumn

otro,-a other, another *(pl. otros,-as)*; *otra vez* again, another time

la **oveja** sheep *8*

oye hey, listen (pause in speech)

P

el **Pacífico** Pacific Ocean

el **padrastro** stepfather *11*

el **padre** father; *(pl. padres)* parents

la **paella** paella (traditional Spanish dish with rice, meat, seafood and vegetables)

pagar to pay

la **página** page

el **país** country *2*

el **paisaje** landscape, scenery

el **pájaro** bird *8*

la **palabra** word; *palabra interrogativa* question word; *palabras antónimas* antonyms, opposite words

el **pan** bread

la **panadería** bakery *5*

Panamá Panama

panameño,-a Panamanian *7*

el **pantalón** pants

la **pantalla** screen *15*

la **pantera** panther *7*

las **pantimedias** pantyhose, nylons

la **pantufla** slipper *2*

el **pañuelo** handkerchief, hanky

la **papa** potato

el **papá** father, dad *11*

los **papás** parents

la **papaya** papaya *9*

el **papel** paper; role; *haz el papel* play the role; *hoja de papel* sheet of paper

la **papelería** stationery store *5*

para for, to, in order to; *para que* so that, in order that

el **parabrisas** windshield *6*

el **parador** inn *16*

el **paraguas** umbrella

el **Paraguay** Paraguay

paraguayo,-a Paraguayan *7*

parar to stop *5*; *ir a parar* to end up *10*

parecer to seem; *¿Qué (te/le/les) parece?* What do/does you/he/she/they think? *10*

la **pared** wall

la **pareja** pair, couple

el **pariente, la pariente** relative

el **parque** park; *parque de atracciones* amusement park

la **parte** place, part *9*

participar to participate *13*

el **partido** game, match; *partidos empatados* games tied; *partidos ganados* games won; *partidos perdidos* games lost

el **párrafo** paragraph

pasado,-a past, last; *pasado mañana* the day after tomorrow

el **pasaje** ticket *15*

el **pasajero** passenger *16*

pásame: see *pasar*

el **pasaporte** passport *15*

pasar to pass, to spend (time); to happen, to occur; *pásame* pass me;

pasar la aspiradora to vacuum; *¿Qué te pasa?* What is wrong with you?

el **pasatiempo** pastime, leisure activity

la **Pascua** Easter

el **paseo** walk, ride, trip; *dar un paseo* to take a walk

el **pastel** cake, pastry *12*

la **pata** paw *8*

el **patinador, la patinadora** skater

patinar to skate; *patinar sobre hielo* to ice-skate; *patinar sobre ruedas* to in-line skate

el **patio** courtyard, patio, yard

el **pato** duck *8*

el **pavo** turkey *8*

el **payaso** clown *8*

la **paz** peace *3*

el **pecho** chest *4*

pedir (i, i) to ask for, to order, to request; *pedir perdón* to say you are sorry; *pedir permiso (para)* to ask for permission (to do something); *pedir prestado,-a* to borrow

peinar(se) to comb *3*

el **peine** comb *3*

la **película** movie, film

pelirrojo,-a red-haired

el **pelo** hair *3*; *tomar el pelo* to pull someone's leg *10*

la **pelota** ball *14*

el **peluquero, la peluquera** hairstylist *17*

la **pena** punishment, pain, trouble; *pena máxima* penalty *14*

pensar (ie) to think, to intend, to plan; *pensar de* to think about (i.e., to have an opinion); *pensar en* to think about (i.e., to focus one's thoughts on); *pensar en* (+ infinitive) to think about (doing something)

peor worse; *el/la/los/las peor/peores* (+ noun) the worst (+ noun)

pequeño,-a small

la **pera** pear *9*

perder (ie) to lose; *partidos perdidos* games lost

perdidos: see *perder*

perdón excuse me, pardon me; *pedir perdón* to say you are sorry

perezoso,-a lazy

perfecto,-a perfect

el **perfume** perfume

el **periódico** newspaper

el **periodista, la periodista** journalist *13*

el **período** period

la **perla** pearl

el **permiso** permission, permit; *con permiso* excuse me (with your permission), may I; *pedir permiso (para)* to ask for permission (to do something)

permitir to permit

pero but

la **persona** person

el **personaje** character *13*

personal personal; *pronombre personal* subject pronoun

el **Perú** Peru

peruano,-a Peruvian *7*

el **perro, la perra** dog

la **pesca** fishing *17*

el **pescado** fish

pescar to fish *4*; *pescar (un resfriado)* to catch (a cold) *4*

el **petróleo** oil

el **piano** piano

el **picnic** picnic *2*

el **pie** foot; *a pie* on foot

la **pierna** leg

la **pieza** piece *16*

el **pijama** pajamas

el **piloto** pilot *16*

el **pimentero** pepper shaker *10*

la **pimienta** pepper (seasoning)

el **pimiento** bell pepper

pintar to paint *2*

la **piña** pineapple *9*

la **pirámide** pyramid

la **piscina** swimming pool

el **piso** floor; *primer piso* first floor

la **pista** clue

la **pizarra** blackboard

la **placa** license plate *6*

el **placer** pleasure *16*

el **plan** plan *12*

la **plancha** iron *12*

planchar to iron *12*; *mesa de planchar* ironing board *12*

la **planta** plant; *planta baja* ground floor

el **plástico** plastic *7*

la **plata** silver

el **plátano** banana

el **plato** dish, plate; *plato de sopa* soup bowl

la **playa** beach
la **plaza** plaza, public square
la **pluma** feather 8; pen
la **población** population
pobre poor 8
poco,-a not very, little; *un poco* a little (bit)
poder (ue) to be able
el **policía, la policía** police (officer) 5
políticamente politically
el **pollo** chicken
el **polvo** dust 2
poner to put, to place, to turn on (an appliance); *poner la mesa* to set the table; *poner(se)* to put on 3
popular popular
un **poquito** a very little (bit)
por for; through, by; in; along; *por ejemplo* for example; *por favor* please; *por fin* finally 18; *por la mañana* in the morning; *por la noche* at night; *por la tarde* in the afternoon; *por teléfono* by telephone, on the telephone; *por todos lados* everywhere
¿por qué? why?
porque because
el **portero, la portera** goaltender, goalie 14
el **Portugal** Portugal 18
portugués, portuguesa Portuguese 18
la **posibilidad** possibility
posible possible 10; *lo más (+ adverb) posible* as (+ adverb) as possible; *lo menos (+ adverb) posible* as (+ adverb) as possible
la **posición** position 16
el **postre** dessert
potable drinkable 16
la **práctica** practice; *La práctica hace al maestro.* Practice makes perfect.
practicar to practice, to do 17
el **precio** price
preciso,-a necessary 12
preferir (ie, i) to prefer
la **pregunta** question; *hacer una pregunta* to ask a question
preguntar to ask; *preguntarse* to wonder, to ask oneself 4
el **premio** prize 13
la **prenda** garment 10
preocupar(se) to worry 3
preparar to prepare

el **preparativo** preparation
la **presentación** introduction
presentar to introduce, to present; *le presento a* let me introduce you (formal, *s.*) to; *les presento a* let me introduce you (*pl.*) to; *te presento a* let me introduce you (informal, *s.*) to
presente present
presento: see *presentar*
prestado,-a on loan; *pedir prestado,-a* to borrow
prestar to lend
la **primavera** spring
primer first (form of *primero* before a *m., s.* noun); *primer piso* first floor
primero first (adverb)
primero,-a first
el **primo, la prima** cousin
la **princesa** princess 15
principal principle, main 9
el **príncipe** prince 15
la **prisa** rush, hurry, haste; *tener prisa* to be in a hurry
probable probable 9
probar(se) (ue) to try (on) 10; to test, to prove
el **problema** problem
el **produce** produces
el **producto** product
el **profe** teacher
el **profesor, la profesora** teacher
el **programa** program, show 1; *bajar un programa* to download a program 1; *programa de concurso* game show
el **programador, la programadora** computer programmer 17
prometer to promise
el **pronombre** pronoun; *pronombre personal* subject pronoun
el **pronóstico** forecast
pronto soon, quickly; *hasta pronto* see you soon
la **pronunciación** pronunciation
la **propina** tip 10
el **propósito** aim, purpose; *a propósito* by the way 18
la **protesta** protest 13
próximo,-a next 5
la **publicidad** publicity
el **público** audience 13
público,-a public
puede ser maybe 15

el **puente** bridge 5
el **puerco** pig 8; pork 8
la **puerta** door
el **puerto** port
Puerto Rico Puerto Rico
puertorriqueño,-a Puerto Rican 7
pues thus, well, so, then (pause in speech)
el **pulpo** octopus, squid 9
la **pulsera** bracelet
el **punto** dot, point 1
la **puntuación** punctuation
el **pupitre** desk
puro,-a pure, fresh 11

Q

que that, which; *lo que* what, that which; *más (+ noun/adjective/adverb) que* more (+ noun/adjective/adverb) than; *que viene* upcoming, next
¿qué? what?; *¿a qué hora?* at what time?; *¿Qué comprendiste?* What did you understand?; *¿Qué hora es?* What time is it?; *¿Qué quiere decir...?* What is the meaning (of)...?; *¿Qué tal?* How are you?; *¿Qué (te/le/les) parece?* What do/does you/he/she/they think? 10; *¿Qué quiere decir...?* What is the meaning (of)...?; *¿Qué te pasa?* What is wrong with you?; *¿Qué temperatura hace?* What is the temperature?; *¿Qué (+ tener)?* What is wrong with (someone)?; *¿Qué tiempo hace?* How is the weather?
¡qué (+ adjective)! how (+ adjective)!
¡qué (+ noun)! what a (+ noun)!; *¡Qué lástima!* What a shame!, Too bad!; *¡Qué (+ noun) tan (+ adjective)!* What (a) (+ adjective) (+ noun)! 8
quedar(se) to remain, to stay 3; *quedarle bien a uno* to fit, to be becoming
el **quehacer** chore
quemar to burn 3; *quemarse* to get burned 3

querer (ie) to love, to want, to like; *¿Qué quiere decir...?* What is the meaning (of)...?; *querer decir* to mean; *quiere decir* it means; *quiero* I love; I want

querido,-a dear

el **queso** cheese

quien who, whom *13*

¿quién? who?; *(pl. ¿quiénes?)* who?

quienquiera whoever *17*

quiere: see *querer*

quiero: see *querer*

la **química** chemistry

quince fifteen

quinientos,-as five hundred

quinto,-a fifth

quisiera would like *2*

quitar(se) to take off *3*

quizás perhaps

R

el **rabo** tail *8*

el **radio** radio (apparatus)

la **radio** radio (broadcast)

rápidamente rapidly

rápido,-a rapid, fast

el **rascacielos** skyscraper

el **ratón** mouse *8*

la **raya** stripe *10*; *a rayas* striped *10*

rayado,-a scratched, striped *11*

la **razón** reason *10*; *tener razón* to be right *10*

real royal; real *17*

la **realidad** reality *18*

realizar to attain, to bring about

la **recepción** reception desk *16*

el **recepcionista, la recepcionista** receptionist *16*

la **receta** recipe

recibir to receive

el **recibo** receipt *10*

recoger to pick up; *recoger la mesa* to clear the table

recordar (ue) to remember

la **Red Mundial de Información** World Wide Web *1*

redondo,-a round

referir(se) (ie, i) to refer *11*

el **refresco** soft drink, refreshment

el **refrigerador** refrigerator

el **regalo** gift

regañar to scold

regatear to bargain, to haggle

registrar to check in *16*

la **regla** ruler; rule *12*

regresar to return, to go back, to come back *12*

regular average, okay, so-so, regular

la **reina** queen *15*

reír(se) (i, i) to laugh *9*

la **reja** wrought iron window grill *11*; wrought iron fence *11*

relacionado,-a related

el **reloj** clock, watch

remoto,-a remote

repasar to reexamine, to review

el **repaso** review

repetir (i, i) to repeat; *repitan (Uds.* command) repeat; *repite (tú* command) repeat

repitan: see *repetir*

repite: see *repetir*

reportando reporting

el **reportero, la reportera** reporter *13*

la **República Dominicana** Dominican Republic

resbaloso,-a slippery *13*

la **reservación** reservation *15*

el **resfriado** cold *4*; *pescar un resfriado* to catch a cold

resolver (ue) to resolve, to solve

el **respaldar** seat-back *16*

responder to answer

la **respuesta** answer

el **restaurante** restaurant

el **resumen** summary; *en resumen* in short

la **reunión** meeting, reunion *13*

reunir(se) to get together *4*

revisar to check *16*

la **revista** magazine

el **rey** king *15*

rico,-a rich, delicious *10*

el **riel** rail

el **río** river *18*

la **risa** laugh *13*; *morirse de la risa* to die laughing *13*

el **ritmo** rhythm

el **robo** robbery *13*

la **rodilla** knee *4*

rojo,-a red

romper to break, to tear *13*

la **ropa** clothing; *ropa interior* underwear

rosado,-a pink

el **rubí** ruby *10*

rubio,-a blond, blonde

la **rueda** wheel *6*

el **rugido** roar *8*

rugir to roar *8*

el **ruido** noise *16*

Rusia Russia *18*

ruso,-a Russian *18*; *montaña rusa* roller coaster *11*

la **rutina** routine

S

sábado Saturday; *el sábado* on Saturday

saber to know; *No sé.* I do not know.; *sabes* you know; *sé* I know

sabes: see *saber*

el **sabor** flavor *10*

saborear to taste, to savor *15*

saca: see *sacar*

el **sacapuntas** pencil sharpener

sacar to take out; *saca (tú* command) stick out *4*

la **sal** salt

la **sala** living room

la **salchicha** sausage *9*

el **salero** salt shaker *10*

la **salida** departure, exit *15*

salir to go out; *siempre salirse con la suya* to always get one's way *18*

la **salsa** salsa (dance music); *salsa de tomate* ketchup *10*

saltar to jump *8*

saludar to greet, to say hello

el **saludo** greeting

salvadoreño,-a Salvadoran *7*

salvaje wild *7*

el **sandwich** sandwich *9*

la **sangre** blood

el **santo** saint's day; *Todos los Santos* All Saints' Day

saudita Saudi, Saudi Arabian *18*

el **saxofón** saxophone

se *¿Cómo se dice...?* How do you say...?; *¿Cómo se escribe...?* How do you write (spell)...?; *¿Cómo se llama (Ud./él/ella)?* What is (your/his/her) name?; *se considera* it is considered; *se dice* one says; *se escribe* it is written; *Se habla español.* Spanish is spoken.; *se llaman* their names are; *(Ud./Él/Ella) se llama....* (Your [formal]/His/Her) name is....

la **sección** section *14*
el **secretario, la secretaria** secretary *17*
el **secreto** secret *10*
la **sed** thirst; *tener sed* to be thirsty
la **seda** silk
seguir (i, i) to follow, to continue, to keep, to go on, to pursue *1; sigan (Uds.* command) follow; *sigue (tú* command) follow
según according to
el **segundo** second
segundo,-a second
la **seguridad** safety *6; cinturón de seguridad* seat belt, safety belt *6*
seguro,-a sure *12*
seis six
seiscientos,-as six hundred
selecciona (tú command) select
la **selva** jungle *7; selva tropical* tropical rain forest
la **semana** week; *fin de semana* weekend; *Semana Santa* Holy Week
sentar (ie) to seat (someone) *3; sentarse* to sit down *3; siéntate (tú* command) sit down *4; siéntense (Uds.* command) sit down
sentir (ie, i) to be sorry, to feel sorry, to regret; *lo siento* I am sorry; *sentir(se)* to feel *10*
la **señal** sign *6*
señalar to point to, to point at, to point out; *señalen (Uds.* command) point to
señalen: see *señalar*
sencillo,-a one-way *15;* single *16*
el **señor** gentleman, sir, Mr.
la **señora** lady, madame, Mrs.
la **señorita** young lady, Miss
septiembre September
séptimo,-a seventh
ser to be; *eres* you are; *¿Eres (tú) de...?* Are you from...?; *es* you (formal) are, he/she/it is; *es la una* it is one o'clock; *Es medianoche.* It is midnight.; *Es mediodía.* It is noon.; *fue* you (formal) were, he/she/it was (preterite of *ser); fueron* you (pl.) were, they were (preterite of *ser); puede ser* maybe *15;*

¿Qué hora es? What time is it?; *sea* it is; *ser difícil que* to be unlikely that *12; ser fácil que* to be likely that *12; ser listo,-a* to be smart; *son* they are; *son las* (+ number) it is (+ number) o'clock; *soy* I am
serio,-a serious *13*
la **serpiente** snake *7*
el **servicio** service *16; servicio al cuarto* room service *16*
la **servilleta** napkin
servir (i, i) to serve *10*
sesenta sixty
setecientos,-as seven hundred
setenta seventy
sexto,-a sixth
los **shorts** shorts *2*
si if
sí yes
siempre always; *siempre salirse con la suya* to always get one's way *18*
siéntate: see *sentar*
siéntense: see *sentar*
siento: see *sentir*
siete seven
sigan: see *seguir*
el **siglo** century
los **signos de puntuación** punctuation marks
sigue: see *seguir*
siguiente following; *lo siguiente* the following
la **silabificación** syllabification
el **silencio** silence
la **silla** chair
el **sillón** armchair, easy chair *11*
el **símbolo** symbol
similar alike, similar
simpático,-a nice, pleasant
sin without; *sin embargo* however, nevertheless *18*
sino but (on the contrary), although, even though *6*
sintético,-a synthetic
la **situación** situation
sobre on, over; about
la **sobrina** niece
el **sobrino** nephew
el **sol** sun; *hace sol* it is sunny; *hay sol* it is sunny
solamente only
soleado,-a sunny; *está soleado* it is sunny
soler (ue) to be accustomed to, to be used to *10*

solo,-a alone *2*
sólo only, just
la **sombrerería** hat store *5*
el **sombrero** hat
son: see *ser*
el **sondeo** poll
el **sonido** sound
sonreír(se) (i, i) to smile *12*
soñar to dream *15*
la **sopa** soup; *plato de sopa* soup bowl
la **sorpresa** surprise
el **sótano** basement *11*
soy: see *ser*
Sr. abbreviation for *señor*
Sra. abbreviation for *señora*
Srta. abbreviation for *señorita*
su, sus his, her, its, your *(Ud./Uds.),* their
suave smooth, soft *17*
el **subdesarrollo** underdevelopment
subir to climb, to go up, to go up stairs, to take up, to bring up, to carry up; to get in *6*
el **suceso** event, happening *13*
sucio,-a dirty
el **sueño** sleep; dream *17; tener sueño* to be sleepy
la **suerte** luck *15; buena suerte* good luck
el **suéter** sweater
el **supermercado** supermarket
el **sur** south *6; América del Sur* South America *11*
suramericano,-a South American *18*
el **sureste** southeast *6*
surfear to surf *1*
el **suroeste** southwest *6*
el **surtido** assortment, supply, selection *10*
el **sustantivo** noun
suyo,-a his, (of) his, her, (of) hers, its, your, (of) yours, their, (of) theirs *8; siempre salirse con la suya* to always get one's way *18*

T

la **tabla** chart *14*
el **taco** taco *5*
tal such, as, so; *¿Qué tal?* How are you?
el **tamal** tamale
el **tamaño** size

también also, too

el **tambor** drum

tampoco either, neither

tan so; *¡Qué (+ noun) tan (+ adjective)!* What (a) (+ adjective) (+ noun)! *10*; *tan (+ adjective/adverb) como (+ person/item)* as (+ adjective/adverb) as (+ person/item)

tanto,-a so much; *tanto,-a (+ noun) como (+ person/item)* as much/many (+ noun) as (+ person/item); *tanto como* as much as; *Tanto gusto.* So glad to meet you.

la **tapa** tidbit, appetizer

la **taquilla** box office, ticket office *8*

tardar to delay *6*; *tardar en (+ infinitive)* to be long, to take a long time *6*

la **tarde** afternoon; *buenas tardes* good afternoon; *de la tarde* P.M., in the afternoon; *por la tarde* in the afternoon

tarde late *3*

la **tarea** homework

la **tarifa** fare *15*

la **tarjeta** card; *tarjeta de crédito* credit card

el **taxista, la taxista** taxi driver *17*

la **taza** cup

te (to, for) you *(i.o.)*; you *(d.o.)*; *¿Cómo te llamas?* What is your name?; *te llamas* your name is

el **té** tea *9*

el **teatro** theater

el **techo** roof *11*

la **tecnología** technology *1*

la **tela** fabric, cloth *10*

el **teléfono** telephone; *número de teléfono* telephone number; *por teléfono* by telephone, on the telephone; *teléfono público* public telephone

la **telenovela** soap opera

la **televisión** television; *ver (la) televisión* to watch television

el **televisor** television set

el **tema** theme, topic

el **temblor** tremor *13*

temer to fear *12*

la **temperatura** temperature; *¿Qué temperatura hace?* What is the temperature?

temprano early

el **tenedor** fork

tener to have; *¿Cuántos años tienes?* How old are you?; *¿Qué (+ tener)?* What is wrong with (person)?; *tener calor* to be hot; *tener cuidado* to be careful *11*; *tener éxito* to be successful, to be a success *13*; *tener frío* to be cold; *tener ganas de* to feel like; *tener hambre* to be hungry; *tener miedo de* to be afraid; *tener (+ number) años* to be (+ number) years old; *tener prisa* to be in a hurry; *tener que* to have to; *tener razón* to be right *10*; *tener sed* to be thirsty; *tener sueño* to be sleepy; *tengo* I have; *tengo (+ number) años* I am (+ number) years old; *tiene* it has; *tienes* you have

tengo: see *tener*

el **tenis** tennis

el **tenista, la tenista** tennis player

tercer third (form of *tercero* before a *m., s.* noun)

tercero,-a third

terminar to end, to finish

la **ternera** veal *9*

ti you (after a preposition)

la **tía** aunt

el **tiempo** time; weather; verb tense; period, half *14*; *a tiempo* on time *12*; *hace buen (mal) tiempo* the weather is nice (bad); *¿Qué tiempo hace?* How is the weather?

la **tienda** store

tiene: see *tener*

tienes: see *tener*

la **tierra** land, earth

el **tigre** tiger *7*

la **tina** bathtub *3*

el **tío** uncle

típico,-a typical

el **tipo** type, kind *10*

tirar to throw away *6*

el **tiro** shot *14*

el **titular** headline *14*

la **tiza** chalk

la **toalla** towel *3*

toca: see *tocar*

el **tocadiscos** record player

el **tocador** dresser *9*

tocar to play (a musical instrument); to touch; *toca (tú command)* touch *4*; *toquen (Uds. command)* touch

el **tocino** bacon *9*

todavía yet; still

todo everything *11*

todo,-a all, every, whole, entire; *de todos los días* everyday; *por todos lados* everywhere; *todo el mundo* everyone, everybody; *todos los días* every day

todos,-as everyone, everybody

tolerante tolerant

tomar to drink, to have; to take; *tomar el pelo* to pull someone's leg *10*

el **tomate** tomato; *salsa de tomate* ketchup *10*

tonto,-a silly

el **tópico** theme

toquen: see *tocar*

el **toro** bull *8*

la **toronja** grapefruit *9*

la **tortilla** cornmeal pancake (Mexico) *5*; omelet (Spain) *5*

la **tortuga** turtle *7*

la **torre** tower *5*

trabajar to work; *trabajando en parejas* working in pairs

el **trabajo** work

traducir to translate *6*

traer to bring

el **tráfico** traffic *6*

el **traje** suit; *traje de baño* swimsuit

la **transmisión** transmission, broadcast *14*

el **transporte** transportation

tratar (de) to try (to do something)

trece thirteen

treinta thirty

treinta y uno thirty-one

el **tren** train; *estación del tren* train station *11*

tres three
trescientos,-as three hundred
la **tripulación** crew *16*
triste sad
el **trombón** trombone
la **trompeta** trumpet
tu your (informal); *(pl. tus)* your (informal)
tú you (informal)
la **tumba** tomb
el **turismo** tourism
el **turista, la turista** tourist
turístico,-a tourist *15*
tuyo,-a your, (of) yours *8*

U

u or (used before a word that starts with *o* or *ho*)
ubicado,-a located
Ud. you (abbreviation of *usted*); you (after a preposition); *Ud. se llama....* Your name is....
Uds. you (abbreviation of *ustedes*); you (after a preposition)
último,-a last *2*
un, una a, an, one; *a la una* at one o'clock
único,-a only, unique
unido,-a united, connected *17*
la **universidad** university *17*
uno one; *quedarle bien a uno* to fit, to be becoming
unos, unas some, any, a few
urgente urgent *12*
el **Uruguay** Uruguay
uruguayo,-a Uruguayan *7*
usar to use
usted you (formal, *s.*); you (after a preposition)
ustedes you *(pl.)*; you (after a preposition)
la **uva** grape

V

la **vaca** cow *8*
las **vacaciones** vacation
la **vainilla** vanilla *9*
valer to be worth *12*; *más vale que* it is better that *12*
¡vamos! let's go!; *¡vamos a (+ infinitive)!* let's (+ infinitive)!
la **variedad** variety *10*

varios,-as several
el **vaso** glass
vayan: see *ir*
ve: see *ir*
el **vecino, la vecina** neighbor *6*
veinte twenty
veinticinco twenty-five
veinticuatro twenty-four
veintidós twenty-two
veintinueve twenty-nine
veintiocho twenty-eight
veintiséis twenty-six
veintisiete twenty-seven
veintitrés twenty-three
veintiuno twenty-one
vencer to expire *15*
el **vendedor, la vendedora** salesperson *17*
vender to sell
venezolano,-a Venezuelan *7*
Venezuela Venezuela
vengan: see *venir*
venir to come; *vengan (Uds.* command) come
la **ventana** window
el **ventilador** fan *11*
veo: see *ver*
ver to see, to watch; *a ver* let's see, hello (telephone greeting); *No lo/la veo.* I do not see him (it)/her (it).; *veo* I see; *ver (la) televisión* to watch television; *ves* you see
el **verano** summer
el **verbo** verb
verdad true
¿verdad? right?
la **verdad** truth
verde green
la **verdura** greens, vegetables
vertical vertical *16*
ves: see *ver*
el **vestido** dress
el **vestidor** fitting room *10*
vestir (i, i) to dress (someone) *3*; *vestirse* to get dressed *3*
el **veterinario, la veterinaria** veterinarian *17*
la **vez** time *(pl. veces); a veces* sometimes, at times; (number +) *vez/veces al/a la* (+ time expression) (number +) time(s) per (+ time expression); *otra vez* again, another time
viajar to travel

el **viaje** trip; *agencia de viajes* travel agency *15*; *irse de viaje* to go away on a trip *10*
la **vida** life
viejo,-a old
el **viento** wind; *hace viento* it is windy
viernes Friday; *el viernes* on Friday
el **vinagre** vinegar
el **vínculo** link *1*
la **visa** visa *15*
la **visita** visit *7*
visitar to visit *4*
la **vista** view; *hasta la vista* so long, see you later
la **vitrina** store window *5*; glass showcase *5*
vivir to live
el **vocabulario** vocabulary
la **vocal** vowel; *vocales abiertas* open vowels; *vocales cerradas* closed vowels
el **volante** steering wheel *6*
volar (ue) to fly *8*
el **volibol** volleyball
volver (ue) to return, to go back, to come back
vosotros,-as you (Spain, informal, *pl.*); you (after a preposition)
la **voz** voice *(pl. voces)*
el **vuelo** flight *15*; *auxiliar de vuelo* flight attendant *16*
vuestro,-a,-os,-as your (Spain, informal, *pl.*)

W

la **Web** (World Wide)Web *1*

Y

y and; *y cuarto* a quarter past, a quarter after; *y media* half past
ya already; now *14*
yo I

Z

la **zanahoria** carrot
la **zapatería** shoe store *5*
el **zapato** shoe; *zapato bajo* low-heel shoe; *zapato de tacón* high-heel shoe
el **zoológico** zoo *11*; *jardín zoológico* zoological garden *11*

Vocabulary English/Spanish

A

a un, una; *a few* unos, unas; *a little (bit)* un poco; *a lot (of)* mucho, muchísimo; *a very little (bit)* un poquito
about sobre; acerca de *14*
above encima de *8*, arriba *11*
accent el acento
accepted aceptado,-a *17*
accident el accidente *13*
according to según
acrobat el acróbata, la acróbata *8*
activity la actividad *13*
actor el actor, la actriz *13*
actress la actriz *13*
to **add** añadir; agregar *10*
address la dirección *6*
advertisement el anuncio (comercial) *13*; *printed advertisement* el aviso *14*
advice el consejo *10*
to **advise** aconsejar *10*
aerobics los aeróbicos; *to do aerobics* hacer aeróbicos
affectionate cariñoso,-a
afraid asustado,-a; *to be afraid of* tener miedo de
Africa el África *7*
African africano,-a *7*
after después de; detrás de *8*; *a quarter after* y cuarto; *the day after tomorrow* pasado mañana
afternoon la tarde; *good afternoon* buenas tardes; *in the afternoon* de la tarde, por la tarde
afterwards después
again otra vez
age la edad
agency la agencia; *travel agency* la agencia de viajes *15*
agent el agente, la agente *15*
ago hace (+ *time expression*) que
to **agree** convenir *12*, estar de acuerdo *13*
agreeable agradable *10*
agreed de acuerdo

ahead adelante *5*; *straight ahead* derecho *5*
air aéreo,-a *15*
air el aire *11*; *air conditioning* el aire acondicionado *11*; *pertaining to air* aéreo,-a *15*
airline la aerolínea *16*
airplane el avión; *by airplane* en avión
airport el aeropuerto *5*
alarm la alarma *6*; *alarm (clock)* la alarma *11*; *fire alarm* la alarma de incendios *12*; *smoke alarm* la alarma de incendios *12*
algebra el álgebra
all todo,-a; *any at all* cualquiera *12*
to **allow** dejar (de) *11*
almost casi
alone solo,-a *2*
along por; *to get along* llevarse *4*
already ya
also también
although sino *6*, aunque *12*
always siempre; *to always get one's way* siempre salirse con la suya *18*
America la América *7*; *Central America* la América Central *7*; *North America* la América del Norte *5*; *South America* la América del Sur *5*; *United States of America* los Estados Unidos
American americano,-a; *Central American* centroamericano,-a *18*; *North American* norteamericano,-a *18*; *South American* suramericano,-a *18*
to **amuse** divertir *(ie, i) 4*
amusement la atracción; *amusement park* el parque de atracciones; *(amusement) ride* la atracción *7*

an un, una
ancient antiguo,-a *7*
and y; (*used before a word beginning with* i *or* hi) e
animal el animal *7*
to **announce** narrar *14*
announcement el anuncio *13*; *commercial announcement* el anuncio comercial *13*
another otro,-a; *another time* otra vez
answer la respuesta
to **answer** contestar
antique antiguo,-a *7*
any unos, unas; alguno,-a, algún, alguna; cualquier, cualquiera *8*; *any at all* cualquiera *10*; *not any* ninguno,-a, ningún, nunguna
anybody alguien
anyone alguien
anything algo
apartment el apartamento *5*
apparatus el aparato *12*
apple la manzana
appliance el aparato *12*; *to turn on (an appliance)* poner
appointment la cita *4*
April abril
aquatic acuático,-a *17*
Arab árabe
Argentina la Argentina
Argentinean argentino,-a *7*
to **argue** discutir *12*
arm el brazo
armchair el sillón *11*
around alrededor de *14*
to **arrange** arreglar
arrival la llegada *15*
to **arrive** llegar
art el arte
article el artículo *14*
artist el artista, la artista *17*
as tal, como; *as (+ adverb) as possible* lo más/menos (+ *adverb*) posible; *as (+ adjective/adverb) as (+ person/item)* tan (+ *adjective/adverb*) como

(+ *person/item*); *as much as* tanto como; *as much/many* (+ *noun*) *as* (+ *person/item*) tanto,-a (+ *noun*) como (+ *person/item*); *as soon as* en cuanto *12*, luego que *12*

Asia el Asia *18*

Asian asiático,-a *18*

to **ask** preguntar; *to ask a question* hacer una pregunta; *to ask for* pedir *(i, i); to ask for permission* (*to do something*) pedir permiso (para); *to ask oneself* preguntarse *4*

aspiration la aspiración *17*

assortment el surtido *10*

at en; *at* (*the symbol @ used for e-mail addresses*) arroba *1; at home* en casa; *at night* de la noche, por la noche; *at…o'clock* a la(s)…; *at times* a veces; *at what time?* ¿a qué hora?

athlete el deportista, la deportista

to **attain** conseguir *(i, i);* realizar

to **attend** asistir a *17*

attic el ático *11*

attitude la actitud *18*

attraction la atracción *7*

attractive bonito,-a, guapo,-a

audience el público *13*

August agosto

aunt la tía

Australia Australia *18*

Australian australiano,-a *18*

autograph el autógrafo *13*

automatic automático,-a

autumn el otoño

avenue la avenida

average regular

avocado el aguacate

B

back la espalda *4*

bacon el tocino *9*

bad malo,-a; *Too bad!* ¡Qué lástima!

bakery la panadería *5*

bald calvo,-a

ball la pelota *14*

balloon el globo *7*

banana el plátano

band la banda *8*

bank el banco

to **bargain** regatear

to **bark** ladrar *8*

baseball el béisbol

basement el sótano *11*

basketball el básquetbol, el baloncesto; *basketball player* el basquetbolista, la basquetbolista

to **bathe** bañar(se) *3*

bathroom el baño, el cuarto de baño; *bathroom sink* el lavabo *3*

bathtub la tina *3*

to **be** ser; andar *9; to be a success* tener éxito *13; to be able to* poder *(ue); to be accustomed to* soler *(ue) 10; to be acquainted with* conocer *6; to be afraid of* tener miedo de; *to be born* nacer *15; to be called* llamarse *3; to be careful* tener cuidado *11; to be cold* tener frío; *to be familiar with* conocer *6; to be fitting* convenir *12; to be glad* alegrarse (de) *12; to be going to* (*do something*) ir a (+ *infinitive); to be hot* tener calor; *to be hungry* tener hambre; *to be important* importar; *to be in a hurry* tener prisa; *to be lacking* hacer falta; *to be likely that* ser fácil que *12; to be long* tardar en (+ *infinitive) 6; to be necessary* hacer falta; *to be* (+ *number*) *years old* tener (+ *number*) años; *to be on sale* estar en oferta; *to be pleasing to* gustar; *to be ready* estar listo,-a; *to be right* tener razón *10; to be satisfied* (*with*) estar contento,-a (con); *to be sleepy* tener sueño; *to be smart* ser listo,-a; *to be sorry* sentir *(ie, i); to be successful* tener éxito *13; to be thirsty* tener sed; *to be unlikely that* ser difícil que *12; to be used to* soler *(ue) 10; to be worth* valer *12*

beach la playa

bear el oso *8; teddy bear* el oso de peluche *8*

beautiful hermoso,-a *17*

because porque; *because of* a causa de

to **become** cumplir; *to become aware* enterar(se) de *14; to become* (+ *number*) *years old* cumplir

bed la cama; *to go to bed* acostarse *(ue) 3; to put* (*someone*) *in bed* acostar *(ue) 3*

bedroom el cuarto, la habitación

beef la carne de res *9; boneless cut of beef* el filete *9*

before antes de; *a quarter before* menos cuarto; *the day before yesterday* anteayer

to **begin** empezar *(ie);* comenzar *(ie) 12*

behind detrás de *8*

to **believe** creer *2*

bellhop el botones *16*

belt el cinturón; *safety belt* el cinturón de seguridad *6; seat belt* el cinturón de seguridad *6*

bermuda shorts las bermudas *2*

beside al lado (de)

besides además *10*

best mejor; *the best* (+ *noun*) el/la/los/las mejor/mejores (+ *noun*)

better mejor; *it is better that* más vale que *12*

between entre

bicycle la bicicleta

big grande; (*form of* grande *before a m., s. noun*) gran

bike la bicicleta

bill la cuenta *10*

biology la biología

bird el pájaro *8*, el ave *9*

birthday el cumpleaños; *Happy birthday!* ¡Feliz cumpleaños!; *to have a birthday* cumplir años

biscuit la galleta *6*

to **bite** morder *(ue) 13*

black negro,-a

blackboard la pizarra

blender la licuadora *12*

blond, blonde rubio,-a
blouse la blusa
blue azul
to board abordar 16
boat el barco, el bote 2
body el cuerpo
Bolivia Bolivia
Bolivian boliviano,-a 7
boneless cut of beef or fish el filete 9
book el libro
bookstore la librería
boot la bota
to bore aburrir 13
bored aburrido,-a
boring aburrido,-a
to borrow pedir prestado,-a
to bother molestar 7
box office la taquilla 8
boy el chico, el muchacho
boyfriend el novio 2
bracelet la pulsera
brake el freno 6
bravo olé
Brazil el Brasil 18
Brazilian brasileño,-a 18
bread el pan
to break romper 13
breakfast el desayuno 3; to have breakfast desayunar(se) 3
brick el ladrillo 11
bridge el puente 5
briefcase el maletín 16
to bring traer; llevar 14; to bring about realizar; to bring up subir
broadcast la transmisión 14
brochure el folleto 15
broom la escoba 11
brother el hermano
brown (color) café
brunet, brunette moreno,-a
brush el cepillo 3
to brush cepillar(se) 3
building el edificio 5
bull el toro 8
bullfight la corrida 15
to burn quemar 3
burro el burro 8
bus el autobús; bus station la estación de autobuses 5
business la empresa, los negocios 17
businessman el hombre de negocios 17
businesswoman la mujer de negocios 17

busy ocupado,-a
but pero; but (on the contrary) sino 6
butcher shop la carnicería 5
butter la mantequilla
to buy comprar
by por; by airplane en avión; by car en carro, en coche; by (+ vehicle) en (+ vehicle); by telephone por teléfono; by the way a propósito 18

C

cafeteria la cafetería
cage la jaula 8
cake el pastel 12
calendar el calendario
to call llamar
to calm down calmar(se) 3
camel el camello 7
camera la cámara 7
camping el camping 2
can la lata
Canada el Canadá 18
Canadian canadiense 18
candy el dulce 5; candy store la dulcería 5
cantaloupe el melón 9
cap (baseball) la gorra 2
capital la capital; capital letter la mayúscula
car el carro; el coche 6; by car en carro, en coche
card la tarjeta; credit card la tarjeta de crédito; playing card la carta
care el cuidado 11; to take care of cuidar(se) 4, encargarse (de) 11
career la carrera 17
Caribbean el Caribe
carpenter el carpintero, la carpintera 17
carpet la alfombra 11
carrot la zanahoria
to carry llevar; to carry up subir
carry-on luggage el equipaje de mano 16
cash el efectivo; in cash en efectivo
cashier el cajero, la cajera 10; cashier's desk la caja
cassette el casete
cat el gato, la gata
catastrophe la catástrofe 13
to catch coger; to catch (a cold) pescar (un resfriado) 4

cathedral la catedral 5
CD-ROM el disco compacto
to celebrate celebrar
celebration la celebración 13
cellular phone el celular 1
center el centro; el medio 18; in the center of en medio de 18; shopping center el centro comercial
Central America la América Central 7
Central American centroamericano,-a 18
century el siglo
cereal el cereal 9
chain la cadena
chair la silla; easy chair el sillón 11
chalk la tiza
championship el campeonato 14
change el cambio
to change cambiar 12
channel el canal 13
character el personaje 13
to charge cargar 15
chart la tabla 14
chat charla; chat room cuarto de charla 1
chauffeur el chofer, la chofer 17
cheap barato,-a
check la cuenta 10, el cheque 15
to check revisar 16; to check in registrar 16
checkered a cuadros 10
checkers las damas
cheese el queso
chemistry la química
chess el ajedrez
chest el pecho 4
chicken el pollo
child el niño, la niña 4
Chile Chile
Chilean chileno,-a 7
chilly fresco,-a
chimney la chimenea 11
China la China 18
Chinese chino,-a 18
chocolate el chocolate
to choose escoger
chore el quehacer
Christmas la Navidad
church la iglesia 5
cigarette el cigarrillo 4
circus el circo 8
city la ciudad; city block la cuadra 5